AFRICAN AMERICAN FIRSTS IN SCIENCE & TECHNOLOGY

AFRICAN AMERICAN FIRSTS IN SCIENCE & TECHNOLOGY

Raymond B. Webster
Guest Foreword by Wesley L. Harris

GALE GROUP

Detroit
San Francisco
London
Boston
Woodbridge, CT

Raymond B. Webster, *Author*

Gale Group Staff

Kristine M. Krapp, *Editor*

Christine B. Jeryan, *Managing Editor*

Mary Beth Trimper, *Production Director*
Evi Seoud, *Assistant Production Manager*
Wendy Blurton, *Buyer*
Margaret Chamberlain, *Picture Permissions*

Cynthia Baldwin, *Art Director*
Michelle DiMercurio, *Product Design Manager*
Randy Bassett, *Imaging Supervisor*

Library of Congress Cataloging-in-Publication Data

Webster, Raymond B.
African American firsts in science and technology / Raymond B. Webster ; foreword by Wesley L. Harris.
p. cm.
Includes bibliographical references and index.
Summary: Presents capsule accounts of notable first achievements by African Americans, arranged in the categories "Agriculture and Everyday Life," "Allied Health," "Dentistry and Nursing," "Life Sciences," "Math and Engineering," "Physical Sciences," and "Transportation."
ISBN 0-7876-387-5 (hc.)
1. Afro-American scientists Biography Juvenile literature.
2. Afro-American inventors Biography Juvenile literature.
[1. Scientists. 2. Inventors. 3. Afro-American Biography.]
I. Title.
Q141.W43   1999
508.996 073–dc2199-27346

CIP

CONTENTS

FOREWORD

~~~~~~

A critical question that has been generated by the foundation of America's culture is: How does one overcome the adversities invoked by racism and not allow its destructiveness to unduly influence one's destiny? For the African American, this critical question is quickly elevated to a much higher level since African Americans are the minority group most adversely impacted by the poisons of racism. Some useful corollary questions for African Americans are: What enables African Americans to remain focused and motivated in a society that does not recognize the contributions of African Americans? Given the continuous, nearly impenetrable barriers of American racism, what are the factors that have driven African Americans to make fundamental, basic cultural progress for selves and nation? Answers to these questions may generally be classified as either external to the persona of African Americans or internal to the African American soul. The set of answers describing the external agents are of significant value to the improved understanding of American racism. The external set, however, does not codify the diverse qualities possessed by African American *Firsts*—our heroes, champions, leaders, pioneers. It is the internal set of diverse qualities which has nurtured the African American spirit and projected African Americans beyond self survival to path makers for progress.

African American Firsts in Science and Technology is much more than retail cataloguing of African American pioneers in science and technology. These *Firsts* provide the framework to begin the discerning of the various qualities and the intricate complexity of those qualities that have produced the foundation upon which African American progress in science and technology has been made broad, deep, and without intermission. (Kenneth R. Manning's seminal work on the life of Ernest Everett Just for which he won the Pfizer Prize of the History of Science Society may be considered an important contribution to the understanding of the African American scientist persona.) These *Firsts* also stimulate the reader to appreciate both the African American leader and his community. The richness, beauty, and strength of the African American community are constants in the approximately 1,200 entries of this book. These extremely successful African

American scientists and technologists become more visible in the context of the African American community through which and for which they are now and forever more true leaders and pioneers.

The scope of *African American Firsts in Science and Technology* captures the progress and path-making achievements of African Americans over a time period exceeding a century, from medicine to agriculture, from land surveying to space travel, and from engineering to physics. It includes women and men of African lineage who possessed a commitment to excellence without qualification. These *Firsts* are about African Americans in search of scientific truth flavored only by a love for and a dedication to humanity. These *Firsts* are a prescription for a major illness.

—*Wesley L. Harris*
Professor, MIT
Cambridge, MA

INTRODUCTION

There are many different ways to tell the stories of African American history. We all hunger to learn the personal stories of our heroes. However, it is important to keep in mind the progress of history and the way that people and events influence each other through time. One useful way to relate historical events to each other is through a chronology. A chronology can put people and events into perspective by putting them in the order in which they happened. "First" achievements are particularly interesting because they relate the stories of pioneers—those who have accomplished things that no one else has done before.

African American Firsts in Science and Technology is a compilation of the pioneering achievements of African Americans in scientific and technical fields. The entries are records of special "first" achievements made by individuals who faced great adversity. Some of these pioneers are famous names in African American history—Charles R. Drew, Madame C. J. Walker, Elijah McCoy. Their lives are well-documented in the annals of history. Others achieved a "first" that was recorded in the history books, but the details of the rest of their lives have been lost. *African American Firsts in Science and Technology* assembles these stories in a way that enables readers to put events in perspective throughout the course of African American history.

African American Firsts in Science and Technology contains nearly 1,200 entries arranged chronologically in subject chapters. The first chapter, Agriculture and Everyday Life, joins the science of agriculture with the inventions of household use. Contained in this chapter are some of the accomplishments of George Washington Carver, William Purvis's invention of the fountain pen, as well as the first African American woman to receive a patent, Sarah E. Goode. The Allied Health chapter covers medical achievements—including medical inventions—by non-physicians. Dentistry and Nursing includes accomplishments and inventions in those disciplines.

The Life Sciences chapter covers the accomplishments of noted biologists, botanists, and zoologists. Accomplishments of Ernest E. Just and Jewel Plummer Cobb are included. Math and Engineering contains events centering on mathematics and computer science, as well as civil, mechanical, and electrical engineering. Medicine is the largest chapter. African Americans were able to launch their own careers in medicine long before they could overcome racial barriers present in the spheres of academia and industry. Therefore, many medical firsts are recorded in this volume. The Physical Sciences chapter includes the disciplines of physics, chemistry, and geology. Geologist Mack Gipson, physicist and inventor Meredith Gourdine, and Edward Bouchet, the first African American to earn a Ph.D. in the United States, are listed. The chapter on Transportation includes firsts related to travel by automobile, airplane, railroad, ship, and submarine. The chapter contains many inventions related to transportation, such as entries on inventions of Elijah McCoy. It also records, for instance, the accomplishments of the first African American pilots, including Bessie Coleman, the first African American woman to earn a pilot's license.

Of course, it is impossible to perfectly catagorize any specific person or event. Biochemist Emmett Chappelle, for example, has an entry in the Life Sciences chapter and the Physical Sciences chapter. Anatomist W. Montague Cobb is listed for his accomplishments in Medicine and Life Sciences. If the reader is researching a particular individual in a marginal field of study, the index should be consulted.

There are also several types of "firsts" included in *African American Firsts in Science and Technology*. Of course the "first African American" to graduate from a particular university or win a certain honor are included. The book also contains entries that cite an African American as the first woman or first person of any race to accomplish a particular goal. For example, Audrey Manley was the first woman named deputy assistant secretary for health in the U. S. Department of Health and Human Services. Benjamin S. Carson became the first neurosurgeon to successfully separate Siamese twins joined at the head in 1987. The book also includes entries in which an African American discovered, invented, founded, or established something significant as a "first."

About 1,200 entries are featured in *African American Firsts in Science and Technology*. One hundred and eight of these are accompanied by a photo of the individual cited. Each entry is followed by a short list of sources, where the reader can find more information on the person or event listed. The main body of the text is accompanied by a set of three indices. The Index by Year combines accomplishments from all the chapters and lists them in chronological order. The Occupation Index lists the individuals contained in the book according to their respective occupations and directs the reader to the pages of those entries. A General Index is also included.

The book is introduced in a foreword by Wesley L. Harris. Dr. Harris is a professor of Aeronautics and Astronautics at the Massachusetts Institute of Technology. He is also Director of the Lean Sustainment Initiative and Co-Director of the Lean Aircraft Initiative. Previously, Dr. Harris was the first Associate Administrator for Aeronautics at NASA, where he was responsible for all programs, facilities, and personnel in Aeronautics. He has served on the National Research Council and the National Science Foundation, among others. The text itself was created by Raymond B. Webster. Mr. Webster earned a master's degree from Howard University and continued his post-graduate studies at Catholic University. He has over 30 years of experience in human and safety engineering, systems development, basic and applied research, and information technology. He has produced over 180 publications, including articles in professional and technical journals, as well as manuals and technical reports.

African American Firsts in Science and Technology highlights the accomplishments of African American scientists and technologists from 1706 to the present. While it is relatively easy to find information on African American civil rights leaders and literary figures, who did their work in the public eye, the individuals listed in these pages fought their battles outside of the limelight. Too often, their accomplishments have gone unrecognized, making this catalogue of achievements all too important to African American history.

PHOTO CREDITS

~~~~~~

Photographs appearing on the following pages in *African American Firsts in Science and Technology* were used with permission from these sources:

George Alcorn 329; **American Medical Association** 266, 284; **Harold Amos** 96; **AP/Wide World Photos** 5, 29, 30, 74, 75, 82, 84, 87, 100, 151, 183, 192, 202, 210, 228, 231, 232, 237, 246, 252, 254, 270, 271, 280, 284, 292, 294, 307, 319, 323, 339, 371, 377; **Archive Photos** 127, 365; **Argonne National Laboratory Media Center** 341; **AT & T Bell Laboratories** 296; **David Blackwell** (photograph by Jean Libby) 122; **Thomas Cannon** 322; **Jewel Plummer Cobb** 96; **Corbis, Corbis-Bettmann, and UPI/Corbis-Bettmann** 89, 90, 166, 176, 251, 298, 300, 352, 374, 375; **Dillard University Library** 185; **Irvin W. Elliot** 98; **Lloyd Ferguson** 299; **Fisk University Library** 1, 2, 4, 49, 103, 116, 159, 289, 290; **Evan B. Forde** 328; **Ford Motor Company and Ronald Goldsberry** 320; **Henry J. Foster, Jr.** 282; **Solomon Carter Fuller** 171; **Sylvester J. Gates, Jr.** 338; **Granger Collection, New York** 13; **Patricia Kenschaft** 113; **George M. Langford** 99; **Carroll Leevy** 243; **Lawrence Berkeley National Laboratory** 314; **Library of Congress** 7, 19, 51, 92; **Samuel P. Massie** 309; **Meharry Medical College** 89, 164, 167, 237, 278, 287; **Jason Miccolo Johnson Photography and Zora Brown** 44; **National Aeronautics and and Space Administration (NASA)** 114, 369, 372; **National Archives and Records Administration** 368; **Joan Murrell Owens** (photograph by Frank A. Owens) 330; **Jennie Patrick-Yeboah** 326; **Frederick D. Patterson** 197; photograph of Robert Pelham in the public domain 13; **Deborah Prothrow-Stith** 43; **Queens Library, Long Island Division** 3; **Schomburg Center for Black Culture** 180, 201; **Scurlock Studio and Peter Marshall Murray** 186; **Earl D. Shaw** 320; **Jeanne C. Sinkford** 70; **Rodney Slater** 153; **Louis W. Sullivan** 273; **University of Texas at Tyler** 147; **Levi Watkins, Jr.** 260.

AGRICULTURE AND EVERYDAY LIFE

1753 • The first clock constructed in the United States was produced by the African American scientist Benjamin Banneker (1731-1806). The hand-carved clock was made of wood, struck the hours, and was reported to have kept time for 40 years. Born to a free mother and slave father, Banneker was a noted inventor, mathematician, and astronomer. Later in his life, he wrote articles condemning slavery, one of which resulted in a series of correspondence with Thomas Jefferson, who was then George Washington's Secretary of State. In 1980, the United States Postal Service issued a commemorative stamp in Banneker's honor.

Blacks in Science and Medicine (1990), p. 19; *Famous First Facts* (1972), p. 7; *Timelines of African American History* (1994), p. 27

1791 • *Benjamin Banneker's Almanack and Ephemeris* was published for the first time in 1791 with information for the following year. The text was published in Baltimore by William Goddard and James Angell. Twenty-nine editions of Banneker's almanac were issued for the years 1792 through 1797. Banneker's almanac was widely read throughout the states of Maryland, Virginia, Delaware, Pennsylvania, and New Jersey and was printed in the cities of Philadelphia, Baltimore, Richmond Petersburg, Trenton, and Wilmington. Although the almanac for 1797 was the last issue published, Banneker continued to calculate astronomical predictions for each succeeding year through 1804. His almanac contained such items as his lunar and solar eclipse calculations, position of the planets, weather data, tidal information, sunrise and sunset information, moon phases, as well as other general information such as recipes, medical reminders, poems, and essays.

BENJAMIN BANNEKER

Dictionary of American Negro Biography (1982), pp. 22-25; *Men of Mark* (1970), pp. 224-228; *Negro Vanguard* (1959), pp. 24-27

1821 • The first African American to receive a U.S. patent was Thomas L. Jennings (1791-1859) in 1821. Jennings, who operated a dry-cleaning and tailoring business in New York City, acquired a patent for a dry-cleaning process. He used the money that he earned to purchase his family out of slavery. Although Jennings was the first African American to receive a U.S. patent, he was not recorded as being African American on his patent application. The first man so recorded was Henry Blair, who received a patent in 1834.

Created Equal (1993), pp. 17, 181; *Outward Dreams* (1991), pp. 4-5; *The Real McCoy* (1989), p. 31; *Eyewitness: The Negro in American History* (1971), p. 139, (1974), p. 139

1834 • The first African American inventor identified on a patent in the United States was Henry Blair (1804-1860). He was issued a patent on October 14, 1834, for a seed planter. Blair was born a free Black in Maryland and so was able to receive his patent. (Slaves could not hold a patent.) Blair also received a second patent on August 31, 1836, for a cotton planter.

Blacks in Science and Medicine (1990), p. 29; *Famous First Facts* (1964), p. 437; *Negro Year Book* (1918-1919), p. 342, (1931-1932), p. 166

NORBERT RILLIEUX

1843 • The sugar refining process was revolutionized to become an efficient and cost-effective procedure by the invention of African American engineer Norbert Rillieux (1806-1894). His patented vacuum-pan evaporator was the basis of Rillieux's system, which he further improved with a second patent, issued on December 10, 1896. Although born in New Orleans, Rillieux was raised and educated in Paris, attending the Paris L'Ecole Centrale. At the age of 24, he was an instructor in applied mechanics, developing and publishing papers on steam engines and steam economy. Returning to New Orleans, Rillieux developed an interest in sugar production, and his two basic patents of 1843 and 1846, the multiple effect evaporator pan, was the basis of developing a cheaper, better, and automated process for crystallizing sugar. (This same process is basic to the manufacturing of condensed milk, soap, gelatin, glue, and the recovery of wastes in distilleries and paper factories.)

Blacks in Science: Ancient and Modern (1983), p. 222; *Dictionary of American Negro Biography* (1982), pp. 525-526; *Eight Black American Inventors* (1972), pp. 106-119

1848 • The toggle harpoon, known as "Temple's Toggle," became the standard harpoon of the American whaling industry and was also called the "universal whale iron." This harpoon, which revitalized America's whaling industry in the 1850s, was invented by African American Lewis Temple (1800-1854). He was a blacksmith and lived in New Bedford, Massachusetts. Temple's harpoon became the standard harpoon of the American whale fishing and was heavily utilized in Alaskan waters.

Dictionary of American Negro Biography (1982), pp. 582-583; *Eight Black American Inventors* (1972), pp. 32-43; *New England Quarterly* (March, 1953), pp. 78-88

1865 • The first African American woman to receive a patent in the United States was Sarah E. Goode. She received a patent dated July 14, 1885, for a cabinet bed. Goode owned a furniture store in Chicago, and her invention was similar to what is today called a sofa bed.

Black Inventors of America (1989), p. 143; *Black Women in America* (1993), p. 618; *Creativity and Inventions* (1987), p. 12; *The Real McCoy* (1989), p. 67

1876 • An improved double cooking range was invented by Thomas A. Carrington and was patented in 1876. Carrington's cooking range had two parts that were similar in construction and symmetrical in arrangement. The two ovens were arranged on opposite sides of the flue, with two furnaces located on the outside of the ovens. The cooking range had a central common flue. Registers and dampers all had operating rods. With Carrington's system, one or both ovens could be used, and the head could be regulated differently for each of the ovens, enabling preparation of different foods at different temperatures simultaneously.

Black Inventors: From Africa to America (1995), p. 238; *Blacks in Science: Astrophysicist to Zoologist* (1977), p. 77; *Created Equal* (1993), p. 182; *Index of Patents* (1876)

1882 • Electric lighting and lighting systems in the latter 1800s and early 1900s received some of their greatest impetus for development from the technical contribution of the African American inventor, Lewis Howard Latimer (1848-1928). In 1882, Latimer received a patent for a process of manufacturing carbon, which revolutionized the manufacturing of electric lamps with his carbon filament. In 1865, He worked in Boston for patent solicitors Crosby and Gould, where he became chief draftsman, remaining with the company for 11 years. Latimer was hired by the United States Electric Lighting Company in 1880, and in 1881, he and J. V. Nichols received a patent for an electric lamp. Latimer was responsible for the design and implementation of electrical lighting systems in New York, London, Montreal, and Philadelphia. He was the first African American member of the "Edison Pioneers," a group of inventors that worked with Thomas Edison.

LEWIS LATIMER

Afro-American Inventor (1975), p. 35; *Blacks in Science: Ancient and Modern* (1983), p. 222; *Encyclopedia of Black America* (1981), p. 497; *Famous First Facts About Negroes* (1972), p. 82

1882 • The prevalent listings of African American inventors and their patents usually place Albert C. Richardson near the head of their listings. Richardson received a patent on March 14, 1882, for a hame fastener (attachments to the collar of a draft horse). In 1891, he received a patent for a churn, and in 1894, a patent for a coffin-lowering device. Richardson also had several other patents.

Blacks in Science and Medicine (1990), p. 201; *Black Inventors of America* (1969), p. 141; *Negro History Compendium* (1971), p. 47

JAN MATZELIGER

1883 • The most important machine required for the manufacturing and production of shoes is the shoe lasting machine, developed and perfected by African American inventor Jan Ernest Matzeliger (1852-1889) in 1883. He was born in Surinam and in 1871, left there as a sailor on a merchant ship, landed in Philadelphia in 1872, remained there until he migrated to Boston in 1876, eventually settling in Lynn, Massachusetts. Matzeliger was employed in a shoe factory, and after a period of several years assembled, in 1880, his first version of the shoe lasting machine. He continued to improve the model for a three-year period and was eventually granted a patent on March 20, 1883, for the "Lasting Machine." Matzeliger eventually sold his machine to the United Shoe Machinery Company, which eventually increased shoe production by the hundreds of millions of dollars while the general cost of shoe production was reduced by 45%. Matzeliger patented an improved lasting machine. (The patent was issued in September 1891, two years posthumously.) Between 1883 and 1891, Matzeliger received five patents, all contributing to the evolution of shoe production. His development is still the basis of current shoe lasting machines utilized today.

African America: Portrait of a People (1994), pp. 678-679; *Afro-American Inventor* (1975), pp. 35-37; *Journal of Negro History* Vol. 40, (January, 1955), pp. 8-33

1884 • William B. Purvis, an African American inventor, acquired 10 patents during the period 1884-1894 for varied paper bag producing machines. Most of his bag production machine patents were sold to the Union Bag Company of New York. Purvis had a number of patents for other inventions, including three patents on electric railroads, one on a fountain pen, one on a magnetic car-balancing device, and one for a cutter for paper roll holders.

The Black Inventor (1975), p. 45; *Black History and Achievement in America* (1982), p. 89; *Negro Year Book* (1918-1919), p. 342; *Short History of the American Negro* (1939), p. 220

1884 • One of America's most productive inventors was Granville T. Woods (1856-1910). Woods's first invention in 1884 was an improved steam boiler furnace. He also had three other patents issued in 1884. The most important of Woods's inventions was the induction telegraph system, patented on November 29, 1887, which permitted communication between moving trains and between the trains and station. He patented 15 inventions for electric railways, several devices for electrical control and distribution, as well as others for air brakes, telephone and telegraph communications, and transmitters. A number of Woods's inventions were sold to the General Electric Company, Westinghouse Air Brake Company, and American Bell Telephone Company. Thomas Edison had also tried to hire him, but he remained independent.

The Black Inventor (1975), p. 52; *Black American Reference Book* (1976), p. 46; *Blacks in Science: Ancient and Modern* (1983), pp. 220-221; *Men of Mark* (1887), pp. 107-112

1884 • African American inventor J. W. Reed was granted a patent in 1884 for a dough kneader and roller. The apparatus consisted of a wooden case or box containing a pair of corrugated intermeshing metallic cylinders, one being stationery in a lateral position, with a crank to activate the device. The other roller was movable. There was a pair of plain rollers connected to one of the corrugated rollers by a belt. The dough was drawn between the corrugated rollers and plain rollers and fell into a receptacle in a continuous sheet. The pressure of the rolls could be regulated by screws, while elastic plates kept the rolls always in contact.

Black Inventors: From Africa to America (1995), p. 246; *Created Equal* (1993), p. 184; *Index of Patents* (1884); *Outward Dreams* (1991), p. 93

GRANVILLE T. WOODS

1886 • Robert F. Flemming, an African American inventor, patented a specialized guitar in 1886. Flemming called his instrument a "Euphonica." It was similar to a guitar, except that the volume and sweetness of the tone was superior, and the instrument was more sensitive to the touch. Flemming's guitar was substantially similar in shape to the ordinary guitar, but instead of wooden heads, it had vellum heads stretched over the wooden sides. The sides had interior bracing to preclude breakage. It also had a bridge composed of a wooden base portion with a metal strip on the upper edge, which was provided with suitable notches for the strings.

Black Inventors: From Africa to America (1995), p. 240; *Blacks in Science: Astrophysicist to Zoologist* (1977), p. 79; *Created Equal* (1993), p. 184

1888 • Miriam E. Benjamin acquired a patent on July 17, 1888, for a gong and signal chair, which was the principle adopted by the United States House of Representatives for the congressmen to call their particular pages. Benjamin was the second African American woman to be issued a patent.

Black Inventors of America (1969), p. 136; *Created Equal* (1993), pp. 120, 186; *Creativity and Inventions* (1987), p. 73; *Black Women in America* (1993), p. 618

1888 • Robert N. Hyde, who had an established custodial service in Des Moines, Iowa, invented a carpet cleaning process that was patented in 1888. Hyde compounded a mixture of distilled water, pulverized borax, soluble soap, aqua-ammonia, bay-runs, oil of sassafras, and alcohol. This solution was heated and applied to a carpet with a brush. The carpet was then rubbed with a cloth. It was not necessary to take up the carpet from the floor, but only sweep loose dirt from it before applying Hyde's solution. The solution helped preserve the carpet and prevented insects from infesting it.

Black Inventors: From Africa to America (1995), p. 106; *Created Equal* (1993), p. 186

1890 • William B. Purvis was granted a patent in 1890 for his invention of the fountain pen. Purvis's pen was adapted for general use and could be carried in the pocket. The penholder is a reservoir and supports the pen flexibly over an outlet from the reservoir. There is an elastic ink-feeding tube between the reservoir and pen, with a pressure point carried by the holder to compress the elastic tube with each downward stroke of the pen, expending a small quantity of ink from the reservoir-outlet. Purvis also had a number of other patents.

Black Inventors: From Africa to America (1995), pp. 91, 246; *Blacks in Science and Medicine* (1990), p. 196; *Created Equal* (1993), pp. 183, 187, 191; *Outward Dreams* (1991), p. 93

1891 • Philip B. Downing invented a letter box that was patented in 1891. Downing's design incorporated a top provided with a mail slot and a cover for the slot that was hinged to the upper part of the box. The hinged cover had a safety plate, and when the cover was closed, the plate hung vertically in the box, raising to a horizontal position when the cover was raised, providing further protection to the deposited mail. When the cover plate dropped, the mail was delivered into the box. A weather strip, hinged to the cover, preventing rain or snow from entering into the box. Downing received two patents on the same day, October 27, 1891, for his letter box invention.

Black Inventors: From Africa to America (1995), p. 240; *Black Inventors of America* (1969), p. 134; *Blacks in Science: Astrophysicist to Zoologist* (1977), p. 78; *Index of Patents* (1891)

1892 • Anthony L. Lewis received a patent for his invention of a window cleaner in 1892. Lewis's window cleaner had a long handle, body, scraper, and a water-containing reservoir. The reservoir was molded of soft rubber with thin walls and a working surface with a number of minute perforations. The surface was ribbed in order to more effectively remove dirt from a window. The reservoir and scraper attached to the handle. Lewis's device was placed in water so as to saturate it and the window surface was cleaned with the window cleaner. Pressure applied to the handle was sufficient to express water from the reservoir for washing. The scraper portion was then used to remove the dirt and water.

Black Inventors: From Africa to America (1995), p. 243; *Created Equal* (1993), p. 188

1894 • George Washington Carver (1864-1943) became the first African American graduate of Iowa State College of Mechanical and Agricultural Arts when he earned his bachelor's degree in 1894. He earned his master's there two years later. Carver, an agricultural chemist, made great contributions to the development of agricultural science, and he was the largest force in the effort to diversify agricultural crops in the American South. His aim was to revolutionize the Southern economy by relieving it from an excessive dependence on a single cash crop, cotton. He devised and promoted over 300 uses for peanuts, sweet potatoes, and pecans. He also held three patents for processes that produced paints and stains from plants. Carver started working at Tuskegee Institute (Alabama) in 1896 and remained there all his profes-

GEORGE WASHINGTON CARVER

sional life, shunning many offers to even work with Henry Ford and Thomas Edison.

Creativity and Inventions (1987), p. 32; *Dictionary of American Negro Biography* (1982), pp. 92-95; *Famous First Facts* (1972), p. 174

1894–1895 • Two machines patented by African American inventor Joseph Lee (1849-1905), in 1894 and 1895, were the major factors in modernizing the bread baking industry. He invented a bread-kneading machine in 1894 and a bread-crumbing machine in 1895. Lee's machines increased bread production by reducing the number of workers required by 75%. Lee sold the rights to his machines to two manufacturers who quickly produced the machines.

Black Inventors of America (1989), p. 144; *Pathfinders II* (1987), p. 12; *The Real McCoy* (1989), pp. 62, 63

1894 • Roger P. Scott invented a green corn silking machine that was patented in 1894. Scott's apparatus consisted of an open-ended horizontal or inclined cylinder, provided with thin wedge-shaped plates with gathering teeth distributed around the inner surface of the cylinder. The apparatus included a scraper supported on levers at the opposite end of the cylinder, and the scraper removed the silk from the teeth of the plates. Bell-cranked levers, a grooved pinwheel, and actuating levers and pins operated the cylinder and attachments. The gathering teeth did not clog up on Scott's machine by his inclusion of the scraper.

Index of Patents (1894)

1894 • George W. Murray, an African American inventor, was awarded six U. S. patents on the same date, June 5, 1894. The patents included a planter, cotton chopper, fertilizer distributor, another type of planter, combined cottonseed, and a combined planter and fertilizer all issued in 1894. Murray was previously issued two other patents on the same date, April 10, 1894, a combined furrow opener and stalk-knocker, and a cultivator and marker.

Black Inventors of America (1989), p. 144; *Blacks in Science and Medicine* (1990), p. 178; *The Colored Inventor* (1969), p. 9; *Science, Technology and Mathematics* (1988), p. 54; *Created Equal* (1993), p. 189

1895 • Claytonia J. Dorticus acquired patents regarding the photographic development process. She patented a machine for embossing photographs on April 16, 1895, and for a photographic print wash in the same month, on April 23, 1895. She also patented a method for applying coloring liquids to sides of soles or heels of shoes and for a hose leak stop. Dorticus operated her own photographic studio in Newton, New Jersey.

Black Inventors of America (1989), p. 142; *Outward Dreams* (1991), pp. 58, 89

1897 • John Lee Love invented a pencil sharpener that served as a paper-weight or desk ornament and was granted a patent in 1897. Love's device was a chamber open at the top, within which was contained an inwardly directed annular flange or rim which was provided with gear teeth. The chamber bottom was raised with a pivoted arm or plate, and a pencil sharp-ener was mounted to revolve on one end of the arm or plate, which was pro-vided with a pinion or gear wheel. A pencil was sharpened by passing the point downward into the sharpener with pressure, and the sharpener was revolved by means of the pinion or gear wheel.

Black Inventors of America (1989), p. 141; *Created Equal* (1993), pp. 189, 191; *Index of Patents* (1897)

1897 • James Cooper received a patent in 1897 for his elevator safety device, which controlled the door of an elevator. Cooper's system combined the motor mechanism of an elevator and a locking device adapted to lock the motor mechanism in an inoperative position. The connection between the locking device and the elevator doors was placed on each floor, and the locking device was operated before the door became unlocked, preventing the elevator doors from opening between floors.

Black Inventors: From Africa to America (1995), p. 239; *Blacks in Science: Astrophysicist to Zoologist* (1977), p. 77; *Created Equal* (1993), p. 189; *Index of Patents* (1897)

1898 • Alvin Longo Rickman received a patent in 1898 for an overshoe, which was the forerunner of later rubbers. Rickman's light overshoe was designed to cover the shoe sole and heel with a shank provided with a con-tinuous rim edging and a fastening device. The fastening device was a loop-shaped piece of spring metal formed with the sole, shank, and heel. In use, the fastening device distended when the overshoe was applied and con-tracted to fit the space between the sole and upper of the shoe while the heel portion of the device engaged the heel of the shoe. Rickman's over-shoe was made of rubber, rubber and fabric combined, or of any suitable waterproof material.

Black Inventors: From Africa to America (1995), p. 246; *Blacks in Science and Medicine* (1990), p. 201; *Created Equal* (1993), p. 191; *Index of Patents* (1898)

1899 • Joseph Ross invented a knock-down hay press, for which he received a patent in 1899. Ross designed a portable bailing press that could be moved from place to place and taken apart for transportation or storage. It could create two or more bales at the same time, and the compressor could compress two bales while the other end was being filled with material to be baled. The press was comprised of sides, ends, and bottom, a central dividing partition, screw shaft, and T-shaped pieces being concaved to hold antifriction balls and flanges holding them in place. With an antifriction cross head construction, Ross prevented the buckling of the screw, allowing the cross head to carry the compressor.

Black Inventors: From Africa to America (1995), p. 247; *Blacks in Science: Astrophysicist to Zoologist* (1977), p. 86; *Created Equal* (1993), p. 193; *Index of Patents* (1899)

1899 • Joseph Hunter Dickinson received a patent for a reed organ in 1899. Dickinson was famous for his inventions related to musical instruments, primarily the piano and organ. He invented devices for automatically playing the piano, and some of his piano-playing invention mechanisms were adopted in the construction of the finest player pianos. He built two organs for the royal family of Portugal and was awarded a diploma and medal for a large combination organ he constructed and exhibited for the Centennial Exposition of 1876.

Evidences of Progress Among Colored People (1902), pp. 344-347; *Negro Year Book* (1921-1922), p. 318, (1931-1932), p. 167; *Official Gazette* (May 2, 1899), pp. 786-787

1899 • John Albert Burr invented an improved lawn mower that was patented in 1899. Burr invented traction wheels and a rotary cutter or shear for the lawn mower. The shear rotated alongside a fixed bar, the motion of which cut the blades of grass. Burr's invention provided a casing that enclosed the operating gearing to prevent it from clogging. The casing had a circular flange on its inner side extending into the recess of the wheel.

Created Equal (1993), p. 192

1899 • The golf tee, invented by George F. Grant (1847-19??), was patented in 1899. Grant's tee had a base made of wood and tapered to a point at its lower end to be inserted into the ground. At the upper end of the wooden tee, or head, was a rounded shoulder or seat, over which a piece of rubber tubing was stretched. The ball rested in the seat or cup. The tee held the ball firmly and did not interfere with the player's swing if struck by the club. Grant was also a dentist who graduated from Harvard Dental School in 1870 and enjoyed a reputation for dental innovation.

Blacks in Science and Medicine (1990), p. 104; *Journal of Blacks in Higher Education* (Winter 1998/1999), p. 99; *Philadelphia New Observer* (September 16, 1992)

1899 • William J. Nickerson invented a piano attachment that incorporated a tone-modifier and pianissimo device. His invention was patented in 1899. The device, designed for an upright piano, consisted of a bracket connected to the inner side of one end wall of the piano case. A pivotally connected bar was moveable and carried an apron to be placed between the hammers and piano strings. A cord, also connected to the bar, extended out over the walls of the piano case with a counter balance weight. The tone-modifier and pianissimo device were adapted by Nickerson to be used in conjunction with each other.

Black Inventors: From Africa to America (1995), p. 245; *Blacks in Science: Astrophysicist to Zoologist* (1977), p. 84; *Created Equal* (1993), p. 192; *Index of Patents* (1899)

1899 • Albert C. Richardson invented an apparatus to destroy insects dangerous to plants and trees without injuring the plants themselves, for which he was granted a patent in 1899. Richardson constructed a rectangular sheet metal box mounted on a wheel at one end and legs at the other end with handles similar to a wheelbarrow. The box casing had a main chamber in which tobacco or other materials were burned and produce smoke and fumes. There was also a cooling chamber provided with vents that were arranged to pass the smoke through a system of tubes and be discharged on a tree or plant. The apparatus was adapted to work between rows simultaneously, subjecting the plants of two rows to the smoke/fumes treatment.

Black Inventors: From Africa to America (1995), p. 246; *Blacks in Science: Astrophysicist to Zoologist* (1977), p. 85; *Index of Patents* (1899)

1899 • A specialized cot for invalids was developed by Benjamin F. Cargill, and a patent was granted him in 1899. Cargill's invention allowed a patient to be turned easily, preventing problems like bedsores. With Cargill's device, after the patient was turned on his back, the cot could be lowered to a desired position and securely locked. The cot system had a frame and mattress. A series of standards connected to the frame, and their inner faces formed with a rack and bearing blocks, with the cot pivotally mounted in the blocks. A rack and shafts with the bearing blocks could elevate or lower the platform.

Black Inventors: From Africa to America (1995), p. 238; *Blacks in Science: Astrophysicist to Zoologist* (1977), p. 77; *Created Equal* (1993), p. 193; *Index of Patents* (1899)

1900 • Andrew Franklin Hilyer (1858?-1925) was an author, civil rights leader, and inventor who, in 1900, patented a hot air register and a water evaporator attachment for hot air registers. Hilyer earned a B.A. from the University of Minnesota in 1882, a L.L.B. in 1884 and a L.L.M. in 1885, both from Howard University. Hilyer was an accountant and produced studies on the business and social status of African Americans.

Black Inventors of America (1989), p. 143; *Blacks in Science and Medicine* (1990), p. 121; *Dictionary of American Negro Biography* (1982), pp. 314-315

1900 • One of the early African American inventors who successfully manufactured and marketed his own invention was A.C. Howard. He experimented with different formulas for shoe polish. Howard won first prize in both the 1900 Paris Exposition and 1907 Jamestown Exposition for his shoe polish products.

The Real McCoy (1989), p. 91

1900 • The first listing or compilation of inventions patented by African Americans in the United States was produced by the African American assistant examiner of the U.S. Patent office, Henry E. Baker (1859-1928). Baker compiled several listings identifying over 1,000 patents assigned to 400 African American inventors before 1913. Baker was appointed, in 1877, to the position "copyist" in the U.S. Patent Office, where he was ultimately promoted to the position of Second Assistant Examiner. Baker completed research uncovering and identifying African American-assigned patents and developed listings of these findings. He compiled several volumes of patent drawings and specifications of patents awarded to African American inventors. Baker published the volume "The Colored Inventor" (Crisis, 1913) listing his identified inventors and their patents.

Black Firsts (1994), p. 347; *Outward Dreams* (1991), p. 54; *The Real McCoy* (1989), pp. 77-78; *Twentieth Century Negro Literature* (1969), pp. 399-413

1900 • J. W. Benton received a patent on October 2, 1900, for a device he invented for hoisting heavy weights. Benton walked from Kentucky to Washington, D.C. carrying his invention on his back to obtain his patent.

The Black Inventor (1975), p. 91; *Jet* (October 4, 1982), p. 19; *Blacks in Science: Astrophysicist to Zoologist* (1977), p. 90; *Official Gazette* (October 2, 1900), p. 82

1905 • Robert A. Pelham Jr. (1859-1943), an African American inventor, was employed by the United States Census Bureau from 1900 until his retirement in 1937. While employed at the Census Bureau, Pelham received a patent in 1905 for a tabulating machine and in 1913, a patent for a tallying machine used in the Bureau's work production effort. Pelham's tabulating machine was used in the census of manufacturing, while his tallying machine was used in the population division. Pelham received a L.L.B. from Howard University in 1904.

Blacks in Science and Medicine (1990), p. 187; *Dictionary of American Negro Biography* (1982), pp. 487-488; *Negro Year Book* (1918-1919), pp. 343-344, (1921-1922), p. 319, (1931-1932), pp. 167-168

ROBERT A. PELHAM, JR.

1905 • Madame C. J. Walker (Sarah Breedlove) (1867-1919) invented a metal heating comb in 1904 and a conditioner for straightening hair in 1905. Walker led an impoverished younger life, being orphaned at the age of seven, marrying at the age of 14, and having a daughter by the age of 20. At age 37, Walker and her daughter moved to Denver, Colorado and joined her widowed sister-in-law and her four daughters. In Denver, Walker developed her hair conditioner and metal heating comb and started selling her products. She developed her company headquarters in 1910 in Indianapolis, Indiana, then moved part of the business operations to New York City. Walker established a chain of beauty parlors throughout the United States, Caribbean, and South America. By 1910, she had over 5,000 African American agents selling her products on a commission basis and by 1919, the total was 25,000 agents. Some claim that Walker became the first self-made female millionaire.

MADAME C. J. WALKER

Blacks in Science and Medicine (1990), p. 240; *Biographical History of Blacks in America* (1971), pp. 435-437; *Notable Black American Women* (1992), pp. 1184-1188

1907 • A cotton-picking machine was invented by Albert P. Albert in 1905 and was patented in 1907. His pneumatic device was comprised of a conduit and a number of fixed projections forming a grid at the end of the conduit and adapted to engage the cotton. His device actually picked the cotton balls, delivering them into a bag via the conduit. Albert was an attorney with a law degree from Howard University. He won his case to get his cotton picker patented by preparing a brief and appearing before a Board of Examiners-in-Chief who were legal and technical experts.

Blacks in Science and Medicine (1990), p. 4; *Index of Patents* (1907)

1911 • Shelby J. Davidson (1868-1931), who received a B.A. from Howard University in 1893, patented an automatic fee device that helped postal clerks assess fees. His first invention was a rewind device for adding machines, which was used on many government adding machines. One of Davidson's mechanical tabulators may have been a forerunner of the modern adding machine.

Blacks in Science and Medicine (1990), p. 68; *Created Equal* (1993), p. 72; *The Real McCoy* (1989), pp. 87-88

1916 • In 1916, George Washington Carver (1864-1943), became the first African American named a fellow of the Royal Society of London. Carver, an agricultural chemist and former slave, worked at the forefront of the newly developing discipline of scientifical agriculture. Through his long career at Tuskegee Institute (Alabama), he received numerous honors. He won the 1923 Springarn Medal from the National Association for the Advancement of Colored People (NAACP) and was bestowed an honorary doctorate degree from Simpson College (Iowa), where he had once attended classes. In 1957, a nuclear-powered Polaris submarine was named in his honor. Upon his death in 1943, President Franklin D. Roosevelt paid tribute to Carver in an address before Congress, and Carver's Missouri birthplace was made a national monument.

Blacks in Science: Astrophysicist to Zoologist (1977), pp. 18-19; *Dictionary of American Negro Biography* (1982), pp. 92-95; *Famous First Facts* (1972), p. 174

1916 • Madeline M. Turner's invention of a fruit press was patented in 1916. Her press was designed to extract juice from such fruits as oranges and lemons. It consisted of a pair of horizontally moving presser plates, one concave and the other convex, which move in a reciprocating motion, one at a higher speed and with greater movement than the other. Fruit fed between the plates is severed by a cutter. When the fruit is passed through the apparatus and cut, the presser plates with their associated plungers are brought together with the fruit between them so that the fruit is thoroughly compressed, extracting the juice from it.

Black Inventors: From Africa to America (1995), p. 249

1918 • Joseph Hunter Dickinson (1855-19??) received a patent in 1918 for his invention of an improved expression device for a phonograph. Dickinson constructed his device with a sound passage, telescoping plug valve, and an elastic throat. The throat controlled the sound passage, and the surface of the valve was recessed to permit the sound to pass when the valve contacts the mouth of the throat. The sound continues to pass in a diminished extent as the valve is telescoped into the throat, closing completely when the valve is fully telescoped. Dickinson also acquired several patents for piano player mechanisms and reed instruments. He also constructed organs, some on a custom basis.

Black Inventors: From Africa to America (1995), p. 95; *Created Equal* (1993), pp. 19, 192; *Index of Patents* (1918); *Negro Year Book* (1918-1919), p. 343; *Negro Year Book* (1921-1922), p. 318

1919 • Alice H. Parker, a creative African American inventor, acquired a patent in 1919 for a heating furnace. Parker's furnace provided regulated heat transferred to various rooms of a building using gas as a fuel. Her system had several heating units branching from a common cold air box, each of which was independently controlled with individual hot air ducts leading to different parts of the structure.

Creativity and Inventions (1987), pp. 19, 75; *Official Gazette* (December 23, 1919), p. 627

1920 • Walter H. Sammons invented a comb for straightening hair with a heat application that was patented in 1920. Sammon's comb had a cylindrical head with curved teeth projecting from it and a cylindrical extension at one end of the comb. A handle connected to the cylindrical extension could be removed. This handle had a small opening for insertion of a thermometer and another for viewing the temperature as recorded. The comb head had a central chamber, which housed the lower part of the thermometer. As the comb was heated for hair treatment, the temperature of the comb was visible, so the comb could be applied to the hair only at a desired temperature.

Black Inventors: From Africa to America (1995), p. 247; *Index of Patents* (1920)

1922 • Jack A. Johnson (1878-1946), who was the first African American heavyweight boxing champion when he won the title in 1908, also invented a wrench tool for which he was issued a patent in 1922. Johnson's wrench was of simple and durable construction, reliable in operation, and easy and inexpensive to manufacture. The wrench was also easily adjustable and adapted to exert a powerful gripping action on the work. Johnson's wrench could also be easily disassembled for purposes of replacement or repair.

Black Inventors: From Africa to America (1995), pp. 127, 232; *Index of Patents* (1922)

1922 • Arthur L. Macbeth received a patent in 1922 for his invention of a daylight moving picture theater. Macbeth's theater was a house-like structure with three rooms, all located in front of each other. The rear room was the projection operation room, which was divided from the middle room by an opaque transverse partition. A second transverse partition divided the middle and front rooms, and the opaque partition had an opening through which pictures were projected onto the screen. The front room had an alcove with an open front, through which the pictures were viewed on the projection screen. The front room had a forward and downward slanting top wall with a restricted opening at the front of the alcove, providing clear vision of the screen from the exterior of the theater, with external light being excluded from the screen.

Index of Patents (1922), p. 318; *Negro Year Book* (1921-1921), p. 33

1926 • A patent was granted to Ambrose Caliver in 1926 for his invention of a work cabinet. Caliver's cabinet, in the open position, supported all the necessary articles of equipment and supplies required by a hairdresser while performing her work operations. When closed, Caliver's work cabinet took on the appearance of an article of furniture. The cabinet included comfortable seats for both the customer and hairdresser. The door to the cabinet had a towel rack secured to it and could hold a removable shelf to house supplies used by the hairdresser.

Index of Patents (1926), p. 104; *Notable Black American Men* (1998), pp. 160-162

1927 • George Washington Carver (1864-1943), who developed 508 food products and many other types of products during his career as a chemurgist, only acquired three patents. His 1927 patent related to producing paints and stains from clay. Carver's process involved boiling 25 pounds of clay of a desired color, 25 pounds of commercial sulfuric acid, 25 pounds of commercial hydrochloric acid, and three pounds of iron turnings with sufficient water to make a thin paste. The resultant compound is then dried and mixed with linseed oil or its equivalent as a pigment to provide a paint. Many different colors of fillers and stains were produced by Carver's technique.

Black Inventors: From Africa to America (1995), pp. 107, 139-141; *Blacks in Science and Medicine* (1990), pp. 50-51; *Created Equal* (1993), pp. 75-83; *Index of Patents* (1925), p. 115, (1927), p. 108

1928 • Marjorie Stewart Joyner (1896-1994) was the first African American inventor to patent a permanent hair-waving machine in 1928. Joyner was working for the famed Madame C. J. Walker when she invented her waving machine and assigned the patent to Walker's company. Joyner enrolled in the A. B. Molar Beauty School (a white-owned school) and in 1916, became its first African American graduate. She first opened her own beauty shop that catered to a white clientele, but later joined Madame C. J. Walker and remained there many years. The Smithsonian Institution, as part of its 1987 Black migration exhibit, displayed Joyner's permanent wave machine.

Beauty Classic Vol. 4, (1987), pp. 30-31, 52; *Feminine Ingenuity* (1992), pp. 297-301; *Notable Black American Women* Book II (1996), pp. 366-370; *Black Firsts* (1994), p. 274

1929 • Virginia Scharschmidt invented a safety window-cleaning device adapted to cleaning the outer side of a window without having to sit on the windowsill or lean out of the window. Her invention was patented in 1929. Her device was basically a frame over which a towel or absorbent cloth was stretched. The frame, at its opposite edges, was provided with straps or tapes, whereby the frame was moved back and forth across the window to clean it. A mop device was used to swab the outside windowpane. The device had an extended handle, eliminating the need to sit on the window sill to wash the window.

Black Inventors: From Africa to America (1995), pp. 109, 216; *Index of Patents* (1929); *Negro Year Book* (1931-1932), p. 166

1930 • Solomon Harper (1895-1980) invented an electrical hair comb that was patented in 1930. His thermostatically controlled comb operated so that the electric current to the heater was automatically cut off to prevent burning or overheating of the hair or skin of the user. Harper had several other inventions and eventually patented a series of thermostatically controlled hair combs and hot curlers. He was a member of the American Association for the Advancement of Science, which he joined in 1956.

The Black Inventor (1975), p. 91; *Creativity and Inventions* (1987), p. 66; *Index of Patents* (1930), p. 300; *Negro Year Book* (1931-1932), p. 166

1931–1932 • Benjamin F. Thornton patented two inventions, one in 1931 and the other in 1932, in the area of telephonic communications. One invention was an apparatus for automatically recording telephone messages. The other related invention was an apparatus for automatically transmitting messages over a telephone line. Thornton's devices could be attached to any telephone. He also deviced a clock to record the time of all messages.

Index of Patents (1931, 1932)

1935 • The first African American to earn a Ph.D. in agronomy was Major Franklin Spaulding (1900-1964), who took the degree in 1935 at Massachusetts State College. Spaulding earned a B.S.A. in 1925 from North Carolina State College, and then a B.S. in 1927 and M.S. in 1928 from Cornell University (New York). He taught at North Carolina State from 1928 to 1937, and from 1937 to 1945 at Prairie View State College, Tuskegee Institute (Alabama), and Langston University (Oklahoma). Spaulding joined the Tennessee A&I State College faculty in 1945, heading the agronomy department from 1946 to 1958. He became dean of the School of Agronomy and Home Economics in 1958, remaining in that post until his death in 1964.

Blacks in Science and Medicine (1990), pp. 217-8; *Journal of Blacks in Higher Education* (Spring 1997), p. 92

1937 • The carborundum method of printmaking was invented by African American artist Dox Thrash (1892-1965). Thrash pursued formal art training in 1919 at the School of the Arts Institute of Chicago. From 1935 to 1942, Thrash worked in the Graphic Arts Division of the WPA (Works Progress Administration) where he invented and developed the carborundum print technique. The Philadelphia Graphic Art Division of the WPA was the only art division of the WPA devoted entirely to the development and production of fine art prints. Carborundum is the trade name of an industrial product traditionally used to clean lithographic stones. When used on a copper plate, its hard granular crystals create an overall pitted surface. The artist then scrapes and burnishes the image on a plate so that the pitted areas will hold ink and print darker than the smooth, burnished sections, creating strong contrasts.

Bulletin (Philadelphia Museum of Art) Vol. 90 (Winter 1995), p. 12; *Philadelphia Inquirer* (April 15, 1989), p. 3C; *Negro Year Book* (1947), p. 29

1939 • Frederick McKinley Jones (1893-1961), who held over 60 patents, invented a ticket-dispensing machine that was patented in 1939. The machine was developed by Jones for ticket dispensing in movie houses. It could be operated by an unskilled person and shifted, severed, and tabulated a strip of tickets to be vended. Jones's machine virtually precluded jamming. If this did occur or if a spring should fail, the machine would continue to operate.

Black Inventors: From Africa to America (1995), p. 107; *Blacks in Science and Medicine* (1990), p. 137; *Index of Patents* (1939), p. 371; *Created Equal* (1993), pp. 149-150

1945 • Cyril Fitzgerald Atkins (1899-19??), an African American inventor, with assistance from Ulysses Simpson Brooks, patented, in 1945, a new paper-producing process for the manufacture of corrugated shipping containers from cotton stems usually left in fields after cotton harvesting.

Blacks in Science and Medicine (1990), p. 16; *Negro Year Book* (1947), p. 30

1948 • George Washington Carver (1864-1943) was the first African American scientist commemorated on a United States postage stamp when it was issued on January 15, 1948. He was a pioneer in the field of agricultural chemistry (finding new uses for agricultural products), and he used his knowledge to improve the lives of poor farmers in the American South. Carver started working at Tuskegee Institute (Alabama) in 1896 and remained there for rest of his professional life, where he established the Agricultural Experimental Station. He received many honors in his long career, including an invitational to serve on the advisory board of the National Agricultural Society in 1916. He was well-respected by Henry

Ford, who built a memorial cabin in his honor at Greenfield Village in Dearborn, Michigan.

African American Firsts (1994), p. 243; *Created Equal* (1993), p. 83; *Jet* (July 14, 1997), p. 19

1948 • An improved foot warmer, which circulated heated air into and through the bottom of a boot or shoe, was invented by Joseph A. Thompson, Jr. and patented in 1948. Thompson's technique consisted of a compartment between the inner and outer soles of a shoe, with a heat-penetrating process in the form of a catalyst such as a spongy platinum or platinum black brought into contact with alcohol vapors mixed with air, generating heat. The generated heat is circulated into and through the compartment and into the sole of the shoe to warm the foot.

Creativity and Inventions (1987), p. 69; *Index of Patents* (1948)

1953 • The first federal monument to an African American was dedicated to George Washington Carver (1864-1943) on July 14, 1953. The monument is located near Diamond, Missouri, the birthplace of Carver. He was a pioneer in the field of agricultural chemistry (finding new uses for agricultural products), and he used his knowledge to improve the lives of poor farmers in the American South. He demonstrated uses for cheap and locally avail-

GEORGE WASHINGTON
CARVER

able materials, such as swamp muck. He searched for new, cheap foods to supplement farmers' diets.

African American Firsts (1994), p. 243; *Created Equal* (1993), p. 83; *Jet* (July 14, 1997), p. 19

1956 • The first African American to earn a Ph.D. in dairy technology was Emmett Bassett (1921-), who received the degree in 1956 from Ohio State University. He had previously received a B.S. degree from Tuskegee Institute (Alabama) in 1942 and a M.S. degree from the University of Massachusetts in 1950. Bassett conducted research and taught at Columbia University (New York) from 1955 to 1967. He then worked as a senior scientist at Ortho Research Foundation for the years 1967 to 1969. Immediately following, he started teaching at the College of Medicine and Dentistry in New Jersey.

Blacks in Science and Medicine (1990), p. 21

1956 • Virgil A. Gant (1897-19??), who received a Ph.D. in pharmacology from the University of Illinois in 1938, was granted a patent in 1956 for his invention of a hair treating composition and method for setting hair. In Gant's process, hair straightening or permanent hair arrangement was achieved quickly and safely. The hair was treated with a composition containing an organic lubricant in combination with an organo-silicon polymer (polipiloxane) adapted to be set in contact with the surface of the hair.

Blacks in Science and Medicine (1990), p. 97; *Index of Patents* (1956)

1956–1987 • The first African American woman to receive five patents in the United States was Mary Beatrice Kenner, who received her first patent in 1956 and her second in 1959, both for personal hygiene devices for women. Her third patent was issued in 1976 for a carrier attachment for invalid walkers and a fourth, in 1982, for a bathroom tissue holder. Kenner's fifth patent was in 1987, for a back washer mounted on a shower wall or bathtub.

Creativity and Inventions (1987), pp. 21-22, 67; *Ebony* (February, 1990), p. 134

1958 • George Benjamin Davis Stephens (1904-) patented his invention of a cigarette holder and ashtray in 1958. Stephens's invention was a combined cigarette support and ashtray to be worn on the wrist or hand, permitting the smoker a convenient safe place to hold and locate the cigarette. The device was also a receptacle for cigarette ashes. Stephens received a B.S. degree from Hampton Institute in 1924 and his M.D. from Howard University Medical College in 1930. He began practicing as a physician in

1935. Stephens also acquired a patent in 1980 for a blank for a box structure which folded into a box or a box with a tray.

Index of Patents (1956); *Who's Who Among African Americans* (1998-1999), p. 1231; *Who's Who Among Black Americans* (1990-1991), p. 1197

1959 • Maurice William Lee Sr. was awarded a patent for an aromatic pressure cooker and smoker in 1959. Lee's cooker allowed wood smoke or other aromatic flavors to impregnate foods being cooked under pressure. It used two heating elements, one in connection with a smoke and steam generator and the other to maintain a constant temperature above the point of condensation of steam vapor at the required pressure. The cooker cooked principally by steam, and its lid had a vent opening for reasonably maintaining a constant pressure in the cooking chamber.

Black Inventors: From Africa to America (1995), p. 121; *Creativity and Inventions* (1987), p. 67; *Index of Patents* (1959), p. 551

1962 • Thomas J. Carter, an African American chemist employed by the United States Department of Commerce, Bureau of Standards, was the recipient of a patent in 1962, for his invention of a leather testing machine specifically designed for testing the water penetration of sole leather. Carter's device would bend a leather specimen in contact with water at an angle similar to that of a shoe in actual service and also provided a means whereby the water-resisting effects of various impregnating materials applied to the sole leather could be evaluated.

Blacks in Science and Medicine (1990), p. 50; *Ebony* (May 1954), p. 4; *Index of Patents* (1962)

1962 • An improvement for scouring pads by Alfred Benjamin was patented in 1962. The invention was a two-ply scouring pad made of interwoven or intermeshed stainless steel wool. One side or ply of the pad had one grade of coarseness, and the other side or ply had a different grade of coarseness. A plastic disc was placed between the two plies. Woven steel wool arms extended from the pad, and the arms formed into a loop for holding the pad on the hand of the user.

Creativity and Inventions (1987), p. 63; *Index of Patents* (1962)

1963 • Charles A. Bankhead received a patent in 1963 for an assembled composition printing process. Bankhead's invention was a new and useful method of preparing a silk screen for printing on any type of surface, such as paper, wood, plastic, or glass. His invention provided an inexpensive method of producing identical signs and posters as are presently used by churches, schools, or small businesses.

Index of Patents (1963)

1963 • Robert T. Allen invented a vertical coin counting tube that was patented in 1963. Allen experimented with several designs before patenting his tube. It had steps that hold five coins in each, and since only five coins fit in each step, the count is quick and accurate. Allen's device had sections that were filled as coins were accumulated. The coins were guided into their respective stacks by shifting to the next free step or stack area as soon as one stack was filled. These were then made available for packaging when discharged by inversion of the tube.

Black Enterprise (July, 1975), p. 35; *Index of Patents* (1963)

1966 • Leonard J. Julien's invention of a sugar cane planter was patented in 1966. His invention eliminated the need to plant cane by hand. Julien's device had a number of parallel overhead conveyors positioned above a cane cart, with each conveyor having an endless chain with a number of grabs for gripping the cane. The chains were continuously driven, and the grabs were periodically opened to receive a stalk. They closed to carry the stalk past the rear of the cart and then reopened to release the stalk and drop it in the furrow. The conveyors were mounted so that they could be progressively lowered.

Black Inventors: From Africa to America (1995), p. 242; *Index of Patents* (1966), p. 685

1968 • A stair-climbing wheelchair was developed by African American inventor Rufus J. Weaver and patented in 1968. Weaver's apparatus is used to mount stairs automatically and includes a self-propelling drive, which can, in reverse, carry the wheelchair down the staircase. The stair-climbing mechanism includes a set of rails forming a track shaped to conform alternately to risers and treads. A wheelchair housing, a driving motor, and gearing, coupled to an output drive with actuating controls, is provided. When the wheelchair unit has ascended a stairway, it can be wheeled away as normal.

Black Inventors: From Africa to America (1995), p. 126; *Blacks in Science and Medicine* (1990), p. 244; *Creativity and Inventions* (1987), p. 69; *Index of Patents* (1968), p. 1266; *Jet* (May 1, 1969), p. 51

1969 • Frank Eugene Sessoms (1947-) is a patent holder for a high-protein, fruit-flavored, fat-stabilized spread. He received the patent in 1969. Sessoms has been a physician in private practice since 1979 and a professor of family medicine at the University of Pittsburgh since 1994. Sessons earned a B.S. in 1970 at Tennessee State University and a M.D. in 1974 from Meharry Medical College.

Who's Who Among African Americans (1998-1999), p. 1338

1970 • James A. Bauer invented a coin-changer mechanism that was patented in 1970. His system was a coin-operated control circuit using binary logic register stages and adapted to register and collect nickels, dimes, and quarters. It initiated a signal on receipt of coins equal to or greater than the selected price of an item and was capable of paying out change accurately. The machine had the added advantage of a simple construction that was easily manipulated by a relatively unskilled serviceperson.

Black Inventors: From Africa to America (1995), p. 122; *Creativity and Inventions* (1987), p. 63; *Index of Patents* (1970), p. 103

1970 • Paul Brown (1917-) was granted a patent in 1970 for his invention of a spinable stringless top. The toy, first marketed by Mattel and now by Duncan, was a friction-activated spinning top that became a bestseller. The top was a gyroscope with a rotatable shaft, a flywheel or rotor secured to the shaft, bearing, and friction roller. The stringless top, with its shaft and rotor secured to it, had a moment of inertia capable of sustaining the angular momentum of the shaft for an extended period of time. The friction roller, at the projecting end section of the shaft, could be briskly rolled on a rigid surface and would revolve at a substantially greater peripheral speed. The top was made of a high impact synthetic polymer.

Created Equal (1993), p. 172; *Creativity and Inventions* (1987), p. 64; *Ebony* (October, 1998), p. 162; *Index of Patents* (1970)

1971 • Howard L. Scott received a patent in 1971 for his invention for a process of treating human, animal, and synthetic hair with a waterproofing composition. With Scott's method, synthetic fiber could be made to have the appearance of human hair and could be straightened. In order to achieve these objectives, a composition containing water-repellent agent and hardening and adhesive agent was applied to the hair. A slipping agent, such as a fluororesin, and an emollient, such as lanolin, was also preferably included.

Black Inventors: From Africa to America (1995), p. 126; *Creativity and Inventions* (1987), p. 68; *Index of Patents* (1971)

1972 • The first African American to earn a Ph.D. from Clemson University (South Carolina) was James Edward Bostic Jr. (1947-), who received the degree in 1972. He also received his B.S. in 1969 from Clemson. Bostic joined the U.S. Department of Agriculture in 1972 as a special assistant, and in 1973 was promoted to deputy secretary of agriculture, in which position he remained until 1977. He was employed from 1977 to 1981 as director of technical analysis for Riegel Text Corporation, and then with its convenience products division until 1985. Bostic served as member of the board of trustees of the U.S. Department of Agriculture Graduate School from 1976-7, and as vice chair and then chair of the South Carolina Commission on Higher Education from 1978 to 1983. Bostic was appointed to the Clemson University Board of Trustees in 1983.

Who's Who Among African Americans (1998-1999), p. 139

1973 • Gertrude E. Downing, tired of getting on her knees in order to scrub floor corners and baseboard junctions, devised an attachment for rotary floor-treatment machines. She was granted a patent for the device in 1973. Her invention was a brush or pad of wedge shape at its outer end to facilitate the cleaning or polishing of corners. The sides of the attachment diverge outwardly and rearwardly with the sides providing with a rubbing surface such as bristles, pads, etc. for cleaning bases. The attachment connected to the machine's bell-shaped housing and was detachable.

The Black Inventor (1975), p. 91; *Black Inventors: From Africa to America* (1995), pp. 213, 214; *Index of Patents* (1973), p. 462

1975 • Virgie M. Ammons was granted a patent in 1975 for a fireplace damper actuating tool she invented. Her invention opened and closed a fireplace damper and secured it, preventing fluttering due to wind. Fireplace dampers had levers to control their positions. Ammons developed a tool that could be wedged against the inner surface of the fireplace lintel to lock the damper in the closed position.

Black Inventors: From Africa to America (1995), p. 122; *Creativity and Inventions* (1987), p. 73; *Index of Patents* (1975)

1975 • A patent was granted Joseph Ausbon Thompson in 1975 for the invention of a moist/dry toilet tissue. The moist and dry sheets are conveniently arranged in the same roll or package in an alternating sequence. Dry tissues are used to dry away any moisture that may remain on the body after using a sheet of moist toilet tissue. Detergents, antiseptics, or aromatic solutions may be added to the water in the moist sheets of tissue. The design considered varied tissue size and shape configurations such as rolls, rectangular packages, round sheets, or packages.

Black Inventors: From Africa to America (1995), p. 126; *Creativity and Inventions* (1987), p. 69; *Index of Patents* (1975), p. 1932

1975 • An emergency fire escape mechanism was invented by James B. Huntley, and the device was patented in 1975. Huntley's invention was a portable, self-contained emergency fire escape mechanism for use in hotels, apartments, or office buildings. His mechanism had an anchoring bar that could be mounted on a windowsill or balcony of the building structure. The anchoring bar was connected with a lowering assembly, having a flexible cable connected to it. The cable was contained in a canister, which was provided with a harness to hold the body of the person escaping the building. The lowering assembly was constructed to controllably pay out cable from the canister.

Black Inventors: From Africa to America (1995), p. 123; *Index of Patents* (1975), p. 863; *Creativity and Inventions* (1987), p. 66

1975 • Dave Bondu invented and patented a slant golf tee in 1975. Bondu's tee is 3 inches (7.5 cm) long and resembles an inverted hollowed out cone that tapers into the usual spike-like point. Bondu and his associates, working with the DuPont Company, developed a bright red, yellow, orange, and white nylon from which to make the tee. In October 1977, he opened his company and has sold franchises in a number of states and several countries. Bondu's invention is a take-off from the first golf tee invented in 1899 by African American dentist George F. Grant of Boston, Massachusetts.

Philadelphia Tribune (April 6, 1979), pp. 13-14

1978 • Christian C. L. Reeburg received a patent, on August 14, 1978, for his invention of a grease gun rack. His invention allows an operator to use the grease gun with one hand instead of two, as previously required.

Created Equal (1993), p. 173

1978 • A patent for a portable luggage carrier was awarded in 1978 to the African American inventor Deborah Ratchford. Ratchford's carrier consists of an 8 inch (20 cm) J-shaped aluminum hook and a removable carriage with four nylon plastic wheels. Ratchford is an attendant for United Airlines and intends to produce and sell the products herself.

Philadelphia Tribune (September 12, 1978), p. 7

1978 • The first African American appointed to the position of Assistant Secretary for Administration at the U.S. Department of Agriculture (USDA) was Joan Scott Wallace (1930-) in 1978. Wallace earned an A.B. degree at Bradley University (1952), a M.S.W. degree from Columbia University (1954), and a Ph.D. degree in 1973 from Northwestern University. In July

1981 the USDA appointed Wallace as administrator of the Office of International Corporation and Development (the first African American in that position). She remained there until 1989, when she was appointed representative of the Inter-American Institute for Cooperative Agriculture (IICA) of Tacarigua, Trinidad, and Tobago. Wallace has represented the USDA in bilateral and multilateral conferences and as a consultant to more than 30 countries in Africa, Asia, Australia, Europe, and Latin America. She has also represented the USDA at various International Food and Agricultural Organizations the United States/Indo Subcommittee, World Food Council, United States/Saudi Joint Commission, among others.

Essence (November 1978), p. 56; *Notable Black American Women* (1992), pp. 1195-1197

1981 • African American horticulturist Booker T. Whatley (1915-), who became a leading expert on small scale farming, founded and edited the journal, *The Small Farm Technical Newsletter,* a kind of *Poor Richard's Almanac* for the small farmer. Whatley's main interest was the development of a program for small farms that combined the best of contemporary farming technology and generations of traditional farming experience. He convinced almost 1,000 farmholders to convert to his program. Whatley earned a B.S. in 1941 from Alabama A&M University and a Ph.D. in horticulture from Rutgers University in 1957. He taught horticulture at Southern University from 1957 to 1969 and then became professor of horticulture at Tuskegee Institute. His primary research interest there was to develop a roster of high-yield, disease-resistant crops. Whatley has a number of publications and is active in regional and national horticultural societies and organizations.

African and African American Contributions (1990), pp. 5-81; *Who's Who Among African Americans* (1998-1999), p. 1585

1982 • Jerome L. Wicks, Sr. patented several safety devices for the home, of which his major invention was a door security device patented in 1982. Wicks's device allowed a person to open a outside door and look out while still being able to resist unauthorized entry, withstanding up to 2,000 pounds of pressure on the door and bar. He also patented a door-guard for securing patio doors and a safety guard for window security. Wicks also patented an automated gasoline dispensing mechanism.

Black Inventors: From Africa to America (1995), pp. 191-193; *Index of Patents* (1982)

1982 • Godfrey A. Gayle received a Ph.D. in biological and agricultural engineering from North Carolina State University in 1982, making him the first African American to receive this degree from that institution. At the time, he was only the fifth African American to receive a Ph.D. in that discipline in the United States. Gayle received a bachelor's degree in agricultural engineering from North Carolina A&T University. He is professor of agricultural and biosystems engineering and chair of the Department of Natural Resources and Environmental Design at North Carolina A&T State University. Gayle is also the chair-elect of the North Carolina Chapter of the American Society of Agricultural Engineers (The Society for Engineering in Agricultural, Food and Biological Systems). Under Gayle's leadership, A&T, in 1991, became the only accredited agricultural engineering program at a historically African American college or university.

Resource (March 1997), p. 29, (February 1996), p. 19

1985 • African American woman inventor June Meredith Horne (1936-) had her invention for an emergency escape apparatus patented in 1985. Horne attended Kennedy King Junior College and was employed as a psychiatric technician for the Veterans Administration from 1964 to 1994. Horne's apparatus was adapted to be used with a staircase of a building in case of an emergency. The device included a slide apparatus installed at the staircase and a slide member extending at an incline over the stairs when disposed in its use position. Mounting devices fixed the slide member to the staircase, and a latching device maintained the slide member in its upright storage position in a releasable manner.

Index of Patents (1985); *Who's Who Among African Americans* (11th Edition), p. 622; *Who's Who Among Black Americans* (1990-1991), p. 613

1987 • Melvin McCoy patented his invention for a vehicle support-type backpack. McCoy's device crossed a standard back-pack and a Native American travois and was equipped with a wheel and two brakes. It allowed a male or female five feet, four inches tall or more to easily carry weight in excess of 100 pounds. His device was called the M.U.L.E. —the Multipurpose Uniaxial Litter Engineering device. McCoy felt that firefighters and military personnel, as well as walkers and hikers, benefited from his invention.

Index of Patents (1993); *Philadelphia Tribune* (June 17, 1994)

1988 • A bubble machine was invented by Phillip A. Collins, and he received a patent for it in 1988. Bubble machines found use in discos, amusement devices, and advertising. Collins's machine produced either large bubbles or small bubbles, a combination of sizes, or even bubbles of different shapes. It was operated by batteries or AC electricity. The system was safe for use by children, but was primarily designed for use in places of entertainment or in film-making.

Black Inventors: From Africa to America (1995), pp. 127, 235, 239; *Index of Patents* (1988)

1990 • Dawn Francis, an African American woman inventor, received a patent in 1990 for a fertilizer called "Way-T-Gro!" It was a single molecule compound comprised of non-toxic, all-organic compounds. Francis's fertilizer was comprised of dried, finely ground deciduous leaves, dried and powdered skim milk, and water in an amount to produce a kneadable mass. The finished product was dried and granular. It was cost-effective, readily manufactured, and did not contaminate or burn the soil and plant life. The fertilizer provided improved plant growth and improved seed and product yield.

Ebony (October, 1998), p. 162; *Index of Patents* (1990)

1990 • Sylvester James Fletcher (1934-) invented a modular-stackable front loading container, which he patented in 1990. Fletcher received a B.A. in 1956 from Virginia State University. He was employed from 1956 to 1976 as a supervisory soil scientist for the U.S. Department of Agriculture and has been self-employed since. Fletcher also has several publications in the field of agronomy and soil science.

Who's Who Among African Americans (1998-1999), p. 487

1990 • The National Inventors Hall of Fame was created in 1973, and the first two African Americans honored by election to the Hall were Percy Lavon Julian (1899-1975) and George Washington Carver (1865-1943) when selected in 1990. The National Inventors Hall of Fame was established by the National Council of Intellectual Property Law Associations and the U. S. Patent and Trademark Office. The purpose of the National Inventors Hall of Fame is to honor the individuals who conceived the great technological advances and to foster continued innovative progress.

Notable Black American Scientists (1999), p. 183

1992 • Billie J. Becoat invented a dual-wheel driven bicycle that was patented in 1992. Becoat developed his concept over a six-year period. It has an extra ring gear on the rear wheel and a sheathed rotating cable that connects to another gear on the front wheel. By shifting power from the back wheel to the front wheel, the Becoat bicycle provides better traction and handling on slippery surfaces and rough terrain. The bicycle makes for easier pedaling on hills and easier steering on turns because the front wheel does not slide on sharp turns. Becoat's invention is applicable to multispeed and single speed bicycles.

Black Enterprise (November 1993), pp. 68-70, 73, 75; *Ebony* (June 1993), pp. 69-70, 72-73; *Emerge* (June 1992), p. 18; *Index of Patents* (1992), p. 237

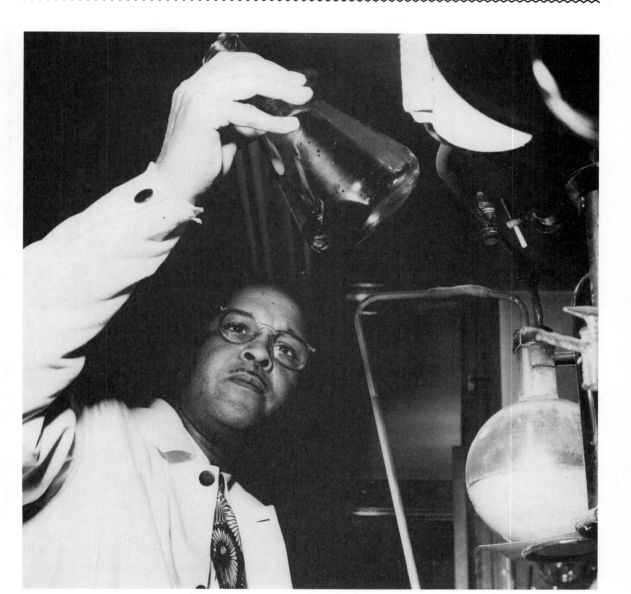

1993 • The appointment of Alphonso Michael Espy (1953-) as Secretary of the U.S. Department of Agriculture in 1993 marked the first time an African American held that office. Espy was a member of the U.S. House of Representatives prior to his selection as Secretary. Espy received a B.A. degree from Howard University in 1975 and a J.D. from Santa Clara School of Law in 1978. He practiced law and managed Central Mississippi Legal

PERCY LAVON JULIAN

ALPHONSO
MICHEAL ESPY

Services until 1980, when he became assistant secretary of state for public lands, a division of the Mississippi State Secretary's Office. In 1984 he became assistant attorney general for consumer protection. The Agriculture Department is the country's fourth largest with 120,000 employees and a $62 billion budget.

African America: Portrait of a People (1994), p. 148; *Jet* (February 1, 1993), pp. 8-9.

1998 • Ronald Demon was granted a patent in 1998 for his invention of a shoe with an adjustable support pattern, making it more comfortable for the wearer. Demon was a senior electrical engineer and computer science major at the Massachusetts Institute of Technology. He started working on his idea while at Palmetto High School in Miami, Florida, in 1993. He developed a software program and eventually a prototype of the shoe. Demon's shoe was designed with sensors to make adjustments, regulating the flow of a fluid from strategically placed bladders to adjust the cushion in a number of zones beneath the user's foot.

Index of Patents (1998); *Jet* (November 23, 1998), p. 32

ALLIED HEALTH

1706 • The slave Onesimus, owned by the Puritan leader Cotton Mather, in 1706 first revealed to his master the concept of inoculation as a preventative against the contraction of smallpox. Onesimus had himself been inoculated against smallpox, one of several medical practices derived from African medical tradition. Mather tried to encourage New Englanders to utilize the inoculation procedure against smallpox and published letters and treatises promoting it in 1721. However, the practice of inoculation was not accepted in the United States until 1777, when George Washington issued orders that all continental army troops be inoculated.

Blacks in Science and Medicine (1990), p. 182; *Black Firsts* (1994), p. 350; *The Real McCoy* (1989), pp. 24-5

1846 • David Ruggles (1810-1849), who did not attend medical school, was the first African American to set up a facility for hydropathic treatment (water therapy) in the United States, which he did in Northampton, Massachusetts in 1846. Ruggles had earlier suffered from a serious illness which made him partially blind. While recuperating, he learned of the successful treatment of disease through hydrotherapy. After an 18-month natural regimen of water, diet, and rest, he returned to good health with improved vision. He then constructed his own hydropathic facility with 20 treatment rooms and began to treat others. His program had a high degree of success, which was reported in newspapers and journals. Some of his successes included Sojourner Truth and William Lloyd Garrison. Ruggles's practice was flourishing when he took ill again and died in 1849.

African American Breakthroughs (1995), pp. 215-216; *Dictionary of Black Culture* (1973), p. 386; *Journal of the National Medical Association* (January 1957), pp. 67-72, (March 1957), pp. 130-134

1858 • The first African American homeopathic practitioner in the United States was Robert Boyd Leach (1822-1863). He established his practice in Cleveland in 1858 after completing a two-year course of study at the Western Homeopathic College in Cleveland (Ohio). Leach was considered a man of high reputation, both professionally and socially, and was an active advocate of civil rights at both local and state levels.

Bulletin of the History of Medicine Vol. 17, (January, 1945), p. 62; *Dictionary of American Negro Biography* (1982), p. 388

1870 • The first degree awarded by Howard University Medical School (Washington, D.C.) to an African American student, James T. Wormley on March 3, 1870, was the Pharm.D. (Doctor of Pharmacy). The Howard University Medical School was established in 1868, and its first five M.D. graduates were awarded degrees in 1871.

African-American Medical Pioneers (1994), p. 9

1892 • Alonzo C. McClennan (1855-??) opened the first African American-owned pharmacy in Charleston, South Carolina, People's Pharmacy, in 1892. McClennan earned his M.D. in 1880 at Howard University, opened a medical practice in Augusta, Georgia, and moved to Charleston in 1884.

Black Women in White (1989), p. 15; *Journal of the National Medical Association, Volume 33* (1941), pp. 15-16

1896 • Jonah Emanuel (1858-19??), who was a chiropodist practicing in New York City, was only African American charter member, in 1896, of the New York State Pedic Society. A former farm hand from Georgia, Emanuel apprenticed to a chiropodist, learned the profession, and eventually bought out the business.

Blacks in Science and Medicine (1990), p. 85; *Who's Who in Colored America* (1933-1937), p. 175, (1938-1940), p. 175

1907 • Clara Frye (1872-19??), who was a practicing nurse in Tampa, Florida, received a patent in 1907 for her invention of a combination bed and bedpan. She studied nursing in Chicago and moved to Florida, with her husband, in 1900. Leading physicians in Tampa and Hot Springs, Arkansas, endorsed her idea. Frye converted her home to a makeshift hospital, and by 1915 she added another wing to the house. In 1930, a hospital was built for African Americans on the banks of the Hillsborough River in West Tampa, and was named for Clara Frye.

Black Inventors: From Africa to America (1995), pp. 209-211

1916 • The first African American woman to graduate from the University of Pittsburgh School of Pharmacy (Pennsylvania), in 1916, was Ella Phillips Stewart (1893-1987). Stewart graduated from Stover College, in West Virginia, in 1910. After she received her Ph.C., she opened a pharmacy in Pittsburgh, which she operated from 1918 to 1920. After moving to Ohio, Stewart owned and operated the first African American-owned pharmacy in Toledo, which was in operation from 1922 to 1945. Stewart utilized her talents as a businessperson, organizer, editor, and community worker throughout her life on a local, national, and international level. She also received appointments to federal and international committees in recognition of her work as a community activist.

Blacks in Science and Medicine (1990), p. 222; *Contributions of Black Women to America* (1982), p. 398; *Notable Black American Women* (1992), pp. 1079-1083; *Philadelphia Tribune* (February 18, 1983)

1920 • Emily C. Charlton (1882-19??) was the first African American woman to graduate from the First Institute of Podiatry in 1920. Charlton had studied at the College of the City of New York prior to her attending the Institute of Podiatry. She also served as vice president and secretary of the New York County Pedic Society.

Blacks in Science and Medicine (1990), p. 53; *Who's Who in Colored America* (1941-1944), pp. 115, 117

1932 • Paul E. Johnson developed improvements in therapeutic lamps for the treatment of diseases. The application for his invention was filed in 1927, and a patent was granted in 1932. The apparatus contained a reflecting chamber that was curved and had a telescoping mast mounted on a spider arm so that the lamp's position could be adjusted. A resistance element that cut down the amount of current necessary to produce a good arc was incorporated. The element transformed electrical energy into heat and generated infrared rays.

Blacks in Science: Astrophysicist to Zoologist (1977), p. 90; *Black Inventors: From Africa to America* (1995), pp. 103, 108; *Index of Patents* (1932), p. 451; *Negro Year Book* (1931-1932), p. 166; *Negro Year Book* (1947), p. 27

1936 • Rose Marie Pegues-Perkins (1913-1992), who was a registered nurse and a graduate of the Kansas City General Hospital No. 2 School of Nursing, was the first African American x-ray technician registered by the ARRT. Pegues-Perkins was not allowed, after successfully completing training under the famous radiologist William E. Allen at the St. Mary's Infirmary School of X-ray Technology in St. Louis, to take the examination due to her race. Several months later, she was allowed to take the certification examination, which she passed without difficulty. Pegues-Perkins completed a 41-year career as an x-ray technologist and in 1940, was the first

African American elected president of the Mound City (St. Louis) Society of X-Ray Technicians.

A Centennial History of African Americans in Radiology (1996), pp. 7-8, 111

1940 • Jesse O. Thomas (1883-1972), when he joined the staff of the American National Red Cross, was the first African American to be employed by the organization in a professional and policy-making position. Thomas earned a B.A. at Tuskegee Institute in 1911 and from 1919 to 1920 and in 1923 did postgraduate study at the New York School for Social Work. He was employed by the National Urban League in 1919, where he remained until 1940. While with the League, Thomas organized several branches, including those in Tampa, Miami, Little Rock, Richmond, Atlanta, and New Orleans. He also completed a number of surveys on African American living conditions in the urban South. Thomas helped organize the Atlanta University School of Social Work.

Encyclopedia of Black America (1981), p. 816; *Black Firsts* (1994), p. 341

1947 • The first African American to receive a Ph.D. in pharmacy was Roy Clifford Darlington (1908-), who received the degree in 1947 from Ohio State University. He had also received a B.S. (1941) and M.S. (1943) from Ohio State. Darlington taught at Howard University, became a professor of pharmacy in 1949, served as the pharmacy department chairman, then as associate dean from 1973 to 1976. He was elected chair of the *Journal of the National Pharmaceutical Association* editorial board and contributed to the widely used pharmaceutical reference text *Handbook of Non-Prescription Drugs.*

Blacks in Science and Medicine (1990), p. 68; *Encyclopedia of Black America* (1981), pp. 301-302.

1949 • Jane Hinton (1920-), along with Alfreda Webb, was one of the first two African American women to receive the doctor of veterinary medicine degree, in 1949. Hinton received her D.V.M. degree from the University of Pennsylvania. After graduation, she returned to her home in Canton, Massachusetts and was employed as a small animal practitioner in Framingham, Massachusetts. Hinton was the daughter of William Augustus Hinton, the famed researcher who developed the accurate serological test for syphilis known as the Hinton test. Jane Hinton also worked as a federal government inspector in Framingham and performed regulatory veterinary work.

African American Women: A Biographical Dictionary (1993), pp. 250-251

1949 • Alfreda Johnson Webb (1923-), an anatomist, was one of the first two African American women to earn a doctor of veterinary medicine degree. Webb received her degree from Tuskegee Institute Veterinary School in 1949, while Jane Hinton received the D.V.M. from the University of Pennsylvania the same year. Webb earned a B.S. degree from Tuskegee Institute in 1943 and a M.S. degree from Michigan State University in 1951. She returned to Tuskegee Institute as an instructor in 1951, and then became an associate professor of anatomy, remaining there until 1959. At that time, she joined the faculty at North Carolina A&T College as professor of biology until 1978, when she became professor of laboratory animal science. Her research areas of interest are histology, embryology, and cytology. Webb was an active member of the American Association of Veterinary Anatomists, the American Veterinary Medical Association, and Sigma Xi.

African American Women: A Biographical Directory (1993), p. 551-552; *Ebony* (August, 1949), p. 42

1951 • Etnah R. Boutte was the only woman of the first three African Americans elected to the Board of Directors of the New York City Cancer Commission in 1951. Boutte was a pharmacist at the time. The other two African Americans elected to the board were John E. Moseley and Louis T. Wright. The New York City Cancer Commission, at the time, was a division of the American Cancer Society.

Negro Year Book (1952), p. 371

1951 • Bessie Virginia Griffin was granted a patent in 1951 for her invention of a device for supporting receptacles on the chest or neck of a user in a prone position. The device, useful for invalids and convalescents, consisted of a base, hanging bar, and receptacle. The hanging bar had one end that was hooked and fit comfortably around the neck of the user while the other end of the hang bar was attached to the base. The hanging bar was adjustable in length and had a holder for a glass, cup, or other container to hold liquids that were consumed by a straw, depending on the physical capability of the patient. The holder was safe, steady, and comfortable.

Black Inventors: From Africa to America (1995), pp. 121, 214; *Index of Patents* (1951)

1953 • The first African American elected president of the National Health Council was Albert Walter Dent (1904-), who assumed the post in 1953. Dent received a B.A. from Morehouse College (Georgia) in 1926. He became president of Dillard University (Louisiana) and director of the National Tuberculosis and Respiratory Disease Association. In 1969, he became the first African American to receive an honorary degree from Tulane University (Louisiana).

Encyclopedia of Black America (1981), p. 307; *Famous First Facts About Negroes* (1972), p. 60; *Timelines of African-American History* (1994), p. 222

1960 • The first African American appointed to the District of Columbia Pharmacy Board was Henry R. Peters, who was selected in 1960. Peters has served as vice president and president, and served on the executive committee of the National Pharmaceutical Association. He was also a past president of the Washington Pharmaceutical Association.

Blacks in Science and Medicine (1990), p. 189; *Jet* (September 8, 1960), p. 50, (August 23, 1962), p. 38

1960 • Viola Gambrill Lewis (1939-) was the first African American woman appointed to the faculty post as research assistant in the psychohormonal unit of the Johns Hopkins University School of Medicine. Lewis received her B.S. from Morgan State College in 1959 and a M.A. from Loyola College in 1978. She is currently an assistant professor of medical psychology at the Johns Hopkins Medical Institute.

Journal of Blacks in Higher Education (Winter 1998/1999), No. 22, p. 103; *Who's Who Among African Americans* (1998-1999), p. 925

1961 • Raleigh H. Allen was the first African American licensed to practice veterinary medicine in the state of Alabama in 1961, after passing a three-day examination. He was also the first African American to pass the test. Allen currently practices in Rolla, North Dakota.

Blacks in Science and Medicine (1990), p. 8; *Jet* (November 9, 1961), p. 18

1962 • C. Kermit Phelps (1908-) became the first African American to teach at the department of psychology at the University of Kansas, serving as an assistant professor of psychology from 1962 to 1965. Phelps was best known for developing a test for detecting mild cortical lesions or other brain pathology. He received an A.B. in 1933, M.A. in 1949, and Ph.D. in 1953, all from the University of Kansas. He began work as a psychologist in 1949 at the Veteran's Administration in Topeka, Kansas. In 1952, he took up practice in Kansas City. He had an active academic career, teaching from 1962 to 1978 at Avila College (Missouri), University of Kansas, and Kansas University Medical Center. Phelps published and presented scientific papers, both nationally and internationally, and received several honorary degrees.

The Story of Kappa Alpha Psi (1967), p. 250; *Who's Who Among African Americans* (1998-1999), p. 1187; *Who's Who Among Black Americans* (1990-1991), pp. 1004-5

1964 • The U. S. Veterans Administration's first long-range program on geographic epidemiology was initiated in 1964 under the direction of African American Andrew Z. Keller. The purpose of such a study was to examine the geographic pattern of disease and relationships between diseases. Keller was a graduate of Morehouse College, Harvard School of Dental Medicine, and Johns Hopkins University.

Jet (May 28, 1964), p. 23

1964 • Rogers W. Griffin, an African American podiatrist, was the first to be named "Foot Specialist of the Year" by the American Association of Foot Specialists in 1964. Griffin received his formal degrees from New York's School of Chiropody and Long Island University and was vice president of Foot Clinics in New York City.

Jet (July 2, 1964), p. 53

1965 • Charles E. Burbridge (1910-), who was superintendent of Washington, D.C.'s Freedmen's Hospital, was the first African American elected regent to the American College of Hospital Administration. Burbridge, who earned a Ph.D. in 1950 in hospital administration from the University of Iowa, started as assistant superintendent at Freedmen's Hospital in 1942 and became its first non-medical chief superintendent in 1948.

Jet (June 10, 1965), p. 42

1968 • In 1968 Louis B. Levy (1934-) became the first African American certified in radiologic physics by the American Board of Radiology. Levy received his Ph.D. from the University of Texas in 1974 and joined the U.S. Army, where he achieved the rank of colonel. After retiring from the army, he went into private practice in San Antonio, Texas.

A Centennial History of African Americans in Radiology (1996), p. 114

1969 • Royce T. Osborne was the first African American radiologist to become president of the American Society of Radiologic Technologists. He was elected to the office in June 1968 and installed in July 1969. Prior to his election, he had served the Society as both Secretary-Treasurer and Vice-President. Osborne was also the first African American elected President of the New Orleans Society of Radiologic Technologists in 1968. Osborne was also a member of the Louisiana Society of Radiologic Technologists. He was, in 1981, the first African American radiologist to be named president of American Hospital Radiology Administrators, Inc. Osborne authored the text *Professional Approach to Radiology Administration* (Thomas, 1980).

A Centennial History of African-Americans in Radiology (1996), p. 9

1969 • The District of Columbia appointed its first African American commissioner of public health in 1969, when Raymond Linwood Standard

(1925-1990) was selected for the position. Standard earned a B.S. in 1948 and M.D. in 1952 from Howard University (Washington, D.C.). He also was awarded the M.P.H. in 1967 from Johns Hopkins University (Maryland) School of Hygiene and Public Health. Standard was clinical director of external medicine from 1956 to 1960 at Provident Hospital, then chief of clinical services from 1960 to 1966 at the Northwest Central Clinic in Washington, D.C. He served as the District of Columbia's chief of the bureau of chronic disease control from 1968-9, and then assumed the post of commissioner of public health until 1980. In 1969, Standard also became clinical associate professor at the Howard University, Georgetown, and George Washington Medical Schools.

African American Medical Pioneers (1994), p. 175; *Who's Who Among Black Americans* (1990-1991), pp. 1193-4

1970 • A urinalysis machine for handling several urine specimens for physical and chemical analysis was patented by African American inventor Dewey S.C. Sanderson in 1970. Sanderson's system provides an apparatus for automatically and simultaneously processing a number of urine samples for purposes of conducting physical analyses for color, appearance, specific gravity, and microscopic examinations. The machine also detects the levels of pH, albumin (protein) content, sugar, acetone, and blood in the samples.

Creativity and Inventions (1987), p. 68; *Index of Patents* (1970), p. 1335

1971 • African American pharmacologist Ira Charles Robinson (1940-) patented a sustained-release pharmaceutical tablet in 1971. Robinson's tablet included: 1) a medicament; 2) a hydrophobic dissolution retardant; 3) an acid-insoluble release agent; and 4) a water soluble or dispersible binder. Robinson was professor of pharmacology at Howard University. He received a B.S. from Florida A&M University in 1961 and a Ph.D. from the University of Florida in 1966. He was a registered pharmacist in Florida and Alabama. He worked as a pharmacist manufacturer from 1963 to 1966, at which time he began employment at the Medical Products Research and Development Division of Pfizer, Inc. and remained there until 1969. Robinson served as professor and dean at Florida A&M from 1969 to 1973 and then dean at Howard University until 1976. Robinson served as executive director of the National Pharmaceutical Foundation, Inc. and has been a professor at Howard University since 1973.

Index of Patents (1971); *Who's Who Among African Americans* (1997), p. 1282; *Who's Who Among Black Americans* (1990-1991), p. 1086

1972 • Agricultural scientist Ferdinand D. Wharton Jr. patented, in 1972, a medical treatment of diarrhea. His treatment was for gastroenteritis diarrhea syndrome in animals, and was composed of polyelectrolyte polymers. Wharton earned a B.S. in agricultural education in 1939 from North Carolina A&T College and a M.S. in poultry nutrition from the University of Connecticut in 1948. He was a college lecturer from 1940 to 1943, and then head of the poultry department of the Avon Training School from 1944 to 1946. Wharton joined the Monsanto Company as a senior project manager in 1964 and was employed there until 1977. He then joined Continental Diversified Industries in 1977 and remained there until 1985. Wharton is active in many scientific and technical organizations and has authored or co-authored 45 scientific publications.

Index of Patents (1972), p. 2107; *Who's Who Among African Americans* (1998-1999), p. 1585; *Who's Who Among Black Americans* (1990-1991), p. 1333

1973 • Albert E. Hopkins (1928-) in 1973, was the first African American appointed a member of the Texas State Board of Pharmacy, where he served until 1992. Hopkins received a B.S. in pharmacy in 1949 from Xavier University. He served as a chief pharmacist in the United States Army and after the military, started his own pharmacy business. Hopkins was active in local, regional, state, and national pharmaceutical associations.

Jet (August 24, 1992), p. 13; *Who's Who Among Black Americans* (1992-1993), p. 680; *Who's Who Among African Americans* (1998-1999), p. 716

1973 • The first woman veterinarian employed by the Los Angles Zoo, the third largest zoo in the United States, was Rosalie A. Reed (1945-). The appointment made her the first woman veterinarian at a major American zoo. Reed graduated from Tuskegee Institute in 1972, passed the written and oral examinations, and was hired in 1973. The Los Angeles Zoo had over 3,000 mammals, birds and reptiles. Reed's daily responsibilities included maintaining good health among the zoo animals, performing surgery, and quarantining and examining new arrivals.

African American Women: A Biographical Dictionary (1993), pp. 417-418; *Ebony* (March, 1974), p. 64; *Sepia* (October, 1973), p. 36-41

1975 • Winton Dennis Jones earned patents for anti-ulcer medications and cardiotonics (used in heart medications) in 1975. Jones earned a B.S. in pharmacology in 1963 and a M.S. in pharmacological chemistry in 1966 from Butler University. He then earned a Ph.D. in medicinal chemistry in 1970 from the University of Kansas, after which he became employed by Merrell Dow Research Institute, a subsidiary of Dow Chemical. So far, Jones has acquired 29 patents in a variety of medical products and processes. He is active in local and national professional chemistry organizations, was a member of the board of directors of the American Chemical Society in 1979, and was a charter member of the National Organization of Black Chemists and Chemical Engineers, Cincinnati Chapter.

Black Enterprise (February 1985), pp. 51-52; *Who's Who Among Black Americans* (1990-1991), p. 717; *Who's Who Among African Americans* (1998-1999), p. 842

1976 • The first African American appointed to the Louisiana Board of Pharmacy was James Davis Wilson (1937-), who was made a member in 1976. Wilson received a B.S. in 1963 from Xavier University (Louisiana) College of Pharmacy. He was pharmacist and manager of Walgreens Drug Store from 1963 to 1969 in New Orleans. Wilson then formed Wilson Surgical Supplies, the first African-American-owned surgical supply company in New Orleans.

Who's Who Among Black Americans (1990-1991), p. 1387; *Who's Who Among African Americans* (1998-1999), p. 1646

1977 • A disposable syringe invented by Calvin R. Mapp was patented in 1977. The invention was also collapsible for ease of transport. The syringe consisted of a collapsible bag descending from a hook, which was attached to an integral ring. The bag may be filled with a liquid and hung from a convenient support and a flexible hose adapted to be connected to a side wall of the bag. Mapp earned a B.A. from Morris Brown College and a L.L.B. from Howard University. He holds four patents, is an author, and is currently a retired court judge of Dade County, Florida.

Index of Patents (1977), p. 1097; *Who's Who Among African Americans* (1998-1999), p. 965

1979 • The first woman and first African American selected to head the American Pharmaceutical Association was Mary Munson Runge, when she was elected in 1979. The Association was comprised of 60,000 pharmacists and students throughout the United States. Runge was a practicing pharmacist from Oakland, California. She was also one of the first African American women to serve as president and board chair of a major national professional medical association. Runge was speaker of the Association's House of Delegates from 1977 to 1978 and is an Association trustee.

Jet (August 30, 1979), p. 6

1979 • The first African American selected Chair of the Board of Governors of the American National Red Cross was Jerome Heartwell Holland (1916-1985), when he was appointed in 1979. Holland received a B.S. in 1939 and M.S. in 1941, both from Cornell University, where he was also an All-American football player for two years. He earned a Ph.D. in 1950 from the University of Pennsylvania. Holland's professional career included the presidency of Delaware State College from 1953 to 1960 and of Hampton Institute from 1960 to 1970. He was appointed U. S. Ambassador to Sweden from 1970 to 1972, when he resigned to become the first African American director of the American Stock Exchange.

Encyclopedia of Black America (1981), p. 443; *Jet* (May 3, 1979), p. 28, (May 6, 1985), p. 54

1982 • The first African American elected a fellow of the American Occupational Therapy Association was William Lofton, Jr. when he was selected in 1982. Lofton was director of occupational therapy at Fitzsimons Army Medical Center in Colorado.

Black Firsts (1994), p. 297; *Jet* (August 16, 1982), p. 21

1982 • Sally Thimms-Kelly, a licensed occupational therapist, and her husband Alfred B. Kelly III own and operate Kelly Rehabilitation Service Center. They patented, in 1982, two health-related products, the Surefit and Versaport wrist support braces for carpal tunnel syndrome sufferers. They started Kelly Manufacturing in 1991 in order to manufacture the wrist supports themselves. Two major corporations, Keebler Company and General Electric, have bought wrist braces from the Kellys.

Black Enterprise (July 1994), p. 32

1983 • The first African American academic dean at San Diego State University was Peter A. Dual (1946-), who was appointed to the position of Dean of College Health and Human Services in 1983. He remained in that position until 1993. Dual received an A.A. degree in 1966 from Lake Michigan College, a B.S. degree in 1969 and M.A. in 1971 from Western Michigan University, a Ph.D. in 1973 from Michigan State University, and a M.P.H. in 1975 from the University of Texas. Dual was assistant professor of health behavior from 1975 to 1980 at the University of Michigan and then, in 1980, became dean of health and human services and professor of health administration at Eastern Michigan University until 1982. He is currently vice president for academic affairs at California Polytechnic Institute in Pomona, California.

Who's Who Among African Americans (1998-1999), p. 363

1984 • Neville A. Baron invented, and then patented in 1984, an apparatus and process for recurving the cornea of the eye. Previously, recurving the cornea by a surgical procedure, called radial keratotomy, was available, but the procedure was difficult to control precisely. Baron's apparatus for cornea recurving disposed light-absorbing color bodies in a cornea. A laser vaporized the targeted color bodies according to a predetermined design, and recurving scars were generated in the cornea in a predetermined design.

Black Inventors: From Africa to America (1995), p. 128; *Index of Patents* (1984)

1985 • Pennsylvania State University College of Health, Physical Education and Recreation hired its first African American woman faculty member to have earned a Ph.D. in exercise physiology and cardiac rehabilitation in 1985, when Barbee Myers was appointed to the faculty. Myers, who earned her doctorate at the University of Tennessee at Knoxville, was the first African American woman to receive a Ph.D. in exercise physiology and cardiac rehabilitation. Myers earned her undergraduate and master's degrees in exercise science at Wake Forest University. She is a member of the American College of Sports Medicine and the American Alliance for Health, Physical Education, Recreation, and Dance.

Philadelphia Tribune (October 22, 1985), p. 5B

1986 • Wilbert Murdock, an African American inventor, acquired a patent in 1986 for a knee alignment monitoring device. Murdock's knee alignment device employs a number of sensors that are positioned at various areas of a wearer's knee. The device monitors the knee and indicates if the knee joint was aligned or if it was being subjected to extreme forces which could result in an injury. Murdock received a degree from Polytechnic University. He headed his own company, Motintronics for Science, founded to develop and manufacture computer-based sports simulators and biomechanical analysis instruments that could be used for training and physical rehabilitation. Murdock also developed a computerized device to help golfers improve their swing and a computerized shadow boxing system.

Index of Patents (1986); *New York Times* (March 19, 1992)

1987 • Deborah B. Prothrow-Stith (1954-) was the first woman—and also the youngest person—ever appointed Commissioner of Public Health for the state of Massachusetts. She served in that position from 1987 to 1989. Prothrow-Stith established the first state office of violence prevention and expanded treatment programs on acquired immunodeficiency syndrome (AIDS), drug rehabilitation, and other urban health issues. Prothrow-Stith received her M.D. from Harvard University in 1979, and in 1982, became a diplomat in internal medicine. When she interned at Boston

City Hospital, she was horrified by the many young victims of violence she saw. This eventually led her to publish, in 1991, the text, *Deadly Consequences,* which was the first book for the general public presenting a public health perspective on violence. Prothrow-Stith was the Secretary of Health and Human Service Award recipient in 1989. She has also received three honorary doctoral degrees from various universities.

DEBORAH
PROTHROW-STITH

Notable Black American Women Book II, (1996), pp. 530-532; *African-American Medical Pioneers* (1994), pp. 103-105, 133; *Journal of the National Medical Association* (1993), Vol. 85, pp. 790-791

1988 • The first African American president of the American Speech-Language-Hearing Association was Sandra Cavanaugh Holley (1943-), who was elected to the position in 1988. Holley received her A.B. degree in 1965 and an A.M. degree in 1966, both from George Washington University, as well as a Ph.D. from the University of Connecticut in 1979. She was a speech pathologist from 1966 to 1970 for the Rehabilitation Center of Eastern Fairfield County (Connecticut) and, from 1970, a professor of speech/language pathology at Southern Connecticut State University. She was vice president for administration of the American Speech-Language-Hearing Association from 1983 to 1985 and has been active in several local and national professional organizations.

Jet (December 19, 1988), p. 22; *Who's Who Among Black Americans* (1992-1993), p. 670; *Who's Who Among African-Americans* (1998-1999), p. 705

1989 • Roscoe Michael Moore, Jr. (1944-) was the first African American to serve as chief veterinary officer in the United States Public Health Service, which he joined in 1989. He earned a B.S. in 1968 and a D.V.M. in 1969 from Tuskegee University (Alabama). He also earned a M.P.H. in 1970 from the University of Michigan, and a M.H.S. in 1972 and a Ph.D. in 1985 from Johns Hopkins University. Moore was a veterinarian for the National Institute for Health from 1970 to 1971, epidemic intelligence officer for the Center of Disease Control from 1971 to 1973, senior veterinarian for the Center for Veterinarian Medicine from 1973 to 1974, and senior epidemiologist for the National Institute for Occupational Safety and Health from 1974 to 1981. Moore was chief veterinary medical officer for the Public Health Service from 1989 to 1993 and became associate director of the Office of International and Refugee Health of the Public Health Service in 1992. He is also a fellow of the American College of Epidemiology.

Jet (October 30, 1989), p. 29; *Who's Who Among Black Americans* (1992-1993), p. 1018; *Who's Who Among African Americans* (1998-1999), p. 1078

1989 • African American physician Henry Scott patented his invention for a spinal traction and support unit for use while seated in 1989. Scott's device is a sedentary traction and support unit for supporting the lumbosacral spine, and is comprised of a girdle with a U-shaped frame secured to it. The unit provides relief to patients while they are sitting in a chair or a vehicle seat.

Howard University Alumni News (April, 1988), p. 16; *Index of Patents* (1989)

1990 • The first African American to receive a Ph.D. from the University of Arkansas, College of Medicine was George Blevins, Jr. (1949-), who was awarded the degree in 1990. Blevins earned his B.S. in 1986 from the University of Arkansas.

African American Medical Pioneers (1994), p. 184

ZORA BROWN

1991 • Zora Kramer Brown (1949-) was the first African American female to be appointed to the National Cancer Advisory Board. She was appointed for the period 1991 to 1998. Brown received a B.S. degree in 1969 from Oklahoma State University and worked in industry upon graduation from 1969 to 1976. She then worked in the federal government administration from 1976 to 1986. Brown joined the Broadcast Capital Fund, Inc. as public affairs director in 1989 and in 1995, became the Fund's vice president and chief operating officer. Brown has been an active member of local and national breast cancer-related boards and commissions since 1989.

Who's Who Among African Americans (1998-1999), p. 165

1992 • Robert M. Williams developed a method and apparatus for disinfecting contaminated medical supplies that was patented in 1992. Williams's invention was ideally suited for disinfecting a large number of disposable items, including syringes, garments, hemostats, and speculums. The device had a cavity for holding the items to be disinfected. The cavity was formed by a wall of sheet material, which was impervious to liquids and gases. The device had an opening by which the items were inserted into the cavity and also contained a dispensing conduit for introduction of the disinfectant solution. A sealing technique closed the cavity. The disinfectant solution flowed into the cavity, and the disinfectant solution and its vapors disinfected the contaminated objects in the device.

Black Inventors: From Africa to America (1995), p. 235; *Index of Patents* (1992)

1992 • Margaret M. Patterson-Townsend (1951-) was the first African American woman to successfully own and operate a sleep disorder clinic. Patterson studied business administration at Bakers Business College, which she finished in 1987. She then studied health care administration and polepomnography at the University of Michigan Medical Center. She was assistant coordinator there from 1991 to 1992 before setting up her clinic in 1992 in Flint, Michigan.

Who's Who Among African Americans (1998-1999), pp. 1162-63

1993 • Winton Dennis Jones (1941-), an African American chemist, patented three chemicals used in the treatments of cancer and heart disease in 1993. Jones joined the staff of Merrill Dow Research Institute, a subsidiary of Dow Chemical Corporation, in 1970. He has done research in organic medicinal chemistry and helds an extensive number of patents related to medical products and processes, including anti-ulcer medications and cardiotonics (utilized in heart medication). Jones earned a B.S. degree in pharmacy from Butler University in 1963 and then a Ph.D in organic medicinal chemistry in 1970 from the University of Kansas. Jones's 1993 patents involved specialized chemicals, one used in the treatment of multi-drug resistant tumors and the other useful in treating cardiac failure.

Black Enterprise (February, 1985), pp. 51-52; *Index of Patents* (1993); *Who's Who Among African Americans* (1998-1999), p. 842

1993 • The first African American to head the Dallas-based American Heart Association (AHA), when selected in 1993, was Clyde Johnson. Johnson oversaw the AHA business operations with a budget of 300 million dollars. He had volunteered for the AHA for over 20 years and had also served as chairman of the board of its Louisiana affiliate.

Philadelphia Tribune (June 29, 1993), p. 8B

1993 • Beverly Parson, when named the National Program Director of the Year in 1993 by the Arthritis Foundation, was the first African American awarded the honor. She is director of programs and services for the Arthritis Foundation, Eastern Missouri Chapter in Saint Louis.

Jet (September 6, 1993), p. 20

1993 • Winton D. Jones (1941-) an African American research chemist for Merrell Dow Pharmaceuticals in Cincinnati, Ohio, has a number of patents in a range of medical products and processes. One of Jones's patents, issued in 1993, relates to pyridyloxazole-2-ones, which are useful in the treatment of multi-drug resistant tumors. The pyridyloxazole-2-ones act to prevent drug resistance, allowing conventional chemotherapeutic agents to kill tumor cells. Jones earned a B.S. in pharmacy in 1963 and a M.S. in pharmacological chemistry in 1966, both from Butler University, and a Ph.D. in medical chemistry in 1970 from the University of Kansas. Jones has been a senior research chemist at Dow since 1970. He has a number of publications in scientific literature relating to drug chemistry.

Black Enterprise (February 1985), pp. 51-52; *Index of Patents* (1993), p. 1335, 2846; *Who's Who Among African Americans* (1998-1999), p. 842; *Who's Who Among Black Americans* (1990-1991), p. 717

1993 • Frances Christian Gaskin (1936-), a nurse and college professor, formed her own company, Frances Christian Gaskin, and has obtained two patents. Her 1993 patent is a melanin-based solution that can be applied to the skin or hair. It acts as a sunscreen. Her 1991 patent is for a melanin-based composition that when applied to the hair and scalp strengthens the hair. Gaskin received a nursing diploma from Fordham Hospital School of Nursing in 1957, a B.S. in 1962 from Hunter College, and a M.S. in 1970 from Adelphi University. She then earned a Ph.D. from Fordham University in 1982. Gaskin has been a college professor from 1978 to 1995 and a research scientist at Brookhaven National Laboratory since 1993.

Index of Patents (1991); *Index of Patents* (1993), p. 845; *Who's Who Among African Americans* (1998-1999), p. 533

1995 • The first African American woman appointed Health Commissioner for the City of Philadelphia was Estelle B. Richman, who was appointed to the post in 1995. Richman earned a B.A. in psychology from Case Western Reserve University and a M.S. in clinical and community psychology at Cleveland State University. Prior to joining Philadelphia's Department of Public Health, Richman was the Southeast Area Director of Mental Health for the Pennsylvania Department of Public Health. In 1991, she became Deputy Health Commissioner for Mental Health, Mental Retardation, and Substance Abuse, the position she held before becoming commissioner in 1995. Some of Richman's duties included: operation of a network of eight primary health care centers; managing prenatal, maternal outreach, and child care services; managing the medical examiners office, drug and alcohol abuse prevention and treatment services, mental health, and mental retardation programs; and oversight of prison health services.

Philadelphia New Observer (November 20, 1996)

1996 • Jennifaye V. Brown was the first African American in the state of Georgia certified by the American Physical Therapy Association as a clinical specialist in neurology in 1996. She was only the second person in the nation to receive that certification. Brown has a bachelors degree in psychology and a masters degree in physical therapy. She is currently a therapist with the Rehab Results Group at the DeKalb Medical Center in Decatur, Georgia. She treats patients with neurological disorders and performs research.

Ebony (March, 1996), p. 9

1997 • Christopher P. Adams (1958-) patented, in 1997, a method of performing amplification of nucleic acid with two primers bound to a single solid support. Adams invented methods and apparatus for performing nucleic acid hybridization and amplification processes on a support. Such methods were useful for synthesizing nucleic acid and detecting target nucleic acid for diagnostics and therapeutics. Adams developed a DNA probe that detects infectious organisms in blood, and started Mosaic Technologies, Inc. to market his product. His probe quickly detected bacteria in blood platelets and increased the safety of platelet transfusions. Adams earned a B.A., worked in the cancer department of the University of Massachusetts Medical School, and in biology research at the Massachusetts Institute of Technology.

Black Enterprise (March, 1999), p. 38; *Index of patents* (1997)

1997 • The first African American physician named to the post of public health director of the Fulton County Health Department in Atlanta, Georgia was Adewale Troutman in 1997. He was formerly the director of Emergency Medical Services at United Hospitals Medical Center in Newark, New Jersey, and an assistant clinical professor at the University of Medicine and Dentistry of New Jersey.

Jet (October 13, 1997), p. 19

1997 • The first FDA-approved drug test available without a prescription is "Dr. Brown's Home Drug Testing System," developed by J. Theodore Brown, Jr. (1956-), an African American clinical psychologist. His system was approved by the U.S. Food and Drug Administration in January 1997. Brown's system detects the use of marijuana, cocaine, methamphetamine, PCP, amphetamine, heroin, morphine, and codeine. The kit contains paper cups to collect urine and test tubes to send the samples to designated laboratories for testing. The samples are coded for anonymity. Brown markets the test kit through his Baltimore-based company, Personal Health and Hygiene.

Emerge (1997), p. 16; *Jet* (February 17, 1997)

1998 • Floyd Benjamin was the first African American promoted to chief executive officer (CEO) of Akorn, Inc. in Chicago, in 1998. At the time he was the only African American CEO of a pharmaceutical company in the United States. Akorn's extensive product line included diagnostic, surgical, therapeutic, pharmaceutical, and over-the-counter ophthalmic products. Benjamin earned both his B.S. and M.S. degrees in microbiology at North Carolina Central University. He had over 25 years of technical and managerial experience in pharmaceuticals and devices. He was CEO and president of the Akorn affiliate, Pasadena Research Laboratories, Inc., prior to his becoming CEO of Akron.

Jet (March, 1999), p. 17

1998 • The United States Occupational Safety and Health Administration appointed the first African American commissioner to the Occupational Safety and Health Review Commission when Thomasina Rogers was appointed in 1998. The Review Commission is a three-member commission that rules on disputes resulting from Department of Labor safety inspections completed in adherence to the 1970 Occupational Safety and Health Act. Rogers received a bachelor's degree from Northwestern University and a law degree from Columbia University School of Law. She was previously legal counsel to the Equal Employment Opportunity Commission for seven years, primarily dealing with the development of the Americans with Disabilities Act employment regulations. She was then appointed Chair of the Administrative Council of the United States for the year 1994 to 1995. Rogers is also an officer of the Board of Directors of the Children's National Medical Center.

Jet (November 23, 1998), pp. 38-39

1999 • Carolyn B. Lewis became the first African American to serve as chair-elect designate of the Board of Trustees of the American Hospital Association (AHA) in 1999. Lewis will assume chairmanship of the AHA Board in 2000, making her the organization's first African American chairperson. As chair-elect, she presides over the Strategic Planning Committee. The American Hospital Association is the largest hospital and health system association in the United States. Lewis was previously an at-large member of the AHA Board of Trustees.

Jet (1998), p. 25

DENTISTRY
AND NURSING

1867 • The first African American to receive a dental doctorate was Robert Tanner Freeman (1847-19??), who received the degree in 1867 from Harvard University. In 1907, the Washington Society of Colored Dentists was renamed the Robert Tanner Freeman Dental Society in his honor.

Blacks in Science: Astrophysicist to Zoologist (1977), p. 113; *Blacks in Science and Medicine* (1990), p. 96; *Profile of the Negro in American Dentistry* (1979), p. 69; *Famous First Facts About Negroes* (1972), p. 113

1870 • George F. Grant (1847-19??) was the first African American to hold a faculty position at Harvard Dental School as an instructor in 1870. Grant received his D.D.S. from Harvard and had an international reputation for dental innovation, as indicated by his invention of the oblate palate. He was also a founder and president of the Harvard Odontological Society and was the personal dentist of the Harvard University president Charles W. Elliot. An avid golfer, Grant was also the inventor of a golf tee in 1899.

Blacks in Science and Medicine (1990), p. 104; *Journal of Blacks in Higher Education* (Winter 1998/1999), No. 22, pp. 98-99

1879 • Mary Eliza Mahoney (1845-1926) was the first African American graduate nurse in the United States. She completed her training in 1879 at the New England Hospital for Children in Boston. Mahoney worked primarily in private duty nursing and developed such an outstanding reputation that her services were requested for patients in Washington, D.C., New Jersey, and North Carolina, as well as the Boston area. Mahoney was deeply committed to the professionalization of black nurses and joined the National Association of Graduate Colored Nurses (NAGCN) shortly after its foundation. She worked diligently for the organization, and in 1911, in recognition of her efforts, she was awarded life membership. She was also one of the few African American nurses to become a member of the American Nurses Association (ANA) of that period. In 1936, the NACGN established the Mary Mahoney Award in memory of her efforts on behalf of

MARY E. MAHONEY

African American nurses. The NACGN was dissolved in 1951, and the Mary Mahoney Award was continued by the ANA.

African-Americans in Boston (1991), pp. 139-140; *Black Women in America* (1993), pp. 743-744; *Jet* (March 24, 1955), p. 14; *The Path We Tread* (1986), pp. 17-19

1882 • N. W. Whitcomb, appointed in June 1882, was the first African American permanent professor of dentistry at the Howard University College of Dentistry. The institution opened in October 1881. James B. Hodgkins was the first lecturer there.

Profile of the Negro in American Dentistry (1979), p. 16

1886 • The first African American dentist to practice in the State of Virginia was Charles B. Jackson. He was the first African American dentist to be licensed in Virginia, registering with the Board of Examiners in 1886.

Profile of the American Negro in American Dentistry (1979), p. 12

1890 • Ida Gray Nelson (1867-1953), in June 1890, graduated from the University of Michigan Dental School, becoming the first African American woman dentist in the United States. Nelson returned to Cincinnati in 1890 after graduation and opened a dental office there, where she practiced from 1890 to 1895. She moved to Chicago in 1897 and started a dental practice there, which she maintained until the 1930s. Nelson was also the first African American woman dentist to open practices in the cities of Cincinnati and Chicago.

Blacks in Science: Astrophysicist to Zoologist (1977), p. 23; *Notable Black American Women* Book II (1996), pp. 496-497; *Profile of the Negro in American Dentistry* (1979), pp. 47-48

1895 • Jessie Sleet Scales was the first African American public health nurse. She was a graduate, in 1895, of the fourth class of the newly formed (in 1891) Provident Hospital Training School (Illinois), founded by surgeon Daniel Hale Williams. Scales worked for the Charity Organization Society in New York City for nine years, becoming the first African American nurse working as a paid district nurse and social worker.

Blacks in Science and Medicine (1990), p. 214; *Encyclopedia of Black America* (1981), p. 652

1900 • The first African American dentist to join the Washington Society of Colored Dentists, which was founded in 1900, was George H. Butler. The Washington Society of Colored Dentists was intended to be a national organization. It survived until 1913, when it was disbanded upon the founding of the National Dental Association on July 19, 1913.

Profile of the Negro in American Dentistry (1979), pp. 68-70

1901 • David A. Ferguson (1875-19??) became the first president of the Washington Society of Colored Dentists when he was elected in 1901. The organization was founded the year before. Ferguson was a staunch supporter of the development of a professional African American dental organization. He also was the first African American to take the Virginia State Board's written examination in 1900. Ferguson was president of the National Dental Association from 1913 to 1918.

Blacks in Science and Medicine (1990), p. 89; *Profile of the Negro in American Dentistry* (1979), pp. 68-70

1902 • The first African American to graduate from a New York State school of dentistry was Walter Nathaniel Beekman (1878-1962) when he graduated from New York Dental School (now Columbia University School of Dentistry) in 1902. Before studying dentistry, Beekman spent two years studying pharmacy at Avery Normal Institute. Later in his life, he won a Columbia University Citation for 50 years of dentistry.

Blacks in Science and Medicine (1990), p. 24; *Jet* (August 10, 1962); *Journal of the National Medical Association* Vol. 33, (July 1961), pp. 408-409

1902 • Susie King Taylor (1848-1912), a military nurse, was the only African American woman to publish an account of her experiences in the Civil War. Taylor did not have formal schooling, but learned to read and write before age 14. She then set up a school for children and any interested adults. In 1862, she became affiliated with the South Carolina Volunteers, later called the 33rd U.S. Colored Infantry, the first colored unit organized by the Union Army. Although she started work as a laundress, she also taught the soldiers to read and write and quickly began tending the sick and wounded. Taylor won praise from Clara Barton, the founder of the Red Cross, for her nursing skills. Taylor published her memoirs in 1902, which were reprinted in 1968.

SUSIE KING TAYLOR

Blacks in Science and Medicine (1990), p. 227; *Dictionary of American Negro Biography* (1982), p. 581; *Notable Black American Women* (1992), pp. 1108-1113; *Black Women in America* (1993), pp. 1145-1147

1905 • John E. Washington was the first African American dentist licensed by the District Board of Dental Examiners in Washington, D.C. in

1905. Washington was also one of the founding members of the National Dental Association.

Profile of the American Negro in American Dentistry (1979), p. 70

1907 • The first African American woman appointed to the newly formed Nurses Examining Board of the District of Columbia was Sara Iredell Fleetwood (1849-1908) in 1907. Fleetwood, in 1896, graduated in the first class of Freedman's Hospital Nursing Training School and initially practiced as a private nurse. In 1901, she was appointed as the first African American superintendent of Freedman's nursing training program and held that position until 1904.

Black Women in America (1993), pp. 437-438; *Black Women in America* (1997), pp. 72-73

1908 • The National Association of Colored Graduate Nurses was founded by Martha Minerva Franklin (1870-1968), and she was elected its first president in 1908. Franklin graduated from Philadelphia's Woman's Hospital Training School for Nurses in 1897, the only African American in her class. In 1908, after a three-day meeting regarding the need to form a permanent professional organization to promote racial integration and enhance the status of African American nurses, the National Association of Colored Graduate Nurses was formed. Franklin was named president; she was re-elected in 1909 and was later designated honorary president for life. Franklin spent the majority of her nursing career in New York City.

Black Women in America Vol. I, (1993), pp. 452-453; *Blacks in Science and Medicine* (1990), pp. 94-95; *Black Women in White* (1989), p. 95

1913 • Minnie D. Woodward in 1913 became the first African American to be issued a certificate of registration as a trained nurse by the State Board of Nurse Examiners of Tennessee. Woodward graduated from the nurse-training department of Meharry Medical College.

Famous First Facts About Negroes (1972), p. 149

1915 • Alfred P. Russell, Jr. (1881-19??) was the first African American on the visiting staff of Forsyth Dental Infirmary for Children. He remained in that position until 1923. Russell received a B.S. in 1905 from Harvard University and in 1908, received a D.M.D. from Howard University Dental School. He remained on the visiting staff of the Forsyth Dental Infirmary for Children until 1923. He was invited to give a clinic on the treatment of cleft palette cases, which he did on May 8, 1914, at the

Massachusetts Dental Society in Boston. Russell was a member of the American Dental Society.

Blacks in Science and Medicine (1990), p. 207; *Who's Who in Colored America* (1933-1937), p. 452, (1941-1944), p. 450

1916 • Adah Bell Samuels Thoms (1863-1943) was a driving force behind the improvement of conditions within segregated health delivery systems. Thoms helped organize the National Association of Colored Graduate Nurses and was its first treasurer and president from 1916 to 1923. She campaigned for improved employment opportunities for qualified African American nurses, and was much concerned with nursing school standards. She was instrumental in the integration of African American graduate nurses into the American Nurses Association and the National Organization for Public Health Nursing. She served as the assistant director of nurses and acting director, from 1906 to 1923, of the Lincoln Hospital School for Nurses. Thoms was the first recipient of the Mary Mahoney Award, in 1936, and authored the text, *Pathfinders: A History of the Progress of Colored Graduate Nurses* (1929), concerning the history of African Americans in nursing.

Black Women in White (1989), pp. 96, 42-43, 104-105; *Dictionary of American Negro Biography* (1982), p. 589; *Who's Who in Colored America* (1933-1937), p. 477

1918 • Veda Watson Somerville (18??-19??) was the first African American woman dentist in the state of California in 1918. She scored among the highest on her dental examination. When Somerville earned her D.D.S., she was the only woman and only African American in her class at the University of Southern California Dental School. She graduated in 1918.

Black Women Makers of History: A Portrait (1975), pp. 91-93; *Blacks in Science and Medicine* (1990), p. 217

1919 • The first African American nurse that the American Red Cross officially recognized was Frances (Reed) Elliott Davis (1882-1965), when she received her nurse's pin in 1919. Elliott graduated from Knoxville College (Tennessee) in 1907, and from Freedman's Hospital Training School in Washington, D.C., in 1912. She did three years' private duty nursing and then applied to the American Red Cross, but was told she needed public health or rural nursing training. She acquired these with an additional year of training at Columbia University. Davis started with the Red Cross in 1917 but did not receive her pin until 1919. It had a special inscription on the back specifying she was a "colored" nurse. This practice was not discontinued by the Red Cross until after World War II. Davis also organized the first training school for African American nurses in the state of Michigan, at Detroit's Dunbar Hospital.

Black Women in America (1993), pp. 307-308; *Black Women in White* (1989), pp. 134-136; *Trail-blazer: Negro Nurse in the American Red Cross* (1969), p. 191

1919 • Jessie G. Garnett (1897-1976) was the first African American woman to graduate from Tufts Dental School when she received the D.D.S. in 1919. She was the first African American woman to practice dentistry in Boston, which she did for a period of 50 years.

African-Americans in Boston (1991), p. 145

1926 • The first oral surgery department was organized at Freedman's Hospital in 1926 by the African American dental surgeon Rosean Franklin Lee (1897-). He was appointed oral surgeon at Howard University in 1924. Lee had acquired his B.S. and his D.D.S. in 1922, both from Howard University.

Blacks in Science and Medicine (1990), p. 151

1928 • Many individuals were involved in the effort to professionalize African American nurses in the 1920s and 1930s, and one special contributor was Carrie E. Bullock (18??-1961). Bullock was founding editor of the *National News Bulletin,* the official news organ of the the National Association of Colored Graduate Nurses (NACGN), which released its first issue in 1928. Bullock completed her nursing training in 1909 at Provident Hospital and joined the staff of the Chicago Visiting Nurses Association that same year. In 1919, she was promoted to supervisor of African American nurses. In 1908, in New York City, the NACGN was founded, and Bullock served as its president from 1927 to 1930. Bullock's main purpose for founding the *Bulletin* was to foster a greater sense of professional and organizational involvement among African American nurses.

Blacks in Science and Medicine (1990), p. 42; *Black Women in White* (1989), pp. 94, 95, 97; *Pathfinders* (1929), pp. 17-19; *The Path We Tread* (1986), pp. 151, 152

1932 • Jesse Harrison, in 1932, was granted a patent for his invention of a combination toothbrush and paste holder. Harrison's device was a container having both ends open and a partition extending across the intermediate part, spaced from both ends. A cap closes one end that has a threaded outlet neck. A brush has a socket in its handle for receiving the threaded necks. Paste is stored in the container portion of the device, and when the piston with a small rod in the cylinder is depressed paste is forced from the cylinder through the container neck and onto the brush bristles. The brush is then placed on the neck and the device used in the ordinary manner, the cylindrical container forming a handle for the brush.

Index of Patents (1932), p. 369; *Twentieth Century Black Patentees - A Survey* (1979)

1936 • William B. Jones patented a dental apparatus in 1936 that he developed to be used in the manufacture of false teeth. One of the objectives of Jones's invention was to provide a device for acquiring an accurate impression of the patient's jaw without unpleasantness to the patient in a way that was efficient for the dentist. The invention included an impression tray that was placed in the patient's mouth prior to actual impression-taking, enabling the dentist to determine the amount of impression material to place in the tray. Excess impression material was conveniently taken care of and overflowing and/or dropping of material into the patient's mouth was eliminated.

Black Inventors: From Africa to America (1995), p. 233; *Index of Patents* (1936)

1940 • Eva M. Noles (1919-) became in 1940 the first African American to graduate from the E.J. Meyer Memorial Hospital School of Nursing (New York). She received a B.S. in 1962 from the Nursing University of Buffalo (New York) and a M.Ed. in 1967 from the State University of New York at Buffalo. Noles served as staff and head nurse from 1945 to 1963 at Roswell Park Memorial Institute, and instructor and then clinical associate professor of nursing from 1963 to 1977 for the State University at Buffalo. She became homecare supervisor and staff developer for Medical Personnel, Inc. from 1977 until her 1984 retirement.

Who's Who Among African Americans (1998-1999), p. 1126

1941 • The first African American nurse commissioned in the U. S. Army as a lieutenant was Della Raney, who was commissioned in April 1941. She became a chief nurse in 1942 and was assigned to the Tuskegee Air Field station hospital. Raney graduated from Lincoln Hospital School of Nursing in Durham and completed further studies at Western Michigan University, Wayne State University, University of Michigan, and Virginia State College. She was promoted to captain in 1945 and to major in 1946. She also served a tour of duty in Japan. Raney retired from the U. S. Army in 1978.

Black Women in White (1989), p. 172; *The Path We Tread* (1986), pp. 169-170

1942 • Earl W. Renfroe (1907-) was the first African American to complete training in orthodontics when he received a M.S. degree in orthodontics from the University of Illinois in 1942. He previously received the D.D.S. from that school in 1941. Renfroe taught at the University of Illinois

Medical Campus and was the first African American full professor and first African American department head there. He was named professor emeritus of orthodontics in 1982. Renfroe was also the first African American dentist certified by the American Board of Orthodontics, and he also authored two textbooks.

Profile of the Negro in American Dentistry (1979), p. 40; *Who's Who Among African Americans* (1998-1999), p. 1252

1943 • Ulysses S. Walton received a patent in 1943 for his invention of a denture partially made of plastic. The denture was of lighter construction than was previously possible. The denture had a metallic reinforcing edge, which was formed to the contour of the dental plate. A tie element was embedded in the denture, tying adjacent metallic edge portions together to prevent their movement, which would change the shape of the denture. Walton's denture could be formed in a dental laboratory without additional tools or equipment.

Black Inventors: From Africa to America (1995), p. 117; *Index of Patents* (1943), p. 568; *Negro Year Book* (1947), p. 29

1944 • Mary Elizabeth Carnegie (1916-) established the first African American baccalaureate program in nursing in Virginia at Hampton University in 1944. An acknowledged leader in the fight to gain professional recognition and acceptance, as well as equality, for African Americans in the nursing profession, Carnegie's influence in the field of nursing was national. She earned a B.A. in 1942 from West Virginia State College. Prior to that, Carnegie had graduated in 1937 from the private Lincoln School for Nurses in New York City. She earned a Ph.D. in 1972 in public administration. Carnegie started teaching in 1942. She moved to Florida and became professor and dean at Florida A & M College which, under her guidance, became the first nursing school in Florida to receive accreditation. In 1949, Carnegie became the first African American nurse elected to the Board of Directors of the Florida State Nurses' Association (FSNA). Carnegie was also senior editor of *Nursing Outlook*, editor of *Nursing Research*, as well as editing or authoring other books and articles.

Black Women in America (1993), pp. 218-219; *Dollars & Sense* (Special Issue 1986), p. 108; *Notable Black American Women* (1992), pp. 156-160

1944 • The first African American dentist commissioned in the U. S. Naval Reserve Dental Corps was Thomas Watkins, Jr. Watkins earned his D.D.S. degree in 1944 from the University of Pennsylvania and was an honor graduate.

Profile of the Negro in American Dentistry (1979), pp. 58-59

1945 • The first African American woman commissioned nurse for the U. S. Public Health Service was Alma N. Jackson, who was commissioned in 1945. At that time, Jackson was the assistant sanitarian in the all-Negro Public Health Service Mission to Liberia. The U.S. Department of State, with endorsement of the War Department, requested the U.S. Public Health Service to dispatch a mission to Liberia following a 1944 presidential memorandum for the United States to do everything possible to improve the health conditions of Liberia. A group of medical and dental surgeons and assistant nurse officers was organized and sent, along with Jackson serving as the assistant sanitarian.

The Path We Tread (1986), pp. 192, 215

1945 • The National Association of Colored Graduate Nurses, with a number of concerned civic groups and individuals during the latter part of World War II, were involved in an intense struggle to get the U. S. Navy to accept African American nurses in its ranks. When President Theodore Roosevelt signed the Naval Appropriations Bill in 1908, he also signed into being the Navy Nurse Corps. It was not until March 1945, though, that the U. S. Surgeon General announced that the Navy would accept African American nurses. Phyllis Daley, a graduate of Lincoln School for Nurses in New York, was sworn into the U. S. Navy Nurse Corps as an ensign—the first African American nurse on active duty with the Navy. Three other African American nurses, Ella Lucille Stimley, Helen Turner, and Edith DeVoe, were commissioned as ensigns just before World War II ended.

Black Women in America (1993), pp. 795-796; *Black Women in White* (1989), p. 181; *The Path We Tread* (1986), p. 177

1947 • The first African American to earn a Master of Arts from North Carolina College was Shirley M. Cornwall (1918-) in 1947. She had previously earned a B.S. there in 1946, and went on to receive a D.D.S. degree in 1952. Cornwall completed an internship and residency, and then entered private practice in 1955 in Charlotte, North Carolina.

Who's Who Among African Americans (1998-1999), p. 323

1948 • First Lieutenant Nancy C. Leftenant originally joined the Reserve Corps of the Army Nurse Corps in 1945, and in 1948, became the first African American member of the Regular Army Nurse Corps. Leftenant was a graduate of Lincoln Hospital School for Nurses in New York.

Blacks in Science and Medicine (1990), p. 151; *Black Women in America* Vol. II, (1993), p. 795; *Black Women in White* (1989), p. 182

1948 • The first African American woman dentist to practice in the state of Mississippi was Mavis N. Jones (1918-), who started her practice there in 1948. Jones received her D.D.S. in 1948 from Meharry Medical College. Before she became a dentist, she was a dental hygienist for 10 years, having received her R.D.H. from Meharry.

Who's Who Among Black Americans (1990-1991), p. 710; *Who's Who Among African-Americans* (1998-1999), p. 835

1951 • Thomas Leslie James (1927-) was the first African American dental officer commissioned in the U. S. Navy in 1951. James received a B.S. degree from Fisk University, a B.A. from Morehouse, and his D.D.S. in 1951 for Meharry Medical College. He served in the Navy from 1951 to 1958 and was an assistant professor of oral biology at the University of Miami School of Medicine from 1968 to 1972.

Blacks in Science and Medicine (1990), p. 131; *Profile of the Negro in American Dentistry* (1979), p. 58; *Who's Who Among Black Americans* (1985), p. 436

1951 • Clifton O. Dummett (1919-), who received a D.D.S. in 1941 and M.S.D. in 1942, both from Northwestern University, was an outstanding educator, administrator, and dentist specializing in periodontics. In 1950 and 1951, Dummett made three significant "firsts." He was the first African American to represent the U. S. Veterans Administration as lecturer at the Conference on Periodontal Disease at the Institute of Pathology of Western Reserve University, the first African American to lecture at the Institute of Periodontology, University of Michigan School of Public Health, and the first African American to be the U. S. Correspondent Member of the British Society of Periodontology. Dummett was also the first African American president of the International Association of Dental Research.

Famous First Facts About Negroes (1972), pp. 118-119; *Negro Year Book* (1952), p. 371; *Who's Who Among Black Americans* (1985), p. 239

1951–1982 • Eunice Lewis Smith (19??-1984) was the first African American nurse in a management position at St. Elizabeth's Hospital in Washington, D.C. during her long career there. Smith received a B.S. from Florida A&M University and a M.S. degree from the Catholic University of America. She served at St. Elizabeth's Hospital from 1951 to 1982 and was the first African American head nurse, first African American supervisor, and first African American director of nursing during her tenure.

Blacks in Science and Medicine (1990), p. 215; *The Path We Tread* (1986), p. 187

1951 • Elouise Collier Duncan was the first African American appointed to the executive staff of the American Nurses Association (ANA) in 1951. Earlier, she was also the first African American to graduate from the Yale School of Nursing. Duncan worked for the ANA until 1953, when she resigned to marry the Liberian Secretary of Public Works and Utilities, Henry B. Duncan. She continued to work representing the interests of nurses in many capacities. Duncan was president of the Liberian Nurses Association, member of the Board of Directors of the International Council of Nurses, and advisor to the Liberian delegation to the 19th General Assembly of the United Nations.

The Path We Tread (1986), pp. 73, 74

1952 • Willie Mae Johnson was the first African American nurse elected to the first Board of Directors of the National League of Nurses in 1952. Johnson received a diploma from the Tuskegee Institute School of Nursing and a B.S. from New York University. She was on the staff of the Community Nursing Services of Montclair, New Jersey.

The Path We Tread (1986), pp. 67, 241

1954 • Betty Smith Williams (1929-) received a M.S. degree from the Frances Payne Bolton School of Nursing, Case Western Reserve University in 1954. She was the first African American to graduate from the school. Williams earned her B.S. from Howard University in 1950 and also earned the Dr.P.H. from the School of Public Health, University of California at Los Angeles. She worked as a staff nurse from 1954 to 1956, when she became assistant professor at Charles Drew Post-Graduate Medical School until 1969. She became assistant professor at UCLA in 1969, and then assistant dean from 1974 to 1976. Williams joined the School of Nursing of the University of Colorado Health Science Center as professor and dean in 1979 and served there until 1984. She served as president of the National Black Nurses Association and became professor emeritus of the California State University Long Beach Department of Nursing in 1989. Williams received numerous honors and awards, including the Distinguished Alumna Award from the Case Western Reserve Bolton School of Nursing.

Howard University Magazine (Winter, 1999), p. 35; *The Path We Tread* (1986), pp. 86; *Who's Who Among African Americans* (1998-1999), p. 1395-1396

1955 • The first African-American dentist on the staffs of Norfolk General Hospital and St. Vincent Hospital in Norfolk, Virginia was Booker Thomas Garnette (1930-), in 1955. Garnette earned his B.S. in 1951 and D.D.S. in 1955, both from Howard University (Washington, D.C.). He was in private practice from 1957 to 1995. Garnette has been active in the Virginia Tidewater Dental Association, serving on its commission on dental health, and the Virginia Dental Association, as well as other local and regional dental organizations.

Who's Who Among Black Americans (1990-1991), p. 454; *Who's Who Among African Americans* (1998-1999), p. 530

1955 • Elizabeth Lipford Kent (1919-) was the first African American nurse to earn a Ph.D. in public health when she received the degree from the University of Michigan in 1955. She had earned a M.P.H. from the University of Michigan in 1946. Prior, she completed nurses training at St. Phillips Hospital School of Nursing in Richmond, Virginia in 1945. Kent was Director of Nursing and Psychiatric Nurse Executive at Detroit's Lafayette Clinic and also assistant professor in the Wayne State University College of Nursing.

Blacks in Science and Medicine (1990), p. 142; *The Path We Tread* (1986), pp. 57-58

1956 • The first African American to finish the University of Texas Dental School was Zeb F. Poindexter, Jr. (1929-), in 1956. He received his B.S. in 1945 from Wiley College and a M.S. degree in 1952 from Texas Southern University. Poindexter has a private dental practice in Houston, and since 1973, has taught at the University of Texas as associate professor of community dentistry. He practiced in the state of Texas for a number of years and was considered the outstanding dentist of the year, 1991, by the Texas Academy of General Dentistry.

Who's Who Among African Americans (1998-1999), p. 1202

1956 • The first African American dentist appointed to any state dental board was Walter B. Garvin (18??-1958) when, in July 1956, he was appointed to the District of Columbia Dental Board. The dental board is an administrative agency empowered to regulate the practice of dentistry. Garvin taught at Howard University for 20 years, and began serving on the board of Dental Examiners in 1920.

Blacks in Science and Medicine (1990), p. 98; *Jet* (February 7, 1957); *Profile of the Negro in American Dentistry* (1979), p. 96

1957 • Christopher L. Taylor (1923-) patented his invention for a combination toothbrush and dentifrice (toothpaste) dispenser in 1957. Taylor's invention provided a combination toothbrush and dentifrice dispenser with a removable brush member arranged to apply dentifrice of either liquid, powder or toothpaste to the brush without removing the dentifrice container. Taylor received a B.S. 1945 from Johnson C. Smith University and a

M.D. from Howard University Dental School in 1950. He completed an internship at Jersey City Medical Center from 1950 to 1951. He has been self-employed as a dentist in Los Angeles since 1951.

Index of Patents (1957); *Who's Who Among African Americans* (1998-1999), p. 1260; *Who's Who Among Black Americans* (1990-1991), p. 1226

1958 • Naomi Louise Tunley (1936-) became the first African American to hold the position of associate chief of nursing services in Oklahoma City when she took the position at the VA Hospital in that city in 1958. Tunley received a B.S. in nursing education from Dillard University (Louisiana) in 1958, and received the M.A. from the University of Missouri in 1974. She served at the Oklahoma City VA Hospital until 1965, and then accepted the position of medical and surgical instructor at Iowa Lutheran Hospital in Des Moines, becoming the first African American to hold that position. Tunley worked at Iowa Lutheran until 1966, and then joined the Kansas City VA Hospital in 1967, holding a number of positions there over the next ten years. In 1977, Tunley became nurse manager for the Kansas City (Missouri) VA Medical Center, a position she held until 1994.

Who's Who Among African Americans (1998-1999), p. 1508

1958 • Daniel A. Collins (1916-) was the first African American diplomate of the American Board of Oral Pathology when selected in 1958. Collins earned an A.B. in 1936 at Paine College (Georgia), a D.D.S. in 1941 at Meharry Medical College (Tennessee), and a M.S. in dentistry in 1944 at the University of California. He was active in the California State Dental Association, American Academy of Oral Pathology, International Association of Pathology, La Federation Dentaire International, the San Francisco Dental Society, and other organizations.

Profile of the Negro in American Dentistry (1979), p. 35; *Who's Who Among African Americans* (1998-1999), p. 361.

1960 • The first African American instructor at the Santa Rosa Junior College School of Nursing was Esther Louisa Allen (1912-). She received a diploma in 1940 from the Kansas City General Hospital School of Nursing, a B.S. from the University of Colorado School of Nursing in 1949, and then a M.S. in 1958 from the University of Washington School of Nursing. Allen was assistant supervisor of operating rooms from 1951 to 1958 at San Joaquin County Hospital and then the first and only African American instructor at Santa Rosa Junior College School of Nursing from 1960 until her 1973 retirement.

Who's Who Among African Americans (1998-1999), p. 20-21

1960 • The first African American to graduate from the University of Texas Medical Branch Nursing School was Wilina Ione Gatson, when she received her B.S. in nursing in 1960. Gatson worked in several hospitals and at Galveston College and University of Texas before retiring. She was the first African American to serve as an officer in the University of Texas Nurses Alumni Association from 1961 to 1962 and was the first African American to receive the Distinguished Alumnus Award of the University of Texas School of Nursing in 1989. Gatson was inducted into the University of Texas Medical Branch Nursing Hall of Fame in 1992.

Who's Who Among African Americans (1998-1999), p. 464-465

1961 • Noah Robert Calhoun (1921-), an oral/maxillofacial surgeon, was the first African American dentist accepted into the American Society of Oral Surgery (ASOS) in 1961. The ASOS was founded in 1946. Calhoun was awarded a D.D.S. degree in 1948 from Howard University Dental School and a M.S.D. in 1955 from Tufts Medical and Dental College. He is coordinator of dental research and has been professor of oral maxillofacial surgery at Howard University Dental School since 1982. Calhoun has also been a selection editor and member of the editorial board of the *International Oral and Maxillofacial Surgery Journal.*

Profile of the Negro in American Dentistry (1979), p. 36; *Who's Who Among African-Americans* (1998-1999), p. 228

1961 • Alexander M. Pratt was the first African American certified as a pedodontist by the Illinois Board of Periodontics in 1961. (A pedodontist has a specialty in treating children.) Pratt has a patent on his invention, the simple matrix retainer (a dental instrument). He is also the author of the text *Your children, Their Teeth and Their Health* (1994).

Profile of the Negro in American Dentistry (1979), p. 41

1962 • Gwendolyn Hickey (1920-), a practical nurse supervisor at the Allen Hospital in Waterloo, Iowa was, in 1962, the first African American to be elected secretary of the State Licensed Practical Nurses. Hickey was also secretary of the Central Nursing League.

Jet (July 19, 1962), p. 23

1962 • Marion George Ford, Jr. (1937-) was awarded a Fulbright fellowship in 1946 to study periodontology at the University of Bonn (Germany) and was the first African American dentist in periodontology to receive a Fulbright. He was also the first dentist from Texas to receive a Fulbright fellowship. Ford earned a B.S. in 1958 *magna cum laude* and his D.D.S.

magna cum laude in 1962, both from the University of Texas. He was developer of the *Denture Acrylic Resin and Shade Guide* in 1962.

Profile of the Negro in American Dentistry (1979), p. 41; *Who's Who Among African Americans* (1998-1999), p. 494

1964 • The first African American nurse on staff at the Central Office of the U. S. Veterans Administration was Minnie Lee Jones Hartsfield in 1964. Hartsfield earned a diploma from Burwell Hospital School of Nursing, a B.S. from Tuskegee Institute, and a M.A. from Teachers College, Columbia University. Hartsfield had 25 years experience at various VA facilities. As nursing specialist at the VA Central Office, she gathered and analyzed facility data to justify programs and policy, reviewed and evaluated various health facilities, and assisted in recruitment and placement of nurses in key positions. Hartsfield left the VA Central Office in 1968. She served as chief nurse at Westside VA Hospital in Chicago from 1968 to 1970 and at the VA Medical Center in Downey, Illinois, from 1970 to 1975.

The Path We Tread (1986), p. 217

1964 • Beatrice L. Murray became the first African American chief nurse at an integrated facility when she was appointed to that position at the Veterans Administration Hospital in Pittsburgh, Pennsylvania, in 1964. Murray was enrolled as a chief nurse trainee with the VA in 1963, and the following year, when she completed her training, she was appointed chief nurse there. She had previously received a diploma from the Kansas City General Hospital School of Nursing and a certificate from the University of Minnesota School of Public Health. She then received a B.S. and M.S. in nursing from Wayne State University School of Nursing. Murray held positions with the U. S. Department of Agriculture, Migratory Labor Health Association, and the VA since 1941. She was chief nurse at the Pittsburgh VA from 1964 to 1966. From 1966 to her 1981 retirement, Murray was chief nurse at VA hospitals in Bedford, Massachusetts; Hines, Illinois; and Washington, D.C.

The Path We Tread (1986), p. 217

1965 • James Talmadge Jackson (1921-) was the first African American dentist, in 1965, to be selected a diplomat of the American Board of Prosthodontics. Jackson was associate dean for clinical affairs and visiting professor of prosthodontics at Howard University College of Dentistry. He was also associate professor of prosthodontics at Georgetown University, as well as chief of the Washington VA Hospital Central Dental Laboratory.

Profile of the Negro in American Dentistry (1979), p. 43; *Who's Who Among African-Americans* (1998-1999), p. 761

1967 • Doctor of dental surgery, medical school administrator, educator, and author Juliann S. Bluitt (1938-), was the first African American full-time faculty member at Northwestern University Dental School when she was appointed in 1967. Bluitt received her B.S. in 1958 and dental degree in 1962, both from Howard University. She practiced in Chicago until 1967, when she became director of dental hygiene and full-time instructor at Northwestern. Bluitt's career has been concerned with practicing dentistry on young children, educating older students to become dental professionals, and training dental students. Bluitt was the first woman elected president of the Chicago Dental Society and served in that office from 1992 to 1993. She has published extensively and has served on the editorial boards of the *Journal of Dental Education* and *Journal of the American Dental Hygienists Association,* as well as serving on other professional and community organizational boards.

Chicago Defender (July 13, 1992), p. 13; *Ebony* (March 1973), pp. 84-86, 88, 90, 92; *Black Firsts* (1994), p. 298; *Jet* (July 13, 1992), p. 15

1967 • The first woman in the U.S. Army to be awarded the Expert Field Medical Badge was African American nurse Clara Leach Adams-Ender (1939-) in July 1967. Adams-Ender, in 1982, became the first African American Army Nurse Corps officer to graduate from the U.S. Army War College. She began her active army career as a second lieutenant and a general duty nurse in 1961 and retired with brigadier general rank, serving in the Office of the U.S. Surgeon General as chief of the U.S. Army Nurse Corps. In 1984, she was the first African American chief of the nursing department at Walter Reed Army Medical Center. Three years later, she became chief of the Army Nurse Corps and director of personnel.

Black Women in America (1993), pp. 10-11; *Jet* (November 15, 1982), p. 16; *Notable Black American Women* (1992), pp. 1-2

1967 • Lawrence C. Washington (1936-) was the first African-American man to receive a regular U. S. Army commission in the Army Nurse Corps at Walter Reed Army Medical Center, Washington, D.C. Washington received a diploma from Freedmen's Hospital School of Nursing (Washington, D.C.), a B.S. from the University of Maryland, and a M.S. from Catholic University of America (Washington, D.C.). He also served as assistant chief of the Department of Nursing, William Beaumont Army Medical Center, Texas.

Blacks in Science and Medicine (1990), p. 243; *The Path We Tread* (1986), pp. 173-174

1968 • Alphonso Trottman (1936-) was the first African American dentist to receive a M.S. degree in orthodontics from Saint Louis University in

1968. Trottman received his D.D.S. in 1961 from Indiana University School of Medicine. Until 1977, he was in private practice and an assistant clinical professor of orthodontics at Southern Illinois University. He also published an article on dentistry in African American children in the *Missouri Dental Journal.*

Who's Who Among Black Americans (1990-1991), p. 1268

1969 • The first African American president of the International Association of Dental Research was Clifton O. Dummett (1919-) when he was elected in 1969. Dummett received a B.S. in 1941 from Roosevelt University, a D.D.S. in 1942 from Northwestern University, and a M.P.H. in 1947 from the University of Michigan. He was professor, and then chairman, of the department of periodontics and oral diagnosis for the period 1942 to 1947, then Dean of the School of Dentistry from 1947 to 1949 at Meharry Medical College. He was then chief of dental services from 1946 to 1965 at Tuskegee VA hospital. Dummett was selected professor and chairman of the department of community dentistry and associate dean of extramural affairs at the School of Dentistry of the University of Southern California at Los Angeles. He was the first African American dental department chairman at Southern California.

Famous First Facts About Negroes (1972), pp. 118-119; *Negro Year Book* (1952), p. 371; *Who's Who Among African Americans* (1998-1999), p. 424

1969 • James R. Lewis (1938-) was the first African American member of the Admiral's Commission for the School of Dentistry of the University of North Carolina from 1969 to 1971. Lewis received a B.S. in chemistry in 1963 from North Carolina Central University and a D.D.S. in 1968 from Howard University (Washington, D.C.), then completed a rotating dental internship at McGill University (Montreal, Canada). He was appointed dental director of the Lincoln Health Center in Durham, North Carolina and was also appointed assistant professor in the department of ecology of the University of North Carolina School of Dentistry.

Who's Who Among African Americans (1998-1999), p. 921; *Who's Who Among Black Americans* (1990-1991), p. 782

1970 • Diane M. Lindsay was the first African American nurse in history to receive the Soldier's Medal for Heroism. She received the medal in 1970. Lindsay, a first lieutenant on duty with the 95th Evacuation Hospital in Vietnam, happened upon a violent soldier. Lindsay and a male officer physically restrained the confused soldier, persuading him to give up a grenade and preventing casualties. Lindsay was the second nurse to receive the Soldier's Medal during the Vietnam conflict.

The Path We Tread (1986), pp. 176-177

1970 • Robert Nathaniel Boyd, III (1928-), an African American dentist, patented a dental filling composition that was more like natural tooth enamel in 1970. Boyd's composition was such that thermal expansion of the filler and resin closely approximated that of the tooth enamel over the temperature range existing within the mouth. Boyd earned his B.S. in 1949 at Rutgers University and his D.D.S. from New York College of Dentistry in 1954. He was an associate professor of dental materials from 1969 to 1983 at New York College of Dentistry and also assistant director of admissions there from 1976 to 1983. Boyd formed Boyd International Industries in 1983 and is its president. He participated in a number of professional dental organizations and published papers on dental compositions.

Index of Patents (1970); *Who's Who Among African Americans* (1998-1999), p. 126; *Who's Who Among Black Americans* (1990-1991), p. 126

1970 • The first African-American woman promoted to the rank of colonel in the United States Army was Margaret E. Bailey (19??-). Bailey received nursing training at the Fraternal Hospital School of Nursing in Montgomery, Alabama and a certificate in psychiatric nursing from Brooke Army Medical Center. She also earned a B.A. in 1959 from San Francisco State College (California) and was head nurse of a psychiatric nursing service.

Blacks in Science and Medicine (1990), p. 17; *Ebony* (September, 1966), pp. 50-52; *The Path We Tread* (1986), pp. 171-172

1970 • Byron Lynwood Mitchell (1936-) was the first African American orthodontist to practice in the state of Florida in 1970. He was also only the second African American orthodontist in the South. Mitchell earned a B.S. degree in 1959 at Savannah State College. He received a D.D.S. degree in 1966 and his orthodontics degree in 1969, both from Howard University School of Dentistry. Mitchell was a member of the American Association of Orthodontics.

Who's Who Among Black Americans (1990-1991), p. 896; *Who's Who Among African Americans* (1998-1999), p. 1059

1971 • The first African American woman chosen to head a major teaching hospital in the United States was Florence S. Gaynor (1921-1993), who was appointed executive director of Sydenham Hospital in New York City in 1971. Gaynor graduated as a registered nurse from Lincoln Hospital in New

York in 1946. Gaynor spent several years as a public-health nurse and school nurse, then pursued a career in hospital administration. She became an assistant administrator in 1970 at Lincoln Hospital, then executive director of Sydenham Hospital. She then became executive director of Newark's Martland Hospital. She served from 1976 to 1980 as director of hospital and health services at Meharry Medical College. Gaynor directed, from 1980 to 1984, the West Philadelphia Community Mental Health Consortium in Philadelphia.

Encyclopedia of Black America (1981), p. 403; *New York Times* (October 1, 1993), p. B8

1971 • The National Black Nurses Association (NBNA) was formed in December 1971, and Lauranne Sams was the first president of the organization. Sams, while attending the 1970 national convention of the American Nurses Association, called for a caucus of African American nurses. A series of meetings were held, and it was determined that the American Nursing Association at that time was not really meaningful to the professional development of African American nurses. In 1971, the NBNA was formed and incorporated in 1972, with Lauranne Sams as its first president. The NBNA had ten objectives, of which four were concerned with the obligation of African American nurses acting as advocates for improving the health care of African Americans. The remaining six objectives focused on the professional development of African American nurses.

Black Women in White (1989), pp. 192-193; *The Path We Tread* (1986), pp. 85-86, 127-128

1972 • Vivian O. Lee was the first African American nurse employed by Region X of the Public Health Services, when she began her term there in 1972. Lee has a B.S.N. from the University of Washington and earned a M.P.A. from the University of Puget Sound. She was a program management officer from 1972 to 1975, designing protocols for increasing program efficiency and effectiveness. Lee was a public health advisor from 1975 to 1980. She then served as regional nursing consultant for the Family Planning Program and as a consultant to the Office of the Assistant Secretary for Health. Lee has won numerous honors and awards, including the DHEW Sustained Superior Performance Award for Program Management Skills and the U.S. Department of Health and Human Services Secretary's Award for Excellence.

The Path We Tread (1986), pp. 203-204

1973 • Foster Kidd (1924-), who is in private dental practice in Dallas, Texas, was the first African American dentist appointed to the Texas State Board of Dental Examiners in 1973. Kidd received a B.A. in 1949 from Fisk

University and his D.D.S. from Meharry College of Dentistry in 1953, and set up a private dental practice in Dallas, Texas in 1953. Kidd has been instrumental in developing the professional advancement of African Americans in dentistry. He has been an active member of the National Dental Association, American Dental Association, and the Texas Dental Association. He has completed major surveys related to the status of African Americans in dentistry and in 1979, edited the text, *Profile of the Negro in American Dentistry*, published by Howard University Press. Kidd has also pubished a number of scientific papers and is the founder and president of the Society for the Study of the Negro in American Dentistry.

Profile of the Negro in American Dentistry (1979), pp. 24, 96, 100, 117; *Who's Who Among Black Americans* (1990-1991), p. 734; *Who's Who Among African Americans* (1998-1999), p. 862

1973 • The Board of the American Nurses' Association, in 1973, formed the American Academy of Nursing. Most professions have a body referred to as an academy, usually comprised of scholars in the field who are concerned with current issues relating to the profession and take positions in the name of the academy. The American Nurses' Association formed its Academy in 1973. One of its goals was to recognize substantial achievement and contribution to nursing. Thirty-six Charter Fellows of the Academy were designated from more than 100 nominees. Those selected were clinical practitioners, academicians, administrators, and researchers. Rhetaugh Dumas and Geraldene Felton were the first two African Americans included among the original Charter fellows. The maximum number of nurses in the American Academy of Nursing is now 500.

The Path We Tread (1986), pp. 107-108

1974 • Robert Blackman Ford (1924-) was the first African American dentist to be appointed to the State Dental Board in Ohio in 1974. Ford received his B.S. from Morehouse College in 1948 and his D.D.S. degree in 1952 form Howard University Dental School. He also completed additional study from 1952 to 1953 at the Veteran's Hospital in Tuskegee; he has logged 300 hours of post-graduate study. Ford established a private practice in Ohio and is a member of the American Dental Association and the Ohio State Dental Assocation.

Who's Who Among African Americans (1998-1999), p. 449; *Who's Who Among Black Americans* (1990-1991), p. 423

1974 • Joseph L. Henry was the first African American appointed to a Harvard professorship in its School of Dental Medicine in 1974. Long created the Department of Oral Diagnosis and Oral Radiology during his tenure there and headed the department for many years. In 1978, he became the first African American Associate Dean of the School of Dental Medicine.

African-Americans in Boston (1991), p. 148

1974 • George Calvin McTeer (1938-) was the first African American graduate of the College of Dental Medicine of University of South Carolina, when he received his D.M.D. in 1974. McTeer earned a B.S. degree in 1960 at South Carolina State University and a M.Ed. from the same school in 1968. He was chief of dental services at the Franklin C. Fetter Family Health Center from 1974 to 1976, prior to starting a private practice in 1976. McTeer has been active in a number of professional associations, including the American Dental Association and the South Carolina Dental Association. He presently works as a dental consultant.

Who's Who Among Black Americans (1990-1991), p. 874; *Who's Who Among African Americans* (1998-1999), p. 1033

1974 • The Harvard School of Dental Medicine awarded Dolores Mercedes Franklin her D.M.D. in 1974, making her the first African American woman graduate of that school. Franklin received an A.B. degree in 1970 from Barnard College and a M.P.H. from Columbia University in 1974. From 1974 to 1975, she was the director of dental services for the New Jersey Dental Group, and then was assistant dean for student affairs at New York College of Dentistry, the first African American woman in that position from 1975 to 1979. Since 1985, Franklin has been the Dental Coordinator for the District of Columbia Commission of Public Health. She has contributed a number of articles to the scientific literature, as well as having authored a textbook. Franklin was consultant for the U.S. Department of Health and Human Services' Year 2000 Oral Health Objectives of the Nation.

Who's Who Among Black Americans (1990-1991), p. 434; *Who's Who Among African Americans* (1998-1999), p. 438

1974 • The first African American nurse to join the staff of the Carville, Louisiana, Hospital was Donna Kibble, who joined the staff in 1974. The Carville medical facility primarily evaluates and treats leprosy patients, and it also serves as a research and training center for the disease. Kibble became clinical nurse supervisor at Carville in 1980.

The Path We Tread (1986), p. 198

1974 • The Harvard School of Dental Medicine appointed the first African American professor to its faculty when Joseph L. Henry (1924-) was selected in 1974. He created the department of oral diagnosis and oral radiology, which he still heads. Henry earned a B.S. from Xavier University in 1946 and his D.D.S. from Howard University in 1948. He also earned a M.S. in 1949 and Ph.D. in 1951 from the University of Illinois. Henry rose from instructor to professor during the years of 1946 to 1951 at Howard University and was director of clinics there from 1951 to 1965. He joined the Harvard Dental School in 1974. In 1978, he became the first African American associate dean at the Harvard Dental School. Henry has been a member and office holder of numerous professional dental/medical associations and has over 100 articles published in journals of dentistry, dental education, optometry, and health.

African-Americans in Boston (1991), p. 148; *Who's Who Among African Americans* (1998-1999), p. 676; *Who's Who Among Black Americans* (1990-1991), p. 577

1975 • The National League of Nursing presented at each convention several awards for various achievements. One of these was the Lucille Petry Award, given to an outstanding young teacher of nursing. The first African American nurse to receive the award was Lillian Stokes in 1975. Stokes was on the faculty of the Indiana University School of Nursing, and was a graduate of North Carolina Central University.

The Path We Tread (1986), pp. 69, 243

JEANNE CRAIG
SINKFORD

1975 • The first woman appointed dean of a school of dentistry in the United States was dentist Jeanne Craig Sinkford (1933-) when she was appointed to that position in 1975 at Howard University. Sinkford earned her B.S. in 1953 and her D.D.S. in 1958, both at Howard University. Further educational endeavors resulted in a M.S. degree and Ph.D. degree in physiology from Northwestern University in 1962 and 1963, respectively. Sinkford started teaching as an instructor at Howard University in 1958 to 1960. She returned in 1964 as associate professor and chair of the department of prosthodontics, the first woman to head such a department. In 1974, she became associate dean, and the following year, was appointed dean of Howard University's College of Dentistry, a position she retained until 1991, when she became professor and dean emerita. Sinkford authored 70 publications and a manual for crown and bridge prosthodontics. In 1974, she was inducted into the U.S. Section of the International College of Dentists.

Ebony (July, 1986), p. 134; *Encyclopedia of Black America* (1981), p. 755; *Jet* (July 10, 1958), p. 49; *Profile of the Negro in American Dentistry* (1979), p. 18

1975 • William Keelan Collins (1914-), when elected president of the American Association of Dental Examiners in October 1975, was the first

African American elected to that office in the 94-year history of the organization. Collins earned his B.S. degree in 1935 and a D.D.S. degree in 1939 at Howard University. He also received a D.Sc. in 1974 from Georgetown University College of Dentistry, and has been in private practice since 1939.

Profile of the Negro in American Dentistry (1979), p. 101; *Who's Who Among African Americans* (1998-1999), p. 308

1976 • The first African American professor on the faculty of the University of Cincinnati College of Nursing and Health Care was Carolyn McGraw Carter, when she was appointed in 1976. The same year, Carter was also awarded the prestigious American Nurses' Association Mary Mahoney Award. She received a diploma from St. Francis Hospital School of Nursing in Pittsburgh, followed by a B.S.N., a M.S., and a Ph.D.—all from the University of Pittsburgh. Carter is associate professor of psychiatric-mental health nursing, Graduate School of Nursing, and Assistant Dean of Student Affairs, School of Medicine, University of Pittsburgh. In this particular joint appointment of nursing and medicine, Carter teaches, conducts research, provides consultation to faculty and students, and does interdisciplinary collaborations.

The Path We Tread (1986), pp. 136-137

1976 • Hattie Bessent (1926-) was the first African American appointed to the position of graduate dean at the Vanderbilt University Graduate School of Nursing in 1976. Bessent received a B.S. in 1959 from Florida A & M University School of Nursing, a M.S. from Indiana University in 1962, and an Ed.D. from the University of Florida, Gainesville in 1970. After receiving her M.S. in psychiatric nursing, she returned to her hometown of Jacksonville and became the first African American nurse to head a psychiatric unit in that city. When Bessent received her doctorate, she was the first African American nurse in Florida to do so. She was also the first African American nurse in the South to be inducted into the honorary organizations Phi Delta Kappa, Sigma Theta Tau, and Pi Lambda Theta. Bessent currently is the deputy executive director of the Ethnic/Racial Minority Fellowship Programs of the American Nurses Association.

Blacks in Science and Medicine (1990), p. 27; *Black Women in America* (1993), p. 113; *The Path We Tread* (1986), pp. 60-61

1976 • The first master's degree program in nursing established at a historically African American higher education institution was implemented by Fostine G. Riddick in 1976 at Hampton University. The first master's degree in nursing at Hampton was acquired by Terry Williams Dagrosa two years later. Riddick received both a diploma and B.S. from Tuskegee Institute

School of Nursing and a M.A. from New York University. The master's program started with courses of study in community health and community health nursing and was expanded to include three specialty areas and two graduate head nurse-practitioner programs. Riddick was dean and professor of the Hampton Institute School of Nursing for many years. Included in her many honors is an eight-year Governor's appointment.

The Path We Tread (1986), pp. 39, 118

1976 • Barbara Martin McArthur, a professor of nursing at Wayne State University, established the nurse epidemiology program at the College of Nursing in 1976. At the time, it was the only such program of its kind, and McArthur was its director from 1976 to 1983. She received a diploma in nursing from Provident Hospital School of Nursing in Chicago, a B.S. and M.S. from DePaul University, and a Ph.D. in 1976 from the University of Washington. She also holds certificates from the Centers for Disease Control in surveillance, prevention, and control of nosocomial infections (those originating in a hospital) and from the Oak Ridge Institute of Nuclear Studies. McArthur is a pioneer in research in institutional epidemiology study. She is a member of several nursing, epidemiology, and microbiology organizations and was a member of the first Certification Board of Infection Control. McArthur has published numerous journal articles and book chapters.

Blacks in Science and Medicine (1990), p. 166; *The Path We Tread* (1986), pp. 122-123; *Who's Who Among Black Americans* (1990-1991), p. 842; *Who's Who Among African Americans* (1998-1999), p. 993

1977 • The first African American faculty member at the University of Rhode Island College of Nursing was Grayce Scott Garner (1922-) when she joined the University in 1977. Garner was at Rhode Island University until 1985. While at Rhode Island, she was also the first African American full professor and first African American Coordinator of Programs in the College of Nursing. Garner received a B.S. in nursing in 1954 from Boston University, a M.S. in 1956 from Columbia University, and an Ed.D. in 1963 from Columbia. She joined the University of Massachusetts in 1985 as professor of nursing and coordinator of medical health.

Who's Who Among African Americans (1998-1999), p. 529

1978 • Verdelle B. Bellamy (1928-) became the first African American president of the Georgia Board of Nursing in 1978. Bellamy devoted her professional life to improving the image of professional nursing and increasing minority participation in the field. She received a B.S. in 1958 from Tuskegee University and a M.S.N. from Emory University in 1963. She was a clinical associate at Tuskegee Institute from 1957 to 1958, and then a nursing instructor at Grady Memorial Hospital School of Nursing from 1958 to 1962. Bellamy was then coordinator and supervisor at the VA Medical Center in Atlanta from 1963 to 1982, when she was then promoted to associate chief of nursing. In 1963, Bellamy was one of the first two African American nurses to graduate from Emory University. Ten years later, she was the first African American appointed to the Georgia Board of Nursing. Bellamy was active in many nursing associations, holding office and board positions in many of them.

Black Women in White (1989), p. 191; *Blacks in Science and Medicine* (1990), p. 25; *The Path We Tread* (1986), pp. 84-85; *Who's Who Among Black Americans* (1990-1991), p. 88; *Who's Who Among African Americans* (1998-1999), p. 101

1978 • The American Nursing Association, in 1978, selected Barbara Lauraine Nichols as its first African American president. Nichols received a B.S. from Case Western Reserve University, a M.S. from the University of Wisconsin, Madison, and her diploma from the Massachusetts General Hospital School of Nursing. Nichols was elected president of the American Nursing Association in 1978 and served in the office until 1982. She also became the first African American in the state of Wisconsin to hold a state cabinet-level position, Secretary of the Wisconsin Department of Regulation and Licensing.

Blacks in Science and Medicine (1990), p. 181; *Ebony* (September 1981), pp. 56-57; *Jet* (September 7, 1978) p. 21; *The Path We Tread* (1986), pp. 80-81, 83-84

1978 • The distinction of being the first woman, youngest, and first African American president of the Planned Parenthood Federation of America was given to (Alyce) Faye Wattleton (1943-) when she was appointed to the position in 1978. Wattleton received her B.S. in nursing from Ohio State University in 1964 and her M.S. in maternal and infant health care in 1967 from Columbia University. She first volunteered her services to Planned Parenthood of Miami Valley, and after serving on the board of directors for two years, was asked to assume the executive directorship, a position she held for seven years. Wattleton resigned from Planned Parenthood in 1992. In 1993, she was inducted into the National Women's Hall of Fame.

Black Women in America (1993), pp. 1239-1240; *Dollars and Sense* (Special Issue 1986), p. 52

1979 • The United States Veterans Administration, in 1979, selected from an applicant pool of 254, five people to become National Veterans Administration Scholars in the Chief Medical Director's Office in Washington, D.C.

Liz Johnson was the only African American chosen. Johnson earned a B.S. from Texas Women's University School of Nursing. She had held other positions in the VA system since 1974, including director of nursing at the VA Hospital in Baltimore, Maryland. Johnson earned a certificate in management from the University of Baltimore.

ALYCE FAYE WATTLETON   *The Path We Tread* (1986), p. 218

1979 • Hazel Winifred Johnson (1927-), who joined the U. S. Army in 1955 became, in 1979, the first African American woman promoted to general. At that time, she became the chief of the Army Nurse Corps, a position she held until 1983. After joining the Army, Johnson later completed training as a nurse, and in May 1960 was commissioned a first lieutenant in the U.S. Army Nursing Corps. While in the military, she completed the requirements for a bachelor's degree in nursing from Villanova University, a masters degree in nursing education from Columbia University, and a Ph.D. in educational administration from Catholic University. Johnson retired from the military in 1983, becoming the director of the government affairs division of the American Nursing Association until 1986. Johnson then became professor of nursing at Virginia's George Mason University.

HAZEL WINIFRED JOHNSON

Black Women in America (1993), p. 644; *Ebony* (July, 1995), p. 120; *Jet* (July 17, 1980), p. 16; *The Path We Tread* (1986), pp. 174, 242, 244

1980 • Vernice Ferguson became the first African American chief of the Nursing Department at the Clinical Center, National Institutes of Health in 1973. She had previously been chief nurse at several U. S. Veterans Administration hospitals. Ferguson, in October 1980, became the first nurse appointed deputy assistant chief medical director for nursing programs and director of nursing services for the Veterans Administration. She was elected president of the American Academy of Nursing in 1981.

Black Women in White (1989), p. 191; *The Path We Tread* (1986), pp. 218, 219; *The Timetables of African American History* (1995), p. 323

1981 • The first African American woman certified by the Board of Infection Control was Barbara Martin McArthur in 1981. McArthur received a diploma in nursing from Provident Hospital and Training School, a B.S. in nursing and a M.S. from DePaul University, and a second M.S. and Ph.D. degree in 1976 from the University of Washington. McArthur was initially a nurse and assistant professor of microbiology and immunology at Knoxville College. She then entered the graduate program in institutional epidemiology and became an associate professor at Wayne State University from 1976 until 1984. She was also an adjunct professor of biology from 1980 to 1988 and professor of nursing from 1978 to 1996. McArthur produced a number of publications, book chapters, journal articles, and abstracts, as well as being on the review board of *ABNF Journal*. McArthur is now retired.

Blacks in Science and Medicine (1990), p. 166; *Who's Who Among African Americans* (1998-1999), p. 860; *Who's Who Among Black Americans* (1990-1991), p. 842

1982 • The first African American woman oral and maxillofacial surgeon in the United States was Gladys L. Johnson, who earned that honor in 1982. She is in private practice in Dallas, Texas. Johnson received her education at Ohio State University, the College of Medicine and Dentistry of New Jersey, Yale University, and Rutgers University. She is also a member of and active in several professional dental organizations and is an adjunct assistant professor in the Department of Dental Hygiene at Texas Women's University.

Ebony (August 1982), p. 5

1983 • The first nurse appointed director of the Michigan Department of Public Health—and the first nurse ever appointed head of a state agency in Michigan—was Gloria R. Smith (1934-) when she was chosen in 1983. Smith earned a B.S. degree in 1955 from Wayne State University, a M.P.H. in 1959 from the University of Michigan, a M.A. from the University of Oklahoma in 1977, and a Ph.D. in 1979 from Union College and University. She was a district nursing supervisor from 1968 to 1970 for the Oklahoma State Health Department. She joined the staff of Oklahoma University as an assistant professor from 1971 to 1973, and as dean and professor from 1975 to 1983, when she joined the Michigan State Department of Public Health.

Black Women in White (1989), p. 191; *Who's Who Among African Americans* (1998-1999), pp. 1382-1383; *Who's Who Among Black Americans* (1990-1991), p. 1168

1984 • When Ernest Donald Walker retired from the U. S. Food and Drug Administration (FDA) in May 1984, he was the only African American nurse on the FDA staff. Since 1980, Walker had been in the position of nurse consultant, medical/surgical/anesthesia. He received a diploma from the Delaware Hospital School of Nursing, a B.S. from Arizona State University, and a M.S. from Boston University. Walker is also a certified nurse anesthetist, providing authoritative medical opinions as necessary in the enforcement of the Federal Food, Drug, and Cosmetics Act as applied to medical devices.

The Path We Tread (1986), pp. 191-192

1984 • Ora Strickland, in 1984, became the first African American chair of the Board of Directors of the *American Journal of Nursing* Company. The company, established by the American Nurses' Association in 1900, is the leading publisher of nursing periodicals and multimedia educational programs. It publishes the *American Journal of Nursing, International Nursing Index, MCN,* the *Journal of Maternal Child Nursing,* and *Geriatric Nursing.* Strickland earned a B.S. from North Carolina A&T State University and a M.S. in nursing from Boston University. She then received a Ph.D. from the University of North Carolina at Greensboro. Strickland was an assistant professor at the University of North Carolina at Greensboro and currently holds the position of Doctoral Program Evaluator and associate professor at the University of Maryland School of Nursing, Baltimore.

The Path We Tread (1986), pp. 87-88, 124-125, 245

1984 • The first African American nurse to be appointed chief of the department of nursing at Walter Reed Army Medical Center was Clara Leach Adams-Ender (1939-) in 1984. Three years later, she was appointed chief of the U.S. Army Nurse Corps. At that time, she held the rank of brigadier general. Adams-Ender started her military and nursing career as a second lieutenant in the active army in 1961 as a general duty nurse. She earned a B.S. degree at North Carolina A & T College in 1961 and a M.S. degree in nursing at the University of Minnesota in 1969. She was awarded a M.S. from the U.S. Army Command and General Staff College at Fort Leavenworth, Kansas in 1976, being the first woman to receive that particular degree. In 1981, Adams-Ender was assigned to the U.S. Recruiting Command in Fort Sheridan, Illinois as chief of the Army Nurse Corps division. After her tour of duty in the Office of the Surgeon General, Adams-Ender became an adjunct faculty member of Georgetown University School of Nursing and of Oakland University School of Nursing in Rochester, Michigan.

Black Women in America (1993), pp. 10-11; *Jet* (November 15, 1982), p. 16; *Notable Black American Women* (1992), pp. 1-2

1985 • Robert L. Kimbrough (1922-), became the first African American president of the Chicago Dental Society in 1985. Kimbrough received a D.D.S. in 1951 from the University of Illinois College of Dentistry. He is in private practice in Chicago, Illinois. Kimbrough is an active member of local, state, and national dental and medical associations. Some of his activities include: President of the Kenwood Hyde Park Dental Society, vice president of the Medical Association of Chicago, fellow of the Academy of General Dentistry, member of the American Dental Association, fellow of the American College of Dentists, and chair of the Peer Review Committee of the Illinois State Dental Society.

Jet (April 8, 1985), p. 24; *Who's Who Among Black Americans* (1990-1991), p. 735

1989 • The first African American president of the Society of Pediatric Dentistry was Jerome C. Scales in 1989. Scales earned a B.S. in 1969 from Tennessee State University, a D.D.S. degree in 1973 from Meharry Medical College, and a certificate in pediatric dentistry in 1975 from the University of Alabama School of Dentistry. He has a private practice in Birmingham, Alabama specializing in pediatric dentistry, which he started in 1975. He has been a clinical associate professor at the University of Alabama School of Dentistry since 1975. Scales has been active in a number of professional organizations including the Birmingham Pediatric Dental Society (President), Alabama Society of Pediatric Dentistry (President), Alabama Dental Society (President), American Dental Association, American Academy of Pediatric Dentistry, and American Orthodontic Society.

Jet (September 18, 1989), p. 20; *Who's Who Among African Americans* (1998-1999), p. 1147; *Black Firsts* (1994), p. 298

1989 • The "WIPSS" or "Williams' Intra-Oral Protective Sports System" is a mouthpiece or oral protector invented by an African American dentist, Edward D. Williams. The WIPSS mouthguard protects the teeth from damage after a blow to the jaw and also stabilizes the jaw. This mouthpiece also covers the upper and lower teeth and is clamped together so as to prevent the lower jaw from moving back and jolting the base of the brain.

Philadelphia Tribune (March 31, 1992), p. 4B

1992 • Margaret H. Jordan (1943-) was the first African American and first woman to be elected vice president of Southern California Edison's Health Care Services in 1992. Jordan is a registered nurse. She received a B.S. in nursing from Georgetown University and a M.P.H. from the University of California at Berkeley. She became vice president of the Kaiser Foundation Health Plan of Texas in 1986. At Edison, Jordan oversees the health care and coverage of Edison's employees, dependents, retirees, and program participants, as well as being responsible for workers compensation and disability activities.

Jet (Dec. 14, 1992), p. 14; *Black Enterprise* (August 1994), p. 60

1992 • Paul A. Stephens (1921-) was the first African American president of the Academy of General Dentistry in 1992. He received both his B.S. and D.D.S. degrees from Howard University in 1942 and 1945, respectively. Stephens has been self-employed since 1946, after serving one year as an instructor at the Howard University College of Dentistry. He has been active with a number of professional organizations, including the Gary, Indiana Board of Health (president, 1973-9), Indiana State Board of Dental Examiners (president, 1978-80), Indiana Academy of General Dentistry (president, 1980-1), and American Academy of General Dentistry (vice-president, 1990-1).

Jet (August 24, 1992), p. 36; *Who's Who Among Black Americans* (1992-1993), p. 1335; *Who's Who Among African Americans* (1998-1999), p. 1231; *Black Firsts* (1994), p. 298

1993 • The first African American president of the Virginia State Board of Dentistry, in 1993, was James Darnell Watkins (1949-). The board is responsible for licensing and disciplining dental professionals. Watkins is a 1975 graduate of the Medical College of Virginia, School of Dentistry. He earned a B.S. degree in biology from Virginia Polytechnic Institute in 1971. He has been in private practice since 1977. Watkins is active in a number of dental associations. He was a governor appointee, in 1989, to the Virginia State Board of Dentistry. Watkins is a captain in the U.S. Naval Reserve Dental Corps, and in 1991, was the first African American commanding officer when he was promoted to that rank.

Jet (February 1, 1993), p. 20; *Who's Who Among African Americans* (1998-1999), pp. 1563-1564

1997 • The first African American woman president in the 21-year history of the National Nurses Society on Addictions was Karen Allen, who was elected to the office in 1997. Allen is an associate professor, Department of Psychiatry, Community and Adult Primary Care, at the University of Maryland at Baltimore, MD.

Jet (February 24, 1997), p. 19; *Who's Who Among African Americans* (1998-1999), p. 24

1998 • Martin T. Tyler was the first African American elected president of the American Academy of Oral Medicine when he was elected to the position in 1998. The Academy members are dentists who specialize in diseases of the mouth. Tyler earned a bachelor's degree in zoology from Ohio State University, a D.D.S. from Howard University, and a master's degree in education from George Washington University.

Ebony (January 1999), p. 10

1998 • The first African American elected president of the American Academy of Implant Dentistry was Terry Reynolds, when he was elected in 1998. Reynolds is a diplomate of the American Board of Oral Implant Dentistry and is in practice in Atlanta, Georgia.

Jet (August 31, 1998), p. 18

1998 • Fannie Gaston-Johansson became the first African American woman at the John Hopkins University School of Nursing to earn a full professorship and tenure in 1998. She is director of International and Extramural Affairs at the School of Nursing. In 1993, Gaston-Johansson was an associate professor and the first African American to hold the Elsie M. Lawler Chair at Johns Hopkins. She was associate professor at the University of Nebraska College of Nursing and director of nursing research at the University of Nebraska Medical Center.

Jet (November 30, 1998), p. 20

LIFE SCIENCES
∿∿∿∿∿∿∿∿∿∿∿∿∿∿∿∿∿∿∿∿

1855 • Solomon G. Brown (1829-1903?) delivered his first public lecture on January 10, 1855 in Washington, D.C. Brown was a widely known naturalist in the D.C. area and often lectured on scientific subjects in public and private sessions. He gained his expertise working for the Smithsonian Institution from 1852 to about 1903. His specialty was zoology, particularly insects, and he prepared elaborate color renderings for Smithsonian presentations as well as for his own. During the 1840s, Brown worked with Samuel F.B. Morse on the installation of the first Morse magnetic telegraph system between Washington, D.C. and Baltimore, Maryland.

Blacks in Science: Astrophysicist to Zoologist (1977), p. 90; *Dictionary of American Negro Biography* (1982), pp. 70-71; *Men of Mark* (1970), pp. 193-200

1889 • Alfred Oscar Coffin (1861-) became the first African American to earn a Ph.D. in the biological sciences when he was awarded his degree in zoology in 1889 from Illinois Wesleyan University. He had previously earned his B.A. from Fisk University in 1885.

Blacks in Science and Medicine (1990), p. 58; *Negro Year Book* (1952), p. 96

1907 • Charles Henry Turner (1867-1923) was the first African American to earn the Ph.D. degree in biology from the University of Chicago, which he received in 1907. Turner published 51 papers in scientific journals covering neurology, invertebrate ecology, and animal behavior. He completed many pioneering studies in the field of entomology. Among his discoveries was the fact that bees are attracted to flowers by their particular colors and odors. He was also the first to prove that insects can hear and distinguish pitch and that cockroaches have the ability to learn. He also discovered the characteristic movement of ants when they are disturbed, called "Turner's Circling" in his honor. Turner taught at Clark College from 1893 to 1895 and then at several high schools. He spent the remainder of his career, from 1908 on, teaching high school biology at Sumner High School in St. Louis until his death in 1923.

Blacks in Science and Medicine (1990), p. 235; *Blacks in Science: Astrophysicist to Zoologist* (1977), pp. 24-25; *Dictionary of American Negro Biography* (1983), p. 608; *Seven Black American Scientists* (1970), pp. 68-91

ERNEST EVERETT JUST

1915 • The first recipient of the National Association for the Advancement of Colored People (NAACP) Springam Medal was cell biologist Ernest E. Just (1883-1941) who received the 1915 award for his work in the field of biological research. The Springarn medal is presented annually for the highest achievement by an African American in any field of endeavor. Just was affiliated with Howard University from 1907 until the 1920s and performed most of his research during summers spent at the Marine Biological Laboratory in Woods Hole, Massachusetts, a world-famous research institution. Just graduated from Dartmouth University in 1907 *magna cum laude* and in 1916, became the first African American to earn a Ph.D. degree in physiology/biology, which he received from the University of Chicago. In 1920, he received the first grant awarded to an African American by the National Research Council. Just was the first American invited to be a guest researcher at the Kaiser Wilhelm Institute for Biology of Berlin in 1929. He spent the remainder of his professional career in Europe, where racial discrimination was less widespread. Just published more than seventy papers and two major classic texts, which centered on cell biology and egg fertilization of marine animals.

African-American Almanac (1997), p. 1073; *Blacks in Science: Astrophysicist to Zoologist* (1977), pp. 72-73; *Black Apollo of Science* (1983); *The Timetables of African-American History* (1996), p. 235

1918 • Walter Sterling Wickliffee was the first African American to earn a Ph.D. in forestry, which he received from the University of Michigan in 1918. Wickliffe worked as a private consultant with a specialty in the diagnosis and treatment of individual trees. He also served as a guest lecturer at the University of Michigan's School of Natural Resources.

Blacks in Science: Astrophysicist to Zoologist (1977), pp. 28-29

1920 • African American botanist Charles Stewart Parker (1882-1950) discovered and described a new sub-genus of the genus *Carex* and also discovered and described 39 species of plants. A new species of sweet pea, *Lathyrus parkeri,* and a new variety of rose, *Rosa spaldingii parkeri,* were named in his honor. Parker earned a B.S. in 1905 from Trinity College, a

M.S. in 1922 from State College of Washington, and a Ph.D. in 1932 from Pennsylvania State College. He joined the Howard University (Washington, D.C.) faculty as an associate professor of botany in 1925 and was promoted to professor in 1926. He became head of the botany department in 1936 and remained at Howard University until his 1947 retirement.

Blacks in Science and Medicine (1990), p. 184; *Blacks in Science: Astrophysicist to Zoologist* (1972), p. 17; *Notable Twentieth Century Scientists* (1995), p. 1532

1921 • In 1921, Thomas Wyatt Turner (1877-1978) became the first African American to be awarded a Ph.D. in botany from Cornell University (New York). Turner had earned a B.A. and M.A. in 1901 and 1905 from Howard University (Washington, D.C.), where he served as professor of botany from 1914 to 1924. In 1924, he was appointed professor of biology and head of the department at Hampton Institute (Virginia), which he headed until 1945. Turner was an expert on plant physiology and pathology, the effects of mineral nutrients on seed plants, and the physiological effects of phosphorus and nitrogen on plants. He also conducted 10 years of research on cotton breeding, which resulted in his discovery of a strain of cotton which was practically pure for fine lock balls.

Blacks in Science and Medicine (1990), p. 236; *Dictionary of Black Culture* (1973), p. 442; *Negro Year Book* (1947), p. 36; *Journal of Blacks in Higher Education* (Spring 1997), pp. 94-5

1922 • Leon Roddy (1922-) was the first African American entomologist of note. Roddy has been a leading authority on insects, especially spiders, since about 1950. Roddy received a B.S. degree from Texas College and a Ph.D. degree from Ohio State University. After graduating from Ohio State, Roddy taught at Southern University in Louisiana. Roddy has been consulted by scientists from all over the world to identify thousands of insects, especially spiders. He has identified over 6,000 spiders in his lifetime.

Ebony (March, 1962), pp. 65-70; *Pathfinders* 3, (1988), p. 18

1927 • Roger A. Young (1889-1964) became the first African American woman to do research at the famed Marine Biological Laboratory in Woods Hole, Massachusetts when she came in the summer of 1927. She returned every summer until 1936. Young earned a B.S. in biology from Howard University in 1923, a M.S. in zoology from the University of Chicago in 1926, and a Ph.D. (zoology) from the University of Pennsylvania in 1940. In her research, she studied structures that control salt concentration in *Paramecium*. She also studied the effects or indirect and direct radiation on sea urchin eggs. In addition to her research, Young taught on the college level.

The Book of African American Women (1996), pp. 211-212; *Black Women in America* (1993), pp. 1298-1299

1930 • The first Ph.D. degree in anatomy awarded to an African American was earned by Roscoe Lewis McKinney (1900-1978) in 1930 from the University of Chicago. He received a B.A. from Bates College in 1921. McKinney founded the anatomy department of the Howard University Medical College and served as its chair from 1930 to 1947. He was vice-dean of the School of Medicine from 1944 to 1946 and Emeritus Professor of the Medical School from 1968 to 1978. Through his distinguished career, McKinney taught abroad in such countries as Iraq, India, and Vietnam and established the first tissue-culture laboratory in the Washington D.C. area, at Howard University. His tissue samples were even included in *Gray's Anatomy*, the foremost anatomy text.

African-American Medical Pioneers (1994), pp. 25, 193; *Blacks in Science and Medicine* (1990), p. 170; *Jet* (November 9, 1978), p. 18; *Journal of the National Medical Association* Vol. 71, (May, 1979), p. 518

SAMUEL NABRIT

1932 • Samuel M. Nabrit (1905-) was the first African American to receive a Ph.D. from Brown University. His degree, earned in 1932, was in biology, with an emphasis in zoology. Nabrit earned his B.A. degree from Morehouse College in 1925, and his M.S. degree in 1928 from Brown. He taught at Morehouse College (1925-1931) and at Atlanta University (1932-1947), where he also served as chair of the biology department. He was then selected president of Southern University, where he served until 1967. Nabrit was a noted biologist who spent five summers at the Woods Hole Marine Biology Laboratory, directed numerous projects, and published extensively. He was appointed to a four-year term to the Atomic Energy Commission by President Lyndon Johnson in 1966, the first African American appointed to that commission. He was also the first African American appointed to the National Science Board for a six-year term (1956-1961) by President Dwight Eisenhower.

Blacks in Science and Medicine (1990), p. 179; *Dictionary of Black Culture* (1973), p. 316; *Famous First Facts* (1972), p. 175; *Who's Who Among Black Americans* (1977), p. 662

1933 • The first Ph.D. in bacteriology awarded to an African American woman was earned by Ruth Moore, when she received the degree in 1933 from Ohio State University. Moore had previously received a B.S. in 1926 and a M.S. in 1927 from Ohio State. Moore was an instructor of hygiene from 1927 to 1930 while in graduate training. Moore joined the Howard University faculty as an instructor in bacteriology in 1933 and was promoted to assistant professor of bacteriology in 1939. She was named acting head of the university's department of bacteriology, preventive medicine, and public health in 1948. In 1955, she was appointed head of the department of bacteriology where she remained until 1960, when she became associate professor of microbiology. Moore remained in that department until her 1973 retirement, whereupon she became associate professor emeritus of microbiology. During her career, she conducted research in the areas of blood groupings and Enterobacteriaceae, a family of disease-causing bacteria.

African-American Medical Pioneers (1994), pp. 25, 193; *Blacks in Science and Medicine* (1990), p. 176; *Notable Black American Scientists* (1999), pp. 235-236; *Notable Twentieth Century Scientists* (1995), p. 1413

1934 • Moses Wharton Young (1904-1986) became in 1934 the first African American to earn a Ph.D. in anatomy from the University of Michigan. Young earned his B.S. in 1926 from Howard University (Washington, D.C.), and then the M.D. in 1930 and the Ph.D. in 1934, both from Michigan. He joined the Howard University faculty in 1934 as an assistant professor of anatomy. He was promoted to associate professor in 1941, and to professor in 1947. In 1973, Young was appointed professor of anatomy at the University of Maryland College of Medicine. Young's research specialty was in hypersensitive deafness and the structure of the inner ear, and he received a number of awards and honors for his medical contributions.

African American Medical Pioneers (1994), pp. 25, 176; *Blacks in Science and Medicine* (1990), p. 260

1939 • Amanda E. Peele (1908-), born in Jackson, North Carolina, was the first African American woman to present a research paper before the Virginia Academy of Science, making the presentation in 1939. Peele earned a B.S. degree from Hampton Institute in 1930 and a M.S. degree from Cornell University in 1934. She was a professor of biology at Hampton Institute, having started teaching there in 1930. Peele was active in the Virginia Conference of College Science Teachers, American Association for the Advancement of Science, Virginia Academy of Science, and the Virginia Research Society.

Blacks in Science and Medicine (1990), p. 187

1941 • Western Reserve University (Ohio) awarded the first Ph.D. in anatomy earned by an African American woman to Ruth Smith Lloyd (1917-) in 1941. She had previously earned a B.A. degree in zoology from Mount Holyoke College in 1937 and a M.S. degree in zoology from Harvard University. Lloyd studied under the world famous biologist Ernest E. Just while at Howard University and was a Rosenwald Fellow in anatomy at Western Reserve, where she co-authored several publications with Boris Rubenstein, her major advisor. Lloyd taught one year at Hampton Institute and joined the Howard University College of Medicine in 1942 as a teaching assistant in physiology. She rose through the academic ranks to assistant professor in anatomy in the Graduate School of Howard University in 1958. Lloyd retired in 1977 but continued to be active in educational, religious, and social affairs in Washington, D.C.

African-American Medical Pioneers (1994), pp. 25, 84-86, 133; *Journal of the National Medical Association* Vol. 85, (1983), p. 787; *Blacks in Science and Medicine* (1990), p. 155

1943 • Biologist Charles Wesley Buggs (1906-1991), who developed a unique method for the treatment of burns and wounds from under the skin, was the first African American full-time faculty member at Wayne State University when he was appointed instructor in bacteriology in 1943. Buggs earned a B.S. degree from Morehouse College in 1928, majoring in zoology. He then earned a M.S. in 1931 and a Ph.D. in 1934, both from the University of Minnesota. Buggs taught biology and became chairman of the natural sciences division at Dillard University during the period 1935 to 1943. He then taught at Wayne State until 1949, when he returned to Dillard and taught until 1956. Buggs held a professorship in microbiology at Howard University from 1956 to 1971. He was associated with the Drew Postgraduate Medical School and University of California until 1973, when he became professor of microbiology at California State College, Long Beach where he retired in 1983. Buggs wrote many scientific articles and published a text on biology.

Blacks in Science and Medicine (1990), p. 41; *Negro Year Book* (1941-1946), p. 35; *Who's Who Among Black Americans* (1990-1991), p. 176

1945 • The first African American to earn a Ph.D. in entomology from Cornell University (New York) was Vivian Murray Chambers (1903-1984), who received the degree in 1945. He received a B.S. in 1928 from Shaw University (North Carolina), a B.A. in 1931 from Columbia University (New York), and then a M.S. from Cornell in 1935. In 1937, Chambers began teaching in the biology department at Alabama A&M University. After receiving his Ph.D. in 1945, Chambers was the first faculty member at Alabama A&M to hold a doctorate degree. During an early work experience at the American Museum of Natural History, Chambers developed an interest in entomology that led to his pioneering research in the ecological impact of pesticides such as DDT. He was also instrumental in the development of the School of Arts and Sciences at Alabama A&M, and became the first dean of the school in 1970, serving in that position until he retired in 1973.

Blacks in Science and Medicine (1990), p. 52; *Notable Black American Scientists* (1999), pp. 62-3

1949 • Charles Wesley Buggs (1906-1991) authored the first significant text by an African American bacteriologist. The book, *Premedical Education for Negroes: Interpretations and Recommendations Based Upon a Survey in*

HAROLD WEST (LEFT) WITH COLLEAGUE AT MEHARRY MEDICAL COLLEGE.

Fifteen Selected Negro Colleges, was published in 1949 and was based on a study that was partially funded by the federal government. Buggs earned a B.A. degree at Morehouse College in 1928, and a M.S. degree in 1932 and Ph.D. degree in 1934 from the University of Minnesota. He taught chemistry for one year at Bishop College (1934-35) and then was professor and chairman of the Division of Natural Sciences at Dillard University from 1935 to 1943. In 1943, he became an instructor at the School of Medicine of Wayne University (Detroit, Michigan) and stayed with the university until 1949. Buggs's primary research areas were in the treatment of wound infections and burns, and he devised a method for treating these traumas from under the skin. He was also an expert on skin grafting. Buggs was a professor of microbiology at California State University at Long Beach from 1973 to 1983.

Black Americans in Science and Engineering (1974), p. 21; *Blacks in Science and Medicine* (1990), p. 41; *Negro Year Book* (1947), p. 35; *Who's Who Among Black Americans* (1990-1991), p. 176

1952 • Harold Dadford West (1904-1974) first joined the faculty of Meharry Medical College (Tennessee) in 1927 as associate professor of physiological chemistry, and in 1952 was appointed the first African American president of that institution. In 1963, West became the first African American appointed to the Tennessee State Board of Education. He completed a B.A. in 1925 at the University of Illinois, where he learned the M.S. in 1930 and the Ph.D. in 1937. He was a recipient of a Julius Rosenwald Fund fellowship and was a Rockefeller Foundation Fellow while working on his advanced degrees. West's teaching and research careers from 1927 through 1973 were devoted to Meharry Medical College. He did extensive research in tuberculosis and other bacilli, the antibiotic biocern, and aromatic hydrocarbons. He was also the first to synthesize threonine. West retired as Meharry's president in 1965, but continued in the position of professor of biochemistry there until 1973.

Blacks in Science and Medicine (1990), p. 246; *Journal of the National Medical Association, Vol. 66* (September 1974), pp. 448-9; *Notable Black American Scientists* (1998), pp. 311-2; *Who's Who Among African Americans* (1998-1999), p. 1582

1956 • Percy L. Julian (1899-1975) patented his process for preparation of the drug cortisone in 1956. His original patent application was filed in September 1950. Research from the Mayo Clinic in 1948 indicated that synthetic cortisone was useful in combating the inflammation symptoms of arthritis, but that the drug was too costly. Julian perfected an economical method of synthesizing cortexolone from soya beans. He determined that the difference between cortisone and cortexolone was one oxygen atom, which he called Substance S. Julian devised a process to add the missing atom to cortexolone, resulting in synthetic cortisone. The drug was just as effective in the treatment of arthritis as the organic form. Julian's invention resulted in the cost of a dose of cortisone dropping from hundreds of dollars a dose to pennies per dose.

Created Equal (1993), pp. 153-162; *Index of Patents* (1956); *Notable Black American Scientists* (1999), pp. 183-185

1956 • The first African American to hold a teaching assistantship at George Washington University, in 1956, was William C. Branche, Jr. (1934-). He received a B.A. in 1956 from Wesleyan University (Ohio), his M.S. from George Washington University in 1959, and then the Ph.D. from the Catholic University of America in 1969. Branche started work for the Walter Reed Army Institute for Research in 1971 and then in 1979, joined the National Institutes of Health (NIH) Bacteriology and Mycology Division. He is currently the Executive Secretary of the Division of Research Grants in the Health Science Administration at NIH.

Who's Who Among African Americans (1991), p. 134, (1997), p. 154

1957 • The American Association of Physical Anthropologists elected its first African American president, W. Montague Cobb (1904-1990), in 1957. Cobb received his A.B. from Amherst College (Massachusetts) in 1925, his

M.D. from Howard University (District of Columbia) in 1929, and a Ph.D. in anatomy and physical anthropology from Western Reserve University (Ohio) in 1932. He joined the Howard University faculty in 1928, where he remained as an active faculty member for 48 years. By 1942, Cobb had been promoted to full professor and served as chairman of the department of anatomy from 1947 to 1969. In 1969 he was elevated to the rank of distinguished professor, and in 1973 he was named professor emeritus. He was visiting professor of anatomy at Stanford University (California), University of Maryland and University of Arkansas, as well as visiting professor of orthopedic surgery at Howard University. Cobb published over 500 scientific articles and 200 biographies of African American physicians.

WILLIAM MONTAGUE COBB

A Century of Black Surgeons (1987), pp. 470-472; *Journal of the National Medical Association* Vol. 85, (August,1993), p. 641

1958 • Theodore E. Bolden (1920-) was the first African American to receive the Ph.D. degree in pathology in 1958 from the University of Illinois. Bolden received his B.A. from Lincoln University (Pennsylvania) in 1941 and his D.D.S. from Meharry Medical College in 1947. He was an associate professor at Seton Hall University College of Medicine (New Jersey) from 1957 to 1962 and chair of the Oral Pathology Department at Meharry from 1962 to 1977. He also conducted research and contributed to over 200 scientific publications, including 10 textbooks. Bolden has been affiliated with the University Medical and Dental School of New Jersey since the 1970s; he was named Professor Emeritus in 1991.

Blacks in Science and Medicine (1990), p. 31; *Profile of the Negro in American Dentistry* (1979), p. 35; *Who's Who in America* (1986-1987), p. 281

THEODORE E. BOLDEN

1961 • The first African American horticulture inspector for the District of Columbia government, appointed in 1961, was Allen Henry Wilkins (1934-). Wilkins earned a B.S. from Tuskegee Institute in 1957 and a M.S. from Catholic University in 1973. He held, until 1973, various positions as a horticultural inspector and landscape designer for various federal agencies. In 1973, Wilkins was appointed professor of horticulture and landscaping at the University of the District of Columbia. He has developed master plans for several projects under the U.S. Department of Defense and completed several landscape and urban design plans for parks and schools.

Who's Who Among African-Americans (1998-1999), p. 1606

1965 • Clarence William Wright (1912-1968) was the first African American to receive a Ph.D. in anatomy from Ohio State University when he was awarded the degree in 1965. Wright was only the seventh African American in the nation to achieve that milestone. He had previously earned his B.S. degree in 1932 from Wilberforce University (Ohio) and a M.S. degree from Ohio State University in 1936. Wright was professor of anatomy at Meharry Medical College from 1946 to 1968.

African-American Medical Pioneers (1994), p. 199; *Blacks in Science and Medicine* (1990), p. 258; *Jet* (January 14, 1965), p. 27

1966 • Harold Eugene Finley (1905-1975) was the first African American elected president of the American Society of Protozoologists in 1966. He was also the first African American elected president of the American Microscopic Society in 1971. Finley received a B.S. degree from Morehouse College in 1928 and an M.S. and Ph.D. in zoology in 1929 and 1942, respectively, both from the University of Wisconsin. Finley was a professor and Zoology Department Head at Howard University from 1947 to 1969. He was also editor of the *Transactions of the National Institute of Sciences* and on the editorial board of the American Society of Protozoologists.

Blacks in Science and Medicine (1990), p. 90; *Encyclopedia of Black America* (1981), p. 745; *Journal of the National Medical Association* Vol. 67 (September, 1974), p. 414

1966 • African American biochemist Emmett W. Chappelle (1925-) co-discovered a method for detecting bacteria in drinking water. Chappelle received a B.S. in 1950 from the University of California Berkeley and a

EMMETT CHAPPELLE
(RIGHT) READING
RESULTS FROM A
BACTERIA DETECTOR.

M.S. in 1954 from the University of Washington. His career has centered on the property of bioluminescence, by which living organisms emit light. He discovered that by introducing chemicals derived from fireflies, he could induce living organisms to emit light. Thus, the amount of bacteria present in drinking water could be measured by the amount of light emitted by water's bacteria. Chappelle also applied his work to detecting life on Mars, when he worked for Hazelton Laboratories (who contracted with NASA) from 1963 to 1966. Chappelle began working for NASA in 1966, where he was able to expand further on his work to monitor agricultural practices and assess acid rain damage to red spruce trees. With 13 patents on his record, he now works for the U.S. Department of Agriculture.

Blacks in Science and Medicine (1990), p. 53; *Ebony* (1961), p. 7; *Ebony Handbook* (1974), p. 370

1968 • John T. Wilson Jr. (1924-) was named, on January 12, 1968, head of the Biological Science Research Laboratories at Lockheed Missile and Space Company, the first African American to hold that position. He had technical and administrative responsibility for the biochemistry, histopathology, microbiology, physiology, and toxicology laboratories. Wilson earned a B.S. *cum laude* from Howard University (Washington, D.C.) in 1946 and an M.D. from Columbia University (New York) in 1950. He also earned a Sc.D. in industrial medicine from the University of Cincinnati (Ohio) in 1956. Wilson was chief of the Bureau of Occupational Health for the Santa Clara County Health Department from 1957 to 1961, when he became life sciences advisor for Lockheed Aircraft Corporation until 1969. Wilson was then, from 1971 to 1974, professor and chairman of Howard University's Department of Community Health Practice. In 1974, he was appointed professor and chairman of the Department of Environmental Health at the University of Washington.

Journal of the National Medical Association, Volume 60 (March, 1968), p. 151; *Who's Who Among African Americans* (1998-1999), p. 1646; *Who's Who Among Black Americans* (1990-1991), p. 1387

1969 • Emmett W. Chappelle developed an invention relating to the storage of bioluminescent compounds, which were used in life detection studies. His invention was patented in 1969. Chappelle (1925-) received a B.S. in 1950 from the University of California, Berkeley and a M.S. in 1954 from the University of Washington. Chappelle taught biochemistry at Meharry Medical College from 1950 to 1952 and was a research associate at Stanford University from 1954 to 1958. He worked as a scientist and biochemist for the Research Institute of Advanced Studies from 1958 to 1963 and as a biochemist at Hazleton Laboratories from 1963 to 1966. He joined the Goddard Space Flight Center in 1966 as a remote sensing scientist. Chappelle has 13 patents and continues to study how living plants give off light. He is now working with agriculture scientists from the U. S. Department of Agriculture developing tests to tell farmers and crop specialists when plants need more water or fertilizer.

Blacks in Science and Medicine (1990), p. 53; *Distinguished African American Scientists of the 20th Century* (1996), pp. 46-49; *Ebony* (November 1961), p. 7; *Index of Patents* (1969), p. 264, 1640

ALFRED DAY HERSHEY

1969 • The first African American to share the Nobel Prize in Physiology or Medicine was Alfred Day Hershey (1908-1997), who was awarded the prize in 1969 with Max Delbruck and Salvador Edward Luria. They were awarded the Nobel Prize for their work in molecular biology. Hershey earned a B.S. in 1930 from Michigan State College and then a Ph.D. from Michigan in 1934. He spent the period 1934 to 1950 as researcher and professor at Washington University in St. Louis (Missouri). In 1950, Hershey assumed work as staff scientist at the Genetics Research Unit of the Carnegie Institute at Cold Spring Harbor, New York, where he remained until 1974, when he retired. Hershey made several discoveries relating to deoxyribonucleic acid (DNA) important to the development of modern molecular genetics. Hershey's most important study was his demonstration in 1952 that DNA, not protein, was the genetic material of life.

Chemical and Engineering News (October 17, 1969), p. 16; *Los Angeles Times* (May 24, 1997); *New York Times* (May 24, 1997); *Notable Twentieth Century Scientists Supplement* (1998), pp. 199- 201

1970 • Microbiologist James Monroe Jay's (1927-) text, *Modern Food Biology,* was published in 1970. It was the first internationally acclaimed and utilized text on food technology written by an African American. Jay's book (after five editions) was widely referenced in the United Kingdom, South Africa, and Israel, and was published in Spanish, Chinese, and Hindi. It remained the preferred textbook at the college level. Jay earned a B.A. from Paine College in 1950, and a M.S. in 1953 and Ph.D. in 1956, both from Ohio State University. He taught at Southern University from 1957 to 1961, when he associated with Wayne State University. There he rose to full professor and was named Professor Emeritus in 1994. He also became, in 1994, adjunct professor at the University of Nevada, Las Vegas. Jay received national and worldwide acclaim and was recognized internationally as an authority in spoilage and food microbiology.

Blacks in Science and Medicine (1990), pp. 131-132; *Encyclopedia of Black America* (1981), p. XI; *Notable Black American Scientists* (1999), pp. 174-175; *Who's Who Among African Americans* (1998-1999), p. 777

1970 • Joseph St. Clair Wiles (1914-), an African American research pharmacologist, patented his invention of an injection pistol for intramuscular implantation of encapsulated liquid or solid chemicals into animals. Wiles's instrument provided intramuscular implantation by an individual without the excessive bleeding and trauma of a surgical procedure. It did not require any special skill or technique on the part of the person administering the drug, and it accomplished the implantation with speed, accuracy, and minimal wound size. Wiles earned an A.B. in biology from Morris Brown College in 1941 and took graduate courses at Atlanta University, Columbia University, and the University of Maryland. He worked for the U.S. Army Corps of Engineers as a bacteriologist from 1942 to 1945. He joined the staff of the Edgewood Arsenal Medical Research Laboratory in 1945, working there until 1980. Wiles was a consultant from 1980 to 1985 for the National Academy of Science.

Index of Patents (1970); *Who's Who Among African Americans* (1998-1999), p. 1389-1390; *Who's Who Among Black Americans* (1990-1991), p. 1349

1971 • The first African American woman to earn a Ph.D. in biology from Tulane University was Joyce M. Verrett (1932-), who received the degree in 1971. She previously received a B.A. degree in 1957 from Dillard University and a M.S. degree in 1963 from New York University. Varrett is a professor at Dillard University, on the faculty of the Division of Nutrition Science.

Who's Who Among African Americans (1998-1999), p. 1526

1972 • The disease in children called CoA transverse deficiency was discovered by the African American scientist James Tyson Tildon (1931-). His discovery related to his earlier findings that ketone bodies are an energy source for the central nervous system in infants. Tildon received his B.S. from Morgan State College in 1954 and then a Ph.D. in biochemistry from Johns Hopkins University in 1965. He was also a Fulbright Scholar at the University of Paris from 1959 to 1960. He was a research assistant at Sinai Hospital in Baltimore from 1954 to 1959 and an assistant professor at Johns Hopkins from 1967 to 1968. He was director of pediatric research at the University of Maryland School of Medicine and also professor of biochemistry. Tildon's research interest was developmental biochemistry and metabolic control processes.

Blacks in Science and Medicine (1990), p. 232; *Encyclopedia of Black America* (1981), p. 817

1972 • Benjamin F. Hammond (1934-) was the first African American appointed chair of the department of microbiology of the University of Pennsylvania School of Dental Medicine when he was selected in 1972. Hammond earned a B.A. degree in 1954 at the University of Kansas. He then received the D.D.S. from Meharry Medical College in 1958 and a Ph.D. from the University of Pennsylvania in 1962. Hammond joined the faculty at the University of Pennsylvania Dental School in 1958, working his way up the ranks from instructor in microbiology to professor, in 1970. Hammond then became chair of the department in 1972 and associate dean for academic affairs in 1984. Hammond's research interest is oral microbiology, with an emphasis on physical and molecular biology of oral lactic acid bacteria.

Blacks in Science and Medicine (1990), p. 110; *Who's Who Among Black Americans* (1985), p 348; *Encyclopedia of Black America* (1981), p. 745

1973 • Luvenia C. Miller (1909-), an African American biological photographer, was the first African American woman to be named director of the Biological Photographers Association, serving in the position from 1973 to 1976. Miller received a B.S. in 1934 from Hampton Institute and acquired certification from the New York Institute of Photography in 1939, Army Air Field Photo Laboratory in 1945, and the Progressive School of Photography in 1949. She served as chief of gross photography for the Armed Forces Institute of Pathology from 1951 to 1975. Miller was also the first African American woman photographer in the Armed Forces Institute of Pathology Association in 1972, as well as the first African American woman registered photographer in North Carolina in 1943.

Who's Who Among Black Americans (1990-1991), p. 888

1974 • In 1974, William Rodney Wiley (1931-1996) became the first African American to be appointed manager of the biology department at the Pacific Northwest National Laboratory (Washington). Wiley received a B.S. in chemistry in 1954 from Tougaloo College (Mississippi), a M.S. in microbiology in 1960 from the University of Illinois, and a Ph.D. from Washington State University in 1965 in bacteriology. After serving for five years as manager at Pacific Northwest National Laboratory, he was appointed director of research, over a staff of 1,500 scientists and engineers. He was named, in 1985, director of the Pacific Northwest Laboratories and senior vice president of Battelle Memorial Institute, which manages the Laboratory for the United States Department of Energy. Wiley was named senior vice president for science and technology at Batelle in 1994.

Blacks in Science and Medicine (1990), pp. 249-50; *Notable Black American Scientists* (1999), pp. 315-6; *Who's Who Among African Americans* (1998-1999), p. 1604

1974 • The first African American to receive a Ph.D. from Wake Forest University was Herman Edward Eure (1947-), which he was awarded in 1974. He received a B.S. degree in 1969 from Maryland State College (now University of Maryland Eastern Shore). Eure was appointed to the faculty of Wake Forest in 1974 as professor of biology and was the first African

American tenured professor there. The primary focus of his research has been the interactions of parasites and aquatic vertebrates, including frogs, toads, turtles, and fish. He has also participated in the effort to recruit minorities into scientific occupations.

Who's Who Among African Americans (1997), p. 459

1977 • The first African American appointed registrar of a major scientific museum was Margaret Santiago. She became registrar, in 1977, of the Smithsonian's National Museum of Natural History. Santiago held the position until her January 1, 1991 retirement. As registrar, she was the responsible for maintaining records on the museum's donations, loans, and other access to collections, which date back to 1834.

Black Firsts (1994), p. 357

1978 • Gerald Virgil Stokes (1943-), a microbiologist, became the first African American to teach graduate-level science courses at George Washington University (Washington, D.C.) School of Medicine and Health Sciences when appointed assistant professor in 1978. Stokes's first degree was an A.A. received in 1962 from Wilson Junior College, followed in 1967 by a B.A. from Southern Illinois University, culminated by a Ph.D. from the University of Chicago (Illinois) in 1973. Stokes was associated with the University of Colorado faculty from 1973 to 1976, and then with Meharry Medical College (Tennessee) from 1976-1978. An active leader in the American Society for Microbiology, Stokes developed an interest in the chlamydia class of micro-organisms, and demonstrated that chlamydia produced a specific chemical when a colony prospered. Stokes continued his studies of chlamydia toward discovering a vaccine against the microorganism.

Distinguished African American Scientists of the 20th Century (1996), pp. 301-4; *Who's Who Among African Americans* (1998-1999), p. 1428

1979 • Jacqueline Minette Jacobs (1936-), an African American inventor, received a patent in 1979 for a biocontamination particulate system. Jacobs has a B.S. in biology and math from Alabama State University, which she earned in 1957, as well as a M.A. in science education, which she received from the University of Washington in 1962. She earned a Ph.D. in botany from the University of Washington in 1974. Jacobs is a senior member of the teaching staff of the California Institute of Technology.

Who's Who Among Black Americans (1990-1991), p. 654

1979 • The first African American to chair the Department of Microbiology at Harvard Medical School was Harold Amos (1919-), when he was

HAROLD AMOS

appointed in 1979. Amos received a B.S. degree in 1941 from Springfield College, as well as a M.A. (1947) and a Ph.D. in bacteriology (1952) from Harvard University. In 1957, he became associate professor of bacteriology at Harvard Medical School and was promoted to full professor in 1969. In 1975, he was named Maude and Lillian Presley Professor of Microbiology and Molecular Genetics, and he now serves as an emeritus professor. Amos was a member of national professional organizations and societies, including membership in the National Academy of Sciences.

African-American Medical Pioneers (1994), p. 184; *Blacks in Science and Medicine* (1990), p. 10

1981–1990 • Jewel Plummer Cobb (1924-) established the first privately funded gerontology center in Orange County, California during her tenure as president of California State College at Fullerton, 1981 to 1990. Cobb earned her B.A. from Talladega College (1944) and both her M.S. (1947) and Ph.D. (1950) degrees in cell biology from New York University. A biologist who spent summers doing research at the famed Marine Biological Laboratory in Woods Hole, Massachusetts, she studied melanin, a pigment that protects human skin from sun damage, and melanomas, or skin cancers. Cobb published 35 papers on her cancer research. She was the dean of Douglas College at Rutgers, the State University of New Jersey, prior to her appointment at Fullerton. During her presidency, she initiated the expansion of university buildings and brought increased funding to the institution. Cobb's contributions have been immortalized by the hanging of her photograph in the National Academy of Sciences. In 1990, Cobb was named president emeritus of California State University, Fullerton. She also works with programs to bring women and minorities into the math and science disciplines.

JEWEL PLUMMER COBB

Blacks in Science and Medicine (1990), pp. 56-57; *Ebony* (August, 1982), pp. 97-98, 100; *Notable Black American Women* (1992), pp. 195-198; *Who's Who in America* (1986-1987), p. 527

1981 • Mary Styles Harris (1949-), African American biologist with a specialty in genetics, was the first State Director of Genetics Services for the Georgia Department of Human Resources in 1981. She had won a National Science Foundation Science Residency Award and upon completion of the residency, was appointed to the new position of Director of Genetics Services in 1981. Harris earned a B.A. from Lincoln University in 1971 and a Ph.D. in genetics in 1975 from Cornell University. She completed a two-year postdoctoral fellowship, studying virus structures at the New Jersey University of Medicine and Dentistry. She was executive director of the Sickle Cell Foundation of Georgia from 1977 to 1979. She also served as an assistant professor at Morehouse College and later at

Atlanta University. Harris later founded her own consulting company after moving to California.

Distinguished African American Scientists of the 20th Century (1996), pp. 140-144; *Notable Black American Scientists* (1999), pp. 148-149; *Who's Who Among African Americans* (1998-1999), p. 642; *Who's Who Among Black Americans* (1990-1991), p. 548

1982 • Thomas P. Fraser (1902-) served as teacher and administrator for 30 years at Morgan State University (Maryland) and was head of the department of science there. Fraser retired and in 1982 was inducted into the South Carolina Hall of Science and Technology, the first African American to receive the honor, and at the time, only the fifth person so honored. He received a B.S. in 1926 from Claflin College (South Carolina), an M.A. from there in 1930, and a Ph.D. from Columbia University (New York). Fraser was also the 26th president of the National Association for Research in Science Teaching, and co-authored the widely used science textbook series, *Concepts in Science.* Fraser was a consultant to the National Science Foundation and was twice interim president at Morgan. He was a member and office holder in several national science education organizations and received many honors and awards for his contributions to science education.

Jet (March 13, 1958), p. 58, (May 3, 1982), p. 38; *Who's Who Among Black Americans* (1980), p. 240; *Blacks in Science and Medicine* (1990), p. 95

1985 • The newly discovered species of bacteria, *Enterobacter taylorae* was named after microbiologist Welton Ivan Taylor (1919-), the first African-American microbiologist to have such a discovery named after him. Taylor received the A.B. degree (1941), M.S. (1947), and Ph.D. in bacteriology (1948) all from the University of Illinois. He was an assistant professor of bacteriology at the University of Illinois from 1948 to 1954, research bacteriologist from 1954 to 1959 for Swift and Company, and supervisor of clinical biology from 1959 to 1964 at Children's Memorial Hospital. Taylor then became consultant and microbiologist until 1977, when he started his own firm, Micro-Palettes, Inc. He has published extensively, authoring more than 50 articles and book chapters, and has several patents. Taylor also formulated a method to detect *Salmonella* and *Shigella* bacteria, which cause foodborne illnesses. It became the standard practice used by the U.S. Food and Drug Administration as well as several other Western nations. Taylor's inventions and patents relate to microbiological detection kits he developed.

Blacks in Science and Medicine (1990), pp. 227-228; *Ebony* (May, 1954), p. 24; *Who's Who Among Black Americans* (1997), p. 1426

1988 • African American research scientist Carolyn Branch Brooks (1946-) was a recipient of the First Annual White House Initiative Faculty

Award for Excellence in Science and Technology in 1988. The Ohio State Ph.D. graduate, 1977, served as a department chairman of biology at the University of Maryland, Eastern Shore. Brooks earned her B.S. at Tuskegee University in 1968 and received a M.S. from that school in 1971. Brooks was a science teacher from 1968 to 1972. She then became a research technician at the Tuskegee VA Hospital for the year 1972, and from 1975 to 1977 was a graduate teaching assistant at Ohio State University. Brooks was principal investigator and program director at Kentucky State University from 1978 to 1988. She was appointed research assistant professor in 1981 at the University of Maryland, Eastern Shore. She was promoted to associate professor in 1987 and became department chair in 1992. Brooks won awards for her research and teaching efforts and has published in professional journals. She has also completed research in Togo, Senegal, and Capon.

Who's Who Among African Americans (1998-1999), p. 142; *Who's Who Among Black Americans* (1990-1991), p. 145

IRVIN WESLEY ELLIOT

1991 • Irvin Wesley Elliott (1925-) is professor emeritus of the department of chemistry at Fisk University and patented a new anti-HIV compound in 1991. He received a B.S. in 1947, a M.S. in 1949, and a Ph.D. in 1952, all from the University of Kansas. He has taught chemistry from 1949 at Southern University, Florida A & M College, Howard University, Wellesley College, and Fisk University where he became professor emeritus in 1996.

Who's Who Among African Americans (1998-1999), p. 449

1991 • The first African American director of the National Institute of Environmental Health Sciences and the National Toxicology Program was biochemist Kenneth Olden (1938-). Olden had been doing research on the possible links between the properties of cell-surface molecules and cancer for more than 20 years. He earned a bachelor's degree in 1960 from Knoxville College, followed by a M.S. in genetics from the University of Michigan in 1964. He then received a Ph.D. in biology and biochemistry from Temple University in 1970. From 1970 to 1991, Olden worked in academia and the government developing a reputation as a leading authority on the structure and function of the extracellular matrix glycoprotein fibronectin. In 1980, two of Olden's published articles on cell biology were listed among the 100 most cited papers of 1978 and 1979. During his NIH tenure, he has devoted particular attention to the anticancer drug Swainsonine. Olden was also appointed by President Bush to the National Cancer Advisory Board in 1991.

Notable Twentieth Century Scientists (1995), pp. 1504-1505

1992 • African American cell biologist George M. Langford (1944-) and his colleagues became in 1992 the first investigators to demonstrate that special filaments responsible for muscle cell movement were also responsible for nerve cell particle movement. Langford graduated from Fayetteville State University (North Carolina) in 1966, receiving a B.S. in biology. He then earned both his M.S. and Ph.D. in cell biology in 1969 and 1971, respectively, from Illinois Institute of Technology. Langford was initially intrigued by the study of intracellular motility, or living cell component movement, while studying at the Illinois Institute of Technology. From 1968 to 1991, he taught at several colleges and continued his research. In 1991, he joined the faculty of biology at Dartmouth College (New Hampshire), where he was appointed the E.E. Just Professor of Natural Sciences.

Notable Black American Scientists (1999), pp. 195-6

1993 • Roderick A. Wells (1952-), in 1993, was the first African American appointed to the board of the Louisiana Mosquito Central Association and

GEORGE LANGFORD

is president of the board. Wells is the assistant director of the local mosquito abatement agency in Baton Rouge. He graduated from Southern University with a B.S. in 1975 and a M.Ed. in 1981.

Jet (November 29, 1993), p. 20

1994 • The first African American to become a regional forester for the U. S. Department of Agriculture Forest Service was Charles "Chip" Cartwright (1948-). He has a B.S. in forestry and wildlife management, which he earned in 1970 at Virginia Polytechnic Institute and State University. Cartwright started with the Forest Service in 1967 and during his employment there, he was the first African American District Forester in 1979 and the first African Amerian Forest Supervisor in 1988. Cartwright is a member of several professional organizations and has received awards for his management of natural resources on public lands.

Who's Who Among African Americans (1997), p. 254

1995 • Francine Essien, a professor of biology, was the first African American to receive one of academia's highest honors—the 1994-1995 U.S. Professor of the Year Award from the Carnegie Foundation for the Advancement of Teaching. Essien earned her undergraduate degree from Temple University and her Ph.D. degree in genetics at the Albert Einstein College of Medicine at Yeshiva University. She is a professor of biology at Rutgers University and director of Rutger's Office of Minority Undergraduate Science Programs, which she established in 1986. One of Essien's research areas concerns the development of models that can be utilized to help understand basic developmental processes such as how muscle cells differentiate or how spinal cords form.

Philadelphia Inquirer (March 27, 1995); *Journal of the National Technical Association* Vol. 70 (Summer, 1960)

ERNEST EVERETT JUST

1996 • The first African American biologist commemorated on a U. S. postage stamp was Ernest Everett Just (1883-1941). The stamp was issued February 1, 1996. Just was an internationally known zoologist primarily known for his work in marine biology. He received a B.A. degree in 1907 from Dartmouth University. In 1916, he was the first African American to earn a Ph.D. in biology when he received his in zoology and physiology from the University of Chicago. Just also received the first Spingarn Medal from the NAACP in 1915, for his research in biology. Just taught at Howard University from 1907 until the 1920s, in addition to spending summers at the Marine Biological Laboratory in Woods Hole, Massachusetts. Just published over 50 scientific papers and authored two classic texts on cell biology, both published in 1939.

Black Pioneers of Science and Invention (1970), pp. 112-121; *Journal of the National Medical Association* Vol. 49, (September, 1957), pp. 349-351; *Philadelphia Inquirer* (February 1, 1996); *Philadelphia New Observer* (January 24, 1996)

1996 • African American biologist Jill Bargonetti, a cancer research specialist, discovered a correlation between a specific gene's ability to bind with DNA and its ability to suppress tumors. Bargonetti earned a B.A. and M.S., and then received a Ph.D. in biology from New York University. This was followed by postdoctoral research at Columbia before accepting the position of assistant professor of biology at Hunter College. Her research primarily focuses on the gene p53, which has the ability to bind to particular DNA sites in a cell and while doing so suppresses tumor cell growth. Bargonetti's research focuses on breast cancer and AIDS. She received a $300,000 three-year grant from the American Cancer Society and a $200,000 four-year award from the Department of Defense for furtherance of her study of breast cancer.

African American Almanac (1997), p. 1063; *Black Enterprise* (February 1996), p. 66

1997 • The first African American woman to receive a Ph.D. in toxicology from the Massachusetts Institute of Technology (MIT) was LaCreis Kidd in 1997. The dissertation completed by Kidd was concerned with the relationship between the heterocyclic amines produced by high temperature cooked muscle-containing foods and colorectal cancer.

Jet (July 21, 1997), p. 24

1997 • Jerry Belson was the first African American to be selected head of the National Park Service's southeast region when appointed in 1997. Belson's responsibility includes 62 parks in nine southeastern states, Puerto Rico, and the U.S. Virgin Islands. Parks such as the Everglades and the Great Smoky Mountains National Park are included in Belson's domain. He is responsible for 2,775 employees and has an operational budget of 214 million dollars.

Ebony (October, 1997), p. 13

1997 • The fifteenth person to hold the position of director of the National Park Service was also the first African American appointed to that position. Robert G. Stanton's appointment was confirmed by the U.S. Senate on July 31, 1997. He earned a B.S. degree from Huston-Tillotson University and undertook graduate work at both Boston University and George Washington University. Stanton's responsibilities as NPS director include a $1.6 billion budget, 20,000 employees, and 83 million acres comprising 375 units. Upon his appointment, Stanton expressed his hope to extend youth programs and increase park accessibility for the physically impaired.

Ebony (June, 1998), p. 8

MATH AND ENGINEERING

1849 • The first African American to become a faculty member of a predominantly white college was Charles Lewis Reason (1818-1893) when he was appointed by Central College (McGrawville, New York) in 1849, where he taught mathematics and French until 1852. Reason then became principal, from 1852-1855, of the Institute for Colored Youth in Philadelphia, where he dramatically increased enrollment, developed a library, and organized a popular lecture series. Reason then taught for the next 37 years in New York City schools. He also worked diligently in the areas of slavery abolition, suffrage, and industrial education.

CHARLES L. REASON

Dictionary of American Negro Biography (1982), pp. 516- 7; *Famous First Facts About Negroes* (1972), p. 50; *Men of Mark* (1887), pp. 1105-12; *Negro History Compendium* (1971), p. 61

1872 • Thomas J. Martin, an early African American inventor, acquired patents on several items, including a fire extinguisher in 1872. He also invented a gun fired remotely by electricity and a four-monkey-motion crank attachment for locomotives that enabled the engine to pull up a grade without losing speed. The crank attachment was purchased by the American Locomotive Company.

Official Gazette (March 26, 1872), p. 294

1883 • Samuel E. Thomas had several patents related to pipes and pipe construction, and in 1883, he was granted a patent for his invention of a waste-trap to be inserted in a line of pipe. Thomas's trap was constructed with an upper portion having the inlet pipe, and a bottom portion having the exit pipe and cleaning plug. The cup portion of Thomas's trap was cast with a cross partition, the upper portion of which was free from the side walls. The partition extended above the top of the cup with the end rounded, and the cup portion and partition were cast together in lead or a similar metal.

Similar waste traps were available, but Thomas's trap was the only one that could be adapted to be placed in a line of pipe and also cast in lead molds.

Blacks in Science: Astrophysicist to Zoologist (1977), p. 88

1884 • John P. Parker (1827-1900) was one of the few African-American inventors to acquire patents before 1890. Parker patented, in 1884, a screw press for tobacco and in 1885, received a patent for a similar press. He was sold to a slave agent at the age of eight years and remained in slavery until 1845, when he was able to pay the full amount for his freedom. While in slavery, Parker became a competent ironworker and molder. In 1854, he erected a small foundry in Ripley, Ohio, producing special and general castings. He remained in the foundry business until his death in 1900. Parker was also active on the Underground Railroad and served in the Civil War.

Blacks in Science and Medicine (1990), p. 184; *Dictionary of American Negro Biography* (1982), pp. 480-481; *Created Equal* (1993), pp. 19, 184; *The Real McCoy* (1989), p. 48

1885 • William Francis Cosgrove received a patent in 1885 for his invention of an automatic stop-plug for gas and oil pipes. The device was primarily used to prevent fires from being fed by gas or oil escaping from broken pipes. Cosgrove's invention consisted of a coupling provided with a tapering socket with an apertured removable cap, a plug passing through the aperture of the caps, and a fusible key passing through the stem on the outside of the cap. In the automatic stop-plug, Cosgrove's combination cap and stem did not conduct heat away from the key. When the fusible key melted, the plug was drawn firmly into place.

Black Inventors: From Africa to America (1995), p. 239; *Blacks in Science: Astrophysicist to Zoologist* (1977), p. 77; *Index of Patents* (1895); *Created Equal* (1993), p. 184

1887 • Alexander Miles received a patent in October 1887 for an elevator he designed. Previous elevators were operated on traditional ropes, which broke after some use. Miles's invention, a platform attached to a structure, used wire ropes.

Jet (October 13, 1997), p. 20

1890 • Inventor Frank J. Ferrell acquired 10 patents, one of which was for a snow-melting apparatus that was patented in 1890. Ferrell's apparatus for melting snow and ice was a box with a removable cover adapted to form the bed or bottom of a gutter. There was a perforated tray in the box with flanges and a ledge for a pipe connected to a source of heated fluid. The box has an opening for the escape of the water as the snow or ice melted. Ferrell provided an automatic steam trap in which the steam used as the melting fluid was not allowed to escape until it condensed to water. The entrance duct of the box was connected to the steam supply source and the exit opening of the box connected to the street sewer or sewer pipes of the building.

Blacks in Science and Medicine (1990), p. 90; *Blacks in Science: Astrophysicist to Zoologist* (1977), p. 78; *Index of Patents* (1890); *Negro Year Book* (1918-1919), p. 343; *Negro Year Book* (1921-1922), p. 220

1891 • J. Standard was issued a patent in 1891 for a refrigerator. The refrigerator had originally been invented in 1834, but Standard's refrigerator had several improvements. His device had cold-air ducts and perforations, providing a constant circulation of air maintained through several chambers, where water for drinking purposes was always kept cool. His refrigerator contained improved compartments for the storage of food articles. It also had a unique grate and bar arrangement where larger cakes of ice could be used for cooling, and prevented glass breakage if the large cake of ice or larger pieces of ice broke off the cake.

Blacks in Science and Medicine (1990), p. 220; *Created Equal* (1993), p. 187; *Index of Patents* (1891)

1896 • A mechanism for overcoming what is known as "dead-center" in mechanics, which occurs in machines where a shaft is driven by a crank, was invented by Willie Harry Johnson and patented in 1896. Johnson's invention applied to a steam engine that had a horizontally moving piston and crank arm. The key to Johnson's apparatus was a two-part, or compound, crank rod constructed so that the parts were automatically locked together at the proper point in the stroke, so as to act as a single rod. At other intervals of its travel, the arm was automatically unlocked so that each part acted independently of the other.

Blacks in Science and Medicine (1990), p. 135; *Index of Patents* (1896)

1897–1917 • Benjamin F. Jackson, an African American inventor, acquired at least 12 patents during the period 1897 to 1917. Some of Jackson's patents acquired during that period included a heating apparatus, gas burner, electrolysers' furnace, steam boiler, trolley-wheel controller, and a hydrocarbon burner system. Jackson patented his invention of a gas burner in 1899. The burner maintained an even combustion and was more efficient than previous models by supplying air under pressure to all the burner-tubes in an equal amount.

Blacks in Science and Medicine (1990), p. 129; *Blacks in Science: Astrophysicist to Zoologist* (1977), p. 80; *Negro Year Book* (1918-1919), p. 343; *Negro Year Book* (1921-1922), p. 318; *A Short History of the American Negro* (1939), p. 221

1900 • James Benton was granted a patent in 1900 for his invention of a lever-derrick. Benton's device was for raising and lowering heavy weights such as stoves, lumber, or other heavy objects. The device comprised a base and uprights, with levers pivotally mounted in the uprights. Gripping levers were also pivotally mounted on the levers and adapted to bind a rope in slots on a notched bar. When Benton completed the model for his invention he could not raise enough money to travel from Kentucky to Washington, so he walked the total distance carrying his baggage and lever-derrick model.

The Black Inventor (1975), p. 91; *Blacks in Science: Astrophysicist to Zoologist* (1977), p. 90; *Blacks in Science and Medicine* (1990), p. 26; *Jet* (October 4, 1982), p. 18

1905–1911 • Brinay Smart, an African American inventor, acquired several patents on reversing valves. He received patents in 1905, 1906, 1909, and 1911 for reversing valves, one in 1913 for a wheel, and another for a shock absorber in 1922. Smart's invention for a rotary valve, patented in 1905, was the combination of a cylinder and a steam chest. A removable, unattached steam-valve seat within the steam chest was provided with supporting flanges. His device had a valve mechanism reciprocating on the steam valve seat and operating to alternatively uncover the exposed halves of the two port-bearing regions with the mechanism.

Blacks in Science and Medicine (1990), p. 215; *Blacks in Science: Astrophysicist to Zoologist* (1977), p. 91; *Index of Patents* (1905, 1906, 1909)

1908 • Hugh M. Browne invented a mechanism for regulating the positions of furnace dampers. The device, which was patented in 1908, was used to regulate the draft to the furnace. Browne's invention provided a reliable means for controlling the furnace dampers from a distance, since a furnace in the basement, for example, could be controlled from the parlor on the first floor. The system consisted of a series of pulleys, ropes, and a cylinder. The cylinder connected to the dampers, which was connected to the rope. An indicator pinpointed the positions of the dampers.

Black Inventors: From Africa to America (1995), pp. 135, 238; *Index of Patents* (1908)

1914 • Garrett A. Morgan (1875-1963) invented what he called a safety hood, or breathing device, in 1912 and was awarded a patent in 1914 for his device. Morgan's device was designed as a portable attachment enabling a fireman to enter an area with thick smoke and breathe safely for a period of time. His device comprised a hood placed over the head. The hood had an extended tube long enough to enter a lower layer of air underneath the smoke. The tube end was lined with absorbent material, which was moistened before use to cool the air and prevent dust and smoke from being sucked up into the helmet. The device had a second tube to handle exhaled air. Morgan later modified the helmet to carry its own air supply. The concept was further improved and used successfully by the U. S. Army during World War I.

Black Inventors: From Africa to America (1995), pp. 103, 107; *Blacks in Science and Medicine* (1990), p. 176; *Created Equal* (1993), pp. 94-96, 113-114, 194

1917 • William D. Polite invented an anti-aircraft gun that was patented in 1917. Polite's gun used a breechblock and an adjustable shell magazine as a unit longitudinally along the barrel of the gun. An artillery shell lifter, supported within the block, automatically adjusted its position along the block in one direction. Then the magazine automatically fed the shells singly onto the lifts. Polite's gun had the means to elevate the lifts at predetermined intervals during adjustment of the block. The upward movement of the lifter was limited when the shell was properly positioned relative to the barrel of the gun.

Index of Patents (1917); *Negro Year Book* (1917-1918), p. 5

1917 • An automatic stopping and releasing device for mine cars invented by George M. Johnson was patented in 1917. Johnson's release device operated automatically by the movement of the mine cars in the mine cage. The device also had an operating mechanism to prevent injury on the ascent of the mine cage. Johnson's device had an actuating rod with a series of anti-friction rollers to provide for uniform travel of the rod. Also, the invention incorporated a means for locking the cars on the mine cage when it was mounted on supports or landers.

Negro Year Book (1918-1919), p. 7; *Twentieth Century Black Patentees - A Survey* (1979)

1918 • A machine gun capable of discharging a number of cartridges in such a manner as to effect the sweeping motion of the bullets was invented by Clarence Gregg and patented in 1918. Gregg's machine gun had a base with a frame holding a number of gun barrels. He then placed a vertically moving magazine adapted to align cartridges with the breech of the gun barrels. A lever, lever socker, and pivoting ratchet bar engaged with the magazine.

Black Inventors: From Africa to America (1995), p. 106; *Negro Year Book* (1921-1922), p. 32; *Twentieth Century Black Patentees - A Survey* (1979)

1919 • African American mathematician Robert T. Browne authored the first text on space by an African American in 1919. Browne contended that humankind was entering into a new period of intellectual development and supported his thesis with mathematical evidence. In the book, he discussed the origins and nature of space, non-Euclidean geometry, the fourth dimension, and the concept of hyperspace. Browne's text was highly praised in 1920 by *The New York Times*.

Western Journal of Black Studies Vol. 16 (1992), p. 51

1919 • African American inventor Alice Parker was granted a patent in 1919 for her invention of a heating furnace for houses and other buildings. Parker's system provided an apparatus and mechanism for regulated heat to be carried to various rooms of a building. It had a number of heating units that branched from a common cold air box, with each unit independently controlled. The system also had individual hot air ducts leading to different parts of the building. The system was designed to use gas as the fuel.

Index of Patents (1919); *Negro Year Book* (1921-1922); *Philadelphia Tribune* (March 23, 1993)

1920 • Mary H. Toland, in 1920, received a patent for her invention of a float-operated circuit closer. Her invention provided a float-operated alarm to be used in conjunction with refrigerators, so that the filling of the drip pan may later serve to operate a satisfactory signaling device. The invention also provided an adjustable means to ensure the operation of the signaling device when the water in the drip pan had risen to a predetermined level.

Black Inventors: From Africa to America (1995), pp. 107, 208, 249; *Index of Patents* (1920), p. 521

1920 • African American inventor Mary Jane Reynolds received a patent, in April 1920, for a hoisting and loading mechanism. Reynolds's device was for the purpose of moving loads from a platform to a truck. The device could hoist items through a second story window and deposit them on a truck.

Negro Year Book (1921-1922), p. 33; *Official Gazette* (April 20, 1920), p. 506

1925 • Elbert Frank Cox (1895-1969) was the first African American to receive the Ph.D. degree in mathematics, which he earned in 1925 from Cornell University. He had received a B.A. in 1917 from Indiana University. Cox taught mathematics at Shaw University from 1921 to 1923, and mathematics and physics at West Virginia State College, where he was department head, from 1925 to 1929. He was an associate professor of mathematics at Howard University from 1929 to 1947, when he was promoted to full professor. Cox also held the position of department head from 1947 to 1961. He retired from Howard University in 1966. He specialized in interpolation theory and differential and difference equations.

African-American Almanac (1997), p. 1068; *Black Firsts* (1994), p. 96; *Blacks in Science and Medicine* (1990), p. 63

1925 • The first African American to earn the Ph.D. degree in civil engineering was George Maceo Jones (1900-19??), who was awarded the degree by the University of Michigan in 1925. He previously earned both his B.A. and M.A. degrees from the University of Michigan. Jones was assistant to the dean and then dean at Florida A&M College from 1927 to 1929. He taught at Howard University from 1930 to 1937, and then was employed as an architect and engineer from 1937 to 1955. In 1955, Jones became an engineer for the federal government. He was an expert in the stress analysis of structures.

Blacks in Science and Medicine (1990), p. 137; *Crisis* Vol. 46, (1939), p. 187; *Negroes in Science: Natural Science Doctorates* (1876-1966), pp. 52-53

1929 • A vacuum heating system for buildings that operated by steam at controlled subatmospheric pressures was invented by David Nelson Crosthwait, Jr. (1891-1976) and patented in 1929. Crosthwait's system involved two or more separate radiating or condensing systems for different parts of the building, with all of the systems being supplied from the same source of steam. A single exhaust system mechanism was used to maintain required subatmospheric pressures throughout the various parts of the system. A reducing valve regulated the pressure of the steam in the radiator.

Blacks in Science and Medicine (1990), pp. 64-65; *Blacks in Science: Astrophysicist to Zoologist* (1977), p. 45

1930 • Theodore Harry Miller (1905-), majoring in electrical engineering, was the first African American to graduate from the University of Nevada. He earned a B.S. in 1930. Miller worked in commercial refrigeration sales for Westinghouse Electric from 1935 to 1941. He was then employed by the U.S. Mare Island Naval Shipyard from 1941 to 1946 as a supervisor of electrical design. After, he served as assistant head of the VA engineering division from 1946 to 1951. Miller became chief electrical engineer for the U.S. General Services Administration 9th Region in 1951, and held that position until 1971, when he became a consulting engineer. Miller also taught part time at Stanford University (California).

Black Engineers in the United States (1974), pp. 140-1; *Journal of Blacks in Higher Education* (Autumn 1996), p. 81; *Who's Who Among African Americans* (1998-1999), p. 1052

1932 • The first African American to earn a degree from the California Institute of Technology was Grant Delbert Venerable (1904-1986), who received a B.S. in civil engineering from there in 1932. Venerable worked as an insurance agent and on several mining engineering projects until 1945. In that year, he and his brother-in-law purchased and began operating a manufacturing company that produced and distributed chalkboard erasers to school districts across the country from 1945 to 1986.

Journal of Blacks in Higher Education (Autumn 1998), p. 125

1934 • David N. Crosthwait (1898-1976) invented a technique for improving a method and apparatus for steam heating from central station mains, which was patented in 1934. His technique increased the operating efficiency of the steam supply main by increasing the number of heating systems or the size of the connected load that could be satisfactorily supplied with steam from a main or supply pipe of any given size. Crosthwait earned a B.S. in 1913 and a M.E. in 1920 from Purdue University. He was the first African American honored by the American Society of Heating, Refrigeration and Air Conditioning Engineers in 1971 and was a designer of the heating system for New York's Radio City Music Hall. Crosthwait held 39 U. S. patents and 80 foreign patents.

Blacks in Science: Astrophysicist to Zoologist (1977), p. 45; *Blacks in Science and Medicine* (1990), pp. 64-65; *Crisis* Vol. 46 (June 1939), p. 187; *Famous First Facts About Negroes* (1972), pp. 64-65; *Index of Patents* (1934), p. 161

1937 • James Matthew Allen invented a remote controlled apparatus that was designed to connect with radio receiving sets and was patented in 1937. Allen's apparatus included a time-controlled circuit closing technique that automatically cut in a selected broadcasting station to a radio receiver. Allen used an alarm clock mechanism, a knife switch, cam, rod spring, fixed post, spring-actuated bar, collar, gear, and other items. With the system connected to a radio receiver, a selected broadcasting station could be automatically cut in and out at designated times.

Black Inventors: From Africa to America (1995), p. 109; *Index of Patents* (1937); *Negro Year Book* (1941-1946), p. 27

1938 • Cap B. Collins invented a portable pocket flashlight that burns without a battery and was patented in 1938. His device was comprised of two cylindrical tubular sections, one the handle section and the other, a generator section. A generator comprised spaced end plates, bars, pole pieces, shaft, bar magnets, and gear unit. A lamp supported in a reflector was at the end of the section. Wires connected the generator to the center contact of the lamp bulb.

Index of Patents (1938), p. 126; *Negro Year Book* (1937-1938), p. 13

1939 • An optical apparatus allowing a machine operator to view the position of the machine with respect to the work being done was invented by

Darnley E. Howard and patented in 1939. Howard's device let the user follow the outline of projected image of a completed article showing the position of the tool with respect to the piece of work being done. The patented device allowed such work to be done more easily and accurately.

Index of Patents (1939), p. 342; *Negro Year Book* (1937-1938), p. 13

1941 • The first African American to earn a Ph.D. in engineering was Walter T. Daniels (1908-1991), who received the degree in civil engineering from Iowa State University in 1941. He had received a B.S. in 1929 from the University of Arizona. After receiving his degree from Iowa State University, Daniels taught one year at Southern University (Louisiana), and in 1943 became the first African American engineer licensed in the state of Louisiana. In that same year, he joined the Howard University (Washington, D.C.) civil engineering faculty, later becoming chair of the civil engineering department and then dean of the School of Engineering for a short period of time. Daniels resigned his position as department chair in 1971, but continued to teach until 1976.

Black Collegian (January/February 1979), pp. 136-8; *Notable Black American Scientists* (1999), pp. 91-2; *Black Engineers in the United States* (1974), p. 47

1942 • A machine was invented by Asa J. Taylor for assembling and/or disassembling the parts of spring-tensioned devices, and he received a patent in 1942 for his invention. Taylor's invention was primarily for use on parts of spring-tensioned valve assemblies for internal combustion engines. The device comprised a base with a number of independently movable slides having projections extending from them. The projections allowed the slides to be maneuvered in such a way that the parts could assembled automatically. The parts could also be disassembled upon removal from the engine.

Creativity and Inventions (1987), p. 69; *Index of Patents* (1942), p. 651

1942 • The first African American commissioned officer in the Women's Army Auxiliary Corps (WAAC), which was renamed Women's Army Corps (WAC) was Charity Adams Earley (1918-) in 1942. Earley earned a scholarship to Wilberforce University, from which she graduated in 1938. She taught math and science in Columbia South Carolina until she was selected for membership in the first officers candidate class of the WAAC. She completed training and received her commission on August 29, 1942. Earley remained in the army until 1946. She received many honors for her pioneering military services, including two honorary doctorates. The book

One Woman's Army: A Black Officer Remembers the WAC was authored by Earley and published in 1989.

The Book of African-American Women (1996), pp. 205-206; *Black Women in America* (1993), pp. 375-376; *One Woman's Army: A Black Officer Remembers the WAC* (1989)

1943 • Stephen H. Davis invented a combined load weighing and totaling device for cranes, hoists, and the like, which was patented in 1943. Davis's device could be readily connected with a crane or hoist and showed the weight of each load as it is handled by the crane. The device also provided the total weight of a number of loads handled consecutively.

Black Inventors: From Africa to America (1995), p. 121; *Creativity and Inventions* (1987), p. 65; *Index of Patents* (1943), p. 138

1944 • In 1938, David N. Crosthwait, Jr. (1898-1976) invented a window thermostat designed to function in a system by controlling the internal temperature of a building. The window thermostat measured the temperature adjacent to the inner surface of an outside window pane as a function of outside weather conditions and room temperature. Crosthwait's invention was granted a patent in 1944. Crosthwait mounted the temperature-sensitive resistance element within an enclosed casing, shielding the element from rapid response to room temperature changes. A technique was adapted to vary an electric current in response to temperature changes.

Blacks in Science and Medicine (1990), pp. 64-65; *Blacks in Science: Astrophysicist to Zoologist* (1977), p. 45; *Index of patents* (1944)

1945 • A method and apparatus for polishing glass was invented by John R. Turner and patented in 1945. The Turner procedure provided an apparatus for mechanically polishing glass and similar substances, especially optical elements. His method uses a measurement of the amount of friction between the tool and the work object to automatically add a lubricant to the work when it begins to dry.

Index of Patents (1945), p. 445; *Official Gazette* (July 10, 1945), p. 300

1945 • Henrietta Mahim Bradberry (1900-1979) patented a torpedo discharge device in 1945. This apparatus operated pneumatically and was adapted to discharge torpedoes below the water surface. It could be located in submarines or in subterranean forts. Her discharge device prevented water from entering the effective mechanism. Prior to that, Bradberry patented a bed rack in 1943.

Black Women in America (1993), pp. 618; *Creativity and Inventions* (1987), pp. 21, 63; *The Technological Woman* (1983), p. 61

1949 • Marjorie Lee Browne (1914-1979) was one of the first two African American women to earn a Ph.D. in mathematics when she received hers from the University of Michigan. (The other woman was Evelyn Boyd Granville, from Yale University). She received her B.S. in mathematics in 1935 from Howard University and a M.S. in mathematics from the University of Michigan in 1939. Browne taught mathematics at North Carolina Central University from 1949 to 1979 and became the first mathematics department chair from 1951 to 1970. Under her leadership, North Carolina Central University was awarded a National Science Foundation grant for summer institutes for secondary teachers. She directed the mathematics section of these institutes from 1957 to 1970. Browne also won a Ford Foundation fellowship and National Science Foundation Faculty Fellow award for advanced mathematical studies. She was the first recipient of the W.W. Rankin Memorial award for Excellence in Mathematics Education given by the North Carolina Council of Teachers of Mathematics. In 1960, she received a $60,000 grant from IBM to establish one of the first computer centers at a predominantly minority university.

MARJORIE LEE BROWNE

African America: Portrait of a People (1994), pp. 665-666; *African American Almanac* (1997), p. 1066; *Black Women in America* (1993), pp. 186-187

1949 • Evelyn Boyd Granville (1924-) became one of the first two African American women to earn a Ph.D. in mathematics when she received her degree from Yale University in 1949. (The other woman was Marjorie Lee Browne, from the University of Michigan.) Granville had previously graduated with a bachelor's degree *summa cum laude* from Smith College in 1945, then earned a M.A. in 1946 from Yale University. She worked as an applied mathematician for the Diamond Ordnance Fuze Laboratories from 1952 to 1956, when she joined IBM working on Project Mercury and Project Vanguard, doing orbit computation methods, celestial mechanics, numerical analysis, and digital computer techniques. In 1967, she joined the California State University in Los Angeles faculty, from which she retired in 1984. Granville taught mathematics and computer science from 1985 to 1988 at Texas College, and in 1990, was appointed to the Sam A. Lindsey Chair at the University of Texas at Tyler. In 1989, she was awarded an honorary doctorate from Smith College, making her the first woman mathematician to receive an honorary doctorate degree.

African America: Portrait of a People (1994), p. 673; *Black Women in America* (1993), pp. 498-499; *The Book of African-American Women* (1996), pp. 264-266

1949 • The first African-American building inspector for the City of Detroit was Everod A. Coleman (1920-) when appointed in 1949. Coleman received his B.S. in 1947 from Lincoln University (Pennsylvania) and went to work for White and Griffin Architects and Engineers as a steel designer until 1949. He was then hired by the City of Detroit, where he worked until 1980 as coordinator of the physical development and community and economic development department. Coleman also served as interim chief building inspector and consultant in 1982 for the City of Inkster, Michigan.

Who's Who among African Americans (1998-1999), p. 297

1949 • Clinton Jones invented an electric release for an artillery trainer that was patented in 1949. Jones's simple device could be used by students in classrooms under simulated battle conditions to receive training in setting large artillery pieces. The trainer had an adjustable plane element carrying a support for a projectile and a firing bolt. Jones's system had an internal electromagnet mounted on the incline plane and connected with the latch arm in an inoperative position. The device would release the bolt when the circuit to the electromagnetic device was closed.

Index of Patents (1949), p. 309; *Negro Year Book* (1947), p. 29

1949 • Robert Sherwood Dorsey (1923-), who received a B.S. in mechanical engineering from Ohio State University in 1949, was the first African American member of the Tau Beta Pi, a national honorary engineering fraternity at Ohio State University, and became a charter member of the Pi Tau Sigma national honorary mechanical engineering fraternity in 1949. Upon graduation, Dorsey became employed by the General Electric Company in Cincinnati, Ohio. He received the Distinguished Alumnus Award from the College of Engineering of Ohio State University in 1970, and was also elected to the Ohio State University Board of Trustees.

Black Engineers in the United States (1974), p. 53; *The Story of Kappa Alpha Psi* (1967), p. 245

GUION BLUFORD

1951 • Guion S. Bluford (1942-) received a patent in 1951 for his invention of an artillery ammunition training round. His invention was for a training round simulating artillery ammunition in its physical and ballistic characteristics, but which employed less expensive small arms ammunition components as its expendable materials. Bluford's artillery round had muzzle velocity and time of flight characteristics similar to that of conventional heavy-caliber ammunition. The rounds provided a relatively inexpensive means of training military personnel in the technique of loading and firing artillery weapons of the older recoil and more modern recoilless types.

Black Inventors: From Africa to America (1995), p. 121; *Index of Patents* (1957)

1953 • Katharine Coleman G. Johnson (1918-), in 1953, was the first African American woman electrical engineer hired at the National Aeronautical and Space Administration's Langley Research Center. Johnson's extensive work for NASA included calculating interplanetary trajectories and orbits of spacecraft and satellites. She worked in the first space mission and the Earth resources satellite mission, as well as analyzing data gathered during lunar missions. Johnson and her colleagues won the NASA Group Achievement Awards in 1967 and 1970. She also won special achievement awards in 1970, 1980 and 1985. Additionally, she studied new navigation procedures, determining more practical ways to track manned and unmanned space missions. Johnson retired from NASA in 1992.

Black Contributions to Science and Energy Technology (February 1979); *Blacks in Science and Medicine* (1990), p. 135; *Notable Twentieth Century Scientists* (1995), pp. 1031-1032

1955–1970 • John B. Christian (1927-) patented a variety of revolutionary lubricants during the period 1955 to 1970. He earned a B.S. in chemistry in 1950 at the University of Louisville and was employed by Dupont and the Naval Ordnance Laboratory before joining the U. S. Air Force Materials Laboratory in 1955. Christian has developed a number of lubricants used for a variety of purposes, including lubricants withstanding wide temperature ranges, those used in helicopter oil liner, astronaut back-pack life support systems, the "moon-buggy" four-wheel drive vehicle, and many other applications related to aircraft and spacecraft. Christian has a large number of patents on lubricants, greases, grease compositions, and lubrication stabilizers, and has generated a number of scientific and technical publications.

Black Americans in Science and Engineering (1984), p. 28; *Black Engineers in the United States* (1974), pp. 36-37; *Creativity and Inventions* (1987), p. 64

1956 • Yvonne Young Clark (1929-), who is associate professor in the department of mechanical engineering at Tennessee A & I University, was the first African American woman on the engineering faculty at Tennessee A & I University. She received a B.S. degree in mechanical engineering at Howard University in 1952. Clark was an equipment designer from 1952 to 1955 for the RCA Tube Division. She was hired by Tennessee A & I University in 1956, and was head of the mechanical engineering department until 1970. In 1971, she was hired by the Ford Motor Company Glass Plant, where she worked until 1972, when she then went back to the engineering department of Tennessee A & I. Clark is a licensed mechanical professional engineer and is active in many engineering organizations and associations.

Black Engineers in the United States (1974), p. 38; *Ebony* (July, 1964), pp. 75-76,78,80,82; *Blacks in Science and Medicine* (1990), p. 55

1956 • Tony W. Helm invented a universal joint that was patented in 1956. Helm's universal joint virtually eliminated various problems of previous designs. The apparatus functions like many mechanic's tools, applying and removing nuts, applying a turning force to any parts in positions that are difficult to access, and driving two angularly positioned shafts for transmitting power. Another asset of Helm's joint is the number of angularly arranged widened faces, each at its opposite ends, having a tapered position which symmetrically meets the adjacent tapered portion of the adjacent face.

The Black Inventor (1975), p. 91; *Blacks in Science: Astrophysicist to Zoologist* (1977), p. 90; *Black Inventors: From Africa to America* (1995), p. 120; *Index of Patents* (1956), p. 353; *Twentieth Century Black Patentees - A Survey* (1979)

PAUL R. WILLIAMS

1957 • Los Angeles architect Paul Revere Williams (1894-1980), an African American architect who designed over 3,000 buildings, was the first African American architect to be elected to the American Institute of Architects (AIA) College of Fellows in 1957. Known as the "Architect to the Stars," Williams was licensed in the state of California in 1921 and established his own firm in 1923 in Los Angeles. He was one of the first African Americans elected to membership in the AIA when he became a member in 1923. Williams designed the homes of the very rich and famous, some of which were, at that time, valued up to $600,000. He was also famous for his design of a number of commercial and pubic buildings. Homes were designed by Williams for Frank Sinatra, Bill "Bojangles" Robinson, Lucille Ball and Desi Arnaz, and Tyrone Power. Some of his public or commercial works include part of the the Los Angeles International Airport, the Saks Fifth Avenue and W. J. Sloane department stores, Beverly Hills Hotel, MCA Building, Los Angeles County Court House, U.S. Naval Station, Long Beach, and many churches.

Ebony (March, 1994), pp. 57-58, 60, 100, 102; *Emerge* (January, 1994), pp. 74-75; *New York Times* (June 1, 1995); *Philadelphia New Observer* (1997, February 5)

1959 • Robert Arthur Bland (1938-) was the first African American student to graduate from the University of Virginia, where he earned a B.S.E.E. in 1959. He also earned a M.A. in 1975 from California State University and an Ed.D. degree from Nova University in 1979. Bland was employed as a project engineer from 1959 to 1971 at the Naval Weapons Center and then as an instructor at the Oxnard Community College from 1977. He has also worked as a division head at the Naval Ship Weapons Systems Engineering Station.

Who's Who Among African-Americans (1998-1999), p. 124; *Journal of Blacks in Higher Education* (Autumn 1996), p. 84

1959 • Philip G. Hubbard (1921-), an African American engineer, joined the faculty of the University of Iowa in 1954 as an assistant professor of mechanics and hydraulics and in 1959 was appointed professor, making him the first tenured African American professor at the University. Hubbard earned a B.S. in chemical engineering from the University of Iowa in 1943 and second B.S. in electrical engineering in 1946. He then earned a M.S. in 1949 and a Ph.D. in 1951, with both degrees in mechanics and hydraulics and all degrees awarded by the University of Iowa. Hubbard was an expert in fluid dynamics with a specialty in the measurement and analysis of turbulence in fluid flow. In 1966, he was appointed dean of academic affairs at Iowa, a position he held until his retirement. Hubbard published articles and books on the mechanics of fluids and also invented an anemometer, an instrument for the measurement of fluid turbulence.

Black Engineers in the United States (1974), p. 98; *Blacks in Science: Astrophysicist to Zoologist* (1977), p. 331; *Blacks in Science and Medicine* (1990), p. 124; *Created Equal* (1993), p. 177; *Ebony* (August, 1959), p. 6

1959 • Otis Boykin (1920-1982) was granted a patent in 1959 for his invention of a wire type precision resistor. Wire type resistors have minimum inductance and capacitance effects and can be handled so that resistance values can be uniformly controlled. Boykin's resistor wire wound into a number of separated sections with the wire being looped in opposite directions in adjacent sections, which are folded over into each other. The wire is wound on a flat tape of insulating material, and the sections are formed of flat loops with the wire held together by plastic or waxy adhesive material for convenient handling. Boykin's resistor is used in guided missiles, computers, artificial heart stimulator control units, and other electronic devices.

Blacks in Science: Astrophysicist to Zoologist (1977), p. 90; *Blacks in Science and Medicine* (1990), p. 34; *Created Equal* (1993), p. 174; *Index of Patents* (1959), p. 108; *Jet* (April 12, 1982), p. 13

1959 • Nathelyne A. Kennedy, president and owner of Nathelyne A. Kennedy & Associates, was the first woman to be awarded an engineering degree by Prairie View A&M University in 1959, and the first African American woman to earn an engineering degree from any university in the state of Texas. Kennedy earned a B.S. in architectural engineering from Prairie View. Following graduation, she worked for 12 years at Alfred Bensch & Company in Chicago, Illinois, where she was the first woman to be hired as an engineer at the firm, and the only woman engineer during her 12 year tenure. Later, Kennedy worked for Bernard Johnson, Inc., in Houston, Texas, as a bridge design engineer. In 1981, the licensed professional engineer started her own company, Nathelyne A. Kennedy & Associates, Inc., a civil and structural consulting engineering firm. Kennedy's firm has been instrumental in a number of highway, roadway, bridge, public transit, and parking facility projects. The firm has also completed water and waste-water systems, marine terminals, and other varied special projects. Some of Kennedy's clients include the City of Austin, City of Houston, Harris County Engineering Department, Texas Department of Transportation, the Houston Port Authority, and Tampa, Florida. She has received many honors, including awards from government agencies and professional organizations.

Ebony (December 1984), p. 34; *The Informer* (December 1997), p. 3A; *Houston Chronicle* (September 28, 1997), Focus on Engineering, p. 2; *US Black Engineer* (Conference 1996), p. 46

1960 • Steven Smith Davis (1910-1977) was an African American mechanical engineer who acquired a patent in 1960 for his design of a supersonic wind tunnel nozzle. Prior to his invention, engineers, in order to change the wind speed of supersonic wind tunnels, had to physically remove the nozzle and replace it with another. Davis's flexible nozzle allowed engineers to change the shape of the nozzle, varying the wind speed of the tunnel as required. Davis also contributed to the development of air compressors. He earned a B.S. in 1936 and a M.S. in 1947, both in mechanical engineering from Howard University. Davis worked at the U.S. Naval Ordinance Laboratory from 1953 to 1963 and became a professor of mechanical engineering at Howard University in 1956. He was made department chair in 1962, and Dean of the School of Engineering and Architecture in 1964. He served as dean until 1970, but continued to teach until 1977.

Blacks in Science and Medicine (1990), p. 70; *Black Engineers in the United States* (1974), pp. 50-51; *Notable Black American Scientists* (1999), pp. 92-94

1960 • Robert F. Bundy (1912?-1989) received a patent in 1960 for a signal generator that was one of a number of significant inventions developed by him. He also designed an x-ray system for detecting weapons and small wires leading to explosives and filed a patent for a traveling wave tube principal.

Creativity and Inventions (1987), p. 64; *Philadelphia Tribune* (December 19, 1989), p. 2B

1960 • The first African American woman to receive a Ph.D. from the University of Texas was Lillian Katie Bradley (1921-). She earned her 1960 degree in mathematics education. Bradley earned her B.A. in mathematics in 1938 at Texas College and a M.A. in mathematics education at the University of Michigan in 1946. She has taught mathematics in Texas colleges since 1946 and has authored a text for elementary mathematics instruction, as well as a college algebra text and other publications on mathematics and education.

Blacks in Science and Medicine (1990), pp. 34-35

1960 • One of the more prolific authors of mathematical textbooks is the African American mathematician Albert Turner Bharucha-Reid (1927-1985). His first text, published in 1960, was entitled *Elements of the Theory of Markov Processes and their Applications* (McGraw Hill). It was later translated into Russian. Bharucha-Reid taught at Wayne State University (Michigan) from 1961 to 1981. Afterward, he held appointments at the Georgia Institute of Technology and Atlanta University. He was awarded several major research grants, including two from the National Science Foundation. His last book, with M. Sambandham, was entitled *Random Polynomials* and was published posthumously in 1986.

Blacks in Science and Medicine (1990), p. 27; *Western Journal of Black Studies* (1992), Volume 16, p. 52

1960 • A quick disconnect valved coupling, having a plug check valve in each of a pair of coupling members, was invented by Vincent A. Gill and patented in 1960. Gill's device permitted an improved seal between and within the coupling members, allowing a relatively high fluid pressure within the coupling with a minimum of leakage. The valves of the coupling structure had a high level of safety by having the valves locked in their closed position to prevent inadvertent opening. However, Gill provided the capability for the valves to automatically unlock for rotation in phase to their open position when the coupling members are protected. When the coupling was securely locked, though, the locking mechanism indicated whether or not the valves were fully open.

Black Inventors: From Africa to America (1995), p. 123; *Creativity and Inventions* (1987), p. 65; *Index of Patents* (1960), p. 324

1961 • A transistorized multivibrator circuit for computers, adapted to oscillate for only a predetermined time, was invented by Phillip Emile, Jr. in 1959 and patented in 1961. Emile adapted the circuit to oscillate for a predetermined time by generating a predetermined number of pulses in response to each trigger pulse. In a variety of electronic applications, it was required that a predetermined number of pulses be generated in response to trigger pulse, but the techniques for generating such pulses were quite complex and not compact as required in computer circuitry. Emile's technique provided simple and compact circuitry that was able to reliably and accurately generate a predetermined number of pulses and provide oscillation for a predetermined time.

Black Inventors: From Africa to America (1995), p. 123; *Creativity and Inventions* (1987), p. 65; *Index of Patents* (1961)

1961 • The African American inventor Adolphus Samms patented a rocket engine pump feed system in 1961. This system aided the flow of liquid fuel or solid fuel to rocket engines. He also patented, in 1965, a multiple stage rocket and an air-breathing booster, and in 1967, patented a rocket motor fuel feed system. Samms' work has been commended by NASA and the President's Office of Science and Technology.

The Black Inventor (1975), p. 48; *Creativity and Inventions* (1987), p. 68

1962 • Kenneth C. Kelly filed a claim for a patent for his invention of a linearly polarized monoplus lobing antenna in 1959, and a patent was granted for the antenna in 1962. Kelly's invention had an improved lobing antenna that was small and provided a linearly polarized beam. An improved monoplus antenna, which provided pointing error information with extremely simple wave energy feed structure, was provided. The lobing antenna could be flush-mounted with a planar surface.

Black Inventors: From Africa to America (1995), p. 125; *Creativity and Inventions* (1987), p. 67; *Index of Patents* (1962)

1962 • The first African American engineering student at LTV Aerospace Corporation was David Leon Ford, Jr. (1944-), when he was hired on in 1962. He retained his position there for five years. Ford graduated from Iowa State University in 1967, receiving a B.S. degree. He then earned a M.S. in 1969 and a Ph.D. in 1972, both from the University of Wisconsin at Madison. Ford was an assistant professor at Purdue University from 1972 to 1975, and in the 1980-81 school year, was a visiting assistant professor at the Yale School of Organization and Management. He has been president of D.L. Ford and Associates management consultants in Dallas, Texas since 1977.

Who's Who Among African Americans (1998-1999), p. 492

1962 • Allen H. Turner's invention of an electrostatic paint system was patented in 1962. His process continuously electrostatically atomized the paint through a painting tube. The tube has a number of small openings arranged at a substantial angle to the horizontal, which establishes an electrical potential between the painting tube and a receiver. The paint liquid is slightly pressurized to push it through the openings in the painting tube.

Black Inventors: From Africa to America (1995), p. 126; *Creativity and Inventions* (1987), p. 69; *Index of Patents* (1962), pp. 43, 517, 1056

1963 • Harvey Gantt (1943-) became the first African American student at Clemson University (South Carolina) when he started classes in 1963. Two years later, he also became the first African American student to graduate from that institution, and he was the third ranking student in the architecture program. Gantt went on to earn a M.S. in urban planning from the Massachusetts Institute of Technology in 1970. He worked for architectural firms in North Carolina from 1965 to 1970. He then went into his own partnership and started the architectural firm Gantt-Huberman in 1971 in Charlotte, North Carolina. In 1974, Gantt was appointed to the Charlotte City Council. He became the first African American mayor of the city of Charlotte in 1983.

Contemporary Black Biography (199), pp. 73-74; *New York Times* (May 8, 1990), (June 7, 1990), (November 8, 1990)

1963 • John W. Blanton (1922-) invented a hydromechanical control system for which a patent was granted in 1963. Blanton's set of servomechanisms employed hydraulic and pneumatic fluids for the control of mechanical motions. The device provided a simplified technique for mechanical control, incorporating dynamic time lead or rate anticipation, which eliminated complex electromechanical and electronic elements. Blanton's technique provided error rate damping, as well as actuator output velocity and acceleration proportional to server valve input error. He earned a B.S. degree in mechanical engineering from Purdue University in 1943. He managed the General Electric Jet Propulsion Laboratory and was responsible for preliminary designs of advanced engine propulsion systems.

Blacks in Science: Astrophysicist to Zoologist (1977), p. 38; *Blacks in Science and Medicine* (1990), p. 30; *Index of Patents* (1963); *Negro Year Book* (1941-1946), p. 30

1963 • A self-propelled lawn mower, which moved in a predetermined pattern without any manual control, was patented by Clarence Nokes in 1963. The lawn mower has steerable wheels for guiding the mower through a given area in a rectangular, square, or polygonal path. The mower is comprised of a frame, drive wheels mounted longitudinally and spaced in relation to the mower assembly, a power assembly connected to the drive wheels, and a control means. The control means is connected with the steerable wheels for pivoting about a generally vertical axis at predetermined timed intervals, causing the mower to travel in a predetermined pattern.

Creativity and Inventions (1987), p. 68; *Index of Patents* (1963), p. 629; *Twentieth Century Black Patentees - A Survey* (1979)

1964 • Henry Thomas Sampson (1934-) received a patent in 1964 for his invention for a binder system for propellants and explosives. Sampson received a B.S. in chemical engineering from Purdue University in 1956, a M.S. in engineering from the University of California at Los Angeles in 1961, and a Ph.D. in nuclear engineering from the University of Illinois in 1967. Sampson has several other patents for propellants and a number of publications in the scientific literature.

Black Engineers in the United States (1974), pp. 174-175; *Blacks in Science and Medicine* (1990), p. 208; *Who's Who Among Black Americans* (1985), p. 736

1964 • Wesley Lee Jordan (1941-) became the first African American full-time faculty member at a Southern, traditionally white college when began teaching mathematics at Belmont Abbey College in 1964. Jordan earned a B.S. degree in 1963, then a M.S. in 1965 from Fordham University. He taught at Belmont College from 1964 to 1967, then joined the faculty at Pace University in 1969.

Who's Who Among African Americans (1998-1999), p. 848

DAVID BLACKWELL

1965 • In 1965, David H. Blackwell (1919-) became the first African American elected to the National Academy of Sciences. Blackwell received his B.S. (1938), M.S. (1939), and Ph.D. (1941) in mathematics from the University of Illinois. He specializes in set theory and game theory, and his research was key to the development of statistical decision theory as it related to games. He coauthored the statistical textbook, *Theory of Games and Statistical Decisions,* with Abe Girshick in 1954. Blackwell has been professor of statistics at the University of California at Berkeley since 1954, and was chair of the department from 1956 to 1961. In 1955, he was elected president of the Institute of Mathematical Statistics, and he received the R.A. Fisher Award from the Committee of the Presidents of Statistical Societies, the most prestigious award in the field of statistics, in 1986.

Encyclopedia of Black America (1981), p. 183; *Philadelphia Tribune* (April 15, 1983); *Western Journal of Black Studies* Vol. 16, No. 1 (1992), p. 52; *Who's Who Among Black Americans* (1992-1993), p. 115

1966 • Donald E. Jefferson invented a triggered exploding wire device for electroexplosive apparatus that was patented in 1966. Jefferson's invention initiated certain types of explosives with exploding wire and an improved triggered spark gab-bride wire arrangement, which was specially adapted for use in an electrical firing circuit. Jefferson's apparatus required fewer components than prior systems and achieved a high degree of safety with regard to the inadvertent firing of the bridge wire.

Black Inventors: From Africa to America (1995), p. 125; *Index of Patents* (1966), p. 665

1966 • The first full-time African American woman professor on the Baylor University (Texas) faculty was Vivienne Lucille Malone Mayes (1932-1995), appointed in 1966. Mayes received her Ph.D. in mathematics from the University of Texas in 1966, making her the first African American woman to earn the doctorate from that institution. She earned a B.A. in mathematics in 1952 at Fisk University (Tennessee) and then the M.A. in mathematics also at Fisk in 1954. Mayes taught at Paul Quinn College (Texas) from 1954 to 1961. After joining the Baylor faculty in 1966, she remained as a professor there until her retirement in 1994. Mayes was very active in the Association of Women in Mathematics and was the first African American elected to its executive committee.

American Mathematical Monthly, Vol. 88 (October 1981), pp. 596-7; *Blacks in Science and Medicine* (1990), p. 165; *Black Women in America* (1993), pp. 499, 757; *Notable Black American Scientists* (1999), pp. 300-1

1966 • John G. King (1925-), an African American inventor, patented an invention for a burglary alarm for portable electrically powered equipment in 1966. King also patented his invention for an electronically operated alarm system for the prevention of illicit entry into protected environments. The system generated an alarm whenever a protected item was being moving. It operated by detecting vibrations. King was owner of King Research Laboratory, Inc. in Maywood, Illinois.

Index of Patents (1966), p. 1972; *Who's Who Among African Americans* (1998-1999), p. 752

1966 • Victor Llewellyn Ransom (1924-) acquired a patent for traffic data processing in 1966. Ransom earned a B.S. in electrical engineering in 1948 from the Massachusetts Institute of Technology and a M.S. in electrical engineering from Case Western Reserve University in 1952. He was an electrical engineer for NACA from 1948 to 1953 and an instructor at Newark College of Engineering from 1956 to 1968. He has published a number of technical documents in the area of switching system design.

Black Engineers in the United States (1974), p. 165

1966 • Wilbert Leroy Jones, Jr. (1927-) invented a duplex capstan (lifting machine) for use in a two-unit handling and storage-type hoist system. Jones's system, which was patented in 1966, met the needed heavy hoisting equipment with long length cable storage capacity. The duplex capstan was comprised of two simultaneously driven, axially slotted cylinders with their bars, intermeshed such that they rotate through substantially the same space on an axis. A cable that was wound about the capstan contacted only one of the cylinders while being laterally advanced. Jones, who was a supervising mechanical engineer for the Naval Research Laboratory, received a B.S. in mechanical engineering from Howard University in 1951.

Black Engineers in the United States (1974), p. 115; *Index of Patents* (1966)

1967 • Robert Roosevelt Brooks (1930-) patented his invention, a line blanking apparatus for color bar-generating equipment, in 1967. Brooks received a B.S. in electrical engineering from Howard University in 1959 and a M.S. from the University of Pennsylvania in 1964. Brooks was employed by the RCA Corporation as a senior electrical design and development engineer.

Blacks in Science and Medicine (1990), p. 38; *Black Engineers in the United States* (1974), p. 26

1967 • Delores Elaine Robinson Brown (1945-) was the first woman to graduate with an engineering degree from Tuskegee Institute. She earned her B.S. in electrical engineering there in 1967. Brown began work with General Electric Company as an associate engineer from 1967 to 1968. For the next two years, she worked for the Florida Power Corporation, then became an associate engineer at the Honeywell Aerospace Corporation from 1971 to 1975. Brown then was employed from 1975 to 1978 as a quality engineer for E-Systems ECI Division, followed by an engineering positon with Sperry Univac until 1990. Since 1990, she has been a minister at Lakeview Presbyterian Church.

Black Engineers in the United States (1974), p. 27; *Blacks in Science and Medicine* (1990), p. 38; *Who's Who Among African-Americans* (1998-1999), p. 176

1968 • The first African American general foreman and superintendent of the Sharon Steel Corporation was William J. White (1935-), when he became general foreman of degassing in 1968. White was initially hired at Sharon Steel in 1957. After a number of promotions with increasing responsibilities, White became general foreman in 1968 and, in 1985, manager of the primary rolling and plant support services. He earned a B.A. degree in 1957 at Westminster College and completed additional courses and advanced training at both the Alexander Hamilton Business Institute and

Youngstown State University. White served as logistics administrator for Weirton Steel Corporation.

Who's Who Among African Americans (1998-1999), p. 1383; *Who's Who Among Black Americans* (1990-1991), p. 1342

1968 • An arithmetic unit for digital computers was invented by Marvin C. Stewart and patented in 1968. Stewart's mechanism was a serial-parallel arithmetic unit for digital computers utilizing m-generating means and operating on signals in bit pairs that selectively interconnected operand and operator storage means. The unit performed all arithmetic functions and used substantially fewer components then was previously required.

Index of Patents (1968), p. 1134; *Twentieth Century Black Patentees - A Survey* (1979)

1968 • A patent was issued Andrew R. Johnson (1934-) in 1968 for his invention of a precision digital delay circuit. Johnson's circuit includes a logical AND circuit having a pair of input terminals, of which one receives the input signal that is delayed. It was precisely controlled and was uniform from circuit to circuit. In Johnson's system the circuit was not dependent on a resistor-capacitor or a resistor-inductor time constant. There were low overall variations in the circuit delay without substantial problems. Johnson's specialty areas are nonlinear magnetics and analysis and digital memory technology. Johnson received a B.S. in electrical engineering from North Carolina A&T State University in 1956 and a M.S. in electrical engineering from Syracuse University in 1961.

Black Engineers in the United States (1974), p. 107; *Index of Patents* (1968)

1968 • Charles A. Peterson invented a power generator that used the flow of water between reservoirs of dissimilar levels to drive a turbine that in turn powered the electrical generator. Peterson's invention was patented in 1968. In Peterson's system, a tower is mounted in a large body of water connected by a supply conduit to a reservoir containing water. A method for harnessing the flow of water, such as a turbine, is mounted in the tower. The water siphoned out of the reservoir is continuously replenished by waves in the large body of water splashing over the sides.

Black Inventors: From Africa to America (1995), p. 125; *Index of Patents* (1968), p. 913

1968 • James Earl Lewis (1931-), an African American physicist and engineer, invented and patented, in 1968, a microwave antenna feed for two coordinated radars. Lewis received a B.S.E.E. in 1955 and a M.S. in physics in 1976, both from Howard University. He worked for the U.S. Naval Research Laboratory from 1957 to 1966, and then was employed by Lockheed Electronics from 1966 to 1969, before joining Westinghouse Electric Company as senior electronics engineer in 1969, where he remained until 1975. In 1972, Lewis received an invention award from Westinghouse for developing a technique for reduced sidelobes on radar antennas.

Blacks in Science and Medicine (1990), pp. 152-153; *Black Engineers in the United States* (1974), p. 125; *Creativity and Inventions* (1987), p. 67; *Who's Who Among African-Americans* (1998-1999), p. 921

1969 • Charles W. Tate, Sr. designed a flexible and transparent lubricant housing for a universal joint, receiving a patent for the device in 1969. The housing provided protection from failure of the universal joint during high speed operation and permitted observation of the universal joint while in operation. The housing enabled the universal joint to operate visibly in a bath of oil, preventing damage to nearby equipment and injury to personnel from the joint if it failed, especially during high-speed operations. The housing was made of high strength elastomeric synthetic plastic, which was flexible, enabling considerable latitude of shaft angles within the hollow confines of the housing and providing for stress reaction, primarily in the terminal walk and stem portions of the housing.

Black Inventors: From Africa to America (1995), p. 126; *Index of Patents* (1969)

1969 • Lonnie George Neal (1928-) patented his invention, an electro-magnetic gyroscope float assembly, in 1969. Neal earned a B.S. in industrial arts from Langston University in 1950 and a B.S. in mechanical engineering from Marquette University in 1966. Neal was employed as a senior project engineer for the General Motors Corporation Delco Electronics Division.

Black Engineers in the United States (1974), p. 149

1969 • M. Lucius Walker (1936-) patented the invention of a laminar NOR element, in 1969. (A NOR is a type of computer logic circuit.) Walker received a B.S. in mechanical engineering in 1957 from Howard University, as well as a M.S. in mechanical engineering in 1958 and a Ph.D. in 1966 from the Carnegie Institute of Technology. Walker was assistant dean of the Howard University School of Engineering from 1965 to 1966, acting department of mechanical engineering chairman from 1968 to 1973, associate dean from 1973 to 1974, and then dean in 1978. Walker has a number of scientific publications and was active in many engineering and scientific organizations.

Black Engineers in the United States (1974), p. 198; *Blacks in Science and Medicine* (1990), p. 239; *Who's Who Among Black Americans* (1985), p. 857; *Creativity and Inventions* (1987), p. 69

1969 • In 1969, George R. Carruthers (1940-) received a patent for a magnetically focused image converter. This device converted electromagnetic waves, such as ultraviolet waves, into an electron image that could be recorded, or into a visible light image, which could be observed. In Carruthers' device, light entered an internal optic image converter and was focused by an internal mirror onto the photocathode. Then emitted electrons were accelerated and focused by a magnetic field produced by a coil. The electron image was focused onto a phosphor screen or nuclear track emulsion. This was nearly an exact reproduction of the optical image on the photocathode. The phosphor screen converted the incident electrons into light, which were then detected by a camera on the electrons and recorded directly on a nuclear track plate or film.

African American Almanac (1997), p. 1066; *Ebony* (June, 1991), p. 48; *Index of patents* (1969)

1969 • Marie Van Brittan Brown, an African American woman inventor, received a patent in 1969, for her invention of a home security system. The system included a device that enabled a homeowner to use a television set to view a person at the door and hear the caller's voice. There was a video-scanning device outside the door and audio intercommunication equipment both inside and outside the door for conversing. A lock was provided for the door, with the releasing mechanism for the lock manually controlled by the occupant.

Black Inventors: From Africa to America (1995), p. 214; *Creativity and Inventions* (1987), p. 64

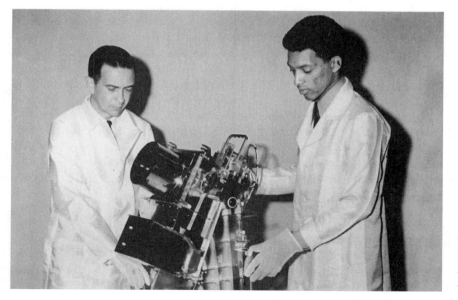

GEORGE CARRUTHERS (RIGHT) AND COWORKER WILLIAM CONWAY WITH THE APOLLO 16 CAMERA THEY DEVELOPED.

1969 • Darnley Mosely Howard patented a method of making a radome (a housing unit for a radar antenna) with an integral antenna in 1969. Howard acquired a B.S. in mechanical engineering from Howard University in 1947. He was a mechanical engineer for the National Bureau of Standards from 1948 to 1954 and an engineer from 1954 to 1962 for Emerson Research Laboratory. Howard then joined Litton Systems as a department head in 1962, following that with the position of senior mechanical engineer at Johns Hopkins University Applied Physics Laboratory in 1964. Howard contributed a number of items to the scientific literature in the areas of engineering mechanics, vibrations, and engineering management.

Black Engineers in the United States (1974), pp. 97-98; *Creativity and Inventions* (1987), p. 66

1969 • Irvin S. Frye was issued a patent in 1969 for his invention of an adjustable shackle for use in carpentry. Frye's shackle was a connector for joining two members of different widths without the use of shims or other adjustment devices. The invention was used for joining apertured members such as eyebolts, plastic, and chains having various thicknesses. His linkage arrangement was readily adaptable to either fixedly secure two members together or to permit relative movement between them. His shackles could be manufactured from simple castings.

Black Inventors: From Africa to America (1995), p. 123; *Index of Patents* (1969)

1970 • The founder and dean of the School of Architecture and City Planning at Howard University was Howard Hamilton Mackey, Sr. (1901-1987), who started the school in 1970. Mackey earned a B.Arch. in 1924 and a M.Arch. in 1972 from the University of Pennsylvania. Mackey was a registered architect in five Eastern states. He started teaching architecture in 1924 at Howard University. Mackey was the acting head of the architecture department from 1930 to 1937 and head from 1937 to 1970. He was also associate dean of the School of Engineering and Architecture for the academic year 1964-5. He was a fellow of the American Institute of Architects and consulted to Guyana, Surinam, Ghana, Nigeria, and India. Mackey received several national awards for his contribution to architecture, and was instrumental in the development of professional African American architects on a local and national level.

Blacks in Science and Medicine (1990), p. 158

1970 • A procedure entry for a data processor employing a stacking system was invented by Benjamin A. Dent and patented in 1970. The two top storing positions in the stack were two registers external to the memory. An additional memory had individually selectable display registers, each containing a different absolute memory address of a base of a stack area to store parameters, variables, and other references for a particular level of a program. Control words contained information, which created an address environment list. Gating and timing caused the system to automatically update the display registers. An address input was provided to add parameters, generating absolute addresses for locating data.

Black Inventors: From Africa to America (1995), p. 123; *Creativity and Inventions* (1987), p. 65; *Index of Patents* (1970), p. 99, 237, 354

1970 • Robert Roosevelt Brooks (1930-) invented an improved apparatus for restoring detail to a video signal, which he patented in 1970. Robinson's device was a television system including a source of video signals. The system reproduced an image in successive fields, having interfaced horizontal lines and an apparatus for correcting the video signals in both horizontal and vertical directions. Brooks was a senior design and development engineer for the RCA Corporation. He received a B.S. degree from Howard University in 1959 and a M.S. degree from the University of Pennsylvania in 1964, with both degrees in electrical engineering. Robinson has other inventions in the electronics field, as well as a number of scientific publications.

Black Engineers in the United States (1974), p. 26; *Blacks in Science and Medicine* (1990), p. 38; *Index of Patents* (1970)

1970 • Clyde Edward Gurley, an African American inventor, patented an automatic telephone alarm system in 1970. The device was external to a telephone unit and line for automatically detecting occurrences of fires and for notifying authorities of occurrences of burglaries, robberies, and fires. The system was readily adaptable to a rotary or push button telephone system and made direct contact with a police or fire department. Gurley also patented on the same date, April 7, 1970, a programmable (automatic) telephone dialing system which was applicable to either a rotary or push-button telephone.

Creativity and Inventions (1987), p. 66; *Index of Patents* (1970), pp. 601, 813

1970 • A microwave phase shift device was an invention of Osborne C. Stafford, patented in 1970. In Stafford's invention, there was a pair of flexible conductors extending from input and output terminals to separate take-up sports. The two conductors were in adjustable conductive engagement, so that the length of the transmission path formed between the terminals could be varied to shift the phase of microwave signal from input to output. The conductors were grounded at a distance of one-quarter wavelength, at the frequency of operation, from the point of conductive engagement to isolate the trailing ends of the conductors from the transmission path.

Black Inventors: From Africa to America (1995), p. 126; *Creativity and Inventions* (1987), p. 69; *Index of Patents* (1970)

1970 • Lawrence Randolph Kelly, Jr. was granted a patent in 1970 for his invention of an automatic telephone alarm apparatus. Kelly's device was external to a telephone unit and line and notified the proper authorities of burglaries, robberies, and fires. The system was activated by various detectors. To operate the alarm, the telephone receiver was lifted from its switchoff position, allowing the selection of modes of operation. The system detected the dial tone signal and then dialed a pre-programmed telephone number. If it detected a busy signal, it automatically re-dialed the number and played back into the telephone a pre-recorded message notifying key personnel of real-time occurrences of fire or crime.

Black Inventors: From Africa to America (1995), p. 242; *Creativity and Inventions* (1987), p. 67; *Index of Patents* (1970)

1970 • James H. Porter (1933-) patented, in 1970, the technique for gas well sulfur removal by diffusion through polymeric membranes. He has a bachelor of chemical engineering from Rensselaer Polytechnic Institute (1955) and a doctorate of science (1963) from Massachusetts Institute of Technology. Porter started as a senior research engineer at Chevron Corporation from 1963 to 1967, then several other corporations until becoming chairman and chief executive officer of U.V. Technologies in 1994. Porter also was an associate professor at MIT from 1971 to 1976 and won the outstanding professor award there in 1974 and 1975.

Blacks in Science and Medicine (1990), p. 193; *Who's Who Among Black Americans* (1985), p. 677; *Who's Who Among African Americans* (1998-1999), p. 1207

1970 • Winser Edward Alexander (1942-) received a patent on November 7, 1970, for a system for enhancing fine detail in thermal photographs. Alexander received a B.S. in mechanical engineering from North Carolina A&T State University in 1964, a M.S. in electrical engineering from the University of New Mexico in 1966, and a Ph.D. from the University of New Mexico in 1974.

Black Engineers in the United States (1974), pp. 4-5; *Blacks in Science and Medicine* (1990), p. 6

1971 • Charles M. Blackburn was granted a patent for his invention of an electronic counting device in 1971. The invention is a parts-handling unit for a high-speed, accurate counting out of parts or pieces equal to a predetermined number. It incorporates the electronic controller, feeder source of the parts, and bagging or boxing provisions for the batches. In the automatic mode, all the units cooperate to convey out batches of the proper number of pieces. Selectable controls can change the rate of materials fed into the machine and the number of parts comprising a batch.

The Black Inventor (1975), p. 91; *Index of Patents* (1971), p. 180; *Twentieth Century Black Patentees - A Survey* (1979)

1971 • Marvin C. Stewart was granted a patent in 1971 for his invention of a system for interconnecting electrical components. Stewart, in his system, used a stack of standard business machine cards for mounting individual components and providing electrical interconnection between cards, without the use of separate connectors and electrical wiring. Individual systems could be changed without destruction of the cards, and the component cards could be reused. Each card in Stewart's system had a matrix of paired conductive pads that were electrically connected. Electricity could be conducted between cards by means of the conductive paths interconnecting pad pairs.

Black Inventors: From Africa to America (1995), p. 248; *Index of Patents* (1971), p. 1810; *Twentieth Century Black Patentees - A Survey* (1979)

1972 • Yvonne Young Clark (1929-) is credited with several pioneering achievements in engineering as an African American and as a woman. Clark was the first woman to earn a B.S. in mechanical engineering at Howard University (Washington, D.C.) in 1952, and became the first woman faculty member and department head in the College of Engineering and Technology at Tennessee State University, where she served from 1956 to 1970. In 1972, she became the first woman to earn a M.S. in engineering management from Vanderbilt University (Tennessee). Clark worked for the Ford Glass Motor Company from 1971-2, the first woman engineer hired at the plant. She remained associated with Tennessee State for over 40 years, teaching engineering and computer graphics. Clark also undertook applied research for the Department of Energy on refrigerants and electricity use in the home.

Blacks in Science and Medicine (1990), p. 55; *Black Engineers in the United States* (1974), p. 38; *Journeys of Women in Science and Engineering* (1997), pp. 63-7

1972 • Ernest L. Walker (1941-), an African American electrical engineer employed by IBM, patented his invention for a shift register memory in 1972. Walker's invention relates to shift registers, particularly shift registers used to store a large amount of data. His register provides a magnetic shift register storage in which pages of data are arranged in order of use so that the most recently accessed page may be shifted into the access position on a priority basis. Walker received his B.S.E.E. in 1967 from Indiana Institute of Technology and his M.S.E.E. from Syracuse University in 1973. He then earned a Ph.D. from North Carolina State in 1982. Walker was initially employed as an associate engineer from 1969 to 1972 by IBM, and in 1973 he was promoted to a staff engineer. Walker became an advisory engineer for IBM in 1985, acquired five patents, and published several technical papers.

Black Engineers in the United States (1974), p. 198; *Index of Patents* (1972); *Who's Who Among African Americans* (1998-1999), p. 1535

1972 • A system for the use of faulty storage circuits by position coding was an invention of Frank S. Green, Sr. (1938-) that was patented in 1972. The computer device was a memory system which made use of a molithic semiconductor memory array having defective rows or columns (or both). This makes possible the wiring of all of the connector pads of each integrated circuit regardless of the existence of bad bits, rows, or columns. Greene received a B.S. in 1961 from Washington University, a M.S. from Purdue University in 1962, and a Ph.D. in 1970 from Santa Clara University. All his degrees were in electrical engineering. From 1965 to 1971 he was a technical staff member of Fairchild Research and Development, becoming president of Technology Development of California in 1971. Green had many technical publications and was active in a number of scientific and technical organizations. He has been a trustee of the Santa Clara University since 1990.

Black Engineers in the United States (1974), pp. 81-82; *Blacks in Science and Medicine* (1990), pp. 105, 106; *Who's Who Among Black Americans* (1990-1991), p. 587

1972 • James W. Cobb, an African American inventor, was co-owner of Pilot Machine Designers of South Norwalk, Connecticut. A graduate engineer, he patented several labor-saving devices, including, in 1972, a method and system for attaching a pocket to a portion of a garment. Cobb designed machinery for making mattress pads, and held a patent for a process of manufacturing paper lollypop sticks.

Black Enterprise (September, 1974); *Index of Patents* (1972)

1972 • Donald E. Jefferson received a patent award in 1972 for his invention of a special purpose data processor that is capable of performing one or more specific processing jobs. The system, a method and machine for processing data, combines the advantages of both special and general-purpose computers, yet avoid the disadvantages of each. Jefferson's system uses a programmable special purpose computer in which stored programs cooperate with hardware circuits to execute multiple programming tasks. The system also has interchangeable data processing circuits.

Index of Patents (1972), p. 158, 924; *Twentieth Century Black Patentees - A Survey* (1979)

1972 • James Battle (1937-) invented a variable resistance resistor assembly, which was patented in 1972. As electronic equipment became more complex, an increasing variety of resistance elements were required, and Battle's system related to that need. His was a variable resistance resistor assembly comprising a resistance element in a sheet form, a pair of electrodes on one side of the resistance element sheet, and a number of resistance variance electrodes on the other side. The resistance electrodes could short, either temporarily or permanently, to vary the resistance of the resistor assembly. Battle earned a B.S. in electrical engineering from the State University of New York, Buffalo and was employed by Carborundum Company in Niagara, New York.

Black Engineers in the United States (1974), p. 14; *Index of Patents* (1972)

1972 • Joel Morton Morris (1944-), while employed as an electrical engineer at Bell Telephone Laboratories, invented a switching system charging arrangement that was patented in 1972. Morris's switching system was able to concurrently provide and disable a video and audio connection between stations. The system was capable of controlling billing equipment to record the completion and duration of each connection. Morris earned a B.S. at Howard University in 1966 and a M.S. at Polytechnic Institute of Brooklyn in 1970. He then received a Ph.D. degree from Johns Hopkins University in 1975. Morris was employed by both the Bendix Corporation and Bell Telephone Laboratories as an electrical engineer. He also was a research engineer for the Naval Research Laboratory and was a science officer for the Office of Naval Research.

Index of Patents (1972); *Who's Who Among Black Americans* (1990-1991), p. 921

1972 • John G. King (1925-), the African American owner of King Research Laboratory, Inc. in Maywood, Illinois, received a patent for his invention for tamperproof auto alarm in 1972. King studied industrial electronics at Chicago City College and completed other industrial training. The primary component of King's alarm was a vibration response transducer. The transducer had an always-closed leaf contact switch and provided a variable resistor for triggering a latching switch to enable an alarm device. An attempt to short circuit it would also trigger the latching switch by way of a shunt path leading from the transducer. The transducer and alarm arrangement was provided in a complete tamperproof automobile alarm construction.

Index of Patents (1972); *Who's Who Among African Americans* (11th Edition), p. 752

1973 • A resistor sensing bit switch was invented by Joseph M. Redmond, a computing specialist at IBM, and was patented in 1973. The basic invention is a data storage circuit utilizing a bitable memory cell and a resistor sensing bit switch pre-amplifier for performing read and write operations. The cell contains two double-emitter semiconductor elements having their bases and collectors cross-coupled to form a bitable circuit. The amplifying transistors are concurrently biased on and off by a gating transistor under selective control of a bit driver decoding circuit. In read operations, the stored data is sensed at the bit sense line resistor by a final sense amplifier.

Index of Patents (1973), p. 189, 1557; *Twentieth Century Black Patentees - A Survey* (1979)

1973 • Charles Austin Dyer (1936-), a computer manager employed by Digital Equipment Incorporation, patented a teaching aid in 1973. Dyer's teaching aid was a mathematical calculator for adding, subtracting, multiplying, and dividing. It illustrated specific numbers divisible by a divisor, the remainder after division, and in more complicated embodiments set up for logarithmic or other relationships. Dyer earned a B.S. from Pratt Institute for Industrial Design in 1957. He then received a M.S. in 1962 from Yeshiva University and a Ph.D. from City College of New York City in 1980. Dyer published papers on artificial intelligence and computer-aided instruction.

Index of Patents (1973); *Who's Who Among African Americans* (1998-1999), p. 432

1973 • Albert G. B. Prather invented a gravity-operated escape means for which he was granted a patent in 1973. Prather's device was a mechanism for escaping from danger at an elevated level to safety at a lower level. It had a post extending between levels and vertically extending roller and brake tracks. It also had carriers and suspended load platforms slide-mounted on the post with rollers and brake shoes. There was a means responsive to the weight of the platform bracing it against the tracks, holding the carrier in a braked position. An adjustable brake release regulated the speed of descent of the carrier.

Black Inventors: From Africa to America (1995), p. 122; *Created Equal* (1993), p. 196; *Creativity and Inventions* (1987), p. 68; *Index of Patents* (1973)

1974 • Robert L. Engram was granted a patent in 1974 for his invention of a shock falsing inhibitor circuit for a plural tone receiver, one of his several patents. Engram's system applied the differential pulse and detected second tone to an AND gate. If both signals were simultaneously applied, the operation of the receiver was inhibited. If the second tone appeared at any time after the differentiated pulse was removed, the receiver operated in a normal fashion. Engram also developed, in 1975, a growable memory system while employed by Bell Laboratory.

Blacks in Science: Ancient and Modern (1983), p. 283; *Index of Patents* (1974), pp. 538, 2291

1974 • A patent was issued to Isadore Small III, in 1974, for his invention of a universal on-delay timer. Small's on-delay timer was comprised primarily of solid state elements for energizing a load at timed intervals after the pilot switch was closed. Upon switch reopening, the load was immediately de-energized and the timer automatically reset. The timer was universal in that it could operate on a wide range of voltages of either direct or alternating current with the load current range limited by the capabilities of the components used.

Index of Patents (1974), p. 1792, 1875; *Who's Who Among Black Americans* (1990-1991), p. 1160

1974 • William L. Muckelroy (1945-) invented a ceramic inductor, for which he received a patent in 1974. Muckelroy's device was a monolithic microminiature inductor comprising a helical conductive path of deposited metal film immersed in a rectangular block of magnetic refractory material with metal caps at each end of the block as terminators. Muckelroy earned a B.A. from the University of Texas in 1967, a M.S. from American University in 1970, and a J.D. in 1974 from American University. He worked as a patent advisor for the Harry Diamond Laboratories and as patent counsel for the RCA Corporation. He was also employed by the Litton Industries division of patent and licensing. Muckelroy was granted seven patents and was patent counsel for the U.S. Patent Society Incorporated. He was also past president of the International Society for Hybrid Microelectronics, Capital Chapter.

Creativity and Inventions (1987), p. 68; *Index of Patents* (1974); *Who's Who Among African Americans* (11th Edition), p. 950

1975 • Curtis Cole, Jr. (1953-) was the first African American athlete to receive an engineering degree at Old Dominion University when he earned his B.S. in civil engineering in 1975. Cole worked as a civil engineering technician for the City of Portsmouth, Virginia from 1975 to 1977, and then in 1977, joined Turner Construction as a project engineer. He has been president of Curtex Corporation since 1983.

Who's Who Among Black Americans (1990-1991), p. 256

1976 • Gerald O. Burnham invented a direction-coded digital stroke generator that allowed arbitrary symbols to be defined in real time and in which the symbols consisted of an unlimited number of discrete signals in 1973. His invention was patented in 1976. Burnham's stroke generator allowed for the selection of different segment lengths for writing symbols of different sizes and of different levels of detail. His generator developed complex display patterns and symbols, while only requiring a minimum memory capacity. Burnham earned an A.A. in mathematics, a B.A. in mathematics from California State College in 1967, and a M.S. in mathematics from CSU in 1968, followed by a M.S. in computer science from the University of Southern California in 1970.

Black Engineers in the United States (1994), p. 31; *Index of Patents* (1976)

1976 • Emmett Paige, Jr. (1931-) was the first member of the U. S. Army Signal Corps promoted to a general when he received the appointment in 1976. Paige received a B.A. degree in 1972 from the University of Maryland and a M.A. degree in 1974 from Penn State University. He also graduated from the Army War College in 1974. Paige was commander of U.S. Army Communication and Systems Agency from 1976 to 1979, when he then became commander of the U.S. Army Communications Research and Development Command in 1979, advancing to the rank of lieutenant general in 1984.

Blacks in Science and Medicine (1990), p. 184; *Ebony* (May, 1986), pp. 64, 66, 68, 70; *Who's Who Among Black Americans* (1985), p. 645; *Who's Who Among African Americans* (1998-1999), p. 995

1976 • Clarence L. Elder (1935-) has acquired 12 U. S. and foreign patents for various electronic devices. He received a patent in 1976 for a bi-directional monitoring and control system, a patent for a sweepstake programmer in 1971, and one for a non-capsizable container in 1968. Elder also developed a system that electronically raises and lowers building temperature as people walk in and out of a building, achieving an energy savings of 30 percent. Elder was honored in 1969 by the New York International Patent Exposition for outstanding achievement in the field of electronics.

Blacks in Science and Medicine (1990), p. 83; *Pathfinders* (1984), p. 12; *Black Contributions to Science and Energy Technology* (1979); *Creativity and Inventions* (1987), p. 65; *Official Gazette* (December 28, 1976), p. 1701

1976–1978 • African American IBM electrical engineer Ernest L. Walker (1941-) patented a number of inventions related to acoustical wave filters, detection of magnetic bubble domains, and analog-to-digital conversion. Walker's 1978 patent was for his invention providing an improved surface acoustic wave device having a frequency response paraband about a center frequency. Walker earned his B.S.E.E. in 1967 from Indiana Institute of technology, M.S.E.E. in 1973 from Syracuse University, and Ph.D. from North Carolina State University in 1982. He was an engineer with the IBM Corporation from 1969 to 1990. He joined the faculty of West Virginia State University Department of Electrical and Computer Engineering as assistant professor in 1990.

Index of Patents (1976, 1978); *Who's Who Among African Americans* (1998-1999), p. 1331

1977 • Arnold F. Stancell (1936-) became Mobil Oil's first African American vice president when he was named Vice President of the company's Plastic Film Division. Stancell received a B.S. in chemical engineering *magna cum laude* from City College of New York in 1958 and a doctorate in chemical engineering from Massachusetts Institute of Technology in 1962. He joined Mobil in 1962 as a scientist and research manager. As vice president of the Plastic Film Division, he expanded the manufacture and marketing of new, petroleum-based plastic film, which now almost completely replaces cellophane. In 1980, Stancell became Mobil's Vice President of Exploration and Producing, U. S. operations, and was responsible for 5,000 employees and managing a $5 billion business. In 1983, he was promoted to Vice President of International Exploration and Production. Stancell has won many honors and awards and is a member of several professional societies. He now teaches at both MIT and Georgia Institute of Technology.

Chemical Engineering Progress (April 1990), pp. 70-75; *Daily Gulf Times* (August 30, 1992); *New York Times* (February 27, 1992); *US Black Engineer* (Conference Issue 1992), pp. 36-38, 40; *Who's Who Among African Americans* (1998-1999), p. 1414

1978 • Henry Fairfax Henderson (1928-) was granted a patent in 1978 for his invention of a weight control system used in transporting large quantities of goods. The system was a continuous loss bin system having a separate weight-measuring device and using digitally monitored weights to track potential losses. Henderson attended the State University of New York, Seton Hall University, and New York University and received engineering certification in 1950. He was employed as an engineer from 1950 to 1967 by Howe Richardson Scale Company and started his own firm, H.F. Henderson Industries, full time in 1967. Henderson has been a member of the Port Authority Commission of New York and New Jersey and other trade commissions and has received several honors, including an honorary doctorate of engineering from Stevens Institute of Technology.

Blacks in Science and Medicine (1990), p. 116; *Index of Patents* (1978), p. 795, 2205; *Ebony* (February 1977), pp. 72-74, 76-78; *Who's Who Among African Americans* (1998-1999), pp. 670-671

1978 • Lois Louise Cooper (1931-) was the first African American woman to earn a license in civil engineering in California in 1978. Cooper received a B.A. in mathematics in 1954 from Los Angeles State University and also completed postgraduate studies in civil engineering at California State University during the period 1975 to 1981. She was employed in 1953 as an engineering aide with the California Division of Highways (CAL-TRANS). She first worked as an aide, then as a junior civil engineer (1958-61), assistant transportation engineer (1961-84), associate transportation engineer (1984-88), and senior transportation engineer (1988-91).

Blacks in Science and Medicine (1990), p. 61; *Black Engineers in the United States* (1974), p. 41; *Who's Who Among African Americans* (1997), p. 318

1980 • The National Science Foundation's first African American director was John Brooks Slaughter (1934-), who served in the position from 1980 to 1982. Slaughter received a B.S. degree in electrical engineering in 1956 from Kansas State University, a M.S. degree in engineering from the University of California at Los Angeles in 1961, and a Ph.D. degree in engineering science from the University of California at San Diego in 1971. He worked as an electronics engineer for General Dynamics from 1956 to 1960, then for the Naval Electronics Laboratory Center from 1960 to 1975. Following his appointment with the National Science Foundation, he became chancellor of the University of Maryland, College Park, remaining in the position from 1982 to 1988. Brooks is currently president of Occidental College, after he was selected to that position in 1988.

Blacks in Science and Medicine (1990), p. 214; *Black Engineers in the United States* (1974), p. 181; *Who's Who Among African Americans* (1998-1999), p. 1370

1980 • Valerie Thomas invented a real-time, three-dimensional television system for the production of three-dimensional images of an object at a remote site. Her invention was patented in 1980. In Thomas's system, a parabolic mirror located at the transmission site disposed an object field illuminated by conventional light sources. At a second site a concave mirror contained an image projector within the center of curvature and was adaptable to produce an illuminated image after reception by a transmitter and processing by a video processor. A viewer observing an image reflected from the surface of the parabolic mirror could observe the image disposed beyond it.

Black Inventors: From Africa to America (1995), p. 216; *Index of Patents* (1980)

1980 • Norma Merrick Sklarek (1928-) become the first African American woman to be made a fellow of the American Institute of Architects in 1980. Sklarek received her bachelor's in architecture from Barnard College of Columbia in 1950. In 1985 she formed, with two other women, her own architectural firm, one of the largest female-owned firms. Some of Sklarek's works include San Bernardino's City Hall, San Francisco's Fox Plaza, Los Angeles Airport's Terminal One, Pacific Design Center in Los Angeles, the Los Angeles Courthouse Center, and the American Embassy in Tokyo. Since 1989, she has been principal architect at Jerde Partnership in California.

African American Firsts (1994), pp. 309-311; *The Book of African-American Women* (1996), pp. 317-318; *African America: Portrait of a People* (1994), pp. 645-646; *Black Women in America* (1993), pp. 1042-1043

1980 • Gary Lynn Harris (1953-), in 1980, was one of the first two African Americans to receive the Ph.D. degree in electrical engineering from Cornell University (the other was Michael Spence). Harris also received both the B.S. and M.S. degrees in electrical engineering, in 1975 and 1976 respectively, from Cornell University. He was an associate at the National Research and Resource Facility for Sumicron Structures from 1977 to 1980 and then a visiting scientist at the Naval Research Laboratory from 1981 to 1982. Harris then joined the faculty of Howard University in 1980 as associate professor. He has also been a consultant to the Lawrence Livermore National Laboratory since 1984. Harris has contributed several publications to the scientific literature.

Blacks in Science and Medicine (1990), p. 112; *Ebony* (August, 1985), p. 64; *Who's Who Among African-Americans* (1998-1999), p. 638; *Who's Who Among Black Africans* (1990-1991), p. 545

1980 • The first African American woman to serve on the board of governors of the Mathematical Association of America was Gloria Gilmer, who served on the board from 1980 to 1982. Gilmer earned a B.S. from Morgan State University (Maryland), the M.S. from the University of Pennsylvania, and a Ph.D. from Marquette University (Wisconsin). Gilmer served on the mathematics faculties of various African American colleges and universities, and also taught in the Milwaukee public schools. She served from 1981 to 1984 as a research associate with the U.S. Department of Education, having formerly served as an exterior ballistics mathematician for the U.S. Army. Gilmer was appointed as president of Math-Tech in Milwaukee, which specializes in developing effective mathematics education programs.

Black Women in America (1993), pp. 486-7

1981 • Joseph S. Gordon, II, (1945-) an African American engineer of interfacial chemistry and structure at IBM's Almaden Research Center, developed new electronic circuitry. Gordon's research often required him to develop special optical instruments, some of which he has patented. In 1981, he patented a projection display device in which the variation in the index of refraction was used to modulate the device's attenuated total reflection. The reflective element was responsible for modulating the light intensity. Gordon has an A.B. earned at Harvard in 1966 and a Ph.D. earned in 1970 at Massachusetts Institute of Technology. He taught at California Institute of Technology from 1970 to 1975, at which time he joined IBM. He became the interfacial science manager in 1984 and in 1988, the interfacial chemistry and structure manager. Gordon also published over 50 professional journal articles.

Black Enterprise (February, 1990), p. 96; *Index of Patents* (1981); *Who's Who Among African Americans* (1998-1999), p. 490-491; *Who's Who Among Black Americans* (1990-1991), p. 484

1981 • A technique for removing surface and high-volume charges from thin high-polymer films was invented by James E. West (1931-) in 1978 and patented in 1981. West's technique involved temporarily increasing the conductivity of the polymer, permitting trapped electrons to combine or move freely out of the polymer. The technique involved subjecting the polymer to penetrating radiation, thereby generating secondary carriers and creating a conductive path for the residual charges. The polymer's low conductivity was restored by annealing it for several hours at elevated temperatures. West had a bachelor's degree from Temple University and pursued further studies at Hampton Institute and Rutgers University. He joined the Acoustics Research Department at Bell Laboratories in 1957 and has specialized in electroacoustics. West has over 20 patents and 60 technical and scientific publications.

Blacks in Science: Ancient and Modern (1983), pp. 289-292; *Black Inventors: From Africa to America* (1995), pp. 122, 153; *Index of Patents* (1981)

1981 • A computer-generated image simulator providing a wide angle visual display to a pilot trainee was the invented by John Henry Allen, Jr. (1938-) and was patented in 1981. With Allen's simulator, a visual image of the target was displayed on a reflective display screen visible to a user. One tracker monitored the user's head, and an eye tracker monitored the user's eyes. Then the head and eye orientation signals were processed electronically so that the target, projected on the reflective display screen by the helmet mounted projector, was oriented on the screen in accordance with the user's head. Allen earned a B.S. and M.S.E.E. in 1964 and 1969, respectively, at California State University. He worked in industry from 1959 to 1970 and was professor at California State College from 1969 to 1978. Allen also held several other patents in electronics.

Black Engineers in the United States (1974), p. 5; *Blacks in Science and Medicine* (1990), p. 8; *Index of Patents* (1981); *Who's Who Among African Americans* (11th Edition), p. 24; *Who's Who Among Black Americans* (1990-1991), p. 21

1982 • David R. Hedgley Jr. (1937-), a computer analyst, solved a decades-old problem in 1982, giving programmers the ability to exhibit any three-dimensional object despite its complexity. His complex solution, called Hedgley's Algorithm, involves a mathematical formula that would tell which lines on a computer screen could and could not be seen from various perspectives. Hedgley's program was challenged for over a year; after it was finally accepted, he received numerous accolades for his innovation, which is used by both the government and private industry. He earned a B.S. in biology from Virginia Union in 1958, a B.S. in math from Michigan State University in 1964, an M.S. in math from California State University in 1970, and a Ph.D. from Somerset University (England) in 1988. Hedgley started with the National Aeronautics and Space Administration in 1966, and in 1984, he was given the Space Act Award, the first person at the NASA Ames Research Center so honored. In 1984, he received the Ames Research Center's H. Julian Allen Award for pure research innovation.

Ebony (March, 1986), pp. 62-66; *Who's Who Among African Americans* (1998-1999), p. 667

1982 • Samuel Fredrick Lambert (1928-), when selected in 1982, became the first African American elected president of the National Association of Power Engineers. Lambert earned a marine engineer's license in 1953 and a bachelor's degree, in 1978, from Pace University. He was a marine engineer with the Military Sea Transport Service from 1956 to 1960, then a custodian engineer from 1962 to 1974 with the New York City Board of Education before becoming supervisor of custodian engineers in 1974.

Jet (July 19, 1982), p. 21; *Who's Who Among Black Americans* (1992-1993), p. 839; *Who's Who Among African-Americans* (1997), p. 885

1982 • Paul E. Belcher (1933-), an African American electronics engineer, invented electronic devices relating to pulse magnifiers and remote AC power controls. Belcher received a B.S. degree in electronics engineering from the Michigan School of Engineering in 1957 and a M.S. degree in electronics engineering from the West Coast University in 1967. He was a senior applications engineer for Hughes Aircraft Corporation before starting his own firm.

Black Engineers in the United States (1974), p. 16; *Index of Patents* (1982); *Who's Who Among Black Americans* (1990-1991), p. 82

1983 • Virgil Thomas Pattman, Sr. (1940-) was the first African American appointed as a senior safety engineer at the General Motors Technology Center in 1983. Pattman earned a B.S. from Lawrence Institute of Technology in 1969, a B.S. from Detroit Institute of Technology in 1981, and a M.S. in 1983 from Central Michigan University. He started at General Motors in

1964 as an electronics technician, moving up to electronics engineer in 1967. He became a safety engineer in the General Motors Technical Auto Manufacturing Division in 1978, and in 1983 was promoted to senior safety engineer, a position in which he was responsible for a staff of 1,500 people.

Who's Who Among African Americans (1998-1999), p. 1164

1983 • The first woman engineering professor at the U. S. Naval Academy's Nuclear Power School was Laura Stubbs (1956-). She graduated in 1979 from the University of Pennsylvania with a B.S. in mechanical engineering. She was accepted at the Naval Academy in 1983. Now a lieutenant, Stubbs teaches naval officers mechanical and nuclear engineering at the Academy.

Philadelphia Tribune (October 8, 1985), p. 7C

1983 • A patent was granted to Richard L. Saxton in 1983 for his invention of a pay telephone with a sanitized tissue dispenser. Saxton's system was developed for the commercial pay telephone. A special housing within the telephone box had a roll of individual, interconnected, sanitized tissues mounted on a rotating spindle. When a coin was deposited into the telephone, an electrical motor rotated the spindle, dispensing a tissue through an opening in the telephone. The tissues were arranged in a stack, wherein a pusher arm forced the uppermost tissue through the opening of the telephone.

Created Equal (1993), pp. 173, 196; *Index of Patents* (1983)

1983 • The first African American appointed deputy director of the Department of Pubic Works for the state of Ohio was Carl L. Wilson (1921-), when he took on that position in 1983. Wilson earned a B.S. in architecture in 1951 from Ohio State University. He worked as a project engineer at the Wright-Patterson Air Force Base in Dayton, Ohio, from 1951 to 1962. He then completed projects for the U.S. Corps of Engineers in Ethiopia and Korea from 1962 to 1967. Wilson worked on a number of government projects in Canton, Covington, Baltimore, Cincinnati, Dayton, and Montgomery City prior to his 1983 appointment.

Who's Who Among Black Americans (1990-1991), p. 1384; *Who's Who Among African Americans* (1998-1999), p. 1642

1983 • Vallerie Denise Wagner (1959-) was the first African American woman to earn the M.S. degree in engineering from Tuskegee University, which she received in 1983. Wagner had received a B.S. in mechanical engineering from Southern University in 1981. She worked as a technical engineer for Diesel Allison and General Motors in Detroit, then joined Jet Propulsion Laboratory as an engineer in 1981. Following the receipt of her master's degree, she became a member of the technical staff there.

Who's Who Among African Americans (1997), p. 1530

1984 • Queen F. Randall, in 1984, became the first African American and first woman president of American River College in Sacramento, California. When Randall started teaching as a math instructor at the college in 1970, she was the first African American appointed to the faculty. She remained at American River College until 1976, when she took the position of dean of instructional systems and student development at Pioneer Community College in Missouri. Randall was appointed president there in 1978, then took over the presidency of El Centro College in Dallas in 1981, where she remained until 1984.

Dollars and Sense (Special Issue 1986), p. 69

1984–1986 • African American automotive engineer Michael D. Griffin (1958-) acquired several patents for his inventions. In 1984 and 1986, he received patents for a throttle positioning system for automotive engines to provide the desired control over air flow to the engine. Griffin was a mechanical engineering graduate of Rensselaer Polytechnic Institute, receiving his B.S. in 1980. He also received a M.B.A. in 1988 from the University of Pennsylvania. He joined the technical staff of the General Motors Corporation in 1980, working as a senior design engineer until 1988, when he became a senior analyst. Griffin became assistant program manager for vehicle systems engineering in 1990.

Index of Patents (1984, 1986); *Who's Who Among African Americans* (1998-1999), p. 594

1985 • Albert M. Ware (1952-), an African American automotive engineer with the General Motors Corporation, developed a forged aluminum design for use in a high volume automotive application in 1985. He won the 6th Annual Aluminum Association Design and Fabrication Seminar Award for that pioneering achievement. Ware, who received a B.S.M.E. degree in 1977 from Wayne State University, worked as a suspension system engineer for the Ford Motor Company from 1977 until 1981, when he joined the staff of General Motors Corporation as a chassis systems engineer. He worked in the area until 1991, when he became vehicle systems integration manager. Ware, in 1996, became the director of full size truck plant integration engineering.

Who's Who Among African Americans (1998-1999), p. 1334

1986 • Samuel Dixon Jr. patented his monolithic, planar-doped, barrier subharmonic mixer on January 7, 1986. This device is designed for use in lightweight radar or "smart" artillery projectiles. Dixon is a senior electronics engineer at the Electronics Technology and Devices Laboratory at the Fort Monmouth Electronics Command. He has worked in the areas of radar, communication, electronic warfare, and satellite system development. Dixon has been presented with 20 patent awards and has published over 40 papers on solid state ferrite and semi-conductor devices.

Index of Patents (1986), p. 438

1986 • James E. Young (1926-) obtained a patent, in 1986, for his invention of a battery performance control. His device is a system for controlling a multi-cell battery. The system also provides read-outs of the amount of charge remaining in the battery and of the battery's remaining useful life. Young obtained a B.S., then a M.S. from Howard University in 1949, followed by a Ph.D. from the Massachusetts Institute of Technology in 1953. He has been a professor of physics at MIT since 1970 and a research associate at Tufts University Medical School since 1986.

Index of Patents (1986); *Who's Who Among African Americans* (1998-1999), p. 1686; *Who's Who Among Black Americans* (1990-1991), p. 1421

1986 • Betty Wright Harris (1940-), an African American research chemist employed by the Los Alamos National Laboratory, patented, in 1986, a spot test for an explosive called TATB. Harris received a B.S. from Southern University in 1961 and a Ph.D. from the University of New Mexico in 1975. Harris was initially employed at Los Alamos National Laboratory in 1972 and took a leave of absence from 1982 to 1984, when she served as chief of chemical technology at Solar Turbines, Inc. She then returned to Los Alamos as a research chemist. Harris has published in the professional journals and is considered a pioneer in explosives and nuclear weapons.

Ebony (October, 1998), p. 162; *Who's Who Among African Americans* (1998-1999), p. 635; *Who's Who Among Black Americans* (1990-1991), p. 542

1986 • John L. Mack (1942-) patented an invention for a participant-identification recording and playback system in 1986. Mack's invention was especially useful for recording and subsequently transcribing conferences and the like. His invention could also be used with wireless microphones. Participants engaged in free-flowing discussions without a need to identify themselves verbally when they spoke, and the system allowed a reporter to provide a verbatim transcript without identification of the speakers. Mack earned a B.S. in 1973 from Massachusetts Institute of Technology and a

M.B.A. in 1978 from Suffolk University. He was coordinator of the regional administrative management centers of the U.S. State Department.

Index of Patents (1986); *Who's Who Among African-Americans* (1998-1999), p. 954

1986 • African American inventor Harry C. Hopkins patented his device for a power controller in 1986. Hopkins's device used motor drive circuits to control the power, saving energy. His motor drive circuit controlled the period of each cycle of line voltage, which was supplied via an electronic switch to a motor winding. Misfiring of switches was avoided by the use of an alternating current-coupled power supply to power the control circuits, and a varistor was located across the line. Fuses were used by to protect the circuitry. Resistive dividers in current and voltage sensing circuits triggered the switches of each phase.

Black Inventors: From Africa to America (1995), p. 128; *Index of Patents* (1986)

1986 • Lewis Walker invented a furnace system that was patented in 1986. Walker's efficient hot water furnace was capable of being used as a primary heating furnace. His furnace has an elongated, cylindrical combustion chamber surrounded by a water jacket. Fire-tubes are located in the top portion of the water jacket, through which the combustion products flow in heat exchange with the water in the jacket. Second fire tubes in heat exchange with the outlet water lead the combustion gases to a stack. A special band of scraper deflectors is provided on at least some of the fire tubes.

Index of Patents (1986); *Who's Who Among African Americans* (1998-1999), p. 1538

1986 • Everett T. Draper, Jr. (1939-) was the first African American named a mathematics department head in the publishing industry when he was hired for the position by Prentice Hall in 1986. Draper received a B.A. in 1960 at Miles College (Alabama) and a M.Ed. at North Adams State (Massachusetts) in 1969. He taught high school mathematics from 1963 to 1969, when he became the first African American math editor at Harcourt Brace. He has since held a variety of positions in the publishing industry and maintained an adjunct professorship at LaGuardia Community College from 1974 to 1985. He is currently executive editor and product manager of mathematics at Prentice Hall.

Who's Who Among Black Americans (1998-1999), p. 361

1987 • The first African American and the first women's dean in an engineering school was Carolyn Ruth Armstrong Williams (1944-), who was appointed assistant dean for Minority Affairs and Women Engineering Programs at Vanderbilt University in 1987. She held an associate professorship there concurrently. Williams earned a B.S. from Tennessee State University in 1966, an M.A. from Northwestern University in 1972, and both an M.A. and a Ph.D. from Cornell University in 1978. She also spent time as a post-doctoral fellow at Harvard University between 1981 and 1983. She taught in high school from 1967 to 1970, then moved on to teaching college classes in 1970 as an instructor at Union College. She taught at the college level until 1983, when she became assistant to the vice chancellor for university relations at North Carolina Central University until 1987. In addition to her position as assistant dean and associate professor, Williams took on the responsibilities of Biomedical Coordinator in 1993. Currently, Williams maintains her positions at North Carolina Central, as well as holding an adjunct professorship at Tennessee State University.

Who's Who Among African Americans (1997), p. 1611

1988 • Em Claire Knowles (1952-) became the first African American assistant dean of the Graduate School of Information Sciences at Simmons College in 1988. Knowles earned a B.A. in 1973 at the University of California at Davis and a M.L.S. in 1974 at the University of California at Berkley. She also earned an M.P.A. at California State University at Sacramento and a Doctorate of Arts in 1988 from Simmons College. Knowles worked at the University of California at Davis from 1972 to 1985 and then as coordinator there until 1988. She joined Simmons as associate dean in 1988. She was active in professional associations and published several articles, including the report "Black Women in Science and Medicine: A Bio-Bibliography" in 1977 with Mattie T. Evans. Besides her administrative teaching activities, Knowles also mentored advanced students in research projects. She also engaged in activities to encourage minorities to enter the information sciences as a profession.

Official Correspondence, Dean of Graduate School, Simmons College (1999); *Who's Who Among African Americans* (1998-1999), p. 878; *Who's Who Among Black Americans* (1990-1991), p. 746

1988 • The first woman to lead a university system in the United States was Delores Margaret Richard Spikes (1936-). She was named president of Southern University Systems in 1988, remaining in that position until 1996. Spikes received her B.S., *summa cum laude*, from Southern University in 1957, a M.S. from the University of Illinois at Urbana in 1958, and her Ph.D. in 1971 from Louisiana State University. All her degrees were in mathematics. She joined the faculty of Southern University in 1961. After she left Southern in 1996, Spikes became president of the University of Maryland Eastern Shore.

Black Women in America (1993), pp. 1097-1098

1988 • Shannon L. Madison (1927-) invented an electrical wiring harness termination system that was patented in 1988. Madison's system can be used with a replaceable electrical component, which has a terminal that can be connected to the component and a free distal portion that can be electrically connected to a terminal of a replacement component. Madison earned a B.S. from Howard University and worked as a development engineer for the York Division of Borg Warner Corporation from 1954 to 1959, and then for Emerson Radio as chief test engineer from 1959 to 1961. Madison then became, in 1961, senior project engineer for the Delco Appliance Division of General Motors.

Index of Patents (1988), p. 442, 1456; *Who's Who Among African Americans* (1998-1999), p. 957; *Who's Who Among Black Americans* (1990-1991), p. 812

1988 • Raymond L. Coleman, an African American electrical engineer, patented a method and apparatus for testing electrical equipment in 1988. He received another patent in 1989 for transformer testing. Coleman was a member of the key team responsible for the design, fabrication, and final checkout of power converters used to supply current to the vital control areas of the *Nimbus,* a satellite which assists meteorologists in predicting the weather.

Blacks in Science: Astrophysicist to Zoologist (1977), p. 67; *Index of Patents* (1988, 1989)

1989 • The first African American woman mathematician to receive an honorary doctorate degree was Evelyn Boyd Granville (1924-), when Smith College, her undergraduate alma mater, bestowed her the degree in 1989. Granville graduated from Smith *summa cum laude* and Phi Beta Kappa in 1945, then earned a M.A. in 1946 and a Ph.D. in mathematics in 1949 from Yale University, becoming one of the first two African American women to earn a Ph.D. in mathematics. Granville worked as an applied mathematician for the Diamond Ordnance Fuze Laboratories from 1952 to 1956, when she joined IBM working on Project Mercury and Project Vanguard, doing orbit computation methods, celestial mechanics, numerical analysis, and digital computer techniques. In 1967, she joined the California State University in Los Angeles faculty, from which she retired in 1984. Granville taught mathematics and computer science from 1985 to 1988 at Texas College, and in 1990, was appointed to the Sam A. Lindsey Chair at the University of Texas at Tyler.

EVELYN BOYD
GRANVILLE

The Book of African-American Women (1996), pp. 264-266; *Notable Black American Scientists* (1999), p. 133

1990 • The first African American faculty member of Duke University's School of Engineering was Theda Daniels-Race, when she joined the Department of Electrical and Computer Engineering as assistant professor in 1990. Daniels-Race was promoted to associate professor in 1997 and then to associate research professor. She received tenure in 1998. Daniels-Race earned a B.S. in 1983 at Rice University and a M.S. in 1985 at Stanford University. She acquired a Ph.D. in electrical engineering at Cornell University in 1989. Beside her teaching activity, Daniels-Race has been responsible for the design, installation, and development of Duke's first molecular beam epitaphy (MBE) laboratory and subsequent program in electronic materials. Results of her research have all been reported in first-tier journals in the fields of physics, materials science, and electrical engineering. Daniels-Race has been invited to give presentations at a number of national conferences and has an extensive-funded-research experience.

Chronicle (September 28, 1989), p. 31; *Graduating Engineer: Minorities Issue* (October 1992), pp. 74, 77-78; *Who's Who Among Students in American Colleges and Universities* (1982), p. 308; *Who's Who in Science and Engineering* (1994), p. 192

1990 • Janet C. Rutledge was the first African American woman to earn a Ph.D. in electrical engineering from Georgia Institute of Technology in 1990. Rutledge received the M.S. in electrical engineering there in 1984. She earned the B.S. in electrical engineering from Rensselaer Polytechnic Institute in 1983. Rutledge was the program director of the Division of Engineering and Education Centers for the National Science Foundation since 1997, and was an associate professor, Division of Otolaryngology—Head and Neck Surgery, of the University of Maryland School of Medicine. Rutledge was adjunct assistant professor of the Audiology and Hearing Sciences Department, and assistant professor of the Electrical and Computing Engineering Department at Northwestern University from 1990 to 1997. She had much experience in audiology, hearing, and signal processing, and was issued a patent in 1993 for an apparatus and method for modifying a speech waveform to compensate for recruitment of loudness. Rutledge was a thesis and dissertation advisor for a number of students and published extensively. She was an invited speaker at many conferences, chairing many of these, and was a member of scientific review panels. She also received a number of awards and honors for her work.

Official Correspondence, Office of the Dean of Graduate Affairs, Georgia Institute of Technology (February, 1999); *Index of Patents* (1993)

1991 • Clay Samuel Gloster, Jr. (1962-) patented a method and apparatus for high-precision weighted random pattern generation in 1991. Gloster was an assistant professor of electrical and computer engineering at North Carolina State University. He earned a B.S. in 1985 and a M.S. in 1988, both in electrical engineering from North Carolina A&T State University. Gloster then received the Ph.D. in computer engineering in 1993 from North Carolina State University. He developed several CAD (Computer Aided Design) tools that were part of the MCNC OASIS (Open Architecture Silicon Implementation Software) system, an automated hardware design system currently in use at over 75 universities worldwide. Gloster joined the North Carolina State University Department of Electrical and Computer Engineering as an instructor in 1993, and in the same year was promoted to assistant professor. His research focused on the identification of a potential application and development of automated tools that assisted scientists in mapping these applications onto adaptive computing resources. Gloster published articles in professional journals, as well acting as a reviewer for several journals.

Great Discoveries and Inventions by African Americans (1998), pp. 98-102; *Index of Patents* (1991); *Personal Correspondence* (February 14, 1999)

1991 • Valerie E. Taylor, who received her Ph.D. in electrical engineering in 1991, was the first African American woman to receive that degree from the University of California at Berkeley. Taylor was an associate professor in the Electrical Engineering and Computer Science Department at Northwestern University since 1991 and held a joint appointment with Argonne National Laboratory. She received her B.S. in computer and electrical engineering and M.S. in electrical engineering in 1985 and 1986 respectively, both from Purdue University. Her research interests were in the area of high performance computing, with particular emphasis on the performance of scientific applications executed on uniprocessors and parallel processors. Taylor published articles on enhancing the performance of scientific computer applications such as the element analysis and transportation. Her work involved high performance systems that included supercomputer visualization and distributed computers. Taylor held a U.S. patent for her dissertation research. She also held a copyright for a RAB tool developed at Purdue University. This tool was installed at Hughes Research Laboratories in Malibu, California, for research related to systolic arrays. Taylor was an active member of several professional and technical computing and electrical organizations.

Official Correspondence, Dean of the Graduate School, University of California at Berkeley (February, 1999); *Index of Patents* (1993)

1992 • John W. Webster, III (1961-) patented a method of comparing computer files to each other in 1992. The patented process allowed a user to visually compare two files or portions thereof, and it showed areas of differences between the items being compared. Another invention was a method of displaying a document on an all-points addressable display system, which provided smooth scrolling and fast response time while being stored efficiently. Webster's patents resulted in his receiving an IBM Achievement Award. Webster was a development manager for IBM at its Research Triangle Park, North Carolina facility. He earned both the B.S.C.S. in 1983 and M.S.C.S. in 1987 at the Massachusetts Institute of Technology. He joined IBM in 1983 as a member of the scientific staff and was promoted to scientific project manager in 1987, then development manager in 1989.

Index of Patents (1991, 1992); *Who's Who Among African Americans* (1998-1999), p. 1576

1992 • The National Aeronautics and Space Administration's first administrator for aeronautics was African American aerospace engineer Wesley Leroy Harris Sr. (1941-), who was appointed to the position in 1992. Harris received a B.E. in aerospace engineering in 1964 from the University of Virginia and then earned the M.A. in 1966 and Ph.D. in 1968, both in aerospace engineering, from Princeton University (New Jersey). He served as assistant professor in engineering at the University of Virginia for 1968-1970, the first African American professor of engineering at the University. From 1972-1979, 1980-1985, and presently, Harris has served as professor of aeronautics, astronautics, and ocean engineering at the Massachusetts Institute of Technology (MIT). From 1985-1990, Harris served as dean of the engineering school at the University of Connecticut. In 1990, he was appointed vice president of the University of Tennessee Space Institute. Harris, who initially worked for the organization in 1979-1980, rejoined NASA as administrator for aeronautics in 1992, where he assumed responsibility for the NASA Langley, Lewis, and Ames Research Centers and the Ames-Dryden Flight Research Facility.

Blacks in Science and Medicine (1990), p. 113; *Black Engineers in the United States* (1974), pp. 89-90; *Notable Black American Scientists* (1999), pp. 149-50; *Who's Who Among African Americans* (1998-1999), p. 646

1992 • Wanda Anne A. Sigur (1958-), an African American engineer, patented a method of fabricating composite structures in 1992. Sigur's invention concerned the fabrication of high-strength, low-weight laminated structures of unlimited size. Her process precluded the use of high-cost autoclaves by applying internal pressure to the structure while providing an external pressure restraint. Sigur received a B.S. in engineering in 1979 from Rice University. She joined the General Electric Company as a laboratory technician in 1977. In 1979, she became employed by Martin Marietta Space Systems as section chief of composites technology.

Index of Patents (1992); *Who's Who Among African Americans* (1998-1999), p. 1174

1992 • Ricky Charles Godbolt (1959-) is an engineer who, in 1992, was the first mechanic and the first African American to win the Instructor of the Year Award from the U. S. Army. Godbolt studied at Central Texas College and received a B.S. *magna cum laude* from Park College. From 1978 to 1980, he was a track mechanic, then became an electrician from 1981 to 1986. He was a mechanic from 1986 to 1990, when he became an instructor.   WESLEY L. HARRIS

Godbolt was an instructor until 1993, when he became chief engineer. He has won numerous awards for his engineering experiences and is a licensed power engineer. Godbolt is active in national engineering associations.

Who's Who Among African Americans (1998-1999), p. 557

1992 • A patent was issued in 1992 to Thomas L. Cosby for his invention of an energy conversion system with a maximum ambient cycle. The system consisted of a high-pressure gas reservoir, a turbine, a compressor, a low-pressure reservoir, a heat exchanger, and flow control structures such as valves. The high-pressure reservoir was in heat exchange with ambient air and delivered fluid at ambient temperature to a turbine. The spent fluid from the turbine exhausts was brought into heat exchange with the compressor. The exhaust, which was heated by the compressor, was then delivered to a low pressure reservoir, and from there the exhaust heated by the compressor was delivered to the compressor inlet. Cosby also patented other closed cycle energy conversion systems in his career.

Creativity and Inventions (1987), p. 64; *Index of Patents* (1992)

1993 • Gloria Jean Jeff (1952-) was the first African American woman to hold the position of associate administrator for policy at the Federal Highway Administration (FHA) when she received her presidential appointment in 1993. This made her the highest-ranking woman in the U. S. Department of Transportation. Jeff received a B.S.E. and M.S.E. in civil engineering (both 1974) and a master's in urban planning (1976), all from the University of Michigan. Jeff worked for the Southeast Michigan Transportation Authority from 1976 to 1981, then took a division administrator position with the Michigan Department of Transportation from 1981 to 1985. She became assistant deputy director in 1985, then deputy director in 1990. Jeff has also been an adjunct professor at the University of Michigan College of Architecture and Urban Planning since 1988. Jeff's responsibilities concern the strategic placement of roads and highways, based on the study of employment, economic, medical, and recreational needs.

Black Enterprise (April, 1997), pp. 118, 120; *Who's Who Among African Americans* (1998-1999), p. 777

1993 • Joe N. Ballard was appointed commanding general of the U. S. Army Engineering Center located at Fort Leonard Wood, Missouri in 1993, and was the first African American to hold that position. Ballard was promoted to major general when installed as facility commander. Prior, he was special assistant to the director of management for the Total Army Basing Study, Office of the Chief of Staff.

Jet (September 20, 1993), p. 38; *ENR* (October 28, 1996), p. 19

1993 • President William Clinton selected the first African American head of the U. S. Federal Highway Administration (FHA) when he appointed Rodney K. Slater (1955-) to head that agency in 1993. In his position Slater was responsible for over 800,000 miles of roads, 4,000 employees, and an $18 billion annual budget. He earned a B.S. degree in 1977 from Eastern Michigan University in 1977 and his J.D. degree in 1980 from the University of Arkansas. Slater was appointed the first African American member of the Arkansas State Highway Commission in 1987 before becoming its head in 1992. He was also director of governmental relations at Arkansas State University before heading the FHA. In 1997, Slater became a member of President Clinton's cabinet, when he was made Secretary of Transportation.

RODNEY SLATER

Jet (July 12, 1993), pp. 26-27; *Philadelphia New Observer* (September 18, 1996)

1994 • The first woman from any branch of the U. S. military to command an ocean-going commissioned United States ship was Lieutenant Commander Evelyn Fields of the National Oceanic and Atmospheric Administration (NOAA). Fields has a B.S. in mathematics, which she earned at Norfolk State University. She first worked as a cartographer for the Atlantic Marine Center in Norfolk, Virginia. She became a ranking officer with NOAA in 1973, just one year after it first admitted women. Fields has been executive officer and operations officer on other ships.

Journal of the National Technical Association (Summer 1996), p. 22

1994 • Philip A. Carswell, an African American software engineer, patented in 1994 a technique and programmable encryption device capable of executing a variety of classified and commercial cryptographic public key and signature algorithms. Encryption software is used to ensure the security of information on the Internet. Carswell was a Tuskegee University graduate and was employed as a software engineer for the Motorola Corporation.

Index of Patents (1998); *US Black Engineer* (August, 1998), p. 12

1995 • Moses T. Asom (1958-), an African American electrical engineer, was a member of the staff of AT&T and acquired patents in the field of semiconductor devicesin 1995. Asom earned a B.S. in physics *magna cum* *laude* from the University of D.C. in 1980 and a Ph.D. in electrical engineering from Howard University in 1985, as well as a M.B.A. from the University of Pennsylvania in 1994. He worked as a research assistant from 1981 to 1985 at Howard University, and then joined AT&T Bell Laboratories in 1986 as a member of the technical staff. Asom became manager of AT&T Microelectronics of Asia/Pacific, Japan, and South America in 1994. He published over 70 technical papers and was a member of technical organizations.

Index of Patents (1995); *Who's Who Among African Americans* (1998-1999), pp. 49-50

1995 • Gilbert Bryant Chapman II (1935-), an African American advanced products consultant, acquired a patent for an integrated utility/camper shell for a pick-up truck in 1995, while working for the Chrysler Corporation Liberty Concept Vehicle Development and Technical Affairs. Chapman earned a B.S. degree from Baldwin Wallace in 1968 and a M.S. degree from Cleveland State University in 1973. He then earned a M.B.A. degree from Michigan State University in 1990. Chapman was a propulsion test technician from 1953 to 1958 for the NACA Lewis Research Center and then worked for NASA from 1961 to 1977 as a materials characterization engineer. He began his career in the auto industry as a project engineer leader for the Ford Motor Company in 1977. He remained at Ford until 1986, when he joined Chrysler as an advanced material-testing specialist. In 1991, Chapman became an advanced materials consultant at Chrysler. Chapman also acquired a patent in 1983 for a method and apparatus for testing the quality of an ultrasound weld in thermoplastic material.

Index of Patents (1983, 1995); *Who's Who Among African Americans* (1998-1999), p. 262

1995 • Carolyn G. Morris was the first woman and first African American to hold the position of assistant director of the Federal Bureau of Investigation (FBI). Morris graduated from North Carolina Central University in 1960, and then received a M.S. from Harvard University (Massachusetts) in mathematics in 1963. Morris joined the FBI in 1980 in the systems development section. She was appointed director of the Information Resources Division in 1995, with responsibility for all of the FBI's data processing operations and mainframe computer operations, as well as the FBI's engineering and research facility in Quantico (Virginia).

Journal of Blacks in Higher Education (Autumn 1998), p. 31; *Who's Who Among African Americans* (1998-1999), p. 1085

1995 • The first conference for African American Research in the Mathematical Sciences was held in 1995. The event was co-organized by African American mathematician Raymond Lewis Johnson (1943-), who was professor of mathematics at the University of Maryland, College Park. Johnson also organized the first Applied Mathematics and Minorities, Connections to Industry conference, which was held in 1996. Johnson was a Phi Beta Kappa graduate of the University of Texas, where he received his B.S. degree in 1963. He earned a Ph.D. from Rice University in 1969. Johnson joined the University of Maryland mathematics department in 1968 as an assistant professor. He received a promotion to professor in 1980 and became department chair in 1991. Johnson held a number of positions in various mathematical associations, including membership on the scientific advisory committee of the Mathematical Science Research Institute and board membership of the National Association of Mathematicians.

Who's Who Among African Americans (1998-1999), p. 701

1996 • A universal wireless radiotelephone system was invented by Jesse E. Russell in 1994, and he was granted a patent for his system in 1996. Russell's radiotelephone operated in two ways. The system could operate with a wide area of coverage, transmitting signals at a first band of frequencies. It could also be used with a second base station, having a localized area of coverage and transmitting signals at a frequency higher than the first band of frequencies. Russell had a B.S. from Tennessee State University and a M.S. from Stanford University, with both degrees in electrical engineering. He was the director of AT&T wireless systems and services architecture center. Russell held several patents, and had a number of technical publications in the field of wireless communications.

Black Futurists in the Information Age (1997), p. 97; *Index of Patents* (1996); *Blacks in Science: Ancient and Modern* (1983), pp. 280-282

1996 • The first African American promoted to General Manager of the Electronic Systems Division of the Aerospace Corporation was Wanda M. Austin, Ph.D. in 1996. She was the youngest person to reach the general manager level at the company, as well as the first woman. Austin was responsible for managing a staff of more than 200 engineers and scientists with expertise in communications and telemetry systems, antennas, digital and analog electronics, infrared and microwave systems, electro-optics, and imagery exploitation. Austin earned a B.A. in mathematics from Franklin and Marshall in 1975, a M.S. in systems engineering and mathematics from the University of Pittsburgh in 1977, and in 1988, received a Ph.D. in systems engineering from the University of Southern California. She joined the Aerospace Corporation in 1979 as a member of the technical staff in the Engineering Analysis and Programming Department. Austin was an instructor at the University of Southern California, the University of Pittsburgh, and Carlow College. She published a number of papers on intelligent simulation environments and quantitative modeling.

Jet (November 11, 1996), p. 20; *Minority Employment Journal* (Spring, 1998), pp. 30-31, 40; *Who's Who Among African Americans* (1998-1999), p. 54

1996 • The first African American elected president of the Society of Automotive Engineers (SAE) was Claude A. Verbal, when he was elected to head the SAE in 1996. As president, Verbal represents over 68,000 automotive engineers and scientists nationwide, promoting the interests of the group in the United States and abroad. During his tenure as SAE chief, he wants to strengthen the organization's efforts to encourage quality science and math education. Verbal earned a B.S.M.E. from North Carolina State University in 1964 and started working for the Buick Motor Division of General Motors (GM) in engineering research and development that same year. He has worked in engineering, experimental engineering, lab testing, quality control, and manufacturing for GM, and has been manager of GM's Service Parts Operations plant in Lansing, Michigan, since 1987.

Ebony (May, 1996), p. 9; *Detroit Free Press* (Dec. 15, 1995); *Emerge* (May, 1996), p. 12; *Who's Who Among Black Americans* (1998-1999), p. 1526

1997 • The first African American to become a member of the Department of Defense civilian-based Senior Executive Service in Engineering was William A. Brown, Sr., when he was appointed in 1997. Brown has a bachelor's degree in architectural engineering. With his appointment, he became responsible for seven billion dollars of design and construction projects for the Defense Department and other federal agencies.

Ebony (June, 1997), p. 8

1997 • Dixie Tyran Garr was the first African American to become a Level 3 director at Texas Instruments in 1997, where she was a software engineering director responsible for a team of over 800 professionals developing real-time, embedded defense systems. Garr was also vice-president of Cicco Systems, a leader in Internet networking.

US Black Engineer (July/August, 1998), p. 9

1998 • Mark Dean (1958-) directed the IBM Research Lab in Austin, Texas, which produced the first 1000 MHz computer chip, the world's fastest. At the time, the fastest chips commercially available operated at a speed of 300 MHz. Dean was also the lead designer on IBM's team that in 1986 created the PCAT architecture, the standard for IBM-compatible PCs. Dean's leadership and technical contributions in this area resulted in his being inducted into the Inventor's Hall of Fame in 1997. At the IBM facility in Austin, he is team leader of 40 scientists working on the development of high-frequency hardware and software technologies. He also has 20 patents, three of which are among the eight basic patents for IBM's personal computer design. Dean was the first African American appointed an IBM fellow.

Black Enterprise (March, 1998), pp. 50-51; *Jet* (February 23, 1998), p. 23

1998 • The first African American woman to earn a Ph.D. in electrical engineering from Polytechnic University was Ruthie D. Lyle, who received the degree in June 1998. Lyle received a B.S. in electrical engineering in 1992 from Northeastern University and a M.S. in electrophysics in 1994 from Polytechnic University. From 1987 to 1992, she participated in the Cooperative Education Program at Northeastern University and completed an internship at Eastman Kodak Company and Grumman Corporation. Lyle was employed by KeySpan Energy as a system planning engineer in the electrical business unit. She was responsible for performing analysis and developing comparisons of study alternatives necessary for the planning of the electric resource, bulk transmission, and interconnected system, and for overall coordination of the various elements that constitute the power system. Lyle also designed upgrades to the Long Island Power Authorities' transmission system.

Newsday (June 7, 1998, June 10, 1998); *National Society of Black Engineers* (November/December, 1998), p. 13

1998 • The first African American vice president and chief information officer for the *New York Times* was Michael G. Williams, who assumed the post in 1998. Prior, Williams was chief technology officer and vice president for information technologies at Seagram Company's Spirits and Wine Group.

Jet (October 26, 1998), p. 20

1998 • The United States Coast Guard's first African American admiral was Erroll M. Brown (1951-) who was commissioned in 1998. Brown is the first African American flag officer in the 207-year history of the Coast Guard. Brown, who is an engineer, has a B.S. degree in marine engineering from the U.S. Coast Guard Academy, two M.S. degrees from the University of Michigan, a M.S. degree in business administration from Rensselear Polytechnic Institute, and a M.S. degree from the Naval War College. Brown is stationed at the Maintenance and Logistics Command Atlantic, and he is responsible for the entire U.S. Coast Guard's activity on the East Coast.

Ebony (August, 1998), pp. 68-69, 70, 72

MEDICINE

1793 • The first African American physician in the United States was James Derham (1762-1824). Although born a slave, Derham worked for various owners as a nurse, medical assistant, and apothecary in Philadelphia and New Orleans, enabling him to earn money to buy his freedom in 1783. He secured a license and set up a business in New Orleans. Assisted by his fluency in French and Spanish as well as English, Derham developed a fine private practice, and was very knowledgeable in the medical practices of the day. On one occasion, Benjamin Rush, one of America's most venerated doctors of that era, consulted with Derham and later commented that he had learned more from Derham than he had taught him about medicine. Rush presented a paper authored by Derham to the College of Physicians of Philadelphia (Pennsylvania) in 1789, the first African American-authored technical paper presented to a medical organization in the United States.

Dictionary of American Negro Biography (1982), pp. 205-206; *Negro Vanguard* (1959), pp. 24-26; *History of the Negro Race in America* Vol I, (1883), pp. 400-401; *Pennsylvania's Black History* (1975), p. 98

1837 • The first African American to receive a medical degree was James McCune Smith (1811-1865). He received a M.D. from the University of Glasgow in 1837. He had previously earned a B.A. (1835) and an M.A. (1836), also at Glasgow. Smith was born in New York City in 1811 and attended the New York African Free School until 1824, when he left for Scotland to further pursue his education. He returned to New York in 1837 and started a private medical practice and two pharmacies (apothecary shops), thereby becoming the first African American to own a pharmacy in the United States. Smith was also a well-known statistician; he specialized in vital statistics and did work on developing mortality tables and computing rates for insurance companies. Smith handsomely prospered from his businesses, and his position enabled him to devote time to his interest in

JAMES MCCUNE
SMITH

promoting civil rights and freedom for African Americans; he became a prominent abolitionist.

Encyclopedia of Black America (1981), pp. 797-798; *Famous First Facts About Negroes* (1972), p. 111; *Journal of the National Medical Association* Vol. 73, (1981), p. 1205; *Negro Year Book* (1918-1919), p. 422

1854 • The Massachusetts Medical Society admitted John V. DeGrasse (1825-1868) in 1854, making him the first African American physician admitted as a member of a medical society in the United States. DeGrasse received his M.D. from Bowdoin College (Maine) in 1849. He practiced medicine first in New York City, then in Boston, where he gained significant prominence. DeGrasse served in the U.S. Army as an assistant surgeon with the 35th U.S. Colored Troops in 1863, and was one of the first eight African Americans commissioned a surgeon in the U.S. Army.

African-American Medical Pioneers (1994), pp. 29, 187; *Dictionary of American Negro Biography* (1982), p. 169; *History of the Negro in Medicine* (1967), p. 38; *Negro Year Book* (1918-1919), p. 422

1858 • Alexander Thomas Augusta (1825-1890) was the first African American faculty member of the Howard University Medical School (Washington, D.C.), as well as the first African American faculty member of any medical school, when he was appointed in 1858. Later, in 1863, he was appointed head of Freedmen's Hospital in Washington, D.C., the first African American to fill that position also. Augusta was the first African American physician to hold a medical commission in the U.S. Army when he was appointed a major on April 14, 1863, and was also the highest-ranked of the eight African Americans appointed. Augusta received his M.D. in 1856 from Trinity Medical College of the University of Toronto (Ontario, Canada).

African-American Medical Pioneers (1994), pp. 9, 24, 33; *Blacks in Science and Medicine* (1990), p. 17; *Bulletin of the History of Medicine* (1945), pp. 61-62; *Journal of the National Medical Association* Vol. 44, (1952), pp. 327-329, Vol. 32, (1947), pp.10-80.

1864 • Rebecca Lee Crumpler (1833-19??) was the first African American woman to earn a medical degree in the United States when she graduated from New England Female Medical College (Boston, Massachusetts) in 1864, fifteen years after Elizabeth Blackwell became the first woman to complete medical school in the United States. She also wrote *A Book of Medical Discourses in Two Parts*, published by Cushman, Keating & Co. in

Boston in 1883. This was the first medical text written by an African American woman in the United States.

African American Almanac (1997), p. 90; *African-American Firsts* (1993), p. 239; *African-Americans in Boston* (1991), p. 139; *Famous First Facts* (1964), p. 451

1865 • The first African American to receive a M.D. degree from Case Western Reserve University School of Medicine was Charles B. Purvis in 1865. He was an undergraduate at Oberlin College. It was 103 years later, in 1965, when the first African American women, Doris A. Evans and Lorna K. Brown, were to receive a M.D. from there. Evans finished undergraduate work at the University of Chicago, while Brown received her B.S. from Case Western Reserve University.

African-American Medical Pioneers (1994), p. 147; *Blacks in Science and Medicine* (1990), p. 196

1867 • The Women's Medical College of Pennsylvania, now known as the Medical College of Pennsylvania, graduated its first African American student, Rebecca J. Cole (1846-1922), in 1867. (She was the second African American woman to earn a M.D. in the United States.) Cole graduated from the Institute for Colored Youth (Philadelphia, Pennsylvania) in 1863 before enrolling at Women's Medical College. Her early career was spent in New York City, where she practiced at the New York Infirmary for Women and Children, a hospital wholly owned and operated by women. She later practiced in Columbia, South Carolina, before settling in Philadelphia, where she established a practice and a center for the aid of impoverished women and children.

Black Women in America (1993), pp. 261-262; *Encyclopedia of Black America* (1981), p. 671; *Notable Black American Women* (1992), pp. 201-202

1870 • When Susan M. Smith McKinney Steward (1847-1918) received her M.D. from the New York Medical College for Women in 1870, she became the first African American female to graduate from a New York State medical school. She practiced medicine in Brooklyn from 1870 to 1895 and also maintained an office in Manhattan. Steward was active in the Kings County Homeopathic Medical Society and the New York State Medical Society, before which she presented medical papers in 1883 and 1886, the first African American woman to do so. She also presented a paper at the First Universal Race Congress in London in 1911, and one at the National Association of Colored Women's Clubs in Wilberforce, Ohio, in 1914. Steward left New York later in her career; she moved to and practiced medicine in Montana, Nebraska, and Ohio from 1896 to1906, and joined the faculty of Wilberforce University (Ohio) in 1896.

African-American Medical Pioneers (1994), pp. 152, 193, 196; *Black Women in America* (1993), pp. 1109-1112; *Journal of the National Medical Association* Vol. 67, (March, 1995), pp. 173-175; *Notable Black American Women* (1992), pp. 1077-1079

1871 • The first two African Americans to receive a M.D. from Howard University College of Medicine were James L. N. Bowen and George W. Brooks, who received their degrees in 1871. Bowen and Brooks were two of only five graduates in 1871. The first African American woman to receive a M.D. from Howard University was Eunice P. Shadd, who received the degree in 1897. Shadd also completed her undergraduate training at Howard University. (The first woman graduate of Howard University Medical College was Dora Spackman, a white, who earned the degree in 1872.)

African-American Medical Pioneers (1994), pp. 149

1872 • William Henry Fitzbutler (1842-1901) was, in 1872, the first African American recipient of a M.D. from the University of Michigan Medical School. He went on to set up a medical practice in Louisville, Kentucky, becoming, in 1872, the first African American physician to practice medicine in that state. In 1888, Fitzbutler founded the Louisville National Medical College (Kentucky), where he was dean until his death in 1901. The college continued to operate until 1911.

African-American Medical Pioneers (1994), pp. 150, 188; *Encyclopedia of Black America* (1981), p. 388; *Journal of the National Medical Association* Vol. 44 (September, 1952), pp. 403-407

1877 • The first African American to receive a M.D. from Meharry Medical College (Tennessee) was James Monroe Jamison, who received the degree in 1877. (At the time, Meharry was called the Medical Department of Central Tennessee College.) Jamison received his undergraduate degree from Central Tennessee College.

African-American Medical Pioneers (1994), p. 151

1883 • The first African American to receive a M.D. from Wayne State University school of Medicine was Robert J. Boland, who received the degree in 1883. (When Boland received the degree, Wayne State University School of Medicine was known as Detroit Medical College.) Helen Marjorie Peebles-Meyers (1915-) was the first African American woman to earn the same degree at Wayne State when she graduated in 1943, 63 years after Boland. Peebles-Meyers earned a B.A. in 1937 from Hunter College and a M.A. in 1938 from Columbia University. After completing an internship and residency at Detroit Receiving Hospital, she set up and maintained a private practice from 1947 to 1977. Peebles-Myers was then employed at Ford Motor Company as chief physician until she retired in 1985.

African-American Medical Pioneers (1994), p. 156

1885 • Robert Reyburn was the first African American president of the Medico Chisurgical Society of the District of Columbia. This was the first African American medical society, which was incorporated in January, 1885 and had been started in April, 1884.

Famous First Facts About Negroes (1972), p. 113

1888 • The first woman to practice medicine in the State of Mississippi was Verina Morton Jones (1869-1943) who started her practice there in 1888. Jones completed her undergraduate work at Columbia, South Carolina State Normal School and then received her M.D. in 1888 from the Women's Medical College of Pennsylvania. Jones left Mississippi after her second marriage and set up private practice in both Brooklyn and in Nassau County on Long Island, where she was the first African American woman physician to practice in Nassau County. She also headed the Lincoln Settlement House in Brooklyn for a number of years, which saw such activities as a clinic, day nursery, free kindergarten, lectures on health and hygiene, and other classes develop under Jones's leadership.

African American Medical Pioneers (1994), p. 191; *Black Women in America* (1993), pp. 656-657, 924, 925; *Black Women in America* (1997), pp. 91-93; *Blacks in Science and Medicine* (1990), p. 139

1888 • The first African American physician to establish a medical practice in Durham, North Carolina was Aaron McDuffin Moore (1863-1923) in 1888. Moore received a M.D. in 1888 from Leonard Medical College of Shaw University (North Carolina). He was also founder and superintendent of Lincoln Hospital in Durham.

Blacks in Science and Medicine (1990), p. 175; *Journal of the National Medical Association* Vol. 16 (1924), pp. 72-4

1889 • The first drugstore operated by an African American in Petersburg, Virginia was opened in 1899 by Edward Parker Reed (1868-19??). Reed received a M.D. in 1889 from Baltimore University (Maryland), having studied under private tutors. He received a Doctor of Refraction in 1899 from the Philadelphia Optical College (Pennsylvania), and a Ph.D. in 1914 from Princeton (New Jersey) Normal and Industrial University. Reed's practice emphasized women and children, and he served as a medical examiner for the Consolidated Benefit Association and Provident Life Association. Reed also opened a drugstore in Philadelphia in 1891.

Blacks in Science and Medicine (1990), pp. 198-9

MONROE ALPHEUS MAJORS

1889 • Monroe Alpheus Majors (1864-1960) was the first African American to pass the California Board of Medical Examiners. He was certified by the state of California on January 26, 1889, although he spent little time there until much later in his career. Majors received a B.S. in 1886 from Central Tennessee College and a M.D. in 1886 from Meharry Medical College (Tennessee). He practiced medicine in Waco, Texas from 1890 to 1895, and later from 1899 to 1901; in Decatur, Illinois from 1895 to 1889; in Chicago until 1923; and in California until possibly as late as 1955. In 1894, he helped to organize and was subsequently elected president of the Lone Star State Medical Association (later, the Lone Star State Medical, Dental and Pharmaceutical Society). Majors was active in medical organizations throughout his career, and was also an outspoken political activist, speaking and writing on the rights of African Americans wherever he lived.

Blacks in Science and Medicine (1990), p. 159; *Dictionary of American Negro Biography* (1982), pp. 421-422; *Journal of the National Medical Association* Vol. 47, (March, 1995), pp. 139-141

1889 • Spencer Cornelius Dickerson (1871-1948), physician and military officer, was the first student, in 1889, to complete the Northwestern University Medical School two-year program in one year. Dickerson received a B.S. degree in 1897 from the University of Chicago and completed medical studies, receiving the M.D. degree, in 1901 at Rush Medical College in Chicago. He completed an internship at Freedman's Hospital in Washington, D.C. and established a medical practice in New Bedford, Massachusetts, which he maintained until 1907. Dickerson joined the staff of Chicago's Provident Hospital in 1907 and was affiliated with the hospital until 1948. He was from 1907 to 1912 the first African American pathologist at Provident. Dickerson joined the Illinois National Guard in 1914 as a private and in 1934, retired from the National Guard with the rank of brigadier general.

Blacks in Science and Medicine (1990), p. 74; *Dictionary of American Negro Biography* (1982), pp. 176-177; *Journal of the National Medical Association* Vol. 34, (1942) p. 119

1891 • The first woman and the first African American admitted on examination to medical practice in Alabama was Hallie Tanner Johnson (1864-1901). Johnson passed the medical exam in 1891, the same year she received her M.D. from the Philadelphia (Pennsylvania) Woman's Medical

College. She accepted the position as resident physician at Tuskegee University (Alabama), where she served as resident physician at Tuskegee from 1891 to 1894, establishing the Nurses Training School and the Lafayette Dispensary.

Afro-American Encyclopedia, Vol. 5 (1993), p. 1339; *Notable Black American Women* (1992), pp. 584-7; *Hine Sight: Black Women and the Reconstruction of American History* (1994), p. 151; *Blacks in Science and Medicine* (1990), p. 134

1892 • The first medical journal published by an African American in the United States was the *Medical and Surgical Observer,* first published in 1892 in Jackson, Tennessee, by physician Miles Vandahurst Lynk (1871-1957). The first issue of the *Observer* appeared in 1892, was 32 pages long, and appeared regularly for 18 months. Lynk also founded, and served as president of, the School of Medicine of the University of West Tennessee. Over 250 African American physicians were awarded degrees from this institution from 1904 to 1923. Lynk was also one of the founders of the National Medical Association.

African-American Medical Pioneers (1994), p. 180; *Journal of the National Medical Association* Vol. 44, (1952), pp. 475-476; *Negro Year Book* (1918-1919), p. 422

1892 • Julia R. Hall (1865-??) was appointed resident to the gynecology clinic at Howard University (Washington, D.C.) in 1892, becoming the first African American woman to receive that appointment. Hall, who earned the M.D. at Howard University in that same year, also served as medical advisor to the Howard women at Miner's Hall.

Black Women in America (1993), p. 517

1892 • Charles Burleigh Purvis (1842-1929) was the first African American to head a civilian hospital when he was appointed surgeon-in-chief of Washington's Freedman's Hospital in 1892. Purvis was not permitted to study medicine in any of Philadelphia's medical schools because of his race, so went instead to Cleveland, Ohio, to attend the Medical College of Western Reserve. He received his M.D. in 1865 and then went to Washington, D.C., where he served as a surgeon in the U.S. Army. In 1869, he was appointed assistant surgeon of Freedman's Hospital. He served in this capacity until 1882, when he was appointed surgeon-in-chief. He remained in this position until 1894. Purvis achieved other firsts as well during his career. He came to the aid of President James Garfield when the President had been shot in 1881, becoming the first African American physician to administer to a U.S. president. Later, in 1897, he was the first African American appointed to serve on the District of Columbia's Board of Medical Examiners.

Dictionary of American Negro Biography (1982), pp. 507-508; *History of the Negro in Medicine* (1967), pp. 51-52; *Men of Mark* (1970 ed.), pp. 476-479

DANIEL HALE
WILLIAMS

1893 • Daniel Hale Williams (1856-1931) was a pioneer in cardiac surgery. On July 9, 1893, he performed the first successful heart surgery, closing stab wounds of the heart and pericardium. His patient made a full recovery and lived another 50 years. Williams received his M.D. in 1883 from Chicago Medical College (now the Medical School of Northwestern University [Illinois]), and taught anatomy there for four years after receiving his degree. He established himself in Chicago, and in 1891, started Provident Hospital, the world's first interracial hospital for both patients and staff. He was also the first African American to introduce a training program for African American nurses, which was affiliated with the hospital. In 1894, Williams accepted a position at Freedman's Hospital in Washington, D.C., and later, in 1913, became the first African American appointed associate-attending surgeon at St. Luke's Hospital. In his later career, from about 1913 to 1923, Williams spent much of his time traveling around the United States; he visited 20 states and was instrumental in establishing 40 hospitals, serving primarily African Americans.

Black Pioneers of Science and Invention (1970), pp. 123-138; *Dictionary of American Negro Biography* (1982), pp. 654-655; *Famous First Facts* (1972), p. 114; *Seven Black American Scientists* (1970), pp. 28-43

1893 • Sarah Garland (Boyd) Jones (1865-1905) was both the first African American and the first woman physician to be licensed by the Virginia State Board in 1893. Jones graduated from the Richmond Normal School in 1883 and received her M.D. from Howard University Medical School in 1893, the same year that she passed the Virginia State Board examination. Jones and her physician husband established a successful practice in Richmond, and in 1898, they founded Women's Central Hospital and Richmond Hospital, a patient-care facility serving primarily female patients. In 1901, a nurse's training school affiliated with the hospital was established. Jones was still the only African American woman physician practicing in Virginia when she died in 1905.

Black Women in America (1993), pp. 653-654; *Blacks in Science and Medicine* (1990), p. 139; *Send Us a Lady Physician* (1985), p. 111; *Notable Black American Women* (1992), p. 600

1893 • Georgia Esther Lee Patton (later Washington) (1864-1900) was one of the first two African American women to earn a M.D. from Meharry Medical College (Tennessee). (The other was Anna D. Gregg.) Patton earned her undergraduate degree at Central Tennessee College. She was also the first African American woman to receive a license to practice medicine and surgery in the state of Tennessee. Patton was a medical missionary to Liberia from 1893-1895, then returned to the United States and established a medical practice in Memphis, Tennessee.

African-American Medical Pioneers (1994), p. 151; *Blacks in Science and Medicine* (1990), p. 186; *Notable Black American Women* (1992), pp. 828-830

GEORGIA ESTHER LEE PATTON

1894 • Lucy Hughes Brown (1863-1911) became, in 1894, the first African American woman to practice as a physician in the state of South Carolina. She established her first practice in Charleston after graduating from Women's Medical College (South Carolina). In 1896, along with eight other African American physicians (all men), including Alonzo McClellan, Brown founded the Cannon Hospital and Nurses Training School in Charleston.

African-American Medical Pioneers (1994), p. 185; *Blacks in Science and Medicine* (1990), p. 39; *Hine Sight: Black Women and the Reconstruction of American History* (1994), pp. 154-155; *Send Us a Lady Physician* (1985), p. 113

1894 • Edward Davis Williston (1865-1928) became in 1894 the first intern at Freedman's Hospital in Washington, D.C. He was also the first African American physician to successfully pass the Medical Examining Board of Washington, D.C. Williston graduated from Fayetteville Normal School in 1881, and then earned the B.A. in 1890 and the M.D. in 1894 from Howard University (Washington, D.C.).

African American Medical Pioneers (1994), p. 176; *Blacks in Science and Medicine* (1990), p. 255; *Journal of the National Medical Association* Vol. 20 (October/December 1928), pp. 193-4

1895 • Nathan Francis Mossell (1856-1946), an African American physician, founded Philadelphia's first hospital for African Americans, the Frederick Douglass Memorial Hospital and Training School for Nurses, in 1895. Mossell received his B.A. from Lincoln University (Pennsylvania) in 1879 and his M.D. from the University of Pennsylvania Medical School in 1882, becoming the first African American to receive a M.D. from that institution. He also studied at the famous British hospitals, Guy's and St. Thomas's in London. In 1908, he enlarged the hospital to a 100-bed capacity. By 1912, the hospital had about 3,500 inpatients and 40,000 outpatients. Mossell practiced medicine until 1944, when he retired. In addition to his long and distinguished medical career, he was also active in promoting human rights and equal justice for the African American citizens of Philadelphia.

Dictionary of American Negro Biography (1982), pp. 457-458; *Journal of the National Medical Association* Vol. 46, (March, 1954), pp. 118-130; *The Negro in Pennsylvania History* (1970), p. 56; *Pennsylvania's Black History* (1975), p. 7

1895 • Marcus F. Wheatland (1868-1934), who received a M.D. in 1895 from Howard University Medical College, was the first African American radiologic specialist. He was granted a license to practice in 1895 in Rhode Island. Wheatland's 1902 publication discusses his radiation therapy techniques. In 1909, at the National Medical Association meeting, he presented the first radiologic paper presented by a recognized African American radiologist.

A Centennial History of African Americans in Radiology (1996), pp. 33, 58-59; *Blacks in Science and Medicine* (1990), p. 246

1895 • Robert Fulton Boyd (1858-1912) was one of the founders of the National Medical Association in 1895, and served as its first president, from 1895 to 1898. Boyd graduated from Fisk University (Tennessee) and received a M.D. from Meharry Medical College (Tennessee) in 1882. He then received a D.D.S. in 1887, and a P.H.C. (certificate in pharmacy) in 1890, both from Meharry as well. In 1887, Boyd established a private medical practice in Nashville, Tennessee. He also did post-graduate study in general and gynecological surgery at the University of Michigan and at the Post Graduate Medical School and Hospital of Chicago. Boyd had a long career at Meharry Medical College; during his tenure there, he chaired the departments of surgery, medicine, anatomy, chemistry, hygiene, physiology, and gynecology. In 1900, he established the 33-bed Mercy Hospital in South Nashville; he later opened Boyd Infirmary, after Mercy Hospital was destroyed by fire.

African-American Medical Pioneers (1994), pp. 29, 178; *Century of Black Surgeons* (1987), pp. 110-111; *Encyclopedia of Black America* (1981), pp. 188, 633-634; *Journal of the National Medical Association* Vol 45, (May, 1953), pp. 233-234

1896 • Austin Maurice Curtis Sr. (1868-1939) was the first African American to be appointed to the surgical staff of Cook County Hospital (Chicago) in 1896. This was the first such African American appointment to a non-segregated hospital. Curtis received his M.D. from Northwestern University (Illinois) in 1891. After two years at Cook County Hospital, he was named surgeon-in-chief at Freedman's Hospital, Washington, D.C., in 1898 and remained in that position for four years. His career continued as professor of surgery at Howard University Medical School (Washington, D.C.) and professor of surgery, head of the department, and chief of surgical service at Freedman's Hospital. Curtis also was consultant surgeon at Provident Hospital and Richmond Hospital (Virginia) and was elected president of the National Medical Association in 1911.

African-American Medical Pioneers (1994), p. 24; *Blacks in Science and Medicine* (1990), p. 66; *Journal of the National Medical Association* Vol. 46, (1954), pp. 294-298

1897 • Matilda Anabella Evans (1872-1935), an African American, became in 1897 the first woman to practice medicine in South Carolina. Evans attended Oberlin College (Ohio) from 1887 to 1891, and enrolled at Women's Medical College (Pennsylvania) in 1893, graduating with the M.D. in 1897. Evans developed a very successful practice with both white and African American patients. She was interested in public health and founded the Columbia Clinic Association, which taught families proper health maintenance and provided a variety of health services. Evans founded the Taylor Lane Hospital and Training School in Columbia in 1901, suspending her private practice to act as superintendent of Taylor Lane Hospital, where a number of Columbia's leading surgeons performed medical work.

Black Women in America (1993), pp. 401-2; *Blacks in Science and Medicine* (1990), p. 87; *Notable Black American Women* (1992), pp. 327-9; *Philadelphia Tribune* (January 11, 1994)

1897 • Rivers Frederick (1873-1954) was the first African American to earn a M.D. from the University of Illinois College of Medicine when he received the degree in 1897. He received his undergraduate degree in 1893 from New Orleans University. Frederick was from 1901 to 1904 the surgeon-in-chief for the Government Hospital in El Roi Tan, Honduras. In 1904, he joined the staff at Flint-Goodrich Hospital, New Orleans, where he remained until 1953. He was the chief surgeon at Flint-Goodrich in 1904 when appointed. Frederick was heavily involved in teaching and in the improvement of the facilities and service of Flint-Goodrich, in addition to his surgical practice. He was active in both national and international medical associations, and in 1951, was the first African American awarded an honorary degree by a European university—the University of Florence.

African-American Medical Pioneers (1994), p. 149; *Journal of the National Medical Association, Volume 46* (November 1954), pp. 434-435; *Negro Year Book* (1952), p. 371; *Who's Who in Colored America* (1941-1944), p. 195

1897 • Eliza Anna Grier (1864-1902) was the first African-American woman to become licensed to practice medicine in the state of Georgia. Grier graduated from Fisk University (Tennessee) in 1891, then taught for one year at the Paine Normal School and Industrial Institute (now known as Paine College) in Georgia. She enrolled at Women's Medical College of Pennsylvania and earned her M.D. in 1897.

Black Women in America (1993), pp. 502-503; *Blacks in Science and Medicine* (1990), p. 107; *Philadelphia New Observer* (February 14, 1996); *Philadelphia Tribune* (January 11, 1994); *The Book of African American Women* (1996), pp. 213-214

1898 • The first African American woman to pass the State Board and register as a practicing physician in the state of Kentucky was Artishia Garcia Gilbert (1869-19??) in 1897. Gilbert received an initial degree in 1892 from the State University of Kentucky and a M.D. from Louisville National Medical College (Kentucky) in 1893. She also attended Howard University Medical School (Washington, D.C.), graduating with her M.D. in 1897. Gilbert served as assistant to the professor of obstetrics in the medical department of the State University and superintendent of the Red Cross Sanitarium in Louisville.

African-American Medical Pioneers (1994), pp. 171, 188; *Blacks in Science and Medicine* (1990), p. 100

1898 • Arthur McKimmon Brown (1867-1939) was the first African American commissioned in the U. S. regular army when he was commissioned a lieutenant on July 21, 1898. He was appointed, at the same time, as a surgeon for an immune regiment in Santiago, Cuba and was the only African American surgeon to serve in Cuba during the Spanish-American War. Brown remained in the military until April 1899. He earned an A.B. in 1888 from Lincoln University and then received a M.D. in 1891 from the University of Michigan. Brown initially set up private practice in Bessemer and Birmingham, Alabama, and Chicago, and then returned to Birmingham to continue his practice.

Blacks in Science and Medicine (1990), p. 38; *Dictionary of American Negro Biography* (1982), pp. 64-65

1898 • William Fletcher Penn was the first African American to earn a M.D. from Yale University Medical School, in 1898. Penn practiced as a physician and surgeon and for a period, was associated with the departments of medicine and surgery at Tuskegee Veterans Administration Hospital. He performed a large number of surgical procedures at Tuskegee, beginning in 1926, and was popularly regarded as the chief surgeon until 1930. Penn was the stepfather of Louis Tompkins Wright, whom he encouraged and closely supported during his educational/medical training, to become a world-renowned physician and surgeon. He was also the grandfather of the famed cancer researcher, Jane Cooke Wright.

African American Firsts (1994), p. 246; *Blacks in Science and Medicine* (1990), p. 188; *Black Pioneers of Science and Invention* (1970), p. 141; *A Century of Black Surgeons* (198), pp. 161, 353; *Journal of the National Medical Association* (March, 1953), p. 131

1899 • The first African American psychiatrist was Solomon Carter Fuller (1872-1953). Fuller received his B.A. in 1893 from Livingstone College (North Carolina) and his M.D. from Boston University School of Medicine (Massachusetts) in 1897. Fuller completed a two-year internship at Westborough State Hospital in 1899 and in that year was simultaneously appointed as a pathologist at Westborough State and instructor in neurology and psychiatry at the Boston University School of Medicine. He served in various capacities at Boston University School of Medicine until he retired as a professor of neurology in 1937. Fuller also studied in Germany under Emile Kraspelin and was the first African American to edit the "Westborough State Hospital Papers" in 1913. He is well known for his research and writings on dementia and Alzheimer's disease. His theory that Alzheimer's disease was not caused by arteriosclerosis was supported by medical researchers in 1953.

SOLOMON CARTER
FULLER

African Americans in Boston (1991), p. 142; *Dictionary of Black Culture* (1973), p. 177; *Encyclopedia of Black America* (1981), p. 400; *Journal of the National Medical Association* Vol. 40, (1954), pp. 37-42

1901 • Algernon B. Jackson (1878-1942) became in 1901 the first African American to earn a M.D. from Jefferson Medical College (Pennsylvania). Jackson completed his undergraduate work at Indiana University. He was, from 1900 to 1912, assistant surgeon at Philadelphia Polyclinic Hospital, later serving as superintendent and surgeon-in-chief at Philadelphia's Mercy Hospital and School for Nurses. Jackson was then appointed as professor of bacterial and public health and director of the School of Public Health at Howard University (Washington, D.C.). Jackson is noted for describing a new treatment for acute rheumatism by injection of magnesium sulfate.

African American Medical Pioneers (1994), pp. 150, 190; *Blacks in Science and Medicine* (1990), p. 129; *Jet* (October 23, 1958), p. 11

1901 • James Webb Ames (1864-19??) was the first African American appointed Diagnostician of Contagious Diseases for the Detroit Board of Health in 1901. Webb received a B.S. in 1888 from Straight (now Dillard) University (Louisiana), his M.D. from Howard University Medical School (Washington, D.C.) in 1894, and established a medical practice in Detroit.

Blacks in Science and Medicine (1990), pp. 9-10; *Who's Who in Colored America* (1938-1940), p. 27, (1941-1944), p. 25

1904 • The first African American woman licensed to practice in Lexington, Kentucky, in 1904, was Mary Elizabeth Britton (1858-1925). She completed her medical training in 1904 at the American Missionary Medical

College in Chicago (Illinois) and at the Battle Creek Sanitarium (Michigan). Britton's specialties were hydrotherapy, electrotherapy, and massage. Britton was well-known in the Lexington community not only for her medical expertise, but also for her social and religious work.

Notable Black American Women Bookl II, (1996), pp. 55-57; *Appalachian Heritage* Vol. 15, (1987), pp. 111-116

1906 • Georgia R. Dwelle (1884-1977) was the first African American woman to practice medicine in Atlanta, Georgia, when she moved there and set up practice in 1906. Dwelle graduated with a B.A. from Spelman Seminary in Atlanta and then in 1904, received her M.D. from Meharry Medical College. She practiced in Atlanta and started Dwelle Infirmary, which was officially established in 1920 as an obstetrical hospital. It became the first successful private hospital for African Americans in Atlanta, and it was also the first birthing hospital for African American women in Atlanta.

Notable Black American Women, Book II (1996), pp. 196-197; *Send Us a Lady Physician* (1985), p. 116

1906 • The first African American to graduate from Jefferson Medical College (Pennsylvania) was Henry McKee Minton (1870-1946), who received his M.D. in 1906. Prior to that, Minton was the first African American in the city of Philadelphia to operate a pharmacy, which he established in 1897. He graduated from Phillips Exeter Academy in 1891 and received a Ph.G. from Philadelphia College of Pharmacy and Science (Pennsylvania) in 1895. He was also one of the co-founders, along with Eugene T. Hinson and Algernon B. Jackson, of Mercy Hospital in Philadelphia in 1907. Minton became superintendent of Mercy Hospital in 1910; he remained in this post until 1934, and retained his staff membership there until his death in 1946. He also worked as a clinician in the Henry Phipps Institute of the University of Pennsylvania; he was a specialist in tuberculosis, and from 1923, he was also supervisor of the Negro Tuberculosis Bureau in Philadelphia.

African-American Medical Pioneers (1994), p. 193; *Dictionary of American Negro Biography* (1982), pp. 440-441; *Journal of the National Medical Association* Vol. 47, (July, 1965), pp. 285-286

1907 • Edward Albert Carter (1882-1958) was the first African American to receive a M.D. from the University of Iowa College of Medicine in 1907. Carter also completed his undergraduate studies at the University of Iowa. He was a partner in private practice with R.O. Early, whose interest in the practice he bought out in 1913. He also provided medical services to local townships and businesses. He was active in local and state medical associations and in 1915, was the only African American member of the Monroe County Medical Society. Florence Battle Shafig, in 1976, became the first African American woman to earn a M.D. from the University of Iowa, 69 years later. Shafig completed her undergraduate studies at Coe College.

African-American Medical Pioneers (1994), p. 149; *Blacks in Science and Medicine* (1990), p. 50

1908 • Cornelius N. Garland, an African-American physician who earned his M.D. in 1901 from Leonard Medical College (North Carolina), was the founder of Plymouth Hospital and Nurse's Training School in Boston, Massachusetts in 1908, which served a major portion of Boston's African-American community until 1928. Garland earned a B.S. in 1897 from Livingstone College (North Carolina). After he earned his M.D., he did postgraduate medical study at University of London Medical College, (England). Garland was a member of the National Medical Association, Massachusetts Medical Society, and the Boston Society for Medical Improvement.

African Americans in Boston (1991), p. 143; *Blacks in Science and Medicine* (1990), pp. 97-98

1908 • Clarence A. Lucas, Sr. was the first African American to receive the M.D. degree from Indian University School of Medicine when he received the degree in 1908. Deborah Lynne McCullough was one of the first two African American women to receive the M.D. degree from Indiana University School of Medicine when she graduated in 1975. McCullough completed her undergraduate degree at Howard University. The other first African American woman was Beverly J. Perkins, who graduated with a bachelors degree from Butler University.

African American Medical Pioneers (1994), p. 149

1908 • Milton Augustus Francis (1882-1961) was born in Washington, D.C., in 1882, and completed his medical studies in 1906 at Howard University. He served a genito-urinary internship at Freedmen's Hospital, which he completed in 1908, becoming the first African American physician to specialize in genito-urinary diseases. Upon completion of his internship, Francis joined the genito-urinary department at Freedmen's, working under and assisting the department head until 1917, when he took charge of genito-urinary services until 1922. In 1923, Francis split this responsibility, and the position was handled in this manner until 1933, when he resigned from Freedmen's and concerned himself with his private practice.

African-American Medical Pioneers (1994), p. 171; *Blacks in Science and Medicine* (1990), p. 93; *Journal of the National Medical Association, Volume 70* (December 1978), pp. 945-946

1909 • Walter Gilbert Alexander (1880-1953) founded the New Jersey Medical Society in 1909 and the New Jersey State Medical Association in

1939. Alexander, who became the first African American physician to be elected to the New Jersey Senate, also co-founded the *Journal of the National Medical Association* in 1909 and served as president of the National Medical Association in 1925. He received a B.A. in 1899 from Lincoln University (Pennsylvania) and a M.D. in 1903 from the College of Physicians and Surgeons in Boston, Massachusetts. Alexander practiced medicine in West Virginia from 1903-4, and then took up practice in Orange, New Jersey. In 1934, he was appointed a city physician in Orange.

African American Medical Pioneers (1994), p. 183; *Blacks in Science and Medicine* (1990), p. 6; *Famous First Facts About Negroes* (1972), p. 186; *Encyclopedia of Black America* (1981), p. 98

1909 • The first editor of the *Journal of the National Medical Association* (1909-1919) was African American physician Charles Victor Roman (1864-1934). Roman received his M.D. from Meharry Medical College (Tennessee) in 1890 and practiced medicine from 1890 to 1904, when he traveled to London for further study at the Royal Ophthalmic Hospital and Central Nose, Throat, and Ear Hospital. After his return to the United States, he was appointed to a teaching position at Meharry, where he remained for 27 years. Additionally, Roman held a position at Fisk University (Tennessee) for 14 years, served as the fifth president of the National Medical Association in 1904-5, and was a prominent advocate for self-determination and the equality of African Americans.

African-American Medical Pioneers (1994), p. 33; *Dictionary of American Negro Biography* (1982), pp. 532-533; *History of the Negro in Medicine* (1967), pp. 68-70; *Journal of the National Medical Association* Vol. 45, (July, 1953), pp. 301-305

1910 • John Edward Perry (1870-1962) established the first African American Hospital in Kansas City, Missouri—the Perry Sanitarium—in 1910. The hospital eventually became the Wheatley-Provident Hospital in 1915. Perry earned a B.A. in 1891 from Bishop College and a M.D. in 1895 from Meharry Medical College. He set up practice after graduation until 1897, when he enrolled in the Chicago Postgraduate Medical School. Perry and Thomas C. Unthank combined efforts during the period 1910 to 1915, leading to the establishment of Kansas City General Hospital No. 2. In 1911, a Negro School of Nursing was opened at City Hospital No. 2, which had white supervisors until 1914. At that time, an African American staff assumed supervision, and the hospital became the first municipal facility and school of nursing completely managed by African Americans. Perry was also a dominant player in the development of the surgery program at Kansas City General Hospital No 2.

African-American Medical Pioneers (1994), p. 180; *Blacks in Science and Medicine* (1990), p. 188; *A Century of Black Surgeons* (1987), pp. 434-440; *Journal of the National Medical Association, Volume 54* (September 1962), p. 526

1910 • Josie E. Wells was the first African American woman physician to teach at Meharry Medical College in 1910. She was also the first woman to attain a position of leadership as superintendent of George W. Hubbard Hospital in Nashville, Tennessee, the teaching hospital affiliated with Meharry, when she became hospital's secretary in 1910. Wells received her M.D. from Meharry Medical College in 1904.

African American Medical Pioneers (1994), p. 182; *Black Women in America* (1993), p. 924; *Notable Black American Women* Book II (1996), p. 157

1911 • Grossi Hamilton Francis (1885-1963) was the first African American intern appointed at Hubbard Hospital in Nashville, Tennessee, in 1911. He received his B.S. in 1907 from the Berkeley Institute of Bermuda and then earned his M.D. from Mercy College of Medicine in 1911. Francis also founded, in 1935, the National Medical Association House of Delegates.

African-American Medical Pioneers (1994), pp. 29, 179; *Blacks in Science and Medicine* (1990), p. 93; *Journal of the National Medical Association* Vol. 41, (September, 1949), p. 232, Vol. 55, (September, 1963), p. 461

1911 • The first scientific paper in the *Journal of the National Medical Association* illustrated by x rays was published in 1911. It was authored by African American radiologist Claudius DeWitt Bell (1875-1918). Bell received his M.D. from Jenner (Chicago) in 1907 and had a private practice in Chicago. He was on the staff of Provident Hospital there until 1918, when he died. Bell was also, in 1901, the first African American certified by the Colorado State Board of Pharmacy. He was a consultant on the x ray of President Theodore Roosevelt in 1912 in Chicago, after an assassination attempt was made on the president in Wisconsin.

A Centennial History of African Americans in Radiology (1996), pp. 60-61; *Journal of the National Medical Association* Volume 3, (1911), pp. 229-232, Volume 87, (July 1995), pp. 505-507

1913 • Jaspar Tappan Phillips (1884-19??) became in 1913-4 the first African American to serve as monitor over medical school applicants for the Tennessee State Medical Board of Examiners. Phillips earned a B.A. in 1907 from Fisk University (Tennessee) and his M.D. in 1913 from Meharry Medical College (Tennessee).

African American Medical Pioneers (1994), p. 180; *Blacks in Science and Medicine* (1990), p. 190

1913 • Daniel Hale Williams (1856-1931) was the only African American among the one hundred organizers of the American College of Surgeons, as well as the first African American to be selected as a fellow in 1913. He

DANIEL HALE
WILLIAMS

was also the first African American to serve on the Illinois State Board of Health and a founder, in 1895, and first vice-president of the National Medical Association.

African-American Medical Pioneers (1994), p. 29; *Blacks in Science and Medicine* (1990), pp. 251-252; *A Century of Black Surgeons* (1987), pp. 311-344; *Journal of the National Medical Association* Vol. 34, (1942), pp. 118-119

1915 • Cornell University Medical School's (New York) first African American graduate was Roscoe Conkling Giles (1890-1970), who received his M.D. in 1915. He became the first Diplomate of the American Board of Surgery in 1938, and was one of the first African Americans to become a member of the American College of Surgeons when he was elected in 1945. He was also invited in 1945 to become a founding fellow of the International College of Surgeons. Giles's professional life was spent primarily in Chicago with Provident Hospital, Cook County Hospital, and Chicago Medical School. He also served as president of the Cook County Physicians Association and was elected to membership of the Chicago Institute of Medicine, the Chicago Medical Society, and several other national medical associations. Giles was the driving force behind the movement to have the designation "Col." (for colored) removed from the American Medical Association Directory, which finally succeeded in 1940.

Blacks in Science and Medicine (1990), pp. 100-101; *Century of Black Surgeons* (1987), pp. 297-309; *Encyclopedia of Black America* (1981), p. 404; *Journal of the National Medical Association* Vol. 62, 1970, pp. 254-256

1915 • In 1915, Catherine Deaver Lealtad (1886-1989) was the first African American graduate of Macalester College. She received a degree in chemistry and pursued a career in medical science. Lealtad worked as a laboratory technician for three years prior to going to medical school. She spent one year at Cornell Medical School and then completed her medical training in Lyon and Berlin. Lealtad returned to the United States and completed specialized training in pediatrics. After an internship in Chicago, she established a medical practice in Harlem and worked in various health clinics.

African American Women: A Biographical Dictionary (1993), p. 324-325

1915 • African American physician John E. Perry (1870-1962) founded the Wheatley-Provident Hospital in Kansas City in 1915. (He had previously founded Perry Sanitarium in 1910 on the same site.) Perry was rebuffed in his attempts to gain access to practice in white hospitals, and the experience convinced him African American-owned hospitals were an absolute necessity, both for services and professional development of African American physicians. Perry graduated from Bishop College in 1891 and received a M.D. in 1895 from Meharry Medical College. He practiced until 1897, when he enrolled in the Chicago Postgraduate Medical School. Perry was also instrumental in the development of post-graduate medical education. One of his efforts resulted in development of the surgery program at Kansas City Hospital No. 2.

African American Medical Pioneers (1994), p. 180; *Blacks in Science and Medicine* (1990), p. 188; *Jet* (May 31, 1962), p. 52

1915 • Emma Rochelle Wheeler (1882-1957) founded the first hospital to be owned and operated by an African American in Chattanooga, Tennessee, in 1915. Wheeler's husband was an attending physician at the hospital, while she was the manager and superintendent. Their hospital, Walden Hospital, was also a nurse's training school for 20 years. Wheeler graduated in 1905 from Walden University's medical program, the Meharry Medical, Dental and Pharmaceutical College. She also introduced, in 1925, a prepaid plan covering hospitalization costs that was unique in its time. Wheeler's plan, called the Nurse Service Club, entitled members to two weeks of hospitalization at no cost, as well as home nurse care afterward.

Notable Black American Scientists (1999), pp. 314-315

1916 • The first African American gynecologist on the staff of Provident Hospital (Chicago), appointed in 1916, was Carl Glennis Roberts (1886-1950). He would remain on staff until 1980. Roberts was also was one of the first African Americans admitted to the American College of Surgeons in 1945, and the first African American graduate of Valparaiso University Medical Department (Indiana) when he received his M.D. from there in 1911.

Blacks in Science and Medicine (1990), p. 201; *African-American Medical Pioneers* (1994), p. 195; *A Century of Black Surgeons* (1987), pp. 273-276; *Journal of the National Medical Association* Vol. 52, (1960), pp. 146-147

1917 • Ulysses Samuel Wharton (1885-1934) was the first African American physician to practice medicine in Altoona, Pennsylvania when he set up practice there in 1917. Wharton attended Hampton Institute and Oberlin

College prior to his receiving his M.D. from Howard University Medical College. He established an outstanding reputation for his successful treatment of influenza during the 1917 influenza epidemic in Altoona.

Encyclopedia of Black America (1981), p. 852

1917 • The first African American to receive a M.D. and a Ph.D. was Julian H. Lewis (1891-19??). His M.D. was earned at Rush Medical College [Illinois] in 1917. He was also the first African American to earn a Ph.D. in physiology, which he received in 1915, from the University of Chicago. Lewis received a B.A. from the University of Illinois in 1911 and an M.A. from the University of Chicago in 1912. Lewis was a pathologist and was on the faculty of the department of pathology at the University of Chicago from 1917 to 1943. He conducted extensive research on immunity and contributed a number of publications to the scientific literature. He was also the author of the first text by an African American author to receive national attention, *The Biology of the Negro*.

African-American Medical Pioneers (1994), pp. 25, 192; *Blacks in Science and Medicine* (1990), p. 153; *Journal of National Medical Association* (1941), Vol. 33, pp. 174-175

1918 • Eslanda Goode Robeson (1896-1965) was the first African American employed as an analytical chemist and technician in the surgery and pathology department at Columbia Presbyterian Hospital. Robeson received a B.S. in chemistry from Teachers College of Columbia University (New York) in 1923, working at Presbyterian Hospital from 1918 to 1925. She married Paul Robeson in 1921 and in 1925, she resigned from Presbyterian Hospital to manage the career of her husband, who was an internationally known singer, actor, and political activist, and to become an well-known political activist in her own right.

Black Women in America Book II, (1996), pp. 986-987; *Notable Black American Women* (1992), Vol. 2, pp. 942-947; *Dictionary of American Negro Biography* (1982), pp. 527-528

ESLANDA GOODE
ROBESON

1918 • Clyde Donnell (1890-1971), who received his M.D. in 1915 from Harvard Medical School (Massachusetts), founded the Durham, North Carolina Academy of Medicine in 1918. Donnell earned a B.S. from North Carolina A&T College in 1907 and a B.A. from Howard University (Washington, D.C.) in 1911. He worked as junior house officer on medical service of Boston City Hospital for the period 1915-6. From 1918 to 1921, he completed postgraduate work in internal medicine and physical therapy, pursuing additional postgraduate work in x ray and physiotherapy from 1922 to

1924, all at Harvard. Donnell, a pioneer in the research of the causes of mortality and morbidity in the African American population, held several executive positions with the North Carolina Mutual Life Insurance Company, including chair of the board.

African American Medical Pioneers (1994), p. 187; *Who's Who Among African Americans* (1990), p. 75; *Jet* (October 28, 1971), p. 28; *Journal of the National Medical Association, Vol. 52* (September 1960), p. 382

1918 • The first African American physician to intern at a major U. S. hospital was Ubert Conrad Vincent (1892-1938), who was accepted to intern at Bellevue Hospital in New York in 1918. Vincent received a B.A. in 1914 from Shaw University (North Carolina), attended Leonard Medical College of Shaw University from 1914-5, and received his M.D. from the University of Pennsylvania in 1918. After completing his internship, he established a private practice in New York. He was successful enough to establish the Vincent Sanitarium in New York in 1929, which unfortunately fell victim to the stock market crash and the Great Depression. His medical innovations included the development of a surgical relief procedure, the Vincent Varicocele Operation, named in his honor.

African American Medical Pioneers (1994), pp. 25, 197; *Blacks in Science and Medicine* (1990), pp. 238-9; *Journal of the National Medical Association, Vol. 67* (January 1975), pp. 73-80

1919 • William Samuel Quinland (1885-1953) was the first African American to win a Rosenwald Fellowship for postgraduate study in 1920. With his fellowship, he worked on a specialization in pathology and bacteriology at Harvard from 1920 to 1922. Quinland received a B.S. in 1918 from Oskaloosa College and a M.D. from Meharry Medical College in 1919. He also earned a Harvard Medical School Graduate Certificate in pathology and bacteriology in 1921. Quinland was appointed professor of pathology at Meharry Medical College (Tennessee) in 1922 and remained there for 25 years, eventually becoming head of the department of pathology. He had several other medical firsts as an African American: he was the first to become a member of the American Association of Pathologists and Bacteriologists (1920); the first to be certified by the American Board of Pathology (1937); and the first to be elected a fellow by the College of American Pathologists (1947). Following his tenure as department head at Meharry, Quinland became, in 1947, the chief of laboratory service of the Veterans Administration Hospital in Tuskegee.

African-American Medical Pioneers (1994), pp. 25, 180-181; *Journal of the National Medical Association* Vol. 33, (1941), p. 89, Vol. 45, (1953), pp. 298-300; *Negro Year Book* (1941-1946), pp. 43-4

LOUIS TOMPKINS
WRIGHT

1919 • Harlem Hospital, in New York City, had an all-white medical staff until the African American surgeon Louis Tompkins Wright (1891-1952) was appointed to the staff in 1919. He became director of surgery in 1942 and president of the Medical Board of Harlem Hospital in 1947, both firsts for an African American. Wright earned a B.S. from Clark College (Georgia) in 1911 and his M.D. from Harvard (Massachusetts), *cum laude*, in 1915. Wright was appointed police surgeon for the New York City Police in 1929, the first African American to hold that position. He was the first African American elected a fellow of the American College of Surgeons in 1935, and he also founded the Cancer Research Center of Harlem Hospital. Wright headed the team that was the first to experiment with the antibiotic aureomycin on humans, and originated the intradermal method of vaccination against smallpox. Wright published 89 scientific papers, of which 30 dealt with Aureomycin and eight with terramycin.

Blacks in Science and Medicine (1990), p. 259; *Black Pioneers of Science and Invention* (1990), pp. 201-18; *A Century of Black Surgeons* (1987), pp. 160-71; *Journal of the National Medical Association* Vol. 45, (1953), pp. 130-148

1920 • Clilan Bethany Powell (1894-1977) was the first African American radiologist to train at Bellevue Hospital in 1920. He was also the first African American radiologist in New York City. Powell earned a B.S. at Virginia Normal University in 1913 and received a M.D. from Howard University in 1920. After his internship, he joined the staff of Harlem Hospital, where he remained eight years. He then started a private x-ray practice. Powell left the medical practice to become a businessman and publisher-editor of the newspaper the *Amsterdam News*.

A Centennial History of African Americans in Radiology (1996), pp. 66-67; *Blacks in Science and Medicine* (1990), p. 194

1920 • The first African American physician to become a member of the staff of the genito-urinary department of Lakeland Hospital and faculty of Western Reserve University (Ohio) was Charles Herbert Garvin (1890-1968), in 1920. Garvin received his B.A. in 1911 and his M.D. in 1915, both from Howard University (Washington, D.C.). He started his private practice of medicine and genito-urinary surgery in Cleveland in 1916, after completing an internship at Freedman's Hospital in Washington, D.C. He spent his entire career in Cleveland, interrupted only by a stint in the armed forces, where he was the first African American physician commissioned in the U.S. Army in World War I in 1917. Garvin published numerous articles for medical journals and was a member of several medical organizations, including the Cleveland Urological Society, Cleveland Academy of Medicine, Ohio State Medical Association, American Medical Association, and National Medical Association.

African-American Medical Pioneers (1994), p. 171; *Jet* (October 30, 1969); *Journal of the National Medical Association* Vol. 49, (1957), pp. 257-8, Vol. 56, (1964), p. 208; *Who's Who in Colored America* (1941-1944), p. 201; *Notable Black American Scientists* (1999), p. 125-6

1920 • The first African American director of radiology at Meharry Medical College, in 1920, was Samuel M. Utley (1868-1934) who taught at Meharry from 1920 to 1930. Utley had received his M.D. from Meharry in 1912.

A Centennial History of African Americans in Radiology (1996), pp. 4, 72, 73, 125-126

1920 • William Samuel Quinland (1885-1953), an African American physician and pathologist with a distinguished career as a pathologist and a member of the medical faculty of Meharry Medical College (Tennessee), also had several pioneering achievements in his particular field. He was the first African American physician admitted to the American Association of Pathologists and Bacteriologists in 1920, the first to be admitted to the level of diplomate by the American Board of Pathology in 1937, and the first to be elected a fellow of the College of American Pathologists. Quinland received a B.S. from Oskaloosa College (Iowa) in 1918, and a M.D. in 1919 from Meharry Medical College. He also received a graduate certificate in 1921 from Harvard Medical School in pathology and bacteriology. He was associate medical director of the George Washington Hubbard Hospital from 1931 to 1937, and then professor and head of the department of pathology at Meharry Medical College from 1922 to 1947.

African-American Medical Pioneers (1994), pp. 23, 30, 180-181; *Blacks in Science and Medicine* (1990), pp. 196-197; *Journal of the National Medical Association, Volume 45* (July, 1953), pp. 298-300

1921 • John Patrick Turner (1885-1958) became the founder and first president of the Pennsylvania State Medical, Dental, and Pharmacy Association in 1921. Turner also was appointed president of the National Medical Association for the term 1921-2, serving also on the editorial board of its *Journal*. He earned a bachelor's degree in 1903 from City College of New York and his M.D. in 1906 from Shaw University (North Carolina). Turner worked as medical examiner for the public schools of Philadelphia for a number of years, and in 1931 became the first African American police surgeon for the city, a post he held until 1941.

African American Medical Pioneers (1994), pp. 29, 33, 197; *Blacks in Science and Medicine* (1990), p. 235; *Journal of the National Medical Association, Vol. 51* (March 1959), pp. 160-1

1924 • Joseph H. Ward (1870-1956), who received his M.D. from Indiana Medical College, was the first African American to head a U. S. Veterans Administration Hospital when he was appointed head of the Tuskegee Veterans Administration Hospital in 1924. Ward had previously been a military officer before his appointment. He was originally placed at the Tuskegee facility as chief of surgical service, but after two weeks was made head of the hospital. Ward headed Tuskegee Veterans Hospital from 1924 to 1936. He was a capable administrator and continued to perform surgeries with his other duties.

African-American Medical Pioneers (1994), pp. 33, 35, 198; *Blacks in Science and Medicine* (1990), p. 242; *A Century of Black Surgeons* (1987), pp. 346-347, 348, 353; *Journal of the National Medical Association, Volume 16* (July-September 1924), pp. 203-204

1925 • James Lowell Hall, Sr. (1892-1965) was the first African American to graduate from the University of Chicago Division of the Biological Sciences, Pritzker School of Medicine, when he received his M.D. in 1925. Hall received a B.A. in 1911 from Prairie View College and a B.S. in 1923 from the University of Chicago. He was director of clinics at Chicago's Provident Hospital from 1936 to 1941 and Director of Medicine at Howard University Medical School from 1941 to 1944. He maintained a private practice from 1947 to 1965. Prior to starting his private practice, Hall was Superintendent of Washington, D.C.'s Freedman's Hospital for the period of 1944 to 1947.

African American Medical Pioneers (1994), p. 147; *Blacks in Science and Medicine* (1990), p. 109; *Journal of the National Medical Association* (January, 1966), pp. 82-83

1925 • Neville C. Whiteman (1899-19??) was one of the first three African Americans to receive M.D.s, in 1925, from New York University School of Medicine. (Arthur M. Williams and Vivian L. Williams were the other two.) Whiteman earned a B.S. from the College of the City of New York (New York) in 1921. Whiteman was, from 1926-1930, an assistant physician in the outpatient department of New York's Harlem Hospital and in 1930 was appointed chief of the medical clinic at Harlem Hospital. He was also a member of five medical associations.

African-American Medical Pioneers (1994), p. 152; *Blacks in Science and Medicine* (1990), p. 248

1925 • Virginia M. Alexander (1900-1945), who obtained her M.D. from Women's Medical College of Pennsylvania, was the first woman to be appointed a member of the staff of Kansas City (Missouri) General Hospital when appointed in 1925. She received her bachelor's degree from the University of Pennsylvania. Alexander returned to Philadelphia in 1928, where she set up a general practice. She also earned a M.S. in public health in 1937 from Yale University and worked in public health for nine years in

Washington, D.C. as a member of the U.S. Department of Health. She also was a staff physician at Howard University Medical School, and later at Schlorsfield Hospital in Birmingham, Alabama.

African-American Medical Pioneers (1994), p. 52-3; *Black Women in America* (1993), pp. 19-20; *Black Women in America* (1997), pp. 34-35

1926 • May Edward Chinn (1896-1980) became the first African American woman to receive a M.D. from Bellevue Hospital Medical College (known as University Medical College, New York University) in 1926, and became the first African American woman to hold an internship at Harlem Hospital the same year. She was also the first woman to ride in ambulances on emergency calls. Chinn developed an interest in cancer early in her career, and specialized in the field of cancer research from 1930 until her retirement in 1977. She was a member of numerous professional organizations, including holding life member status in the American Academy of Family Physicians and fellow status in the American Geriatrics Society.

Black Firsts (1994), p. 355; *Black Women in America* (1993), pp. 235-236; *Blacks in Science and Medicine* (1990), p. 53; *New York State Journal of Medicine* (1985), pp. 145-146

MAY EDWARD CHINN

1926 • Harlem Hospital, in New York City, accepted its first African American intern in 1926, when Ira McCown (1900-19??) was appointed. McCown was also the only African American gynecological advisor to the New York Workmen's Compensation Board after he received the highest marks in a run-off oral examination.

Blacks in Science and Medicine (1990), p. 168; *A Century of Black Surgeons* (1987), p. 172

1927 • The American Board of Otolaryngology was organized in 1924, and in 1927, certified its first African American physician, William Harry Barnes (1887-1945). Barnes was the first African American physician certified by any medical specialty board in the United States. He received a B.S. in 1908 and a M.D. in 1912, both from the University of Pennsylvania. Barnes interned at Douglas Hospital and in 1921, took a postgraduate course in operative surgery of the ear, nose, and throat at the University of Pennsylvania, and also traveled abroad for further study. In 1922, he announced that he would specialize in otolaryngology, and in 1931, he became the first African American physician to master bronchoscopy. He organized the Department of Bronchoscopy at Mercy Hospital, and also invented the hypohyscope, used for visualizing the pituitary gland through the sphenoid sinus. He also devised a medical record system and developed a modification of the Myles lingual tonsillectomy. Barnes was also founder and executive director of the Society for the Promotion of Negro Specialists in Medicine.

Blacks in Science and Medicine (1990), pp. 20-21; *Century of Black Surgeons* (1987), pp. 485, 504-508; *Journal of the National Medical Association* Vol. 47, pp. 64-66, (1955), Vol. 62, (1970), p. 435; *Negro Handbook* (1949), p. 31

1928 • Austin Maurice Curtis Sr. (1868-1939) was the first African American appointed a professor in the Surgery Department of Howard University Medical School (Washington, D.C.) in 1897. He eventually became the fourth physician and first African American to head the department in 1928. Curtis earned his B.A. at Lincoln University (Pennsylvania) in 1888, and his M.D. from Northwestern University (Illinois) in 1891. He was the first African American intern at Chicago's Provident Hospital in 1891, and also the first African American physician surgeon appointed to the staff of Cook County Hospital in Chicago in 1896. Curtis was professor of surgery at Howard University for 25 years and chaired the surgery department until 1928. He was also chief surgeon at Freedman's Hospital from 1898 to 1938.

Blacks in Science and Medicine (1990), p. 66; *African-American Medical Pioneers* (1994), pp. 24,186; *A Century of Black Surgeons* (1987), pp. 270-272; *Journal of the National Medical Association* Vol. 46, (1954), pp. 294-298

1928 • The first medical director at Baltimore's Provident Hospital in 1928 was African American physician Robert L. Jackson (1894-19??). Jackson was a recipient of a M.D. in 1921 from Meharry Medical College, and he also completed postgraduate medical courses at Cook County Graduate School of Medicine, Presbyterian and Mount Sinai Hospitals in New York City, New York University, and George Washington University Postgraduate Schools of Medicine. Jackson practiced medicine in Baltimore for 41 years and was one of the founders of Provident Hospital there. He was, in 1931, Junior Consultant in Surgery, Associate Chief of Surgery in 1935, Chief of Staff in 1940, and Chief of Surgical Services in 1950, while with Provident. He was also an attending surgeon at Lutheran Hospital in Baltimore. Jackson was a recipient of awards and honors for his pioneering work to get African American physicians into professional medical societies and for his development of Provident Hospital.

Blacks in Science and Medicine (1990), p. 130; *Journal of the National Medical Association, Volume 55* (November 1963), pp. 549-550

1929 • The first African American dean of the Howard Medical School (Washington, D.C.), appointed in 1929, was Numa P.G. Adams (1885-

1940). Adams received his B.A. from Howard in 1911, his M.A. from Columbia University (New York) in 1912, and his M.D. from Rush Medical College of the University of Chicago (Illinois) in 1923. He taught chemistry at Howard from 1912 to 1919. After receiving his M.D., Adams interned at Homer G. Phillips Hospital (St. Louis, Missouri) in 1924 and practiced medicine in Chicago from 1925 to 1929, when he received the appointment as medical school dean at Howard. Adams served as dean until 1940, and in this role he reorganized the curriculum in the Medical School, raised salaries, recruited promising African American students and instructors, and encouraged young graduates working toward M.D.s to acquire Ph.D.s as well.

African-American Medical Pioneers (1994), pp. ; *Dictionary of Black Culture* (1973), p. 13; *Journal of the National Medical Association* Vol. 32, (1940), pp. 257-258, Vol. 43, (1951), pp. 42-54

1929 • Theodore K. Lawless (1892-1971) was the first African American physician awarded the Harmon Award for Outstanding Achievement in Medicine (dermatology) in 1929 and was the first African American certified by the American Board of Dermatology and Syphilology in 1935. Lawless received a B.A. from Talladega College (Alabama) in 1914, a M.D. in 1919, and an M.S. in 1920, both from Northwestern University School of Medicine (Illinois). From 1920 to 1924, he also studied at Columbia (New York) and Harvard (Massachusetts) Universities, as well as in Paris, Freiburg, and Vienna. He did special research in Freiburg and Paris, where he made valuable contributions to the scientific treatment of syphilis and leprosy. Lawless taught at Northwestern University School of Medicine from 1924 to 1941 and for many years was senior attending physician at Provident Hospital. He was extremely successful in the treatment of skin diseases and was known worldwide for his specialty while directing his own dermatological clinic and private practice in Chicago.

THEODORE K.
LAWLESS

Blacks in Science: Astrophysicist to Zoologist (1977), pp. 22-23; *History of the Negro in Medicine* (1967), pp. 109-110; *Negro Year Book* (1947), p. 43; *Journal of the National Medical Association* (1970), Vol. 62, pp. 310-312

1931 • Peter Marshall Murray (1888-1969), who received his M.D. from Howard University Medical School (Washington, D.C.) in 1914, was the first African American physician to become a certified Diplomate of the American Board of Obstetrics and Gynecology in 1931. He established a medical practice in New York City in 1921, working there until

PETER MARSHALL
MURRAY

1928 when he joined the staff of Harlem Hospital. He worked there until 1954. Murray was the first African American, in 1949, to sit in the House of Delegates of the American Medical Association, representing the Medical Society of the County of New York. He was also the first African American physician appointed to serve on the Board of Hospitals of the City of New York, the nine-member board directing New York's 29 municipal hospitals. Murray was active in several other professional organizations and contributed a number of publications to the scientific literature from 1922 to 1965.

African-American Medical Pioneers (1994), p. 30; *Timelines of African-American History* (1994), pp. 214, 224

1931 • Estelle Massey Riddle Osborne (1901-1981) was one of the most dynamic individuals in pursuit of the nursing profession at all levels. When she earned a M.A. from Teachers College, Columbia University in 1931, she became the first African American nurse to earn a M.A. in nursing education. Osborne graduated from the Homer G. Phillips Hospital School of Nursing in 1923 and received a B.S. in nursing education in 1930. In 1927, when she entered college, Osborne was the first African American recipient of a Rosenwald Fund fellowship for nurses. Osborne was a driving force in the National Association of Colored Graduate Nurses (NACGN), serving as president from 1934 to 1939. Osborne returned to her alma mater, the Homer G. Phillips Hospital School of Nursing, as the first African American superintendent of nurse training while also serving her NACGN duties. She also held an elective office in the American Nurses' Association in 1948.

American Women of Nursing (1947), pp. 96-118; *Black Women in White* (1989), pp. 118-119; *Negro Almanac* (1989), pp. 1389, 1426; *The Path We Tread* (1986), pp. 137-139

1931 • The first African American professor of pharmacology in the United States was Arnold Hamilton Maloney (1888-1955), who became a professor at Howard University Medical School (Washington, D.C.) in 1931. He was appointed head of the department there during the 1930s. Maloney received his B.S. from Naparima College (Trinidad) in 1909, his M.S. from Columbia University (New York) in 1910, his M.D. from Indiana University in 1929, and a Ph.D. in pharmacology from the University of Wisconsin in 1931. While at Howard from 1931 to 1953, he published over 20 scientific papers in the United States and Belgium. He was the first to discover the antidotal action of Picrotoxin to poisoning by barbiturates, a group of sleep-inducing drugs.

African-American Medical Pioneers (1994), p. 193; *Blacks in Science and Medicine* (1990), p. 160; *Journal of the National Medical Association* Vol. 47, (1955), pp. 424-426; *Negro Builders and Heroes* (1937), pp. 230-231

1931 • R. Wellesley Bailey was the first African American physician admitted to membership in the Philadelphia Neurological Society in 1931. Wellesley was the only African American neurologist practicing in the city of Philadelphia at that time.

Negro Year Book (1931-1932), p. 181

1932 • The first African American to earn a Ph.D. in pathology was Robert Stewart Jason (1901-1984), who received his degree from the University of Chicago (Illinois) in 1932. Jason earned a B.A., *magna cum laude*, at Lincoln University (Pennsylvania) in 1924 and a M.D. at Howard University Medical School (Washington, D.C.) in 1928. He served as professor of pathology at Howard University from 1932 to 1937, as vice-dean from 1946 to 1953, and as dean from 1955 to 1965. He was emeritus professor of pathology at Howard University Medical School from 1970 to 1984 and also served as a pathologist at Freedman's Hospital from 1932 to 1970. Jason's research specialty areas were in the histopathology of the palatine tonsils and pathology of syphilis of the aortic valve.

Encyclopedia of Black America (1981), p. 470; *Jet* (May 19, 1955), p. 49; *Journal of the National Medical Association* Vol. 62, (1970), p. 60, Vol. 76, (1984), p. 934; *Blacks in Science and Medicine* (1990), p. 131

1932 • Mattie E. Coleman (1870-1942) was the first graduate of Meharry's dental hygiene program. One of Tennessee's first African American woman doctors, Coleman was influential during her career not only in her medical practice but also in her social involvement. Coleman studied medicine at Meharry Medical College (Tennessee), graduating in 1903. She then received a second degree, in 1932, from Meharry's dental hygiene program. In 1909, she became the first dean of women and medical advisor at Lane College in Jackson, Tennessee. She was appointed medical examiner of the Court of Calanthe in Tennessee, where she served for 20 years and was the first African American woman physician to serve as a state tuberculosis advisor and counselor in 1922. From 1939 until her death in 1942, Coleman headed the State Vocational School for girls in Nashville. She was also active in church affairs and in women's suffrage concerns.

Notable Black American Women Book II (1996), pp. 125-129

1933 • Chester W. Chinn (1899-1978) was the first African American ophthalmologist certified by the American Board of Ophthalmology in 1933. Chinn received a M.D. in 1925 from the University of Michigan. He completed his internship at Howard University Medical College and then returned to Michigan, completing ophthalmologic training as well as training in ear, nose, and throat. Chinn set up practice in New York City and was a consultant and the director of ophthalmology at Sydenham Hospital. He was also certified by the American Board of Otolaryngology in 1937 and was a fellow of the American College of Surgeons.

A Century of Black Surgeons (1987), pp. 500-502; *African-American Medical Pioneers* (1994), pp. 29, 185

1933 • N. Louise Young, in 1933, became the first African American woman physician to practice in the state of Maryland. Young received her M.D. in 1930 from Howard University Medical College. After interning and completing a residency at Freedmen's Hospital in Washington, D.C., she joined the staff of the Maryland Training School for Girls in 1933, where she served until 1940. Young was a visiting physician, assistant chief, and then acting chief of obstetrics at Baltimore's Provident Hospital. She also had a private practice in obstetrics and gynecology in Baltimore.

Encyclopedia of Black America (1981), p. 873

1933 • The first public venereal disease clinic in the United States was established in 1933 by African American physician David Wellington Byrd (1868-1945). His clinic was an approved clinic with ties to the U.S. Marine Hospital at Norfolk, Virginia. Byrd was also a special consultant to the U.S. Public Health Service in 1938.

Journal of National Medical Association (1916), p. 190-191, Vol. 37, (1945), p. 206; *Who's Who in Colored America* (1941-1944), p. 97; *Blacks in Science and Medicine* (1990), p. 44

1935 • Lucy Oxley, in 1935, was the first African American to receive a M.D. from the University of Cincinnati College of Medicine. Oxley had previously completed her undergraduate work at the University of Cincinnati. The first African American man to earn the M.D. from the University of Cincinnati was Emmett Campbell (1927-), who received the degree in 1953. He earned a B.S. from the University of Dayton in 1948. Campbell was the assistant director, Temporal Bone Laboratory, of the New York Eye and Ear Infirmary and a consultant to the Cleft Palate Clinic of the North Shore University Hospital.

African-American Medical Pioneers (1994), p. 148; *Who's Who Among Black Americans* (1990-1991), p. 970, 203

1935 • The first African American certified by the American Board of Obstetrics and Gynecology in both obstetrics and gynecology was Julian Waldo Ross (1884-1961) in 1935. Ross earned a B.A. at Lincoln in 1907 and a M.D. at Howard University in 1911. He was head of the department of obstetrics and gynecology at Howard University College of Medicine and taught a total of 44 years at Howard.

A Century of Black Surgeons (1987), p. 487; *Jet* (April 20, 1961), p. 50; *Journal of the National Medical Association* Vol. 48, (1956), p. 430, Vol. 52, (1960), pp. 220-222

1935 • William E. Allen Jr. (1903-1982), when certified in roentgenology in 1935 by the American Board of Radiology, became the first African American radiologist certified in the field. He earned a B.S. at Howard University in 1927 and then a M.D. in 1930 from the same institution. Allen volunteered for active military service in the U. S. Army and was the first African American radiologist in the country, in 1939, to do so. Most of his military service was at the Ninth Service Command Regional Hospital at Fort Huachuca, Arizona where he primarily trained medical officers in roentgenology and remained in the service until 1945. Allen became the Medical Director of the Radiology Department of the Homer G. Phillips Hospital (St. Louis) in 1945 and served in that position until 1973. He was also, in 1940, the first African American accepted into the American College of Radiology (ACR) and became in 1945 the first African American fellow of the ACR. He was a pioneer provider of approved training opportunities for African Americans in radiology.

African-American Medical Pioneers (1994), pp. 29, 169; *Blacks in Science and Medicine* (1990), pp. 8-9; *A Centennial History of African Americans in Radiology* (1996), pp. 9-10, 11-13, 26-27

1936 • The first African American physician elected a diplomate of the American Board of Urology was Richard Francis Jones (1904-1979), when he was certified on December 6, 1936. Jones received his B.S. and M.D., in 1922, both from Howard University. Jones was appointed clinical assistant professor in urology at Howard University College of Medicine in 1937 and instituted a urology training program, which he continued to develop through 1947. Jones was appointed clinical associate professor in 1942 and clinical professor in 1945. He was named professor in 1945 and then medical director at Freedmen's Hospital in 1958. Jones also published a number of professional journal articles. Jones, in 1939, began one-stage suprapubic prostactectomies as a routine and was the first American urologist to report the procedure. He also pioneered the therapeutic utility of the antibiotic Terramycin in 1950. Jones also received appointments by Presidents Kennedy, Johnson, and Nixon.

A Century of Black Surgeons (1987), pp. 516-520; *African-American Medical Pioneers* (1994), pp. 29, 30, 172; *Journal of the National Medical Association* Vol. 64, (1972), pp. 276-279, Vol. 71, (1979), p. 908

1937 • The first African American member of the University of Illinois Medical School faculty was Roosevelt Brooks (1902-1985), who was appointed in 1937. Brooks received his M.D. in 1930 from Illinois. He was certified by the American Board of Ophthalmology and became a fellow of that organization.

African American Medical Pioneers (1994), p. 184; *Blacks in Science and Medicine* (1990), p. 38; *A Century of Black Surgeons* (1987), p. 502

1937 • Jesse Jerome Peters (1895-1966) was the first African American radiologist certified by the American Board of Radiology in 1937. Peters earned a M.D. in 1920 from Indiana University School of Medicine. He initially practiced medicine in St. Louis and joined the Tuskegee Veterans Administration Hospital in 1926, where he remained until 1958. He also became associated with Tuskegee's John A. Andrew Hospital in 1926, becoming the first African American radiologist there. Peters was a diplomate of the Pan American Medical Association and also published in a number of medical journals.

African-American Medical Pioneers (1994), pp. 30, 194; *A Centennial History of African Americans in Radiology* (1996), pp. 35, 41, 92; *The Story of Kappa Alpha Psi* (1967), p. 387; *Journal of the National Medical Association* Vol. 51, (1957), pp. 67-68

1938 • Frederick Douglass Stubbs (1906-1947) became the first African American thoracic surgeon in 1938. He received a M.D. from Harvard Medical School in 1931, *cum laude*, and although he lived only 41 years, established a reputation as one of the finest surgeons of his time. Stubbs received an A.B. from Dartmouth College, *magna cum laude*, in 1927. He was the first African American elected to the Harvard Chapter of Alpha Omega Alpha Honor Medical Society in the same year he received his M.D. Stubbs was the first African American to intern (1931-2) and to complete a thoracic fellowship (1932-3) at Cleveland City Hospital. He then did a residency of one year in surgery at Douglass Memorial Hospital in Philadelphia and remained there until 1937. Then he undertook one year training in thoracic surgery at Sea View Hospital in New York City, earning his the honor of being the first African American thoracic surgeon. Stubbs was an outstanding trainer of young African American surgeons, was certified by the American Board of Surgery in 1943, and gained fellowship status in the American College of Surgeons in 1946.

A Century of Black Surgeons (1987), pp. 529-557; *Journal of the National Medical Association* Vol. 40, (1948), pp. 24-26

1938 • William H. Sinkler (1906-1960) who received his M.D. in 1932 from Howard University, was the first African American, in 1938, appointed consultant in chest surgery at Koch Hospital in St. Louis. After completing an internship and then a two-year residency, he set up a private practice in St. Louis. Sinkler was appointed medical director of Homer G. Phillips Hospital in St. Louis in 1941, where he remained until he died in 1960. He was also, in 1956, appointed director of surgery at Homer G. Phillips. Sinkler was the first African American surgeon appointed to the surgical service and faculty of Washington University Medical School. Sinkler was also the first African American to operate at Cardinal Glennon Children's Hospital, Barnes Hospital of Washington University, and St. Louis' Jewish Hospital.

Blacks in Science and Medicine (1990), pp. 213-214; *A Century of Black Surgeons* (1987), pp. 251-264; *Journal of the National Medical Association* Vol. 52, (November 1960), p. 455

1938 • Paul Timothy Robinson (1898-1966) founded and edited the *Journal of New Orleans Medical, Dental and Pharmaceutical Association* in 1938. Robinson earned a B.A. in 1921 from Bishop College and a M.D. in 1931 from Meharry Medical College. He completed a three-year residency at Flint-Goodridge Hospital from 1932 to 1935 in pathology and during that period, set up a pathology at Flint-Goodridge. Robinson served on the staff of Flint-Goodridge from 1937 to 1952. He was junior associate in general surgery from 1937 to 1939, then senior associate in surgery until 1952. In 1950, he also founded and was the Medical Director of the Robinson Infirmary and Clinic in New Orleans. Robinson was a member of state and national medical associations and a diplomate of the National Board of Medical Examiners.

African-American Medical Pioneers (1994), p. 181; *Blacks in Science and Medicine* (1990), p. 204; *Journal of the National Medical Association, Volume 58* (July 1966), pp. 321-323

1939 • Roland Boyd Scott (1909-) was one the first two African Americans admitted to the American Academy of Pediatrics in 1939. The clinical and research skills, as well as the mentoring contributions, of Scott are known nationally and internationally, especially his achievements in pediatrics and the study of sickle cell disease. His other achievements include becoming the first African American physician selected for American Pediatric Society membership in 1952, as well as admission to the Society for Pediatric Research the same year. Scott was the second African American, in 1939, to become a diplomate of the American Board of Pediatrics.

African-American Medical Pioneers (1994), pp. 108-110, 133, 174; *Blacks in Science and Medicine* (1990), p. 210; *Black Enterprise* (February 1975), pp. 22-23

1940 • Henry Arthur Callis (1887-1974) was the first African American physician selected a diplomate of the American Board of Internal Medicine when selected in 1940. He earned a B.A. in 1909 at Cornell University and received his M.D. in 1922 from the University of Chicago School of Science, Rush Medical College. Callis worked as a chemist and laboratory technician from 1915 to 1919, a physician from 1923 to 1927, then for three years as a pathologist. He was associate professor of medicine at Howard University for the period 1930 to 1939, when he set up a private practice, which he maintained until his 1963 retirement. Callis was one of the founders of Alpha Phi Alpha Fraternity and a member of several national medical and historical organizations.

African-American Medical Pioneers (1994), p. 30, 185; *Blacks in Science and Medicine* (1990), p. 45; *Ebony* (October 1958), pp. 58, 59; *Journal of the National Medical Association* Vol. 21, (April/June 1929), pp. 64-65, Vol. 67, (July 1975), pp. 333-334

1940 • Clarance H. Payne (1892-1965), an African American surgeon and chest specialist, was one of the first three African American physicians to get the prefix "col.," for "colored," removed behind their names in the American Medical Association Directory. The designation was removed from the 16th edition of the AMA Directory in 1940. The other two physicians were Roscoe Giles and Carl Roberts. Payne received his M.D. in 1920 from the University of Chicago Medical School. He was one of the first two African American physicians appointed to the staff of the Municipal Tuberculosis Sanitarium of Chicago.

African American Medical Pioneers (1994), pp. 33, 194; *Blacks in Science and Medicine* (1990), p. 186; *Jet* (July 22, 1965), p. 24, (January 26, 1987); *Journal of the National Medical Association, Volume 57* (November, 1965), p. 525

CHARLES R. DREW

1940 • The 200-page doctoral thesis "Banked Blood: A Study in Blood Preservation" established the African American physician Charles R. Drew (1904-1950) as a pioneer in blood preservation in 1940. Drew discussed in his thesis the evolution of the blood bank, changes in preservation of blood, and organization and operation of a successful blood bank. His thesis was the guide for setting up blood banks in the United States and Europe. Drew received a B.A. from Amherst College in 1926, received a M.D. and C.M. (master of surgery) from McGill University in 1933, and also received a M.D.Sc. from Columbia University. He supervised the 1940 British blood plasma collection effort and in 1941, was appointed the first American Red Cross Blood Bank Director and Assistant Director of Blood Procurement for the National Research Council in charge of blood use by the United States Army and Navy. He was appointed an examiner by the American Board of Surgery, the first African American to hold the position. Drew was also professor and head, Department of Surgery, of Howard University College of Medicine from 1941 to 1950.

A Century of Black Surgeons (1987), pp. 63-102; *Journal of the National Medical Association* Vol. 71, (September 1979), pp. 893-895, Vol. 85, (October 1993), pp. 780-781; *The Timetables of African-American History* (1995), p. 255

1940 • The first African American graduate of the University of Minnesota Medical School, Minneapolis was Paul Boswell (1905-), who received a M.D. in 1940. Boswell received an A.B. in 1930 from Lincoln University and then a B.S. and M.B. from the University of Minnesota. Boswell was a practicing dermatologist.

African-American Medical Pioneers (1994), p. 151; *Who's Who Among African-Americans* (1998-1999), p. 140

1941 • The first African American dean of Meharry Medical College, Michael J. Bent, was appointed in 1941. Bent received his M.D. from Meharry Medical College in 1921 and studied at Columbia and Harvard Universities. He was initially hired at Meharry as a professor of bacteriology.

African American Medical Pioneers (1994), pp. 25, 28, 178; *Dictionary of Black Culture* (1973), p. 42

1941 • Edward V. Williams (1903-1995) was the first African American to graduate from the University of Kansas Medical School when he received his M.D. in 1941. When Williams entered Kansas Medical School in 1936, African American students were only accepted for a two-year period. However, the Kansas Board of Regents voted, in 1938, that African Americans with the appropriate scholastic standing were eligible to graduate. Williams had completed his undergraduate studies at the University of Kansas. Marjorie Ransome Cates, in 1958, became the first African American woman to earn her M.D. at Kansas State. She also earned her bachelors degree from Kansas State University.

African American Medical Pioneers (1994), p. 150; *Philadelphia Tribune* (March 3, 1995)

1941 • The first medical research presentation by an African American physician at an American Medical Association convention was given in 1941 by Leonidas Harris Berry (1902-). Berry received his B.S. in 1924 from Wilberforce University (Ohio) and then a B.S. in 1925 from the University of Chicago (Illinois). He earned a M.D. in 1929 from Rush Medical School (Illinois) and a M.S. in pathology from the University of Illinois in 1933. Berry was an expert in gastrointestinal surgery, treating patients with stomach diseases and other digestive problems. At the time of his invited AMA presentation, he had examined more patients with the gastroscope (a special device allowing a physician to look into a patient's stomach) in the United States than any other doctor, and had also written more scientific papers on the use of the gastroscope than anyone except his co-worker, Rudolph Schindler. Berry developed the fiberoptic endoscope, a device that can detect cancers not seen by x rays, and was the prime author of the definitive textbook on its use.

Blacks in Science and Medicine (1990), pp. 26-7; *Century of Black Surgeons* (1987), p. 284; *Distinguished African American Scientists of the 20th Century* (1996), pp. 9-12

1942 • Midian Othello Bousfield (1885-1948) was the first African American physician to establish a military hospital for the U. S. Army when he set up the 100-bed Station Hospital Number One at Fort Huachuca, Arizona in 1942. He later became the first African American colonel in the United States Army Medical Corps. Bousfield earned an A.B. at the University of Kansas in 1907 and received a M.D. degree from Northwestern University School of Medicine in 1909. He started a private practice in Chicago in 1914, where he practiced and was active in public affairs. He was a consultant to the U. S. Children's Bureau and to the Chicago Board of Health. Bousfield was also president of the National Medical Association from 1933 to 1934.

African-American Medical Pioneers (1994), p. 184; *Dictionary of American Negro Biography* (1982), pp. 51-52; *Encyclopedia of Black America* (1981), p. 187; *Journal of the National Medical Association* (1948), Vol. 40, p. 120

1942 • The first African American to become a commissioned officer in the U. S. Navy was Bernard W. Robinson (1918-1972) in 1942. He received a M.D. from Harvard University in 1945 and began his medical career, after the service, as a radiologist in the VA hospital system, and became the first African American appointed to the position of chief-of-service in a Chicago-area VA hospital. Robinson passed away in 1972, and his obituary was the first of an African American to appear in the journal *Radiology.*

A Centennial History of African Americans in Radiology (1996), p. 94; *Blacks in Science and Medicine* (1990), p. 203; *Famous First Facts* (1964), p. 407

1942 • The first African-American pharmacist mate to serve in the U. S. Coast Guard was Horace James McMillan (1919-), who served as chief pharmacist mate from 1942 to 1946. McMillan received a B.S. from Prairie View A&M College in 1942 and then, after his Coast Guard duty, entered the University of California at Los Angeles. He earned his M.D. in 1950 and started his private medical practice in 1952 in Santa Barbara. McMillan was vice president of the Santa Barbara Family Medical Center and a staff member of St. Francis, Santa Barbara Cottage, Goleta Valley Community, and Pine Crest Hospitals. He was also a founder of, and from 1967 to 1977 a member of, the board of directors of Goleta Valley Community Hospital. McMillan was also an active member of the Santa Barbara Academy of Family Practice and the National Academy of Family Practice.

Who's Who Among African Americans (1998-1999), p. 1025; *Who's Who Among Black Americans* (1990-1991), p. 869

1943 • Helen Marjorie Peebles-Meyers (1915-) was the first African American woman to graduate from Wayne State University School of Medicine when she received her M.D. in 1943. She received a bachelor's degree in 1937 from Hunter College and a M.A. in 1938 from Columbia University. She completed her internship and residence from 1943 to 1947 and was the first African American woman to do so at Detroit Receiving Hospital. Peebles-Meyers set up a private practice in Detroit, which she maintained from 1947 to 1977. She then became the first African American physician to be the chief medical officer for salaried personnel at the World Headquarters of the Ford Motor Company from 1977 until 1985, when she retired.

African-American Medical Pioneers (1994), pp. 156, 194; *Blacks in Science and Medicine* (1990), p. 187; *Ebony* (December 1986), pp. 68, 70, 72, 74; *Who's Who Among Black Americans* (1985), p. 657

1943 • Guy O. Saulsberry (1909-) was the founder and medical director of Kirkwood General Hospital, in October, 1943, in Detroit, Michigan. Kirkwood had 50 beds at its opening in 1943 and grew to 161 beds, and was the largest African American-owned hospital in Detroit. The hospital's staff grew to 134 medical staff members, had 12 departments, and was the largest employer of African Americans in Detroit at that time. Saulsberry received his M.D. in 1927 from Howard University Medical College (Washington, D.C). He was active in city, state, and national medical associations, and received a number of awards including the Physician of the Year Award, Detroit Medical Society, 1968, and General Practitioner of the Year Award, National Medical Association, 1972

Blacks in Science and Medicine (1990), p. 209; *Ebony* (October, 1950), p. 38; *Journal of the National Medical Association, Volume 61* (September, 1969), pp. 446-448

1943 • The ninth open-heart surgery was performed in 1943 by Myra A. Logan (1908-1977), an African American who became the first woman to perform the procedure. Logan received a B.A. in 1927 from Atlanta University (Georgia) and a M.S. from Columbia University (New York). She earned her M.D. in 1933 from New York Medical College, completing her internship and residency in surgery at Harlem Hospital in New York. An active surgeon and medical researcher, she developed an interest in antibiotic drugs, completing extensive research on aureomycin. Logan also worked in the area of breast cancer, developing a process of slower x-ray procedures that could more accurately detect differences in tissue density, leading to the earlier detection of tumors. She maintained a private practice while performing as a surgeon at both Harlem and Sydenham Hospitals.

African American Medical Pioneers (1994), p. 192; *Blacks in Science and Medicine* (1990), p. 156; *Black Women in America* (1993), p. 731; *Notable Twentieth Century Scientists* (1995), pp. 1267-8

1944 • Eugene Heriot Dibble Jr. (1893-1968) served from 1936 to 1946 as the second African American manager of the Tuskegee (Alabama) Veterans

Administration Hospital. During his tenure there, the managers of all Veterans Administration hospitals were considered as on duty with the U.S. Army, following congressional action resulting in all VA hospital managers being given the rank of colonel. Dibble, in 1944, thus became the first African American medical officer commissioned at this rank. Dibble received a B.A. in 1915 from Atlanta University (Georgia) and the M.D. in 1920 from Howard University (Washington, D.C.). He served as assistant medical director of J.A. Andrew Memorial Hospital from 1920 to 1923, then as chief of surgery at Tuskegee Veterans Hospital from 1924-5, where he later returned as manager and medical director. From 1946 to 1965, Dibble served as medical director of John A. Andrew Memorial Hospital.

African American Medical Pioneers (1994), p. 170; *Blacks in Science and Medicine* (1990), p. 74; *A Century of Black Surgeons* (1987), pp. 346-7; *Journal of the National Medical Association, Vol. 60* (September 1968), p. 446

1944 • The first African American medical officer in the United States Navy was Arthur Lee Thompson, who was appointed in July 1944. Thompson was an instructor at Meharry Medical College when he transferred from the United States Army medical reserve corps to the United States Navy.

National Negro Health News, Vol. 12 (July-September 1944), p. 16; *Washington Afro-American* (July 22, 1944)

1945 • Huerta C. Neals (1914-), an African American cardiologist, was the first African American military officer assigned to a general hospital in Italy during World War II. Neals received his B.S. degree from Morehouse College in 1936 and his M.D. degree from Howard University in 1942. Although in private practice, Neals was an attending physician with the Jersey City Medical Center and a clinical associate professor of internal medicine at the University of Medicine and Dentistry of New Jersey. He received the Liberty Achievement Award from the Liberty Healthcare System, Inc. in 1996, in recognition of his pioneering career of more than 45 years. Neals was active in many state and national professional associations, but is now retired.

Jet (October 14, 1996), p. 22; *Who's Who Among African-Americans* (1998-1999), p. 1111

1945 • Alida Cooley Daily graduated from the Harlem Hospital School of Nursing in 1927 and received a Red Cross scholarship to do postgraduate work at Columbia University. Daily was appointed as the first African American director of nursing and superintendent at Harlem Hospital School of Nursing in 1945 and at the same time, became the first African American woman to hold those positions in any New York municipal institution. Prior, Daily had worked ten years as a public-health nurse in Montclair, New Jersey and was an administrator for five years before becoming the director at Harlem School.

Black Women in White (1989), p. 45

1945 • The first school of veterinary medicine located at an African American educational institution was established in 1945 at Tuskegee Institute by Frederick Douglas Patterson (1901-1988). Patterson joined the Tuskegee Institute faculty in 1928 and remained there for 30 years. Patterson received a B.A. in 1919 from Prairie View College, a D.V.M. and M.S. from Iowa State College in 1923 and 1927 respectively, and then in 1932, he received a Ph.D. in veterinary medicine from Cornell University. Patterson taught from 1923 to 1928 at Virginia State College before joining Tuskegee in 1928, where he started as an instructor then became head of the veterinary division. He became director of the school of agriculture before being appointed President. Patterson, in 1943, was also the founder of the United Negro College Fund.

FREDERICK D. PATTERSON

Blacks in Science and Medicine (1990), p. 186; *Ebony* (November 1985), p. 72; *Encyclopedia of Black America* (1981), p. 665

1945 • Joseph G. Gathings (1898-1965) was the first African American, in 1945, to be certified in dermatology and syphilology. Gathings received his M.D. in 1928 from Howard University College of Medicine. He maintained a private practice in Washington, D.C., and from 1946 to 1965, was a member of the clinical faculty in dermatology and syphilology at Howard University Medical College. Gathings was an active member of a number of professional organizations. He was a Rosenwald fellow, a diplomate of the American Board of Dermatology and Syphilology, and a fellow of the American Academy of Dermatology and Syphilology.

African-American Medical Pioneers (1994), p. 171; *Blacks in Science and Medicine* (1990), p. 99; *Journal of the National Medical Association, Volume 57* (September 1965), pp. 427-428, Volume 85, (August 1993), p. 641

1946 • Leonidas H. Berry (1902-1995) was the first African American physician on staff at Michael Reese Hospital and Medical Center when he was appointed in 1946. By that time, Berry had become of the first African American physicians to specialize in the area of digestive disorders and endoscopy, eventually becoming recognized as an international expert. He received his B.S. from Wilberforce College (Ohio) in 1924 and then earned a M.D. from the University of Chicago (Illinois) in 1929 and an M.S. (in pathology) from the University of Illinois in 1933. He was an international authority on digestive diseases and endoscopy (the visual examination of the digestive tract through a long fiberoptic scope). He was the first doctor to perform gastroscopics (operation involving instruments with which doctors can view the digestive tract) at several Chicago Hospitals in the 1930s and 1940s. Berry also invented the gastrobiphyscope. He was a Diplomate of the American Board of Internal Medicine and Gastroenterolgy and the first African American internist at Cook County Hospital. He also served as a mentor, training hundreds of physicians.

Blacks in Science and Medicine (1990), pp. 26-27; *Blacks in Science: Astrophysicist to Zoologist* (1977), p. 30; *Journal of the National Medical Association* Vol. 56, (November, 1964), pp. 538-539

1946 • The first African American to join the staff of Newark (New Jersey) City Hospital was E. Mae McCarroll (1898-19??), appointed in 1946. She also in 1953 became the first deputy health officer in Newark. McCarroll earned a B.A. in 1917 from Talladega College (Alabama), and her M.D. in 1925 from the Medical College of Pennsylvania. She was primarily concerned with the field of public health and was an active leader in local, state, and national medical associations.

African American Medical Pioneers (1994), p. 193; *Blacks in Science and Medicine* (1990), p. 168; *Journal of the National Medical Association, Vol. 65* (November 1973), pp. 544-5

1946 • John E. Moseley (1909-1996) was the first African American radiologist to become a member of the Society for Pediatric Radiology when he was elected in 1946. Moseley received his M.D. from the University of Chicago in 1936 and completed residencies in radiology at Bellevue Hospital and Mt. Sinai Hospital of New York. He joined the staff of Mt. Sinai hospital in 1944 as an assistant radiologist in diagnosis, culminating a 35-year career as Emeritus Associate Professor in the Mt. Sinai Medical School. Also during that period, Moseley became director of the radiology department of Sydenham Hospital. Moseley retired in 1980 and then served as medical director of the Washington Heights Medical Group until 1989.

A Centennial History of African Americans in Radiology (1996), pp. 14, 137-141; *Negro Year Book* (1952), p. 371; *New York Times* (November 29, 1996), p. B19

1947 • Clotilde Dent Bowen (1923-) received her B.A. from Ohio State University in 1943, and in 1947, became the first African American woman to receive a M.D. from Ohio State University Medical School. Bowen interned at Harlem Hospital (1947-8) and also completed a residency (1948-9) there. She did a residency in psychiatry at Albany Veterans Administration Hospital from 1959 to 1962. In her military career, Bowen, in 1965, became a lieutenant colonel and, in 1968, became a medical colonel in the U.S. Army. She practiced psychiatry during her military career at various installations, including Tripler Hospital, Vietnam, Fitzsimons Army Medical Center, Ft.

Benjamin Harrison, and VA medical centers in Cheyenne and Denver. She is currently staff psychiatrist with the Veterans Affairs Medical Center in Denver. Bowen has contributed numerous publications to the scientific literature.

African American Medical Pioneers (1994), pp. 153, 184; *Blacks in Science and Medicine* (1990), p. 33; *Ebony* (December, 1968), pp. 100-101, 104, 106, 108; *Who's Who Among African Americans* (1998-1999), p. 141

1947 • J. Edmond Bryant (1901-1955) was the first African American selected to become a member of the American College of Chest Physicians in 1947. Edmonds was a 1923 graduate of Jamestown College and earned a M.S. degree in 1930 from the University of North Dakota in physiology. He received, in 1937, the M.D. degree from Howard University and interned at Chicago's Provident Hospital. Bryant was head of the Science Department at Paine College from 1928 to 1929 and also taught physiology at Howard University Medical College from 1930 to 1934. He was active in local and national medical associations and served on the editorial board of the *Journal of the National Medical Association*.

Blacks in Science and Medicine (1990), p. 41; *Journal of the National Medical Association, Volume 48* (1956), pp. 137-139

1947 • The first African American certified by the American Board of Physical Medicine and Rehabilitation was Harvey F. Davis (1896-19??) in 1947. Davis earned his undergraduate degree in 1918 from Howard University and then received his M.D. in 1923 from Boston University School of Medicine.

African-American Medical Pioneers (1994), p. 186

1948 • Margaret Morgan Lawrence (1914-) was the first African American student in psychoanalytic training admitted to the Columbia Psychoanalytic Center, in 1948. Lawrence graduated from Cornell University in 1936 with a B.A., and then earned a M.D. from Columbia University in 1940, followed by a two-year pediatric internship at Harlem Hospital. She taught pediatrics and public health at Meharry Medical College from 1943 to 1947 and received her Certificate in Psychoanalytic Medicine in 1951. Lawrence worked for many years in the mental health field from 1951 to 1984. She was associate clinical professor of psychiatry from 1963 to 1984 at Columbia University's College of Physicians and Surgeons and for the same period was supervising child psychiatrist and psychoanalyst at Harlem Hospital Center. Lawrence also maintained a private practice.

Black Women in America (1993), p. 927; *Blacks in Science and Medicine* (1990), p. 148; *Notable Black American Women* (1992), pp. 658-660; *Who's Who Among African Americans* (1998-1999), pp. 897-898

1948 • The first African American physician appointed to the West Virginia State Board of Health was Peyton Randolph Higginbotham (1902-19??) when he received the appointment in 1948. Higginbotham received his B.S. in 1923 and M.D. in 1926 from Howard University. He served as college physician for women at Bluefield State College from 1934 and as a public health clinician for Mercer County (West Virginia) from 1937.

African-American Medical Pioneers (1994), p. 172; *Blacks in Science and Medicine* (1990), p. 118; *Who's Who Among Black Americans* (1985), p. 385

1948 • Walter Anderson Adams (1900-1959) was the first African American psychiatrist appointed chief of the Provident Hospital (Chicago) Medical Counseling Clinic for Narcotic Addicts in 1948. Anderson earned a M.D. from Howard University Medical College in 1926. He completed a residency at Boston Psychopathic Hospital and did postgraduate work at the Chicago Institute for Psychoanalysis and was licensed in both the District of Columbia and state of Illinois. Adams was consulting psychiatrist for the Chicago Welfare Department from 1948 to 1955.

Blacks in Science and Medicine (1990), p. 3; *Jet* (March 19, 1959), p. 29

1948 • Walter Scott Brown (1906-1985) established, in 1948, the first outpatient surgical facility in the United States. Brown's clinic, located in Seattle, Washington, was the model for and was toured by plastic surgeons for several years. Brown received a bachelors degree from Talladega College, and in 1931, earned his M.D. from the University of Illinois School of Medicine. Brown established a plastic surgery practice in Seattle in 1946 and in the same year performed the first dermabrasion procedure for acne in the Northwest. Brown was the first plastic surgeon in King County to surgically correct bedsores by covering them with a full flap of skin. Brown also directed the first free outpatient plastic surgery clinic at Harborview Hospital, now a part of the University of Washington School of Medicine.

A Century of Black Surgeons (1987), pp. 615-623

1948 • The antibiotic aeromycin was first used to treat humans in 1948 by the African-American physician Louis Tompkins Wright (1891-1952). Wright was also the first physician to introduce the intradermal method of smallpox vaccination in 1918. Wright received his M.D. in 1915, *cum laude,* from Harvard University (Massachusetts). He had an amazing career as a physician, surgeon, scientific researcher, and educator. Wright was a pioneer in varied aspects of medicine, and was associated with New York's Harlem Hospital for most of his professional life. He formed the Harlem Surgical Society in 1937 and the Harlem Hospital Bulletin in 1948. Wright, as a function of his cancer research activities, also established the Harlem Hospital Cancer Research Foundation in 1948 and was also a founder-member of the American Academy of Compensation Medicine. In 1949, he was made medical advisor to the Director of Selective Service for New York City. Wright also received numerous awards and honors and held memberships in local, regional, and national medical associations.

Blacks in Science and Medicine (1990), p. 259; *Journal of the National Medical Association, Volume 45* (March, 1953), pp. 130-148; *Century of Black Surgeons* (1987), pp. 160-171; *Dictionary of American Negro Biography* (1982), p. 670-671

LOUIS TOMPKINS
WRIGHT

1949 • The first African American physician certified by the American Board of Orthopaedic Surgery was J. Robert Gladden (1911-1969) in 1949. He was the first African American elected to fellowship in the American Academy of Orthopaedic Surgeons in 1951. Gladden received a bachelors degree from Long Island University and a M.D. in 1938 *magna cum laude* from Meharry Medical College. He completed his internship at Freedmen's Hospital and became the first resident in Freedmen's orthopedic residency program. Gladden became a member of the Howard University College of Medicine staff in 1945, became chief of the Division of Orthopaedic Surgery in 1950, and held that position until 1964.

A Century of Black Surgeons (1987), pp. 502-504; *African-American Medical Pioneers* (1994), pp. 30, 179

1949 • James Richard Laurey (1907-1964), professor of thoracic surgery at Howard University College of Medicine and chief of the Division of Thoracic Surgery at Freedmen's Hospital, was the only African American member of the Founder's Group of the American Board of Thoracic Surgery when the group was established in 1949. Laurey received an A.B. in 1929, a M.B. in 1932, and a M.D. in 1933, all from Wayne State University (Michigan). He interned at Chicago's Provident Hospital and completed an additional year as senior assistant in surgery there. Laurey joined the Howard University medical faculty in 1935, attained the rank of full professor in 1947, became chief of thoracic surgery in 1950, and held the post of Chairman of the Department of Surgery until 1955. He became a diplomate of the American Board of Surgery in 1942 and was a member of the American Association for Thoracic Surgery.

African-American Medical Pioneers (1994), pp. 30, 192; *A Century of Black Surgeons* (1987), pp. 513-515; *Journal of the National Medical Association* Vol. 56, (1964), pp. 548-550

1949 • The first African American physician selected a member of the Missouri State Medical Society, in 1949, was William D. Morman (1901-1951). Morman received a B.S. in 1925 from Morehouse College and then earned a M.D. in 1929 from Howard University College of Medicine. He was also one of the first two African Americans, in 1949, (with Walter A. Younge) selected members of the St. Louis Medical Society. Morman was a diplomate of the American Board of Otolaryngology (1940), a fellow of the American Academy of Otology, Rhinology and Laryngology (1941), and the American College of Surgeons (1948).

African-American Medical Pioneers (1994), pp. 30, 173; *Blacks in Science and Medicine* (1990), pp. 176-177; *Journal of the National Medical Association* Vol. 44, (January 1952), pp. 70-73

1949 • The first African American physician appointed to the medical staff of Boston City Hospital was Charles D. Bonner (1917-1990) in 1949. Bonner was later appointed medical director of Cambridge's Youville Hospital. He was elected president of the Massachusetts Heart Association in 1979. Bonner developed an expertise in stroke victim rehabilitation for which he was nationally known.

African-Americans in Boston (1991), pp. 146-147

1949 • The first four African American doctors who integrated the medical staff at Washington University School of Medicine (St. Louis, Missouri) in 1949 included Helen E. Nash (1921-), a pediatrician. Nash graduated from Spelman College, received her M.D. from Meharry Medical College, and completed a rotating internship at Homer G. Phillips Hospital in St. Louis. Nash developed a thriving pediatric practice and is active in child advocacy, with a particular interest in reducing rates of infant mortality.

Black Women in America (1993), pp. 836-838

WILLIAM AUGUSTUS
HINTON

1949 • Harvard University appointed its first African American professor when William A. Hinton (1883-1959) was appointed clinical professor of bacteriology and immunology in 1949. Long one of the world's authorities on venereal diseases and rabies, Hinton was the first to develop a reliable method for detecting syphilis, in 1927, which is known as the Hinton Test. He also collaborated with Dr. J.A.V. Davies in the development of the Davies-Hinton Test also utilized in the detection of syphilis. Hinton received his B.S. in 1905 and his M.D. in 1912, both from Harvard University. He started teaching at Harvard in 1918 as an instructor in preventive medicine and continued teaching there until his 1950 retirement. Hinton published the text, *Syphilis and Its Treatment,* a first and classic medical text on the subject authored by an African American.

Hinton was also the director of the famous Wassermann laboratory from 1915 to 1953.

Blacks in Science and Medicine (1990), pp. 121-122; *Dictionary of American Negro Biography* (1982), pp. 315-316; *Harvard University Gazette* (July 16, 1960), pp. 243-244; *Journal of the National Medical Association* Vol. 49, (1957), pp. 427-429

1950 • Ethel L. Nixon was the first African American appointed assistant psychiatrist in the outpatient department of Johns Hopkins University Hospital in 1950. Nixon was also a recipient of the Commonwealth Fellowship in psychiatry from Johns Hopkins University.

Negro Year Book (1952), p. 372

1950 • Charles D. Watts, who received an undergraduate degree from Morehouse College and his M.D. from Howard University School of Medicine, was the first African American surgeon in North Carolina certified by any surgical specialty board in 1950. He completed an internship and surgical residency at Washington's Freedmen's Hospital and was a member of the Howard University medical school faculty until 1950, when he went to Durham, North Carolina to practice surgery. He was selected a diplomate of the American Board of Surgery in 1950 and a fellow in the American College of Surgeons in 1956. Watts was on the staff of Durham County General Hospital and was an adjunct associate clinical professor at the Duke Medical Center.

A Century of Black Surgeons (1987), pp. 440, 441-442; *Negro Year Book* (1952), p. 372

1950 • Edward Estes Holloway (1909-1993), a cardiologist who received his M.D. in 1935 from Howard University College of Medicine, was the first African American elected a Fellow of the American College of Physicians in 1950. He also was the first African American certified by the American Board of Cardiovascular Diseases in 1955. He had previously been certified as a diplomate of the American Board of Internal Medicine in 1946. Holloway taught several years at the Medical College of Pennsylvania. He was an assistant chief at Philadelphia General Hospital, where he also taught students, interns, and residents. Holloway was the last chief of medicine at the former Frederick Douglass Hospital and the only chief of medicine at Mercy-Douglass Hospital.

Philadelphia Tribune (April 13, 1993), p. 5D

1950 • Hilda G. Straker, in 1950, was the first African American woman physician certified by the American Board of Dermatology and Syphilology.

Straker was also the first African American dermatologist to become a member of the mid-Manhattan Postgraduate Hospital.

Negro Year Book (1952), p. 372

1950 • Helen Octavia Dickens (1909-), who received her M.D. from the University of Illinois in 1934, was the first African American woman admitted to the American College of Surgeons in 1950. Dickens completed an obstetrical residency at Chicago's Provident Hospital. Settling in Philadelphia, she became a staff member and eventually chief of obstetrics and gynecology at Mercy-Douglass Hospital and an associate clinical professor at the Medical College of Pennsylvania. She was certified by the American Board of Obstetrics and Gynecology in 1946. She started as an instructor in obstetrics and gynecology at the University of Pennsylvania and was eventually promoted to full professor. Dickens was later appointed associate dean for minorities at the University of Pennsylvania School of Medicine. Dickens was also president of the Pan American Women's Alliance from 1970 to 1973.

Black Women in America (1993), pp. 335-336; *Blacks in Science and Medicine* (1990), p. 74; *Ebony* (April 1951), p. 5; *Who's Who Among Black Americans* (1985), p. 224

1950 • The first African American urologist to practice in the state of Virginia, in 1950, was Silas Odell Binns (1920-). Binns received his B.S. in 1942 from Virginia Union and M.D. from Howard University in 1945. From 1945 to 1949, he undertook his internship and residencies in urology at Homer G. Phillips Hospital. Binns later maintained a private practice in urology.

Who's Who Among Black Americans (1990-1991), p. 100

1950 • The first Rockefeller Fellow in Surgery, appointed in 1941 at the Strong Memorial Hospital of the University of Rochester, was African American physician Burke Syphax (1910-). He received his B.S. in 1932 and a M.D. in 1936 from Howard University. Syphax completed a residency in general surgery at Howard from 1937 to 1940 and became a surgical assistant until 1941. He also was certified by the American Board of Surgery in 1943, one of the first African Americans certified by that board. Howard University Medical College appointed Syphax its first chief of general surgery in 1950, and in 1957, he became the acting head of surgery. He became professor and head of the department from 1958 to 1970. Howard University awarded its first Department of Surgery Distinguished Surgeon's Award to Syphax in 1974, and in 1985, Howard awarded him with an honorary doctor of science degree.

A Century of Black Surgeons (1987), pp. 636-639; *African-American Medical Pioneers* (1994), pp. 56, 116-118, 134, 175; *Journal of the National Medical Association* Vol. 70, (1978), p. 605, Vol. 85, (October 1993), p. 793

1951 • An eminent researcher in cardiovascular physiology, Edward William Hawthorne (1921-1986) was the first African American to earn a Ph.D. in physiology from the University of Illinois, which he received in 1951. He earned a B.S. in 1941 and a M.D. in 1946 from Howard University, as well as a M.S. from the University of Illinois. He completed an internship and residency at Freedmen's Hospital in Washington, D.C. from 1946 to 1948. Hawthorne served as head of the physiology department at Howard University Medical College from 1951 to 1969, became assistant dean in 1962, and was named associate dean in 1967. In 1971, Hawthorne became vice-president at-large of the American Heart Association.

African-American Medical Pioneers (1994), p. 172; *Ebony* (February 1966), pp. 73-76, 78, 80, (August 1972), p. 124; *Encyclopedia of Black America* (1981), pp. 423-424

1951 • Mildred Fay Jefferson (1925-), who received a B.A. from Texas College and a M.S. from Tufts College, was the first African American woman to earn a M.D. from Harvard Medical School, which she received in 1951.

African-American Medical Pioneers (1994), p. 149; *African-Americans in Boston* (1991), p. 148; *Blacks in Science and Medicine* (1990), p. 132; *Who's Who Among Black Americans* (1985), p. 438

1951 • Hughenna L. Gauntlett was the first African American woman to earn a M.D. from Loma Linda University School of Medicine when she received the degree in 1951. Gauntlett completed her internship at New York's Mount Sinai Hospital in 1951 and then practiced in Los Angeles with an emphasis on obstetrics and gynecology until 1960, when she took a year of postgraduate courses in physiology, pathology, pharmacology, and anatomy. She then undertook surgical training at California Hospital in Los Angeles, completed training in general surgery at Kaiser Sunset, and continued to practice surgery in Los Angeles. Gauntlett became vice-chair and chair of the Department of Surgery at California Hospital. She became the first African American woman to become certified by the American Board of Surgery in 1968.

African-American Medical Pioneers (1994), pp. 150, 188; *A Century of Black Surgeons* (1987), pp. 593-597, 608

1951 • Howard Marshall Payne (1907-1961), physician and pathologist, was the first African American elected vice-president of the National Tuberculosis Association and served in the position from 1951 to 1952. Payne received a B.A. in 1928 from Dartmouth College and a M.D. in 1931 from Howard University Medical College. He was a member of the medical faculty at Harvard University from 1937 to 1953 and was Tuberculosis Specialist and Superintendent from 1958 to 1961 of the Middlesex County Sanitarium in Waltham, Massachusetts.

African-American Medical Pioneers (1994), pp. 34, 174; *Blacks in Science and Medicine* (1990), pp. 186-187; *Jet* (September 28, 1961), p. 54; *Journal of the National Medical Association* Vol. 53, (November 1961), pp. 653-655

1951 • The first African American physician trained in the United States as a surgical oncologist was Jack E. White (1921-1988) who finished a cancer fellowship at Memorial Hospital for Cancer and Allied Diseases in 1951. White received his M.D. from Howard University College of Medicine in 1944. He joined the Howard Faculty in 1951 as an assistant professor and was the driving force in upgrading the instruction in cancer treatment in the medical school. White also performed a number of cancer operations for the first time at Freedmen's Hospital, including radical neck dissection, pelvic exenteration, and hemipelvectomy. White was the first chairman of the department of oncology at Howard (1974-85) and also was named director of the Howard Cancer Research Center of Freedmen's Hospital in 1972.

A Century of Black Surgeons (1987), p. 42; *Blacks in Science and Medicine* (1990), pp. 247-248; *Ebony* (April 1978), p. 129; *Journal of the National Medical Association* Vol. 73, (1981), pp. 67-69

1951 • Marie Metoyer, in 1951, was the first African American woman to earn a M.D. from Cornell University. Metoyer completed her undergraduate education at Fordham University. Thirty-six years prior, the first M.D. awarded by Cornell was earned by Roscoe Conkling Giles in 1915, who had also completed undergraduate work at Cornell University. Giles became a diplomat of the American Board of Surgery and was one of the first four African American members of the American College of Surgeons.

African-American Medical Pioneers (1994), p. 148; *Journal of the National Medical Association, Volume 62* (1970), pp. 254-256

1952 • The first full-time African American member of the University of Michigan faculty was Albert Harold Wheeler (1915-) when appointed in 1952. Wheeler was a public health specialist who received a B.A. in 1936 from Lincoln University, a M.S. in 1937 from Iowa State College, and a M.S.P.H. in 1938 and a Ph.D. in 1944, both from the University of Michigan. Wheeler was a clinical technician at Howard University College of Medicine from 1938 to 1940 and a research associate from 1944 to 1952, when he became assistant professor of bacteriology at the University of Michigan. He was associate professor, then professor, in the Department of Microbiology and Immunology starting in 1959. Wheeler subsequently ran for mayor of Ann Arbor, Michigan, and served from 1975 to 1978.

Blacks in Science and Medicine (1990), pp. 246-247; *Who's Who Among Black Americans* (1985), p. 882; *Who's Who Among Black Americans* (1990-1991), p. 1334

1952 • Calvin C. Sampson (1928-), after receiving his M.D. from Meharry Medical School in 1951 and interning one year at Philadelphia's Mercy-Douglass Hospital became, in 1952, the first African American resident at Philadelphia's Episcopal Hospital. Sampson completed his residency in 1957 and became one of the first African Americans certified in clinical pathology. He joined Howard University in 1958 as director of laboratories and hospital pathologist at Freedmen's Hospital. Howard University Medical College named Sampson the first pathologist director of Howard's new Department of Medical Technology in 1963. In 1971, he became the first acting chairman of the newly established Department of Allied Health Professions. Sampson became a full professor and vice-chairman of the pathology department and retired in 1990. He was not only a medical administrator and clinician but an outstanding researcher, having contributed over 100 publications to the scientific literature.

African-American Medical Pioneers (1994), pp. 26, 34, 105-108, 133; *Journal of the National Medical Association* Vol. 73, (1981), p. 1235, Vol. 85, (October 1993), p. 791; *Who's Who Among African Americans* (1998-1999), p. 1313

1952 • De Haven Hinkson (1891-19??) was the first African American, along with Edward Holloway, elected to membership into the Philadelphia College Surgeons in 1952. Hinkson received his M.D. in 1915 from the Medico-Chirurgical College of Philadelphia (Pennsylvania). He was a staff member of Philadelphia General Hospital, where he played a key role in the implementation and development of the surgery teaching program. After being discharged from the U.S. Army in 1919, Hinkson set up practice in Philadelphia until 1932, when he received a Barnes Foundation Fellowship for advanced training in gynecology and endocrinology at the Faculties of Medicine in Paris. He returned to Philadelphia to practice until he returned to military duty from 1941 to 1945. He then served in the gynecologic departments of both Douglas Hospital and Mercy Hospital until their merger as Mercy-Douglas Hospital, where he continued until 1967, when he was granted staff emeritus status.

Blacks in Science and Medicine (1990), p. 121; *A Century of Black Surgeons* (1987), p. 447; *Journal of the National Medical Association*, Vol. 66 (July, 1974), pp. 339-342

1953 • The first African American appointed to the staff of a Louisville (Kentucky) hospital was Grace Marilyn James (1923-), who was appointed instructor in child health in 1953 at the University of Louisville School of Medicine. James, a pediatrician, served at the Louisville University School of Medicine until 1962. She received a B.A. in 1944 from West Virginia State College and her M.D. from Meharry Medical College (Tennessee) in 1950. James was a public health physician from 1962-3. She served from 1966-7 as director of diagnostic and evaluation services for the Division of Mental Retardation in Frankfort, Kentucky, and from 1968 to 1983 served on the staff of Kentucky Kosair Crippled Children's Hospital. James was an active leader in many medical associations and was a fellow of the American Academy of Pediatrics.

Blacks in Science and Medicine (1990), p. 131; *Ebony* (February 1955), p. 4; *Who's Who Among Black Americans* (1955), p. 4

1953–1958 • W. Lester Henry Jr. (1915-), internist and endocrinologist, was the first African American John and Mary Markle Scholar in medical science from 1953 to 1958. Henry earned an A.B. from Temple University in 1936 and a M.D. in 1941 from Howard University College of Medicine and, during his medical career, achieved a number of African American firsts. He was the first African American governor of the American Board of Internal Medicine (1971-8), first African American member of the Residency Review Committee in Internal Medicine (1971-8), first African American representative from the American Board of Internal Medicine to the American Board of Medical Specialties (1974-8), first African American regent of the American College of Physicians (1974-80), and the first African American master of the American College of Physicians (1987). Henry had been associated with Howard University as assistant, associate, and full professor and department of medicine chairman from 1953 to 1988.

African-American Medical Pioneers (1994), pp. 68-71, 97, 132, 168; *Blacks in Science and Medicine* (1990), p. 117; *Journal of the National Medical Association* Vol. 54, (July 1962), pp. 494-495, Vol. 85, (October 1993), pp. 784-785

1953 • Emmett Earle Campbell (1927-), in 1953, was the first African American man to receive a M.D. from the University of Cincinnati College of Medicine. Campbell is a Fellow of the American College of Surgeons (1969) and the American Academy of Ophthalmology and Otolaryngology (1966), as well as a diplomate of the American Board of Otolaryngology (1966). He was the assistant director of the Temporal Bone Laboratory of the New York Eye and Ear Infirmary before becoming consultant to the Cleft Palate Clinic N. Shore University Hospital in New York.

African-American Medical Pioneers (1994), p. 148; *Who's Who Among African Americans* (1998-1999), p. 232

1953 • The first African American to receive a M.D. from the University of Texas Medical School at Galveston was Herman Aladdin Barnett (1926-1973) who received the degree in 1953. He received a B.S., with honors, from Huston Tillotson College in 1949. Barnett was inducted into the U. S. Army Air Corps and became a pilot in World War II. After his military service, he entered private practice in surgery and after several successful years, completed a residence in anesthesiology and started a practice. Barnett died while flying his own aircraft in 1973 at the age of 47.

A Century of Black Surgeons (1987), pp. 613-615; *African-American Medical Pioneers* (1994), p. 155

1953 • Clarence Sumner Greene (1901-1957) was the first African American physician elected a diplomate of the American Board of Neurosurgery in 1953. Greene received a B.A. in 1932 from the University of Pennsylvania and a M.D. in 1936 from Howard University. He did a surgical residency (1937-1939) at Douglass Hospital and then an assistant residency in surgery at Freedmen's Hospital in Washington, D.C. After a period of teaching at Howard University, Greene did a two-year residency in neurosurgery, from 1947 to 1949, at McGill University and then became chief of Howard's Division of Neurosurgery. He was a diplomate of the National Board of Medical Examiners and the American Board of Surgery. In 1943, he became the first Howard graduate certified by the surgical board.

A Century of Black Surgeons (1987), pp. 493-496; *African-American Medical Pioneers* (1994), pp. 26, 30, 171; *Journal of the National Medical Association* Vol. 60, (1968), pp. 253-255

1954 • John Edward Lowery (1898-19??) was the first African American physician elected president of the Queens (New York) Medical Society when he took the post in 1954. Lowery received a B.S. from the University of Pennsylvania and a M.D. from Howard University Medical School in 1923.

Blacks in Science and Medicine (1990), pp.156-157; *Journal of the National Medical Association* Vol. 67, (1975), pp. 404-407, Vol. 85, (August 1993), p. 642

1954 • The first African American physician appointed chief of surgery at any United States military hospital was Webster Clay Brown (1923-) when he was assigned to the 7520th USAF Hospital in London, England in 1954. Brown earned a B.S. *magna cum laude* from Wiley College in 1942, a D.D.S. in 1945 from Meharry Dental School, and a M.D. from Meharry Medical School in 1950.

Who's Who Among Black Americans (1990-1991), p. 165

1954 • The first African American to join any Kaiser-Permanente health organization was Raleigh C. Bledsoe (1919-1996), who also became the first

African American partner in that organization. He retired from that organization in 1986 after setting a record of 32 years as chief-of-service. Bledsoe received his M.D. from Meharry Medical College in 1944. Beside being an outstanding radiologist, he introduced the "fat pad sign" of elbow trauma to the American scientific medical literature.

A Centennial History of African Americans in Radiology (1996), p. 100

1954 • Frances Justina Cherot was the first African American woman to receive a M.D. from the State University of New York Health Science Center at Brooklyn College of Medicine when she received the degree in 1954.

African-American Medical Pioneers (1994), p. 154

1954 • Cardiologist John B. Johnson Jr. (1908-1972) was one of the two first African American physicians appointed to the staff of Georgetown University Hospital in 1954. (The other physician was R. Frank Jones.) Johnson was a pioneer in the diagnostic use of angiocardiography and cardiac catherization. He earned a B.A. in 1931 from Oberlin College and a M.D. in 1935 from Western Reserve University, followed by an internship at Cleveland City Hospital. Johnson joined Howard University in 1936 as a laboratory assistant and then joined the Department of Medicine in 1937, where he remained until his retirement. In addition to his work in angiocardiography, he also studied the problem of hypertension. Johnson served on the board of directors of the American Heart Association from 1958 to 1961 and published 64 scientific papers.

Journal of the National Medical Association (March 1973), pp. 166-170; *Notable Twentieth-Century Scientists* (1995), pp. 1029-1030

DOROTHY LAVINIA
BROWN

1954 • The first African American woman surgeon to practice in the South, in 1954, was Dorothy Lavinia Brown (1919-). Brown earned a B.A. in 1941 at Bennett College and in 1948, received a M.D. from Meharry Medical College. She interned one year at New York's Harlem Hospital and then completed a residence in surgery at Meharry in 1954. Brown started her practice in Nashville, Tennessee in 1954 and was the first African American woman to become a fellow in the American College of Surgeons. Brown was also educational director of Riverside-Meharry Clinical Rotation Program and chief of surgery at Riverside until the facility closed in 1983. She was the attending surgeon at George W. Hubbard Hospital and professor of surgery at Meharry Medical College.

Notable Black American Scientists (1999), p. 47; *Ebony* (September 1958), pp. 92-96; *Notable Black American Women* (1992), pp. 114-116; *Southern Medicine* Vol. 61, (August 1973), pp. 11-14

1954 • In 1954, John Beauregard Johnson Jr. (1908-1972) became one of the first two African Americans appointed to the staff of Georgetown University Hospital (the other was R. Frank Jones). Johnson also became one of the first African Americans to become a department chair of the Howard University (Washington, D.C.) Medical College when he served as acting chair of the Department of Medicine from 1944 to 1949. Johnson earned a B.A. from Oberlin College (Ohio) in 1931, and his M.D. in 1935 from Western Reserve University (Ohio). He completed a one-year internship at Cleveland City Hospital before joining the Howard University staff in 1936, where he served until his retirement. Johnson was a cardiologist and was an early practitioner of angiocardiography, and also pioneered the technique of cardiac catherization. He also studied hypertension and its disproportionate effects on African Americans. Johnson received many national awards and honors, and Howard University named the John Beauregard Johnson Professor of Medicine Chair in recognition of his teaching and research contributions.

African American Medical Pioneers (1994), pp. 34, 191; *Journal of the National Medical Association, Vol. 65* (March 1973), pp. 166-70; *Notable Twentieth Century Scientists* (1995), pp. 1029-30

1954 • The first African American member of the Mecklenburg County (North Carolina) Medical Association was Emery Louvelle Rann Jr. (1914-), who was elected to the post in 1954. He also in 1958 became the first African American to serve as vice president of that organization. Rann received a B.S. in 1934 from Johnson C. Smith University (North Carolina), a M.S. from the University of Michigan in 1963, and his M.D. from Meharry Medical College (Tennessee) in 1948.

African American Medical Pioneers (1994), p. 181; *Blacks in Science and Medicine* (1990), p. 198; *Journal of the National Medical Association, Vol. 54* (January 1962), p. 116

1955 • Roderick Edward Charles (1927-) was one of the first two African Americans to receive a M.D. from the University of Maryland School of Medicine when he received the degree in 1955 (the other was Donald Wallace Stewart). Charles earned a B.S. at Howard University in 1951. He completed an internship and residency during the period 1956 to 1959 and became an attending psychiatrist from 1960 through 1966 at Erie County Medical Center. From 1966 to 1996, he was assistant clinical professor at the SUNY Brooklyn School of Medicine. Charles also established a private practice in psychiatry in 1966.

African-American Medical Pioneers (1994), p. 150; *Who's Who Among African Americans* (1998-1999), pp. 264-265

1955 • Doris Shockley was the first African American woman to earn a Ph.D. in pharmacology in the United States. She received the degree in

1955 from Purdue University. Shockley received a B.S. from Louisiana State University in 1951 and a M.S. from Purdue in 1953. She served as assistant professor of pharmacology at Meharry Medical College in 1955, and was promoted to associate professor in 1967. Shockley has undertaken research in the measurement of non-narcotic analgesics, effects of drugs on stress conditions, and the effects of hormones on connective tissue.

African-American Medical Pioneers (1994), pp. 26, 196; *Ebony* (August 1977), p. 116; *Journal of the National Medical Association* Vol. 55, (1963), pp. 246-247, Vol. 85, (September 1993), p. 718

1955 • Jean Louise Harris (1931-) was the first African American woman to receive a M.D. from the Medical College of Virginia when she received the degree in 1955. She had received a B.S. in 1951 from Virginia Union University. Harris was the director of the bureau of research and development of the District of Columbia Department of Health from 1967 to 1969 and then executive director of the National Medical Association Foundation from 1969 to 1973. She was the first African American Director of the Medical College of Virginia Department of Community Medicine from 1973 until 1978, when she became the Secretary of Human Resources of the state of Virginia, a post she held until 1982. Harris was senior associate director of medical affairs of the University of Minnesota Hospital and Clinics. Harris was elected mayor, in 1994, of the city of Eden Prairie, Minnesota.

African-American Medical Pioneers (1994), pp. 156, 189; *Who's Who Among African Americans* (1998-1999), p. 640

1955 • Matthew Walker (1906-1978) was one of the first three African Americans elected to the Nashville Academy of Medicine in 1955. (The other two physicians were Edward P. Crump and Alex Hansen, both graduates of Meharry Medical College.) Walker earned his B.S. from Louisiana State University in 1929 and his M.D. from Meharry Medical College in 1934. He interned for a year at George W. Hubbard Hospital in Nashville, then completed a three-year residency in surgery and gynecology there in 1938. Walker was an instructor in surgery, physiology and pathology from 1936 to 1943. He was assistant professor of surgery and gynecology from 1939 to 1942 and then associate professor from 1942 to 1944, when he was named professor and chair of the department of surgery, a position he held until 1973. He was also provost for external affairs until 1973. Walker was well respected as a teacher of medicine and surgery and was a pioneer in raising the quality surgery department staff, facilities, and resources to the levels necessary for surgery specialty board certification.

African American Medical Pioneers (1994), pp. 30, 56, 179, 182; *Blacks in Science and Medicine* (1990), pp. 239-240

1955 • The first physician named General Practitioner of the Year in 1955 by the New Jersey Medical Society was the African American woman physician Ernest Mae McCarroll (1898-1990). McCarroll earned a B.A. in 1917 from Talladega College and a M.D. in 1925 from the Woman's Medical College of Pennsylvania. She then interned at Kansas City General Hospital No. 2 and practiced in Philadelphia until 1929, when she set up her practice in Newark, New Jersey. She was the first African American physician to practice at Newark City Hospital in 1946. She also received a M.S. in public health from Columbia University in 1939 and did postgraduate work at the Harvard School of Public Health. McCarroll pioneered the fight against sexually transmitted diseases in Newark and the rest of New Jersey.

Black Women in America (1993), p. 764; *African-American Medical Pioneers* (1994), p. 193; *Journal of the National Medical Association* (November 1973)

1956 • Charles F. Whitten (1922-) was the first African American physician appointed Chief of Pediatrics at Detroit Receiving Hospital in 1956. He held this position until 1962. Whitten graduated from the University of Pennsylvania in 1942 with an A.B. and then received his M.D. from Meharry Medical College (Tennessee) in 1945. He was appointed Pediatric Chief at Detroit Receiving Hospital before becoming, in 1962, a professor at Wayne State University from 1962 to 1970. Whitten then became professor of pediatrics from 1976 to 1992, and from 1973 to 1992 was the director of the comprehensive Sickle Cell Center at Wayne. He became the first African American associate dean for special programs at Wayne in 1992. He founded, in 1972, the National Association for Sickle Cell Disease (NASCD). Whitten's Sickle Cell Center received over seventeen million dollars in grants from the National Institute of Health.

Blacks in Science and Medicine (1990), pp. 248-249; *African-American Medical Pioneers* (1994), pp. 27, 182; *Who's Who Among African Americans* (1998-1999), p. 1386

1956 • In 1956, Julius Wanser Hill (1917-1983) was the first African American physician to set up a practice in orthopedic surgery in California. Hill earned a B.A. in 1933 at Johnson C. Smith University (North Carolina), then got a Ph.D in physics from the University of Illinois. He went on to earn a M.D. in 1951 from Meharry Medical College (Tennessee) and completed postgraduate work in orthopedic surgery at the University of California in 1956. He was the first African American to complete a residency in orthopedic surgery at Los Angeles County/USC Medical Center. Hill was a member of the Los Angeles City Health Commission from 1961 until his death. A building was dedicated to him at the Martin Luther King, Jr. Hospital in Los Angeles in 1974.

Blacks in Science and Medicine (1990), p. 120; *Jet* (November 7, 1983), p. 55; *Journal of the National Medical Association* Vol. 76, (1984), p. 390

1957 • The University of Virginia School of Medicine awarded its first African America M.D. graduates, Edward B. Nash and Edward T. Wood, with degrees in 1957. Barbara Starks Favazza was the first African American woman, in 1966, to receive a M.D. from the University of Virginia. Nash was an undergraduate of Virginia Union University, and Wood was an undergraduate of Dartmouth College. Barbara Farazza earned her undergraduate degree from Beaver College.

African American Medical Pioneers (1994), p. 156

1957 • Elroy Young (1923-) was the first African American orthopedic surgeon to practice in the state of Maryland when he set up practice in Baltimore in 1957. Young received a B.S. from the University of Illinois in 1947 and a M.D. in 1951 from Meharry Medical College. He interned at Lincoln Hospital from 1951 to 1952 and completed residencies at Lincoln Hospital from 1952 to 1953 and at Freedmen's Hospital from 1953 to 1957. Young has maintained a private practice, been an active member of several professional organizations, and served as a board member of James Kerman Hospital in Baltimore.

Who's Who Among African Americans (1998-1999), p. 1685

1957 • Lloyd Charles Elam (1928-) was the first African American, in 1957, to graduate from the University of Washington School of Medicine. He received a B.S. in 1950 from Roosevelt University. Eighteen years later, Blanch Marie Chavers and Robin Eleanor Wragg were the first African American women, in 1975, to earn M.D.s from the University of Washington. Blanche Chavers was an undergraduate of the University of Washington, while Robin Wragg completed her undergraduate degree at Stanford University. Elam served as president of Meharry Medical College from 1968 to 1981.

African-American Medical Pioneers (1994), p. 156; *Blacks in Science and Medicine* (1990), p. 83; *Journal of the National Medical Association, Volume 60* (March, 1968), pp. 150-151

1957 • The first African-American physician elected president of the Gary (Indiana) Board of Health was G. Kenneth Washington, when elected in 1957. He had been a member of the board for two years prior to his selection as board president. Washington completed pre-medical studies at the University of Chicago (Illinois) and received his M.D. from Indiana University Medical School. The board supervises the operation of the Gary Health Department (city nurses, department of vital statistics, clinics, and sanitation) with about 35 employees.

Jet (June 13, 1957), p. 29; *Blacks in Science and Medicine* (1990), pp. 242-243

1957 • The first African American physician to obtain a surgical residency at Temple University (Pennsylvania) was Charles A. Tollett, who completed the residency in 1957. Tollett was awarded a D.Sc. degree by Temple at the same time for his work on thyroid carcinoma. He previously earned a B.S. at Howard University (District of Columbia) in 1950, *cum laude,* and a M.D. at Temple University in 1952. Tollett, after completing military service in 1957, set up private practice in surgery in Oklahoma City. He was the first African American surgeon in the state of Oklahoma to be certified, in 1958, by the American Board of Surgery, and he is a fellow also in the American College of Surgeons. Tollett was guest examiner, in 1973, 1978, and 1985 for the American Board of Surgery.

A Century of Black Surgeons (1987), pp. 931-932; *Who's Who Among African Americans* (1998), p. 1598

1958 • The first African American to become a member of the International Skeletal Society was Gadson Jack Tarleton, Jr. (1920-) in 1958. Another first for Tarleton was his participation at the 1956 Mexico City 8th International Congress of Radiology. He was the first African American radiologist ever to participate in the international event. Tarleton achieved eminence during his professional career as an educator of African American radiologists. A graduate of Meharry Medical College (Tennessee) in 1944, Tarleton later taught at his alma mater, as well as practicing in Norfolk, Virginia.

A Centennial History of African Americans in Radiology (1996), pp. 89-91

1958 • The first African American woman to earn a M.D. from Saint Louis University School of Medicine (Missouri) was Maceola L. Cole (1934-), in 1958. She received a B.S. in 1954 from Saint Louis University.

African-American Medical Pioneers (1994), p. 154

1958 • Among many other achievements, Asa G. Yancey (1916-) was the first African American board-certified surgeon in Georgia in 1958. Yancey also accomplished a number of other "firsts" as an African American in his career. He was the first African American member of the Southern Surgical Association (1985), first African American medical director of Grady Memorial Hospital (1972), first African American full professor at Emory Medical School (1975), and first African American associate dean at Emory

Medical School (1975). While doing research at Tuskegee, Yancey developed a procedure that modified the Swenson technique for congenital megacolon. He published a report in 1952 on his findings, 10 years before the traditional procedure, now commonly referred to in standard medical text books, was described.

African-American Medical Pioneers (1994), pp. 127-130; *A Century of Black Surgeons* (1987), pp. 934-936; *Who's Who Among African Americans* (1998-1999), p. 1456

1959 • Edward James Mason (1923-) was the first African American chief resident on the staff of the Pittsburgh Veterans Administration Hospital in 1959. Mason received his M.D. from the Howard University College of Medicine in 1949. He was in private practice and was a diplomat of the American Board of General and Abdominal Surgery. He was also a member of the Board of Directors of the Forrest Avenue Hospital of Dallas.

Who's Who Among African Americans (1998-1999), p. 980

1959 • James Edwin Jackson was the first African American, in 1957, to receive a M.D. from George Washington University School of Medicine and Health Sciences (Washington, D.C.). The Georgia native earned his undergraduate degree at Morehouse College.

African-American Medical Pioneers (1994), p. 149

1959 • In 1959 Dorothy L. Brown became the first African American woman selected to be a fellow of the American College of Surgeons. Brown, who received her B.S. from Bennett College (North Carolina) in 1941, received her M.D. in 1948 from Meharry Medical College (Tennessee). She interned one year at Harlem Hospital, then undertook a five-year residency in surgery at Meharry Medical College/Hubbard Hospital. She was appointed chief of surgery at Riverside Hospital (Nashville), a position she held from 1957 through 1983. She also served on the National Advisory Board of the National Institute of Health. Brown was the first single woman in the state of Tennessee to adopt a child. In 1966, she ran for a seat in the Tennessee state legislature and became the first African American woman to serve in it.

Black Women in America (1993), pp. 174-175; *Journal of the National Medical Association* V. 60 no. 2 (March, 1968), pp. 136-137, 163

1959 • George Washington University School of Medicine and Health Sciences awarded its first M.D. to an African American named James Edwin Jackson in 1959, who had completed undergraduate training at Morehouse College. In 1968, Joan R. Sealy (1942-) became the first African American woman to receive a M.D. at George Washington. Sealy finished her undergraduate work at the University of Chicago, where she received her B.A. She completed an internship at the Washington Hospital Center and undertook a psychiatric residency from 1969 to 1972 at Yale University Medical Center. Sealy was in private practice and an associate clinical professor at George Washington University Medical School.

African-American Medical Pioneers (1994), p. 149; *Who's Who Among African Americans* (11th Edition), p. 1156; *Who's Who Among Black Americans* (1990-1991), p. 1128

1959 • Vivian Moon Sanford Lewis received a M.D. from the University of Oklahoma College of Medicine in 1959, the first African American woman to do so. Lewis, prior to that, had received a B.A. from Fisk University in 1952. After receiving her medical degree, Lewis completed a rotating internship and pediatric residency at Hurley Hospital between 1959 and 1963. She served Mott Children's Health Center on the pediatric staff and as chairperson from 1963 to 1969. She began a private pediatrics practice in 1970. Daniel W. Lee, prior to Lewis, was the first African American man to receive a M.D. from Oklahoma in 1955. Lee completed his undergraduate work at Langston University.

African-American Medical Pioneers (1994), p. 153; *Who's Who Among African Americans* (11th Edition), p. 801; *Who's Who Among Black Americans* (1990-1991), p. 784

1959 • The first African American named as an examiner for the American Board of Ophthalmology was Howard Phillip Venable (1913-) who received his M.D. from Wayne State University in 1940. Venable was the director of the department of ophthalmology from 1943 to 1965 at Homer G. Phillips Hospital in St. Louis, and served as the hospital's medical director beginning in 1965. When Venable was appointed a fellow of the American Board of Ophthalmology, he scored one of the highest grades ever on the examination.

African American Medical Pioneers (1994), p. 30; *Encyclopedia of Black America* (1981), p. 826; *Journal of the National Medical Association* Vol. 53, (1961), p. 551, Vol. 58, (1966), p. 220

1959 • Samuel L. Bullock (1913-1994), who taught on the faculty of Howard University College of Medicine for more than 30 years, was the first African American physician to be appointed an associate member of the District of Columbia Board of Police and Fire Surgeons in 1959. Bullock earned his undergraduate degree at Lincoln University (Pennsylvania) in 1931 and then the M.D. degree from Howard University (District of Columbia) in 1937. He later became the chief medical officer of the District of Columbia jail and physician at the District of Columbia women's detention center. He was also a chief medical officer of the D.C. Department of Corrections pension service. Bullock specialized in abdominal and proctological surgery. He retired from Howard University in 1971, from surgery in 1977, and from medicine in 1990.

Howard University Magazine (Fall, 1994), p. 47

1959 • Edith Mae Irby Jones (1927-) became in 1952 the first African American to be awarded the M.D. from the University of Arkansas. Jones earned a B.S. in 1947 at Knoxville College (Tennessee). She practiced in Hot Springs, Tennessee from 1953 to 1959. From 1959 to 1962, Jones participated as the first African American in the Baylor (Texas) Affiliated Hospital's internal medicine resident program. She then established a private practice in Houston, which she maintained throughout her career. Active in state and national medical organizations, Jones became the first woman to chair the National Medical Association's Council on Scientific Assembly in 1975, and served as that organization's first female president from 1984 to 1986.

Blacks in Science and Medicine (1990), p. 136; *Jet* (May 1986), p. 42; *Ebony* (May 1986), p. 42; *Notable Black American Scientists* (1999), pp. 181-2

1960 • The University of Medicine and Dentistry of New Jersey/New Jersey Medical School graduated its first African America M.D. recipients, Marjorie Earline Jones, Albert Paul Knott, and David Roland Snead, in 1960. Marjorie Jones earned her undergraduate degree from St. John's University. Albert Knott earned his bachelors degree from Yale University, and David Snead received his B.S. from Seton Hall University.

African-American Medical Pioneers (1994), p. 152

1960 • Fletcher Pearl McBroom (1926-), an African American cardiologist, discovered in 1960 a new method of observing changes in coronary blood vessel tissue affected by hardening of the arteries. McBroom earned her B.A. in 1946 at the University of Chicago and in 1953 received her M.D. from Columbia College of Physicians and Surgeons (New York). She completed residencies from 1954 to 1955 at Columbia University Wing Goldwater Hospital. From 1955 to1957 she was a resident at the University of California at Los Angeles. She was the first African American resident accepted at UCLA. McBroom was then a NIH research fellow from 1958 to 1962. She later engaged in private practice, consulting, and independent research in cardiovascular and preventive medicine.

African American Medical Pioneers (1994), p. 193; *Blacks in Science and Medicine* (1990), p. 167; *Ebony* (May, 1964), p. 70; *Jet* (February 11, 1960), p. 18

1960 • The first African American woman to receive a M.D. from Albert Einstein College of Medicine of Yeshiva University was Carol E. Burnett in

1960. Edwin Markham Jallah and Ernest Preston Porter were the first African American men to receive a M.D. from the same college when they graduated in 1961. Burnett was an undergraduate of Hunter College. Jallah earned his B.S. from the University of Pennsylvania, while Porter received his B.S. from Ohio State University.

African American Medical Pioneers (1994), p. 146

1960 • The first African American physician to be named General Practitioner of the Year by the Pennsylvania State Medical Society, in 1960, was Whittier Atkinson (1893-1991). Atkinson received a B.S. from Howard University (District of Columbia) in 1922 and then his M.D. from Howard in 1925. He practiced in central Pennsylvania for most of his career and in 1932, founded a small interracial hospital, Clement Atkinson Memorial Hospital, in Coatesville, Pennsylvania. It began as a five-bed hospital adjacent to his home, and he treated at least half of his patients for free. He gradually expanded the number of beds, and in 1946 Atkinson gave his hospital to the city of Coatesville, to run as a non-profit community hospital.

African-American Medical Pioneers (1994), pp. 34, 35, 169; *Journal of the National Medical Association* Vol. 48, (1956), p. 206, Vol. 53, (1961), p. 85

1960 • Middleton H. Lambright, Jr. (1908-) was the first African American physician appointed assistant dean at the Medical University of South Carolina in 1960. Lambert received his M.D. in 1938 from Meharry Medical College (Tennessee). He interned and then completed a residency at Cleveland City Hospital and remained there, being eventually appointed as an assistant clinical professor of surgery at what is now Case Western Reserve School of Medicine. Lambert's appointment also included staff privileges at the University and Mount Sinai hospitals, thus making him in 1946 the first African American physician having full staff appointment in Cleveland's hospitals. In 1960 he accepted the positions of associate professor of surgery and assistant dean at the Medical University of South Carolina, where he remained until 1979. In 1984, Lambert became Vice-President of Medical Affairs for Blue Cross and Blue Shield of Northern Ohio.

African-American Medical Pioneers (1994), pp. 26, 179; *Blacks in Science and Medicine* (1990), p. 145; *Century of Black Surgeons* (1987), pp. 625-628

1961 • Aubre De L. Maynard (1901-19??), in 1961, became the first African American professor of surgery at a predominantly white medical school when he was appointed clinical professor of surgery at Columbia University. He was also the first African American to be named full-time director of surgery at Harlem Hospital. Maynard was born in Georgetown, Guyana, and educated in Barbados. He received a B.S. in 1922 from the City College of New York and in 1926 earned his M.D. from New York University Medical College. Maynard set up a private practice in New York in 1926 and in 1928 was appointed to the surgical staff of Harlem Hospital, where he spent 50 years of service. He was appointed to the position of directory of surgery in 1952. In 1958, Maynard was called in to handle an emergency involving a prominent person who had been stabbed. Police escorted the doctor past an anxious crowd. In the operating room he found Martin Luther King with a dagger protruding from his chest. Maynard removed the knife, and the reverend quickly recovered.

African-American Medical Pioneers (1994), p. 193; *Blacks in Science and Medicine* (1990), p. 165; *Century of Black Surgeons* (1987), pp. 171-176

1961 • Augustus Aaron White, III (1936-), internationally known orthopedic specialist, was the first African American to receive a M.D. from Stanford University College of Medicine in 1961. White received his B.A. *cum laude* from Brown University in 1957. He completed his internship and orthopedic residency during the years 1961 through 1969. He went on to become chairman and orthopedic surgeon-in-chief at Boston's Beth Israel Hospital, affiliated with Harvard Medical College. An outstanding scholar, he published several medical books and over 150 scientific articles. In 1973, Sharon Ann Bogerty graduated from Stanford and became the first African American woman to receive a M.D. from that institution.

African-American Medical Pioneers (1994), p. 154; *Blacks in Science and Medicine* (1990), p. 247; *Ebony* (June, 1979), pp. 44-52; *Who's Who Among African Americans* (11th Edition), p. 1376-1377; *Who's Who Among Black Americans* (1990-1991), p. 1336

1961 • The Department of Psychiatry of Meharry Medical College (Tennessee) was established in 1961 and the African-American psychiatrist, Lloyd Charles Elam (1928-), was the department's first head. He was department head from 1961 to 1968, when he became president of Meharry, an office he held until 1981. Elam earned a B.S. in 1950 from Roosevelt University (Illinois) and a M.D. from the University of Washington in 1957. He also received the American Board of Neurology and Psychiatry Diploma in 1965. After receiving his M.D., he interned at the University of Illinois Hospital and completed a residency in psychiatry at the University of Chicago (Illinois) from 1958 to 1961, before joining the medical staff of Meharry Medical College in 1961. Elam was active in medical associations and received a number of honors and awards.

Blacks in Science and Medicine (1990), p. 83; *Ebony* (October, 1976), p. 31; *Journal of the National Medical Association, Volume 60* (March, 1968), pp. 150-151; *Who's Who Among Black Americans* (1980-1981), p. 237; *Who's Who Among African Americans* (1998-1999), p. 447

1961 • Samuel L. Kountz (1930-1981) was the first African American physician to perform a kidney transplant. He performed over 500 transplants during the course of his career. In 1961, he performed the first transplant in which an unidentical donor (non-twin donor) was used. This surgery was performed at Stanford University (California) in conjunction with Dr. Roy Cohn. He also participated, in 1959, in the first West Coast kidney transplant. Kountz received his B.S. from the University of Arkansas, Pine Bluff in 1952 and completed his medical studies at the University of Arkansas, Fayetteville, in 1958. He was a professor at the University of California School of Medicine, San Francisco, where he started the largest kidney transplant research and training program in the country. Kountz's last appointment was that of professor and chairman of the department of surgery, State University of New York, Downstate Medical Center, Brooklyn.

African-American Medical Pioneers (1994), p. 191; *Blacks in Science and Medicine* (1990), pp. 144-145; *Black Enterprise* (February, 1985), p. 51

1961 • The first African American appointed assistant director of the New York State Department of Mental Hygiene, Harlem Valley Psychiatric Center, was Richard L. Francis (1919-) who held the position from 1961 to 1967. Francis received his B.S. from Howard University (District of Columbia) in 1941 and his M.D. from there in 1944. He interned at New York's Sydenham Hospital in 1945, then completed a psychiatric residency at Tuskegee VA Hospital from 1947 to 1951. Francis practiced in upper New York state from 1955 until 1988, when he became a psychiatric consultant.

Blacks in Science and Medicine (1990), p. 94; *Who's Who Among African Americans* (1998), p. 437

1962 • The first African American to earn a M.D. from Washington University School of Medicine was James Leonard Sweatt, III, in 1962. He received his B.S. from Middlebury College. Sweatt was a highly regarded thoracic surgeon with a practice in Dallas. In 1995, Sweatt became the first African American selected president of the Dallas County Medical Society in the group's 119-year history. In 1973, Karen LaFrance Scruggs became the first African American woman to earn a M.D. at Washington University. Scruggs completed her undergraduate work at Macalester College.

African-American Medical Pioneers (1994), p. 156; *Jet* (May 22, 1995), p. 24

1962 • The first African American and first woman in the United States hired to head a state department of mental health was Mildred R. Mitchell-Bateman (1922-) when she was appointed full-time director of the West Virginia State Department of Mental Health in 1962. Mitchell-Bateman was also, in 1962, the first female health chief in the country. She graduated with a B.S. in 1941 from Johnson C. Smith University (North Carolina) and in 1946 received her M.D. from Women's Medical College of Pennsylvania. She completed a one-year internship at New York's Harlem Hospital and then completed a fellowship from 1952 to 1955 at the Menninger School of Psychiatry in Topeka, Kansas. Mitchell-Bateman next worked at Lakin State Hospital in West Virginia as physician, clinical director and superintendent until 1960, when she joined the West Virginia State Department of Mental Health.

Notable Black American Women Book II, (1996), p. 479; *Who's Who Among African-Americans* (1998-1999), p. 921

1962 • Sarah Ewell Payton was the first African American woman to be certified by the American Board of Radiology in 1962. She received her M.D. in 1957 from Howard University College of Medicine (District of Columbia). Payton completed residencies and was affiliated with such medical facilities as Mary Hitchcock Memorial Hospital, Hanover, New Hampshire; Children's Hospital, Mt. Zion Hospital and St. Mary's Hospital, all in San Francisco; and Albert Einstein Medical Center, Northern Division, Philadelphia. She was certified by the Radiology Board in 1962.

A Centennial History of African Americans in Radiology (1996), pp. 13, 18

1962 • John William Lathen (1916-), a psychiatrist, was the first African American to be elected president of the the Bergen County (New Jersey) Mental Health Association in 1962. Lathen earned a B.S. in 1938 from Virginia State College and a M.D. from Howard University College of Medicine (Washington, D.C.). He started a private practice in psychiatry in 1949, which he maintained until 1980, and was also an adolescent psychiatrist for Essex Co. from 1980 to 1984. Lathen became the first African American medical director of Greystone State Hospital in 1977, when he was named assistant medical director. He was also the first African-American intern at Hackensack Hospital in 1949.

Blacks in Science and Medicine (1990), p. 146; *Jet* (February 22, 1962); *Who's Who Among Black Americans* (1990-1991), p. 759

1963 • John E. Moseley (1909-) authored *Bone Changes in Hematologic Disorders*, the first radiology textbook by an African American. The book was published in 1963 by Grune & Stratton. Mosely received his B.S. (*cum laude*) from Harvard (Massachusetts) in 1932 and then his M.D. from the University of Chicago in 1936. He completed residences in radiology at Bellevue Hospital, New York from 1941 to 1943 and at Mt. Sinai in New York in 1943. Moseley became particularly interested in the bone changes recurring in sickle cell disease, then in anemia in general, and then radiographic manifestation of bone changes in all hemotologic disorders, ultimately writing the classic text in the area. Moseley was the first African American radiologist to become a member of the New York Roentgen Ray Society and the first African American member of the Society of Pediatric Radiology. He published over 40 scientific articles.

A Centennial History of African-Americans in Radiology (1996), pp. 81, 137-140

1963 • Jesse Balmary Barber, Jr. (1924-), in 1963, was the first African American certified by the American Board of Neurosurgery. Barber was also the founder and first director of Howard University's Medical Stroke Project, which he started in 1968. In 1983, the first professor of social medicine at Howard University College of Medicine. Barber completed his undergraduate studies at Lincoln University and received his M.D. from Howard University Medical College in 1948. He completed his internship and a residency from 1948 to 1954 at Freedman's Hospital in Washington, D.C., as well as a two-year residency at McGill University Montreal Neurological Institute. In 1961, he became chief of the division of neurosurgery and professor of surgery at Howard University. Barber was a member of many national medical organizations and received many awards for his medical contributions.

Blacks in Science and Medicine (1990), pp. 19-20; *African-American Medical Pioneers* (1994), pp. 35, 169; *Notable Twentieth-Century Scientists Supplement* (1999), pp. 106-107; *Who's Who Among African Americans* (1998-1999), p. 73

1963 • William E. Matory (1927-) received his B.S. in 1949 and M.D. in 1953, both from Howard University (Washington, D.C). Matory dedicated his professional service to the Howard University Medical College as a physician and surgeon. Matory made several significant pioneering achievements during his tenure at Howard, including founding the Howard University College of Medicine (HUCM) Trauma Center in 1963, founding the HUCM Hemodialysis Service in 1963, founding the Department of Family Practice and its residency program in 1969, and initiating the HUCM Continuing Medical Education Program in 1976. Matory also received the first D. Hale Williams Award for Outstanding Achievement in 1960.

African-American Medical Pioneers (1994), pp. 27, 173; *Blacks in Science and Medicine* (1990), p. 164; *Century of Black Surgeons* (1987), pp. 629-631

1964 • The first African American woman to receive the Presidential Medal of Freedom was Lena F. Edwards (1900-1986), who was presented the medal by President Lyndon B. Johnson in 1964. She received the award for her devotion in providing medical services to migrant workers and low-income women. The award is the highest civilian award for service. Also, Edwards was the first obstetrician-gynecologist to ever receive the award. Edwards received her B.S. in 1921 and M.D. in 1924, both from Howard University (District of Columbia). Edwards gave up a lucrative private practice in New Jersey in 1961 and built a maternity clinic, with her own funds, for migrant Mexican workers in Hereford, Texas.

African-American Medical Pioneers (1994), pp. 34, 170; *Black Women in America* (1993), pp. 387-388; *Ebony* (February, 1962), pp. 59-60, 62, 64, 66, 68; *Journal of the American Medical Women's Association* Vol. 39, pp. 192-195

1964 • Alvin H. Crawford (1939-), was the first African American to receive a M.D. from the University of Tennessee College of Medicine in 1964. He was the first African American pediatric orthopedic fellow at Boston Children's (Harvard) Medical Center in 1971. Crawford earned his B.S. in 1960 at Tennessee A&I. In 1981 Crawford was the first African American appointed professor of orthopedic surgery at the University of Cincinnati College of Medicine. He was also the first African American appointed editor of the *Journal of Pediatric Orthopaedics*, a post he held starting in 1987.

African-American Medical Pioneers (1994), p. 186

1964 • Carl Weber Watson was the first African American to earn a M.D. from the University of Kentucky in 1964. Doris L. Clowney and Marsha C. Miller were the first African American women, both graduating in 1978, to receive M.D.s from the University of Kentucky College of Medicine. Watson's B.S. was earned at the University of Kentucky. Clowney earned her B.S. from South Carolina State College, while Miller earned hers from Kentucky State University.

African American Medical Pioneers (1994), p. 150

1964 • O.T. Ayer was the first African American chief of the division of general practice at Mound Park Hospital and Mercy Hospital in St. Petersburg, Florida, in 1964. Ayer was one of five African American doctors in St. Petersburg at that time and was elected division chief for both hospitals by his peers. Both medical facilities were city-operated hospitals.

Jet (January 28, 1965), p. 23

1964 • The first African American selected as a member of the Federal Hospital Benefits Advisory Council was Kenneth Witcher Clement (1920-1974), who was appointed by President Lyndon Johnson in 1964.

Clement's main effort on the Council was to assist in the formulation of Medicare legislation. He received a B.A. in 1942 from Oberlin College (Ohio) and in 1945 was awarded a M.D. from Howard University (District of Columbia). Clement was president of the National Medical Association from 1963 to 1964. He published over 36 papers and articles in professional journals.

African-American Medical Pioneers (1994), p. 170; *Blacks in Science and Medicine* (1990), p. 56; *Journal of the National Medical Association* Vol. 57, (November, 1965), pp. 505-506; Vol. 67, (May, 1975), pp. 252-255

1964 • The first African American pathologist elected president of the D.C. Society of Pathologists was Marvin Alexander Jackson (1927-) when he was selected in 1964. Jackson earned a B.S. from Morehouse College in 1947 and a M.D. in 1951 from Meharry Medical College. He interned at the U.S. Naval Hospital from 1951 to 1952, and undertook his residency from 1953 to 1956 at the University of Michigan, followed by a residency at the Hospital for Joint Diseases of New York from 1956 to 1957. Jackson taught at the University of Michigan from 1955 to 1968. He was a consultant pathologist for the National Institute of Health, National Naval Medical Center, and the Armed Forces Institute of Pathology, as well as the U.S. Veterans Administration. Jackson won awards from both national and foreign scientific organizations, and was an active member of a number of national scientific and professional organizations.

African American Medical Pioneers (1994), pp. 107, 179; *Who's Who Among African Americans* (1998-1999), p. 763

1964 • The first African American physician in Memphis, Tennessee elected a fellow in the American College of Surgeons was George William S. Ish, Jr. (1919-1965). Ish earned a B.S. at Talladega College in 1944 and then received the M.D. in 1944 from Howard University Medical College. He completed his residency in surgery at the Tuskegee Veterans' Administration Hospital and at Chicago's Hines Hospital. Ish was chief of surgery at Collins Chapel Hospital in Memphis from 1962 to 1965.

African-American Medical Pioneers (1994), p. 172; *Blacks in Science and Medicine* (1990), p. 128; *Jet* (May 28, 1964), p. 23

1964 • The first African American physician to be certified by the American Board of Pathology as a forensic pathologist was John Frederick Burton (1913-) who received certification in 1964. Burton received his M.D. in 1933 from Meharry Medical College (Tennessee) in 1941. He was staff pathologist from 1952 to 1955 for the Dearborn (Michigan) VA Hospital, an instructor in cytology at Wayne University in 1955 and in 1970, was a pathologist with the Wayne County Medical Examiner's Office. At the time he received his forensic pathology certification, less than 100 physicians in the United States held that honor. Burton also trained with Scotland Yard, the famed London police bureau, in 1970.

African-American Medical Pioneers (1994), p. 178; *Blacks in Science and Medicine* (1990), pp. 42-43; *Journal of the National Medical Association* Vol. 58, (May, 1966), p. 223

1965 • The first Director of Health Services for the Head Start Program, appointed in 1965, was the African American physician Gertrude Cera T. Hunter (1926-), who served in that position until 1971. Hunter received her M.D. from Howard University (District of Columbia) in 1950, interned at the Homer G. Phillips Hospital (St. Louis), and completed pediatric residencies at both Homer G. Phillips and Freedman's Hospital (Washington D.C.). Her career primarily concerned the activities of teaching and research at Howard's department of pediatrics. Other firsts for Hunter include being the first African American Region One Health Administrator for the U.S. Public Health Services from 1972 to 1976 and the first African American woman on the Board of Trustees of the Massachusetts College of Pharmacy and Allied Health Sciences. Hunter retired from her professorship at Howard University in 1988.

African-American Medical Pioneers (1994), pp. 71-74, 133; *Journal of the National Medical Association* Vol. 85, (1993), p. 642

1965 • The first African American to earn a degree from Tarkio College (Missouri) was Walter C. Gough (1934-) who received his A.B. from there in 1965. He then earned a M.D. in 1970 from Meharry Medical College (Tennessee). Gough interned from 1970 to 1972 at Pittsburgh's Mercy Hospital and was then medical director from 1974 to 1981 at various medical services and hospitals in Mississippi. In 1984, Gough set up private practice in a family and pediatric clinic setting. Gough is also certified by the American Board of Physicians and American Board of Emergency Medicine.

Who's Who Among African Americans (1998-1999), p. 493

1965 • Russell L. Miller (1939-) received his M.D. from Howard University Medical College (District of Columbia) in 1965 and then undertook a residency in internal medicine at the University of Michigan Medical School, becoming the first African American internal medicine resident there. Miller earned his B.S. with honors at Howard University in 1961. He returned to Howard University College of Medicine as a member of the faculty in 1974 in the department of internal medicine. In 1977, he became the first African American Burroughs-Wellcome Scholar in Clinical Pharmacology. Miller was professor of internal medicine and pharmacology for five years and in July 1979 was appointed dean of the medical school. In 1988, he was appointed vice president for health affairs and in 1990, senior vice president of Howard University.

African-American Medical Pioneers (1994), pp. 95-97; *Blacks in Science and Medicine* (1990), p. 173

1966 • Virginia Elizabeth Stull (1939-) was the first African American female to earn a M.D. from the University of Texas Medical School at Galveston in 1966. Stull earned a B.S. in 1960 from Texas Southern University and studied one year at American University (District of Columbia). She has been in private practice since 1967. Stull was a field medical consultant for the Bureau of Vocational Rehabilitation from 1968 to 1975 and school physician for the Columbus, Ohio Board of Education, as well as president and owner since 1975 of Medical Diagnostic Service, Inc.

African-American Medical Pioneers (1994), p. 155; *Who's Who Among African Americans* (1998-1999), p. 1246

1966 • The first African American submarine doctor in the 66-year history of the U. S. Submarine Service was William A. Ross (1937-) when commissioned in 1966. Ross was assigned to the submarine *George C. Marshall* out of Newport News in 1966. He received a B.S. from Wayne State University in 1960 and his M.D. in 1964 from Meharry Medical College. Ross is currently an orthopedic surgeon at Arlington Medical Group in Oakland, California.

Blacks in Science and Medicine (1990), p. 206; *Ebony* (November, 1966), pp. 112-114, 116, 118; *Who's Who Among African Americans* (1998-1999), p. 1299

1967 • The first African American graduate of Emory University School of Medicine was Hamilton Holmes (1941-1995), who received his M.D. in 1967. Holmes received his bachelor's degree in 1963 from the University of Georgia and was also elected to Phi Beta Kappa. He and Charlayne Hunter (later known as Charlayne Hunter-Gault, a prominent journalist) were the first two African American students to integrate the University of Georgia in 1961. Holmes and Hunter were only two admitted to the university when the United States Supreme Court intervened. The governor of Georgia had shut down the campus to prevent their enrollment. After years of bitterness toward his alma mater, Holmes, in 1983, went on to become the first African American trustee of the University of Georgia. He was an orthopedic surgeon in Atlanta and was medical director of that city's Grady Hospital.

New York Times (October, 1995)

JANE COOKE WRIGHT

1967 • An outstanding contributor to the field of cancer therapy, Jane Cooke Wright (1919-) was the first African American woman to serve as associate dean of a major medical school—New York Medical College, when she was appointed to that position in 1961. Cooke had previously earned her M.D. from the school in 1945 and a B.A. from Smith College (Massachusetts) in 1942. Wright served her internship and residency at Bellevue and Harlem hospitals, specializing in internal medicine. Her first employment in 1949 was as a school physician and clinician at the Harlem Hospital Cancer Research Foundation. In 1952, she became its director. She worked there until 1955, when she joined the faculty of New York University Medical Center as director of cancer chemotherapy research and instructor in surgery. In 1967, Wright became associate dean, still contributing significantly to research on cancer. She has published more than 75 treatises on cancer research, and received many awards in recognition of her work.

Crisis Vol. 60, (January, 1953), pp. 4-5; *Ebony* (May, 1968), pp. 72-74, 76-77

1967 • Wilhelm Delano Merriwether was the first African American, in 1967, to receive a M.D. from Duke University School of Medicine. Merriweather completed his undergraduate degree at Michigan State University. Joanne A. Pebbles-Wilson and Jean Gaillard Spaulding were the first two African American women to receive their M.D.s from Duke University School of Medicine in 1973. Pebbles-Wilson received her B.S. from the University of North Carolina, while Spaulding received her undergraduate degree from Columbia University.

African American Medical Pioneers (1994), p. 148

1967 • Robert Lee Gamble and John Nabwangu were the first two African Americans to earn M.D.s from Johns Hopkins University School of Medicine in 1967. Patricia Ann Jenkins and Edwina Margaret Barnett were the first two African women to receive their M.D.s from Johns Hopkins University School of Medicine in 1973. Nabwangu earned a B.S. from Johns Hopkins, and Gamble earned his undergraduate degree from Howard University. Barnett received her B.S. from Ohio State University, while Jenkins received her B.S. from Morgan State University.

African American Medical Pioneers (1994), p. 150

1967 • Walter James Tardy, Jr. (1941-) was the first African American to earn a M.D. from the University of Wisconsin, which he received in 1967. He earned a B.A. degree in 1962 from Tennessee State University and a M.P.H. degree from the Harvard School of Public Health in 1969. Tardy was the director of psychiatry at the Long Island Jewish Medical Center from 1978. He was an active member of at least 10 professional medical organizations on a state, regional and national level and has received professional recognition awards from national medical associations. In 1975, Ada M. Fisher became the first African American woman to receive a M.D. from the University of Wisconsin. Fisher completed her undergraduate work at the University of North Carolina.

African American Medical Pioneers (1994), p. 156; *Blacks in Science and Medicine* (1990), p. 226

1968 • Theresa Greene Reed (1923-) became the first African American female epidemiologist in 1968, when she took the post of medical epidemiological officer with the U. S. Food and Drug Administration. Reed received her B.S. in 1945 from Virginia State College and then her M.D. from Meharry Medical College (Tennessee) in 1949. She also received the M.P.H., in 1967, from Johns Hopkins University (Maryland). She served as a staff and public health physician from 1950 to 1958 at the Homer G. Phillips Hospital and then as assistant clinical director there from 1958 to 1966. Reed joined the FDA in 1968 as a medical epidemiological officer and remained there until 1992, when she retired. She was also the first African American president of the Mound City (St. Louis) Women Physicians Association in 1963. Reed published numerous articles in medical journals.

African-American Medical Pioneers (1994), p. 181; *Who's Who Among African Americans* (1998-1999), p. 1080

1968 • The first African American to earn a M.D. from the University of California, Irvine, College of Medicine was John Richard Crear, Jr., who received the degree in 1968. Crear completed his undergraduate work at the University of Texas.

African-American Medical Pioneers (1994), p. 147

1968 • Louis Joseph Bernard (1925-), who received his M.D. from Meharry Medical College (Tennessee) in 1950, became the first African American physician to be elected president of the Oklahoma City Surgical Society when he took office in 1968. Bernard received a B.A. from Dillard University (Louisiana) in 1946. After receiving his M.D., Bernard completed an internship and two residencies between 1950 and 1958. In 1959, he began private practice in Oklahoma City with a specialty in surgery, which he maintained until 1969. Bernard then joined the staff of Meharry Medical College, holding the positions of dean of medicine from 1987 to 1990 and vice-president for health services from 1988 to 1990. Bernard also served as the director of the Drew/Meharry/Morehouse Consortium Cancer Center from 1990 to 1996.

African American Medical Pioneers (1994), p. 178; *Who's Who Among African Americans* (1998-1999), p. 108

1968 • Vincent Porter (1926-1980), who earned his M.D. at Howard University (District of Columbia) in 1954, was the first African American certified, in April 1968, by the American Board of Plastic Surgery. Porter interned at Queens General Hospital in New York from 1954 to 1955 and then served junior and senior surgical residencies at Pennsylvania Hospital from 1955 to 1959. He was a teaching fellow from 1954 to 1961 at the University of Pittsburgh Medical Center. He was certified in 1967 by the American Board of Surgery. From 1967 to 1975, Porter served at Beckman Downtown Hospital, Columbia College of Physicians and Surgeons and Mount Sinai Medical School. He was then appointed director of plastic surgery at Harlem Hospital, where he served until his death in 1980.

African-American Medical Pioneers (1994), pp. 30, 174; *Century of Black Surgeons* (1987), pp. 511-512

1968 • Loma K. Brown Flowers was one of the first two African American women to receive a M.D. from Case Western Reserve University School of Medicine (Ohio). The other was Doris A. Evans. They received their degrees in 1968. Flowers (1944-) received an A.B. (*magna cum laude*) in biology in 1965 from Case Western. She interned at San Francisco General Hospital from 1968 to 1969 and then completed a residency in psychiatry, in 1972, at Stanford University Medical Center (California). Flowers was director of mental health at East Palo Alto Community Health Center from 1969 to 1973, then served from 1973 to 1977 as chief of the mental health clinic of the San Francisco Veterans Administration Hospital. She started a private practice in psychiatry in San Francisco in 1977. Flowers authored several books on psychotherapy and dream interpretation.

African American Medical Pioneers (1994), p. 147; *Who's Who Among African Americans* (1998-1999), p. 422

1968 • Joan R. Sealy was the first African American woman to earn a M.D. from George Washington University School of Medicine and Health Sciences (District of Columbia) in 1968. Sealy (1942-) received her B.A. in 1964 from the University of Chicago. She interned, from 1968 to 1969, at Washington Hospital Medical Center and then undertook residency in psychiatry from 1969 to1972 at Yale University. Sealy is in private practice and is an associate clinical professor at George Washington University Medical School.

African-American Medical Pioneers (1994), p. 149; *Who's Who Among Black Americans* (1990-1991), p. 1128

1969 • The first M.D. degree awarded by the University of Miami School of Medicine was earned by George Sanders (1942-) in 1969. Sanders completed his undergraduate schooling at Morehouse College in 1965. Between the period of 1969 through 1976, Sanders completed his internship, a residency, and a fellowship in cardiology. He maintained a private practice in internal medicine and cardiology. Sanders was a physician in internal medicine and cardiology for the U.S. Air Force and since 1992 has been the director of the U.S. Air Force Cardiopulmonary Laboratory at Elgin Air Force Base.

African-American Medical Pioneers (1994), p. 151; *Who's Who Among African Americans* (11th Edition), p. 1139

1969 • The first African American associate dean for students at Yale University School of Medicine was James Pierpont Comer (1934-). Comer received his B.A. from Indiana University in 1956, the M.D. in 1960 from Howard University (District of Columbia), and then a Masters in Public Health from the University of Michigan in 1964. Comer received training in psychiatry from 1964 through 1968 and in 1969, was appointed to his Yale

JAMES PIERPONT COMER

Medical School position. He has published numerous articles for professional journals and has authored several textbooks, mostly concerned with African American childcare. Comer also cofounded, in 1968, an organization called Black Psychiatrists of America.

African-American Medical Pioneers (1994), pp. 45-47; *Black Enterprise* (October, 1988), p. 95; *Journal of the National Medical Association* Vol. 85, (1993), p. 779

ALVIN FRANCIS
POUSSAINT

1969 • Alvin Francis Poussaint (1934-) was the first African American appointed assistant dean of students at Howard Medical School. He also holds the title of professor of clinical psychiatry there. Poussaint received a B.A. from Columbia University (New York) in 1956, a M.D. in 1960 from Cornell University Medical College (New York), and an M.S. in 1964 from the University of California at Los Angeles. He was associated with Tufts University Medical School (Massachusetts) from 1965 to 1969. He joined Harvard Medical School in 1969 as associate dean of students and clinical professor of psychiatry. Poussaint specialized in the emotional and psychological problems of African Americans and developed the "aggression-rage" theory. He has published numerous scholarly articles and texts.

African-American Medical Pioneers (1994), pp. 26, 1195; *Encyclopedia of Black America* (1981), p. 697; *Who's Who Among African Americans* (1998-1999), p. 1049

1969 • Jeanne Spurlock (1921-) was the first African American woman to head a department of psychiatry at an American medical school when she joined the faculty and headed the psychiatry department at Meharry Medical College (Tennessee) in 1969. Spurlock completed her M.D. requirements at Howard University Medical College (District of Columbia) in 1947 and then completed an internship at Provident Hospital in Chicago in 1948 and residency training in general psychiatry at Cook County Psychopathic Hospital in Chicago in 1950. Spurlock became certified in adult and child psychoanalysis at the Chicago Institute of Psychoanalysis in 1962. Spurlock was, from 1960 to 1968, an attending psychiatrist and chief of the Child Psychiatry Clinic at Chicago's Michael Reese Hospital and maintained a private practice in Chicago from 1951 to 1958. In 1971, she was the first woman and first African American to receive the Edward A. Strecker M.D. Award from the Institute of Pennsylvania for outstanding contributions in psychiatric care and treatment.

Blacks in Science and Medicine (1990), p. 219; *Encyclopedia of Black America* (1981), p. 808; *Jet* (May 27, 1971), p. 49

1969 • The first African American physician tenured at the University of Nebraska Medical School was Melvin Earl Jenkins (1922-), when he was appointed in 1969. Jenkins received his B.A. in 1944 from the University of Kansas and a M.D. from the University of Kansas School of Medicine in 1946. Jenkins did a rotating internship (1946-47) at Washington, D.C.'s Freedman's Hospital. From 1963 to 1965, he completed a research fellowship in pediatric endocrinology at Johns Hopkins Hospital, becoming the first African American pediatric endocrinologist in the United States. He worked at Nebraska from 1969 to 1973, when he came to Howard University as chairman of the department of pediatrics. He held this position until his 1986 retirement. Jenkins was also the first African American physician member of the governing body of the American Board of Pediatrics, where he served from 1983 through 1989.

Blacks in Science and Medicine (1990), p. 133; *Ebony* (July, 1995), p. 124; *Journal of the National Medical Association* Vol. 79, (1987), pp. 1104-1106; Vol. 85, (1993), p. 785

1969 • Mitchell W. Spellman (1919-) was the first dean of the Charles R. Drew Postgraduate Medical School in Los Angeles in 1969. Spellman simultaneously filled the position of assistant dean at the University of California at Los Angeles School of Medicine and a clinical professorial appointment in surgery at the University of Southern California. He received a B.A. from Dillard University (Louisiana) in 1940, a M.D. from Howard University School of Medicine (District of Columbia) in 1944, and a Ph.D. in surgery in 1955 from the University of Minnesota. He was also certified by the American Board of Surgery in 1953 and was appointed a John and Mary Markle Foundation Scholar in Medical Science in 1954. Prior to his joining the Drew Postgraduate Medical School, Spellman was associated with Howard University since 1950, where he was full professor and chief medical officer of the Howard University Division of Surgery at the District of Columbia General Hospital. In 1978 Spellman became dean for medical services at Harvard Medical School, as well as executive president of the Harvard Medical Center in Boston.

A Century of Black Surgeons (1987), pp. 633-636; *Journal of the National Medical Association* Vol. 53, (July, 1961), p. 429, Vol. 70, (August, 1978), p. 606

1969 • Walter F. Leavell (1934-) was the first African American president of the Minority Affairs Section of the Association of American Medical College (AAMC) when he was selected to the position in 1969. Leavell received a B.S. from the University of Cincinnati College of Pharmacy (Ohio) in 1957 and then a M.D. in 1964 from Meharry Medical College (Tennessee). He then completed postgraduate work at St. Joseph's Hospital and at SUNY-Upstate Medical Center, both located in Syracuse, New York. Leavell's pioneering medical efforts were in the area of medical education administration. He originated and developed the Upstate Medical Education Development Program at SUNY-Upstate, was a founding member of the National Association of Minority Medical Educators (NAMME) and was primarily responsible for establishing the Minority Affairs Section of the AAMC. Since 1993, Leavell has been senior associate vice president for Health Affairs at Howard University (District of Columbia).

African-American Medical Pioneers (1994), pp. 31, 79-81, 130

1969 • The first African American woman appointed vice-president for health affairs at Howard University (District of Columbia) was Angella D. Ferguson (1925-), who, in 1969, became the highest ranking woman in health affairs there. Ferguson was the prime mover behind the construction of Howard University's new $43 million hospital facility, as well as the Seeley G. Mudd Building, the Animal Research Center, Child Care Center, and Cancer Center. Ferguson acquired a B.S. in 1945 and M.D. in 1949, both from Howard. Ferguson had been a researcher in sickle cell anemia since the early 1940s, and in 1962 and 1963, received certificates of merit from the American Medical Association for her research papers in that area. In 1964, the New York-based Association for Sickle Cell Anemia, Inc. awarded Ferguson with a bronze plaque for outstanding work in the field. Ferguson is the author or co-author of over 35 publications involving sickle cell anemia and the growth and development of African American children.

Ebony (September, 1963), pp. 86, 92; *Journal of the National Medical Association* Vol. 85, (1993), p. 783

1969 • Anna Cherrie Epps (1930-) became in 1969 the first African American woman professor at the Tulane University (Louisiana) School of Medicine. She earned a B.S. from Howard University (Washington, D.C.) in 1951, the M.S. from Loyola University (Louisiana) in 1959, and the M.D. from Howard in 1966. Epps was program director and assistant professor of microbiology at Howard from 1960 to 1969, when she joined the Tulane University School of Medicine as a U.S. Public Health Service faculty fellow. She served at Tulane as assistant and then associate professor of medicine from 1971 to 1975, and then as professor and medical director from 1975 to 1980. In 1980, Epps became assistant dean of student services, holding that position until 1986, when she was appointed associate dean and professor of medicine at Tulane. She founded the Medical Education Reinforcement and Enrichment Program for Minorities in the Health Professions (MevREP) at the Tulane Medical Center.

Blacks in Science and Medicine (1990), p. 85; *African American Medical Pioneers* (1994), pp. 26, 170; *Who's Who Among African Americans* (1998-1999), p. 455; *Who's Who Among Black Americans* (1985), p. 256

1970 • The first African American to be appointed full professor of radiology in a predominately white medical school was Leslie L. Alexander (1917-), when he was appointed full professor of radiology at the State University of New York, Downstate Medical Center, Brooklyn, in January 1970. He first joined that institution in July 1956 as an instructor in the department of radiology. Alexander earned a B.A. (1947) at New York University, and a M.A. (1948) and M.D. (1952) at Howard University. He has completed extensive research in radiology, covering such topics as radiation therapy, nuclear medicine, radiobiology, and cancer, and has published over 100 scientific papers. In 1963, Alexander became the first African American physician elected president of the Brooklyn Radiological Society. He has lectured across the country and worldwide and has been a long-term member of the editorial board of the National Medical Association (NMA). In 1974, he was honored by the NMA, who awarded him the Distinguished Service Medal.

A Centennial History of African Americans in Radiology (1996), pp. 14-15, 18, 50, 97; *African-American Medical Pioneers* (1994), p. 169; *Blacks in Science: Astrophysicist to Zoologist* (1977), p. 56; *Blacks in Science and Medicine* (1990), pp. 5-6

1970 • The first African American appointed State Commissioner of Health for the State of New Jersey was James Rankin Cowan (1919-) when he was appointed to the position in 1970. Cowan served as Commissioner until 1974. He received a B.S. from Howard University in 1939, a M.A. from Fisk University in 1940, and a M.D. from Meharry Medical College in 1944. After completing his commissioner post in New Jersey, Cowan was the first African American to be appointed to the post of assistant secretary for Health and Environment of the United States Department of Defense in 1974. He held the post until 1976. Cowan then became senior vice-president of Blue Cross and Blue Shield of Greater New York. Cowan has been active in a number of medical associations, as well as being selected as a member of several national medical task forces, by the White House, and by other national medical councils and commissions.

African-American Medical Pioneers (1994), pp. 34, 179; *Ebony* (April 1972), p. 96; *Journal of the National Medical Association* Vol. 63, (March 1971), p. 151, Vol. 66, (July 1974), pp. 336-338; *Who's Who Among African Americans* (1998-1999), p. 327

1970 • Charles Ireland was the first non-physician and first African American appointed an officer at Temple University's School of Medicine in 1970. Ireland joined Temple in 1966 as Chief Social Worker and Assistant Professor of Social Work in the School of Medicine. In 1970, Ireland initiated his Recruitment, Admissions and Retention Programs (RAR) at Temple's School of Medicine. The program seeks minority students with medical school potential, supports and encourages students to stay in the medical program, and provides seminars, counseling, and other guides to help students graduate on time. Ireland also founded the Medical Minority Educators, the National Alliance of Black Social Workers, and the National Alliance on Graduate and Professional-Level Education.

Philadelphia Tribune (February 4, 1997), p. 8A

1970 • John A. Kenney Jr. (1914-), who received his M.D. from Howard University College of Medicine in 1945, was the first African American to become a member of the American Dermatology Association in 1970. He also achieved several other firsts as an African American in the field of medicine. Kenney received his bachelor's degree from Bates College in 1942 prior to entering Howard University Medical College. He became, in 1950, the first African American resident in dermatology at the University of Michigan from 1950 to 1953. Kenney then, in 1971, became the first African American selected a board member of the American Academy of Dermatology. When he received the Finnerwood Award of the Dermatology Foundation in 1988, he was the first African American recipient of that award.

African-American Medical Pioneers (1994), pp. 172-173; *Blacks in Science and Medicine* (1990), p. 142

1970 • The first African American selected president of the American Public Health Association, in 1970, was Paul B. Cornely (1906-) who received his M.D. in 1931 from the University of Michigan. He had also received his B.A. in 1928 from there. When Cornely received his M.D., he was the first African American elected to Michigan's Alpha Omega Alpha honor society. After he completed his internship at Lincoln Hospital in Durham, North Carolina, he returned to the University of Michigan where, in 1934, he became the first African American to earn a Dr.P.H. Cornely then associated with the Howard University College of Medicine. In 1943, he became head of the public health department, in 1950, chairman of its community health practice department, and professor emeritus in 1973. Cornely was selected the first president (1962) of the D.C. Public Health Association and the first African American president of the Physician's Forum.

History of the Negro in Medicine (1967), pp. 99-100; *Journal of the National Medical Association* Vol. 85, (October 1993), pp. 779-780; *Encyclopedia of Black America* (1981), p. 288

1970 • Effie O'Neal Ellis (1913-1994), a national leader of the quality of life movement and child medical care specialist, was the first African

American woman to hold an administrative position with the American Medical Association. In 1970, Ellis was appointed to the newly created AMA post of special assistant for health services—a special advisor on child and national health matters and health care of the poor. She served in the position from 1970 to 1975. Ellis received a B.A. in 1933 from Spelman College and a master's degree from Atlanta University in 1935. She then received a M.D. in 1950 from the University of Illinois College of Medicine. Ellis was a specialist in preventive health, family planning, and pre- and postnatal care.

Black Women in America (1993), pp. 391-392; *Ebony* (August 1974), p. 38; *Jet* (July 25, 1994), p. 54; *Notable Black American Women* (1992), pp. 324-325

EFFIE O'NEAL ELLIS

1970 • David Satcher (1941-) was the first African American to earn both a M.D. and a Ph.D. from Case Western Reserve University in 1970. Satcher's doctorate is in the field of genetics, and he has worked on sickle-cell disease. He was president of Meharry Medical College when he was appointed by President Clinton, in 1993, as the first African American director of the Centers for Disease Control (CDC). Satcher was confirmed in 1998 as President Clinton's nominee for Unit-

DAVID SATCHER

ed States Surgeon General, the first African American man appointed to that office.

Philadelphia Tribune (September 16, 1997), pp. 1A, 3A; *Who's Who Among African Americans* (1998-1999), p. 1320

1970 • Ruben Earl Brigety and Henry Earl Coteman were the first two African Americans to earn M.D.s from the University of Florida College of Medicine, in 1970. Brigety was awarded his undergraduate degree from Morehouse College, while Cotman received his undergraduate degree from Florida A&M University. Two years later, in 1972, Cassandra J. Ndiforchu became the first African American woma M.D. recipient from the University of Florida. Ndiforchu received her B.S. from Fisk University.

African-American Medical Pioneers (1994), p. 149

1970 • Chester Middlebrook Pierce (1927-) was the first African American member of the American Board of Psychiatry and Neurology in 1970 and in 1978, was elected president of that board. Pierce was also the founding national chairman, in 1969, of the Black Psychiatrists of America. He received his B.A. in 1948 and M.D. in 1952, both from Harvard University. He was an instructor from 1957 to 1960 at the University of Cincinnati and then assistant professor and professor from 1960 to 1969 at the University of Oklahoma. Pierce joined the Harvard University faculty as professor in 1969. He has held active membership and offices in national medical associations, both domestic and foreign, and has acquired numerous honors for his work in psychiatry.

African-American Medical Pioneers (1994), p.194; *Who's Who Among African Americans* (1998-1999), p. 1192

1970 • The first M.D. awarded to an African American by Louisiana State University School of Medicine in New Orleans was received by Claude Jenkins Tellis in 1970. Tellis completed his undergraduate education at Michigan State University. In 1974, Louisiana State University awarded M.D.s to Charleta Guillory, who received her bachelors degree from Southern University, Baton Rouge, and Critty Lillette Hymes, who earned her bachelors degree at Xavier University of Louisiana. Guillory and Hymes were the first African American women to receive M.D.s from Louisiana State University.

African-American Medical Pioneers (1994), p. 150

1970 • The first two African American men to graduate from the University of Alabama Medical School were Richard Charles Dale and Samuel William Sullivan, Jr., who received their M.D.s in 1970. Patience Hodges

Claybon was the first African American woman to receive a M.D. in 1974. Both Dale and Sullivan received their B.S. degrees from Howard University, while Claybon earned her B.S. from Tuskegee University.

African-American Medical Pioneers (1994), p. 146

1970 • Charles Harry Epps (1930-), an orthopedic surgeon who received his M.D. from Howard University in 1955, has been an outstanding pioneer in organized medicine. Among other pioneering achievements, Epps was the first African American oral examiner for the Board of Orthopaedic Surgery in 1970, first African American president of the Washington Orthopaedic Society from 1967 to 1968, first African American president of the D.C. Medical Society in 1979, first African American governor of the American College of Surgeons from 1982 to 1988, first African American president of the Association of Children's Prosthetic and Orthotic Clinics, and first African American member of the AMA House of Delegates representing the American Academy of Orthopaedic Surgeons from 1982 to 1987. Since 1988, Epps has been dean of the Howard University College of Medicine and has a national reputation as an outstanding orthopedic surgeon, medical educator, and administrator. He has authored numerous scientific articles, edited textbooks, and maintained an active practice specializing in work with handicapped children.

African-American Medical Pioneers (1994), pp. 57-60; *Blacks in Science and Medicine* (1990), pp. 85-86; *Journal of the National Medical Association* Vol. 85, (October 1993), pp. 781-782; *Philadelphia New Observer* (November 23, 1994)

1970 • The first African-American woman to be an administrative officer at Howard University College of Medicine (Washington, D.C.) was Eleanor L. Franklin (1929-), who was appointed associate dean for Academic Affairs in 1970. Franklin earned a B.S. in 1948 from Spellman College (Georgia) and an M.S. in zoology in 1951 from the University of Wisconsin. She then earned a Ph.D. in endocrinology from Wisconsin in 1957. Franklin taught physiology and pharmacology at the Veterinary School of Tuskegee Institute for six years, and then joined the faculty of Howard University College of Medicine as an endocrinologist. In 1970, she was appointed associate dean for academic affairs, becoming the first woman administrative officer in the Medical School and holding the position for 10 years. Franklin was responsible for curriculum development, academic support service, and educational administration. She played a key role in the development of a combined B.S.-M.D. program and in the establishment of the Office of Medical Education.

African-American Medical Pioneers (1994), pp. 65-68, 188; *Blacks in Science and Medicine* (1990), p. 94

1971 • The first two African American males to receive the M.D. degree from the Medical College of Georgia School of Medicine were John Harper and Frank Rumph, who earned their degrees in 1971. Harper earned his bachelors degree from Morehouse College, and Rumph received his bachelors degree from Fort Valley State College. In 1975, the Medical College of Georgia awarded M.D.s to its first two African American woman, Angelica Valencia Sims and Elizabeth Hawkins Woods. Sims was a Morris Brown College undergraduate, while Woods completed her undergraduate studies at Clark College.

African-American Medical Pioneers (1994), p. 149

1971 • Claude H. Organ (1928-), a surgeon, was the first African American chair of a surgery department at a predominately white medical school when he served in that capacity at Creighton College from 1971 to 1982. Organ was also the first African American selected chairman of the Southwestern Surgical Congress (1984-1985) and first African American physician to serve as chairman of the American Board of Surgery (1984-1986). He was selected a member of the Surgery Residency Review Committee, and in 1985, was elected president of the California Medical Association. Organ became the first African American fellow of the Royal College of Surgeons of South Africa in 1986. In 1989, he also became the first African American physician in the Royal Australian College; that same year, he was the first African American physician selected editor of the *Archives of Surgery*, the largest surgical journal in the English-speaking world.

African-American Medical Pioneers (1994), pp. 27, 31, 97-100; *A Century of Black Surgeons* (1987), pp. 775-780, 884-914; *Ebony* (January, 1987), pp. 88, 90, 92, 95; *Journal of the National Medical Association* Vol. 85, (1993), p. 789

1971 • In 1971, Bobby J. Harris (1936-) became the first African American physician to be certified in colorectal surgery. Harris received a B.S. in 1958 from Union College and the University of Nebraska, and his M.D. in 1962 from Nebraska.

African American Medical Pioneers (1994), p. 189

1971 • Roland Boyd Scott (1909-), recognized worldwide as an outstanding author, educator, researcher and medical practitioner, established at Howard University, in 1971, the first major research center for sickle cell disease. He served as its director until 1990. Scott acquired a B.S. in 1931 and a M.D. in 1934, both degrees from Howard University. He started as assistant professor of pediatrics at Howard University in 1939. In 1945, he was appointed chief of the division of pediatrics, and then from 1949 to 1973, was chairman of the department of pediatrics. Scott has won numerous honors and awards for his leadership and pioneering efforts in directing national and international attention to the study of sickle cell disease.

He is highly respected for his development and training of research techniques for medical students and researchers, especially in the areas of pediatrics and the study of diseases.

African-American Medical Pioneers (1994), pp. 108-110, 133, 174; *Jet* (May 29, 1952), p. 15, (March 20, 1958), p. 11; *Journal of the National Medical Association* Vol. 85, (October 1993), pp. 791-792

1971 • John Andrew Kenney Jr. (1914-) was the first African American physician elected a board member of the American Academy of Dermatology, where he served from 1971 to 1973. He was also, in 1970, the first African American physician selected as a member of the American Dermatology Association. He was, in 1974, the first African American board member of the Society for Investigative Dermatology. Kenny received his M.D. in 1945 from Howard University Medical College.

African-American Medical Pioneers (1994), pp. 172-173; *Blacks in Science and Medicine* (1990), p. 142

1971 • Cora LeEthel Christian, in 1971, was the first African American woman to earn a M.D. at Jefferson Medical College of Thomas Jefferson University. Christian (1947-) earned a B.S. from Marquette University in 1967 and then a M.D. from Jefferson Medical College in 1971. She also earned a M.P.H. in 1975 from Johns Hopkins University. Christian was chief resident, then instructor from 1973 to 1975 at Howard University Family Practice. She worked for public health agencies in the Virgin Islands from 1975 to 1992, when she became medical director for the Hess Oil Virgin Islands Corporation. Christian has also been a medical instructor for Meddar/PCC Virgin Islands since 1994.

African-American Medical Pioneers(1994), p. 150; *Who's Who Among African Americans*(1998-1999), p. 272

1971 • Lemuel W. Diggs (1899-1995), an African American hematologist and researcher, was the first to develop a comprehensive research center, in 1971, dedicated primarily to the study of sickle-cell anemia. It was located at the Memphis campus of the University of Tennessee. Diggs had been a member of the faculty there since 1929. He received both his undergraduate and master's degrees from Randolph Macon College, and in 1925, he received a M.D. from Johns Hopkins University School of Medicine. Diggs also helped establish the first blood bank in the South in 1938. (It was located in Memphis, Tennessee.) This was only the fourth blood bank in the United States at the time. Diggs was the author of the text *Morphology of Human Blood Cells,* a reference classic which is still widely used. He also played a prominent role in the development of the famed St. Jude's Children's Hospital as a research hospital, as well as a treatment center for children with leukemia.

Jet (February 27, 1995), p. 46; *New York Times* (January 28, 1995), p. 10

1972 • The first blind African American psychiatrist in the United States was Edwin Nii Adom (1941-). Adom received a B.A. in 1963 from the University of Pennsylvania and a M.D. from Meharry Medical College in 1968. He undertook an internship in 1968 to 1969 at Pennsylvania Hospital and then completed a residency, from 1969 to 1972, at Thomas Jefferson University. Adom has been a staff psychiatrist for the West Philadelphia Consortium since 1972 and a clinical assistant professor of psychiatry since 1972 at the University of Pennsylvania School of Medicine. Adom has also been a consulting psychiatrist for the Pennsylvania Bureau of Visual Handicapped and Blindness since 1974 and Bureau of Disability Determination since 1975. Adom has consulted for a number of community and medical organizations and institutions and since 1991, has been the medical director of the West Philadelphia Community Mental Health Consortium and also maintains a private practice.

Blacks in Science and Medicine(1990), p. 3; *Who's Who Among Black Americans*(1990-1991), p. 10; *Who's Who Among African Americans*(1998-1999), p. 11

1972 • The first African American named president of the Golden State Medical Association was Arthur H. Coleman (1920-) in 1972. Coleman received his M.D. in 1944 from Howard University College of Medicine and a L.L.B in 1944 from Howard, also followed by a J.D. in 1968 from Golden State College. Coleman was co-founder of the American Health Care Plan in 1973, the first African American founder of a major HMO (health maintenance organization).

African-American Medical Pioneers(1994), pp. 31, 170; *Journal of the National Medical Association*Vol. 67, (1975), pp. 481-482, Vol. 85, (September 1993), p. 719

1972 • Carol Coleman Gray (1946-) was the first African American woman to earn a M.D. from the University of Texas Medical School at San Antonio, which she received in 1972. She previously received a B.S. in 1967 from the University of Texas, Austin. Gray completed pediatric residences at Walter Reed Army Medical Center and University of Maryland Hospital. She was the medical coordinator for the Dallas Independent School District Project Find from 1979 to 1983. Gray has been in private practice as a pediatrician in Dallas, Texas since 1981.

African-American Medical Pioneers(1994), p. 155; *Who's Who Among African Americans*(1998-1999), p. 577

1972–1976 • Samuel L. Kountz (1930-1981), a specialist in kidney transplantation, developed during the years 1972 to 1976 the first standards for administering tolerable dosages of the drug methylprednisolone (used to prevent rejection in transplanted organs). Kountz also developed, with his partner, Folkert O. Belzer, a machine able to preserve kidneys up to fifty hours from the time they are taken from the body of a donor. The machine is called the Belzer Kidney Perfusion Machine.

African-American Almanac(1997), p. 1073; *Black Enterprise*(February 1985), p. 51

1972 • World-renowned liver disease specialist Carroll M. Leevy (1920-) organized the first known multidisciplinary clinic in the country for alcoholics with liver disease in 1971. Leevy is author of over 400 scientific articles and editor of six books focusing on liver disease in alcoholics. He received an A.B. from Fisk University in 1941 and a M.D. from the University of Michigan in 1944. He also received a Sc.D. in 1989 from the University of Nebraska. Leevy helped establish the former Seton Hall College of Medicine and Dentistry, New Jersey and has trained over 40 hepatologists and nutritionists, over half of whom hold positions in academic medicine. Leevy was the first African American chair, in 1966, of internal medicine at a predominately white medical school when he headed internal medicine at Seton Hall. He is also a member of the editorial board of the American Journal of Medicine and holds two patents.

CARROLL M. LEEVY

African-American Medical Pioneers(1994), p. 26; *Black Enterprise*(February 1975), pp. 22; *Journal of the National Medical Association*Vol. 63, (1971), p. 499, Vol. 65 (1973), p. 259; *Encyclopedia of Black America*(1981), pp. 503-504.

1972 • Asa G. Yancey (1916-) was the first African American associate dean at the Emory University School of Medicine when appointed to the post in 1972. Yancey was a graduate of Morehouse College with a B.S., and he obtained a M.D. from the University of Michigan Medical School in 1941. He interned at Cleveland City Hospital, completed a surgical residency at Freedmen's Hospital, then completed a surgical training program at the Marine Medical College in Boston. He was also an instructor in surgery at Meharry Medical College. Yancey was instrumental in training young African American doctors. He was chief of surgery at Tuskegee V.A. hospital where he directed the first accredited training program for African American surgeons in Alabama from 1948 to 1958. He was chief of surgery at Hughes Spalding Pavilion (Atlanta), where residents were trained in general surgery, the first accredited training program for African American surgeons in Georgia (1958-1972). He is a diplomate of the American Board of Surgery and a fellow of the American College of Surgeons.

Blacks in Science and Medicine(1990), p. 259; *African-American Medical Pioneers*(1994), pp. 127-130; *Ebony*(February 1974), p. 94

1973 • The University of Texas Southwestern Medical Center at Dallas Southwestern Medical School awarded M.D.s to its first African American graduates in 1973. Charles Douglas Foutz and Johnny Lee Henry were the first African American men, and Kathryn Haley Flangin, in 1974, was the first African American woman to receive a M.D. Foutz completed his undergraduate education at Lamar University, and Henry finished undergraduate work at the University of Texas, Austin. Flangin received her bachelor's degree from North Texas State University.

African-American Medical Pioneers (1994), p. 155

1973 • The Michigan State University College of Human Medicine awarded its first African American-earned M.D.s in 1973 to two women, Janice Marie Fox and Judith Ann Ingram, and to two men, Donald Gregory Weathers and Roger O'Niel Whitmire. Fox earned her B.S. from Michigan State University, while Ingram earned hers from Eastern Michigan University. Weathers received the B.S. from St. Augustine's College, while Whitmore received his B.S. from Prairie View A&M University.

African-American Medical Pioneers (1994), p. 151

1973 • John Alexander Anderson (1937-), an African American physician and radiologist, founded the Southwest Medical Society in 1973. Anderson earned a B.S. in 1958 from the University of Chicago (Illinios), and in 1962 received his M.D. from Howard University (Washington, D.C.) College of Medicine. He interned from 1962-3 at Wright-Patterson Air Force Base hospital, followed by a residency in radiology from 1963 to 1965 at Wilford Hall U.S.A.F. Medical Center at Lackland Air Force Base, Texas. He served as a radiologist from 1963 to 1971 at varied U.S.A.F. medical facilities. Alexander then served as radiologist with Southwest Detroit Hospital and Boulevard Hospital until 1974, when he became radiologist and chief of radiology at Detroit's Highland Park General Hospital.

African American Medical Pioneers (1994), pp. 31, 169; *Blacks in Science and Medicine* (1990), p. 12; *Who's Who Among African Americans* (1998-1999), p. 34

1973 • Clarence G. Robinson, Jr. (1920-) was the first African American chief surgeon (1973-1985) and first full-time police surgeon and supervisory chief surgeon (1980-1985) for the New York City Police Department. Robinson received a B.S. degree in 1942 from the University of Chicago and his M.D. degree in 1945 from Meharry Medical College. He was clinical assistant professor of medicine at the College of Medicine, State University of New York Downstate Medical Center and served as director of medicine at Coney Island Hospital, Brooklyn from 1967 to 1971. He was chair of the police physician section of the International Association of Chiefs of Police from 1986 to

1989 and then a consultant in quality assurance at Coney Island Hospital in Brooklyn from 1990 to 1993. Robinson was a founding member and president of the American Academy of Police Medicine from 1981 to 1985.

Encyclopedia of Black America (1981), p. 733; *Who's Who Among African Americans* (1998-1999), p. 1109

1973 • Clive Orville Callender (1936-) was the first African American member of the National Task Force on Organ Procurement and Transplantation when he was appointed in 1973. That same year, Callender established a kidney transplant center located at Howard University Hospital. The center was designated a transplant center by the United States Department of Health, Education and Welfare in 1977, with federal funding support retroactive to 1973. It was the first African American transplant center in a minority institution and one that has the only African American histocompatibility laboratory in the world. Callender received a B.A. from Hunter College in 1959 and a M.D. from Meharry Medical College in 1963. Callender entered the area of organ transplantation via a NIH postdoctoral fellowship from 1971 to 1973 in transplant immunology at the University of Minnesota. He then returned to Howard University, establishing the kidney transplant program.

Blacks in Science and Medicine (1990), p. 45; *Black Enterprise* (October 1988), p. 80; *Journal of the National Medical Association* Vol. 85 (October 1993), pp. 777-778

1973 • Mark Ivey, III (1935-), practicing physician and pharmacist in Lakeland, Florida, became the first African American resident in the department of obstetrics and gynecology at Akron General Medical Center in 1973. Ivey received his B.S. in 1958 in pharmacy from Florida A & M University and a M.D. in 1973 from Meharry Medical College. He completed his residency in 1978. He served as an Akron City Health Department deputy health officer from 1974 to 1978. In 1985, Ivey was the first African American appointed chief of the Gynecological Service of the Lakeland (Florida) Regional Medical Center. He was the medical director of the Planned Parenthood of Central Florida from 1978 to 1994 and is active in a number of medical associations.

Blacks in Science and Medicine (1990), pp. 128-129; *Who's Who Among Black Americans* (1985), p. 422; *Who's Who Among African Americans* (1998-1999), p. 752

1973 • John Lawrence S. Holloman (1919-), public health services administrator, was the first African American to become president of the New York City Health and Hospital Corporation when appointed to the position in 1973. Holloman earned a B.S. *cum laude* in 1940 at Virginia Union University, a M.D. in 1943 at the University of Michigan School of Medicine, and a D.Sc. in 1983 at Virginia Union University. He started his private practice in 1947. Holloman served as a vice-president of the Health Insurance Plan from 1972 to 1974, as president of the New York City Health and Hospital Corporation, and as a trustee and/or advisor for a dozen health organizations. He was a medical officer for the United States Food and Drug Administration from 1980 to 1985 and has been medical director of the W.F. Ryan Health Center and assistant attending physician at St. Lukes/Roosevelt Hospital. Holloman's research interests included clinical, pharmaceutical, social, and administrative medicine.

Blacks in Science and Medicine (1990), p. 123; *Encyclopedia of Black America* (1981), p. 443; *Journal of the National Medical Association* Vol. 57, (November 1965), pp. 507-508; *Who's Who Among African Americans* (1998-1999), p. 706

1974 • The first African American to receive a M.D. from Vanderbilt University in 1974 was Levi Watkins, Jr. (1944-) in 1974. Darlene Dailey and Janis Adelaide Jones were the first African American women, in 1978, to receive M.D.s from Vanderbilt. Dailey completed her undergraduate work at Ohio State University, while Jones completed her undergraduate education at Smith College. Watkins earned his B.S. from Tennessee State University in 1966. In 1980, he became internationally known as the first surgeon to implant the life-saving automatic implantable cardiac defibrillator.

African-American Medical Pioneers (1994), p. 155; *Journal of the National Medical Association, Volume 85* (1993), pp. 793-794

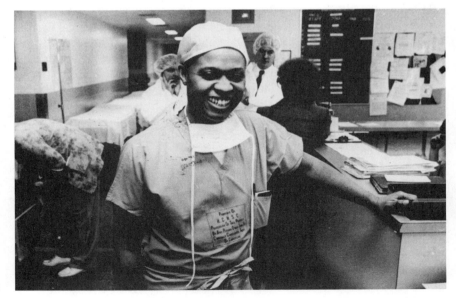

CLIVE O. CALLENDER

1974 • The Pennsylvania State University College of Medicine awarded M.D.s to its first five African American recipients in 1974. The first four men graduates were James F. Byers, Theodore R. Densley, Wade A. Johnson, and Lewis E. Mitchell, while Janice C. McIntosh was the first woman graduate. McIntosh received her B.S. from the University of California. Byers earned a B.S. at the State University of New York at Buffalo, while Densley received his B.S. from Michigan State University. Johnson received a B.S. from Morgan State University, and Mitchell received his B.S. from Muskingum College.

African-American Medical Pioneers (1994), p. 153

1974 • The first African American physician to be awarded the Gold Medal of the American College of Radiology was William E. Allen, Jr. This gold medal is the highest honor awarded by the American College of Radiology. Allen served as Director of the Homer G. Phillips Hospital, St. Louis, Radiology Department from 1945 to 1973. He established the internationally renowned School of Radiology Technology at Homer G. Phillips Hospital. Allen was the first African American elected to membership in several other professional radiological societies. He is also engaged in extensive research activities regarding nuclear medicine, radiation therapy-carcinoma of the prostate, and simplified radiation dosimetry-carcinoma of the cervix, while contributing over 30 publications to the scientific literature.

A Centennial History of African Americans in Radiology (1996), pp. 25-27, 38-39, 50, 61-62; *African-American Medical Pioneers* (1994), pp. 29, 169; *Blacks in Science and Medicine* (1990), pp. 8-9

1974 • Samuel L. Kountz (1930-1981) was the first African American elected president of the Society of University Surgeons in 1974. This was an expression of the appreciation his colleagues had for both his clinical and research work. Kountz was an international authority in kidney transplantation and published numerous scientific papers in the area. He was also a member of several editorial boards including: *The Kidney, Surgery, Journal of Hypertension and Renal Disease,* and the *New York State Medical Journal.*

African-American Medical Pioneers (1994), pp. 31, 191; *A Century of Black Surgeons* (1987), pp. 661-695; *Blacks in Science and Medicine* (1990), pp. 144-145; *Journal of the National Medical Association* Vol. 70, (September 1978), pp. 683-684

1974 • The first major hospital in New York City named in honor of an African American was the Knickerbocker Hospital, which was formally named the Arthur C. Logan Memorial Hospital in 1974. Arthur C. Logan (1909-1973) received an A.B. in 1930 from Williams College, having been elected to Phi Beta Kappa the previous year. He then earned a M.D. from Columbia University College of Physicians and Surgeons in 1934 and completed a two-year internship in Harlem Hospital. He undertook graduate study in surgery from 1941 to 1946 at New York Postgraduate Medical School and Hospital. Logan was associate-visiting surgeon at Harlem Hospital and associate surgeon there from 1936 to 1961. He had a long association with Sydenham Hospital, from 1954 to 1973, being acting director of surgery there from 1972 to 1973. He had been associate surgeon at Knickerbocker Hospital since 1964. Logan originated the plan to build Manhattanville Health Park, which included a new hospital to replace Sydenham Hospital, a municipal hospital in Harlem.

Blacks in Science and Medicine (1990), p. 155; *Journal of the National Medical Association, Volume 66* (May 1974), pp. 272-273; *Jet* (February 28, 1974), p. 41

1974 • The first African American graduate of the University of Utah School of Medicine to earn a M.D. was William Anthony Robinson, who received the degree in 1974. Denise L. Capel and Marjorie S. Coleman, in 1979, were the first African American women to receive M.D.s from there in 1979. Robinson received his undergraduate degree from Hunter-Lehman College. Both Capel and Coleman completed their undergraduate education at the University of Utah.

African American Medical Pioneers (1994), p. 155

1975 • The first partial artificial heart (LVAD) implantation in a human was completed by African American cardiac surgeon John C. Norman (1930-) and Denton Cooley on December 23, 1975. The pair have implanted 22 such devices. Norman designed, staffed, and directed the Cardiovascular Surgical Research Laboratories at the Texas Heart Institute. He remained at the Heart Institute from 1971 through 1981, authored or co-authored more than 450 articles, edited five books, and applied rigorous hemodynamic evaluation to the usage of the intra-aortic balloon pump and devices to assist a failing heart. He also taught and advised more than 1,000 fellows and residents from all parts of the world while at the Texas Heart Institute.

Century of Black Surgeons (1987), pp. 733-774

1975 • The first African American physician promoted to the rank of brigadier general in the U. S. Army Medical Reserve Corps was Marion Mann (1920-) when he was promoted in 1975. While in the position, Mann was in active command of the 2290th U. S. Army Hospital in Rockville, Maryland. While in the service, he graduated from the U. S. Army Command and General Staff College, the Industrial College of the Armed

Forces, and the Army War College. Mann received his B.S. in 1940 from Tuskegee Institute and his M.D. from Howard University Medical College in 1954. He also earned a Ph.D. in pathology in 1961 at Georgetown University. Mann was a member of the Howard faculty from 1957, starting as an assistant in pathology until 1979, when he retired as dean. He retired from full-time teaching at the medical school in 1983.

Blacks in Science and Medicine(1990), pp. 160-161; *Black Enterprise*(February 1975), pp. 23-24; *Journal of the National Medical Association*Vol. 62, (1970), pp. 368-369, Vol. 85, (October 1993), p. 788

1975 • James Herman Mabrie III (1948-) was the first African American otolaryngology resident at Baylor Affiliated Hospitals in 1975. He completed his residency in 1978, becoming the first African American otolaryngologist. Mabrie is engaged in private practice in Houston, Texas.

African-American Medical Pioneers(1994), pp. 177, 180; *Blacks in Science and Medicine*(1990), p. 158; *Who's Who Among Black Americans*(1985), p. 535

1975 • Donna P. Davis (1947-) was the first African American doctor in the U. S. Navy Medical Corps when appointed in 1975. Davis earned her B.A. in 1969 at Cornell University and a M.D. in 1973 from Meharry Medical College. She was a physician for Heffner Medical Clinic from 1977 to 1978 and for Cigna Health Plan from 1978 to 1987. Davis is currently in private practice.

African American Almanac(1997), p. 99; *Timelines of African-American History*(1994), p. 285; *Who's Who Among Black Americans*(1992-1993), p. 352

1975 • The first African American deputy commissioner of the New York State Department of Mental Hygiene was Hugh F. Butts (1926-). He received a B.S. in 1949 from the City College of New York and a M.D. from Meharry Medical College in 1953. Butts has worked for a number of medical institutions as a psychiatrist beginning in 1958, including Columbia University Psychoanalytic Clinic, Beth-Israel Hospital, Bronx State Hospital, and Albert Einstein College of Medicine, and joined the New York State Department of Mental Hygiene in 1974. Butts has also consulted with numerous organizations and published a number of articles.

Who's Who Among African Americans(1998-1999), pp. 219-220

1975 • Samuel Blanton Rosser (1934-), who received a M.D. in 1960 from Howard University College of Medicine, was the first African American to be certified, in 1975, in pediatric surgery. Rosser received a B.S. from Clark College in 1954 and in 1956, earned a M.S. in parasitology from Wayne State University. He completed a rotating internship at Freedmen's

Hospital in Washington, D.C., as well as residencies at Staten Island United States Public Health Service Hospital and Memorial Sloan-Kettering Cancer Center. In 1970, Rosser became the first African American to enter pediatric surgery residency at Washington, D.C.'s Children's Hospital. After completing that residency in 1972, he returned to Howard University's Department of Surgery as chief of the Pediatric Surgery Service. Rosser has published in a number of journals and is active in several professional medical organizations.

African-American Medical Pioneers (1994), pp. 31, 174; *Century of Black Surgeons* (1987), pp. 484, 508-510; *Who's Who Among African Americans* (1998-1999), p. 1300

1975 • Maurice Rabb (1932-), chief of the division of ophthalmology at Mercy Hospital and Medical Center in Chicago, was the first African American president of the Chicago Opthalmological Society. Rabb received his B.S. in 1954 and M.D. in 1958 from the University of Louisville. He did postgraduate training at Kings County Hospital in Brooklyn and the University of Illinois Eye and Ear Infirmary. Rabb started private practice in Chicago in 1965 and joined the staff of Illinois Central Hospital. Rabb became, in 1969, the first African American medical director of the Illinois Eye Bank. In 1993, he received the Senior Honor Award from the board of directors of the American Academy of Ophthalmology. Rabb has published extensively, including the authoring of five texts in the field. He is a professor of ophthalmology at the University of Illinois and was one of the pioneers of retinal photography.

Black Enterprise (October, 1998), p. 78; *Blacks in Science and Medicine* (1990), p. 197; *Jet* (February 27, 1993), p. 20

1975 • The first two African American women to graduate from the University of Colorado School of Medicine were LaRae H. Washington and Deborah Green, who received their M.D.s in 1975. In 1907, Samuel L. Raines was the first African American man to receive a M.D. from the University of Colorado. Green received her B.S. from Grinnell College, and Washington earned hers at the University of Colorado.

African-American Medical Pioneers (1994), p. 148

1975 • Sandra Dian Battis and Diane Loren Pemberton were the first two African American women to earn a M.D. from the University of California at Davis School of Medicine, in 1975. Otis Gladdis was the first African American man to receive his M.D. from the that school in 1953. Battis received a B.S. from Fisk University, while Pemberton received her B.S. from Drexel University. Gladdis received a B.S. from Sacramento State College.

African-American Medical Pioneers (1994), p. 147

1975 • The first African Americans to receive M.D.s from the State University of New York at Stony Brook were Janice C. Lark, Mitchelene J. Morgan, Paul J. Fox, and Johnson B. Murray in 1975. Lark earned her undergraduate degree at Howard University, and Morgan earned her undergraduate degree at Dennison University. Fox earned his bachelors degree at the City College of New York, and Murray received his bachelors degree from New York University.

African-American Medical Pioneers(1994), p. 154

1975 • Paul J. Fox and Johnson B. Murray were the first two African American men to receive M.D. degrees from the State University of New York at Stony Brook Health Sciences Center School of Medicine when they received their degrees in 1975.

African-American Medical Pioneers(1994), p. 154

1976 • First African American inducted as an Honorary Fellow of the College of Physicians of Philadelphia was W. Montague Cobb (1904-1990), then a professor emeritus of anatomy at Howard University. The College of Physicians of Philadelphia, founded in 1787, is the oldest medical society in the United States. Cobb's induction was on December 15, 1976. Cobb earned a M.D. from Howard University in 1929 and a Ph.D. in anatomy and physical anthropology from Western Reserve University in 1932. It is estimated that Cobb helped train more than 6,000 physicians and wrote more than 625 scientific papers. He was the editor of the *Journal of the National Medical Association* for 28 years and was the 64th president of the National Medical Association. Cobb has been on the board and chaired a number of prestigious organizations and has received many awards and citations.

WILLIAM MONTAGUE COBB

Journal of the National Medical Association, Volume 69, No. 4(1977); *A Century of Black Surgeons*(1987), pp. 470, 471, 472

1976 • The first African American to have his portrait hung in the gallery of scientists at the Clinical Center of the National Institutes of Health was Charles Richard Drew (1904-1950), who was awarded this honor in 1976. Drew was a renowned teacher, surgeon, and researcher who was a world authority on blood plasma and the developer of two of the world's largest blood banks. He earned his undergraduate degree in 1926 at Amherst Col-

CHARLES R. DREW

lege (Massachusetts), the M.D. in 1933 at McGill University (Canada), as well as a medical degree at Columbia University (New York) in 1940. He became a diplomate of the National Board of Medical Examiners in 1934, a diplomate of the American Board of Surgery in 1941 (becoming the first African American surgeon to serve as an examiner on that board), and was elected a Fellow to the International College of Surgeons in 1946. Awarded the Spingarn Medal of the NAACP in 1944, Drew received many varied honors during his relatively short lifetime, as he died in an auto accident at the age of 45. A number of medical and college buildings and facilities were later named in his honor, and in 1981 he was honored with a U.S. postage stamp commemorative.

Blacks in Science and Medicine(1990), pp. 78-9; *Journal of the National Medical Association*Vol. 42 (July 1950), pp. 239-245, (March 1971), pp. 156-7; *Ebony*(February 1974), pp. 88-96

1976 • Texas Tech University Health Sciences Center School of Medicine awarded M.D.s to its first African American graduates in 1976. The group included two women, Stella Pinkney Jones and Johnnie Paris Frazier, and one man, Charles Edward Mathis, III. Jones and Frazier both completed their undergraduate work at Texas Southern University. Mathis received his undergraduate degree from Texas Tech University.

African-American Medical Pioneers(1994), p. 155

1976 • Alexa Canady (1950-) was the first woman and first African American neurosurgical resident at the University of Minnesota when appointed in 1976. Canady received a B.S. in 1971 from the University of Michigan and a M.D. in 1975 from the College of Medicine at Michigan. Her residency at Minnesota was completed in 1981, after which she completed a two-year fellowship in pediatric neurosurgery at Philadelphia's Children's Hospital while also teaching at the University of Pennsylvania. Canady settled in Detroit, joining the neurosurgery department of Henry Ford Hospital and later joining Children's Hospital of Michigan, becoming the department head. She was certified by the American Board of Neurological Surgery in 1984 and is also clinical associate professor at Wayne State University.

Black Firsts(1994), p. 357; *Ebony*(September 1983), pp. 72-74, 76; *Notable Black American Women*(1992), pp. 155-156

1977 • Deborah Maxine Hyde (1949-) was the first woman in neurosurgical training at Case Western Reserve University School of Medicine in 1977. She had received a B.S. in biology *cum laude* in 1970 and a M.S. in biology, also from Cleveland State University, in 1973. Hyde completed an internship from 1977 to 1978 and a neurosurgery residence from 1978 to 1982 at Case Western Reserve University Hospitals. She then served on the neurosurgical staff of Guthrie Clinic from 1982 to 1987, when she set up private neurosurgical practice in Canoga Park, California. Hyde has been featured in the first edition of *Medica* (1983), *Ebony* (1983), *First Register of Yearly Article on Young Professional Esquire* (1984), and *American Medical News* (1984). She has published a number of professional articles and is an active member of several medical societies.

Emerge(March 1995), p. 9; *Who's Who Among African Americans*(1998-1999), p. 745

1977 • Muriel Marjorie Petioni (1914-) organized African American women physicians into the national organization, Medical Women of the National Medical Association, in 1977. This was the first women physicians' organization officially recognized as a component of the National Medical Association, formed in 1895. Petioni earned a B.S. in 1934 and a M.D. in 1937 from Howard University. She completed her internship at Harlem Hospital and residency at St. Louis' Homer Phillips Hospital. Petioni was a college physician for several years, then set up private practice in New York in 1951, where she practiced until her 1990 retirement. She also started, in 1974, the New York-area Susan Smith McKinney Steward Medical Society and continued as its first president until 1984.

Black Women in America(1993), p. 916; *Who's Who Among African Americans*(1998-1999), p. 1185

1977 • The first African American woman to earn the M.D. from Southern Illinois University School of Medicine was Elizabeth Bertram, who received her diploma in 1977. Bertram had also earned a B.S. from Southern Illinois University.

African American Medical Pioneers(1994), p. 149

1977 • The first African American woman to graduate from the University of Southern Alabama School of Medicine was Patricia Ann Sanders, while the first African American man to graduate from there was John Henry Wagner III. They both received the M.D. in 1977.

African-American Medical Pioneers(1994), p. 146

1978 • Herman James Mabrie III (1948-) was the first African American to complete a three-year residency in otolargynology at Baylor Affiliated Hospitals, and in 1978, became the first African American otolaryngologist in the United States. Mabrie is in private practice in Houston, Texas. He had received the B.S. degree in 1969 from Howard University his M.D. in

1973 from Meharry Medical College. He is a member of the American Council on Otolaryngology.

African-American Medical Pioneers(1994), pp. 177, 180; *Blacks in Science and Medicine*(1990), p. 158; *Who's Who Among African Americans*(1998-1999), p. 952

1978 • Augustus A. White III (1936-), when he became orthopedic surgeon-in-chief at Boston's Beth Israel Hospital in 1978, became the first African American to serve as chairman of a clinical department in a major teaching hospital. The hospital is affiliated with Harvard Medical School. White received his B.A. *cum laude* in 1957 from Brown University and his M.D. in 1961 from Stanford University. He was the first African American to complete an internship at Presbyterian Medical Center (1961-2) and the first African American to complete an orthopedic residency at Yale-New Haven Hospital (1963-5). He was consulting orthopedic surgeon at the New Haven VA Hospital and Hill Health Center from 1969 to 1978. White joined Harvard School of Medicine in 1978 as professor of orthopedic surgery. He has been visiting orthopedic surgeon at Massachusetts General Hospital and senior associate in orthopedic surgery at Children's Hospital Medical Center since 1979 and serves as orthopedic surgeon-in-chief at Brigham and Women's Hospital, as well as Beth Israel Hospital in Boston. White has consulted extensively and received numerous local and national honors.

African Americans in Boston(1991), p. 48; *Blacks in Science and Medicine*(1990), p. 247; *Ebony*(June 1979), pp. 44-46, 48, 50, 52

LASALLE D. LEFFALL

1978 • The contribution of Dr. LaSalle D. Leffall, Jr. (1930-) to medicine has been primarily as a teacher and clinician with a specialty in surgical oncology. He was the first African American physician elected president of the Society of Surgical Oncology in 1978. In 1985, Leffall was elected secretary of the Board of Regents of the American College of Surgeons. He has held positions of leadership in the Washington Academy of Surgery, Medical Chirurgical Society of the District of Columbia, and the National Task Force on Colon and Rectal Cancer of the American Cancer Society. He is a director on the American Board of Surgery.

A Century of Black Surgeons(1987), pp. 693-731, 884-913; *Blacks in Science and Medicine*(1990), p. 151; *Ebony*(April 1978), pp. 127-130, 132, 134, 136; *Journal of the National Medical Association*Vol. 62, pp. 248-249

1978 • Mitchell W. Spellman (1919-), appointed dean for medical services at Harvard University Medical Center in 1978, was the first African American to hold that position. Spellman earned a B.A. from Dillard University in 1940, a M.D. from Howard University in 1944, and a Ph.D. in surgery from the University of Minnesota in 1955. He interned at Cleveland General

Hospital, was assistant resident in surgery there, and then became assistant resident in surgery at Washington's Freedmen's Hospital. From 1947 to 1969, Spellman held teaching and directorships in surgery when he became dean and professor, in 1969, at the Charles R. Drew Postgraduate Medical School. He remained there until his 1978 Harvard appointment, which position he held until 1990. Spellman has been a member of professional organizations and has received a number of honorary degrees and other awards.

African-American Medical Pioneers(1994), pp. 27, 175; *Blacks in Science and Medicine*(1990), p. 218; *Journal of the National Medical Association, Vol. 85*(August 1993), p. 643, Volume 70, (1978), p. 606

1978 • Alvin J. Thompson (1924-) was the first African American physician to serve as president of the Washington State Medical Association, in which position he served from 1978 to 1979. Thompson received his M.D. from Howard University College of Medicine in 1946 and interned at St. Louis City Hospital from 1946 to 1947. He has maintained a private practice in internal medicine since 1957. Thompson has achieved other pioneering firsts in medicine. He was the first African American president of the Seattle Academy of Internal Medicine (1972-3), the first African American president of the King County (Washington) Medical Society (1974), and first African American governor (for Washington and Alaska), American College of Physicians (1974-8). Thompson has produced a number of journal articles and editorials and has been active in medical and professional organizations.

African-American Medical Pioneers(1994), p. 175; *Who's Who Among African Americans*(1998-1999), p. 1479; *Who's Who Among Black Americans*(1990-1991), p. 1246

1978 • Kenneth C. Edelin (1939-) was the first African American physician to direct a major clinical department at Boston City Hospital when, in 1978, he was named the director of obstetrics and gynecology. Edelin earned a B.A. in 1961 at Columbia University and a M.D. in 1967 from Meharry Medical College. He served as chairman and professor of obstetrics and gynecology at Boston University School of Medicine, holding that position from 1979 to 1989. Edelin was then appointed chairman of the board of Planned Parenthood Federation of America in 1989, being the first African American selected to that post.

African-Americans in Boston(1991), pp. 148-149; *Who's Who Among African-Americans*(1998-1999), p. 438

1978 • Augustus Aaron White III (1936-) was the senior author of the text *Clinical Biomechanics of the Spine,* the first text of its kind (1978).

White is one of the most renowned orthopedic surgeons in the United States and maintained his practice in the Boston area. He is an alumnus of Stanford Medical School (1961) and has been affiliated first with Yale Medical School, then Harvard's Medical School. While maintaining a heavy practice and a clinical and instructional program, White has also performed research and published numerous scientific articles.

African-American Medical Pioneers(1994), pp. 154, 198; *African Americans in Boston*(1991), p. 148; *Blacks in Science and Medicine*(1990), p. 247

1978 • The first African American women to earn M.D.s from the University of Massachusetts Medical School were Marcia Clair Bowling and Vernette Jones Bee, in 1978. Bowling received her bachelors degree from Brandeis University, and Bee received her B.S. from Radcliff College. The next year, 1979, saw the first two African American men, George Chidi Njoku and Harold F. Tate, receive a M.D. from Massachusetts. Nyoku earned the bachelors degree from Worcester State College, and Tate earned his undergraduate degree from Cornell University.

African American Medical Pioneers(1994), p. 150

1979 • The first African American to serve as president of the American Cancer Society was LaSalle D. Leffall Jr. (1930-) when he was elected president in 1979. Leffall earned a B.S. (with greatest distinction) in 1948 from Florida A&M University and his M.D. in 1952 from Howard University. He interned at Homer G. Phillips (St. Louis) (1952-3), then did his junior residency (1953-6) and senior residency (1956-7) at Freedmen's Hospital, Washington, D.C. Leffall was assistant professor (1962-6), associate professor (1966-70), and then from 1970, professor and chairman of the department of surgery at Howard University College of Medicine. Leffall has been visiting professor at 75 institutions and has authored more than 80 articles and chapters in six textbooks. He has, under sponsorship of professional organizations, produced 15 surgical movies covering topics mainly in surgical oncology.

African-American Medical Pioneers(1994), pp. 81-84; *Black Enterprise*(October 1988), p. 76; *Philadelphia Tribune*(June 26, 1984), p. 13; *Who's Who Among Black Americans*(1985), p. 511

1979 • Leroy Maxwell Graham (1954-) was the first African American student elected to Alpha Omega Alpha Honor Medical Society at Georgetown University School of Medicine in 1979. Graham received his B.S. *cum laude* from St. Joseph College and his M.D. from Georgetown in 1979. Graham did a pediatric residency from 1979 to 1982 at Fitzsimmons Army Medical Center and completed additional pediatric services at other military installations until 1986. He continued his duties at the University of

Colorado Health Sciences Center and Children's Hospital and from 1989 has been director of the pediatrics intensive care unit at Fitzsimmons Army Medical Center. Graham was certified by the American Board of Pediatrics in 1983.

Who's Who Among African Americans(1998-1999), p. 571

1979 • Roland A. Gandy, Jr. (1924-1996), who received his M.D. from Temple University in 1951, was a founding member of the Toledo Surgical Society in 1979, and served as its president in 1990. Gandy also served on the Ohio State Medical Board from 1974 to 1980 and was its president in 1980. He received his B.A in 1947 from Lincoln University prior to entering Temple University's Medical School. Gandy served an internship and general surgery residency at Cleveland's City Hospital and Philadelphia General Hospital from 1951 to 1956. From 1968 to 1974, Gandy was chief of surgery and later chief of staff at Mauamee Valley Hospital and was associated with Mercy Hospital in Toledo as director of the Surgery Residence Program from 1974 through 1990. He also served as chair of the Surgery Department from 1977 to 1989. Gandy was team physician for Scott High School for 33 years and was a team physician for the University of Toledo for 29 years.

Who's Who Among African Americans(1998-1999), p. 1700; *Philadelphia Tribune*(May 14, 1996), p. 6D

1979 • The first African American chief of gynecology of the University of Chicago (Illinois) Medical School was Robert Charles Stepto (1920-1994), appointed in 1979. He earned a B.S. in 1941 from Northwestern University (Illinois), the M.D. from Howard University (Washington, D.C.) Medical School in 1944, and a Ph.D. in 1948 from the University of Chicago. He was professor of obstetrics at the Chicago Medical School from 1970 to 1975, and professor at Rush Medical School from 1975 to 1979. Stepto also served as chair of the Cook County Hospital department of obstetrics from 1972 to 1976, chair of the Mount Sinai Hospital department of obstetrics and gynecology from 1969 to 1979, and president of the Chicago Board of Health in 1988. Active in many professional organizations, he was president of the International College of Surgeons from 1978-9, and president of the Association of Gynecological Oncologists in 1983.

African American Medical Pioneers(1994), p. 175; *Blacks in Science and Medicine*(1990), p. 221; *Who's Who Among Black Americans*(1985), p. 795; *Who's Who Among Black Americans*(1990-1991), p. 1199

1979 • Surgical oncologist LaSalle Doheny Leffall Jr. (1930-) held in February 1979 the first national conference on cancer among African Americans, under the auspices of the American Cancer Society, of which he was president in 1978. Leffall received a B.S. in 1948 from Florida A&M University, and the M.D. in 1952 from Howard University (Washington, D.C.) College of Medicine. From 1957 to 1959, he was a senior fellow in cancer surgery at Memorial Sloan-Kettering Cancer Center (New York). Leffall joined the Howard University medical faculty in 1962, serving as assistant dean of the College of Medicine from 1964 to 1970, before being appointed professor and chair of the Department of Surgery. Leffall's research interests and clinical studies were cancer of the breast, head, neck, and colorectum, with a specialty in educating both the lay public and medical professionals about cancer risks for minorities.

A Century of Black Surgeons (1987), pp. 697-731, 884- 913; *Journal of the National Medical Association, Vol. 62* (May 1970), pp. 248-9; *Ebony* (April 1978), pp. 127-30, 132, 134, 136; *Notable Black American Scientists* (1999), pp. 205-6

1979 • Doris Louise Wethers (1927-), an African American pediatrician with a specialty in sickle-cell disease, founded the comprehensive Sickle Cell Program at New York's St. Luke's/Roosevelt Hospital, and was its first director in 1979. Wethers received a B.S. *magna cum laude*, from Queens College in 1948 and then earned her M.D. in 1952 from Yale University School of Medicine. She was director of pediatrics at St. Luke's Roosevelt Hospital Center from 1973 to 1979 and attending pediatrician there from 1973. In 1987, Wethers became attending pediatrician at Columbia Presbyterian Medical Center and clinical professor of pediatrics at Columbia University College of Physicians and Surgeons. She published extensively and was a reviewer of the *American Journal of Pediatric Hematology/Oncology* and a member of many boards and commissions, as well as a very active member in professional organizations.

Blacks in Science and Medicine (1990), p. 246; *Notable Black American Scientists* (1999), pp. 312-313; *Who's Who Among African Americans* (1998-1999), p. 1584

1980 • The first African American elected to the Alpha Omega Alpha Medical Honor Society at Tulane University was Patrice T. Gaspard when elected in 1980. Gaspard received her B.S. from Tulane in 1976. She completed a pediatric residency at Fitzsimmons Army Medical Center, as well as a fellowship there in adolescent medicine. Gaspard was certified by the American Board of Pediatrics in 1984 and is a member of the American Academy of Pediatrics.

Who's Who Among African Americans (1998-1999), p. 534

1980 • Vernal Gordon Cave (1918-1997) received his B.S. in 1941 from City College of New York and his M.D. in 1944 from Howard University, and in 1980, he became the first African American physician elected president of the Medical Society of Kings County (New York). Cave was also the first African American dermatologist in Brooklyn. Cave also had been a founding father of the New York City Health and Hospitals Corporation and had worked for almost 50 years in behalf of African American medical and social causes.

African-American Medical Pioneers(1994), p. 169; *Blacks in Science and Medicine*(1990), p. 51; *Philadelphia Tribune*(May 20, 1997)

1980 • Guthrie Turner (1930-) was the first African American to attain the rank of brigadier general in the United States Army Medical Corps when he achieved the rank. He served in the position from 1980 to 1983. During the same period, Turner was the Hospital Commander of the Madigan Army Medical Center. Turner received a B.S. from Shaw University in 1949 and then a M.D. degree from Howard University Medical College in 1953.

African-American Medical Pioneers(1994), pp. 175

1980 • Leslie L. Alexander (1917-), when selected chancellor in 1980 of the American College of Radiology (ACR), was the first African American physician to be elected to that office, which he served through 1985. He was also the first African American elected vice-president of the ACR, which position he held for the period 1984-5. Alexander was treasurer of the National Medical Association from 1969 to 1974 and in 1978, delivered the first William E. Allen, Jr. Lecture of the Radiology Section of the National Medical Association. Two other firsts for Alexander include being the first African American radiologist to become chief of a service at the Jewish Hospital, Greenpoint Hospital Center of Brooklyn, and first African American consultant in radiotherapy at the Brooklyn Veterans Administration Hospital.

A Centennial History of African Americans in Radiology(1996), pp. 14-15, 97; *African-American Medical Pioneers*(1994), p. 169; *Black Enterprise*(February 1975), p. 27; *Journal of the National Medical Association*Vol. 57, (1965), p. 426

1980 • Maurice C. Clifford (1920-), in 1980, was the first African American selected president of the Medical College of Pennsylvania. He was appointed vice president for medical affairs in 1978, acting president in 1979, and president in 1980. Clifford earned a B.A. in 1941 at Hamilton College, a M.A. in 1942 at the University of Chicago, and a M.D. in 1947 at Meharry Medical College. He served as president of the Medical College of Pennsylvania from 1980 to 1986, then became commissioner of the

Department of Public Health of the City of Philadelphia. He is currently with Lomax Health Systems.

African-American Medical Pioneers(1994), pp. 27, 178; *Who's Who Among African Americans*(1998-1999), p. 287

1980 • The Scott Spiral Knee Brace was patented by an African American orthopedic surgeon, Linzy Scott (1934-), in 1980. Scott is currently in private practice in Atlanta, Georgia. He received a B.A. in 1957 from Lincoln University, a M.A. from Fisk University in 1959, and a M.D. from Howard University in 1963. He completed a residency at New Jersey Orthopedic Hospital and another at Columbia Presbyterian Hospital. Scott is an active member of a number of medical and orthopedic organizations. He was an Olympic team physician in 1981 and in 1983, team physician for the Gold Medalist National Amateur Basketball Team.

Who's Who Among African Americans(1998-1999), pp. 1124-1125

LEVI WATKINS, JR.

1980 • The first surgeon to implant the life-saving Automatic Implantable Defibrillator in a human was Levi Watkins, Jr. (1944-) when he performed the operation in 1980. Watkins received his M.D. from Vanderbilt University in 1970 and was the first African American student to receive the M.D. from Vanderbilt. He had received his B.S. in biology from Tennessee State University in 1966 with highest honors. Watkins applied for an internship at the Johns Hopkins University School of Medicine and in 1977, became Hopkins' first African American chief resident in surgery and cardiac surgery. Johns Hopkins promoted him to full professor in 1991, making him the first African American to hold that rank at the medical school. In the same year, Watkins was appointed the first African American assistant dean of Johns Hopkins Medical School, being responsible for all accredited postdoctoral programs, and faculty development.

African-American Medical Pioneers(1994), pp. 27, 121-124, 134; *Blacks in Science and Medicine*(1990), p. 243; *Century of Black Surgeons*(1987), pp. 932-933; *Ebony*(January 1982), pp. 96-98, 100

1980 • Pauline Y. Titus-Dillon (1938-), who received her M.D. from Howard University College of Medicine in 1964, was the first African American woman physician administrator in the dean's office of the Howard University College of Medicine when appointed in 1980. After receiving her M.D. degree, Titus-Dillon completed her internship and residency (in internal medicine) requirements at Freedmen's Hospital in Washington.

From 1977 to 1980, she was the first woman chief of the Howard University medical services at the District of Columbia General Hospital. Titus-Dillon also developed a five-year medical curriculum, which was approved by the dean, faculty, and trustees in 1988 as a type of support program. It was designed to meet the needs of students who required additional support to stay in school.

African-American Medical Pioneers (1994), pp. 119-120; *Journal of the National Medical Association* Vol. 85, (October 1993), p. 793; *Who's Who Among African-Americans* (1998-1999), p. 1492

1981 • The first African American appointed Director of the Michigan Department of Public Health, in 1981, was Bailus Walker, Jr. (1932-). Walker received his undergraduate degree in 1971 from the University of Kentucky and his M.D. in 1975 from the University of Minnesota. He was appointed Commissioner of Public Health and Chair of the Massachusetts Public Health Council, in which position he served from 1983 to 1987. Walker was also the first African American physician to hold these positions.

African-American Medical Pioneers (1994), p. 197; *African-Americans in Boston* (1991), p. 149

1981 • Sabrina Ann Benjamin was the first African American woman to receive a M.D. from the Uniformed Services University of the Health Sciences (Maryland) when she graduated in 1981. The Maryland native received her undergraduate degree from Howard University.

African-American Medical Pioneers (1994), p. 155

1981 • Natalear R. Collins and Brenda Mills Klutz were the first African American students to graduate with M.D.s from East Carolina University School of Medicine in 1981. Collins completed her undergraduate work at the University of North Carolina, Chapel Hill, while Klutz finished her undergraduate work at North Carolina A&T State University. In 1982, East Carolina School of Medicine awarded M.D.s to Julius Q. Mallette and James Reid, who were the first two African American men to receive degrees from that institution. Mallette received his bachelors degree from North Carolina State University, and Reid completed undergraduate work at East Carolina University.

African-American Medical Pioneers (1994), p. 148

1981 • In 1981, African American biomedical engineer Raphael C. Lee (1949-) became the first surgeon to win the prestigious MacArthur Prize Fellowship. Lee contributed unique research developments in surgery, biomedical engineering, and electrical shock trauma. Lee received an electrical engineering degree in 1971 at the University of South Carolina, and then in 1975 obtained a joint M.S. in electrical engineering from Drexel University and M.D. from Temple University (Pennsylvania) School of Medicine. He completed a surgical internship at University of Chicago (Illinois), then completed his Sc.D. at Massachusetts Institute of Technology in 1979, followed by a surgical residency at the University of Chicago and a residency in plastic and reconstructive surgery at Massachusetts General Hospital. Lee began a dual faculty appointment in 1983 at Harvard University (Massachusetts) and MIT, where he discovered an unrecognized cause of tissue injury in electrical shock victims, resulting in the advancement of a new therapy. Lee also developed new pharmaceutical approaches for excessive scar formation control.

African American Voices of Triumph (1994), p. 70; *Notable Twentieth Century Scientists* (1995), pp. 1208-9; *Science Digest* (December 1984), p. 49

1982 • The first African American female to earn a M.D. from Wright State University (Ohio) School of Medicine, in 1982, was Carol Jean Hubbard. The Ohio native received her undergraduate degree from the University of Cincinnati.

African-American Medical Pioneers (1994), p. 156

1983 • Kenneth A. Forde (1933-), a surgeon with a specialty in endoscopy, was a founding member of the Society of American Gastrointestinal Endoscopic Surgeons (SAGES). In 1983, he was the first African American elected president of the group. Forde earned a B.S., with honors, from the City College of New York in 1954 and received a M.D. in 1959 from the College of Physicians and Surgeons of Columbia University. He completed his residency at Columbia in 1966 and was appointed to the faculty in the Department of Surgery. Forde developed a reputation in endoscopy, and he was instrumental in promoting the importance of surgical endoscopy in surgery teaching programs. He has authored four chapters in textbooks, 43 journal articles, and developed educational materials and scientific exhibits. Forde also served as president of the New York Surgical Society.

A Century of Black Surgeons (1987), pp. 623-625; *African-American Medical Pioneers* (1994), p. 188

1983 • Howard University (Washington, D.C.) College of Medicine's first professor of social medicine was Jesse Belmary Barber Jr. (1924-), who assumed the post in 1983. Barber received his B.A. at Lincoln University (Pennsylvania), and in 1948 received the M.D. from Howard. He then undertook internship and residency programs in general surgery at Freedmen's Hospital from 1948 to 1954. Barber was instructor in surgery and pathology at Howard from 1956 to 1958, and then a resident at McGill University (Canada) Montreal Neurological Institute from 1958 to 1961. Taylor returned to Howard in 1961, holding the position of chief of the division of neurosurgery and professor of surgery until 1991. In 1968, Barber founded the Medical Stroke Project at Howard. In 1994, he became been president of the medical dental staff and associate professor of community medicine at District of Columbia General Hospital.

African American Medical Pioneers (1994), pp. 34, 1169; *Blacks in Science and Medicine* (1990), pp. 19-20; *Who's Who Among African Americans* (1998-1999), p. 73

1983 • Lori Margaret Campbell was the first African American woman and Paul Jeffrey Smith was the first African American man to receive, in 1983, M.D. degrees from the University of Hawaii, John A. Bumi School of Maui. Campbell also earned her undergraduate degree from the University of Hawaii, while Smith received his undergraduate degree from Howard University (D.C.).

African-American Medical Pioneers (1994), p. 149

1983 • The first African American woman to head a hospital's gastroenterology department was Doreen P. Palmer (1949-), who held that position at Manhattan's Metropolitan Hospital from 1983 to 1986. Palmer received her B.A. in 1972 from Lehman College and her M.D. in 1976 from New York Down State Medical School. She pursued a specialization in gastroenterology at Johns Hopkins Hospital from 1979 to 1981. In 1981, Palmer became an assistant professor of medicine at New York Medical College in Valhalla and assistant chief of the division of gastroenterology at Metropolitan Hospital in Manhattan, becoming division chief two years later. She is an adjunct physician at Lenox Hill Hospital and attending physician at Cabrini Hospital and Doctors' Hospital, both in New York.

Black Enterprise (October, 1988), p. 64; *Who's Who Among African Americans* (1998-1999), p. 1149

1983 • Melvin E. Jenkins, Jr. (1923-) was the first African American selected as a governor of the American Board of Pediatrics in 1983, serving in that position until 1989. Jenkins received his B.A. degree from the University of Kansas in 1944 and earned the M.D. degree in 1946. He completed a rotating internship at Freedman's Hospital in Washington, D.C. from 1946 to 1947 and a pediatric residency there until 1950. He became a clinical instructor in pediatrics, assistant professor in 1957, and associate professor in 1959. Jenkins trained from 1963 to 1965 as a research fellow in pediatric endocrinology at Johns Hopkins Hospital, becoming, in 1965, the first African American pediatric endocrinologist in the United States. He also became the first African American tenured faculty member at the University of Nebraska's Medical School, where he served from 1969 to 1973. Jenkins then returned to Howard University in 1973 and chaired the department of pediatrics and child health until he retired in 1987.

African-American Medical Pioneers(1994), pp. 28, 31, 74-77; *Blacks in Science and Medicine*(1990), p. 133; *Journal of the National Medical Association*Vol. 79, (October, 1987), pp. 1104-1106

1983 • In 1983, John D. Lewis became the first African American man and Rochelle A. Broome, Yvonne A. Patterson and Margo Shamberger Prade were the first African American women to receive M.D.s from Northeastern Ohio University College of Medicine. Lewis and Patterson earned their undergraduate degrees from the University of Akron (Ohio), while Broome and Prade received theirs from Kent State (Ohio).

African-American Medical Pioneers(1994), p. 153

1983 • The first African American to receive a M.D. degree from East Tennessee State University, James H. Quillen College of Medicine, was Gregory Patterson, who earned the degree in 1983. Patterson received his undergraduate degree from Fisk University (Tennessee).

African-American Medical Pioneers(1994), p. 154

1984 • Clive Orville Callender (1936-) was the first and only African American physician out of 18 distinguished scientists selected to the National Organ Transplant Task Force in 1984. Callender earned his M.D. from Meharry College (Maryland) in 1963. He is an internationally known expert in the field of organ transplantation and founder of the Howard University Hospital Transplant Center in 1973. In 1993, the center was awarded funding from the National Institutes of Health for the National Minority Organ and Tissue Transplant Education Program aimed at increasing pubic awareness and minority participation in organ/tissue transplant activities. Callender in now professor and chair of the surgery department at Howard University. He holds the chair of the membership committee of the American College of Surgeons.

African-American Medical Pioneers(1994), pp. 34, 178; *Blacks in Science and Medicine*(1990), p. 45; *Ebony*(April, 1977), pp. 59-62, 64-66; *Jet*(November 1, 1993), p. 38

1984 • The first African American appointed Commissioner of Public Health and Chair of the Massachusetts Public Health Council was Bailus Walker, Jr. (1932-) in 1984. He served in that position until 1987. Walker received his undergraduate degree in 1971 from the University of Kentucky and M.D. degree in 1975 from the University of Minnesota. Walker was previously appointed Commissioner of the Michigan Department of Public Health in 1981.

African-American Medical Pioneers(1994), p. 197; *African-Americans in Boston*(1991), p. 149

1984 • The first dedicated comprehensive cardiac MRI (magnetic resonance imaging) acquisition and analysis software package was initially developed in 1984 by Roderic I. Pettigrew (1950-) with the Philips Medical Systems. Pettigrew received his M.D. in 1979 from the University of Miami. Prior, in 1977, he had received a Ph.D. from Massachusetts Institute of Technology in nuclear engineering. Pettigrew is board certified in nuclear medicine and is a major contributor to research related to cardiac MRI. He is also a fellow in cardiovascular radiology of the American Heart Association and was a member of the board of trustees of the Society of Magnetic Resonance in Medicine from 1991 to 1993.

A Centennial History of African Americans in Radiology(1996), pp. 115-116, 146

1984 • Harold P. Freeman (1933-) was the first African American chair of the National Advisory Committees on Cancer, which he served from 1984 to 1988. Freeman earned an A.B. from the Catholic University of America in 1954 and his M.D. from Howard University Medical College in 1958. He completed an internship (1958-9) and a general surgery residency (1959-64) residency at Howard University Hospital, followed by a residency (1964-7) at the Sloane Kettering Cancer Center. Freeman became director of surgery at Harlem Hospital Center in 1974 and professor of clinical surgery at Columbia University in 1989. He is an active member of numerous medical organizations, councils, and task forces, and has lectured extensively in the United States and abroad. Freeman has published extensively and was elected president of the American Cancer Society in 1988.

A Century of Black Surgeons(1987), pp. 193-196; *African-American Medical Pioneers*(1994), pp. 34, 171; *Black Enterprise*(October 1988), p. 95; *Who's Who Among African Americans*(1998-1999), p. 513

1985 • The first African American physician elected to the Council on Medical Services of the American Medical Association, in 1985, was Lonnie R. Bristow (1930-). He also, in 1985, became the first African American elected to the American Medical Association Board of Trustees. Bristow later became the first African American physician elected president of the American Medical Association. Bristow received a B.S. degree in 1953 from

LONNIE BRISTOW

the City College of New York and the M.D. degree from New York University College of Medicine in 1957. He interned at San Francisco City and County Hospital from 1957 to 1958 and then completed a series of residencies at the USVA Hospital in San Francisco, Francis Delafield Hospital, Columbia University Service, and the USVA Hospital in the Bronx until 1961. Bristow has been awarded three honorary degrees.

Ebony (July 1995), pp. 38; *New York Times* (June 22, 1995); *Who's Who Among African Americans* (1998-1999), p. 140

1985 • The first African American female physician certified a gynecological oncologist was Deborah Ann Turner (1950-) who received her certification in 1985. Turner received her M.D. degree in 1978 from Iowa State University, having previously received her B.S. degree in 1973 there.

African-American Medical Pioneers (1994), p. 31, 197

1985 • The American Orthopedic Association selected, in 1985, Charles H. Epps, Jr. (1930-) as president. Epps was the first African American to hold that office. He graduated from Howard University with a B.S. in 1951 (*magna cum laude*) and then received a M.D. degree at Howard in 1955. Epps interned from 1955 to 1956 at Freedman's Hospital and then completed residencies at Freedman's Hospital, D.C. General, and Mount Alto VA Hospitals. He was the first African American physician serving as chief resident in orthopedic surgery during his tenure at D.C. General. He joined the Howard University College of Medicine in 1961 and by 1972, achieved the rank of full professor. He became dean in 1988. Epps is a nationally known orthopedic surgeon and medical educator. He has published extensively and edited three editions of *Complications in Orthopedic Surgery*. He was a member of the Council on Ethical and Judicial Affairs of the American Medical Association from 1982 to 1987 and again from 1989 to 1992.

A Century of Black Surgeons (1987), p. 38; *Blacks in Science and Medicine* (1990), pp. 85-86; *Journal of the National Medical Association* Vol. 49, (1957), p. 341; *African-American Medical Pioneers* (1994), p. 57-60

1985 • Lionel W. Young (1932-) became the first African American chair of the board of the Society for Pediatric Radiology in 1985. Young received his M.D. from Howard University in 1957. He then completed a three-year residency in radiology at Strong Memorial Hospital in Rochester and later a two-year fellowship in pediatric radiology at Cincinnati's Children's Hospital. From 1961 to 1963 he served at the U. S. Naval Hospital at Portsmouth, New Hampshire. Young, in 1984, became the first African American radiologist elected president of the Society for Pediatric Radiology, before being elected chair of the board the following year. In 1969, he was awarded the Society's John Caffey Award, and was the first recipient of the award. Young was well-known for his graphic medical displays, and at the National Association of Medicine's 1970 meeting, won its Gold Certificate of Merit as the best scientific exhibit.

A Centennial History of African Americans in Radiology (1996), pp. 15-16, 112

1985 • The Charles R. Drew University of Medicine and Science (California) awarded its first M.D. degrees to 15 graduates. Founded in 1966, Drew is the only of four historically African American medical schools that is located in the West.

African American Medical Pioneers (1994), p. 148

1985 • Milton E. Brunsen (1947-) was the first African American physician to complete a residency in obstetrics and gynecology at the University of Arkansas Medical School. Brunsen completed the residency in 1985 and finished course work at Philander Smith College and the University of Arkansas, Little Rock prior to his receiving the M.D. in 1980 from the University of Arkansas College of Medicine.

African American Medical Pioneers (1994), p. 185

1986 • Agnes Dolores Lattimer (1928-) became first African American woman to hold the top medical post in a major hospital in a major city when she was appointed medical director of Cook County Hospital (Chicago)in 1986. As medical director, she was responsible for 350 doctors and 475 interns and residents in the 1,200 bed medical facility. Lattimer held the position until 1995. In 1954, she was the first African American woman to earn a M.D. degree from the University of Chicago, having received a B.S. degree, *magna cum laude,* from Fisk University (Tennessee) in 1949. Lattimer was director of ambulatory pediatrics at Michael Reese Hospital in Chicago from 1966 to 1971 and held the same position at Cook from 1971 to 1984. Lattimer is a fellow of the American Board of Pediatrics and also holds a full professorship in the Department of Pediatrics of the University of Chicago. She has also taught at the Illinois School of Public Health.

African-American Medical Pioneers(1994), p. 192; *Black Women in America*(1993), pp. 698-699; *Ebony*(September, 1986), pp. 44, 46, 48

1986 • Rosalyn Sterling (1950-) was the first African American woman certified by the American Board of Thoracic Surgeons in 1986. Sterling received her M.D. from New York University School of Medicine in 1974. She served as director of Surgical Intensive Care Unit at King-Drew Hospital.

African-American Medical Pioneers(1994), pp. 31, 196

1986 • Herbert W. Nickens (1947-) became in 1986 the first African American to be appointed director of the U. S. Department of Health and Human Services Office of Minority Health. Nickens earned a B.S. from Harvard University (Massachusetts) in 1969 and a M.D. in 1973 from the University of Pennsylvania. He held the Office of Minority Health directorship until 1988, when he became vice president of the A.A.M.C. Division of Minority Health Education and Prevention.

African American Medical Pioneers(1994), pp. 34, 194

1986 • John L. Townsend (1932-) and Donald E. Wilson (1936-) founded the Association for Academic Minority Physicians in 1986. Townsend earned his B.S. in 1955 from Fisk University (Tennessee) and the M.D. from the University of Oklahoma College of Medicine in 1959, while Wilson earned a B.S. in 1958 from Harvard University (Massachusetts) and his M.D. from Tufts University (Massachusetts) School of Medicine in 1962.

African American Medical Pioneers(1994), pp. 31, 197, 124- 6

1987 • Beverly Coleman (1948-) was the first African American woman to be appointed a full professor of radiology at the University of Pennsylvania when she was promoted to the position in 1987. Coleman is the author of the text *Genitourinary Ultrasound* (1987).

A Centennial History of African Americans in Radiology(1996), p. 109

1987 • Gayle Smith-Blair, in 1987, was the first African American woman to receive a M.D. from Texas A&M University Health Sciences Center School of Medicine. Smith-Blair also earned her undergraduate degree from Texas A & M.

African-American Medical Pioneers(1994), p. 155

1987 • Benjamin S. Carson (1951-) became the first neurosurgeon to successfully separate Siamese twins joined at the head when he performed the 22-hour operation in 1987. The twins were seven months old. Carson earned his B.A. at Yale University in 1973 and his M.D. at the University of Michigan in 1977. He developed an expertise in brain surgery, performing complex neurosurgical procedures, particularly on children, and is considered an international authority on hemispherectomies (in which the two halves of the brain are separated to prevent seizures). At age 33, Carson was the youngest and the first African American director of pediatric neurosurgery at Johns Hopkins Hospital in Baltimore, Maryland in 1985. Carson also performed the first successful intrauterine shunting procedure for hydrocephalic twins in 1986. He has numerous scientific publications in texts and journals, having started publishing in 1982. He also published his autobiography, *Gifted Hands*, in 1990.

African American Almanac (1997), p. 1066; *African-American Firsts* (1994), p. 251; *Ebony* (January, 1988), pp. 52, 54, 56, 58; *The Timetables of African-American History* (1996), p. 349; *Notable Twentieth Century Scientists* (1995), p. 320-2

1987 • John F. Williams (1948-), who received the M.D. from George Washington University in 1979, was the first African American to become assistant dean of admission and chair of the admissions committee at George Washington University College of Medicine in 1987. Williams completed his undergraduate work at Boston University in 1975.

African American Medical Pioneers (1994), p. 199

1988 • Thomas Ellis Malone (1926-) was the first African American to serve as Vice-President for Biomedical Research of the Association of American Medical Colleges from 1988-1993. Prior to that position, Malone was the first African American to serve as associate vice chancellor for research at the University of Maryland Graduate School, Baltimore, from 1986 to 1988. He received a B.S. degree in 1948 from North Carolina Central University and a Ph.D. from Harvard University in 1952. After receiving his Ph.D., Malone served as professor of zoology from 1952 to 1958 at North Carolina Central University and then was a resident research associate at Argonne Research for the period 1958 to 1959. Malone started working for the National Institutes of Health in 1963 as assistant chief of the research grants section and served in several capacities—including deputy and acting director—there until 1986. Malone is now retired.

African-American Medical Pioneers (1994), pp. 192-193; *Who's Who Among African Americans* (1998-1999), p. 962

1988 • In 1988, Patricia E. Bath (1942-) patented the Laserphaco Probe, a laser device used to remove cataracts from the eyes. This newer device, which she spent five years developing, is less disruptive to the eye than older methods of removing cataracts. Bath received a B.S. from Hunter College in 1964 and her M.D. from Howard University in 1968. She completed a residency in ophthalmology at New York University School of Medicine from 1970 to 1973 and then in 1974, was a co-founder of the ophthalmology residency program at King/Drew Medical Center. In 1975, she became a surgeon on the staff at UCLA Medical Center. Bath was the first African American woman to chair the Department of Ophthalmology at King/Drew Medical Center from 1983 to 1986. She has also been awarded patents in Japan, Canada and Europe.

African-American Medical Pioneers (1994), p. 169; *Ebony* (February, 1997), p. 48; *Journal of the National Medical Association* Vol. 85, (1993), p. 641

1988 • The first African American physician named chief of staff of Halifax Regional Hospital in North Carolina was Raven L. DeLoatch. The hospital serves three rural counties and holds over 200 beds. DeLoatch is an internist serving Roanoke-Amaranth Community Health Center in Jackson, North Carolina.

Jet (June 22, 1998), p. 57

1988 • Eric Arnold Buffong (1951-), in 1988, presented the first eight cases of laparoscopic vaginal hysterectomies in the world at the First North

BENJAMIN CARSON

American/South American Congress of Gynecologic Endoscopy held in Dallas, Texas. Buffong earned the M.D. degree from Howard University College of Medicine in 1977. He was a fellow in reproductive endocrinology at Albert Einstein College of Medicine from 1981 to 1983 and associate professor of gynocology from 1983 to 1984. He then entered private practice and is now a senior partner of the Onslow Women's Health Center in Jacksonville, North Carolina.

Who's Who Among African Americans(1998-1999), p. 202

1989 • The first woman named deputy assistant secretary for health in the U. S. Department of Health and Human Services was African American physician Audrey Forbes Manley (1934-) in 1989. In that position, she was the second ranking person in the public health system. In 1988, Manley had been promoted to the rank of surgeon general (rear admiral) in the U.S. Public Health Service and was the first African American woman promoted to that position. Manley received a B.A. from Spellman College in 1955 and her M.D. from Meharry College in 1959. She completed a residency in pediatrics at Cook County Children's Hospital from 1961 to 1963. She was the first African American woman to be chief resident at Cook's 500-bed Children's Hospital in 1962 and the first African American to hold a faculty appointment at the University of Chicago School of Medicine in 1966. Manley also received a M.P.H. from Johns Hopkins University School of Public Health and Hygiene in 1987.

AUDREY MANLEY

African American Medical Pioneers (1994), pp. 87-89; *Journal of the National Medical Association* Vol. 85, (1993), p. 787; *Philadelphia Tribune* (January 3, 1989); *Who's Who Among Black Americans* (1990-1991), p. 816

1989 • Robert Lee M. Hilliard (1931-) was the first African American elected President of the Texas State Board of Medical Examiners when he was appointed president in 1989. He served in the position until 1990, having been first appointed to the Board in 1984. Hilliard received a B.S. degree in 1951 from Howard University and his M.D. 1956 from the University of Texas, Medical Branch. He was elected president of the National Medical Association in 1982.

African-American Medical Pioneers(1994), p. 189; *Blacks in Science and Medicine*(1990), p. 121; *Who's Who Among African Americans*(1998-1999), p. 695

1989 • Tyshawn M. James was the first African American to earn the M.D. degree from Marshall University School of Medicine when she received the degree in 1989. She had previously received her undergraduate degree from Marshall.

African-American Medical Pioneers(1994), p. 150

1989 • Louis W. Sullivan (1933-) was the first African American in George Bush's presidential administration when he was appointed Secretary of the Department of Health and Human Services in 1989. Sullivan received his B.S. in 1954 from Morehouse as a premedical major. After receiving his M.D. with honors from Boston University Medical School, he became the first African American house staff officer at Cornell Medical School's New York Hospital. From 1961 to 1964, Sullivan was the first African American fellow on the Harvard service of the Thorndike Laboratory at Boston City College. He was appointed the first dean of the new Morehouse Medical Education Program in 1975, and then in 1981 became the first president of the Morehouse School of Medicine. Sullivan has over 70 articles published in numerous journals between 1957 and 1992. He authored a textbook on the education of African American health professionals.

African-American Medical Pioneers(1994), pp. 113-115, 196-197; *Black Firsts*(1994), pp. 165-166; *Blacks in Science and Medicine*(1990), p. 224; *Journal of the National Medical Association*Vol. 85, (1993), pp. 792-793

1989 • The first African American woman to serve as president of the Society of Adolescent Medicine was Renee Rosalind Jenkins (1947-), who held the office from 1989 to 1990. In 1990, she became the first African American to chair a national committee for the American Academy of Pediatrics. Jenkins received her B.A. degree in 1967 and her M.D. in 1971, both from Wayne State University (Michigan). She specialized in pediatrics and completed the residency program at Albert Einstein College of Medicine (New York). Jenkins directs the adolescent medicine program at Howard University Hospital and in 1993, became the first woman and first African American to direct that program.

African-American Medical Pioneers(1994), pp. 77-79; *Journal of the National Medical Association*Vol. 85, (1993), p. 786; *Philadelphia New Observer*(January 29, 1997)

1989 • The Society of Nuclear Medicine selected its first African American president, for the term 1989-90, when Richard A. Holmes (1931-) was named to that position. Holmes received his M.D. in 1958 from Temple University. He was a fellow in nuclear medicine at Johns Hopkins from 1965 to 1967 and, after a career in nuclear medicine at the University of Missouri-Columbia, he was named vice-president for research and develop-

ment at the DuPont-Merck Corporation in 1994. Prior to that, Holmes was instrumental in Charles R. Drew University re-establishing accreditation for its residency program. He was also the developer of the radioisotopic agent, HMPAO.

A Centennial History of African Americans in Radiology(1996), p. 113   LOUIS W. SULLIVAN

1989 • The first African American woman to head the Radiology Section of the National Medical Association was Elizabeth Ann Patterson (1936-) in 1989. She received her B.S. in 1951 from the University of Michigan and her M.D. in 1961 from Howard University College of Medicine. Patterson worked as a radiologist for Mercy Hospital from 1972 to 1980 and was assistant professor of radiology from 1981 to 1985 at the University of Pittsburgh/Magee Women's Hospital. She was then, from 1985 to 1988, diagnostic radiologist at Central Medical Center and Hospital before becoming assistant professor of radiology at the Hospital of the University of Pennsylvania. Patterson has been president of both Pittsburgh and Philadelphia Roentgen Ray Societies and president (1996-7) of the Pennsylvania Radiological Society.

A Centennial History of African Americans in Radiology (1996), pp. 26, 27- 28, 109

1990 • Eddie L. Hoover (1944-) was the first African American appointed chair of the department of surgery at the State University of New York at Buffalo School of Medicine and Biomedical Sciences in 1990. Hoover received his B.S. in 1965 from the University of North Carolina, Chapel Hill in 1965, and was the second African American to receive the M.D. at Duke University School of Medicine when he graduated in 1969.

African American Medical Pioneers (1994), p. 190

1990 • Roselyn Payne Epps (1930-) was the first African American president of the American Medical Women's Association for the term 1990-1991. Epps graduated from Howard University in 1951 with a B.S. majoring in zoology, then acquired her M.D. from Howard University in 1955. She also earned a M.P.H. in maternal and child health from Johns Hopkins in 1973 and a M.A. from American University in 1981 in interdisciplinary studies. Epps has been a practicing pediatrician, educator, administrator, and organizational leader. In all her activities she has been motivated by her belief in advocating adequate and appropriate medical services for poor people. She was the first woman and first African American to become president of the D.C. Chapter of the American Academy of Pediatrics from 1988 to 1991, and she was the first African American woman to be president of the D.C. Medical Society in 1992.

African-American Medical Pioneers (1994), pp. 60-62; *Blacks in Science and Medicine* (1990), p. 86; *Ebony* (June, 1955), p. 124; *Journal of the National Medical Association* Vol. 85, (1993), pp. 782-783

1990 • The first African American to author a text on rational behavior therapy was Maxie C. Maultsby (1932-), when his book, *Rational Behavior Therapy*, was published in 1990. Another book, *Coping Better*, was published the same year. Maultsby received a bachelor's degree in 1953 from Talladega College and a M.D. from Case Western Reserve University in 1957. He completed his internship in 1958 at Philadelphia General Hospital. He was a family practitioner in Cocoa, Florida, from 1958 to 1962. Maultsby completed psychiatric residency training in adult and child psychiatry at the University of Wisconsin Hospitals in Madison, Wisconsin. His major contribution to psychiatry was making emotional self-help a legitimate focus of scientific research and clinical use. Maultsby's technique of cognitive-behavioral therapy, called rational behavior therapy, is the first comprehensive, yet short-term, culture- and drug-free technique of psychotherapy that produces long-term therapeutic results. His books are designed for professional therapists and the knowledgeable lay audience.

African American Medical Pioneers(1994), pp. 92-95, 193; *Journal of the National Medical Association, Volume 85*(October 1993), pp. 788-789

1990 • The first African American physician elected president of the American College of Obstetricians and Gynecologists (ACOG) was Ezra C. Davidson, Jr. (1933-), when he was elected to the position in 1990. Davidson has been a professor and chairman of the obstetrics and gynecology department at Charles R. Drew University of Medicine and Science and department chief at Martin Luther King General Hospital since 1971. He earned a B.S. degree in 1954 from Morehouse College and a M.D. degree in 1958 from Meharry Medical School. He was a professor, from 1971 to 1980, at the University of Southern California School of Medicine and has held a professorship at the University of California since 1979. He was chair of the Federal Advisory Committee for Fertility and Maternal Health Drugs in 1992 and has been a member of the National Academy of Sciences, Institute of Medicine, since 1991.

Blacks in Science and Medicine(1990), p. 68; *Jet*(August 27, 1990), p. 20; *Philadelphia Tribune*(June 26, 1990); *Who's Who Among African-Americans*(1998-1999), p. 362

1990 • James Frederick Littles, Jr. (1960-) was the first African American faculty member in the Department of Radiation Oncology at the University of Michigan Medical School when appointed in 1990. Littles earned his B.S. in 1982 at South Carolina State University and his M.D. in 1986 at Howard University Medical College (D.C.). In 1991, Littles became the first African American Clinical Radiation Oncology Service Chief of the Veterans Affairs Medical Center in Ann Arbor, Michigan. Littles is also a deacon at the Straight Gate Church.

Who's Who Among African-Americans(1998-1999), p. 931

1991 • The first African American physician elected chair of the American Board of Internal Medicine was Gerald E. Thomson (1932-), when he took office in 1991. Thomson earned the M.D. degree from Howard University College of Medicine in 1959. He interned from 1959 to 1960 at State University of New York (SUNY) Kings County Hospital and completed residencies there in internal medicine from 1960 to 1963. He was associated with SUNY Medicine, Brooklyn Hospital, from 1966 to 1970 and Coney Island Hospital also, until 1970. Thomson was president of the Harlem Hospital Center from 1976 to 1978. Since 1970, he has taught at Columbia University and been associated with Presbyterian Hospital. He is currently the Samuel Lambert professor at Columbia and chief of staff at Presbyterian. Thomson has been an active member of several health commissions, both local and national, and a member of the advisory board of the Journal of Urban Health. He is a diplomat of the American Board of Internal Medicine, as well as a fellow of the American College of Physicians. In 1984, he received the National Medical Award from the National Kidney Foundation.

African-American Medical Pioneers (1994), p. 175; *Who's Who Among African Americans* (1998-1999), p. 1486

1991 • Vivian Winona Pinn (1941-) became the first director of the Office of Research on Women's Health at the National Institutes of Health when she was chosen for that office in 1991. The mission of her office is to represent women's issues and to promote those interests within N.I.H. and the biomedical community. Pinn earned her B.A. from Wellesley College and her M.D. from the University of Virginia School of Medicine. She completed her postgraduate training in pathology at Massachusetts General Hospital. Pinn served as professor of pathology at Howard University when she accepted the position as chair of the department in 1982. She was the first African American woman to chair a medical pathology department. Pinn is a past president of the National Medical Association, only the second woman to hold that position.

Blacks in Science and Medicine (1990), p. 192; *Ebony* (April, 1990), pp. 58, 60, (July, 1995), pp. 124, 126; *Journal of the National Medical Association* (1993), Vol. 85, p. 790

1991 • The first African American physician in the United States to develop a specialty in sleep disorder treatment was Alex Adu Clerk in 1991. Clerk is the director of the Stanford University Sleep Disorders Clinic in Stanford, California. Clerk completed studies at the University of Ghana Medical School before completing his residency in psychiatry at Loma Linda (California) University School of Medicine. He then completed a post-doctoral fellowship at Stanford in 1989-90 and was appointed director of the Sleep Disorders Clinic in 1991. Clerk and his staff consult with, diagnose, and treat patients with chronic sleep problems. At the time of his appointment, Clerk was the only African American physician heading one of about 150 sleep clinics in the United States.

Ebony (July, 1992), pp. 60-62

1991 • When Donald E. Wilson (1936-) was appointed dean of the University of Maryland Medical School in 1991, he became the first African American dean of a predominately white medical school. Wilson received his B.S. in 1958 from Harvard College and then received his M.D. from Tufts Medical School in 1962. He completed a residency at the Boston VA Hospital and served a fellowship at Boston's Lemuel Shattuck Hospital, where he also became chief resident. After his postgraduate training and two years of military service, Wilson became an instructor at the State University New York (SUNY) Downstate, Brooklyn from 1968 to 1971 and worked at the University of Illinois School of Medicine in Chicago until 1977. He returned to SUNY Downstate in 1980 as the first African American professor and chairman of its department of medicine until 1991, when he was appointed dean at Maryland. He was the first African American officer elected to the Association of Professors of Medicine in 1990. Wilson was heavily engaged in research during his career, having authored or co-authored over 100 journal articles.

African-American Medical Pioneers (1994), pp. 27, 124-126; *Ebony* (July, 1995), p. 124; *Journal of the National Medical Association* Vol. 85, (1993), p. 794

1991 • The first African American man to receive a M.D. from the University of Nevada School of Medicine was Carl Demardrian Virgil in 1991. He earned his undergraduate degree from the University of Nevada, Las Vegas.

African-American Medical Pioneers (1994), p. 152

1991 • Wilburn Harold Weddington, Sr. (1924-) was the first African American appointed associate dean, Medicine Administration, Ohio State University College of Medicine when appointed to the position in 1991. Weddington joined the staff at Ohio State University College of Medicine in 1970 as staff physician and held the position until 1988. He was clinical associate professor there from 1980 to 1985 and professor of clinical family medicine from 1987. He earned a B.S. degree from Morehouse College (Georgia) in 1944 and a M.D. degree in 1948 from Howard University College of Medicine (D.C.). He also studied radiology at the University of Buffalo (New York), electrocardiography at Harvard University, and obstetrics and pediatrics at the University of Mexico. Weddington is a member of several medical association and organizations, including being a co-founder of the Columbus Association of Physicians and Dentists in

1973. He has authored or co-authored a number of medical publications and editorials.

African-American Medical Pioneers(1994), p. 176; *Who's Who Among African Americans*(1998-1999), p. 1376

1992 • Charles L. Curry (1934-) was the first African American physician appointed to the board of trustees of the American College of Cardiology with his term running from 1992 through 1997. Curry received his B.S. in 1955 from Johnson C. Smith College and a M.D. from Howard University in 1959. Curry, an internist, was a founding member of the American Association of Professors of Cardiology in 1990.

African-American Medical Pioneers(1994), p. 170

EDWARD S. COOPER

1992 • Edward Sawyer Cooper (1926-) was the first African American selected president of the American Heart Association when he took office in 1992. The mission of the Association is to reduce disability and death from cardiovascular stroke and disease. Cooper received his B.A. from Lincoln University (Pennsylvania) in 1946 and a M.D. in 1949 from Meharry Medical College (Georgia). He completed internship and residency activities at Philadelphia General Hospital from 1949 to 1954. He joined the University of Pennsylvania Medical School's medical staff in 1958 and in 1972, became the university's first African American tenured professor. He was later named chief of medical services at the university's hospital. Cooper was a member of numerous editorial boards, as well as acting as consulting editor for *Stroke* magazine

Blacks in Science and Medicine(1990), p. 61; *Ebony*(October, 1992), pp. 25-26 , (July, 1995), p. 126; *Philadelphia Inquirer*(June 25, 1991)

1992 • The University of Alabama School of Medicine appointed its first African American associate vice president for health affairs when Marlon L. Priest (1952-) was selected for the office in 1992. Priest received a B.S. from Florence State University (Alabama) in 1974 and his M.D. in 1977 from the University of Alabama School of Medicine. He was the director of outpatient medicine at the Baptist Medical center in Birmingham from 1980-1, when he assumed the posts of deputy medical director and then medical director of the emergency department of the University of Alabama University Hospital, remaining there until 1990. He became assistant professor of surgery at Alabama in 1985, and was promoted to associate professor in 1986 and full professor in 1994. Priest also served as a member of the president's advisory council for the University.

African American Medical Pioneers(1994), p. 195; *Who's Who Among African Americans*(1998-1999), p. 1220

1993 • The first African American woman to head a U. S. medical school was Barbara Ross-Lee, when she was appointed dean of the Ohio University College of Osteopathic Medicine in 1993. She is also a practicing physician, professor of family medicine, and a naval officer. Ross-Lee received her medical degree in 1973 from Michigan State University College of Osteopathic Medicine. She began teaching at Michigan State and served as associate dean for health policy and professor of family medicine before her tenure at Ohio University. She has been president of the National Osteopathic Medical Association since 1992.

Jet(August 11, 1993), p. 18; *Philadelphia Tribune*(July 9, 1993); *Timelines of African-American History*(1994), p. 344; *Who's Who Among African Americans*(1997), p. 1126

1993 • S. Allen Counter was the first African American physician to be awarded the doctor of medical science degree from the Karolinska Nobel Institute in Sweden (Stockholm), which he received in 1993. Counter is a Harvard University neuroscientist and earned the degree after four years of study.

Jet(May 31, 1993), p. 22

1993 • President William Clinton appointed M. Joycelyn Elders (1933-) as U. S. Surgeon General in 1993, making her the first African American and first woman to hold that position. Elders earned her B.S. from Philander Smith College in 1952 and her M.D. from the University of Arkansas School of Medicine in 1960. She also earned a M.S. degree in biochemistry from the University of Arkansas Medical Center in 1967. After graduation, she was hired as an assistant professor at the University of Arkansas Medical College, then promoted to associate professor in 1971, and finally, in 1976, to professor of pediatrics. As a pediatric endocrinologist, Elder completed extensive research in metabolism, growth hormones, and somatomedia in acute leukemia. In 1987, she was appointed head of the Arkansas Department of Health, making her the first woman and first African American to hold the position. Elders was U.S. Surgeon General from September 8, 1993 until December 10, 1994, when she resigned. During her tenure, she worked to reduce the rate of teen pregnancies and the spread of HIV and AIDS. Elders has, to date, published over 147 scientific papers and monographs.

Black Firsts(1994), pp. 166-167; *Ebony*(February, 1993), pp. 156-160; *Jet*(September 27, 1993), pp. 19-20; *New York Times*(September 8, 1993); *Philadelphia Tribune*(September 8, 1993)

M. JOCELYN ELDERS

1993 • The first African American appointed dean of a predominately white medical school was Haile T. Debas (1937-) when he became dean, in 1993, of the University of California Medical School at San Francisco. Debas earned a B.S. degree at the University College of Addis Ababa, Ethiopia in 1958 and his M.D. at McGill University (Canada) in 1963. He then completed an internship from 1963 to 1964 at Ottawa Civic Hospital and a general surgery residency from 1964 to 1969 at Vancouver General Hospital. He was professor of surgery and chief of gastrointestinal surgery at the University of Washington from 1985 to 1987, then professor and surgery department chairman at University of California, San Fransisco in 1991 until his appointment as dean of the medical school in 1994. Debas, in 1991 to 1992, was president of the International Hepato-Biliary-Pancreatic Association. He has been director of the American Board of Surgery since 1990 and a fellow of the American Academy of Arts and Sciences since 1992.

African-American Medical Pioneers(1994), pp. 27, 28, 186; *Who's Who Among African-Americans*(1998-1999), p. 385

1993 • The U. S. Postal Service appointed the first African American physician as its national medical director when David H. Reid III (1936-) assumed that position in 1993. Reid received his medical degree from Howard University and is a specialist in occupational medicine. He began his tenure with the postal service in 1987, when he was appointed senior medical officer for the Chicago Division. From 1991 to the time of his appointment as national director, he was the Southern Region medical director.

Philadelphia Tribune(July 2, 1993), p. 2B

1993 • L.D. Britt was the first African American physician to be named the Henry Ford Professor of Surgery at Norfolk (VA) State University when he was selected in 1993. Britt was the first African American in Virginia to be appointed a full professor of surgery at the same time. He is chief of the division of trauma and critical care at Eastern Virginia Medical School.

Jet(September 6, 1993), p. 20

1993 • Ross M. Miller Jr. (1928-1996) was the first African American physician, in 1993, elected president of the Los Angeles Surgical Society. This group is comprised of fellows of the American College of Surgeons and surgeons who teach at medical schools and major hospitals in the Los Angeles area. Miller was a member and governor of the surgical section of the National Medical Association to the American College of Surgeons, as well as a fellow of the International College of Surgeons. He completed his internship at Jersey City Medical Center (1951-2) and then surgical residencies at Tuskegee VA Hospital (1952-4), Bronx VA Hospital (1956-8), and then surgical residencies at Emory University and Grady Memorial Hospital (1958-9). Miller was involved in private practice, as well as holding the position of clinical professor of surgery at UCLA and Charles R. Drew Medical School. He also served as president of the Medical, Dental, and Pharmaceutical Association of Southern California and as president of the Southern California Chapter of the American College of Surgeons.

A Century of Black Surgeons (1987), pp. 475, 476; *Howard University Alumni News* (Spring/Summer 1993), p. 37; *Jet* (April 5, 1993), p. 20

HENRY W. FOSTER, JR.

1993 • Henry Wendell Foster, Jr. (1933-), in 1993, was the first African American elected president of the Association of Professors of Obstetrics and Gynecology. Foster graduated from Morehouse College in 1954 with a B.S. degree and in 1958, received his M.D. from the University of Arkansas. He interned at Detroit Receiving Hospital in 1959, then completed a surgery residence in 1962 at Malden Hospital and another residency in obstetrics and gynecology from 1962 to 1965 at George W. Hubbard Hospital. At Meharry Medical College, Foster became professor and department chairman from 1973 to 1990, dean and vice-president for medical affairs from 1990 to 1993, then acting president from 1993 to 1994. He was the presidential nominee for U.S. Surgeon General in 1995 and Senior Advisor to President Clinton for Teen Pregnancy and Youth Issues in 1996. Foster is currently a professor in obstetrics and gynocology at Meharry.

African-American Medical Pioneers (1994), p. 188; *Who's Who Among African Americans* (1998-1999), p. 499

1994 • Osteopathic surgeon William G. Anderson was inaugurated on July 17, 1994 as the first African American president of the American Osteopathic Association (AOA). Anderson is a 1956 graduate of the University of Osteopathic Medicine and Health Sciences, Des Moines, and is a fellow of the American College of Osteopathic Surgeons. He has over 30 years experience in a general and surgical specialty practice. Anderson served as a consultant and senior attending surgeon at the Michigan Health Care Corporation. He also served as chief of surgery, chief of staff, and chairman of the board of directors. Anderson has served as president of both his county and state osteopathic associations and as a trustee of the AOA for over 10 years. He is currently associate director of medical education at the Detroit Riverview Center and president of the LifeChoice Quality Health Plan, a Detroit HMO.

Emerge (July/August, 1994), p. 44; *Philadelphia New Observer* (August 18, 1993); *Philadelphia Tribune* (July 15, 1994)

1994 • Eve Juliet Higginbotham (1953-) became the first African American woman to chair a university-based department of ophthalmology when she was appointed in 1994 as professor and chair of the department of ophthalmology at the University of Maryland, Baltimore. Higginbotham received both a B.S. and M.S. from the Massachusetts Institute of Technology in 1975 and a M.D. from Harvard University Medical School in 1979. She interned in 1979 at the Pacific Medical Center and completed a residency from 1980 to 1983 at the Louisiana State University Eye Center. Higginbotham was an assistant professor from 1985 to 1990 at the University of Illinois, and then assistant professor and assistant dean from 1990 to 1994 at the University of Michigan.

Who's Who Among African Americans (1998-1999), p. 685

1995 • The American Medical Association selected the first African American woman to become a member of the board of trustees in 1995 when it chose Regina M. Benjamin (1956-) to the post. She is only the second African American to be named to the board in the organization's history. Benjamin is a family doctor who runs a small clinic in the isolated town of Bayou LaBatre, Alabama. She earned a B.S. in chemistry from Xavier University in 1979 and her M.D. in 1984 from the University of Alabama at Birmingham. Benjamin worked for the National Health Service Corps from 1987 until 1990, when she took over the operation of the rural health clinic in Bayou LaBatre. She was named Person of the Week by *ABC World News Tonight* in 1995.

New York Times (June 22, 1995); *Philadelphia Tribune* (July 4, 1995, August 1, 1995); *Who's Who Among African Americans* (1998-1999), p. 103; *Jet* (July 10, 1995), p. 38

1995 • The first African American to head a radiation oncology department for the Department of Defense was Darryl C. Hunter in 1995. Hunter is chief of the radiology oncology department at Keesler Air Force Base (Mississippi). Hunter received a B.S. in genetics from the University of California at Davis and a M.D. from the Uniformed Services University of the Health Sciences (Maryland). Hunter's responsibilities as radiation oncology department head includes oversight for radiation treatments and clinical research.

Ebony (January, 1996), p. 6

1995 • James L. Sweatt, III was the first African American, in 1995, elected president of the Dallas County Medical Society, which has a membership of over 5,000 physicians. Sweatt, a thoracic surgeon, was the first African American to receive the M.D. degree from the Washington University School of Medicine in 1962. He received his undergraduate degree from Middlebury College.

African-American Medical Pioneers (1994), p. 156; *Jet* (May 22, 1995), p. 24

LONNIE BRISTOW

1995 • The American Medical Association (AMA) selected an African American physician, Lonnie Robert Bristow (1930-) for the first time in its 140-year history as president. Bristow was as an alternate delegate to the AMA in 1978 and joined its board of trustees in 1985. He received a B.S. in 1953 and a M.D. from the New York University College of Medicine in 1957. He has spent his career as an occupational health specialist in internal medicine. In 1981, Bristow was elected president of the American Society of Internal Medicine. He received a presidential appointment in 1966 as Chairman of the Board of Regents of the Uniformed Services University of the Health Sciences. Bristow was named a fellow of the American College of Physicians in 1977 and a master in 1995. He has received three honorary degrees.

Ebony(April, 1995), pp. 82, 85; *New York Times*(June 22, 1995); *Philadelphia Inquirer*(June 22, 1995); *Philadelphia Tribune*(August 1, 1995)

HELEN GAYLE

1995 • Helen Doris Gayle (1955-) became in 1995 the first African American woman to serve as director of the National Center for HIV, STD, and TB Prevention Centers for Disease Control and Prevention of the U.S. Centers for Disease Control (CDC). Gayle earned a B.A. in 1976 at Barnard College (New York), the M.D. in 1981 from the University of Pennsylvania, and then a M.P.H. from Johns Hopkins University (Maryland) in 1981. She completed her residency and internship in pediatrics at Children's Hospital Medical Center in Washington, D.C. Gayle's association with the CDC from 1984 onward led to her work as coordinator of the AIDS Agency and chief of the HIV/AIDS Division of the U.S. Agency for International Development Office of Health, where she enhanced her reputation as one of the international community's top AIDS scientists. Gayle has received the U.S. Public Health Service Achievement Medal among her many awards.

African American Almanac(1997), p. 1069; *Blacks in Science and Medicine*(1990), p. 99; *Black Enterprise*(October 1988), p. 62; *Ebony*(July 1995); *Who's Who Among African Americans*(1998-1999), p. 537

1996 • Audrey Burnette Rhodes was the first African American president of the South Carolina chapter of the American Academy of Family Physicians. Rhodes acts as spokesperson for the organization's 1,175 members statewide. She earned a B.S. and M.S. in biology and received her M.D. from the Medical College of Toledo. Rhodes is currently director of a community-based immunization program.

Ebony(April, 1996), p. 8

1996 • The newly formed National Institute of Allergy and Infectious Diseases Laboratory of Allergic Diseases appointed the African American physician, Dean D. Metcalfe, as its first chief. Prior to his appointment, Metcalfe was, from 1993, the head of the Asthma, Allergic and Immunologic Diseases Cooperative Intramural Research Center.

Philadelphia Tribune (March 12, 1996), p. 7B

1996 • Debra Holly Ford became in 1996 the first African American woman to be certified in colon and rectal surgery, also becoming the first African American woman diplomate of the Board of Colon and Rectal Surgery. Ford received a B.S. in zoology from Howard University (Washington, D.C.) and her M.D. from the Howard University School of Medicine. She later became chief of the colon and rectal surgery division at Howard.

Ebony (October 1996), p. 8; *Who's Who Among African Americans* (1998-1999), p. 492

1997 • Joyce Carter (1956-) was the first woman and first African American to serve as chief medical examiner for Harris County (Houston area) Texas when appointed in 1997. One of only a handful of African Americans in her field, she has a staff of 80 physicians, chemists, lab technicians, investigators, and secretaries. Carter received her M.D. from Howard University and then served as chief resident in pathology at the university's hospital. She was a fellow in forensic pathology in Dade County, Florida and chief physician and forensic pathologist in the U.S. Air Force Medical Corps. Formerly chief medical examiner in Washington, D.C., Carter also teaches at Howard University and Baylor College of Medicine (Texas).

Black Enterprise (February, 1998), p. 118; *Philadelphia Tribune* (October 14, 1997)

1997 • Robert Shaw Rhodes (1936-) was the first African American physician elected president of the American College of Occupational and Environmental Medicine (ACOEM) when elected in 1997. The ACOEM is an international organization of 7,000 occupational medicine physicians. Rhodes became a member of ACOEM in 1979 and a fellow in 1987. He earned his M.D. at Meharry College (Tennessee) in 1962. He completed his residency at Meharry from 1963 to 1967 and won a fellowship at Vanderbilt School of Medicine from 1967 to 1970. He was then associated with Meharry and Hubbard Hospital from 1972 to 1978, when he affiliated with General Motors. Rhodes held positions as associate medical director from 1978 to 1980, medical director of health services from 1980 to 1982, safety director from 1982 to 1987, and finally regional director of health services since 1988.

Jet (August 4, 1997), p. 19; *Who's Who Among African Americans* (1998-1999), p. 1089

1997 • The first African American named to the post of the director of public health for the Fulton County Health Department in Atlanta, Georgia, was Adewale Troutman, who was appointed in 1997. Previously, Troutman was the director of Emergency Medical Services of Newark, New Jersey's United Hospitals Medical Center, and was former assistant clinical professor at the University of Medicine and Dentistry of New Jersey.

Jet(October 13, 1997), p. 19

1997 • Karen Drake, an African American perinatal obstetrician, was the first American, with her partner, Paula Mahone, to be successful in the delivery of septuplets. The McCaughey septuplets were the first live septuplets, in November 1997, successfully delivered in the United States. Drake received a B.A. from Dillard University and received a M.D. from the University of Illinois Medical School in 1988. She completed a residency in obstetrics and gynecology at the State University of New York, Buffalo in 1992, then completed fellowship training in maternal fetal medicine at Albert Einstein College of Medicine. Drake has been with the Iowa Methodist Medical Center in Des Moines since 1996. She has also been involved in teaching and research, has several publications, and has recently studied HIV disease in pregnancy.

Philadelphia Daily News(November 20, 1997), p. 3; *New York Times*(November 17, 1997); *Philadelphia Inquirer*(November 20, 1997), pp. A1, A18

1998 • David Satcher (1941-), a physician and genetic researcher, was the first African American man to be confirmed as U. S. Surgeon General when he took office in 1998. When he received his M.D. in 1970, Satcher became the first African American to earn both the M.D. and Ph.D. degrees at Case Western Reserve University. He developed an expertise in the study of epidemiology and sickle cell anemia. He became professor and chair of the Department of Family Medicine at Morehouse College School of Medicine from 1974 to 1976 and then in 1982, became president of Meharry Medical College and CEO of Meharry/Hubbard Hospital. Satcher was nominated for and then appointed, in 1993, director of the Centers for Disease Control and Prevention, the first African American to hold that position. While serving in that position, he was then nominated by President Clinton and confirmed as U. S. Surgeon General.

African-American Medical Pioneers(1994), p. 196; *Blacks in Science and Medicine*(1990), p. 209; *Jet*(August 25, 1997), p. 19; *Ebony*(July, 1995), p. 120; *New York Times*(November 11, 1997)

1998 • The first woman and first African American elected speaker of the American Psychiatric Association in 1998, the highest assembly post in the organization, was Donna M. Norris (1943-). She is the first African American to hold the position in the 153-year history of the organization. Norris earned her B.A. in 1964 from Fisk University and a M.D. in 1969 from Ohio State University College of Medicine. Norris completed an internship in 1970 at Mt. Carmel Medical Center in Columbus, Ohio. She then fulfilled residencies in 1972 at Boston University Medical Center and in 1974 at Children's Hospital Judge Baker Guidance Center. She was a psychiatric consultant from 1974 to 1979 for the Massachusetts Rehabilitation Commission of Roxbury and Quincy and then a senior psychiatrist for the Boston Juvenile Court Clinic from 1974 to 1988. Norris was the medical director of the Family Services Association of Greater Boston from 1981 to 1989 and an associate in psychiatry, since 1983, for the Children's Hospital Medical Center and Judge Baker Guidance Center. She has also been an instructor at the Harvard Medical School since 1974. Norris has been active in numerous professional organizations.

Emerge (July/August 1998), p. 16; *Who's Who Among African Americans* (1998-1999), p. 1128

1998 • James W. Bridges (1935-), an obstetrician and gynecologist, was named president, in 1998, of the Dade County Medical Association in Miami, Florida. He is the first African American named president of the organization. Bridges, as president, leads a membership of 2,600 practicing physicians, residents and medical students. He received his M.D. from Meharry Medical College in 1960. He is in private practice and is a clinical assistant professor at the University of Miami. He is also chief of his depart-

DAVID SATCHER

ment at Christian Hospital. Bridges is a diplomat of the American Board of Obstetrics and Gynecology since 1970 and a fellow of the American College of Obstetrics and Gynecology.

Jet (July 13, 1998), p. 20; *Who's Who Among African-Americans* (1998-1999), p. 159

1998 • Reginald P. Dickerson was the first African American physician appointed, in 1998, to the position of chief of the medical staff of Meridian Huron Hospital, part of the Cleveland Health System. Dickerson is a cardiologist with a private practice in Cleveland Heights.

Jet (June 22, 1998), p. 57

1998 • Lauren A. McDonald was appointed president of the medical staff of St. Paul Medical Center in Dallas, Texas in 1998. She is the first woman and youngest appointee to the position. McDonald is also the medical director of the Mockingbird Dialysis Center in Dallas. She has a bachelor's degree from Brown University and M.D. degree from Temple University School of Medicine.

Emerge (June, 1998), p. 16

PHYSICAL SCIENCES

1875 • Alexander P. Ashbourne received a patent for his invention of a process to prepare coconut for domestic use in 1875. Ashbourne's process was to pare the coconut, grate the meat, and sift it through fine screens, adding boiling water at the same time. The meat was steamed for an additional three to four hours until it was thoroughly cooked. Then it was pressed until it was completely dry. White sugar was mixed with the meat in the proportion of one pound to three pounds of meat, with a small quantity of cinnamon being added to preserve the flavor. The compound was then dried gradually until fit for packing.

Black Inventors: From Africa to America (1995), p. 92; *Created Equal* (1993), p. 182; *Index of Patents* (1875)

1876 • The first African American to earn a Ph.D. in the United States was Edward Alexander Bouchet (1852-1918), when he received his 1876 degree in physics from Yale University. His degree was only the sixth Ph.D. in physics ever awarded in the United States. Bouchet had previously earned his undergraduate degree from Yale in 1874. He studied with the most well-known physicists of his day, but was unable to find work as a research scientist. He taught from 1876 to 1902 at the Institute for Colored Youth as an instructor in chemistry and physics. He then taught in various high schools until 1913, when he joined the faculty of Bishop College in Marshall, Texas. He remained there until 1916, when ill health forced him to resign.

EDWARD A. BOUCHET

Black American Reference Book (1976), p. 454; *Blacks in Science and Medicine* (1990), p. 32; *Ebony* (July, 1950), p. 18; *Encyclopedia of Black America* (1981), p. 187

1879 • Josephine Silone Yates (1859-1912) was the first African American woman professor in 1879, teaching chemistry at Lincoln Institute, now Lincoln University, at Jefferson City, Missouri. Yates attended the Rhode Island State Normal School, taking education courses and graduating with honors. She took the state teacher's examination and received the highest score that had been recorded to date. Yates became the first African American certified to teach in the State of Rhode Island. After a period at Lincoln, she became head of the department of natural science and remained at the institution until 1889, when she resigned her position to marry. She continued to write professionally, primarily for newspapers. Yates became the second president of the National Association of Colored Women (NACW), serving from 1901 to 1906.

Black Women in America(1993), p. 1297; *Blacks in Science and Medicine*(1990), p. 259

1916 • The first African American to receive a Ph.D. degree in chemistry was St. Elmo Brady, who received the degree in 1916 from the University of Illinois. Brady received a B.A. in 1908 from Fisk University and in 1914, received a M.S. degree from the University of Illinois. He was a professor of chemistry at Howard University and then professor and head of the chemistry department at Fisk University.

Blacks in Science and Medicine(1990), p. 35; *Crisis*(August, 1916), pp. 190-191; *Negro Year Book*(1952), p. 96; *Famous First Facts about Negroes*(1972), p. 172

ELMER S. IMES

1918 • Elmer Samuel Imes (1883-1941), the first African American astrophysicist of note, received a Ph.D. degree in physics from the University of Michigan in 1918. He had earned his B.A. in 1903 and his M.A. in 1910, both from Fisk University (Tennessee). Imes performed research in atomic and quantum theory, taking the work of Albert Einstein, Ernest Rutherford, and Neil Bohr one step further. He was the first to establish that the quantum theory could be extended to include rotational states of molecules. He also worked in the field of high-resolution spectral studies. The infrared spectrum of hydrogen fluoride polymers was probably reported for the first time by Imes. He worked in the private sector as a consulting and research engineer until 1930, when he took a professorship at Fisk University. As department head, he remained at the university until his death in 1941.

Blacks in Science: Ancient and Modern(1983), pp. 262-265; *Blacks in Science and Medicine*(1990), p. 127; *The Physical Review*Vol. 15, pp. 152-155 (February, 1920)

1921 • Amherst College (Massachussetts) appointed its first African American faculty member in 1921 when Robert Percy Barnes (1898-1990) received the appointment. Barnes had received a B.A. in 1921 from Amherst. He worked at Amherst for one year and then re-established his residency in Washington, D.C., where he joined the faculty at Howard University as an instructor in chemistry. Barnes earned the M.A. in 1930 and a Ph.D. in chemistry in 1933, both from Harvard University (Massachusetts). He taught at Howard University until his retirement in 1967. Barnes published a number of scientific journal articles and did extensive research on diketones. He achieved another African American first when he received a presidential appointment, in 1950, to the first National Science Board of the National Science Foundation, where he served until 1958.

Blacks in Science and Medicine (1990), p. 20; *Negro Year Book* (1947), pp. 36-7; *Notable Black American Scientists* (1999), p. 20; *The Role of the Negro in Science* (1966), p. 48

1927 • James A. Parsons, in 1927, won the first Harmon Award in the category of science and invention for his outstanding work in metallurgy. For a number of years, Parsons was chief chemist and metallurgist for the Duriron Company in Dayton, Ohio. He patented austenitic alloy steels, which are corrosion resistant to sulfuric and nitric acids and other industrial chemicals. In 1943, at the Nineteenth Exposition of Chemical Industries, held at Madison Square Garden, products made possible by Parsons's inventions were displayed.

Blacks in Science: Astrophysicist to Zoologist (1977), p. 91; *Blacks in Science and Medicine* (1990), p. 185; *Negro Year Book* (1931-1932), p. 192, (1941-1946), p. 30

1929 • E. Luther Brookes was the founder of Alpha Delta Alpha Scientific Society of Clark University in 1929. Brookes received a B.A. from Lincoln University *magna cum laude* in 1923 and a M.A. in chemistry in 1928 from Columbia University. He taught chemistry and was acting dean at Clark University from 1928 to 1930. He also taught summers at Alabama State Teachers College from 1927 to 1930. Brookes then became director of the Birmingham Branch of Alabama State Teachers College in 1931. He was a member of the American Chemical Society.

Blacks in Science and Medicine (1990), p. 37

1930 • A method for the preparation of colloidal silver iodide compound was invented by Harry Sanderson Keelan, and was patented by him in 1930. The process subjected an insoluble silver salt in colloidal solution to reaction with an iodide of an alkali-forming metal. Keelan's invention relates to germicidal solutions and to an improved reversible colloidal silver iodide, which can be reduced to a dry form without destroying its capacity to resume the colloidal form when it is again mixed with water. Keelan discovered that an improved colloidal silver iodide can be prepared by a metathetical reaction involving an interchange of ions.

Black Inventors: From Africa to America (1995), p. 106; *Index of Patents* (1930), p. 377

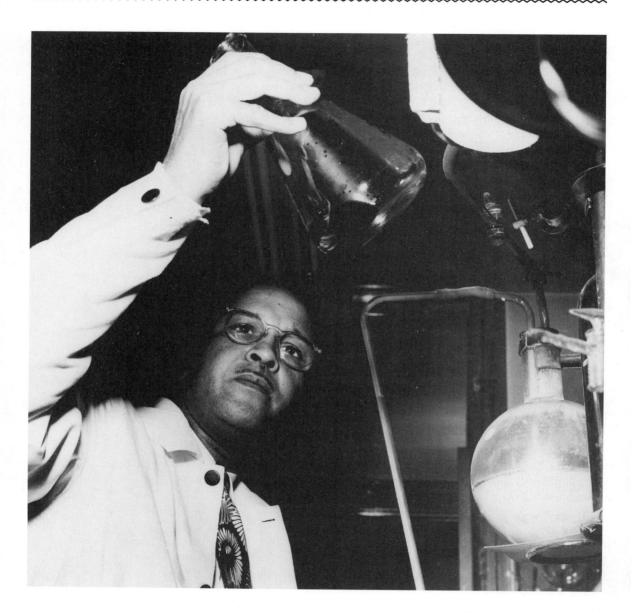

PERCY LAVON JULIAN

1932 • The first African American to earn a Ph.D. from the University of Minnesota was Vernon Alexander Wilkerson (1901-1968), who received the 1932 degree in biochemistry. Wilkerson earned a B.A. in 1921 at the University of Kansas and a M.D. in 1925 from the University of Iowa. Wilkerson completed an internship and residency from 1926 to 1928. He joined the Howard University College of Medicine in 1932 as an associate professor in biochemistry and became professor in 1937, and then headed the department until 1948. Wilkerson was a member of several professional organizations and contributed a number of articles to professional journals.

African-American Medical Pioneers (1994), pp. 25, 198; *Crisis* (May, 1932), p. 163; *Journal of the National Medical Association* Vol. 61, (1968), pp. 344-345

1934 • Dennis Arthur Forbes (1887-19??) acquired a design patent on April 17, 1934, for a cheulls game (chemical card game). Forbes was a chemist who earned a B.A. in 1912 at Howard University. He was an instructor at Livingstone College from 1918 to 1921 and from 1921 to 1924, an instructor at Shaw University. Forbes was a professor of physical science at Tennessee A & I University until 1940, and in 1941 became a vocational educator for the American Youth Administration.

Blacks in Science and Medicine (1990), p. 92; *Creativity and Inventions* (1987), p. 71; *Crisis* (June, 1939), p. 169

1935 • Percy Lavon Julian (1899-1975), an African American research chemist, discovered a method to synthesize physostigmine, a drug used to treat glaucoma, in 1935. Julian received his undergraduate degree in 1920 from DePauw University and a master's degree from Harvard in 1923. He earned a Ph.D. degree from the University of Vienna in 1931. Julian worked for Glidden Company, in Chicago, from 1936 to 1953, as chief chemist and director of research, where he developed products and procedures based on soybean proteins. His efforts turned the company around, from a $35,000 deficit to a $135,000 profit. Julian founded his own company in 1954, which he operated until 1961, at which time he sold to Smith, Kline and French pharmaceutical company. He developed an inexpensive method to manufacture cortisone, a drug used to treat arthritis and certain muscle diseases, as well as the hormones progesterone, testosterone, and cortexolone. He developed a very successful foam fire-smothering agent extensively used in World War II. Julian acquired over 100 chemical patents and published numerous scientific papers.

African American Almanac (1989), pp. 1084-1085; *Black Pioneers of Science and Invention* (1970), pp. 87-101; *Created Equal* (1993), pp. 153-162

1935 • William G. Holly, an African American chemist, was the first to formulate a complete series of interior paints using titanium as the basic pigment, which created a new method for the paint industry. Prior to Holly's work, calcium titanium was considered to be applicable only to finishes. Holly was superintendent and chemist for the Imperial Paint Company of New York, which manufactured print, varnishes, lacquers, and industrial finishes. While superintendent of the Gypsy Paint and Varnish Company, in

1935, Holly formulated his titanium-based pigment paint series, and its acceptance by the industry was immediate.

Blacks in Science and Medicine(1990), p. 123; *Crisis*Vol. 46 (1939), p. 168; *Negro Year Book*(1931-1932), p. 185, (1952), p. 99

1937 • J. Ernest Wilkins, Jr. (1923-) was the youngest student ever admitted to the University of Chicago in 1937, when he was just 13 years old. Wilkins earned his B.S. in 1940 and his M.S. in mathematics in 1941. He earned his Ph.D. in physics from the University of Chicago in 1942, at the age of 19. During 1944 to 1946, he worked in the University of Chicago's metallurgical laboratory on the Manhattan Project, which developed the first atomic bomb for use in World War II. Wilkins spend the bulk of his career in industry, including work at the Nuclear Development Corp. of America and the General Atomic Division of General Dymanics Corp. He also was part owner of a firm that designed and developed nuclear reactors for power generation. Since 1990, Wilkins has been a Distinguished Professor of Applied Mathematics and Mathematical Physics at Clark Atlanta University.

Blacks in Science and Medicine(1990), p. 250; *Blacks in Science: Astrophysicist to Zoologist*(1977), pp. 44-45; *Encyclopedia of Black America*(1981), p. 856

1938 • Flemmie P. Kittrell (1904-1980) was a nutritional chemist who received a B.S. from Hampton Institute in 1928 and a M.S. in 1930 from Cornell University. Kittrell became the first African American woman to

J. ERNEST WILKINS, JR.

earn a Ph.D. degree in nutrition, which she received in 1938 from Cornell University. She taught from 1928 to 1940 at Bennett College and at Hampton Institute from 1940 to 1944. She served as head nutritionist at Howard University from 1944 to 1973 and then became a professor emeritus there until her death. Kittrell was a researcher who not only completed extensive studies in the United States, but became involved in projects in Liberia, India, Japan, Guinea, and Zaire. Among her interests were the protein requirements of adults and the feeding practices of minority infants.

African American Medical Pioneers (1994), pp. 25, 191; *Blacks in Science and Medicine* (1990), pp. 143-144; *Ebony* (January, 1958), p. 59; *Notable Black American Women* (1992), pp. 636-638

1939 • One of the founders of the Institute of Food Technologists in 1939 was African American chemist Lloyd Augustus Hall (1894-1971), who played an important role in the emergence of the industrial science of food chemistry. Hall graduated in 1916 with a B.S. in chemistry from Northwestern University (Illinois), and undertook graduate studies at the University of Chicago. Hall obtained over 105 food patents and developed processes to cure and preserve meat, including the "flash-drying" method, as well as procedures for sterilizing spices. Some of Hall's sterilization processes are still used in hospitals and the hospital supply industry. Hall worked as a consultant until 1924, when he joined Griffith Laboratories in Chicago, where in 1925 he became chief chemist and director of research, remaining in these positions until his retirement in 1959.

Black Pioneers of Science and Invention (1970), pp. 102-11; *Blacks in Science and Medicine* (1990), pp. 109-10; *Journal of Negro History* Vol. 35 (1950), pp. 135-89; *Notable Black American Scientists* (1999), pp. 143-4

1939 • Herman Russell Branson (1914-1995) became the first African American to obtain a Ph.D. in a physical science at the University of Cincinnati when he earned his degree in physics. He had received his B.S. *summa cum laude* from Virginia State College in 1936. In the years 1948-49, Branson received a National Research Council Senior Fellowship for study at the California Institute of Technology, where he worked with chemist Linus Pauling. Branson performed research in which he developed a mathematical analysis of the alpha-helix, the primary structure of proteins in DNA. This analysis led to one of Pauling and Robert B. Corey's first papers on the helical structure of proteins. Branson spent 29 years at Howard University as professor, researcher, and head of the department of physics before he was selected president of Central State University (Ohio) in 1968. He served there until 1970, when he accepted the presidency of Lincoln University (Pennsylvania), where he remained until his 1985 retirement.

Encyclopedia of Black America (1981), pp. 190-191; *The Negro in Science* (1955), p. 189; *New York Times* (June 13, 1995); *Philadelphia Inquirer* (June 11, 1995)

1939 • African American physicist Floyd R. Banks (1913-), when he completed his Ph.D. dissertation in 1939, demonstrated for the first time radioactivity producing self-diffusion in zinc. Banks received a B.S. from Temple University in 1934 in physics, and a M.S. and Ph.D. in physics in 1937 and 1939, respectively, from the University of Pennsylvania. He authored a number of scientific papers in physics and worked as a research associate at the Massachusetts Institute of Technology from 1942 to 1945, when he became a member of the staff of Haskins Laboratories.

Blacks in Science and Medicine (1990), p. 18; *Negro Year Book* (1947), p. 44

1942 • Marguerite Thomas Williams (1895-19??) was the first African American woman to earn a Ph.D. in geology, which was awarded her by Catholic University of America in 1942. She had previously earned a B.S. degree in 1923 at Howard University and a M.A. degree from Columbia University in 1930. Williams was a teacher at Miner Teachers College (Washington D.C.) from 1923 to 1929 and chair of the Division of Geography from 1923 to 1933. She was promoted to assistant professor, then professor, of social sciences during the years 1943 to 1955.

Blacks in Science and Medicine (1990), p. 253; *Black Firsts* (1994), p. 96

W. LINCOLN HAWKINS

1942 • Chemist and inventor W. Lincoln Hawkins (1911-1992) was the first African American member of the technical staff of AT&T's Bell Laboratories when he was hired in 1942. He acquired a B.S. (1932) from Rensselear Polytechnic Institute, a M.S. in chemical engineering (1934) from Howard University, and a Ph.D. in chemistry (1939) from McGill University. He was employed at AT&T until he retired in 1976, when he was the director of Bell's chemistry research laboratory (the first African American in that position). He was then the research director of the Plastics Institute of America from 1976 through 1983. Hawkins was a specialist in the degradation and stabilization of high polymers and research in plastics for telecommunications. His most important contribution to AT&T/Bell was the development of additives that gave an extensive life (70 years) to the plastic coatings used to shield wire cables, saving AT&T hundreds of millions of dollars in cable-laying costs and replacement. Hawkins acquired 18 U.S. patents and 129 foreign patents and published 55 scientific papers and three books. He was awarded the National Medal of Technology by President George Bush in 1992.

African-American Firsts (1994), p. 248; *Jet* (July 20, 1993), p. 24; *Timelines of African-American History* (1994), p. 338; *Who's Who in Engineering* (1985), p. 375

1943 • James A. Parsons, Jr., an inventor and metallurgist, received a patent in 1943 for the invention of a cementation process of treating metal.

In Parsons's process, cementing a ferrous metal article with silicon comprised heating the article at a specified temperature, with flowing gaseous silicon tetrachloride and hydrogen gas in contact with the metal article. The processed article was maintained in a low frequency, alternating current magnetic field, which kept a minimum magnetizing force. Parsons studied at Rensselaer Polytechnic Institute and became chief chemist of the Duriron Company in Dayton, Ohio. He developed a number of patents in austenitic steels and also worked in bronze.

Index of Patents(1943); *Negro Year Book*(1931-1932), p. 192; *Negro Year Book*(1941-1946), p. 30

1943 • The first African American chemist employed by the Bendix Corporation was John William Lathen (1916-). Lathen earned his B.S. degree in 1938 from Virginia State College and a M.D. degree from Howard University Medical School in 1949. Lathen worked for Bendix from 1943 to 1945. After his medical education, he became a psychiatrist in private practice from 1949 to 1980, then worked as an adolescent psychiatrist for Essex Company from 1980 to 1984. Lathen was the first African American elected president of the Bergen County, New Jersey, Mental Health Association. He was also the first African American medical director of Greystone Mental Hospital, a position he held from 1977 to 1980.

Blacks in Science and Medicine(1990), p. 146; *Jet*(February 22, 1962), p. 26; *Who's Who Among Black Americans*(1985), p. 502

1943 • The first Ph.D. in chemical engineering earned by an African American was awarded to Harry James Green Jr. (1911-) by Ohio State University in 1943. Green earned a B.Ch.E. in 1932 from Ohio State University, and a M.S. from the Massachusetts Institute of Technology in 1938. Green taught chemistry from 1934 to 1944 at North Carolina A&T College, when he left to join Stromberg-Carlson Company, where he worked as a senior engineer for 15 years and supervisor of research and development for eight years. Green joined the staff of General Dynamics in 1967 as principal engineer, and then joined the Xerox Corporation in 1970, where he then engaged in broad-base research concerning metals, plastics, and microelectronics.

Blacks in Science and Medicine(1990), p. 105; *Journal of Blacks in Higher Education*(Spring 1997)

1945–1971 • William Jacob Knox, Jr. (1904-1995) was considered the Kodak Corporation's expert on surfactants (chemicals used in the manufacture of photographic film). During the period 1945 to 1971, Knox acquired 21 patents related to surfactants. Surfactants, also known as wetting agents, help film emulsions to wet or cling to underlying film/paper surfaces, promoting good bonding. Proper selection of surfactants produces thin emulsion layers that spread evenly and are free of defects. Knox earned a B.S. degree in chemistry in 1925 from Harvard University and then received a M.S. degree in 1929 and Ph.D. degree in 1935, both in physical chemistry from the Massachusetts Institute of Technology. He worked at Columbia University from 1943 to 1945 on the atomic bomb project and then joined Kodak in 1945, where he remained until his 1970 retirement.

Blacks in Science and Medicine(1990), p. 144; *Notable Black American Scientists*(1999), pp. 191-192; *Who's Who Among Black Americans*(1985), p. 494

WALTER S. MCAFEE

1946 • Walter S. McAfee (1914-1995), an astrophysicist, performed mathematical calculations that enabled a team of scientists and engineers at Fort Monmouth, New Jersey, to bounce high-frequency radar signals off the Moon's surface for the first time in January 1946. The effort was called Project Diana. McAfee earned a B.S. degree in 1934 at Wiley College, a M.S. in 1937 at Ohio State University, and a Ph.D. in 1949 at Cornell University. He joined the staff of the U.S. Army Signals Corps Electronic Research Command in 1942 as a physicist and worked in several areas, including radiation physics, electromagnetic wave preparation, applied physics, and passive sensing. He remained at the facility for 40 years.

Blacks in Science: Astrophysicist to Zoologist(1977), p. 47; *Blacks in Science and Medicine*(1990), p. 166; *Ebony*(June, 1968), p. 8; *Negro Almanac*(1989), p. 1088

1948 • Marie Maynard Daly (1921-) was the first African American woman to earn a Ph.D. in chemistry, which she received in 1948 from Columbia University. Daly earned the B.S. in 1942 from Queens College and a M.S. from New York University in 1943. She was an instructor at Howard University for the academic year 1947-1948 and a research assistant at the Rockerfeller Institute from 1951 to 1955. She was then an associate in biochemistry with Columbia University Research Service at Goldwater Memorial Hospital and taught at Columbia until 1971. Daly joined Albert Einstein College of Medicine, Yeshiva University, in 1971 as an assistant professor, and she remained at the college as associate professor of biochemistry and medicine until 1986. Daly conducted research into the biochemical aspects of metabolism and the role of the kidneys in bodily functions. She also focused her attention on diseases like hypertension and atherosclerosis.

Blacks in Science and Medicine(1990), p. 67; *Blacks in Science: Astrophysicist to Zoologist*(1977), p. 17; *Holders of Doctorates Among Negroes*(1946), p. 151

1950 • The first Ph.D. in metallurgical engineering awarded by the Illinois Institute of Technology (IIT) was received by African American metallurgical engineer Frank Alphonso Crossley (1925-) in 1950. Crossley earned a B.S. degree in chemical engineering and M.S. degree in metallurgical engineering, both from IIT in 1945 and 1947 respectively. Crossley taught at Tennessee A & I State University from 1950 to 1952, then worked for IIT Research Institute from 1952 to 1966. He was employed by the Lockheed Corporation from 1966 to 1986, when he joined the Aerojet Propulsion Research Institute for a year. He held various positions at General Corporation from 1987 to 1991, when he retired. During his career, Crossley developed new commercial grades of the metal titanium and was an expert in high temperature metals. He published 58 scientific articles on metallurgy between 1951 and 1990 and acquired seven patents, primarily in metallurgy, between 1957 and 1983.

Blacks in Science and Medicine(1990), p. 64; *Black Engineers in the United States*(1974), pp. 44-46; *Ebony*(September, 1975), pp. 158, 160-161; *Who's Who Among African Americans*(1998-1999), p. 340

1950 • Robert Percy Barnes (1898-1990) was appointed to the first National Science Board of the National Science Foundation in 1950. He served on the board until 1958. Barnes was an African American chemist who studied alpha and beta diketones. He and his researchers (a great number of them his college students) created a number of new substances and added new processes in synthesizing chemicals. Barnes earned an A.B. in chemistry from Amherst College, where he also made Phi Beta Kappa. He received a M.A. in 1930 and a Ph.D. in 1933, both from Harvard University. Many of Barnes's scientific publications regarding his research had industrial applications.

*Crisis*Vol. 46, no. 6 (June 1939), p. 168; *Negro Year Book*(1947), pp. 36-37; *Negro Year Book*(1952), p. 100; *Negro Vanguard*(1959), p. 316

1952 • Lloyd N. Ferguson (1918-) wrote six major textbooks in the field of chemistry, the first of which, *Electron Structures of Organic Molecules*, was published in 1952. Ferguson earned a B.S. in 1940 and a Ph.D. in chemistry in 1943, both from the University of California. He worked as a research assistant for National Defense research projects at intervals from 1941 to 1944. He then joined the Howard University faculty in 1945, became a full professor in 1955, and held the position of chemistry department head from 1958 to 1965. During this time, he was a National Science Foundation Fellow at the Swiss Federal Institute of Technology in Zurich, Switzerland, in 1961 and 1962. Ferguson then became a member of the faculty at California State University with the rank of professor from 1965 until 1986, when he became professor emeritus. He was also head of the chemistry department from 1968 to 1971. Ferguson wrote his textbooks and con-

LLOYD N. FERGUSON

ducted research in the area of organic chemistry, especially the chemical properties of aromatic compounds. He studied the molecular and biochemical components of taste and the chemistry of compounds called alicycles, which gave the scientific community insight into the function of natural chemicals like steroids, vitamins, and antibiotics.

Blacks in Science and Medicine (1990), p. 90; *Encyclopedia of Black America* (1981), p. 385; *Great Negroes, Past and Present* (1972), p. 60

1953 • Julius Henry Taylor (1914-) was the first African American to receive a research award from the U.S. Army's Office of Ordinance research in 1953. He was awarded the prize consecutively from 1953 to 1957. Taylor was the editor of the popular document "The Negro in Science," published in 1955. He was a physicist with experience in solid-state physics, space flight development, and education. Taylor earned a B.A. in 1939 from Lincoln University, and a M.S. in 1941 and a Ph.D. in 1950 from the University of Pennsylvania. He was professor of physics at West Virginia State College from 1945 to 1947 and became professor of physics at Morgan State University in 1949, where he remained until 1978 as the physics department head. Taylor left Morgan University in 1978 to work on a contract awarded him by the Goddard Space Flight Center.

Encyclopedia of Black America (1981), p. 814; *Who's Who Among African Americans* (1998-1999), p. 1457

EMMETT CHAPPELLE (RIGHT) READING RESULTS FROM A BACTERIA DETECTOR.

1954–1958 • Emmett W. Chappelle (1925-), an African American biochemist with a least 13 patents, has been a pioneer in the field of biochemistry. During the period 1954 to 1958, while a research associate at Stanford University studying amino acids, Chappelle discovered the key enzyme for the production of the amino acid glycine. He also showed that the enzyme for producing glycine is exactly the same in both plant and animal and could be interchanged. Chappelle earned a B.S. in 1950 from the University of California, Berkeley and a M.S. from the University of Washington in 1954. He worked for the Research Institute for Advanced Studies from 1958 to 1963, then he worked as a biochemist for Hazleton Laboratories until 1966. Chappelle joined NASA's Goddard Space Flight Center in 1966, completing numerous studies on light emissions from plants, crops, and trees.

Blacks in Science and Medicine(1990), p. 53; *Distinguished African American Scientists of the 20th Century*(1996), pp. 46-49; *Notable Black American Scientists*(1999), p. 63-65; *New York Times*(August 25, 1975), p. 25

1954 • Alfred E. Martin (1911-) was an African American physicist who completed contributory work in the areas of radiometry and luminescence of inorganic phosphors. In 1954, Martin was head of the photonics section of the Sylvania Electric Products physics laboratory, where he led the group that developed a new television picture tube with the HaloLite principle. The tube reduced eye strain on the television viewer. Martin received a B.S. from City College of New York in 1932 and a M.S. from the University of Michigan in 1933. He taught at Shaw University from 1933 to 1936 and at Fisk University from 1936 to 1942. He then worked in industry until 1967, at such firms as Cardwell Manufacturing, Sylvania, McGraw-Hill Publishing, Polaroid Electronics, Arinc Research, and Grumman Aircraft Engineering Corporation. Martin then returned to academia and became an assistant professor of physics at Manhattan Community College.

Blacks in Science and Medicine(1990), pp. 162-163; *Ebony*(April 1954), p. 5; *Notable Black American Scientists*(1999), pp. 215-216

1954 • The first African American to earn an advanced degree in physics from Rutgers University was James B. Drew (1922-) when he was awarded his M.S. in physics in 1954. Drew previously earned a B.S. from Virginia Union University in 1943 and a M.S. in 1947 from Howard University. He remained at Howard University from 1947 through 1950, where he worked with one of the first interdisciplinary medical research teams (medicine and physics) concerning the use of radioactive materials in the treatment of thyroid cancer. After his graduation from Rutgers, Drew began a 14-year career with Philadelphia's Franklin Institute as a research physicist. His research interests included atomic energy, nuclear isotopes, and thin films. His work led the receipt of awards and fellowships. Drew presented his research finding at national and international conferences. He was active in professional societies.

Distinguished African American Scientists of the 20th Century(1996), pp. 74-77

1955 • Lloyd Augustus Hall (1894-1971), a pioneering industrial chemist, was the first African American elected to the national board of the American Institute of Chemists. Hall earned his B.S. in pharmaceutical chemistry from Northwestern University in 1916 and a D.Sc. from Virginia State College in 1944. He worked in several positions from 1917 to 1921, when he then began to focus on food chemistry. In 1924, Hall joined Chicago's Griffith Labs and became chief chemist and director of research in 1928. He developed the food preservation technique known as flash-drying and other meat preserving processes that revolutionized the meat-packing industry. He also developed seasonings, emulsions, bakery products, antioxidants and protein products. His sterilization method is still utilized worldwide by hospitals for such items as bandages, dressings, drugs, sutures and cosmetics. By his retirement in 1959, Hall had acquired over 105 patents in the United States and abroad.

African-American Almanac(1997), pp. 1070-1071; *Blacks in Science and Medicine*(1990), pp. 109-110; *Created Equal*(1993), pp. 123-126; *Profiles in Excellence*(1994)

1956 • Edward Lee Harris (1902-1974) was an African American chemical engineer who patented, in 1956, his invention for an apparatus for handling corrosive acid substances. Harris was chief chemist for the Rocket Propellant Section, Wright-Patterson Air Force Base. He earned a B.S. degree in 1926 and a Ph.D. in chemical engineering in 1935, with both degrees being awarded by the University of Pittsburgh. Harris's invention was an apparatus for conducting chemical analysis of highly corrosive acid substances such as hydrogen fluorine, hydrofluoric acid, and fuming nitric acid or alkaline mixtures of these chemicals used for neutralization.

Blacks in Science and Medicine(1990), pp. 111-112; *Index of Patents*(1956)

1956 • June Bacon-Bercey (1932-) became the first African American woman meteorologist of prominence in the United States. Bacon-Bercey earned a B.S. in 1954 and a M.S. degree in 1955, both in mathematics and meteorology, from the University of California at Los Angeles. She worked as a meteorologist for the National Weather Service in Washington, D.C. from 1956 to 1962, for the Sperry Rand Corporation from 1962 to 1974, and then did consulting and lecturing from 1974 to 1975. Bacon-Bercey joined the National Oceanic and Atmospheric Agency as a public affairs specialist, and later as chief of television services. From 1982 to 1990, she worked in the state of California with the National Weather Service as a forecasting training officer. Bacon-Bercey was an active leader in organizations such as the American Meteorologist Society, American Geophysical Union, and the New York Academy of Sciences.

Blacks in Science and Medicine(1990), p. 17; *Notable Black American Scientists*(1999), p. 17

1957–1962 • African American chemist Moddie Taylor (1912-1976), who was the head of the chemistry department at Howard University from 1969 to 1976, undertook substantial strides in the chemistry of rare earth metals. In 1957 and 1962, he acquired patents for the preparation of anhydrous alkaline earth halides and preparation of anhydrous lithium salts. Taylor earned a B.S. degree from Lincoln University, Jefferson City, in 1935 and a M.S. degree in 1939 from the University of Chicago. He also received a Ph.D in 1943 from Chicago also. He was professor of chemistry at Lincoln University from 1939 to 1941. Taylor joined the faculty of Howard University's chemistry department as an associate professor in 1948 and became full professor in 1959 and then department head in 1969. He also published a chemistry textbook in 1960 and was named, in the same year, by the Manufacturing Chemists Association as one of the six best college chemistry teachers in the country. Taylor retired from Howard University in 1976.

Blacks in Science and Medicine(1990), p. 227; *Encyclopedia of Black America*(1981), p. 814; *Index of Patents*(1962); *Notable Black American Scientists*(1999), p. 294

1958 • One of the first Ph.D.s in chemistry awarded by Howard University in 1958 was earned by the African American chemist Harold Delaney (1920-1994). Delaney earned a B.S. in chemistry and a M.S. in chemistry in 1943, both from Howard University. From 1943 to 1945, Delaney worked as a chemist on the Manhattan Project and then taught chemistry at North Carolina A&T University from 1945 to 1948. He then became a member of the faculty of Morgan State University, where he taught from 1948 to 1966. He continued from 1969 to 1977 in primarily administrative positions at the State University of New York, University of North Carolina, and Manhattanville College. Delaney then served as executive vice president of the American Association of State Colleges and Universities from 1977 until 1987.

Black Issues in Higher Education(April 2, 1998), p. 13.; *Howard University Magazine*(Fall 1994), p. 47

1958 • The first doctoral program in chemistry developed and operated at any African American college or university was developed at Howard University (Washington, D.C.) in 1958 by Lloyd Noel Ferguson (1918-). Ferguson earned a B.S. in 1940 and a Ph.D. in 1943, both from the University of California, Berkeley, thereby becoming the first African American to earn a Ph.D. in chemistry from Berkeley. Ferguson began teaching chemistry at Howard in 1945 and remained there until 1965, serving as department head from 1958-1965. He won a number of fellowships and completed research at such facilities as the Carlsberg Laboratory in Copenhagen, Denmark and the Swiss Federal Institute of Technology in Zurich, Switzerland. Ferguson joined the faculty of California State University, Los Angeles in 1965 and chaired the chemistry department there from 1968-1971. Ferguson was a prolific author of scientific publications, including six chemistry textbooks, of which three were translated into Japanese and Hindi. Ferguson also wrote many articles for high school teachers and students as part of his effort to recruit young minority people for careers in science.

Distinguished African American Scientists of the 20th Century (1996), pp. 94-9; *Who's Who Among African Americans* (1998-1999), p. 475; *Western Journal of Black Studies* (1992), Vol. 16, p. 52

1960 • The Massachusetts Institute of Technology awarded the first Ph.D. in meteorology ever earned by an African American to Charles Edward Anderson (1919-1994) in 1960. Anderson earned a B.S. in chemistry at Lincoln University (Missouri) and a M.S. in meteorology in 1943 from the University of Chicago. He worked for the atmospheric science branch of Douglas Aircraft from 1961 to 1965. In 1966, he was named professor at the University of Wisconsin, and in 1986, became a professor emeritus. Anderson joined the North Carolina State University faculty as a tenured professor in meteorology and was awarded professor emeritus status there in 1992. His research efforts concerned cloud and aerosol physics and the meteorology of other planets.

Blacks in Science and Medicine (1990), p. 11; *Kappa Alpha Psi Journal* (December, 1994), p. 257

1961 • George W. Reed (1920-) a University of Chicago chemist, was the first African American appointed as the U. S. Representative to the International Atomic Energy Agency in Vienna, Austria, in 1961. Reed earned a B.S. at Howard University in 1942, and a M.S. in 1944 and Ph.D. in chemistry in 1952, at the University of Chicago. He started working for the University of Chicago and Argonne National Laboratory in 1952. His early work was on nuclear fission on uranium-235 and thorium-232 on the Manhattan Project. His interests broadened to the study of halogen and mercury in meteorites and then trace elements in lunar samples by activation analysis. Finally, Reed's work effort was concerned with acid rain and geothermal problems related to permanent storage of radioactive waste.

African-American Baseline Essays (1990), pp. 5-79; *Blacks in Science and Medicine* (1990), p. 199; *Jet* (May 4, 1961), p. 3

1961 • A method of preparing aqueous dispersion of metal oxides with relatively high concentrations of finely divided silica was patented by Kenneth A. Loftman (1925-) in 1961. Loftman determined that up to 40 percent by weight of pyrogenic silica may be incorporated into an aquasol without gelation occurring, provided the silica is agglomerated prior to its addition to water with careful control of its pH. Loftman, who was silicone industrial manager for the Cabot Corporation, earned a B.S. in chemical engineering in 1951 and B.S. in business administration in 1953 from Northeastern University. Loftman was a licensed professional engineer in chemistry in Massachusetts and held several patents and had several publications.

Black Engineers in the United States(1974), p. 127; *Index of Patents*(1961)

1962 • Louis Wright Roberts (1913-) received a patent for his invention of a microwave radio frequency signal device adapted to high-power applications. Roberts's invention was a high-frequency gas discharge tube having magnetic means for regulating the position and structure of the electron discharge plasma. The regulator was able to control the heating characteristics of the tube and also certain non-linear electrical characteristics of the tube. Roberts earned an A.B. in 1935 at Fisk University and a M.S. from the University of Michigan in 1937. He taught in college from 1935 to 1944 and then worked for various industries from 1944 to 1967. He worked for NASA as chief of a microwave laboratory until 1970. Roberts then worked for the U.S. Department of Transportation's Transportation System Center until 1989. He held several other patents, was active in a number of technical organizations, and published a number of journal articles and government reports.

Index of Patents(1959, 1962, 1966); *Who's Who Among African Americans*(1998-1999), p. 1105; *Who's Who Among Black Americans*(1990-1991), p. 1079

1963 • Robert A. Thornton (1902-1982) became the first Dean of the School of Science at San Francisco State University when he was named to that post in 1963. Thornton received a B.S. from Howard University in 1922, a M.S. from Ohio State University in 1925, and a Ph.D. in the philosophy of science from the University of Minnesota in 1946. He joined the faculty of San Francisco State University in 1956 as professor of physics, and held the position of Dean of the School of Natural Sciences from 1963 until 1967. From 1980 until his death, Thornton was a visiting professor of physical science at the University of the District of Columbia. San Francisco State University honored his memory by naming a building in his honor, and dedication services were held in April 1982 at for Robert A. Thornton Hall.

Blacks in Science and Medicine(1990), pp. 231-232

1963 • A high-pressure optical cell for use in spectrum analysis of solid materials was invented by African American physicist Charles E. Weir and patented in 1963. Weir's invention permitted the study of solid materials in spectral regions under pressure. The device was comprised of a casing, first and second holding devices with apertures, a means for movable mounting, and two diamonds positioned in the aperture of the first and second holding means. Such additional items as a spindle, compression spring, thrust plate, and pressure plate were also part of the device. Energy in a selected spectral region was applied to the first diamond and a means for performing a spectral analysis of the energy transmitted through the second diamond was provided.

Blacks in Science and Medicine (1990), p. 245; *Black Inventors: From Africa to America* (1995), pp. 126,251; *Index of Patents* (1963)

1963 • Mack Gipson Jr. (1931-1995) was the first African American to earn a Ph.D. in geology, which he received in 1963 from the University of Chicago. Gipson earned a B.S. in 1953 at Paine College (Georgia) and the M.S. in 1961 from the University of Chicago. He worked as a geologist for the Walter H. Flood Company until 1964, when he began teaching at Virginia State University, becoming professor and chair of the geological sciences department until 1975. Gibson joined the Exxon Company in 1975 as a research associate, implementing oil exploration utilizing the method of seismic stratigraphy. Gibson also worked for ERCO Petroleum and Phillips Petroleum before returning to academia in 1986, when he became professor of geology at the University of South Carolina.

Ebony (May 1976), p. 7; *Blacks in Science and Medicine* (1990), pp. 101-2; *Distinguished African American Scientists of the 20th Century* (1996), pp. 120-3

1964 • Mack Gipson, Jr. (1931-) founded the first geology department in a traditionally African American university when he started this program at Virginia State University in 1964. He led the department from its inception until 1975. Gipson earned a B.A. from Paine College in 1953, a M.S. in 1961 from the University of Chicago, and then the Ph.D. from Chicago in 1963. While at Virginia State, he continued his own research with a major project studying the surface of the planet Mars. Gipson worked for the Exxon Company from 1975 until 1982, investigating lands that might hold petroleum deposits, which included possible oil fields in Alaska, Florida, Mexico, Pakistan, and Czechoslovakia. In 1982 Gipson transferred to ERCO Petroleum Services, working in the area of oil exploration and extraction until 1986, when he joined the faculty of the University of South Carolina. He was a member of many scientific and technical organizations and published numerous professional articles.

Blacks in Science and Medicine (1990), pp. 101-102; *Distinguished African American Scientists of the 20th Century* (1996), pp. 121-123; *Who's Who Among African Americans* (1998-1999), p. 1700

1964 • Herbert Leonard, Jr. received a patent in 1964 for his process for the production of hydroxylamine hydrochloride. Previously hydrochloric acid was excluded in hydroxylamine preparation because its presence resulted in solution of the hydrogenation catalyst under the conditions employed. Leonard's procedure was a single step process for the catalytic hydrogenation of nitric acid in the presence of hydrochloric acid. The yields of hydroxylamine hydrochloride range from about 70 percent upward.

Black Inventors: From Africa to America (1995), p. 125; *Index of Patents* (1964)

1964–1973 • Meredith Gourdine (1929-1998) founded, in 1964, Gourdine Systems, Inc., which did research and development work in the field of electrogasdynamics. (Electrogasdynamics technology is the process concerned with the interaction of charged particles with a moving gas stream.) From 1964 to 1973, Gourdine was listed as inventor or co-inventor on nearly 70 patents of practical applications of electrogasdynamics, magnetohydrodynamics, and plasma physics. His firm has produced unique paint spraying systems, pollutant reduction devices, energy conversion systems, fog dispersion systems, and monitoring devices. Gourdine did not manufacture or sell his inventions, but instead licensed their use to other companies.

MEREDITH GOURDINE

The Black Inventor (1975), p. 31; *Blacks in Science: Ancient and Modern* (1983), pp. 217-278; *Black Engineers in the United States* (1974), pp. 78-79; *Blacks in Science: Astrophysicist to Zoologist* (1977), pp. 50-51

1964 • A process for the preparation of nitroform and the salts of nitroform was invented by Joseph C. Dacons (1912-) and was patented in 1964. Dacons was an organic chemist who earned a B.A. in 1937, a M.S. in 1948, and then a Ph.D. in 1952 from Ohio State University. He taught chemistry at Fisk University from 1950 to 1953 and was professor and chairman of the department of chemistry at North Carolina A&T College from 1953 to 1955. He joined the U. S. Naval Ordnance Laboratory as a research chemist in 1956. Dacons's method for the preparation of nitroform and its salts was a process by which one of the nitro groups of titranitromethane is replaced by a hydrogen, sodium, potassium, or other light metal ion.

Blacks in Science and Medicine (1990), p. 66; *Index of Patents* (1964), p. 201, 343

1965 • A photographic transfer process was invented by James E. Lu Valle and patented in 1965. Lu Valle's technique transferred images of developed silver on a silver halide substrate to a transfer material, forming an essentially silver halide-free image while leaving the substrate substantially silver-free. Novel processing sheets, receiving sheets, and coating composition for protecting silver images were all adapted for use with Lu Valle's transfer process. A single image or a number of successive images, either negative or positive in type, can be obtained from a single latent image by mechanical transfer of developed silver through adhesion. Lu Valle earned a B.A. from the University of California at Los Angeles in 1936, an M.A. in 1937, and a Ph.D. in 1940 from the California Institute of Technology and has conducted research in photochemistry, electron diffraction, and magnetic resonance.

Blacks in Science and Medicine (1990), p. 157; *Index of Patents* (1965), p. 741; *Negro Year Book* (1952), p. 100

1965 • John R. Cooper, a chemist and inventor, was employed by E.I. DuPont de Nemours and was superintendent of the elastomers department. He received a patent in 1965 for a process of reacting an organic polyisocyanate compound with an ether solution and a catalyst. Cooper supervised a staff of chemists and engineers who were concerned with the research and development of new applications of synthetic rubber. He held several patents in the development of fluorine-rubber compounds resistant to heat, with applications for seals in jet engines.

Blacks in Science and Medicine (1990), p. 61; *Ebony* (May, 1970), p. 6; *Index of Patents* (1965)

1965 • A method for the preparation of carbon transfer inks was invented in 1961 by Hansel L. McGee, and he was granted a patent for his invention in 1965. McGee's process incorporated a new amido-ester synthetic wax, which had all the characteristics of natural waxes. The process for preparing carbon transfer inks of the hot melt type contained at least one amino-esther synthetic. This compound was mixed with a portion of paraffin oil and heated to a temperature sufficient to melt the wax constituent. Then it was mixed with a portion of carbon blacks, and heating was continued. Finally, it was milled by adding steel balls and shaking vigorously until the ink mixture was homogenous.

Index of patents (1965)

1966 • An improved process for the preparation of aromatic mono-,di-, and polyisocyanates from the corresponding aromatic amines was developed by John Richard Cooper, an African American chemist and inventor. His invention was granted a patent in 1966. Cooper's technique was a phosgenation process for the preparation of aromatic isocyanates in which improved yields of the isocyanate are obtained for a given concentration of reactant, and the yields are less sensitive to variations in concentration of reactant. The process also reduced the viscosity of the reaction slurry in the first reaction stage. Cooper was employed by E.I. DuPont de Nemours and was appointed superintendent of the elastomers chemical department. He has several patents related to the development of fluorine-rubber compounds resistant to heat, with applications for seals in jet engines.

Blacks in Science and Medicine(1990), p. 61; *Ebony*(May 1970), p. 6; *Index of Patents*(1966), p. 266

1966 • The U.S. Naval Academy in Anapolis, Maryland, appointed its first African American faculty member in 1966, when it selected Samuel P. Massie (1919-) to its chemistry department. Massie received his B.S. in 1938 from the Normal College of Arkansas and his M.A. from Fisk University (Tennessee) in 1940. He was awarded his Ph.D. in organic chemistry from Iowa State University in 1946. In 1960, Massie was associate Program Director at the National Science Foundation, which supports a national science policy by funding science programs. In 1977, 11 years after he was hired, Massie was appointed chairman of the chemistry department at the Naval Academy, the position he held until 1981. He retired in 1993 and was named professor emeritus in chemistry the following year. An expert in organic chemistry, he has presented papers before international conferences in Switzerland, Japan, Brazil, Mexico, as well as across the United States. He has studied the preparation of drugs against malaria, tuberculosis, cancer, sickle-cell anemia, and hypertension. He received, in 1982, a patent and an invention award form the U.S. Army for his studies in compounds against gonorrhea. Massie also received the Lifetime Achievement Award of the White House Initiative on Science and Technology Advisory Committee in 1989.

SAMUEL MASSIE

Jet(February 1, 1993), p. 36; *Kappa Alpha Psi Journal*(February, 1996), p. 35, Vol. 77, (1991), p. 73; *Journal of the National Technical Association*(July, 1987), p. 14

1966 • Louis W. Roberts (1913-), in 1966, was granted a patent for his device for amplifying radio frequency waves. The device used an electron plasma that absorbs negative radiation. Roberts's mechanism amplified electromagnetic waves to a kilomegacycle wave amplifier device. This invention is one of 11 patents for electronic devices that Roberts holds. He earned a B.A. from Fisk University in 1935 and a M.S. in 1937 from the University of Michigan. Roberts taught physics in college from 1935 to 1944 and then worked in industry until 1967, when he joined the National Aeronautics and Space Administration, remaining until 1970. He was appointed deputy director of the U. S. Department of Transportation Systems Center in 1970, retiring from there in 1989 as its director.

Blacks in Science and Medicine(1990), p. 202; *Black Contributions to Science and Energy Technology*(1979); *Index of Patents*(1966), p. 1114; *Who's Who Among African Americans*(1998-1999), p. 1275

1966 • John Perry Jr. patented a biochemical fuel cell he invented in 1966. Perry was a team leader and chemist in the Fort Monmouth Electronics Command's Electronics Technology and Devices Laboratory. His areas of expertise were the development of lithium/thionyl chloride batteries and power sources for communications, electronics, and laser equipment. Perry holds four patents on fuel cells and has published 10 scientific papers. His fuel cell used a lower noble metal catalyst of platinum doped with lead oxide, which reduced the noble metal loading by about 82 percent while providing about the same performance.

Index of Patents (1966), pp. 631, 1026

1967 • In 1967, African American chemist Lloyd Albert Quarterman (1918-1982) became the first to study the x-ray, ultraviolet, and Raman spectra of a given compound by dissolving it in hydrogen fluoride. Quarterman's process, which basically devised a window to view certain molecular phenomena, became known as "the diamond technique." Quarterman earned a B.S. in 1943 from St. Augustine's College (North Carolina) and a M.S. in 1952 from Northwestern University (Illinois). He was hired by the U.S. War Department in 1943 to work on the Manhattan Project—the development of the atomic bomb. He was one of only six African American scientists who worked on the atom bomb project.

Blacks in Science and Medicine (1990), p. 196; *Blacks in Science: Ancient and Modern* (1983), pp. 266- 72; *Notable Twentieth Century Scientists* (1995), pp. 1628-9

1967 • Edwin R. Russell (1913-) invented a technique for the removal of cesium from aqueous solutions by ion exchange, for which he received a patent in 1967. Russell earned a B.S. at Benedict College and a M.S. at Howard University in 1937. Russell has 11 patents on atomic energy processes and has conducted research in bio-assay, radioactive tracer, gas absorption, ion exchange absorption, and radioactive waste treatment.

Blacks in Science and Medicine (1990), p. 207; *Creativity and Inventions* (1987), p. 68; *Who's Who Among Black Americans* (1985), p. 733

1967–1972 • Arnold F. Stancell (1936-), an African American chemical engineer, joined Mobil Oil as a scientist/research manager. He developed a number of patents during the years 1967 to 1972, for various processes for manufacturing polyethylene, polybutylene (now used in plastic pipes), and a key chemical compound used in polyester fiber. He also developed patents for terephthalic acid and thin film deposition. Stancell published in the scientific journals and retired from Mobil Oil in 1993 as Vice-President,

International Exploration and Production. He held professorships at both Massachusetts Institute of Technology and Georgia Institute of Technology.

Blacks in Science and Medicine(1990), p. 6; *Chemical Engineering Progress*(April, 1990), pp. 70-72; *New York Times* (February 27, 1992); *Index of Patents*(1967, 1972)

1967 • The African American organic chemist Henry Aaron Hill (1915-1979) invented a composition and process for curing furfuryl-alcohol-modified urea formaldehyde condensates that was patented in 1967. Hill's process requires a composition of furfuryl-alcohol-modified urea formaldehyde condensate, hexamethylene tetramine, and a nitrite. The hexamethylene and nitrite combination retard the curing process at atmospheric or storage temperature, but not at the elevated temperature used commercially for curing. Hill earned his B.A. in 1936 from Johnson C. Smith University and a Ph.D. from Massachusetts Institute of Technology in 1942. He was a major researcher in industry from 1943 to 1976, with a national reputation for his work in fluorocarbons. Hill was an active member of professional and technical organizations and was the first African American to become president of the American Chemical Society.

African-Americans in Boston(1991), p. 146; *Blacks in Science and Medicine*(1990), p. 119; *Index of Patents*(1967), p. 578; *Jet*(April 19, 1979), p. 53

1967 • Steve B. Latimer (1927-) was the first African American to earn a Ph.D. in chemistry from North Carolina State University when he received the degree in 1967. Latimer earned a B.S. in 1953 and M.S. in 1955, both from Tuskegee Institute. He also completed one year's training at the Federal Executive Institute in 1972. Latimer was the holder of three National Science Foundation scholarships, a Public Health Service traineeship, a National Institute of Health Fellowship, and a Carver Foundation Fellowship. He has held academic positions at Langston University, North Carolina State University, and Shaw University, where he was chairman of the chemistry department from 1955 to 1962. Latimer is a fellow of the American Institute of Chemists, as well as a member of other scientific organizations including the American Chemical Society, National Institute of Science, and the Oklahoma Academy of Science.

Who's Who Among African Americans(1998-1999), p. 894; *Who's Who Among Black Americans*(1990-1991), p. 759

1968 • The patent for an air purification system was assigned to the African American inventor Rufus Stokes (1924-) on April 16, 1968. Stokes's device reduced gases and ash from furnaces and power-plant smoke to a safe level.

Blacks in Science: Astrophysicist to Zoologist(1977), p. 91; *Creativity and Inventions*(1987), p. 69; *Official Gazette*(April 16, 1968), p. 738; *Blacks in Science and Medicine*(1990), p. 222

1968 • Morris Leslie Smith (1933-) received a patent in 1968 for his invention of a printing fluid. Smith's was an aqueous, low-viscosity fluid containing a water-soluble, thermosetting, vinylsulfonium polymer resin and a water-soluble dye, which was compatible with the resin in solution. Smith's printing fluid was useful in high-speed printing processes. The ink made it possible to print designs on paper towels that would not rub off on the hands. Smith was an analytical research chemist with a 1959 B.S. degree from Michigan State University. He worked from 1961 to 1965 for Scott Paper Company, and was promoted to senior research project chemist until 1974, when he became a section leader. In 1978, he started his own firm, The M.L. Smith Group, Inc. Smith also held other patents related to chemically treated paper products.

Black Enterprise(February, 1990), p. 110; *Index of Patents*(1968); *Who's Who Among African Americans*(1998-1999), p. 1391

1968 • Henry T. Brown, an African American research chemist for the Esso Research and Engineering Company, received a patent in 1968 for a process for reactivating hydroforming catalysts, especially in petroleum products. His process related to activating and/or reactivating hydroforming naphthas used in hydroforming. Brown's process employs a platinum group metal catalyst and describes how to maintain the halogen content of the catalyst within desired limits in order to maintain the catalyst at a high activity level. The process uses three or four reactors containing catalyst.

Creativity and Inventions(1987), p. 64; *Index of Patents*(1968), p. 153

1969 • A patent was granted to Jonathan S. Smith II, in 1969, for his process of making a transparent zirconia composition. In his process, Smith developed a high-density, polycrystalline, fully stabilized cubic zirconia body characterized by fine, uniform grain size, negligible porosity, and which was stable in oxidizing environments at temperatures above 2000 degrees Celcius. The process produced a fully stabilized, highly pure material consisting of zirconium oxide and a stabilizing additive, and having improved stability in oxidizing environments at elevated temperatures. The material was capable of transmitting visible and infrared radiation.

Black Inventors: From Africa to America(1995), p. 126; *Index of Patents*(1969), pp. 1018, 1473

1969 • A single axis gyroscope with an electromagnetic system for supporting a float assembly was invented by Lonnie G. Neal (1928-) and patented in 1969. Neal improved the gyroscope by including a primary power input subassembly with the gyro end housing and a secondary or power pickup subassembly with the float. Another improvement was an electrical connection between the secondary or power pickup subassembly and the motor or motors which drive the inertial sensing element carried by the float. The motor was constructed in a way that facilitated mass production. Neal earned a B.S. from Marquette University in 1966 and previously, in 1950, received a B.S. from Langston University, and was a senior project engineer for General Motors Corporation.

Black Engineers in the United States(1974), p. 149; *Index of Patents*(1969), p. 1130, 1148; *Twentieth Century Black Patentees - A Survey*(1979)

1969 • A method and composition for autocatalytically depositing copper was developed by African American Henry Jackson and patented in 1969. This process, developed while Jackson was working for IBM, deposits copper films onto a substrate. The stabilizing composition is composed of five components in an aqueous solution. Its ingredients are a wetting agent, an alkali metal carbonate or bicarbonate, an alkali metal thiosulfate, an alkali metal theocanate, and an active sulfur containing compound. A film of an activating metal, such a palladium, gold, or silver, is applied to the base to be plated and then immersed in the copper solution. In certain instances, the plating operation may then be followed by the electrolytic deposition of a superimposed copper film.

Black Inventors: From Africa to America(1995), p. 125; *Index of Patents*(1969), p. 770

1969–1970 • James Andrew Harris (1932-) was co-discoverer of element 104, rutherfordium, and element 105, now called dubnium, in 1969 and 1970. He was the leader of a group of researchers at Lawrence Berkeley Laboratory that first detected the elements. Harris received a B.S. degree in 1953 from Huston-Tillotson College (Texas), and was employed from 1955 to 1960 as a radiochemist for Tracerlab Inc., where he worked to detect secret Soviet tests of nuclear weapons by studying their radioactive fallout. He then joined the staff at Lawrence Berkeley Laboratory in 1960 as a nuclear chemist. His team's major assignment was discovering elements whose existence had been theorized but that had never been found in nature or created in a laboratory. Harris produced the purified target material of the element californium, which was bombarded with carbon or nitrogen atoms in an effort to produce new elements. Harris retired in 1988.

Blacks in Science: Astrophysicist to Zoologist(1977), pp. 46-47; *Black Contributions to Science and Energy Technology*(February, 1979), p. 10; *Who's Who Among Black Americans*(1991), p 546

1969 • Tralance Obuama Addy (1944-) was the first person to receive B.A. and B.S. degrees simultaneously from Swarthmore College (Pennsylvania). He received both the B.A. in chemistry and the B.S. in mechanical engineering in 1969. He then received a M.S.M.E. and a Ph.D. in 1974 from the University of Massachusetts. Addy worked for Scott Paper Company from 1973 to 1980, starting as a research project engineer, and advancing to program leader. He then started as director of applied research in 1980 for SURGIKOS, Inc., becoming vice-president and general manager of the ASP division from 1988 to 1995, when he became president of that division. Addy has several patents and is the author of a number of technical articles on nonconventional food resources and production.

Who's Who Among Black Americans (1990-1991), p. 9; *Who's Who Among African Americans* (1998-1999), p. 10

1969 • James King, Jr. (1933-), a physical chemist who contributed to diverse fields such as anesthesia, nuclear energy, and solar power, was the first African American named manager of the physics department of the Jet Propulsion Laboratory (California) in 1969. At the Laboratory, King primarily conducted research on the chemistry of natural and artificial gases. He received his B.S. in 1953 from Morehouse College (Georgia), and both his M.S. in 1955 and Ph.D. in 1958 from the California Institute of Technology, becoming the first African American graduate of Morehouse College to receive advanced degrees from Cal Tech. King was employed by the National Aeronautical and Space Administration from 1974 to 1984, where he directed varied space shuttle environmental effects programs. He then taught chemistry from 1984-1986 at Morehouse College, before returning to the Jet Propulsion Laboratory in 1986. In 1988, King became senior technical manager of the Space Science and

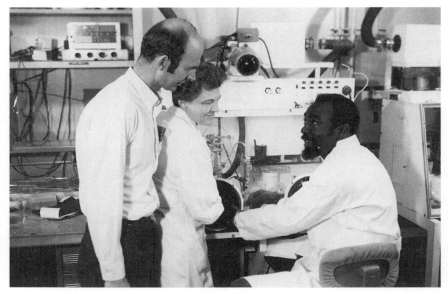

JAMES A. HARRIS (RIGHT)
WITH COLLEAGUES AT
LAWRENCE BERKELEY
NATIONAL LABORATORY.

Application Program at the Laboratory, where in 1993 he was appointed director of science and engineering.

Blacks in Science and Medicine (1990), p. 143; *Distinguished African American Scientists of the 20th Century* (1996); *Notable Black American Scientists* (1999), p. 189; *Who's Who Among African Americans* (1998-1999), pp. 868-9

1970 • John B. Christian (1927-) received a patent on June 30, 1970, for his invention of a grease composition for use at high temperatures and high speeds. Christian earned a B.S. in chemistry in 1950 from the University of Louisville. Christian worked as a chemist for DuPont from 1952 to 1954, and then spent one year as a chemist for the U.S. Naval Ordnance Laboratory. He then started working for the U.S. Air Force at Wright Patterson Air Force Base as a materials research engineer. Christian became a leading specialist in lubricants and grease development, especially lubricants and greases that could withstand temperatures ranging from negative 50 degrees to 600 degrees. He developed and patented a significant number of lubricants and greases and published in a variety of technical journals.

Black Engineers in the United States (1974), pp. 36-37; *Creativity and Inventions* (1987), p. 64; *Blacks in Science and Medicine* (1990), p. 54

1970 • Walter Cooper (1928-) was an African American chemist employed as a research associate by the Eastman Kodak Company. He developed three patents in photographic science and published 25 scientific papers while employed by Kodak. Cooper received one of his patents in 1970 for a polymerization process that initiated polymerization in ethylenically unsaturated monomers. He received a B.A. degree in 1950 from Washington and Jefferson College, earned a Ph.D. in 1956 from the University of Rochester, and a Sc.D. in 1987 from Washington and Jefferson. Cooper began his career with Kodak in 1956 as a research chemist, retiring from there in 1986 and continuing as a consultant for industry.

Index of Patents (1990); *Who's Who Among African Americans* (1998-1999), p. 319

1971 • A high-pressure optical cell for Raman spectrography was invented by Charles E. Weir and patented in 1971. Weir's invention is used to obtain a chemical analysis of materials under high pressures and temperatures. The system includes a laser as a source of radiation, combined with a high pressure cell to permit analysis of a relatively small amount of material.

Black Inventors: From Africa to America (1995), p. 126; *Creativity and Inventions* (1987), p. 69; *Index of Patents* (1971), p.1983, 2043

1971 • The gamma-electric cell was a device that converted nuclear radiation from reactors or isotopes directly into electricity, without going through a heat cycle. This valuable device was invented by African American nuclear physicist Henry T. Sampson (1934-), who patented the cell in July 1971. Sampson earned a B.S. from Purdue University in 1956 and a MSc. from the University of Illinois in 1965. He also earned another MSc. from the University of California at Los Angeles in 1961, and then the Ph.D. from the University of Illinois in 1967. Sampson was a research engineer from 1956 to 1962 for the U.S. Naval Weapons Center. For many years, he was the Director of Mission Development and Operations for the Space Test Program at the Aerospace Corporation. Sampson also had several patents for propellants and published a text about African Americans in the entertainment industry.

Blacks in Science and Medicine(1990), p. 208; *Black Engineers in the Unites States*(1974), pp. 174-175; *Index of Patents*(1971); *Who's Who Among African Americans*(1998-1999), p. 1313

1971 • James Edward Young (1926-19??) became the first African American tenured full professor of physics at Massachusetts Institute of Technology in 1971. Young earned a B.S. in 1946 and the M.S. in 1949 at Howard University (Washington, D.C.), followed by a M.S. in 1951 and a Ph.D. in 1953 from MIT. He served as an instructor in physics at Hampton Institute (Virginia) from 1946 to 1949, and then as a physics research assistant from 1949 to 1953 at MIT. He was a staff member from 1956 to 1969 at the Los Alamos Science Laboratory, and in 1986 was appointed research associate in neuroscience and cell biology at Tufts University Medical School.

Blacks in Science and Medicine(1990), p. 260; *Who's Who Among African Americans*(1998-1999), p. 1686; *Who's Who Among Black Americans*(1985), p. 939

1971 • A patent for production of high impact polystyrene was issued to Herbert Leonard, Jr. in 1971. Leonard's polystyrene composition is a blend of from 50 to 99.5 percent by weight of at least one styrene-type resin and from 0.5 to 50 percent by weight of at least one alfin rubber. The styrene-type resin can be a polymerized monovinyl aromatic hydrocarbon of the benzene series and/or an interpolymer. The alfin rubber was either a butadiene homopolymer or an interpolymer. The impact resistance of Leonard's process was improved if the alfin rubber had a gel content sufficient to render the percentage of gel in the total blend between about one percent and about 25 percent by weight.

Black Inventors: From Africa to America(1995), p. 125; *Index of Patents*(1971)

1971 • Emmett Scott Harrison (1930-) was an African American engineer who patented, in 1971, his invention of a gas turbine air compressor and control generally used to produce snow-like crystals. Harrison received a B.A. in chemistry from Talladega College in 1940 and in 1955, he earned a B.S. in chemical engineering from Polytechnic Institute of Brooklyn. His device was an artificial snow-producing system employing a gas turbine air compressor, which had an air bypass connected to discharge nozzles to deliver compressed air mingled with water, generating snow-like water particles. The compressor had an overload prevention system to avoid excess bypass of compressed air and overheating, which could lead to failure of the combustor and turbine components.

Black Engineers in the United States(1974), p. 90; *Index of Patents*(1971)

1972 • Frank Roger Prince (1941-) invented an improved process for producing chemicals called 2-pyrrolidones, for which he received a patent in 1972. Prince's process used the carbonylation of alkyl chloride, preferably in a two-phase solvent system, in the presence of ammonia at elevated temperature and pressure. The proportion of alkyl chloride and ammonia and the temperature could be adjusted so as to produce 2-pyrrolidone and N-allyl-pyrrolidone simultaneously in equal proportions. Prince earned a B.S. degree from the Philadelphia College of Pharmacy in 1963 and a Ph.D. from Brooklyn Polytechnic Institute in 1968. He was a senior research chemist for Atlantic Richfield Chemical Company from 1967 to 1969, when he joined the Allied Chemical Corporation.

Blacks in Science and Medicine(1990), p. 195; *Ebony*(July, 1970), p. 7; *Index of Patents*(1972)

1972 • In 1970, Arnold Francis Stancell (1936-) invented a process for partially separating components from fluid mixtures that was patented in 1972. Stancell's process involved selective permeation through a permeable membrane, wherein at least one fluid substance diffuses through the membrane at a higher flow rate than one or more other components. The technique was particularly useful for separating hydrogen from mixtures containing methane and other gaseous organic compounds. Stancell earned a Sc.D. from Massachusetts Institute of Technology in 1962. From 1988 to 1993, he was vice president of Mobil Oil's International Exploration and Production. Stancell had a number of technical publications and eight patents in chemical engineering.

Blacks in Science and Medicine(1990), p. 220; *Index of Patents*(1972); *New York Times*(February 27, 1992); *Who's Who Among African Americans*(11th edition), p. 1226

1972 • A method of sealing containers for microelectronics devices was the invention of Harry J. Green Jr. (1911-), patented in 1972. Green, an African American chemical engineer, earned a B.Ch.E. from Ohio State University in 1932, a M.S. from Massachusetts Institute of Technology in 1938, and a Ph.D. in chemical engineering from Ohio State University in

1943. He taught at North Carolina A&T College from 1934 to 1944, when he joined Stromberg-Carlson as a senior engineer in 1944 and stayed until 1967. He was a member of the Xerox Corporation staff after 1970. Green's invention involved coating the surface of the container to be sealed with a gold coating partially dissolved into an eutectic, gold-tin solder preform. The pre-tinned container layers are juxtaposed and fused to form an airtight seal. The process takes place at a temperature below that which would damage the microelectronic device.

Blacks in Science and Medicine (1990), p. 105; *Index of Patents* (1972), p. 698

1972 • Donald E. Jefferson invented, in 1969, resin solution useful for increasing the wet strength of cellulosic material. The chemical mixture was maintained at a specific temperature range to form a solid condensation product. The solid was then separated and reacted with formaldehyde in a mixture of water and a monohydric alcohol.

Black Inventors: From Africa to America (1995), p. 125; *Index of Patents* (1979)

1985 • William L. Wade, Jr., an African American chemist at the US Army Electronics Technology and Devices Laboratory at Fort Monmouth, New Jersey has acquired 10 patents, of which one granted in 1985 was for a porous carbon cathode for use in an electrochemical cell. Wade's process included: wetting carbon black with isopropyl alcohol water and adding a binding agent; smearing the resulting paste on a thin expanded metal screen; pressing and rolling to the desired thickness; drying the cathode sheet while a weight was placed above and below the cathode sheet; and sandwiching the sheet between two pieces of blotting paper in an elevated drying oven at 280 degrees centigrade for one hour. Cathodes prepared following Wade's process were structurally strong maintained their physical integrity with minimal cracking and flaking, and did not crumble when cut.

Black Scientific and Engineering Contributions (1985), p. 13; *Index of Patents* (1985)

1972 • The African American chemist George W. Nauflett received a patent in 1972 for his process for the synthesis of 2-fluoro-2, 2-dinitroethanol (FDNOL). Nauflett's process is for the preparation of this substance that is especially useful as an intermediate in the preparation of a plasticizer, a chemical that adds flexibility. The process basically involves a formation of an alkali metal salt by the reaction of nitromethane and formaldehyde in the presence of an alkali metal base. Fluorinating the alkali metal salt with gaseous fluorine yields the FDNOL.

Creativity and Inventions (1987), p. 68; *Index of Patents* (1972), p. 1371

1973 • Eddie Lomax, Jr. (1923-) became the first technical director of the Puritan Chemical Company when he was promoted to that post in 1973. As technical director, Lomax was responsible for the development and improvement of the company's products. He received a B.S. degree in 1948 from Morehouse College (Georgia) and a M.S. from Atlanta University (Georgia) in 1951. Lomax was hired on at Puritan as a development chemist in 1951.

Blacks in Science and Medicine(1990), p. 156; *Ebony*(December, 1956), p. 5

1973 • The first African American woman to earn a Ph.D. in physics was Shirley Ann Jackson (1946-), who earned that degree from the Massacusetts Institute of Technology (MIT) in 1973. The degree also made her the first African American to earn a Ph.D. in any subject from MIT. Jackson previously received her B.S. in physics in 1968 at MIT. She was resident associate in theoretical physics from 1973 to 1976 with the Fermi National Accelerator Laboratory, visiting science associate from 1975 to 1976 with the European Organization for Nuclear Research, and member of the technical staff of Bell Laboratories for the period 1976 to 1992. She has been a professor of physics at Rutgers University (New Jersey) since 1991. In 1995, she became the first African American and first woman to chair the Nuclear Regulatory Commission. In that position, she oversees a staff of over 3,000 employees and is responsible for a budget of $500 million. Jackson, whose specialty is theoretical elementary particle physics, has published more than 100 scientific articles and abstracts.

SHIRLEY ANN JACKSON

African America: Portrait of a People(1994), pp. 672-673; *Ebony*(March, 1996), pp. 110-111, (May, 1996), p. 110; *Journal of the National Technical Association*(Summer, 1996), Vol. 70, p. 13

1974 • John William Coleman (1929-), an African American molecular physicist, developed advances in electron microscopy and received patents related to the electron microscope in 1974. Coleman received a B.S. from Howard University in 1950, a M.S. from the University of Illinois in 1957, and a Ph.D. in biophysics in 1963 from the University of Pennsylvania. He was a physicist at the National Bureau of Standards from 1951 to 1953 and an instructor in physics at Howard University from 1957 to 1958. Coleman then joined RCA Corporation in 1958 and conducted research in electron optics. He was a Fulbright Scholar and winner of the prestigious David Samoff Award.

Blacks in Science: Astrophysicist to Zoologist(1977), p. 17; *Blacks in Science and Medicine*(1990), p. 58; *Index of Patents*(1974)

RONALD E. GOLDSBERRY

1974–1976 • Ronald Eugene Goldsberry (1942-), an African American organic chemist, acquired patents on a class of polymers in 1974 and 1976. These polymers have a basic chemical composition that stabilizes the chemical and physical properties of the polymers against the degradative effect of ultraviolet light and high temperatures. Goldsberry's inventions produce novel aromatic azines, which are useful in the preparation of these newer polymers. He received a B.S. degree in chemistry in 1964 from Central State University, a Ph.D. in organic chemistry from Michigan State University in 1969, and a MBA in finance and marketing in 1973 from Stanford University. Goldsberry taught chemistry from 1969 to 1971 at the University of California, San Jose. He was employed in the oil industry from 1975 to 1987. Goldsberry joined the Ford Motor Company as general manager of its Plastic Products Division in 1987, and in 1993 was appointed vice president of customer services, becoming only the second African American vice president at Ford Motor Company.

Index of Patents (1974, 1976); *Who's Who Among African Americans* (1998-1999), p. 559

EARL D. SHAW

1974 • Earl D. Shaw (1937-) became the first African American researcher at Bell Laboratories when he was hired on in 1974. Shaw, a son of sharecroppers, had received a B.S. in 1960 from the University of Illinois, a M.S. from Dartmouth University in 1964, and a Ph.D. from the University of California at Berkeley in 1969. Upon receiving the Ph.D., Shaw began work as an adjunct professor of physics at Howard University until the mid-1970s. Through his work at Bell Laboratories, he has developed a reputation as a specialist in laser technology. He was co-inventor of the spin-flip tunable laser, which was patented in 1971. This laser was remarkable in that the user could adjust the wavelength of the laser by turning a knob. In 1991, Shaw retired from Bell and began teaching physics at Rutgers University (New Jersey). He has more than 40 scientific publications to his credit.

Black Genius (1998), pp. 306-327; *Blacks in Science and Medicine* (1990), p. 212; *Blacks in Science: Astrophysicist to Zoologist* (1977), p. 42; *Created Equal* (1993), pp. 165-169

1974 • Frank Eugene Sessoms (1947-), an African American physician, has undertaken research in food chemistry and, in 1974, patented high-nutrition food spreads. Sessoms's process results in the preparation of a high-nutrition food spread that uses a soy protein as the nutritional supplement. This particular food preparation has little or no sticky or gritty feeling in the mouth, which is associated with other such spreads. Sessoms received a B.S. from Tennessee State University in 1970 and a M.D. in 1974 from Meharry Medical College. He completed an internship and residency in family practice from 1974 to 1977 at St. Margaret's Memorial Hospital. Sessoms started his private practice in 1979, and was a professor of Family Medicine at the University of Pittsburgh. He also published a number of scientific articles.

Index of Patents(1974); *Who's Who Among African Americans*(1998-1999), p. 1338

1975 • The invention of a low-cost telemeter for monitoring a battery and DC voltage converter power supply was developed by Floyd Allen and was patented in 1975. In the system, the output information is obtained from a frequency modulated transmitter whose modulation signal is alternatively obtained from the two data channels on a periodic basis. This system and circuit is inexpensive to produce and use in the field, capable of testing fuse battery power supplies on a large scale.

Index of Patents(1975), p. 58; *Twentieth Century Black Patentees - A Survey*(1979)

1975 • Eddie Charles Gay (1940-), a chemical engineer, developed a cathode for a secondary electrochemical cell that was patented in 1975. Gay was the recipient of a B.S. in chemical engineering in 1962 and Ph.D. in 1967 from Washington University. He started working for Argonne National Laboratory in 1968 as an assistant engineer, working his way up to program manager status in 1975. Gay's electrochemical cell is comprised of an alkali metal anode, a molten salt electrolyte, and an improved cathode. To use the cell, the cathode is first electrocharged in a series with the anode, to convert the sulfide reaction product into a useable cathode reactant submerged into molten electrolyte. Gay is active in a number of chemical societies and organizations and has received local and national awards for his technical achievements.

Black Engineers in the United States(1974), pp. 74-75; *Blacks in Science and Medicine*(1990), p. 99; *Index of Patents*(1975), p. 637; *Who's Who Among African Americans*(1998-1999), p. 537

1976 • Edwin Roberts Russell (1913-1996) acquired 11 patents on atomic energy processes. Russell received a B.S. from Benedict College in 1935, a M.S. from Howard University in 1937, and a D.Sc. from Benedict College in 1974 (honorary). He taught in colleges from 1936 to 1953, when he was hired as a research chemist by E.I. Dupont de Nemours & Company. Russell conducted research in bio-assay, radioactive tracer, gas absorption, ion exchange absorption, monomolecular films, and radioactive waste treatment. One of his patents, granted January 3, 1976, was a process for the removal of cesium from an aqueous solution by ion exchange.

Blacks in Science and Medicine(1990), p. 207; *Creativity and Inventions*(1987), p. 68; *Who's Who Among Black Americans*(1985), p. 733

1976 • A patent was issued in 1976 to Joseph L. Russell for his invention of a preparation of tungsten hexafluoride from halogen and hydrogen fluoride. In Russell's procedure, a tungsten compound, a halogen, and hydrogen fluoride were reacted at elevated temperature and pressure in the absence of air or water. The process converted tungsten directly to the hexafluoride without the preparation or isolation of intermediates. The intermediate halides, however, could be employed as a starting material if desired.

Creativity and Inventions(1987), p. 68; *Index of Patents*(1976)

1976 • Albert Y. Garner, an African American research chemist employed by the Monsanto Research Corporation, received a patent in 1976 for inventing a flame-retardant or a flameproofing technique. Garner's flame retardant was for material made from cotton or polyester-cotton having about 30 to 70 percent by weight cotton. The material was treated with an aqueous solution containing a sufficient amount of Garner's specified mixtures and then dried to make the materials self-extinguishing. The treated and dried material was cured at a sufficient temperature to bond the compounds to the material.

Black Inventors: From Africa to America(1995), p. 123; *Index of Patents*(1976)

1976 • A portable hardness tester for thin film plastic was invented by Samuel C. Smith and patented in 1976. The device had a platform for the sample to be tested, an indenter consisting of a straight vertical-placed shaft pointed on the lower end, and a weight for applying a driving force to the indenter. A dial gauge was connected directly to the indenter to measure the vertical displacement of the indenter when the weight was applied. Smith's device provided the capability for reproducible indentation readings to be made.

Black Inventors: From Africa to America(1995), p. 126; *Index of Patents*(1976), p. 1727

THOMAS C. CANNON

1976 • Thomas C. Cannon Jr. (1943-) played a pioneering role in the design and execution of the first commercial fiber optic lightwave system in the United States, installed in Chicago (Illinois) in 1976. Cannon earned a B.S. in 1964 in aeronautical engineering, the M.S. in 1966, and a Ph.D. in 1970, all from Purdue University (Indiana). After completing his academic training, Cannon joined Bell Labs Federal Systems division and helped design a cable system made with the synthetic material Kelvar. He developed mathematical equations necessary to predict the effects of physical forces on fibers, allowing manufacturers to design cables that could be installed without creating harmful stresses on the fibers. Cannon and co-inventors developed the ST Connector, the most widely manufactured optical connector, and also developed the Tactical Fiber Optical Connector (TOFC), the first military-certified optical connector.

Blacks in Science: Ancient and Modern (1983); *Notable Black American Scientists* (1999), pp. 58-9

1977 • Lester A. Lee received a patent in 1977 for his invention of carbon dioxide laser fuels. Lee's procedure provides a composition suitable for use in a thermally pumped laser, as well as a simplified method for generating a laser beam. The process also provides a fuel composition suitable for generating a laser beam. The fuel, when burned with an oxidizer, produces a gas which excites at least one other molecule to laser activity.

Black Inventors: From Africa to America (1995), p. 125; *Creativity and Inventions* (1987), p. 67; *Index of Patents* (1977), p. 1025

1977 • The American Chemical Society, in 1977, elected Henry Aaron Hill (1915-1979) as president. Hill was the first African American to hold that position. During his 38-year history with the ACS, he chaired a committee that produced personnel guidelines for companies employing chemists. He earned a B.A. in 1936 at Johnson C. Smith University, and then a Ph.D. in organic chemistry from MIT in 1942. He worked from 1942 to 1946 for Atlantic Research Association. He became the vice-president of research in 1944, and the company was renamed North Atlantic Research Company in 1945. He was hired by Dewey and Almy Chemical Company as supervisor of research from 1946 to 1952, then became assistant manager for National Polychemicals in 1952 before rising to become the company's vice president in 1956. In 1961, he started his own firm, Riverside Research Laboratory, which was involved in organic chemistry research. Hill was an authority on polymer chemistry and fabric flammability. He was appointed to President Johnson's National Commission on Product Safety.

HENRY A. HILL

African-Americans in Boston (1991), p. 100; *Encyclopedia of Black America* (1981), p. 437; *Ebony* (January, 1977), p. 86; *Negro Year Book* (1952), p. 100

1977 • Waverly J. Person (1927-) in 1977 was the first African American appointed director of the National Earthquake Information Center in Colorado. Person acquired a B.S. in 1949 from St. Paul's College. In 1962, he got a job as a technician at the National Earthquake Information Center through the U.S. Department of Commerce. After his interest in earthquakes was captured and he obtained some further education, he became a geophysicist in 1973. Person is among the first African Americans in his field. Person has published many articles on earthquakes in scientific journals, as well as having contributed to a number of textbooks on earth-quakes. He authored *Significant Earthquakes of the World 1985-1989*, as published by the U.S. Geological Survey.

African American Almanac(1997), p. 1064; *Who's Who Among African Americans*(1997), p. 1182

1977 • A vertical liquid electrode employed in an electrolytic cell was invented by Donald J. Cotton (1939-) in 1975 and patented two years later in 1977. The electrode was used to manufacture chemical products by electrolytic decomposition. In Cotton's system, the cell incorporates the advantage of high current density and efficiency, as well as low space requirement, low liquid electrode requirement, and the convenience of operational diaphragm employment. Cotton received a B.S. from Howard University in 1957 and a M.S. in physical chemistry from Yale University in 1957. He returned to Howard, where he received a Ph.D. in physical chemistry in 1967. Cotton was technical lead for the Department of Energy regarding nuclear research. He lectured in Africa and South America and was involved in technical projects in several European countries. Cotton also published a number of scientific and technical papers.

Black Inventors: From Africa to America(1995), p. 123; *Blacks in Science and Medicine*(1990), p. 62; *Creativity and Inventions*(1987), p. 64; *Index of Patents*(1997)

1977 • The chemist Albert Clifton Stewart (1919-) became the first African American director of sales for the Chemical and Plastics Division of Union Carbide in 1977. Earlier, in 1973, Stewart had become the first African American international business manager for the same division. Stewart was employed by Union Carbide from 1956 through 1984. He obtained his B.S. in 1942 and his M.S. in 1948 from the University of Chicago (Illinois). Stewart then received a Ph.D. in inorganic chemistry in 1951 from the University of St. Louis (Missouri). He worked from 1951-6 for the Oak Ridge National Laboratory, where he was the first African American with a Ph.D. on the staff. While at Union Carbide, he undertook significant consulting roles for the Ford Foundation, NASA, and the Agency for International Development. After Union Carbide, Stewart became associate dean and professor of marketing at Western Connecticut State University. He also holds two U.S. patents.

Blacks in Science and Medicine(1990), p. 222; *Ebony*(July 1959), p. 7; *Notable Black American Scientists*(1999), pp. 284-5; *Who's Who Among African Americans*(1998-1999), p.1423

1978 • Alfred A. Bishop (1924-), an African American chemical engineer, patented a flow distributor in 1978 that was used on nuclear reactor cores. Bishop earned a B.S. in 1950 from the University of Pennsylvania, a M.S. in chemical engineering from the University of Pittsburgh in 1965, and a Ph.D. in mechanical engineering from Carnegie-Mellon University (Pennsylvania) in 1974. Bishop worked for Fischer & Porter, Westinghouse Corporation, and B.B. Nuclear Engineering Consultants prior to joining the University of Pittsburgh in 1981 as a research engineer. He published numerous articles on nuclear engineering, heat transfer, and fluid mechanics.

Black Engineers in the United States(1974), p. 18; *Created Equal*(1993), p. 176

1978 • James C. Letton (1933-) was an organic chemist with the Proctor and Gamble Company in Cincinnati, where he worked on developing biodegradable soap agents. Two patents resulted from that work effort in 1978. Letton was experienced in both the food chemistry and industrial chemistry fields. He earned a B.A. in chemistry in 1955 from Kentucky State University, at which time he started working in steroid production and manufacturing with Julian Laboratories in Chicago. In 1970, he received a Ph.D. in chemistry from the University of Illinois. He taught chemistry at Kentucky State until 1975, when he joined Proctor and Gamble. Letton earned a third patent for his work on enzyme stabilization for laundry products and another for alkyglycosides, chemicals used to make biodegradable agents from sugar. Letton also contributed to work on the fat substitute, Olestra.

Black Enterprise(February 1990), p. 106

1978 • Tralance O. Addy (1944-), an African American chemist, patented his process for minimizing the accumulation of static charges on fibers resulting from fiberization of pulp lap sheets. Addy's technique directed the pulp lap sheets into stacks, directing the stack of sheets in a downstream direction to a fiberizing device for separating fibers from the stack. With Addy's technique, a lower percentage of pump lap sheets were treated directly with an antistatic chemical, without requiring complex, expensive liquid application systems. Addy, who earned both a B.A. and B.S. degree from Swathmore College in 1969, also earned a M.A. and a Ph.D. in 1974 from the University of Massachusetts. He began working in industry in 1973 and became president of ASP, Johnson and Johnson Medical, Inc. in 1995.

Index of Patents(1978); *Who's Who Among African Americans*(1998-1999), p. 9; *Who's Who Among Black Americans*(1990-1991), p. 9

1978 • Kenneth Morgan Maloney (1941-) received a patent in 1978 for his invention of an improved mercury vapor lamp. The key to Maloney's lamp was an ultraviolet reflecting underlayer of alumina particles for the phosphor coating. This reduced the weight of the coating without an accompanying reduction in the lamp brightness. The alumina underlayer was deposited on the interior surface of the lamp glass envelope and was useful in conventional high pressure and low-pressure mercury vapor lamps. Maloney was a physical chemist who earned a B.S. degree from Southern University in 1963, and a Ph.D. from the University of Washington in 1968. Maloney was a research scientist for several organizations from 1963 to 1970, when he joined General Electric Company as a senior scientist in its Lamp Division. He then worked for Xerox and Allied Corporation from 1976 to 1981, when he joined Phillip Morris Research and Development.

Blacks in Science and Medicine (1990), p. 160; *Index of Patents* (1978)

JENNIE R. PATRICK

1979 • Jennie R. Patrick (1949-) earned her Ph.D. in chemical engineering from Massachusetts Institute of Technology in 1979, making her first African American woman to earn that degree. Patrick had previously earned her B.S. degree in chemical engineering in 1973 at the University of California at Berkeley. Patrick worked as a research engineer for General Electric Company from 1979 to 1983, when she transferred to Phillip Morris for the years 1983 to 1985. She then worked in emulsion technology and polymer science for Rohm and Haas Research Lab from 1985 until 1990. In 1993, Patrick joined the faculty at Tuskegee University as a professor in the department of chemical engineering.

Black Collegian Vol. 14, (1984), p. 102; *Ebony* (May, 1981), p. 6; *U.S. Black Engineer* (Fall, 1988), pp. 30-33; *Notable Black American Women* Book II, (1996), pp. 516-518

1979 • The first minority-owned firm in the United States to receive contracts from the U. S. Environmental Protection Agency Laboratory was Energy and Environmental Engineering, located in Cambridge, Massachusetts. The firm was founded by James Hall Porter (1933-) in 1979. Porter earned a B.S. in chemical engineering from Rensselaer Polytechnic Institute (New York) in 1955 and a D.E. in chemical engineering from Massachusetts Institute of Technology in 1963. He was manager of Computer Applications Design from 1967 to 1972 and then associate professor of chemical engineering from 1971 to 1976 at MIT. Porter was a co-founder and president of the National Organization for the Professional Advancement of Black Chemists and Chemical Engineers.

African Americans in Boston (1991), p. 149; *Blacks in Science and Medicine* (1990), p. 193; *Black Engineers in the United States* (1974), p. 162; *Who's Who Among African Americans* (1998-1999), p. 1207

1979 • The invention of a photosensitive composite sheet material useful as a printing plate was patented by African American chemist George Canty in 1979, while he was employed by the 3M Company of St. Paul, Minnesota. The photosensitive sheet material was useful as printing plates, and Canty's process provided a photosensitive composite sheet material having a thin coat of a primer layer between the substrate and the photopolymerizable composition. After irradiation, the primer layer firmly anchored the photopolymerized composition to the substrate, preventing its removal from the plate during the printing process. Such plates could be used for over 100,000 impressions. Canty earned both his B.S. in chemistry in 1954 and M.S. in physics and chemistry in 1966 from the University of Pittsburgh. He was a chemist for the National Institute of Health from 1958 to 1963, and from 1965 to 1973 worked for the Gillate Research Institute and Celanese Research Company. Canty was then employed by the 3M Company in 1973 as supervisor of product development.

Index of Patents(1979); *Who's Who Among African Americans*1998-1999), p. 203; *Who's Who Among Black Americans*(1990-1991), p. 205

1980 • John Spencer Trent (1950-), an electron microscopist, discovered, in 1980, the use of ruthenium telraoxide as a polymer staining agent for use with transmission electron microscopes. Trent earned a B.S. in polymer science in 1974 from Pennsylvania State University, a M.S.E. in macromolecular science from Case Western Reserve University in 1979, and a Ph.D. in mechanics and materials science from Rutgers, the State University of New Jersey, in 1983. Trent was a research chemist, consultant, and visiting and assistant professor in Michigan, New Jersey, and Pennsylvania until 1985. Trent then joined General Electric Plastics in 1986 as lead polymer scientist and microscopist.

Who's Who Among African Americans(1998-1999), pp. 1501-1502

1982 • A toothpaste containing pH-adjusted zeolites was developed by Anthony L. Dent (1943-) and patented in 1982. Dent's toothpaste provided polishing and lustering and had good pasting properties. It was free of other abrasive agents. Dent earned a B.S. at Morgan State University and a Ph.D. from Johns Hopkins University in 1970. He was an associate professor of chemical engineering at Carnegie Mellon University from 1970 to 1978 and joined the PQ Corporation as a principal scientist in 1979, where he is a senior scientist. Dent is active in a number of local, regional, and national chemical associations and organizations.

Black Engineers in the Unites States(1974), p. 52; *Index of Patents*(1982), p. 382; *Who's Who Among African Americans*(1998-1999), p. 393

1982 • Denise Annette Ford was the first African-American graduate of the University of Missouri-Rolla, in 1982, with a degree in geological engineering. Ford's initial employment was as a petroleum engineer trainee with the Gulf Oil Company in Odessa, Texas.

Blacks in Science and Medicine (1990), p. 92; *Jet* (May 31, 1982), p. 21

1982 • The first African American oceanographer to participate in submersible dives aboard research ships (known as research submersibles) was Evan B. Forde (1952-), who began working for the National Oceanic and Atmospheric Administration (NOAA) in 1974, and for NOAA's Ocean Chemistry Division in 1982. Forde earned a B.S. in geology, with a specialty in oceanography, from Columbia University (New York) in 1974, and then in 1976 earned a M.S. in marine geology from Columbia. Forde's extensive research examined how environmental changes affect the ocean and how the environmental process of global warming impacts the content of carbon dioxide in the ocean.

Notable Black American Scientists (1999), p. 119

1983 • Frank Alphonso Crossley (1925-), an African American metallurgical engineer, developed a process for the grain refinement of titanium alloys that was patented in 1983. Crossley's contribution substantially improved the development of the new commercial metal titanium. The

EVAN B. FORDE

process involved inoculating the alloys prior to or during casting with small amounts of at least one composition of a specific type of titanium or a nitrogen-oxygen-titanium compound. Crossley earned his B.S. in 1945, M.S. in 1947, and Ph.D. in metallurgical engineering in 1950 from the Illinois Institute of Technology. From 1966 to 1987, he worked for Lockheed Missiles and Space Company and Aerojet Corporation until 1991. Crossley published 58 articles in various technical journals and acquired seven patents between 1957 and 1983.

Black Engineers in the United States(1974), pp. 44-46; *Blacks in Science and Medicine*(1990), p. 64; *Ebony*(September, 1975), pp. 158, 160-161; *Who's Who Among Black Americans*(1990-1991), p. 294; *Who's Who Among African Americans*(11th Edition), p. 293

1983 • Lois E. Hill was the first African American to graduate with a M.S. in physics from Clark College in 1983, which is now Clark/Atlanta University. She was an environmental engineer with the Environmental Protection Administration.

Journal of the National Technical Association(Summer, 1996), p. 23

1984 • Joan Murrell Owens (1933-) was the first African American woman to earn a Ph.D. degree in geology, which she received in 1984 from George Washington University. She received a B.A. in fine arts *magna cum laude* from Fisk University in 1954, then went on to receive a B.S. in geology in 1973 and a master's degree in 1976, both from George Washington University. Owens joined the faculty of Howard University as an associate professor of geology in 1976, then became became an associate professor of biology in 1991. In 1995, she retired from teaching. She is a specialist in deep-sea corals, and has refined their classification system and even discovered a new species. Owens has published extensively in areas of marine biology and paleontology.

Who's Who Among Black Americans(1990-1991), p. 969; *Who's Who Among African Americans*(1998-1999), p. 1144

1984 • George Edward Alcorn (1940-) patented, in 1984, an imaging x-ray spectrometer using thermomigration of aluminum. He also patented a process of plasma etching, which is utilized by a number of companies manufacturing semiconductors. Alcorn has acquired over 25 patents and is considered a pioneer in the fabrication of plasma semiconductor devices. He received a B.A. in physics from Occidental College in 1962 and a M.S. in nuclear physics in 1963 from Howard University. He earned his Ph.D. in atomic and molecular physics from Howard University in 1967. Alcorn worked 12 years in industry for Philco-Ford, Perken-Elmer, and IBM

GEORGE E. ALCORN

before joining NASA in 1978. While at NASA's Goddard Space Flight Center, he was the recipient of the NASA Goddard NASA/GSFC Inventor of the Year Award. Alcorn is chief of Goddard's Office of Commercial Programs supervising technology transfer, small business innovative research, and commercial use of space programs.

Journal of the National Technical Association (Fall 1988), p. 22; *Notable Black American Scientists* (1999), pp. 2-3

1985–1988 • Anthony Michael Johnson (1954-), an African American physicist who had been employed by AT&T Bell Laboratories since 1974, contributed to the research on lasers and fiber optics. From 1985 to 1988, he acquired patents related to high speed circuit measurements, integrated optical devices, and photodetectors for detecting electromagnetic radiation. Johnson earned a B.S. in physics *magna cum laude* from Polytechnic Institute of New York in 1975 and a Ph.D. in physics in 1981 from the City College of New York. He first joined AT&T Bell Labs in 1974 as a senior technical associate, and became a member of the technical staff in 1981. He was promoted to a distinguished member of the technical staff in 1984. Johnson was active in professional and technical organizations and was co-chair of the 1992 Conference on Lasers and Electro-Optics—the world's largest

JOAN MURRELL OWENS

laser meeting with over 7,000 in attendance. Johnson published extensively and served as technical journal topical editor and board advisor.

African American Voices of Triumph (1994), p. 73; *Index of Patents* (1985, 1987, 1988); *Who's Who Among African Americans* (1998-1999), p. 790

1985 • Lincoln J. Diuguid (1917-), an African American organic chemist, patented a technique in 1985 for increasing the burning efficiency of fuels. His invention was used with gasoline, diesel oil, jet fuels, kerosene, and naphtac, all fuels generally used in piston or rotating turbine-type internal combustion engines. Diuguid achieved higher efficiencies by incorporating alkynol, which was directly added to the fuel in the fuel reservoir or aspirated into systems employing a fuel/air premixing method. Diuguid served as president of his firm, Du-Good Chemical Laboratory and Manufacturers. He earned a B.S. from West Virginia State College in 1938 and a M.S. in 1939 and a Ph.D. in organic chemistry in 1945 from Cornell University. Diuguid taught at the college level, conducted extensive research in organic chemistry, and has published numerous technical scientific papers in the field.

Blacks in Science and Medicine (1990), p. 75; *Index of Patents* (1985); *Negro Year Book* (1952), p. 100; *Who's Who Among African Americans* (11th edition), p. 347; *Who's Who Among Black Americans* (1990-1991), p. 345

1985 • Bobby L. Wilson (1942-), an African American chemist, patented a process for the hydroconversion of carbonaceous materials in 1985. Wilson's technique was a process for hydroconverting carbonaceous materials to lower molecular weight products. This improved process is effective for both solid and liquid carbonaceous materials. Wilson is a professor of chemistry at Southern University. He earned a B.S. in 1966 at Alabama State College, a M.S. at Southern University in 1972, and a Ph.D. in 1976 at Michigan State University. Wilson joined Texas Southern University's faculty as assistant professor in 1976, and he ultimately was appointed chemistry department chairman in 1987. He then became vice president of academic affairs in 1990 and served as provost from 1992 to 1994. Wilson published in both domestic and international journals and co-authored a general chemistry laboratory manual.

Index of Patents (1985); *Who's Who Among African Americans* (1998-1999), p. 1424

1985–1988 • William Frank King (1938-), an African American research chemist, was employed by the Chevron Chemical Company from 1975. He conducted extensive research in pesticides, insecticides, antibacterial and antifungal agents, and related areas. He acquired over 30 U.S.

and foreign patents, most between 1985 and 1988. King earned his B.A. degree in chemistry from Lincoln University in 1961. He then received a M.S. degree in organic chemistry from Fisk University in 1963 and a Ph.D from Utah State University, also in organic chemistry, in 1972. King taught from 1972 to 1975 prior to joining Chevron as a senior research chemist. He transferred to the Oronite Technology Division, Additive Synthesis and Processing, as a senior research chemist in 1992. King was active in professional and technical associations, published extensively, and taught as a chemistry instructor at the College of Marian.

Index of Patents (1985, 1986, 1987, 1988); *Who's Who Among African Americans* (1998-1999), p. 872

1985 • William L. Wade Jr., an African American chemist at the United States Army Electronics Technology and Devices Laboratory at Fort Monmouth, New Jersey, has acquired 10 patents. A 1985 patent was for a porous carbon cathode for use in an electrochemical cell. Wade's process including wetting carbon black with isopropyl alcohol water and adding a binding agent. The resulting paste was smeared onto a thin, expanded metal screen. It was pressed and rolled to a desired thickness, drying the cathode sheet while a weight was placed above and below it. The sheet was then sandwiched between two pieces of blotting paper in an elevated drying oven at 280 degrees Celcius for one hour. Cathodes prepared following Wade's process are structurally strong, maintain their physical integrity with minimal cracking and flaking, and do not crumble when cut.

Black Scientific and Engineering Contributions (1985), p. 13; *Index of Patents* (1985), pp. 183, 2273

1986 • James E. Young (1926-) received a patent in 1986 for his invention of a system for controlling a multi-cell battery. The device had two sets of cells. The first set had an active partition connected to a load, while the second set was not connected to the load and had a passive partition. The controls on Young's device also provided read-outs on the amount of charge remaining in the battery and its remaining useful life. Young completed his undergraduate studies at Howard University and received a Ph.D. from Massachusetts Institute of Technology in 1953. He has been professor of physics at MIT since 1970 and a research associate in neuroscience in the department of anatomy at Tufts University Medical School.

Index of Patents (1986); *Who's Who Among African Americans* (1998-1999), p. 1686; *Who's Who Among Black Americans* (1990-1991), p. 1421

1986 • John L. Carter acquired a patent in 1986 for his invention of a distributed pulse-forming network for a magnetic modulator. It was one of his 26 patents. Carter was a senior scientist and former branch chief in the

Electronics Technology and Devices Laboratory at Fort Monmouth, New Jersey. His major work areas concerned microwave ferrite devices, and he was considered the most prolific African American inventor at Fort Monmouth. Carter also received the Meritorious Civilian Service Award for his work on microwave ferrite devices, which was the U. S. Army's second highest award.

Black Scientific and Engineering Contributors to the US Army at Fort Monmouth, New Jersey(1988); *Index of Patents*(1986)

1987–1991 • Linneaus C. Dorman (1935-) received several patents from 1987 to 1991 for his invention of an artificial bone material composed of an ivory-type compound. The material is similar to bone in its strength and flexibility. Dorman researched other medical applications, including the testing of compounds that might prove useful in the treatment of mental illness, peptides for commercial use, and peptides for slowing down the blood clotting process. Dorman earned a B.S. degree from Bradley University in 1956 and a Ph.D. from the University of Indiana in 1961. He was employed by the U. S. Department of Agriculture during the summers from 1956 through 1959. He started as a research chemist with Dow Chemical in 1960 and progressed to research specialist to associate scientist. In 1994, he was promoted to senior associate scientist. Dorman was named Inventor of the Year by Dow in 1983.

Blacks in Science and Medicine(1990), p. 76; *Index of Patents*(1991,1993); *Notable Black American Scientists*(1999), pp. 95-96; *Who's Who Among African Americans*(1998-1999), p. 409

1987 • Dennis Weatherby created a lemon formula for dishwashing liquid while working as a process engineer at Proctor and Gamble Company in Cincinnati, Ohio. His invention is now the basis for the composition of all lemon cleaning products that contain bleach and was patented in 1987. He discovered a unique category of dyes that successfully gives a non-staining yellow color to detergents that contain bleach. His compound contains detergent-builder materials, chlorine bleach, an optional low-foaming surfactant, and a relatively water soluble dye, which is color stable. Prior to Weatherby's invention, pigments that stained dishes and dishwasher parts were used instead of dyes.

Ebony(October 1998), pp. 158, 159; *Index of Patents*(1987), p. 2122, 2743

1988 • Bertram J. Fraser-Reid (1934-), an African American biochemist on the faculty of Duke University, led a research team that developed a method for linking single sugars together to form oligosaccharides—compounds that are important in regulating various biochemical activities. A patent for the method was issued in 1988. Fraser-Reid received both his

B.S. and M.S. degrees in chemistry from Queen University (Canada) and received his Ph.D. in chemistry in 1964 from the University of Alberta. He has contributed significantly to the study of complex sugars through his research efforts. The Merck, Sharpe and Dohme Award was given for his contribution to organic chemistry in 1977, and in 1989, he was honored as the Senior Distinguished U.S. Scientist by Germany's Alexander Von Humboldt Foundation. He also received the Claude S. Hudson Award in carbohydrate chemistry from the American Chemical Society.

Black Enterprise (February, 1990), p. 86; *Timelines of African-American History* (1994), pp. 322, 326

1988 • A laminate, adapted for manufacturing metal beam leads that are bonded to integrated circuit chips, was patented by African American chemist Michael Molaire in 1988. He is a research associate and project manager at Eastman Kodak in New York. Molaire acquired 28 U. S. patents and over 65 foreign patents. Most of his work has been in the area of laser printing and optical recording. Molaire received the Eastman Kodak Research Laboratories' C.E.K. Mees Award for excellence in scientific research and reporting and was inducted into the Kodak Distinguished Inventor's Gallery.

Ebony (October 1998), p. 160; *Index of Patents* (1988), pp. 1249, 1633

1988 • James E. Millington (1930-), who received a Ph.D. in chemistry from the University of Western Ontario in 1956, received a patent in 1988 for his method of making styrene-type polymers. Millington earned his undergraduate degree from Lincoln University in 1951 and a M.S. in 1953 from Western Ontario. His invention was a procedure for suspension polymerizing a styrene-type monomer composition in an aqueous medium of polyvinyl alcohol (PVA). Millington won the 1964 Allis-Chalmers Science and Engineering award and $5,000 for the invention of an electrical insulating paper.

Blacks in Science and Medicine (1990), p. 173; *Created Equal* (1993), pp. 175-176; *Index of Patents* (1988)

1988 • The first African American to hold the position of manager of the Waste Management Operation of the Argonne National Laboratory was Aubrey Carl Smith, Jr. (1942-), who was promoted to the office in 1988. Smith earned an A.A. in science in 1968 from Thornton Community College (Illinois) and a B.A. in chemistry in 1972 from Illinois Institute of Technology. He started employment with Argonne National Laboratory in 1986 as supervisor of waste management operations, became manager of waste management operations in 1988, and then environmental compliance representative from 1990 to 1992. Smith was then promoted to building manager and environmental compliance representative in 1992. He has been a member of chemical, engineering, and safety professional organizations, as well as being active in the Chicago National Safety Council.

Who's Who Among African Americans(1998-1999), p. 1375

1989 • Two patents were issued for chemically treated paper products to African American inventor Morris Leslie Smith (1933-) in November 1989. His inventions are chemical treatments for facial tissues and paper towels. The added treatments allow the products to soothe human skin while retaining their water-absorbent property and strength.

Index of Patents(1989)

1989 • The first African American elected president of American Association for the Advancement of Science was Walter Eugene Massey (1938-), when he was selected in 1989. Massey received a B.S. from Morehouse College in 1958 and a Ph.D. in physics in 1966 from Washington University. He was director of the National Science Foundation in 1990 and remained there until 1993, when he became provost and senior vice president for academic affairs at the University of California System in Oakland, California until 1995. At that time, he became president of Morehouse College. Massey's personal research efforts were concerned with methods of calculating low-temperature properties of strongly interacting fluids, and he has published numerous scientific papers. He holds membership in many professional and scientific organizations and has received numerous awards and honors, including a number of honorary Doctor of Science degrees.

Black Issues in Higher Education(1989), p. 8; *Blacks in Science and Medicine*(1990), p. 164; *Ebony*(August 1989), pp. 62-63, 65; *Notable Black American Men*(1999), pp. 773-774; *New York Times*(June 4, 1991), p. A25

1989 • Francis E. Levert (1940-), an African American nuclear engineer with the KEMP Corporation, invented a continuous fluid level detector that was patented in 1989. The device detects the level of liquid in a closed tank and uses a measuring apparatus comprising an electrical heater, metallic sheathed thermocouple cable, and an electrical insulant positioned between each thermoelectric element. Levert earned a B.S. from Tuskegee Institute in 1964, and a M.S. in 1966 and a Ph.D. in nuclear engineering in 1971 from Pennsylvania State University. Levert taught one year at Tuskegee Institute in 1972 and worked a year for the Commonwealth Edison Corporation. He was a nuclear engineer for Argonne National Laboratory for several years and is now vice president with KEMP Corporation. Levert has 12 patents, and is the author of two books and 63 technical journal articles.

Index of Patents(1989); *Who's Who Among African Americans*(1998-1999), p. 916

1989 • Meteorologist S. George H. Philander (1942-) published his first text in 1989. The book, *El Nino, La Nina and the Southern Oscillations* was published by Academic Press. Philander earned his B.S. at the University of Cape Town in 1963 and a Ph.D. from Harvard University in 1970. He joined Princeton University as a research assistant in 1971, remaining in that position until 1978. He became a full professor in Princeton University's Department of Geological and Geophysical Science in 1990, when he was also named director of the Atmospheric and Oceanic Sciences Program. In 1994, he became the chair of his department. Philander is an active member of national and international professional organizations and has consulted to such organizations. Philander has published two textbooks, contributed to many others, and written numerous journal articles. He also won the Distinguished Author Award in both 1979 and 1983. In 1985, he was named a fellow of the American Meteorological Society.

*Western Journal of Black Studies*Vol. 16, No. 1, (1992), p. 53; *Who's Who Among African-Americans*(1998-1999), p. 1188

1993 • Shelia K. Nash-Stevens invented an optical fiber holder that was patented in 1993. Her invention provided a simple, reliable means for securing and aligning optical fibers for splicing. Securing and aligning optical fibers by her method was quick and easily achievable. Nash-Stevens is an electronics engineer with the George C. Marshall Space Flight Center.

Index of Patents(1993); *Journal of the National Technical Association*(Summer Edition), Vol. 70, (1996)

1993 • Warren Morton Washington (1936-), an internationally recognized expert on atmospheric and climate research, was the first African American elected president of the 11,000-member American Meteorological Society. Morton earned his B.S. in physics in 1958 at Oregon State University and received the M.S. (1960) and Ph.D. (1964), both in meteorology, from Pennsylvania State University. He joined the National Center for Atmospheric Research (NCAR) in 1963, and in 1987 was appointed director of the Center's Climate and Global Dynamics Division. Washington has performed research on the El Nino/La Nina weather phenomenon and is an expert in computer climate modeling. His book, *Introduction to Three-Dimensional Climate Modeling*, is a standard reference tool. He was appointed to the National Advisory Committee of Oceans and Atmospheres by the President in 1978, and founded the Black Environmental Trust in

1989. He is currently a senior scientist and Climate Change Research Section head (since 1995) at NCAR.

Blacks in Science and Medicine(1990), p. 253; *Ebony*(January, 1974), p. 7; *Western Journal of Black Studies*Vol. 16, (1992), p. 53; *Who's Who Among African Americans*(1998-1999), p. 1560

1994 • Kenneth Dwight Lewis (1949-) was the first African American to help lead a mission to remove a half ton of bomb-grade uranium from Kazakhstan. The secret 1994 mission transferred the metal from Kazakhstan to the United States to be made into safer material. Lewis earned a B.S. in physics in 1971 from Rutgers University, a M.S. in physics in 1972 from Lehigh University, a M.S.E. in nuclear engineering from Stanford University in 1974, an A.M. in applied math from the University of Illinois in 1979, and a Ph.D. in nuclear engineering in 1982 from Illinois as well. Lewis started employment at Lockheed Martin Energy Systems in 1982 as a senior engineer and by 1995 was appointed the corporate nuclear criticality safety manager. He published a number of scientific papers and was a member of several scientific societies. Lewis lectured in foreign countries and received numerous awards and honors.

US Black Engineer(January/February, 1999); *Who's Who Among African Americans*(1998-1999), pp. 921-922

1994–1996 • James E. West (1931-), an African American physicist, acquired more than 20 patents in the field of electroacoustics from 1994 to 1996. West completed the fundamental studies that pioneered the widespread industrial use of electret transducers (microphones) for sound recording and voice communication. He has published over 50 scientific papers. West received an undergraduate degree from Temple University in 1956 and completed further study at Hampton Institute and Rutgers University. He joined the Acoustic Research Department of Bell Laboratories in 1957, where he has specialized in electroacoustics, physical acoustics, and room acoustics. West was also co-inventor of the foil electret, a device used to convert sound into electrical signals in hearing aids, portable tape recorders, and lapel microphones. He was honored with the Electrochemical Society of America Callinan Award and Institute of Electrical and Electronics Engineers Group on Acoustics, Speech and Signal Processing Senior Award.

Blacks in Science: Ancient and Modern(1983), pp. 289-292; *Index of Patents*(1994, 1995, 1996)

1994 • Henry Thomas Chriss (1964-) was the director of account logistics for NIKE, Inc. and received a patent in 1994 for a footwear additive made from recycled materials. Chriss's patent related to an additive used in shoe formation comprising finely divided, recycled footwear materials, which were scraps generated during manufacturing, or defective or used articles of footwear. Chriss studied polymer science at Akron University and business management at Kent State University. He worked for Duramax Johnson from 1985 to 1991 in polydispersions and was a quality control chemistry laboratory supervisor. Chriss joined NIKE in 1991 as a chemistry laboratory manager and became director of account logistics there in 1995. He also received three patents in 1998 for the chemical bonding of rubber to plastic in articles of footwear.

Index of Patents (1994, 1998); *Who's Who Among African Americans* (1998-1999), p. 272

SYLVESTER JAMES GATES

1994 • The first recipient of the American Physical Society Prize for Visiting Minority Professor Lectureship was African American Sylvester J. Gates Jr. (1950-), who was awarded the prize in 1994. The research of Gates, a theoretical particle physicist, emphasized the development of a unified field theory, which would explain the diversity and complexity of the universe in terms of the interactions of a small number of building blocks. Gates earned two B.S. degrees at Massachusetts Institute of Technology in 1973, one in mathematics and one in physics. He also received his Ph.D. in physics in 1977 from MIT. Gates continued postdoctoral studies from 1977 to 1982 at Harvard University (Massachusetts) and California Institute of Technology. He then taught at MIT from 1982 to 1984, when he became affiliated with the University of Maryland's Department of Physics and Astronomy, becoming full professor in 1988 and serving as chair of the department of physics and astronomy from 1991 to 1993. Also affiliated with Howard University (Washington, D.C.), Gates was instrumental in obtaining a $6 million grant from NASA to establish the Howard University Center for the Study of Terrestrial and Extraterrestrial Atmospheres.

Notable Twentieth-Century Scientists (1995), pp. 734-5

1995 • James Winfield Mitchell (1943-), an African American chemist, patented a method of growing continuous diamond films in 1995. Mitchell headed the Analytical Chemistry Research Division of Bell Laboratories. His work included exploiting microwave discharges and plasmas for analysis and synthesis of materials, development of methods for the ultrapurification of analytical reagents and research chemicals, and using spectroscopy and nuclear radiation to develop highly accurate methods for ultratrace analysis. Mitchell received a B.S. degree in chemistry from the Agricultural and Technical State University of North Carolina in 1965 and a Ph.D. in analytical chemistry from Iowa State University in 1970. He joined AT&T Bell Laboratories in 1970 as a member of the technical staff and was promoted to head of the Analytical Chemistry Research Department in 1975. He was made an AT&T Bell Laboratories Research Fellow in 1985. Mitchell lectured internationally and completed 60 scientific publications. He has won the Pharmacia Industrial Analytical Chemistry Award, Percy L. Julian Research Award, and was inducted into the National Academy of Engineering.

Blacks in Science and Medicine (1990), pp. 174-175; *Black Enterprises* (February, 1990), p. 82; *Distinguished African American Scientists of the Twentieth Century* (1996), pp. 259-261; *Index of Patents* (1995, 1996)

1995 • The first African American and first woman appointed to the position of Chair of the Nuclear Regulatory Commission was Shirley Ann Jackson (1946-), who was named to that post in 1995. In that position, she oversees a staff of over 3,000 employees and is responsible for a budget of $500 million. Jackson earned her B.S. in 1968 and her Ph.D. in physics in 1973 at the Massachusetts Institute of Technology (MIT). She was the first African American woman to earn a Ph.D. in physics, as well as the first African American woman to earn a Ph.D. from MIT. She was resident associate in theoretical physics from 1973 to 1976 with the Fermi National Accelerator Laboratory, visiting science associate from 1975 to 1976 with the European Organization for Nuclear Research, and member of the technical staff of Bell Laboratories for the period 1976 to 1992. She has been a professor of physics at Rutgers University (New Jersey) since 1991. Jackson has published more than 100 scientific articles and abstracts.

SHIRLEY ANN JACKSON

African America: Portrait of a People (1994), pp. 672-673; *Ebony* (March, 1996), pp. 110-111, (May, 1996), p. 110; *Journal of the National Technical Association* (Summer, 1996), Vol. 70, p. 13

1995 • Clyde G. Bethea received an A.A.S. degree in electronics technology from the City College of New York in 1970, and then joined the AT&T Bell Laboratories Research Division as a member of the technical staff working in nonlinear optics. He was the first to develop the technique of electric field-induced, optical, second-harmonic generation in liquids and gases in 1995. He was also the first to design and operate a high powered Wd:YAG laser at 1.32 microns, and simultaneously at both 1.06 and 1.32 um. Bethea developed several techniques for picosecond optical sampling of electronic devices. His interest involved the high-speed analog/digital imaging acquisition of the internal functionality of semiconductor lasers, VHF, and microwave devices. He developed real-time diffraction-limited infrared imaging video systems used to map the internal distribution of functioning discrete semiconductor devices and circuits. Bethea won the Best Paper Award of 1988 from the Institute of Electrical Engineers for his work on quantum well detectors and received an award for his work on picosec time domain reflectometers from the Association of Electrical Engineers of Italy. Bethea published over 100 papers and held over 14 U.S. and foreign patents.

Philadelphia Tribune (November 13, 1979); *Index of Patents* (1976, 1988, 1991, 1995)

1996 • Gardy Cadet, African American inventor and chemist, joined Bell Labs in 1988 and became highly respected in the fields of process engineering and chemistry. He received patents for producing and analyzing gases used in semiconductor production and was specifically recognized for developing high-performance control methods for delivering chemical reagents used in the manufacture of optical fibers. Cadet earned both the B.S. and M.S. degrees at Brooklyn College in New York and a Ph.D. in nuclear chemistry from New York University in 1987. In his work at Bell Labs, he was co-developer of a point-of-use arsine generator—a safer way to produce chemical reagents used in the manufacture of integrated circuits. In 1995 and 1996, Cadet patented two inventions, providing an acoustic cell for determining the composition of gas mixtures and an invention for a process and apparatus for generating precursor gases used in the manufacture of semiconductor devices.

Bell Labs Publication (February, 1999); *Index of Patents* (1995, 1996)

1996 • The third director in the 50-year history of New Brunswick Laboratory at Argonne National Laboratories was Margaret Ellen Mayo Tolbert (1943-), who upon appointment in 1996 became the first African American woman to hold this post. Tolbert received her B.S. in 1967 from Tuskegee Institute (Alabama) and a M.S. in analytical chemistry in 1968 from Wayne State University (Michigan). She then earned a Ph.D. in 1974 from Brown University (Rhode Island). Tolbert taught and completed extensive research from 1974 through 1987 at Tuskegee, Florida A&M, and then again at Tuskegee. She became senior planner and senior budget and control analyst for British Petroleum from 1987-1990. Tolbert then directed the Research Improvement in Minority Institutions Programs for the National Science Foundation from 1990 to 1993, helping to strengthen research programs at minority colleges and universities. Tolbert initially joined Argonne National Laboratories in 1994 as the director of the division of educational programs, to coordinate educational and training research activities between the laboratory and colleges, universities, and other national and international organizations.

Blacks in Science and Medicine (1990), p. 233; *Essence* (August 1980), pp. 37-8; *Distinguished African American Scientists of the 20th Century* (1996), pp. 317-20; *Notable Black American Scientists* (1999), pp. 299-301

1998 • Brian G. Jackson is a researcher in semiconductor technology who received a patent for a portable highway warning device in 1998. The device is laid flat on a roadway and produces an audible warning sound when contacted by the wheels of a moving vehicle. Jackson worked at the Advanced Large Scale Integration Development Laboratory of Bell Labs. During the 1980s, he was one of the first scientists to experiment with using the x-ray lithographic technique to create designs for semiconductors. He designed and built a computer to automatically perform the semiconductor inscription task and used mathematical and programming methods to fine-tune the operation.

Blacks in Science: Ancient and Modern (1983), pp. 275-280; *Index of Patents* (1998)

1998 • Rensselaer Polytechnic Institute selected Shirley A. Jackson (1946-) in December 1998 as its new president, making her the first African American woman to head a leading technology university in the United States. Jackson earned a B.S. in 1968 and Ph.D. in 1973 in physics from the Massachusetts Institute of Technology, becoming the first African

MARGARET TOLBERT
(LEFT) WITH U.S.
SECRETARY OF ENERGY
FREDERICO PENA.

American woman to earn a Ph.D. at MIT. Jackson also served as chair of the United States Nuclear Regulatory Commission (another African American first), a visiting scientist at the European Organization for Nuclear Research in Geneva, and as a visiting lecturer at the NATO International Advanced Study Institute in Belgium. She also held posts as a research physicist at the AT&T Bell Laboratories and as a professor of physics at Rutgers University (New Jersey).

New York Times (December 12, 1998); *Who's Who Among African Americans* (1998-1999), p. 767

TRANSPORTATION

1847 • The first steamboat to sail San Francisco Bay was launched by the African American businessman William Alexander Leidesdorff (1810-1841) in November 1847. Leidesdorff settled in the San Francisco area known as Yerba Buena after leaving New Orleans, where he made a goodly amount of money as a cotton merchant. He was a successful merchant and real estate investor in San Francisco and became a well-respected prominent businessperson. Leidersdorff wanted to establish a 24-hour rapid trade line between the Sacramento Valley and San Francisco by way of steamship. His steamship *Sitka* was the first to sail on San Francisco Bay in 1847 but was too slow and ineffective to travel the intended route. Leisdorff was a city councilman, city treasurer, and chair of the school board that opened the state's first public school in 1848.

Dictionary of American Negro Biography(1982), pp. 392-393; *Famous First Facts About Negroes*(1972), p. 121; *I, Too, Sing America*(1992)

1871 • Landrow Bell invented an improved smokestack for locomotives patented in 1871. Bell's device was a cone-shaped device that prevented embers from flying from the locomotive to the passenger compartments. The smokestack had a combination of flues, channels, air funnels, fans, wire screens, and conducting tubes to achieve this. An additional flue created a downward draft in the smokestack of the locomotive. This flue had a supplementary bonnet and pipes leading to the ash pan. A fan wheel and channel, along with wire bonnets, made of sufficiently finely woven wire, arrested objectionable sparks and embers passing up the stack and returned them, without gases and fumes, to the ash pan.

Blacks in Science and Medicine(1990), p. 25; *Index of Patents*(1871)

1872 • Elijah McCoy (1844-1929), one of the most prolific African American inventors, designed many devices to facilitate the lubrication of locomotive machinery and engines efficiently, economically, and in a dependable manner. McCoy patented his first lubricating oil-cup in 1872 for steam cylinders. He developed a cup with a stopcock that could supply oil, drop by drop, to the moving parts of machines automatically, without having to stop locomotives each time oiling was required. McCoy perfected his oil lubricating system for different types of machines and received over 30 patents concerned with machine and engine lubricating. Most of the railroad locomotives between 1872 and 1915, especially in the United States, were equipped with McCoy's lubricators. Many of McCoy's inventions carried patents in England, France, Germany, Austria, and Russia.

The Black Inventor (1975), pp. 39-40; *Creativity and Inventions* (1987), p. 67; *Dictionary of American Negro Biography* (1982), pp. 413-414; *Negro Year Book* (1931-1932) p. 168

1888 • A direct-acting steam engine was invented by Frank Winn and patented in 1888. Winn's engine was designed to operate in an upright or vertical position. The apparatus consisted of a steam chest, a piston rod and piston, valve stem and valves to operate in the steam chest, and a shaft with a gear wheel with a series of rounded teeth. Steam entered the upper side of the steam chest via a pipe, which passed into the cylinder on one side of the piston, moving the rack bar, and turning the cogwheel. The cogwheel operated the main shaft, moving the valves. The piston was almost at the end of its stroke before the steam is reversed, starting the motion in the reverse direction.

Blacks in Science: Astrophysicist to Zoologist (1977), p. 88; *Created Equal* (1993), p. 186; *Index of Patents* (1888)

1888 • Albert B. Blackburn received a patent in 1888 for a railroad signal used to alert engineers to danger along the route. Blackburn's device consisted of a spring-sustained cross-bar, a trip that was pivoted, a rock-shaft connected with a signal, and a link pivotally connected with the trip and with the rock-shaft. When the trip was struck by a wheel moving in one direction, it would merely rock without operating the signal, but when struck by a wheel moving in the reverse direction, it would operate the signal.

Black Inventors: From Africa to America (1995), p. 98; *Blacks in Science and Medicine* (1990), p. 29; *Index of Patents* (1888)

1889 • Arnold Romain invented a public transit passenger register that was patented in 1899. Romain's device automatically registered the entrance and exit of each passenger and was used as a fare register. When a passenger entered the car, he stepped on a trap, causing a lever to tilt on its fulcrum and turning a wheel on a shaft of a box attached to the underside of the car. This device caused a ball to roll down a groove and into a glass receptacle. When a passenger got off the vehicle the same process occurred, so that at the end of a trip, the number of balls in the receiver was double that of the fares collected.

Blacks in Science: Astrophysicist to Zoologist (1977), p. 86

1890 • Humphrey H. Reynolds was awarded a patent in 1890 for his invention of a safety-gate for drawbridges. His device allowed the safety-gates at the approaches of the bridge to be lowered before the draw-section begins to swing to open the bridge, and allows the gates to be raised by the section as it again swings into position in closing the bridge.

Black Inventors of America (1989), p. 144; *Blacks in Science and Medicine* (1990), p. 200; *Created Equal* (1993), p. 184; *Index of Patents* (1890); *The Real McCoy* (1989), p. 72

1891 • Henry Linden invented a piano truck, for either square or upright pianos, which was patented in 1891. The apparatus was a truck body consisting of a bottom, skids, a framework formed of interposed separating pieces, wheel frames, lower axles, cranks, and a stop piece, as well as wheels. The forward and rear wheel frames of the truck body could be raised or lowered and secured in either position. They also had a reversing mechanism. The truck body was also cushioned at suitable points where the piano rested.

Black Inventors of America (1969), p. 134; *Created Equal* (1993), p. 187; *Index of Patents* (1891); *Outward Dreams* (1991), p. 91

1891 • George Toliver was granted a patent in 1891 for his invention of a propeller for boats. Toliver developed a version of the screw propeller with a casing having a funnel-shaped front end and a double conical middle compartment that had side openings with diverging chutes. A shaft was arranged longitudinally in the casing with a hub mounted on the shaft. Toliver placed spiral blades on the front and rear ends of the hub. The front compartment of the casing was provided with wire netting guards to prevent debris from entering the casing.

Black Inventors: From Africa to America (1995), p. 249; *Blacks in Science: Astrophysicist to Zoologist* (1977), p. 88; *Index of Patents* (1891)

1893 • Elbert Robinson (1800s-1925) patented an electric railway trolley in 1893. Robinson's trolley had improvements for overhead electric railway systems which prevented the trolley from jumping off the wire when the car was rounding a curve or going down an incline in the road. His trolley had wheels consisting of three independent pulleys—a central grooved pulley and two outer beveled pulleys mounted on the same axle. It had an improved guide consisting of an open metal loop attached to the top of the car by means of braces, and springs which yielded somewhat to the trolley when the car rounded a curve.

Blacks in Science and Medicine(1990), p. 203; *Blacks in Science: Astrophysicist to Zoologist*(1977), p. 36; *The Negro Yearbook*(1947), p. 27; *Created Equal*(1993), p. 188; *Black Inventors of America*(1989), p. 98

1893 • The chilled groove wheel, later used on all railroads, was invented by African American inventor Elbert R. Robinson (1800s-1925). The invention was stolen and patented by two corporations. Robinson instituted proceedings all the way up to the Supreme Court, which decided in his favor, with a significant monetary award in royalty payments. Robinson also invented an electric railway trolley, patented in 1893, a casting composite patented in 1897, as well as a third rail, concrete pillar mold, and the interlocking switch.

The Black Inventor(1975), p. 92; *Blacks in Science: Astrophysicist to Zoologist*(1977), p. 36; *Blacks in Science and Medicine*(1990), p. 203

1893 • Thomas W. Stewart developed a station and street name indicator system for railway and streetcars which was patented in 1893. The display system comprised two shafts bearing gears at one end, ratchets, radial levers, pivoted bars, and pawls. A belt with street and station names was designed to wind and unwind on the shafts, displaying street and station names. The device was placed near the rail track, which had a block and tripping mechanism actuated by a wheel on the car. When actuated, the display system would wind or unwind, indicating street names and station names through an opening in the display apparatus. Stewart also had patents for a mop, a map, and a metal bending machine.

Blacks in Science: Astrophysicist to Zoologist(1977), p. 87; *Index of Patents*(1893)

1896 • A dust-proof bag for street sweepers was invented by Charles B. Brooks and patented in 1896. As the street sweeper was pushed, brushes would rotate, brushing debris into a hopper with a flange and damper. The elevator casing carried the debris to the bag attached to the hopper, with a tightening strap at the upper end of the bag engaging the hopper. When operated, no dust or dirt flew around, even while the filled bag was being closed.

Blacks in Science and Medicine(1990), p. 37; *Black Inventors: From Africa to America*(1995), p. 238; *Created Equal*(1993), p. 190

1897 • A train alarm for the benefit of trainmen when approaching an overhead bridge was invented by Richard A. Butler and patented in 1897. In Butler's design, the wheels of a passing train depressed a spring on the track. Then through a system of wires and levers, the motion was transmitted to the hammer of the alarm, which hit the alarm gong. The alarm gong was mounted on a post raised to about the height of the top of a freight car, in order to warn any trainmen on the top of the freight car. The unique combination of a curved spring extending above the track rail secured to a plunger by means of a cushion, the bell crank lever, wire from the lever to the base of the post, elbow, rod, spring, and arm comprised the alarm system.

Black Inventors: From Africa to America (1995), p. 238; *Blacks in Science: Astrophysicist to Zoologist* (1977), p. 77; *Created Equal* (1993), p. 191

1897 • The "Jenny Coupler," a device that automatically joins two railroad cars together, eliminated the dangerous job of hooking railroad cars together by hand, saving thousands of limbs and lives of railroad workers. This device was patented in 1897, by African American inventor Andrew Jackson Beard (1850?-1921) who was born a slave and freed at the age of 15. Beard also received a patent in 1892 for a rotary engine. The impact of Beard's automatic coupling device served as the focal point of the Federal Safety Appliance Act, which Congress enacted at the turn of the century.

The Black Inventor (1975), p. 25; *Black Inventors of America* (1989), pp. 23-27; *Creativity and Inventions* (1987), p. 29; *Blacks in Science and Medicine* (1990), p. 23

1899 • William Burr invented a railway-switching device that was patented in 1899. In Burr's system, a rotating roller and spring-supported railway switch were mounted on the side of the tracks. The main track had a portion of its periphery protruding above the rail tread, so that both simultaneously received the weight of the car wheel rim. The main track was provided with two rollers mounted, one in advance of the other. The journal support for the roller was located below the rail, with a supporting spring for the journal support and a housing unit enclosing the spring.

Black Inventors: From Africa to America (1995), p. 238; *Created Equal* (1993), p. 199; *Index of Patents* (1899)

1899 • Leonard C. Bailey, in 1899, patented a folding bed used as an upper berth in the Pullman compartment of trains. Bailey's bed was comprised of a bedpost with an upper and lower section, screw-threaded plugs to secure the upper and lower sections, and sleeves with interlocking non-rotatable connections. It was adaptable for hospital use on account of its hygienic properties, enabling it to be kept clean and antiseptic. It was easily packed for transportation or storage and could be assembled quickly in an emergency.

Blacks in Science and Medicine (1990), p. 17; *Created Equal* (1993), p. 192

1899 • A weather shield for street railroad cars was invented by Edward H. West, which he developed for the protection of the motorman from the weather. West's apparatus was a detachable shield designed to project beyond the car dashboard. It was attached to other parts of the car, providing complete shelter that was quick and easy to remove. The skeleton framework was secured to the roof and floor of the car and had window frames supported by the framework, which held window sashes. The upright, which supported the framework, also formed doorposts to support hinged doors. West provided a vent above the windows so that any moist warm air would be free to rise and escape instead of condensing on the windows.

Black Inventors: From Africa to America(1995), p. 249; *Created Equal*(1993), p. 193; *Index of Patents*(1899)

1899 • Wesley Johnson invented a velocipede, a variation of the bicycle, which was patented in 1899. Johnson's machine was based on a frame of light, tubular construction similar to a bicycle frame. It included a seat, driving mechanism, and two forward and two rear wheels. The two front wheels were mounted between two forks 4-6 inches (10-15 cm) apart, as were the two rear wheels. The forward wheels were provided with stiffening crossbars mounted on a hub, which was secured in the forward forks with intervening ball bearings. The double rear wheels were mounted on a stationery axle between the rear forks, with double rear wheel hubs and sprocket teeth to engage the chains connecting the driving sprocket with the rear driven sprocket wheels. Johnson's machine had increased stability and balance with a more secure corner-turning capability.

Black Inventors: From Africa to America(1995), p. 241; *Blacks in Science: Astrophysicist to Zoologist*(1977), p. 80; *Created Equal*(1993), p. 192; *Index of Patents*(1899)

1900 • An airship invented by John F. Pickering was patented in 1900. Pickering's objective was to invent a ship of strength and durability, powered by an electrical motor, and under the direct control of the operator. The first airship (or dirigible) was developed in France in 1852, but was filled with hydrogen gas. Pickering's airship was powered by an electric motor and was the first to have directional control. The dirigible had an attached car and was driven by a propeller and fans powered by the motor. It had air pipes, movable tubes, and air trunks extending throughout the balloon and the bottom of the car. This was the means for shifting the blast of air from the fan to either the upward or downward air pipes.

Black Inventors: From Africa to American(1995), p. 245; *Blacks in Science and Medicine*(1990), p. 191; *Index of Patents*(1900); *Created Equal*(1993), p. 193

1901 • Benjamin F. Jackson, who had a number of patents for such inventions as heating and lighting devices and transportation devices for trolleys, also received a patent in 1901 for a generator and motor for an automobile. Jackson's generator had an oil burner, oil receptacle, water drum, steam generator tubes, and steam drum, all supported on a portable frame. The oil valve and engine valves were connected by a signal lever so that both the steam and fuel were cut off at the same time when it was necessary to stop the vehicle. The burner was provided with an auxiliary portion, which only used sufficient oil to keep the generator pipes hot. This ensured that the vehicle would start promptly when the main burner was started and the engine connected with the steam generator.

Blacks in Science: Astrophysicist to Zoologist (1977), p. 80; *Blacks in Science and Medicine* (1990), p. 129; *Index of Patents* (1901); *Negro Year Book* (1918-1919), p. 343; *Negro Year Book* (1921-1922), p. 318

1906 • William Hunter Dammond (1874-1956) acquired a patent, in 1906, for a safety light device, which was used in the railroad industry. Dammond's signal system had green go, orange caution, and red stop signals, colors that were initially utilized on the railroad lines which ran from New York City to Washington, D.C. Dammond was also the first African American to graduate from the University of Pittsburgh.

Creativity and Inventions (1987), pp. 12-13, 65; *Index of Patents* (1906)

1909 • The first African American to reach the North Pole, on April 6, 1909, was Matthew A. Henson (1866-1955). Henson was a member of Admiral Robert E. Perry's expedition, and was sent ahead with four Eskimos for the final leg of the journey. Perry himself arrived approximately 45 minutes later. Henson met Perry in 1887 and was hired to help him with his survey of a canal route through Nicaragua. Perry took Henson on his expedition to the Arctic in 1891, 1893, 1896, 1897, 1898, 1905, and the last one to the pole in 1908-1909. Henson was largely ignored in the history books, but received some recognition later in his life. By order of President Taft, he received employment as a clerk in the New York Customs House from 1913 to 1936. The Explorer's Club made him a member in 1937, and he was awarded the Gold Medal by the Geographic Society of Chicago in 1948. Congress awarded him, in January, 1944, one of the joint medals honoring Henson and the five whites of the Arctic expedition.

Black History and Achievement in America (1982), p. 90; *Dictionary of American Negro Biography* (1982), p. 308; *New York Times* (October 12, 1986); *Seven Black American Scientists* (1970), pp. 116-141

1912 • Walter G. Madison invented three improvements in monoplane aircraft, which were patented in 1912. His first invention improved longitudinal and lateral stability and reduced resistance to the ascent of the aircraft. His second improvement provided better horizontal and vertical steering. The third improvement was the addition of propellers for lifting and driving the aircraft.

Blacks in Science: Astrophysicist to Zoologist (1977), p. 91; *Black Inventors: From Africa to America* (1995), pp. 105, 112

1915 • A life preserver, invented by Samuel J. Hines, was patented in 1915. Hines's device was a garment worn by an individual. It sustained a floating person and provided protection from the water. The life preserver was a watertight garment forming a body portion, leg portions, sleeve portions, and hand and feet coverings. A casing was formed at the waistline, with an inflatable buoyant element located within the casing. There were flexible straps mounted on the body portion immediately below the casing, and inflatable buoyant elements at the free ends of the straps.

Black Inventors: From Africa to America (1995), p. 106; *Index of Patents* (1915)

1917 • Eugene Jacques Bullard (1894-1961) was the first African American combat pilot in 1917. He served combat duty for France and was awarded a posthumous commission by the U. S. Air Force on August 23, 1994. Suffering racial persecution in the United States, he left in 1911 and joined the French Foreign Legion at the beginning of World War I. He later transferred to the French Army. He was wounded twice during more than 20 missions after receiving his flying certificate on May 5, 1917. His first flight mission was September 8, 1917. Bullard left the French Air Service in November 1917. In full uniform, Bullard wore 15 French medals and decorations, including the Legion of Honor and Croix de Guerre. A portrait bust of Bullard was unveiled in a private ceremony, in October 1992, at the Smithsonian Institution's National Air and Space Museum and is displayed in the museum's World War I gallery.

Blacks in Science and Medicine (1990), p. 41; *Philadelphia Tribune* (October 13, 1992), p. 8A

1920 • James Sloan Adams was granted a patent in 1920 for a propelling method for airplanes. Adams's improved propeller was designed to use the stored energy of a spring for driving the aircraft. In his system, the propelling wheel was discharged instead of the spring, and a resistance plane connected with the spring. The spring was compressed during the power stroke of a motor and suddenly released during the exhaust stroke. The stored energy of the compressed spring gave a forward propelling impulse to the aircraft.

Creativity and Inventions (1987), p. 63; *Index of Patents* (1920)

1920 • Mary J. Reynolds received a patent in 1920 for inventing a device for moving heavy loads from a platform to a vehicle, usually a truck. Reynolds's system worked with the engine and gears of the truck, upon which a lifting device was mounted. A train rail system was mounted on the truck, which held the load carrier. Lazy tongs raised and lowered the train rail. The tongs operated by cables that wound and unwound from winding drums, and gear connections with the truck shaft of the engine controlled the cables. With Reynolds's system, heavy loads could be hoisted from a platform through a second floor window.

Index of Patents (1920), p. 429; *Negro Year Book* (1921-1922), p. 33

1921 • An airplane parachute device, invented by Hubert Julian, was patented in 1921. The device provided safety for occupants in case of engine trouble or other difficulty. Julian incorporated a shaft into the aircraft that extended above it and had a parachute attachment. A motor was mounted adjacent to the shaft with a fan positioned below the parachute mechanism. Flexible cables connected the parachute attachment to the airplane. The motor, when operated, rotated the fan to drive air against the underside of the parachute, raising it from a closed position. The parachute allowed the aircraft to descend gradually without injury to the occupants.

Created Equal (1993), p. 194; *Creativity and Inventions* (1987), p. 67; *Index of Patents* (1921), p. 271; *Negro Year Book* (1921-1922), p. 33; *Twentieth Century Black Patentees - A Survey* (1979)

1921 • Norman Jackson invented an improved inner tube for pneumatic tires that was patented in 1921. Jackson's pneumatic tire consisted of a set of main circular air tubes, as well as emergency tubes that were arranged in a series between the main air tubes. The emergency tubes displaced the main sections of the tube when the latter were punctured. The emergency sections were automatically inflated when needed.

Black Inventors: From Africa to America (1995), p. 106; *Index of Patents* (1921)

1922 • A gas-filled dirigible flying machine was invented by Oscar Robert Cassell and was patented in 1922. Cassell's machine had a rigid cigar-shaped frame, a propeller for water navigation, and was designed for passenger service. Cassell had boat-shaped cars rigidly secured to the aircraft frame at each end, and a car in the center on the underside of the machine. The rear car had a pushing propeller, while the front car had a pulling propeller. The middle car had a water propeller for driving the machine along the surface of the water. There were rotatable steering posts with rudders mounted in them, a method of balancing the machine longitudinally consisting of a weight, and a longitudinally movable rope to which the weight was attached.

Blacks in Science: Astrophysicist to Zoologist(1977), p. 90; *Index of Patents*(1922)

1922 • Just ten years after the first American man acquired a pilot's license, Bessie Coleman (1893-1926) became the first African American woman to earn a pilot's license. Finding that no American flying school would accept her because of her race, Coleman went to Europe and earned her accreditation from a French flying school. She earned her international pilot's license in 1922, the first African American female to do so. Coleman was a popular stunt pilot and was planning to open a school for African Americans so they could learn to fly and prepare for careers in aviation, but was killed in an accident on April 30, 1926.

Black Wings(1983), p. 3; *Ebony*(May, 1977), pp. 88-90; *Negro Digest*(May, 1950), pp. 82-83; *New York Times*(November 25, 1985); *Timelines of African American History*(1994), p. 160

BESSIE COLEMAN

1925 • William Hale, in 1925, was granted a patent for his invention of an airplane that hovered in the air and ascended and descended vertically, as well as being able to move horizontally. Hale's aircraft could run along the ground the same as a wheeled vehicle and either in a forward or reverse direction, with a means of steering the craft when moving in either direction. The craft patented by Hale had a propeller at each end, one under the body, one at the top, and a propeller at each side of the body. The craft had a motor for driving each propeller and adjustable planes connected with the body. There was a manual means for adjusting each wing and each rudder.

Black Inventors: From Africa to America(1995), p. 114; *Index of Patents*(1925), p. 282

1925 • Oliver L. Thompson invented a vehicle parking attachment that facilitated the parking of a motor vehicle in a small space. His invention was patented in 1925. Thompson's system was an attachment to the underpart of a motor vehicle. The device would elevate the vehicle so as to lift the wheels from the ground. The device would then move the vehicle to the side, either toward or away from the curb. Thompson's device was folded upwardly underneath the body of the vehicle, and when it was required to park, a lever mechanism lowered the apparatus to the ground. The apparatus was connected to the drive mechanism of the vehicle for operation.

Creativity and Inventions(1987), p. 69; *Index of Patents*(1925), p. 677

1927 • David Baker (1881-19??) was granted a patent in 1927 for his invention of a liner for an inner tube. Baker's invention was a circular covering that completely enclosed the inner tube of a tire. The covering was provided with a resilient tread armor that was adapted to protect the outer periphery of the tube from a radial puncture. The liner also connected with the inner tube to prevent the inner tube from creeping relative to a pneumatic tire. Baker's device protected a tube from a puncture and formed reinforcement to the entire exterior surface of the pneumatic tube. Baker also had several other inventions, such as an elevator scale that prevented against overcrowding.

Created Equal(1993), p. 151; *Index of Patents*(1927)

1929 • The first person to invent and patent a practical and efficient refrigeration unit/system for trucks and railroad transportation was the African American engineer and inventor Frederick McKinley Jones (1893-1961). Jones during his 67 years obtained 61 patents, of which 40 were related to refrigeration units and systems. Jones's other major inventions included a self-starting gasoline engine, theater sound system, theater ticket dispenser and changer, military field-hospital air-conditioning unit, portable x-ray machine, military field-kitchen refrigerator, portable air-conditioning and cooling unit, and food containerization/refrigeration systems. Frederick Jones was inducted into the Minnesota Inventors Hall of Fame and was the first African American to receive the National Medal of Technology (posthumously) in 1991.

Black Firsts(1994), pp. 347, 349; *Dictionary of American Negro Biography*(1982), p. 366; *Ebony*(December, 1952), pp. 41-44, 46; *Man with a Million Ideas*(1977)

1930 • James Carmichael Evans (1900-1988) was granted a patent in 1930 for an invention preventing the accumulation of snow and sleet on the wings of an airplane. Evans's invention used the heat generated by the airplane motor(s) and its exhaust gases to raise wing temperature above the freezing point, preventing snow or sleet accumulation. The heat was distributed evenly over a prescribed area. The leading edge of the wing had a heat-insulating member with small openings and pipes connected to the engine, conveying exhaust gases and heat through the pipes throughout the wing's leading edge. Evans received a B.A. from Roger Williams University in 1921, and then earned a B.S. in 1925 and a M.S. in 1926 from the Massachusetts Institute of Technology. During his career, Evans was involved in research in electronics, and in 1926, won the Harmon Award for electronics research. Evans also taught electrical engineering at Howard University from 1946 until his 1970 retirement.

Blacks in Science and Medicine(1990), p. 87; *Index of Patents*(1930), pp. 212, 702; *Negro Year Book*(1937-1938), p. 7; *Notable Twentieth Century Scientists Supplement*(1998), pp. 149-150; *Who's Who Among Black Americans*(1990-1991), p. 395

1931 • Benjamin A. Crenshaw received a patent in 1931 for his invention of a turning signal device for use on a motor vehicle. The device was used to indicate to other vehicles or pedestrians the intended direction of the vehicle. Crenshaw's signal device had a number of lights that could be seen from the front or rear of the car in both the daytime or at night. A pneumatically actuated plunger, powered directly by the engine, operated the signals. The signaling device was located on each side of the vehicle adjacent to the window. Two valves and two control levers or one four-way valve operated the signals. The central portion of the signal contained the light, and colored glass made the signal appear red from the front and green from the rear.

Index of Patents (1931), p. 178; *Negro Year Book* (1931-1932), p. 165

1931 • William S. Hawkins invented an auto seat cape for automobiles with rumble seats. His invention was patented in 1931. The device would accommodate one or two people and was wind-, rain-, and snow-proof. Hawkins's invention was a combined cape and top for the rumble seat compartment in the rear deck of the automobile, with a rain gutter around the margins of the compartment and a cape cover for the compartment and occupants. The cape had an opening for each occupant and each had a zipper to secure the cape around the occupant. The cape, when not in use, could be packaged and conveniently stored in the automobile or used as a cushion.

Index of Patents (1933); *Negro Year Book* (1937-1938), p. 12

1932 • The first transcontinental flight successfully completed by African Americans occurred in 1932 when James Herman Banning (1900-1933) and Thomas C. Allen completed the flight. Banning and Allen obtained a used aircraft and set off on their flight with less than $100 for expenses. They completed the flight in 41 hours and 27 minutes. Born and raised in Oklahoma, Banning migrated to Chicago in the early 1920s, seeking to enter aviation school. No school would accept him because of his race, so he migrated to Des Moines, Iowa, where he learned to fly from an army officer. When Banning moved to the West Coast in the late 1920s, he was one of the very few African American pilots licensed by the U.S. Department of Commerce.

Black Wings (1983), pp. 8-9

1932 • The invention of an improved automatic gear shift was developed by Richard B. Spikes (18??-1962) and patented in 1932. Spikes's invention allowed the driver to operate a lever to change the vehicle speed and then press the automobile clutch pedal to change gears. The various sets of gears are constantly in mesh with no clashing of gears when shifting from speed to speed, making the transmission operate in silence. He also patented, for the automobile, a transmission and shifting mechanism (November 28, 1933), a braking system (January 2, 1962), and such varied items as a Trolley-pole arrester, beer tapper, and a billiard cue rack.

Black History & Achievement in America (1982), p. 89; *Black Inventors: From Africa to America* (1995), pp. 107, 126; *Blacks in Science: Astrophysicist to Zoologist* (1977), p. 87; *Blacks in Science and Medicine* (1990), p. 218; *Index of Patents* (1932), p. 816

1933 • The first round-trip transcontinental flight by African American pilots was undertaken and successfully completed by Charles Alfred Anderson and Albert E. Forsythe in 1933. They flew round-trip from Atlantic City, New Jersey to Los Angeles, California. The trip started July 17, 1933 from Atlantic City, and they arrived in Los Angeles, California on July 19, 1933, with the return flight being completed on July 28, 1933. Anderson trained many cadets during the primary phase of flight training at Tuskegee Air Field during 1941-2. One of his students was Daniel "Chappie" James, the future Air Force general. Anderson also gave a guest flight to First Lady Eleanor Roosevelt when she visited the Tuskegee Air Facility.

Black Firsts (1994), p. 255; *Black Wings* (1983), pp. 16-17, 27; *Philadelphia Tribune* (August 16, 1985); *Famous First Facts* (1964), p 1048; *Jet* (July 19, 1993), p. 39

1933 • Henry F. Stilwell invented a device for delivering mail and other items from an in-flight aircraft, which was patented in 1933. Stilwell's system comprised a cable guide-way with converging sidewalls placed on a relatively stationary surface, with the converging walls spaced apart for the exit of the cable received in the guide-way. When an in-flight aircraft dangled a weighted cable, the cable would spring a cable trap. The trap would release the load of mail, allowing the aircraft to carry it away.

Index of Patents (1933), p. 766; *Negro Year Book* (1937-1938), p. 13

1935 • A device to protect automobiles from harsh weather and dirt was invented by Curtis L. Bryant and patented in 1935. Bryant's device completely covered an automobile when it was not in use. The housing unit was mounted on the top of an automobile with a forward and rear entrance and self-winding rollers. A cover element, made of waterproof material, was carried by the rollers and fed out of the housing by way of the two entrances. The covering was made up of a main strip and side flaps. The main flap was attached to the front and rear bumpers and the side flaps were connected in pairs at the side of the automobile. The cover housing curved to conform to the contour of the top of the automobile and could be easily placed and/or removed from the vehicle top.

Index of Patents (1935), p. 103; *Negro Year Book* (1937-1938), p. 13

1937 • James Thomas Redding invented a convertible seat designed primarily for use in automobiles that was patented in 1937. Redding's convertible seat had a seat and back section with elongated extension pieces. A series of pins in the seat and back sections allowed the seat to be adjustable to various positions. In this manner, the seat could be converted into a bed in the back of the automobile.

Black Inventors: From Africa to America (1995), p. 109; *Index of Patents* (1937)

1938 • The first African American pilot to fly airmail in the United States was Grover C. Nash. He had an intrastate route from Chicago to Mattoon, to Charleston, Illinois. Nash started flying air mail in 1938 during National Air Mail Week.

Black Wings (1983), p. 5

1938 • Robert Lee developed an automobile safety device to prevent sudden swerving, and his invention was patented in 1938. Lee's safety device would be called blowout control today. The device prevents, automatically, the sudden swerving of the vehicle that occurs on a blowout in a front wheel. The device arrests the shifting of the steering connections between the knuckles of the front wheels of the vehicle to prevent the swerving of the vehicle. The safety device was simple in its construction, readily installed on an automobile, and was comparatively inexpensive to manufacture.

Black Inventors: From Africa to America (1995), p. 243; *Index of Patents* (1938), p. 372

1938 • An airplane with folding wings was invented by Hermon L. Grimes and patented in 1938. His machine had wings of extended area and length for a longer flight time. The design also incorporated a change in the ailerons (trailing edges of the wings) that resulted in more efficient control of the aircraft. The controlling mechanism included a geared transmission with hand levers for controlling power from underslung motors outside and laterally of the fuselage. The motors powered the folding and adjustment of the wings. Grimes's folding-wing technology is evidenced today in such aircraft as the F-17 Tomcat and the Boeing 777. Prior military craft with the Grimes design are the Grumman Aircraft Hell Cat, Tiger Cat, and Wild Cat, as well as the Avenger bomber, all World War II aircraft.

Index of Patents (1938), p. 254; *Philadelphia New Observer* (April 10, 1996); *Philadelphia Tribune* (April 16, 1996), p. 1D

1939 • The invention of an auxiliary circulating device for automobile heaters was developed by Lionel F. Page and patented in 1939. Page's system adapted the hot water heater of the automobile to have the heated water from the engine cooling system to circulate while the engine was temporarily shut off, preventing the automobile from getting cold. Page used a water-circulating device in the hot water circuit to accomplish this. There was also a check valve to prevent the flow of water back into the circuit and a technique for starting and stopping the circulating device.

Index of Patents (1939), p. 537; *Negro Year Book* (1947), p. 28

1942 • The first U. S. merchant ship commanded by an African American captain was the *Booker T. Washington,* a Liberty ship launched in 1942 and commanded by the African American captain Hugh Mulzac (1886-1971). Mulzac, in 1920, was the first African American to hold an unlimited mariner's license. He made more than 22 round trips transporting over 18,000 troops to Europe, the Mediterranean, and the Pacific.

Dictionary of Black Culture (1973), p. 311; *Jet* (February 18, 1971), p. 12; *Famous First Facts About Negroes* (1972), p. 119

1942 • Joseph N. Blair (1904-) invented a speedboat in 1942, an aerial torpedo for long range bombing in 1944, and a 75-mm anti-aircraft gun. He offered his invention to the U.S. government but was turned down until 1958.

Blacks in Science and Medicine (1990), p. 29; *Created Equal* (1993), p. 195; *Jet* (March 20, 1958), pp. 22-28

1942 • The pioneer aviatrix Willa Beatrice Brown (1906-1992) was the first African American woman, in 1942, to become an officer in the Civil Air Patrol. Brown earned a B.A. from Indiana Teachers College in 1927 and her M.B.A. from Northwestern University in 1937. She started her flying lessons in 1934 in Chicago. In 1939 Brown and husband-to-be Cornelius Coffey founded the National Airman's Association of America, set up to promote the presence of African Americans in aviation. Brown and Coffey started the Coffey School of Aeronautics in 1940, some of whose students became members of the "Tuskegee Airmen." Brown received her Civil Aeronautics Administration ground school instructor rating in 1940. She later became a training coordinator, and in 1942, became the first African American officer of the Civil Air Patrol. Brown was appointed a member of the Federal Aviation Administration Women's Advisory Commission on Aviation in 1972.

Notable Black American Women Book II (1996), pp. 69-70; *African American Airmen in World War II* (1976); *Black Women in America* (1993), pp. 184-186

1944 • The first African American to complete the U. S. Army Air Corp's Central Instructor's School was James O. Plinton Jr. (1914-). Plinton graduated from Lincoln University with a B.S. in 1935, and in 1942, he received a commercial pilot's certificate and flight instructor's rating. He organized and operated a passenger/cargo airliner in 1948, Quisqueya Ltd., the first such venture outside the United States by an African American. Plinton joined Eastern Airlines as vice president for marketing in 1971, being employed there until 1979. He has received a number of awards and honors including several honorary doctorate degrees.

Black Enterprise (September 1979), pp. 59-60; *Encyclopedia of Black America* (1981), p. 146; *Who's Who Among African Americans* (1998-1999), p. 1200; *Who's Who Among Black Americans* (1990-1991), p. 1016

1944 • Gus Burton developed an emergency landing runway system for airplanes, for which he received a patent in 1944. Burton's system included a number of surface rollers arranged on a plastic runway to provide an efficient landing area for a disabled aircraft. The runway system was constructed of cement, concrete, asphalt, or other road-surfacing material, and placed to embed the frame and anchor the frame in place. A frame construction provided efficient drainage around and adjacent to the traction rollers, which were carried by the runway.

Black Inventors: From Africa to America (1995), p. 238; *Index of Patents* (1944); *Negro Year Book* (1941-1946), p. 29

1945 • A mail bag delivery device for airplanes was developed by Gus Burton in 1941 and patented in 1945. Burton's apparatus enabled a moving airplane to pick up mailbags or other containers from a moving crane or support. A trackway extending longitudinally along a runway had a carriage with a supported crane traversing the trackway. As an aircraft touched the runway, its tires depressed a treadle plate, which activated the carriage apparatus to travel along the trackway, with the mailbag supported by the crane, at a predetermined speed. A pickup device on the aircraft scooped up the bag and was retracted into the body of the aircraft.

Black Inventors: From Africa to America (1995), p. 238; *Index of Patents* (1945); *Negro Year Book* (1941-1946), p. 29

1945 • James H. Crumble received a patent in 1945 for his invention for a float operated by the motion of waves. Crumble's floats could be mounted on the sides of ships close to the bow or aft of the stern. The floats could also be mounted on a dock or pier whereby they would be actuated by usual wave motion or could be raised and lowered by tidal rising and falling. Crumble had other inventions, including an ever-ready battery and a bicycle driving mechanism.

Black Inventors: From Africa to America(1995), pp. 111, 117-119, 239; *Index of Patents*(1945); *Negro Year Book*(1941-1945), p. 29; *Negro Year Book*(1947), p. 27

1950 • Joseph G. Logan Jr. (1920-), an African American physicist and inventor, developed a new small jet engine that had relatively low fuel consumption and was applicable to guided missiles and helicopters in 1950. Logan received a B.S. from D.C. Teachers College and a Ph.D. in physics from the University of Buffalo in 1955. He became vice president of research and development of the West Coast Research Corporation in 1978.

Blacks in Science and Medicine(1990), pp. 155-156; *Ebony*(September, 1950), p. 16

1950–1956 • The first experimental airborne radio beacon for tracking crashed aircraft was developed by a team led by aeronautical engineer O. S. Williams (1921-). Williams attended New York University, where he earned his B.S. in 1943 and his M.S. in 1947. He was working at Greer Hydraulics when he led the development the radar beacon, which, unfortunately, was never produced commercially. He was hired by Grumman International as a rocket propulsion engineer in 1961, where he managed the development of the *Apollo* Lunar Module reaction control subsystem. The rockets he designed helped guide the lunar module during moon landings.

Black Contributions to Science and Energy Technology(1979), p.13; *Pathfinder*(1984), p. 31; *Philadelphia Tribune*(May 31, 1977)

1953 • James C. Evans (1900-19??) was an award-winning African American researcher in electronics, as well as an inventor. In 1953, he acquired a patent on a method of using airplane exhaust gases to prevent ice from forming on aircraft. Evans earned a B.A. from Roger Williams University in 1921. He received a B.S. in 1925 and a M.S. in 1926, both from the Massachusetts Institute of Technology. Evans was a professor of technical industries from 1928 to 1937 at West Virginia State College and then was administrative assistant to the president until 1942. He became a civilian aide to the U.S. Secretary of War in 1943 and remained in that capacity until 1949, when he joined the faculty of Howard University as professor of electrical engineering until his 1970 retirement. In 1926, Evans won the Harmon Award for scientific research in electronics.

Negro Year Book(1931-1932), p. 191; *Negro Year Book*(1937-1938), p. 7; *Notable Twentieth Century Scientists*(1995), pp. 605-606; *Who's Who Among Black Americans*(1990-1991), p. 395

1956 • Perry H. Young (1919-), when hired in 1956 by New York Airways, Inc., became the first African American pilot for a scheduled passenger commercial carrier. Young piloted for New York Airways from 1956 to 1979. Prior, Young had varied flying experiences, including four years as flight instructor with Tuskegee Institute, and corporate pilot flying from 1949 to 1955.

Black Firsts (1994), p. 256; *Famous First Facts* (1972), p. 70; *Who's Who Among African-Americans* (1998-1999), p. 1687

1956 • A parking garage, or building designed specifically for parked cars was the invention of Joseph W. Gilliard, which was patented in 1956. The building was designed with a centrally located elevator system. It had a series of vertically stacked parking platforms that were radially spaced and mounted on vertical columns. Each platform had a number of individual support areas, each of which aligned with a vehicle-receiving portion of the elevator. Each parking platform was also independently rotatable on its column with its own power motor. The elevator platform had a series of spokes corresponding to the number of stacks of parking platforms, and the individual vehicle support areas aligned with the vehicle-receiving portion of the elevator.

Black Inventors: From Africa to America (1995), p. 121; *Creativity and Inventions* (1987), p. 65; *Index of Patents* (1956), p. 299

1961 • Peachy Booker developed a large flying landing platform, which could speed to a disabled aircraft while it was still airborne so that it could be safely landed. The invention was patented in 1961. The flying landing platform was designed so that an aircraft with disabled landing gear could be landed upon it. The landing platform was particularly adapted to recover space vehicles after they re-entered the Earth's atmosphere. A portion of the landing platform was articulated to vary the angle it formed with the path of flight of the flying landing platform.

Black Inventors: From Africa to America (1995), p. 123; *Index of Patents* (1961), p. 97

1962 • Paul E. Williams received a patent in 1962 for helicopter improvements. One improvement was a smooth operating rotor eliminating most, if not all, energy losses due to aerodynamic shift, noise, and air excitation. The rotor also did not require an anti-torque compensation device. Also, the system required a single rotor as opposed to counter-rotating rotors. Williams's design eliminated all of the cyclic pitch control mechanism, saving weight, cost, and mechanical complications. The rotor blade had minimal tip turbulence, which increased the efficiency of the blade and reduced the power necessary to rotate it.

Black Inventors: From Africa to America (1995), p. 126; *Index of Patents* (1962), p. 1138

1962 • John Glenn, when he orbited Earth in the *Friendship 7* space capsule on February 20, 1962, had his vital signs and other physiological functions monitored by several specialists placed at 18 stations around the globe during that history-making Mercury mission. Vance H. Marchbanks, Jr. (1905-1988) was one of the specialists monitoring Glenn, serving on the mission flight control team stationed at Kano, Nigeria. Marchbanks received a B.S. degree in 1931 from the University of Arizona and then earned a M.D. at Howard University in 1937. By 1960, he had been assigned a project physician to Project Mercury, the first manned spacecraft launched by the United States. He also helped design the space suits and monitoring systems the astronauts used for the *Apollo* mission to the Moon. Marchbanks spent much of his medical career researching the sickle-cell genetic trait, which causes sickle-cell anemia.

Blacks in Science: Ancient and Modern (1983), p. 264; *Blacks in Science: Astrophysicist to Zoologist* (1977), p. 28; *Ebony* (July, 1995), p. 126

1962 • A motor fuel composition comprising additive agents adapted to reduce or prevent engine manifold deposits was an invention of William E. Lovett and was patented in 1962. Lovett's process for the preparation of solvent oils was based on the products derived from the reaction between olefin, carbon monoxide, and hydrogen in the presence of a metallic carbonylation catalyst. The process then included combining those products with a carboxylic acylating acid. Lovett's solvent oil composition had an enhanced ability to reduce engine manifold deposits.

Index of Patents (1962), p. 639

1965 • Adolphus Samms invented a multiple stage rocket that was patented in 1965. The variation of a conventional rocket had fuel and oxidizer tanks concentrically arranged about its outer peripheral surface. Automatically detachable fluid connections between the concentric tanks and the motor of the conventional rocket were provided. Samms's invention eliminated airframes and the weight of longer multiple stage rockets that had to be jettisoned in flight by the provision of a single combustion chamber that slid on a pair of supporting frame shafts.

Blacks in Science: Astrophysicist to Zoologist (1977), p. 91; *Creativity and Inventions* (1987), p. 68; *Index of Patents* (1965), p. 1036

1965 • William R. Norwood (1936-) was the first African American pilot to fly for United Airlines when he joined the carrier in 1965. He was a second officer from 1965 to 1968 and then a first officer until 1983. In that year, he became a captain for United, serving in that capacity until he retired in 1996. Norwood earned a B.A. in chemistry in 1959 from Southern Illinois

University and a M.B.A. in 1974 from the University of Chicago. He earned his pilot's license in 1959, when a senior in college. Norwood was in the Air Force from 1959 until he joined United in 1965. While in the Air Force, he piloted B-52s and while at United, captained the DC-10 after 1993.

African-American Firsts(1994), pp. 7-8; *Who's Who Among African Americans*(1998-1999), p. 1130

1966 • Wilson E. Hull was granted a patent in 1966 for his invention of a sublimation timing switch for satellites. The switch used predetermined time delays for sequentially activating various electrical switches. The number of sequential switching operations was determined by the number of aligned positions of the terminals in the switch. Hull increased the number of possible switching operations by using insulated elements to isolate certain fingers, so that a circuit was only connected between any two adjacent terminals. The switch could be used to initiate separation of a payload from a rocket or to separate multiple payloads. The switch could also be used for turning on high voltage for a particular satellite experiment.

Creativity and Inventions(1987), p. 66; *Index of Patents*(1966), pp. 630, 1470

1966 • James T. Whitehead (1934-), pilot and flight engineer, was the first African American U-2 reconnaissance aircraft commander when appointed in 1966. He served in that post for a year. Whitehead earned a B.S. in 1957 from the University of Illinois and was commissioned a second lieutenant in the U. S. Air Force that same year. After completing pilot training in 1958, Whitehead was a co-pilot on the KC-135 and then a KC-135 aircraft commander. He joined Trans World Airlines as a flight engineer in 1967 and became a first officer on the Boeing 707 in 1968. He then moved to flight engineer/instrument flight engineer/check airman on the Boeing 747.

Who's Who Among African-Americans(1998-1999), p. 1596

1968 • Ralph W. Sanderson received a patent, in 1968, for his invention of a type of hydraulic shock absorber. Sanderson's shock absorber dissipated the energy of impact when a vehicle collided with another object. The invention included an incompressible fluid-containing cylinder provided with a piston which could be connected to the vehicle. The cylinder had a cap with a number of concentric blowout plugs of increasingly large diameters. The cap was of continuously decreasing thickness from the outside to the inside to provide, in effect, an infinite number of concentric blowout segments. In this system, the greater the force of a collision, the more plugs were blown.

Black Inventors: From Africa to America(1995), p. 125; *Index of Patents*(1968), p. 1021

1969 • Hugh D. MacDonald invented a rocket catapult that was patented in 1969. MacDonald's invention was a pilot-seat ejection system for emergency aircraft escape. It had a secured launching tube that telescopically received a rocket tube, without complex unlatching devices, flow control valves, or similar moving metal parts. The invention had a minimum overall rocket assembly size and weight for a given amount of propellant, for maximum efficiency and minimum chance for malfunction.

Black Inventors: From Africa to America (1995), p. 125; *Index of Patents* (1969), p. 972

1971 • Raymond Edward Rose (1926-) received a patent in 1971 for an air data sensor for aircraft. Rose earned a B.A. from the University of Kansas in 1951, and then a M.S.A.E. in 1956, and a Ph.D. in 1966 from the University of Minnesota in aerospace engineering. Rose was employed at Rosemont Aero Laboratories, University of Minnesota from 1951 to 1962. He was then employed by Honeywell, Inc., starting in 1966 as a senior principal research scientist until 1984, when he was program manager of general aviation and subsonic aircraft technology. Rose then joined NASA in 1984 as general aviation and commuter aerodynamics coordinator and manager. He has a number of scientific publications and made a number of contributions to the research and development of aviation.

Black Engineers in the United States (1974), p. 172; *Blacks in Science and Medicine* (1990), p. 206; *Who's Who Among African Americans* (1998-1999), p. 1297

1971 • The U. S. Navy appointed the first African American admiral in its history when, in 1971, Samuel Gravely Jr. (1922-) was promoted to the rank of rear admiral. Gravely enlisted in the U.S. Navy in 1942 and after being commissioned as an ensign, served varied naval assignments during World War II. He was discharged from active duty in 1946, returned to college, and received a B.A. in 1948 from Virginia Union University. Gravely decided to make a career of the Navy, rejoining in 1949. In 1962, he became the first African American to command a U.S. warship when he took command of the U.S.S. Falgout. Gravely was again promoted in 1976 to vice-admiral and was placed as commander of the Navy's 3rd fleet. He held that command until 1978. Gravely's last position, before retirement, was that of director of the Defense Communication Agency for the period 1978 through 1980.

African-American Almanac (1997), pp. 97, 99; *African-American Firsts* (1994), p. 175; *Blacks in Science and Medicine* (1990), p. 104; *Timelines of African-American History* (1994), p. 272

1971 • James O. Plinton Jr. (1914-), pilot and business executive, was the first African American corporate executive to work for a major airline when he joined Eastern Airlines in 1971. Plinton graduated with a B.S. from Lincoln University in 1935 and received a commercial pilot's certificate and flight instructor's rating in 1942. In 1944, he became the first African American to complete the Army Air Corp's Central Instructor's School. Plinton organized and operated a passenger/cargo airliner in 1948, Quisqueya Ltd., in Port-au-Prince, Haiti, the first such venture by an African American. He was vice-president for marketing for Eastern Airlines from 1971 to 1979. Plinton was active in aviation, marketing, and economic development organizations.

Black Enterprise (September 1979), pp. 59-60; *Encyclopedia of Black America* (1981), p. 146; *Who's Who Among African Americans* (1998-1999), p. 1200

1972 • The destroyer escort U.S.S. Jesse L. Brown, which was launched in 1972 in Louisiana, was the first U. S. Naval ship named for an African American naval officer, Jesse L. Brown (1926-1950), who was the first African American naval officer killed in action during the Korean War. He was shot down near the Chosin Reservoir in North Korea. After his death, Brown was awarded the Distinguished Flying Cross and Air Medal for Bravery.

Black Firsts (1994), p. 254; *Jet* (April 18, 1963), p. 11; *Timelines of African-American History* (1994), p. 276

1972 • George R. Carruthers (1939-), an African American astrophysicist, was the principal scientist responsible for the development of an ultraviolet astronomical camera, called the far ultraviolet camera/spectrograph, that operated successfully from the Moon's surface during the *Apollo 16* mission. This camera, deployed on April 16, 1972, was Earth's first Moon-based observatory. It obtained ultraviolet images and spectra of Earth's upper atmosphere and the Sun's corona. Carruthers earned his B.S. (1961), M.S. (1962), and Ph.D. (1964) degrees in aeronautical and astronautical engineering from the University of Illinois College of Engineering. Carruthers is a senior astrophysicist at the U.S. Naval Research Laboratory and has over 70 scientific publications in major scientific journals.

Blacks in Science: Ancient and Modern (1983), pp. 258-262; *Blacks in Science: Astrophysicist to Zoologist* (1977), pp. 14-14; *Ebony* (June, 1991), pp. 42, 44, 48, 50; *Journal of the National Technical Association* (April, 1987), p. 35

1972 • A personal restraint system for vehicular occupants was invented by John Leslie Jones Sr. (1913-) and patented in 1972. Jones, who received both a B.S. and M.S. from the University of California, earned a Ph.D. in physical chemistry from Stanford University in 1936. He worked as a research chemist, taught college, and from 1950 to 1959, was a division head for the U. S. Ordnance Test Station. Jones has been a patent agent and industrial consultant since 1959. His personal restraint system had an accordion-pleated impact restraint bag folded flat in a transverse

U-bend in a case, which could be fixed to the instrument panel. An impact sensor discharged an adjacent tank of liquid carbon dioxide. A second impact sensor operated a second carbon dioxide tank, which flooded the gas tank vicinity with carbon dioxide to prevent or extinguish a gasoline fire.

Blacks in Science and Medicine (1990), p. 138; *Index of Patents* (1972), p. 941

1974 • The first African American pilot to fly with the U. S. Air Force Aerial Demonstration Squadron, the Thunderbirds, was Lloyd W. Newton, who joined the elite squadron in 1974. Newton, in 1995, was appointed assistant vice-chief of staff stationed at the Pentagon.

Black Wings (1983), p. 65; *Who's Who Among African-Americans* (1998-1999), p. 1120

1975 • Nathaniel John Mullen received a patent in 1975 for an asphalt-paving vehicle he invented. Mullen's vehicle enabled the operator to lay a uniform layer of asphalt around sharp curves and inclines and to drive the asphalt paver vehicle to another job location on completion. The vehicle contains a hydrostatic motor-driven transmission, four wheel drive, front and rear steering, flotation tires, a floating screed, and a weight distribution system to allow the machine to apply a smoother, more consistent, and uniform layer of asphalt.

Twentieth Century Black Patentees - A Survey (1979); *Index of Patents* (1975), p. 1339

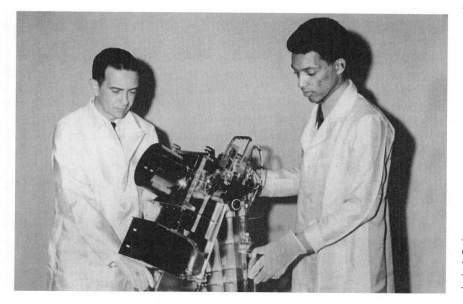

GEORGE CARRUTHERS (RIGHT) AND COWORKER WILLIAM CONWAY WITH THE APOLLO 16 CAMERA THEY DEVELOPED.

1975 • The U. S. Air Force, in 1975, promoted Daniel H. James (1920-1978) to the rank of four-star general, making him the first African American to achieve that rank. James graduated from the Civilian Flying School, Tuskegee Institute and was commissioned in the Air Force in 1943. By 1954, he was commanding a fighter squadron, the 437th Fighter Interceptor Squadron. During the Korean War, James flew 101 combat missions, and in 1957, was appointed air staff officer, Office of the Deputy Chief of Staff for Operations, Air Defense Division. In 1966, he was appointed deputy commander for operations, Eighth Tactical Fighter Wing, Thailand and led 78 missions over North Vietnam. James was promoted to brigadier general in 1970 and then to lieutenant general in 1973. In 1975, he became commander-in-chief of NORAD/ADCOM, the first African American to hold the position, and was appointed a four-star general.

African America: Portrait of a People (1994), p. 759; *Encyclopedia of Black America* (1981), pp. 468-469; *Ebony* (December 1975), pp. 48-51, 54, 58-59, 62; *Who's Who Among Black-Americans* (1977-1978), p. 466

1976 • Joseph A. Garnell invented an internal combustion engine with a turbine-driven supercharger that was patented in 1976. Garnell's system turbine was continuously driven by a pressurized fluid, such as water, which was continuously maintained in a liquid state. The water was stored in a tank and supplied by a pump to the turbine for rotating it, which caused the rotation of the supercharger compressor. The closed fluid system also included a passageway to the intake manifold, permitting the injection of water into the fuel-air mixture.

Black Enterprise (July, 1975), p. 36; *Index of Patents* (1976)

1976 • A patent was granted Samuel A. Clark Jr., in 1976, for his invention of a protective metal shield for plastic fuse radomes. (Radomes protect antenna for radar on aircraft.) Clark's structure is a metal strap-on cap designed to slip on or over the arch of the radome. The cap has two open windows permitting antenna of the fuse electronics to radiate out while being protected from rain damage by the large umbrella at the top. The electronic components are protected from heat by the large metal band at the bottom. The device also includes electrical grounding connections.

Index of Patents (1976), p. 349; *Twentieth Century Black Patentees - A Survey* (1979)

1977 • William Childs Curtis (1914-), an African American engineer and inventor, was a pioneering developer of radar technology and weapon systems development. He patented an airborne moving-target-indicating radar system in 1977. Curtis also created the Black Cat weapons system, the M6-3 fire control system, the 300-A weapon radar system, and the Airborne

Interceptor Data Link, which were all included in the United States military arsenal. A graduate of Tuskegee University, Curtis became the university's first Dean of Engineering, and was a prominent mentor to the famed Tuskegee Airmen.

Created Equal (1993), p. 173; *Index of Patents* (1977)

1978 • Texas International hired the first African American woman pilot to fly for a commercial airline when Jill Brown (1950-) was hired at the age of 28 in 1978. Brown started flying at the age of 17 and in 1976 began working for Warren Wheeler, who had a small commuter airline in North Carolina. While there, she accumulated 1,200 hours of flying time, allowing her to be accepted by Texas International flight training program.

African-American Firsts (1994), p. 10; *Encyclopedia of Black America* (1981), p. 146

1979 • U. S. Army Second Lieutenant Marcella A. Hayes earned her aviator wings in 1979, becoming the first African American woman pilot in the history of the U. S. armed services. Hayes was an Army ROTC program graduate from the University of Wisconsin.

African-American Almanac (1997), p. 100; *Timelines of African-American History* (1994), p. 296

1979 • Frank E. Peterson (1932-), in 1979, became the first African American general in the U. S. Marine Corps. Peterson entered the Naval Reserve as an aviation cadet in 1951 and was commissioned as a second lieutenant in the Marine Corps in 1952, becoming the first African American commissioned as an aviator in the Marines. He flew many combat missions during the Korean War, and in 1968, commanded the Marine Aircraft Group in Vietnam, becoming the first African American to command a tactical air command. Peterson served as senior ranking pilot in both the United States Navy and Marine Corps from 1985 to 1988. Peterson retired from military service in 1989.

African-American Almanac (1997), pp. 1158-1159; *Black Wings* (1983), p. 65; *Ebony* (December 1986), pp. 140, 144, 146; *Jet* (July 14, 1986), pp. 28-29

1980 • Lawrence C. Chambers (1929-) was the first African American U. S. Naval Academy graduate to be commissioned a line officer in 1980 when he was appointed a rear admiral. Chambers was the second African American to graduate from the U. S. Naval Academy, graduating in 1952 with a B.S. in aeronautical engineering. When Chambers became rear admiral, he was the first African American to command the Carrier Group

Three in the Indian Ocean, which was comprised of over 6,000 personnel and 85 aircraft. Admiral Chambers is now retired.

Blacks in Science and Medicine (1990), p. 52; *Ebony* (May 1978), p. 46, (November 1981), pp. 118, 120-122; *Jet* (March 13, 1980), p. 57

1982 • Irene Duhart Long (1951-) was initially hired in 1981 by the National Aeronuatics and Space Administration (NASA) and in 1982, became the first African American woman to be appointed chief of Medical Operations and Human Research Branch of the Biomedical Office. Long was the first African American woman certified in aerospace medicine in 1991. She was named, recently, as director of the Kennedy Space Center Biomedical Operations and Research Office. For the past 16 shuttle missions, Long, the top-ranking African American woman at NASA's Kennedy Space Center, has been a member of the team staffing the Launch Control Center's biomedical console.

African American Medical Pioneers (1994), p. 192; *Blacks in Science and Medicine* (1990), p. 156; *Emerge* (November, 1994) p. 13; *Reference Library of Black America* (1990), p 1100

1983 • Guion S. Bluford (1942-) was the first African American astronaut to fly in space when he served as flight engineer on the four-day space shuttle *Challenger* mission, which lifted off on August 30, 1983 and touched

IRENE D. LONG

down September 5, 1983. Bluford received a B.S. degree in aerospace engineering from Penn State University in 1964 and then earned both the M.S. degree (1974) and Ph.D. degree (1978) in aerospace engineering from the Air Force Institute of Technology. He was the space mission specialist on the 1983 *Challenger* launch and was responsible for the deployment of an Indian communications satellite, as well as collecting data for medical research. He flew two other space shuttle missions, one in 1985, when he spent a week aboard *Challenger*, and the third in 1991, when he went up in *Discovery* as part of the Strategic Defense Initiative. Bluford spent a total of 688 hours in space. He retired from NASA in 1993 to pursue a career in private industry.

GUION BLUFORD

African America Almanac (1997), p. 1065; *African American: Portrait of a People* (1994), pp. 664-665; *Ebony* (March, 1979), pp. 54-62; *Philadelphia New Observer* (December 2, 1982)

1983 • The *U.S.S Houston,* a nuclear submarine, was placed in 1983 under the command of Chancellor A. Tzomes (1944-), the first African American to command such a vessel for the United States. Tzomes graduated from the U. S. Naval Academy in 1967. He attended a nuclear power training program, and in 1969, he was assigned to the *U.S.S. Will Rogers* in order to complete his qualifications in submarines. He served on the *U.S.S. Pintado* and was executive officer on board the *U.S.S. Cavalla* for three years before becoming commander of the *U.S.S. Houston* in 1983. Tzomes commanded the *U.S.S. Houston* until 1986, when he became the Force Operations Officer on the staff of Commander Submarine Force for the U. S. Pacific Fleet.

Ebony (December 1985), pp. 45-46, 48, 50; *Philadelphia Tribune* (August 8, 1989), p. 5A

1984 • Isaac Thomas Gillam, IV (1932-) became the first assistant administrator of commercial programs at the National Aeronuatics and Space Administration (NASA) headquarters in Washington, D.C. Gillam received a B.S. in mathematics from Howard University in 1952, at which time he was commissioned in the U.S. Air Force. Gillam left the Air Force's Strategic Air Command in 1963 when he joined NASA. During 1971-76, he was program manager of small launch vehicles and international projects, in which Delta and Scout launches put satellites in orbit for RCA, Comstat, Western Union, and several foreign companies. He was appointed the director of NASA's Dryden Flight Research Center at Edwards Air Force base in 1978 and remained in that position until 1981. While director there, the critical approach and landing tests of the space shuttle were carried out. He received NASA's highest award, its Distinguished Service Medal, for his foreign satellite launch program directive efforts. Gillam also worked at the White House in the Office of Science and Technology Policy. Since 1987, he has spent his time working in the private sector.

Blacks in Science and Medicine(1990), p. 101; *Blacks in Science: Ancient and Modern*(1983), pp. 246-247; *Ebony*(April, 1977), pp. 124-126, 128-129

1984 • Ida Van Smith (1917-) was the first African American woman inducted into the International Forest of Friendship in recognition of her contributions to aviation. Smith took her first flying lesson at 50 years of age, became a licensed pilot, instrument rated, and a ground instructor. She founded, in 1967, the Ida Van Smith Flight Clubs to introduce children from age three to careers in aviation and space. Some of the graduates of Smith's flight clubs have become U. S. Air Force and Navy pilots, officers, submarine navigators, and airline and private pilots. She also has classes for adults. Ida Van Smith Flight Clubs are in New York, Texas, and North Carolina.

Black Women in America(1993), pp. 1079-1080

1984 • John S. Brooks (1951-) patented an internal combustion engine spark timing control that included a peak combustion sensor in 1984. Brooks earned a B.S. in 1992 at Indiana Wesleyan University and a M.B.A. from Anderson University in 1996. He started working in 1969 as a production worker for Delphi-E in Anderson, Indiana, became supervisor of engineering laboratories in 1983, and in 1992, was promoted to manager of the test facility.

Index of Patents(1984); *Who's Who Among African Americans*(1998-1999), p. 167

1985 • The U. S. Navy's elite special flying squadron, the Blue Angels, accepted its first African American pilot, Lieutenant Commander Donnie Cochran (1954-) in 1985 to fly with the squadron. Cochran has a B.S. degree in civil engineering, which he earned in 1976 from Savannah State College. He was a student aviator from 1976 to 1978 and then engaged in advanced flight training on a variety of aircraft. Cochran became a member of the Blue Angels in 1985, Blue Angels #3 in 1987, and Blue Angels #4 in 1988.

African American Almanac(1997), p. 102; *Who's Who Among African Americans*(1997), p. 291

1985 • Michael D. Griffin (1958-) received a patent for a valve shaft end float control in 1985. Airflow to conventional automotive spark ignition internal combustion engines is controlled by a butterfly throttle valve secured to a valve shaft, which is journaled for rotation in a throttle body.

Griffin's invention is a valve assembly constructed to limit the motion of the valve shaft, preventing substantial wear of the valve on its bore.

Index of Patents (1985), p. 702

1986 • Ronald E. McNair (1950-1986) became the first African American to die during a space mission on January 28, 1986. McNair was a member of the crew aboard the shuttle *Challenger*, which exploded shortly after lift-off and killed all its crew members. McNair earned a B.S. degree in physics from North Carolina A&T in 1971 and a Ph.D. in physics from Massachusetts Institute of Technology (MIT) in 1976. He was a specialist in laser physics and had presented papers on lasers and molecular spectroscopy in both the United States and Europe. He had also been employed, from 1976 to 1978, at Hughes Research Laboratories as a research scientist prior to his entry into the astronaut-training program. McNair was the second African American astronaut to travel in space when he successfully completed a *Challenger* mission in February 1984. On the 1984 flight, he conducted microgravity experiments, monitored space gases, tested solar cells, operated the shuttle's 50-foot mechanical arm, and was responsible for launching a German communications satellite.

RONALD MCNAIR

African American Almanac (1997), p. 1076; *Jet* (October 18, 1993), p. 25; *New York Times* (February 9, 1986); *Reference Library of Black America* (1990), p. 1094

1987 • The first African American woman pilot hired by United Airlines was Shirley Tyus (1950-), who was a former flight attendant for United. Tyus enrolled in Professional Flight School in Friendly, Maryland, in 1977 and earned a pilot's license in 1979. She accumulated more than 2,000 hours flight time as a part-time pilot for the African-American owned Wheeler Airlines, based in Raleigh, North Carolina. Tyus applied for a pilot position with United Airlines in 1986 and was hired in 1987, making her the first African American woman pilot in United Airlines history.

African American Firsts (1994), p. 10; *Ebony* (April 1991), pp. 62, 64, 66

1987 • The flight of the space shuttle *Discovery* on November 22, 1987 was the first space shuttle under the command of an African American astronaut, Frederick D. Gregory (1941-). The seven-member *Discovery* crew had a seven-day space mission. Gregory graduated from the United States Air Force Academy in 1964 with a B.S. degree, and in 1977 received a M.S.A. in information systems from George Washington University. Military service for Gregory included five years as a helicopter and fighter pilot, including two years in Vietnam on rescue missions. He has flown more than 40 different types of military and commercial aircraft. He grad-

FREDERICK D. GREGORY

uated from Naval Test Pilot School in 1971, becoming a research and engineering test pilot until he was selected as a NASA test pilot in 1974. Gregory was then selected as an astronaut candidate in 1978 and completed his training in August 1979. His first space flight was in 1985 as pilot on the *Spacelab 3 Challenger* space shuttle. With that flight, he became the first African American to pilot a space shuttle. Gregory was also responsible for the redesign of the space vehicle cockpit displays and controls layout, making it more efficient and easier to fly. He has also designed other spacecraft pilot controls and flight systems, including a landing system that used microwave instrumentation.

Black Firsts(1994), p. 362; *Blacks in Science: Ancient and Modern*(1983), pp. 239-245; *Ebony*(August, 1985), pp. 62-63; *Black Stars in Orbit*(1995), pp. 55-57; *Jet*(July 15, 1991), p. 26

1987 • William Harwell (1953-) was an African American mechanical engineer employed at the National Aeronautical and Space Administration's Johnson Space Center, Crew Systems Division. In 1994, he patented an apparatus for capturing an orbiting spacecraft. Harwell also acquired patents for a magnetic attachment apparatus for a remote manipulator system and a regulator for condensation tubes in a subcooling system. He has designed special power packs worn by astronauts during space walks.

Blacks in Science and Medicine(1990), p. 114; *Index of Patents*(1987, 1990, 1994)

1989 • Gilbert Allen Cargill (1916-) was the first African American enshrined in the Michigan Aviation Hall of Fame in 1989. Cargill earned an A.B. from Oberlin College in 1937. He attended the Case School of Science from 1959 to 1960 and Wayne State University from 1970 to 1972. Cargill was a flight instructor for the U. S. Army from 1945 to 1946 and then taught for the Detroit Board of Education from 1946 to 1966. He became employed by Berz Aviation as a charter pilot/flight instructor, where he worked until 1985. Cargill was also a Federal Aviation Administration designated pilot examiner and safety counselor from 1972 to 1989. He has received many honors and awards, and the Federal Aviation Administration named the Aviation Radio Station "CARGL" after him in 1981.

Who's Who Among African Americans(1998-1999), pp. 238-239; *Who's Who Among Black Americans*(1990-1991), p. 207

1990 • Gary Holloway, a design engineer with the General Electric Aircraft Engine Group since 1969, led a group of engineers that developed a new film-cooled, high-pressure turbine shroud for aircraft engines in 1990. This shroud is a ceramic or metal material built into the engine's outer casing that prevents the aircraft blade from touching the turbine casing. Holloway currently leads a team of 12 engineers whose goal is to replace the current metal-based turbine shroud system with composites that will increase the overall aero-thermodynamic efficiency of the aircraft engines by using less fuel while maintaining greater thrust. Holloway joined General Electric after earning a B.S. in mechanical engineering from North Carolina A&T State University. Holloway and his group have received three patents for their technical achievements.

Black Enterprise (February 1990), p. 92

1991 • The first African American woman to hold a Missouri Air National Guard squadron command was Colonel Edith P. Mitchell, when she was appointed commander of the Air Guard's 131st Medical Squadron. Mitchell held that position until she was promoted, in 1995, to the position of the Guard's state air surgeon.

Philadelphia Tribune (May 24, 1996), p. 5-B

1992 • Southwest Airlines chose Louis Freeman as chief pilot in August 1992, which made him the first African American chosen as chief pilot for a major United States airline. Freeman was hired by Southwest as a pilot in 1980, the first African American pilot to fly for that airline. Freeman earned his bachelor's degree at East Texas State University in 1974. He also earned his private pilot's license while in college. Freeman joined the U. S. Air Force, where he served until 1980. While in the Air Force, he continued his pilot training and was eventually assigned to piloting 737s. His major Southwest Airlines responsibility was overseeing all flight operations of Southwest's 350-pilot base and ensuring that all flight procedures exceeded F.A.A. requirements.

African-American Firsts (1994), pp. 12-13; *Ebony* (August 1995), pp. 46, 48

1992 • Woodrow W. Crockett was the first African American to be inducted into the Arkansas Aviation Hall of Fame when he entered the Hall in 1992. He was a member of the renowned Tuskegee Airmen, who broke the color barrier by flying in World War II. Crockett retired from the U. S. Air Force as a Lieutenant Colonel in 1970 and was then employed by the National Guard Bureau at the Pentagon.

Southern Living (October 1996), pp. 104, 106; *Who's Who Among African Americans* (1998-1999), p. 1056

1992 • The crew aboard the space shuttle *Endeavor*, launched on December 12, 1992, included mission specialist Mae C. Jemison (1956-), the first African American woman in space. This particular flight was a cooperative effort between the United States and Japan and was a seven-

day endeavor, the purpose of which was to study the varied effects of
zero gravity on human and animals. Jemison earned a B.S. in chemical
engineering and a B.A. in African and Afro-American Studies in 1977 at
Stanford University and then received the M.D. degree from Cornell
University in 1981. She was the first African American woman admitted
into astronaut training when she was selected in June 1987. She completed training in August 1988. Prior to her flight, Jemison's duties
included processing space shuttles for launch and working in the Shuttle Aeronautics Integration Laboratory (SAIL) verifying shuttle computer software. During the *Endeavor* flight she conducted experiments on
weightlessness and motion sickness on the crew members. Jemison
resigned from NASA in 1993 to teach at Dartmouth University and start
her own technology company. She also conducted the first International
Space Camp in 1994.

Black Women in America (1993), pp. 633-635; *Contemporary Black Biography* (1992), pp. 113-
114; *Notable Black American Women* (1992), pp. 571-573; *New York Times* (September 19, 1992)

1993 • The current head pilot for the General Motors' corporate fleet is
William Avery Henderson (1943-), the first African American pilot to head
the fleet when promoted to the position in 1993. Henderson was also the
first African American promoted to the rank of brigadier general in the
Michigan Air National Guard in 1993. He received a B.S. in sociology and

MAE JEMISON ABOARD
THE SPACE SHUTTLE
ATLANTIS.

history in 1964 from Eastern Michigan University. Henderson joined General Motors in 1974 as a pilot and in 1993, was promoted to chief pilot. He was promoted in 1995 to the rank of major general in the Michigan Air National Guard.

Who's Who Among African Americans(1998-1999), p. 673

1993 • Ellwood G. Ivey Jr.(1961-) invented, in 1993, the driver bio-system sensitized steering wheel, which detects whether drivers are intoxicated. Ivey's invention monitors the driver's blood alcohol concentration, detecting whether the driver is intoxicated. Ivey was inspired to create the device after witnessing a fatal automobile accident involving his co-workers. The device disables the vehicle when the driver's blood alcohol concentration exceeds the legal limit. Ivey has developed another device which monitors blood pressure, glucose, and cholesterol levels.

Black Enterprise (September, 1994), p. 22

1994 • United Parcel Service's (UPS) contingent of pilots includes Patrice Clark-Washington, the first African American woman flight captain for an airline service. Clark-Washington commands UPS's DC 8s. She started at the Embry-Riddle Aeronautical University in Florida in 1979, and in 1983, became the first African American woman to graduate from Embry-Riddle with a commercial pilot's license. Clark-Washington joined UPS in 1988 as a flight engineer, then a first officer, before becoming captain for UPS.

Ebony(July 1995), pp. 74, 76, 78; *Jet*(March 6, 1995), p. 34; *Philadelphia Tribune*(March 24, 1995), p. 4B; *Who's Who Among African Americans*(1998-1999), p. 1560

1994 • On February 3, 1994, Charles Frank Bolden, Jr. (1946-) commanded the first joint United States/Russian space shuttle mission as *Discovery* was launched into space. The shuttle crew included five American astronauts and one Russian cosmonaut. Bolden started his career as a second lieutenant in the U.S. Marine Corps, and in 1970 underwent flight training and became a naval aviator. He graduated from the U.S. Naval test Pilot School in 1979 and was assigned to the Naval Test Aircraft Directorates where he logged over 2,600 hours flying time. Previously, he had earned a B.S. from the United States Naval Academy in 1968, then he received the M.S. degree in systems management from the University of Southern California in 1977. Bolden was a veteran of four space flight, including piloting the space shuttle *Columbia* in 1986 and flying on the *Discovery* mission that deployed the Hubble Space Telescope in 1990. He

CHARLES F. BOLDEN, JR.

has received the NASA Outstanding Leadership Medal and three Exceptional Service Medals.

African American Almanac(1997), pp. 1065-1066; *African America: Portrait of a People*(1994), p. 665; *Jet*(February 27, 1997); *New York Times*(February 9, 1994)

1994 • Jim Edwards Sr. and Jim Edwards Jr. are the first African American father and son pair that are pilots for a major airline, both flying for United Airlines. Edwards Sr. joined United in 1978 and is a captain for the airline, while Edwards Jr. joined United in 1994 and is a first officer. Edwards Sr. earned his private pilot's license while in the Air Force and finished flight school in Detroit. Previously, he had resigned from the Air Force Officers Candidate School after receiving many racial threats. Edwards Jr. took private lessons to learn to fly and acquired the hours and certification to become a qualified pilot. He flew three years for American Eagle prior to joining United. Edwards Sr. flies the 747 aircraft, and Edwards Jr. flies the 767 and 757 aircrafts.

Ebony(June 1998), pp. 122, 124, 126

1995 • Bernard A. Harris, Jr. (1956-) astronaut and physician, was the first African American to walk in space. He accomplished that feat on February 9, 1995, when he was the mission specialist on space shuttle *Discovery* mission STS-63. Harris earned his B.S. in 1978 from the University of Houston and in 1982 received the M.D. degree from the Texas Tech University Health Science Center. He later earned a M.S. from the University of Texas Medical Branch in 1996. Harris had a private medical practice until he joined NASA's Johnson Space Center as a clinical scientist and flight surgeon in 1987. He was selected as an astronaut candidate in January 1990 and became an astronaut in July 1991. Harris's first space flight was in August 1991; his second flight was in 1993. His third flight, in February 1995, required him to perform Extra Vehicular Activity (EVA) with astronaut Michael Foals. During that five-hour span of time, the pair tested spacesuit thermal improvements and practiced lifting a 2,800-pound telescope.

African American Medical Pioneers(1994), p. 35; *Jet*(August 28, 1995), p. 47; *Philadelphia Tribune*(February 13, 1996)

1996 • The U. S. Navy promoted an African American officer to four-star rank for the first time when Vice-Admiral Adam J. Paul Reason (1941-) was nominated in 1996. With that rank, Reason became commander-in-chief of the U.S. Atlantic Fleet. Before this he was commander of the Atlantic Fleet surface forces. Reason graduated from the U. S. Naval Academy, completed the nuclear propulsion school of the Navy, and in 1970 earned a M.S. in computer systems management. From 1986 through 1988, he was commander of Naval Base Seattle. In 1994, he was assigned as deputy chief of Naval Operations and remained in that post until his 1996 promotion. Reason is responsible for 195 warships and 1,357 aircraft based on 18 major shore facilities and oversees an annual $19.5 billion budget.

Ebony(April, 1998), pp. 116-118, 120, 122; *Philadelphia New Observer*(June 5, 1996); *Philadelphia Tribune*(May 17, 1996)

1996 • John P. Morris III is president and majority owner of Red River Shipping, which is the first African American controlled company to operate ocean-going vessels under the United States flag. Red River owns the 22,000 ton *Buffalo Soldier* and 27,000 ton *Advantage*. Morris joined the firm in 1988 and in 1993, took over operation at his father's request after 10 years of operations. Morris implemented several joint ventures to keep the business going and in 1996, Morris controlled 51% of the company.

Emerge(February 1996), p. 14

1997 • Air Force Major Robert Henry Lawrence, Jr. (1935-1967) was officially recognized as the first African American astronaut, though he never flew in space. While in astronaut training, Lawrence was killed on December 8, 1967, in the crash of an F-104 fighter aircraft while on a training exercise. At the time of his death, he was a member of the Air Force's Manned Orbiting Laboratory (MOL) program. Lawrence earned his B.A. in chemistry at Bradley University (1956) and received a Ph.D. degree in physical chemistry from Ohio State University in 1965. He joined the Air Force in 1956 and was a test pilot when he was selected as a candidate for the astronaut training program in June 1967, as one of the 16 people chosen out of 500 applicants. He was the ninth fatality of the U.S. astronaut program. Had he lived, he would probably have traveled to space in a *Gemini* B spacecraft.

ROBERT LAWRENCE, JR.

African American Almanac(1997), pp. 1074-1075; *Jet*(December 27, 1997), p. 39; *Philadelphia Inquirer*(December 9, 1997)

1998 • Cheick Diarra was named the 19th Goodwill Ambassador of the United Nations Educational, Scientific, and Cultural Organization in 1998. Diarra was the first African American citizen appointed to the post, as well as the first American. He is the manager of the Mars Exploration Education and Public Outreach Office at NASA's Jet Propulsion Laboratory. Diarra earned a M.S. in 1983 and Ph.D. in 1988, both from Howard University.

Howard University Magazine(Winter, 1999), p. 40

BIBLIOGRAPHY

Aaseng, Nathan. *Black Inventors*. New York: Facts on File, Inc., 1997.

Abram, Ruth J., ed.. *Send Us a Lady Physician: Women Doctors in America, 1835-1920*. New York: W. W. Norton & Company, 1985.

Adams, Russell L. *Great Negroes, Past and Present*. Chicago: Afro-Am Publishing Company, Inc., 1969.

Ambrose, Susan A., et. al. *Journeys of Women in Science and Engineering: No Universal Constants*. Philadelphia, PA: Temple University Press, 1997.

Baker, Henry E. *The Colored Inventor: A Record of Fifty Years*. New York: Arno Press, 1969 (reprint).

Bardolph, Richard. *The Negro Vanguard*. New York: Rinehart & Company, Inc., 1959.

Baskin, Wade and Richard N. Runes. *Dictionary of Black Culture*. New York: Philosophical Library, Inc., 1973.

Bedini, Silvio A. *The Life of Benjamin Banneker*. New York: Charles Scribner and Sons, 1972.

Black Americans in Defense of Our Nation. Washington D.C.: United States Government Printing Office, 1991.

Blockson, Charles L. *Pennsylvania's Black History*. Philadelphia: Portfolio Associates, Inc., 1975.

Bolden, Tonya. *The Book of African American Women*. Holbrook, Massachusetts: Adams Media Corporation, 1996.

Bros, Joseph J., ed. *Who's Who in Colored America*. New York: Who's Who in Colored America Corporation, 1927.

Brame, Herman A. *The World Records of Black People*. Portland: Sudan Publications, 1983.

Brawley, Benjamin. *Negro Builders and Heroes.* Chapel Hill: University of North Carolina Press, 1937.

————. *Short History of the American Negro.* New York: MacMillan and Company, 1974.

Brodie, James Michael. *Created Equal: The Lives and Ideas of Black American Innovators.* New York: Bill Adler Books, Inc., 1993.

Burns, Khephra and William Miles. *Black Stars in Orbit.* San Diego: Harcourt, Brace & Company, 1995.

Burt, McKinley, Jr. *Black Inventors of America.* Portland: National Book Company, 1989.

Carnegie, Mary Elizabeth. *The Path We Tread.* Philadelphia: J.B. Lippincott Company, 1986.

Carwell, Hattie. *Blacks in Science: Astrophysicist to Zoologist.* Hicksville, New York: Exposition Press, 1977.

Cave, Janet B. *African-American Voices of Triumph: Perseverance.* Alexandria: Time-Life Books, 1993.

Cloyd, Iris (Editor). *Who's Who Among Black Americans: 1990-1991.* Detroit: Gale Research, Inc., 1990.

Contemporary Black Biography. Detroit: Gale Research, Inc., 1992-.

Cooper, Charles and Ann. *Tuskegee's Heroes.* Osceolo, Wisconsin: Motorbooks International, 1996.

Cowan, Tom and Jack McGuire. *Timelines of African-American History.* New York: Berkely Publishing Group, 1994.

Culp, Daniel, ed. *Twentieth Century Negro Literature.* Atlanta: J.L. Nichols and Company, 1902.

Daniels, Thomas E. *Selected Contemporary Black Inventors.* Fort Monmouth, New Jersey: United States Army Laboratory Command, 1987.

Davis, Marianna W., ed. *Contributions of Black Women in America.* Columbia, South Carolina: Kenday Press, 1982.

Early, Charity Adams. *One Woman's Army: A Black Officer Remembers the WAC.* College Station, Texas, 1989.

Epps, Charles H. Jr., Davis G. Johnson and Audrey L. Vaughn. *African-American Medical Pioneers.* Rockville, MD: Betz Publishing Co., 1994.

Estell, Kenneth. *African Americans: Portrait of a People.* Detroit: Visible Ink Press, 1994.

Flynn, James J. *Negroes of Achievement in Modern America.* New York: Dodd, Mead and Company, 1970.

Foy, David M. *Great Discoveries and Inventions by African-Americans.* Edgewood, Maryland: Duncan and Duncan, 1998.

Garrett, Romeo B. *Famous First Facts About Negroes.* New York: Armo Press, 1972.

Gibbs, C.R. *The Black Inventor.* Washington, D.C., 1975.

———. *Black Inventors: From Africa to America.* Silver Spring, Maryland: Three Dimensional Publishers, 1995.

Greene, Harry Washington. *Holders of Doctorates Among American Negroes.* Boston: Meador Publishing Company, 1946.

Guthrie, Robert V. *Even the Rat was White.* 2nd ed. Boston: Allyn and Bacon, 1998.

Guzman, Jessie Blackhurst, ed. *Negro Year Book: 1941-1946.* Tuskegee: Tuskegee Institute Department of Records and Research, 1947.

Haber, Louis. *The Role of the American Negro in the Fields of Science.* Washington, D.C.: United States Department of Health, Education and Welfare Office of Education Report ED 013275, 1966.

———. *Black Pioneers of Science and Invention.* New York: Harcourt, Brace and Co, 1970.

Hardesty, Von and Dominic Pisano. *Black Wings.* Washington, D.C.: Smithsonian Institution, 1983.

Harley, Sharon. *The Timetables of African-American History.* New York: Simon & Schuster, 1995.

Harris, Middleton A. *The Black Book.* New York: Random House, 1974.

Haskins, James. *Outward Dreams: Black Inventors and their Inventions.* New York: Walker Publishing Company, 1991.

Hayden, Robert C. *Seven Black American Scientists.* Reading, MA: Addison-Wesley Publishing Company, 1970.

———. *Eight Black American Inventors.* Reading, MA: Addison-Wesley Publishing Company, 1971.

———. *African-Americans in Boston: More than 350 Years.* Boston: Trustees of the Boston Public Library, 1991.

Hine, Darlene Clark. *Black Women in White: Racial Conflicts and Cooperation in the Nursing Profession.* Bloomington: Indiana University Press, 1989.

———, Elsa Barkley Brown, and Rosalyn Terborg-Penn, eds. *Black Women in America.* 2 vols. Bloomington: Indiana University Press, 1993.

———. *Hine Sight: Black Women and the Re-construction of American History.* Bloomington: Indiana University Press, 1994.

———, ed. *Facts on File Encyclopedia of Black Women in America: Science, Health and Medicine.* Vol 11. New York: Facts on File, 1997.

Ho, James K. K. *Black Engineers in the United States: A Directory.* Washington, D.C.: Howard University Press, 1974.

Hudson, Karen E. *Paul R. Williams, Architect: A Legacy of Style.* New York: Rizzoli International Publications, 1993.

Ives, Patricia Carter. *Creativity and Inventions.* Arlington, VA: Research Unlimited, 1987.

Jackson, George F. *Black Women Makers in History: A Portrait.* Sacramento: Fong and Fong, 1977.

James, Portia P. *The Real McCoy: African-American Invention and Innovation, 1619-1930.* Washington, D.C.: Smithsonian Press, 1989.

Kane, Joseph Nathan. *Famous First Facts.* New York: H. W. Wilson, 1964.

Kessler, James H., et. al. *Distinguished African American Scientists of the 20th Century.* Phoenix: Oryx Press, 1996.

Kidd, Foster, ed. *Profile of the Negro in American Dentistry.* Washington, D.C.: Howard University Press, 1979.

Krapp, Kristine M., ed. *Notable Black American Scientists.* Detroit: Gale Research, 1998.

Lerner, Gerdo. *Black Women in White America: A Documentary History.* New York: Pantheon Press, 1992.

Logan, Rayford W. and Michael R. Winston, eds. *Dictionary of American Negro Biography.* New York: W.W. Norton & Company, 1982.

Low, W. Augustus and Virgil A. Clift, eds. *Encyclopedia of Black America.* New York: McGraw Hill, 1981.

Mabunda, L. Mpho, ed. *The African-American Almanac.* 7th ed. Detroit: Gale Research, Inc., 1997.

Manning, Kenneth R. *Black Apollo of Science: the Life of Ernest Everett Just.* New York: Oxford University Press, 1983.

Morais, H.M. *History of the Negro in Medicine.* New York: Publishers Company, 1967.

Newell, Virginia K., et. al., eds. *Black Mathematicians and Their Works.* Ardmore, Pennsylvania: Dorrance Co., 1980.

Oakes, Claudia M. *United States Women in Aviation, 1930-1939.* Washington, D.C.: Smithsonian Institution, 1985.

Oestrich, Alan E., ed. *A Centennial History of African Americans in Radiology.* Tacoma Park, MD: The Section of Radiology of the National Medical Association, 1996.

Organ, Claude H. and Margaret M. Kosiba, eds. *A Century of Black Surgeons.* 2 vols. Norman, Oklahoma: Transcript Press, 1987.

Ott, Virginia and Gloria Swanson. *Man with a Million Ideas.* Minneapolis: Lerner Publications Company, 1977.

Papanek, John L., ed. *African-American Voices of Triumph: Leadership.* Alexandria: Time-Life Books, 1994.

Pederson, Jay P., and Jessie Carney Smith, eds. *African American Breakthroughs: 500 Years of Black Firsts.* Detroit: UXL, 1995.

Peters, J. Jerome, C. Roger Wilson and William L. Crump. *The Story of Kappa Alpha Psi.* Philadelphia: Kappa Alpha Psi Fraternity, 1967.

Phelps, Shirelle (Editor). *Who's Who Among African Americans,* 11th ed. Detroit: Gale Research, Inc., 1998.

Pitrone, Jean Maddern. *Trailblazer: Negro Nurse in the American Red Cross.* New York: Hartcourt, Brace and World Publishing, 1969.

Ploski, Harry A. and James Williams, eds. *The Negro Almanac: A Reference Work On the African American.* Detroit: Gale Research, Inc., 1989.

Potter, Joan with Constance Claytor. *African-American Firsts: Famous, little-known, and unsung triumphs of blacks in America.* Elizabethtown, New Jersey: Pinto Press, 1994.

Richings, G.F. *Evidences of Progress Among Colored People.* Philadelphia: George S. Ferguson Company, 1905.

Russell, Dick. *Black Genius and the American Experience.* New York: Carroll and Graft Publishers, Inc., 1998.

Russell, M. *Black Achievers in Science*. Chicago: Museum of Science and Industry, 1988.

Salem, Dorothy C., ed. *African American Women: A Biographical Dictionary*. New York: Garland Publishing, 1993.

Sammons, Vivian Ovelton. *Blacks in Science and Medicine*. Bristol, Pennsylvania: Taylor and Francis, 1990.

Saunders, Doris E., ed. *Ebony Handbook*. Chicago: Johnson Publications, 1974.

Simmons, William J. *Men of Mark: Eminent, Progressive and Rising*. Chicago: Johnson Printing Company, Inc., 1970 (reprint).

Smith, Jessie Carney, ed. *Notable Black American Women*. Detroit: Gale Research, Inc., 1992.

————. *Notable Black American Women, Book II*. Detroit: Gale Research, Inc., 1996.

————. *Black Firsts: 2000 Years of Extraordinary Achievement*. Detroit: Gale Research, Inc., 1994.

————, ed. *Notable Black American Men*. Detroit: Gale Research, 1999.

Smythe, Mable M., ed. *The Black American Reference Book*. Englewood Cliffs, NJ: Prentice-Hall, Inc., 1976.

Toppin, Edgar A. *A Biographical History of Blacks in America since 1528*. New York: David McKay Company, Inc., 1971.

Thomas, Vivien T. *Pioneering Research in Surgical Shock and Cardiovascular Surgery*. Philadelphia: University of Pennsylvania Press, 1985.

Thoms, Adah B. *Pathfinders: A History of the Progress of Colored Graduate Nurses*. New York: Kay Printing House, 1929.

Van Sertima, Ivan. *Blacks in Science: Ancient and Modern*. New Brunswick: Transactions Books, 1983.

Waddell, William H. *The Black Man in Veterinary Medicine*. Honolulu, HI: 1982.

Williams George W. *History of the Negro Race in America, from 1619 to 1880*. Volume I. New York: G.P. Putnum's Sons, Inc., 1883.

Work, Monroe Nathan, ed. *Negro Year Book: 1912-1937*. Tuskegee, AL: Negro Year Book Publishing Co., Tuskegee Institute, 1913-38.

Young, Robyn V., ed. *Notable Mathematicians*. Detroit: Gale Research, 1998.

Yount, Lisa. *Black Scientists*. New York: Facts on File, Inc., 1991.

Yost, Edna. *American Women of Nursing*. Philadelphia: Lippincott Publishing Company, 1955. Revised Edition.

Zimmerman, Jan, ed. *The Technological Woman: Interfacing with Tomorrow*. New York: Praeger Scientific Publications, 1983.

PERIODICALS

Aerospace Technology Innovation, American Society of Civil Engineering News, A&T Register (North Carolina Agriculture and Technical University),*Black Collegian, Black Enterprise, Black Issues in Higher Education, Black Scholar, Chicago Defender, Chicago Courier, The Crisis* (NAACP), *Daily Gulf Times, Dollars & Sense Magazine, Ebony, Emerge, Essence, Graduating Engineer, Houston Chronicle, Howard University Alumni News, Howard University Gazette, Howard University Magazine, Index of Patents, Jet, Journal of the National Medical Association, Journal of the National Technical Association, Minority Business Journal, NASA Technical Briefs, National Negro Health News, New York State Journal of Medicine, New York Times, News and Observer* (East Carolina University), *Official Gazette* (United States Patent Office), *Philadelphia Business Journal, Philadelphia Daily News, Philadelphia Inquirer, Philadelphia New Observer, Philadelphia Tribune, Resource, Southern Living, Time, US Black Engineer, Western Journal of Black Studies*

INDEX BY YEAR

Robert Boyd Leach was the first African American homeopathic practitioner in the United States 31

1865

Charles B. Purvis was the first African American to receive a M.D. degree from Case Western Reserve University 161

Sarah E. Goode became the first African American woman to receive a patent in the United States 3

1867

Rebecca J. Cole was the first African American woman to graduate from The Women's Medical College of Pennsylvania 161

Robert Tanner Freeman became the first African American to receive a dental doctorate 49

1870

George F. Grant was the first African American to hold a faculty position at Harvard Dental School 49

James T. Wormley received the first degree awarded by Howard University Medical School to African American student 32

Susan M. Smith McKinney Steward was the first African American woman to graduate from a New York State medical school 161

1871

James Bowen and George Brooks were the first two African Americans to receive their M.D.s from Howard University 162

Landrow Bell patented an improved smokestack for locomotives 343

1872

Elijah McCoy received his first patent 343

Thomas J. Martin a patent on a fire extinguisher 103

William Henry Fitzbutler was the first African American recipient of a M.D. from the University of Michigan 162

1875

Alexander P. Ashbourne patented a process for preparing coconut for domestic use 289

1876

Edward A. Bouchet was the first African American to earn a Ph.D. in the United States 289

Thomas A. Carrington patented an improved double cooking range 3

1877

James Monroe Jamison was the first African American to receive a M.D. from Meharry Medical College 162

1879

Josephine Silone Yates was the first African American woman professor at Lincoln Institute 289

Mary Eliza Mahoney was the first African American to earn a nursing degree in the United States 49

1882

Albert C. Richardson received a patent for a hame fastener 4

Lewis Latimer received a patent for a process of manufacturing carbon 3

N. W. Whitcomb was the first African American permanent professor of dentistry at Howard University College of Dentistry 50

1883

Jan Ernest Matzeliger developed and perfected the shoe lasting machine 4

Rebecca Lee Crumpler was the first African American woman to earn a medical degree in the United States 160

Robert Boland was the first African American to receive a M.D. from Wayne State University 162

Samuel E. Thomas patented a waste-trap to be inserted in a line of pipe 103

1906

Georgia R. Dwelle became the first African American woman to practice medicine in Atlanta, Georgia 172

Henry McKee Minton was the first African American to graduate from Jefferson Medical College 172

William Hunter Dammond acquired a patent for safety light 349

1907

Albert P. Albert patented a cotton-picking machine 13

Charles Henry Turner became the first African American to earn Ph.D. degree in biology from the University of Chicago 81

Clara Frye patented a combination bed and bedpan 32

Sara I. Fleetwood was the first African American woman appointed to the Nurses Examining Board of the District of Columbia 52

The first African American to receive a M.D. from the University of Iowa was Albert Edward Carter 172

1908

Clarence A. Lucas was the first African American to receive a M.D. from Indiana University 173

Cornelius N. Garland founded Plymouth Hospital and Nurse's Training School 173

Hugh M. Browne patented a furnace damper mechanism 106

Martha Minerva Franklin was the first president of The National Association of Colored Graduate Nurses 52

Milton Augustus Francis became the first African American physician to specialize in genito-urinary diseases 173

1909

Charles Victor Roman served as the first editor of the Journal of the National Medical Association 174

Matthew A. Henson became the first African American to reach the North Pole 349

Walter Gilbert Alexander founded the New Jersey Medical Society 173

1910

First African American Hospital in Kansas City, Missouri established by John Edward Perry 174

Josie E. Wells was the first African American woman physician to teach at Meharry Medical College 175

1911

Claudius DeWitt Bell authored the first scientific paper in the Journal of the National Medical Association illustrated by x rays 175

Grossi Hamilton Francis was the first African American intern appointed at Hubbard Hospital 175

Shelby J. Davidson patented an automatic fee device 14

1912

Walter G. Madison patented three monoplane improvements 349

1913

Daniel Hale Williams was the first African American selected as a fellow of the American College of Surgeons 175

Jaspar Tappan Phillips became the first African American monitor of medical school applicants for the Tennessee State Medical Board of Examiners 175

Minnie D. Woodward was the first African American registered trained nurse in Tennessee 52

1914

Garrett A. Morgan was awarded a patent for a safety hood, or breathing device 106

1915

Alfred P. Russell, Jr. was the first African American on visiting staff of Forsyth Dental Infirmary for Children 52

Catherine Deaver Lealtad was the first African American graduate of Macalestor College 176

Emma Rochelle Wheeler founded the first hospital to be owned and operated by an African American in Chattanooga, Tennessee 177

First NAACP Springarn Medal awarded to Ernest E. Just 82

John E. Perry founded Wheatley-Provident Hospital in Kansas City 177

Roscoe Conkling Giles was the first African American graduate of Cornell University 176

Samuel J. Hines patented a life preserver in 1915 350

1916

Adah Bell Samuels Thoms was the first treasurer and president of the National Association of Colored Graduate Nurses 53

Carl Glennis Roberts was the first African American gynecologist on the staff of Provident Hospital 177

Ella Phillips Stewart was the first African American woman to graduate from the University of Pittsburgh School of Pharmacy 32

George Washington Carver became the first African American named a fellow of the Royal Society of London 14

Madeline M. Turner patented a fruit press 14

St. Elmo Brady became the first African American to receive a Ph.D. in chemistry 290

1917

Automatic stopping and releasing device for mine cars patented by George M. Johnson 107

Eugene Jacques Bullard became the first African American combat pilot 350

Julian H. Lewis was the first African American to receive a M.D. and a Ph.D. 178

Ulysses Samuel Wharton became the first African American to practice medicine in Altoona, Pennsylvania 177

William D. Polite patented an anti-aircraft gun 107

1918

Clarence Gregg patented a machine gun capable of discharging a number of cartridges 107

Clyde Donnell was the founder of the Durham Academy of Medicine 178

Elmer S. Imes, the first African American astrophysicist of note, earned his Ph.D. 290

Eslanda Goode Robeson was the first African American employed as an analytical chemist and technician in the surgery and pathology department at Columbia Presbyterian Hospital 178

Joseph H. Dickinson patented an improved expression device for a phonograph 14

Ubert Conrad Vincent became the first African American physician to intern at a major U. S. hospital 179

Veda Somerville was the first African American woman dentist in the state of California 53

Walter S. Wickliffee became the first African American to earn a Ph.D. in forestry 82

1919

Alice H. Parker acquired a patent for a heating furnace 15

Alice Parker patented a heating furnace for buildings 108

Frances (Reed) Elliott Davis was the first African American nurse officially recognized by the American Red Cross 53

Jessie G. Garnett was the first African American woman to graduate from Tufts Dental School 54

Louis Tompkins Wright was the first African American surgeon appointed to the medical staff at Harlem Hospital 180

Robert T. Browne authored the first text on space by an African American 107

William Samuel Quinland received the first Rosenwald Fellowship 179

1920

Charles Herbert Garvin was the first African American to become a member of the staff of the genito-urinary department of Lakeland Hospital of Western Reserve University 180

1927

David Baker patented an inner tube liner
352

George Washington Carver was issued a
patent for producing paints and stains
from clay 16

James A. Parsons won the first Harmon
Award for his work in metallurgy 291

Roger A. Young became the first African
American woman to do research at the
Marine Biological Laboratory 83

William Harry Barnes was the first African
American physician certified by a U.S.
medical specialty board 183

1928

Austin Maurice Curtis Sr. was the first
African American to head the Surgery
Department of Howard University Med-
ical School 184

First issue of the National News Bulletin
was released by editor Carrie E. Bullock
54

Marjorie Stewart Joyner became the first
African American inventor to patent a permanent hair waving machine 16

Robert L. Jackson became the first medical
director at Baltimore's Provident Hospital
184

1929

David Nelson Crosthwait Jr. patented a vacuum heating system for buildings 109

E. Luther Brookes was the founder of
Alpha Delta Alpha Scientific Society of
Clark University 291

Frederick McKinley Jones patented the
first practical refrigeration unit/system
for trucks and railroad transportation
353

Numa P.G. Adams was the first African
American dean of the Howard University
Medical School 184

Theodore K. Lawless was the first African
American physician awarded the Harmon
Award for Outstanding Achievement in
Medicine 185

Virginia Scharschmidt patented a safety
window-cleaning device 17

1930

James Carmichael Evans patented an
invention preventing the accumulation of
snow and sleet on the wings of an airplane 353

Method for the preparation of colloidal silver iodide compound patented by Harry
S. Keelan 291

Roscoe McKinney received the first Ph.D.
degree in anatomy awarded to an African
American 84

Solomon Harper patented an electrical hair
comb 17

Theodore Harry Miller became the first
African American to earn a B.S. at the
University of Nevada 109

1931

An auto seat cape for rumble seats was
patented by William S. Hawkins 354

Arnold Hamilton Maloney was the first
black professor of pharmacology in the
United States 186

Benjamin A. Crenshaw patented a turning
signal device for use on a motor vehicle
354

Benjamin F. Thornton acquired patents for
recording and transmitting telephone
messages 17

Estelle Massey Riddle Osborne became
the first African American to earn a M.A.
in nursing education 186

Peter Marshall Murray was the first
African American physician to become a
certified Diplomate of the American
Board of Obstetrics and Gynecology 185

R. Wellesley Bailey became the first African
American member of the Philadelphia
Neurological Society 187

1932

Grant Delbert Venerable became the first
African American to graduate from the
California Institute of Technology 109

James H. Banning and Thomas Allen
became the first African Americans to
successfully complete a transcontinental
flight 354

Jesse Harrison was granted a patent for a
combination toothbrush and paste holder
54

Mattie E. Coleman was the first graduate of Meharry's dental hygiene program 187

Paul E. Johnson patented improvements in therapeutic lamps 33

Richard B. Spikes invented an automatic gear shift 354

Robert Stewart Jason was the first African American to earn a Ph.D. in pathology 187

Samuel Nabrit became first African American to receive a Ph.D. from Brown University 84

Vernon A. Wilkerson became the first African American to earn a Ph.D. degree at the University of Minnesota 292

1933

Charles A. Anderson and Albert E. Forsythe completed the first round-trip transcontinental flight by African Americans 355

Chester W. Chinn became the first African American ophthalmologist certified by the American Board of Ophthalmology 188

David Wellington Byrd established the first public venereal disease clinic in the United States 188

Henry F. Stilwell patented a device for delivering mail from an in-flight aircraft 355

N. Louise Young became the first African American woman physician to practice in Maryland 188

Ruth Moore was the first African American woman to receive a Ph.D. in Bacteriology 84

1934

David N. Crosthwait invented a technique to improve a method and apparatus for steam heating from central station mains 110

Dennis Arthur Forbes acquired a design patent for a cheulls game (chemical card game) 293

Moses Wharton Young was the first African American to earn a Ph.D. in anatomy from the University of Michigan 85

1935

Curtis L. Bryant patented a device to protect automobiles from harsh weather and dirt 355

Julian Waldo Ross became the first African American certified by the American Board of Obstetrics and Gynecology in both obstetrics and gynecology 189

Major Franklin Spaulding became the first African American to earn a Ph.D. in agronomy 17

Percy Lavon Julian discovered how to synthesize physostigmine 293

The first African American to receive a M.D. from the University of Cincinnati was Lucy Oxley 188

William E. Allen Jr. became the first African American radiologist certified in roentgenology by the American Board of Radiology 189

William G. Holly was the first to formulate a series of interior paints with titanium as the basic pigment 293

1936

Richard Francis Jones became the first African American elected a diplomate of the American Board of Urology 189

Rose Marie Pegues-Perkins became the first African American x-ray technician registered by the ARRT 33

William B. Jones patented a dental apparatus for use in the manufacture of false teeth 55

1937

Carborundum print technique invented by Dox Thrash 18

J. Ernest Wilkins, Jr. became the youngest student ever admitted to the University of Chicago 294

James Matthew Allen patented a remote controlled radio receiving set 110

James Thomas Redding patented a convertible seat for use in automobiles 356

Jesse Jerome Peters became the first African American radiologist certified by the American Board of Radiology 190

Roosevelt Brooks was the first African American member of the University of Illinois Medical School faculty 190

1938

Airplane with folding wings patented by Hermon L. Grimes 356

Cap B. Collins patented a portable pocket flashlight 110

Flemmie P. Kittrell became the first African American woman to earn a Ph.D. degree in nutrition 294

Frederick Douglass Stubbs became the first African American thoracic surgeon 190

Grover C. Nash became the first African American pilot to fly air mail in the United States 356

Paul Timothy Robinson founded the Journal of New Orleans Medical, Dental and Pharmaceutical Association 191

Robert Lee patented an automobile safety device to prevent sudden swerving 356

William H. Sinkler became the first African American appointed consultant in chest surgery at Koch Hospital in St. Louis 190

1939

Amanda E. Peele was the first African American woman to present a research paper before the Virginia Academy of Science 85

Darnley E. Howard invented an apparatus allowing a machine operator to see a visual guide of the work 110

Floyd R. Banks demonstrated for the first time self-diffusion by radioactivity in zinc 296

Frederick McKinley Jones patented a ticket dispensing machine 18

Herman R. Branson became the first African American to obtain a Ph.D. in a physical science at the University of Cincinnati 295

Lionel F. Page patented an auxiliary circulating device for automobile heaters 356

Lloyd Augustus Hall helped found the Institute of Food Technologists 295

Roland Boyd Scott became one of the first two African Americans admitted to the American Academy of Pediatrics 191

1940

Charles R. Drew became established as a pioneer in blood preservation 192

Clarance H. Payne was one of the first three African American physicians to get the prefix "COL" removed behind the names of such physicians from the American Medical Association Directory 192

Eva M. Noles became the first African American graduate of the E.J. Meyer Memorial Hospital School of Nursing 55

Henry Arthur Callis became the first African American diplomate of the American Board of Internal Medicine 191

Jesse O. Thomas became the first African American to be employed by the American National Red Cross in a professional and policy-making position 34

Paul Boswell became the first African American graduate of the University of Minnesota, Minneapolis 193

1941

Della Raney became the first African American nurse commissioned in the U. S. Army as a lieutenant 55

Edward V. Williams was the first African American to graduate from the University of Kansas Medical School 193

Leonidas Harris Berry gave the first medical research presentation by an African American physician at an American Medical Association convention 193

Michael J. Bent was the first African American dean of Meharry Medical College 193

Ruth Smith Lloyd received the first Ph.D. in anatomy awarded to African American woman 85

Walter T. Daniels became the first African American to earn a Ph.D. in engineering 111

1942

Asa J. Taylor patented a machine for assembling spring-tensioned devices 111

Bernard W. Robinson was the first African American to become a commissioned officer in the U. S. Navy 194

Charity Adams Earley was the first African American commissioned officer in the Women's Army Auxiliary Corps 111

Earl W. Renfroe was the first African American to complete training in orthodontics 55

Horace James McMillan became the first African-American pharmacist mate in the U. S. Coast Guard 194

Joseph N. Blair invented a speed boat 357

Marguerite Thomas Williams became the first African American woman to earn a Ph.D. in geology 296

Midian Othello Bousfield became the first African American to establish a military hospital for the U. S. Army 194

The Booker T. Washington became the first U. S. merchant ship commanded by an African American captain, Hugh Mulzac 357

W. Lincoln Hawkins became the first African American member of the technical staff at AT&T's Bell Laboratories 296

Willa Beatrice Brown became the first African American officer in the Civil Air Patrol 357

1943

Charles Wesley Buggs was the first African American full-time faculty member at Wayne State University 86

Guy O. Saulsberry founded Kirkwood General Hospital 195

Harry James Green Jr. became the first African American to earn a Ph.D. in chemical engineering 297

Helen Marjorie Peebles-Meyers became the first African American woman to graduate from Wayne State University School of Medicine 194

James A. Parsons, Jr. patented a cementation process of treating metal 296

John W. Lathen became the first African American chemist employed by the Bendix Corporation 297

Myra A. Logan became the first woman to perform open heart surgery 195

Stephen H. Davis patented a combined load weighing and totaling device for cranes, hoists, and the like 112

Ulysses S. Walton patented a denture partially made of plastic 56

1944

Arthur Lee Thompson became the first African American medical officer in the United States Navy 196

David N. Crosthwait, Jr. patented a window thermostat that worked in a system for controlling the temperature of a building 112

Eugene Heriot Dibble Jr. became the first African American medical officer at the rank of colonel in the U.S. Army 195

Gus Burton patented an emergency landing runway system for airplanes 358

James O. Plinton Jr. became the first African American to complete Army Air Corp's Instructor School 357

Mary Elizabeth Carnegie established the first African American baccalaureate program in nursing in Virginia 56

Thomas Watkins, Jr. was the first African American dentist commissioned in the U. S. Naval Reserve Dental Corps 56

1945

Alida Cooley Daily became the first African American director of nursing and superintendent at Harlem Hospital School of Nursing 196

Alma N. Jackson was the first African American woman to be a nurse for the U. S. Public Health Service 57

Cyril Fitzgerald Atkins patented a new paper producing process 18

Frederick Douglas Patterson established the first school of veterinary medicine located at an African American educational institution 197

Gus Burton patented a mail bag delivery device for airplanes 358

Henrietta Mahim Bradberry patented a torpedo discharge device 112

Huerta C. Neals was the first African American military officer assigned to a general hospital in Italy during World War II 196

James H. Crumble patented a float operated by wave power 358

John R. Turner patented for method and apparatus for polishing glass 112

Joseph G. Gathings became the first African American to be certified in dermatology and syphilology 197

U. S. Navy first accepted African American nurses 57

Vivian Murray Chambers was the first African American to earn a Ph.D. in entomology from Cornell University 86

William Jacob Knox, Jr. acquired surfactant patents for Kodak Corp. 297

1946

E. Mae McCarroll became the first African American appointed to the staff of Newark City Hospital 198

John E. Moseley became the first African American radiologist to become a member of the Society for Pediatric Radiology 198

Leonidas H. Berry was the first African American physician at Michael Reese Hospital and Medical Center 197

Walter S. McAfee performed the mathematical calculations that resulted in the first successful attempt to bounce a radar signal off the surface of the Moon 298

1947

Clotilde Bowen became the first African American woman to receive a M.D. from Ohio State University Medical School 198

Harvey F. Davis became the first African American certified by the American Board of Physical Medicine and Rehabilitation 199

J. Edmond Bryant was the first African American member of the American College of Chest Physicians 199

Roy Clifford Darlington became the first African American to receive a Ph.D. in pharmacy 34

Shirley M. Cornwall was the first African American to earn a Master of Arts from North Carolina College 57

1948

George Washington Carver became the first African American scientist to be commemorated on a U.S. postage stamp 18

Joseph A. Thompson Jr. patented an improved foot warmer 19

Louis Tompkins Wright was the first to use the antibiotic aeromycin on humans 200

Margaret Morgan Lawrence became the first African American student in psychoanalytic training at the Columbia PsychoanalyticCenter 199

Marie M. Daly became the first African American woman to earn a Ph.D. in chemistry 298

Mavis N. Jones was the first African American woman dentist to practice in the state of Mississippi 58

Nancy C. Leftenant became the first African American member of the Regular Army Nurse Corps 57

Peyton Randolph Higginbotham became the first African American appointed to the West Virginia State Board of Health 200

Walter Anderson Adams became the first African American psychiatrist appointed chief of the Provident Hospital (Chicago) Medical Counseling Clinic for Narcotic Addicts 200

Walter Scott Brown established the first outpatient surgical facility in the United States 200

1949

Alfreda Johnson Webb was one of the first African American women to receive a D.V.M. degree 34

Charles D. Bonner became the first African American appointed to the medical staff of Boston City Hospital 202

Charles W. Buggs authored the first significant text by an African American bacteriologist 86

Clinton Jones patented an electric release for an artillery trainer 114

Evelyn Boyd Granville became the one of the first two African American women to earn a Ph.D. in mathematics 113

Everod A. Coleman was the first African-American building inspector for the City of Detroit 113

Helen E. Nash was one of the first four African American doctors who integrated the medical staff at Washington University School of Medicine 202

J. Robert Gladden became the first African American certified by the American Board of Orthopaedic Surgery 201

James Richard Laurey was the only African American member of the Founder's Group of the American Board of Thoracic Surgery 201

Jane Hinton was one of the first two African American women to receive a D.V.M. degree 34

Marjorie Lee Browne became one of the first two African American women to earn a Ph.D. in mathematics 113

Robert Sherwood Dorsey was a charter member of the Pi Tau Sigma 114

William A. Hinton became the first African American appointed clinical professor of bacteriology and immunology at Harvard University 202

William D. Morman became the first African American member of the Missouri State Medical Society 202

1950

Burke Syphax became the first chief of general surgery appointed at Howard University Medical College 204

Charles D. Watts became the first African American in North Carolina certified by any surgical specialty board 203

Edward E. Holloway became the first African American Fellow of the American College of Physicians 203

Ethel L. Nixon became the first African American assistant psychiatrist in the out-patient department of Johns Hopkins University Hospital 203

Frank A. Crossley earned the first Ph.D. in metallurgical engineering awarded by the Illinois Institute of Technology (IIT) 298

Helen Octavia Dickens became the first African American woman admitted to the American College of Surgeons 204

Hilda G. Straker became the first African American woman certified by the American Board of Dermatology 203

Joseph G. Logan Jr. developed a low-fuel consumption jet engine 359

O. S. Williams headed team that originated the first experimental airborne radio beacon 359

Robert Percy Barnes was appointed to the first National Science Board 299

Silas Odell Binns became the first African American urologist to practice in the state of Virginia 204

1951

Bessie Virginia Griffin patented a receptacle supporter for convalescents 35

Clifton O. Dummett became the first African American to represent U. S. Veterans Administration as lecturer at the Conference on Periodontal Disease 58

Edward William Hawthorne became the first African American to earn a Ph.D. in physiology from the University of Illinois 205

Elouise Collier Duncan became the first African American appointed to the executive staff of the American Nurses Association 59

Etnah R. Boutte was the only woman of the first three African Americans elected to the Board of Directors of the New York City Cancer Commission 35

Eunice Lewis Smith was the first African American managing nurse at St. Elizabeth's Hospital in Washington, D.C. 58

Guion S. Bluford patented an artillery ammunition training round 114

Howard Marshall Payne became the first African American vice-president of the National Tuberculosis Association 205

Hughenna L. Gauntlett became the first African American woman to earn a M.D. from Loma Linda University 205

Jack E. White became the first African American trained in the United States as a surgical oncologist 206

Mildred Fay Jefferson became the first African American woman to earn a M.D. from Harvard Medical School 205

The first African American woman to earn a M.D. from Cornell University was Marie Metoyer 206

Thomas L. James was the first African American dental officer in the U. S. Navy 58

1952

Albert Harold Wheeler became the first full-time African American member of the University of Michigan faculty 206

Calvin C. Sampson became the first African American resident at Philadelphia's Episcopal Hospital 207

De Haven Hinkson was the first African American member of the Philadelphia College of Surgeons 207

Harold Dadford West became the first African American president of Meharry Medical College 87

Lloyd N. Ferguson publishes the first of his six major textbooks in the field of chemistry 299

Willie Mae Johnson was the first African American member of the first Board of Directors of the National League of Nurses 59

1953

Albert Walter Dent was the first African American president of the National Health Council 35

Clarence Sumner Greene became the first African American diplomate of the American Board of Neurosurgery 209

Emmett Earle Campbell became the first African American man to receive a M.D. from the University of Cincinnati 208

First national monument dedicated to African American George Washington Carver 19

Grace Marilyn James became the first African American appointed to the staff of a Louisville hospital 207

Herman Aladdin Barnett became the first African American to receive a M.D. from the University of Texas Medical School at Galveston 209

James C. Evans patented a method of using airplane exhaust gases to prevent ice from forming on aircraft 359

Julius Henry Taylor was the first African American to receive a research award from the U.S. Army's Office of Ordinance 300

Katharine Coleman G. Johnson was the first African American woman electrical engineer hired at NASA's Langley Research Center 115

W. Lester Henry Jr. became the first African American John and Mary Markle Scholar in medical science 208

1954

Alfred E. Martin led the group that developed a specialized television picture tube 301

Betty Smith Williams was the first African American to graduate from the Bolton School of Nursing, Case Western Reserve University 59

Dorothy Lavinia Brown became the first African American woman surgeon to practice in the South 210

Emery Louvelle Rann Jr. became the first African American member of the Mecklenburg County Medical Association 211

Emmett W. Chappelle discovered a key enzyme for the production of the amino acid glycine 301

Frances Justina Cherot became the first African American woman to receive a M.D. from the State University of New York Health Science Center at Brooklyn 210

James B. Drew became the first African American to earn an advanced degree in physics from Rutgers University 301

John B. Johnson Jr. became one of two first African American staff members of Georgetown University Hospital 210

John Beauregard Johnson Jr. was one of the first two African Americans appointed to the staff of Georgetown University Hospital 211

John Edward Lowery became the first African American president of the Queens Medical Society 209

Raleigh C. Bledsoe became the first African American to join any Kaiser-Permanente health organization 209

Webster Clay Brown became the first African American chief of surgery at any U. S. military hospital 209

1955

Booker Thomas Garnette was the first African-American dentist on the staffs of Norfolk General Hospital and St. Vincent Hospital 59

1956

1957

Steven Smith Davis patented his design of a supersonic wind tunnel nozzle 118

The first African American recipients of M.D.s from the University of Medicine and Dentistry of New Jersey were Marjorie Jones, Albert Knott, and David Snead 218

The first African American to receive a M.D. from Albert Einstein College of Medicine of Yeshiva University was Carol Burnett 218

Viola G. Lewis was the first African American woman appointed research assistant in the psychohormonal unit of Johns Hopkins University School of Medicine 36

Whittier Atkinson was the first African American named General Practitioner of the Year by the Pennsylvania State Medical Society 219

Wilina Ione Gatson was the first African American to graduate from the University of Texas Medical Branch Nursing School 62

1961

Adolphus Samms patented a rocket engine pump feed system 120

Alexander M. Pratt was the first African American dentist certified as a pedodontist by the Illinois Board of Periodontics 62

Allen H. Wilkins was the first African American horticulture inspector for the District of Columbia government 89

Aubre De L. Maynard was the first African American professor of surgery at a predominantly white medical school 219

George W. Reed became the first African American U. S. Representative to the International Atomic Energy Agency 304

Kenneth A. Loftman patented of method of preparing aqueous dispersions of metal oxides 304

Lloyd Charles Elam was first head of the Department of Psychiatry of Meharry Medical College 220

Noah Calhoun was the first African American dentist accepted into the American Society of Oral Surgery 62

Peachy Booker patented a flying landing platform 360

Phillip Emile Jr. patented a transistorized multivibrator circuit 119

Raleigh H. Allen was the first African American licensed to practice veterinary medicine in Alabama 36

Richard L. Francis was the first African American appointed assistant director of the New York State Department of Mental Hygiene, Harlem Valley Psychiatric Center 221

Samuel A. Kountz was the first African American physician to perform a kidney transplant 221

The first African American to receive a M.D. from Stanford University was Augustus White, III 220

1962

Alfred Benjamin patented improved scouring pads 21

C. Kermit Phelps became the first African American to teach in the psychology department at the University of Kansas 36

Electrostatic paint system patented by Allen H. Turner 120

First African American engineering student at LTV Aerospace Corporation 120

Gwendolyn Hickey became the first African American secretary of the State Licensed Practical Nurses 62

John William Lathen was the first African-American president of the Bergen County Mental Health Association 222

Kenneth C. Kelly patented a linearly polarized monoplus lobing antenna 120

Leather testing machine patented by Thomas J. Carter 21

Louis Wright Roberts patented a microwave radio frequency signal device adapted to high-power applications 305

Marion Ford, Jr. was the first African American dentist in periodontology to receive a Fulbright fellowship 62

Mildred R. Mitchell-Bateman was the first African American and first woman to head a state department of mental health 221

Paul E. Williams patented helicopter improvements 360

Sarah E. Payton was the first African American woman certified by the American Board of Radiology 222

The first African American to earn a M.D. from Washington University was James Sweatt, III 221

Vance Marchbanks, Jr., flight surgeon, monitored the first man to orbit Earth 361

William E. Lovett patented a motor fuel to reduce engine manifold deposits 361

1963

Charles A. Bankhead received a patent for an assembled composition printing process 21

Charles E. Weir patented a high-pressure optical cell for use in spectrum analysis of solid materials 305

Clarence Nokes patented a self-propelled lawn mower 121

Harvey Gantt became the first African American student at Clemson University 121

Jesse Balmary Barber, Jr. was the first African American certified by the American Board of Neurosurgery 223

John E. Moseley was the first African American to publish a textbook in the field of radiology 222

John W. Blanton patented a hydromechanical control system 121

Mack Gipson Jr. became the first African American to earn a Ph.D. in geology 306

Robert A. Thornton became the first Dean of the School of Science at San Francisco State University 305

Robert T. Allen patented a vertical coin counting tube 22

William E. Matory founded the Howard University College of Medicine (HUCM) Trauma Center and Hemodialysis Service 223

1964

Alvin H. Crawford was the first African American to receive a M.D. from the University of Tennessee 224

Beatrice L. Murray was the first African American chief nurse at an integrated facility 63

George William S. Ish Jr. was the first African American in Memphis, Tennessee elected a fellow in the American College of Surgeons 225

Henry Thomas Sampson invented a binder system for propellants and explosives 122

Herbert Leonard Jr. patented a process for producing hydroxylamine hydrocholoride 307

John Frederick Burton was the first African American to be certified by the American Board of Pathology 225

Joseph C. Dacons patented a process for the preparation of nitroform and its salts 307

Kenneth Witcher Clement was the first African American selected as a member of the Federal Hospital Benefits Advisory Council 224

Lena F. Edwards was the first African American woman to receive the Presidential Medal of Freedom 223

Mack Gipson founded the first geology department in a traditionally African American university 306

Marvin Alexander Jackson was the first African American president of the D.C. Society of Pathologists 225

Meredith Gourdine invented or co-invented nearly 70 patents 307

Minnie Lee Jones Hartsfield became the first African American nurse on staff at the Central Office of the U. S. Veterans Administration 63

O.T. Ayer became the first African American chief of the general practice division at Mound Park Hospital and Mercy Hospital 224

Rogers W. Griffin became the first podiatrist named "Foot Specialist of the Year" by the American Association of Foot Specialists 37

The first African American to earn a M.D. from the University of Kentucky was Carl Watson 224

The U. S. Veterans Administration's first long-range program on geographic epidemiology was initiated by Andrew Z. Keller 36

Wesley L. Jordan became the first African American full-time faculty member at a Southern white college 122

1965

A photographic transfer process was patented by James E. Lu Valle 307

Adolphus Samms patented a multiple stage rocket 361

Charles E. Burbridge became the first African American regent to the American College of Hospital Administration 37

David H. Blackwell became the first African American elected to the National Academy of Sciences 122

First African American to receive a Ph.D. in anatomy from Ohio State University was Clarence W. Wright 89

Gertrude Cera T. Hunter was the first Director of Health Services for the Head Start Program 226

Hansel L. McGhee patented a method for the preparation of carbon transfer inks 308

James T. Jackson was the first African American dentist to be selected a diplomat of the American Board of Prosthodontics 63

John R. Cooper patented a process for reacting a polyisocyanate compound 308

Russell L. Miller, Jr. was the first African American internal medicine resident at the University of Michigan 226

Walter C. Gough was the first African American to earn a degree from Tarkio College 226

William R. Norwood became the first African American pilot for United Airlines 361

1966

Donald E. Jefferson patented a triggered exploding wire device for electroexplosive apparatus 123

Emmett Chappelle co-discovered method for detecting bacteria in water 90

First African American submarine doctor in the U. S. Submarine Service 227

Harold E. Finley was the first African American elected president of the American Society of Protozoologists 90

James T. Whitehead became the first African American U-2 reconnaissance aircraft commander 362

John G. King patented an alarm device 123

John Perry Jr. patented a biochemical fuel cell 310

John Richard Cooper patented an improved process for preparing aromatic mono-,di-, and polyisocyanates 308

Leonard J. Julien patented a sugar cane planter 22

Louis W. Roberts patented a device for amplifying radio frequency waves 309

Samuel Massie named first African American faculty member at the U.S. Naval Academy 309

Victor Llewellyn Ransom patented a traffic data processing 123

Virginia Elizabeth Stull was the first African American woman to earn a M.D. from the University of Texas at Galveston 227

Vivienne Lucille Malone Mayes became the first full-time African American woman professor at Baylor University 123

Wilbert L. Jones, Jr. patented a duplex capstan 124

Wilson E. Hull patented a sublimation timing switch for satellites 362

1967

Arnold F. Stancell had patents developed for various processes for manufacturing various polymers 310

Clara Adams-Ender became the first woman to be awarded the Expert Field Medical Badge 64

Delores Robinson Brown became the first woman to graduate with an engineering degree from Tuskegee Institute 124

Edwin R. Russell patented a technique for the removal of cesium from aqueous solution 310

Hamilton Holmes was the first African American graduate of Emory University 227

Henry Aaron Hill patented a composition and process for curing furfuryl-alcohol-modified urea formaldehyde condensates 311

Jane Cooke Wright was the first African American woman to serve as associate dean of a major medical school 228

Juliann S. Bluitt became the first African American full-time faculty member at Northwestern University Dental School 64

Lawrence C. Washington was the first African-American male nurse to receive a regular U. S. Army commission in the Army Nurse Corps at Walter Reed Army Medical Center 64

Lloyd Albert Quarterman was the first chemist to study the x-ray, ultraviolet, and Raman spectra of compounds through the "diamond technique" 310

Robert Roosevelt Brooks patented a line blanking apparatus for color bar generating equipment 124

Steve B. Latimer became the first African American to earn a Ph.D. in chemistry from North Carolina State University 311

The first African American to receive a M.D. from Duke University was Wilhelm Merriwether 228

The first African Americans to earn M.D.s from Johns Hopkins University were Robert Gamble and John Nabwangu 228

Walter James Tardy was the first African American to earn a M.D. from the University of Wisconsin 228

1968

A patent was issued to Andrew R. Johnson for a precision digital delay circuit 125

Alphonso Trottman was the first African American dentist to receive a M.S. degree in orthodontics from Saint Louis University 64

Charles A. Peterson patented an electrical generator powered by hydropower 125

Henry T. Brown patented a process for reactivating hydroforming catalysts 312

James Earl Lewis patented a microwave antenna feed 125

Joan R. Sealy was the first African American woman to earn a M.D. from George Washington University 230

John Richard Crear, Jr. was the first African American to earn a M.D. from the University of California, Irvine 229

John T. Wilson Jr. was the first African American to be named head of the Biological Science Research Laboratories at Lockheed Missile and Space Company 91

Loma K. Brown Flowers was one of the first two African American women to receive a M.D. from Case Western Reserve University 230

Louis B. Levy was the first African American certified in radiologic physics by the American Board of Radiology 37

Louis Joseph Bernard became the first African American president of the Oklahoma City Surgical Society 229

Marvin C. Stewart patented a arithmetic unit for digital computers 125

Morris Leslie Smith patented a printing fluid 312

Patent for an air purification system assigned to Rufus Stokes 311

Ralph W. Sanderson invented a hydraulic shock absorber 362

Rufus J. Weaver developed a stair-climbing wheelchair 22

Theresa Greene Reed was the first African American woman epidemiologist 229

Vincent Porter was the first African American certified by the American Board of Plastic Surgery 230

William J. White as the first African American general foreman and superintendent of the Sharon Steel Corporation 124

1969

Alfred Day Hershey was the first African American to share the Nobel Prize in Physiology or Medicine 92

Alvin Francis Poussaint was the first African American appointed assistant dean of students at Howard Medical School 232

Angella D. Ferguson was the first African American woman appointed vice-president for health affairs at Howard University 234

Anna Cherrie Epps became the first African American woman professor at Tulane University School of Medicine 234

Charles W. Tate, Sr. patented a transparent lubricant housing for a universal joint 126

Clifton O. Dummett became the first African American president of the International Association of Dental Research 65

Darnley Mosely Howard patented a radome with an integral antenna 128

Electromagnetic gyroscope with float assembly patented by Lonnie G. Neal 312

Emmett W. Chappelle patented an invention relating to the storage of bioluminescent compounds 91

Frank Eugene Sessoms patented a high-protein, fruit-flavored, fat-stabilized spread 22

George R. Carruthers patented a magnetically focused image converter 127

Henry Jackson patented a method and composition for autocatalytically depositing copper 313

Irvin S. Frye patented an adjustable carpentry shackle 128

James A. Harris led group of researchers who discovered new chemical elements 313

James King, Jr. was the first African American named manager of the physics department of the Jet Propulsion Laboratory 314

James Pierpont Comer was the first African American associate dean for students at Yale University School of Medicine 231

James R. Lewis was the first African-American member of the Admiral's Commission for the School of Dentistry of the University of North Carolina 65

Jeanne Spurlock was the first African American woman to head a department of psychiatry at an American medical school 232

Jonathan S. Smith II patented a process of making a transparent zirconia composition 312

Lonnie Neal patented an electromagnetic gyroscope float assembly 126

M. Lucius Walker patented a laminar NOR element 126

Marie Van Brittan Brown patented a home security system 127

Melvin Earl Jenkins was the first African American tenured at the University of Nebraska Medical School 233

Mitchell W. Spellman was the first dean of the Charles R. Drew Postgraduate Medical School in Los Angeles 233

Raymond Linwood Standard was the first African American to be District of Columbia commissioner of public health 37

Rocket catapult patented by Hugh D. MacDonald 363

Royce T. Osborne was the first African American to become president of the American Society of Radiologic Technologists 37

The first M.D. awarded by the University of Miami was given to George Sanders 231

Tralance Addy became the first person to receive both a B.A. and a B.S. simultaneously from Swarthmore College 313

Walter F. Leavell was the first African American president of the Minority Affairs Section of the Association of American Medical Colleges 233

1970

Benjamin A. Dent patented a procedure entry for a data processor 128

Byron L. Mitchell was the first African American orthodontist to practice in the state of Florida 66

Charles Harry Epps became the first African American oral examiner for the Board of Orthopaedic Surgery 239

Charles Ireland became the first non-physician and first African American appointed an officer at Temple University's School of Medicine 235

Chester Middlebrook Pierce became the first African American member of the American Board of Psychiatry and Neurology 238

Clyde Edward Gurley patented an automatic telephone alarm system 129

David Satcher became the first African American to earn both a M.D. and a Ph.D. from Case Western Reserve University 237

Dewey S.C. Sanderson patented a urinalysis machine 38

Diane M. Lindsay became the first African American nurse to receive the Soldier's Medal for Heroism 65

Effie O'Neal Ellis became the first African American woman to hold an administrative position with the American Medical Association 236

Eleanor L. Franklin was the first African-American woman administrative officer at Howard University College of Medicine 239

James A. Bauer patented a coin-changer mechanism 23

James H. Porter patented a technique for gas well sulfur removal 130

James Monroe Jay wrote the first world-wide acclaimed and utilized text on food technology by an African American 92

James Rankin Cowan became the first African American appointed State Commissioner of Health for the State of New Jersey 235

John A. Kenney Jr. became the first African American to become a member of the American Dermatology Association 236

John B. Christian patented a high-temperature grease composition 315

Joseph St. Clair Wiles patented an injection pistol for intromuscular implantation of encapsulated chemicals into animals 92

Lawrence Randolph Kelly, Jr. patented an automatic telephone alarm apparatus 130

Leslie L. Alexander became the first African American to be appointed full professor of radiology in a predominantly white medical school 235

Margaret E. Bailey was the first African-American woman promoted to the rank of colonel in the U. S. Army 66

Osborne C. Stafford patented a microwave phase shift device 129

Paul B. Cornely became the first African American selected president of the American Public Health Association 236

Paul Brown patented a spinable stringless top 23

Robert Nathaniel Boyd, III patented a dental filling composition 66

Robert Roosevelt Brooks patented an improved apparatus for restoring detail to a video signal 129

The first M.D. awarded to an African American by Louisiana State University in New Orleans was given to Claude Tellis 238

The first two African Americans to earn M.D.s at the University of Florida were Ruben Brigety and Henry Coteman 238

The first two African Americans to graduate from the University of Alabama were Richard Dale and Samuel Sullivan, Jr. 238

The School of Architecture and City Planning of Howard University was started by Howard Hamilton Mackey, Sr. 128

Walter Cooper patented a polymerization process 315

Winser Alexander received a patent for a system for enhancing fine detail in thermal photographs 130

1971

Bobby J. Harris was the first African American certified in colorectal surgery 240

Charles M. Blackburn patented an electronic counting device 130

Claude H. Organ became the first African American chair of a surgery department at a predominately white medical school 240

Cora LeEthel Christian became the first African American woman to earn a M.D. at Thomas Jefferson University 241

Florence S. Gaynor became the first African American woman chosen to head a major teaching hospital in the United States 66

Henry T. Sampson invented the gamma-electric cell 315

Herbert Leonard Jr. received a patent for the production of high impact polystyrene 316

High pressure optical cell for Raman spectrography patented by Charles E. Weir 315

Howard L. Scott patented a process for water-proofing natural and synthetic hair 23

Ira Charles Robinson patented a sustained-release pharmaceutical tablet 38

James Edward Young was the first African American tenured professor of physics at Massachusetts Institute of Technology 316

James O. Plinton Jr. became the first African American corporate executive to work for a major airline 363

John Andrew Kenney Jr. became the first African American physician elected a board member of the African American Academy of Dermatology 241

John Harper and Frank Rumph were the first two African American men to receive their M.D.s from the Medical College of Georgia 240

Joyce M. Verrett became the first African American woman to earn a Ph.D. in biology from Tulane University 93

Lemuel W. Diggs became the first African American hematologist and researcher to develop a comprehensive research center 241

Marvin C. Stewart patented a system for interconnecting electrical components 131

Raymond Edward Rose patented an air data sensor for aircraft 363

Roland Boyd Scott established the first major research center for sickle cell disease 240

Samuel Gravely Jr. became the first African American rear admiral in the U. S. Navy 363

The first African American engineer to patent a gas turbine air compressor and control was Emmett Scott Harrison 316

The first president of the National Black Nurses Association (NBNA) was Lauranne Sams 67

1972

Arnold Francis Stancell patented a process for partially separating components from fluid mixtures 317

Arthur H. Coleman became the first African American named president of the Golden State Medical Association 242

Asa G. Yancey became the first African American associate dean at the Emory University School of Medicine 243

Benjamin F. Hammond became the first African American appointed chair of the Microbiology Department of the University of Pennsylvania School of Dental Medicine 93

Carol Coleman Gray became the first African American woman to earn a M.D. from the University of Texas Medical School at San Antonio 242

Carroll M. Leevy organized the first known multidisciplinary clinic in the country for alcoholics with liver disease 243

Disease in children called CoA transverse deficiency discovered by African American scientist James Tyson Tildon 93

Donald E. Jefferson patented a resin solution for increasing the wet strength of cellulosic material 318

Donald E. Jefferson received a patent for a special purpose data processor 132

Edwin Nii Adom became the first African American blind psychiatrist in the United States 242

Ernest L. Walker patented an invention for shift register memory 131

Ferdinand D. Wharton Jr. patented a medical treatment of diarrhea 38

Frank Roger Prince patented an improved process for producing 2-pyrrolidones 317

Frank S. Greene, Sr. patented a system for the use of faulty storage circuits 132

George Carruthers invented an ultraviolet astronomical camera sent to Moon's surface 364

George W. Nauflett patented a process for the synthesis of 2-fluoro-2, 2-dinitroethyl (FDNOL) 318

Harry J. Green Jr. patented a method of sealing containers for microelectronics devices 317

James Battle patented a variable resistance resistor assembly 133

James Edward Bostic Jr. became the first African American to earn a Ph.D. from Clemson University 23

James W. Cobb patented a system for attaching a pocket to a garment 132

Joel M. Morris patented a switching system charging arrangement 133

John G. King patented a tamperproof auto alarm 133

John Leslie Jones Sr. patented a personal restraint system for vehicular occupants 364

Samuel L. Kountz developed first standards of tolerable dosages of the drug methylprednisolone 242

The Jesse L. Brown became the first United States Naval ship named for an African American naval officer 364

Vivan O. Lee became the first African American nurse employed by Region X of the Public Health Services 67

Yvonne Young Clark became the first African-American woman to earn a B.S. in mechanical engineering at Howard University 131

1973

Albert E. Hopkins became the first African American appointed a member of the Texas State Board of Pharmacy 39

Albert G. B. Prather patented a gravity-operated escape means 134

American Nurses' Association formed the American Academy of Nursing 68

Charles Austin Dyer patented a teaching calculator 134

Clarence G. Robinson, Jr. was the first African American chief surgeon for the New York City Police Department 244

Clive Orville Callender became the first African American member of the National Task Force on Organ Procurement and Transplantation 245

Eddie Lomax, Jr. named first African American technical director of the Puritan Chemical Company 319

Foster Kidd was the first African American dentist appointed to the Texas State Board of Dental Examiners 67

Gertrude E. Downing devised an auxiliary attachment for rotary floor-treatment machines 24

John Alexander Anderson founded the Southwest Medical Society 244

John Lawrence S. Holloman became the first African American to become president of the New York City Health and Hospital Corporation 245

Joseph M. Redmond patented a resistor sensing bit switch 134

Luvenia C. Miller became the first African American woman to be named director of the Biological Photographers Association 94

Mark Ivey, III became the first African American resident in the department of obstetrics and gynecology at Akron General Medical Center 245

Rosalie A. Reed was the first woman veterinarian employed by the Los Angles Zoo 39

Shirley Ann Jackson became the first African American woman to earn a Ph.D. in physics 319

The first African Americans to earn M.D.s from Michigan State University were Janice Fox, Judith Ingram, Donald Weathers, and Roger Whitmore 244

The University of Texas Southwestern Medical Center at Dallas Southwestern Medical School awarded M.D.s for the first time to African American graduates Charles Foutz and Johnny Henry 244

1974

A patent for a ceramic inductor was earned by William L. Muckelroy 135

Dolores M. Franklin was the first African American woman graduate of Harvard School of Dental Medicine 69

Donna Kibble became the first African American nurse to join the staff of the Carville, Louisiana, Hospital 69

Earl D. Shaw became the first African American researcher at Bell Laboratories 320

Frank Eugene Sessoms patented high nutrition food spreads 320

George C. McTeer was the first African American graduate of the College of Dental Medicine of University of South Carolina 69

Herman E. Eure became the first African American to receive a Ph.D. degree from Wake Forest University 94

Isadore Small III invented a universal on-delay timer 135

John William Coleman received a patent related to the electron microscope 319

Joseph L. Henry became the first African American professor appointed to faculty of Harvard School of Dental Medicine 69

Joseph L. Henry was the first African American appointed to a Harvard professorship in its school of Dental Medicine 68

Lloyd W. Newton became the first African American pilot to fly with U. S. Air Force Aerial Demonstration Squadron 365

Robert B. Ford was the first African American dentist appointed to the State Dental Board in Ohio 68

Robert L. Engram was granted a patent for a shock falsing inhibitor circuit 134

Ronald Eugene Goldsberry acquired patents on a class of polymers 320

Samuel L. Kountz became the first African American elected president of the Society of University Surgeons 247

The first African American graduate of the University of Utah was William Robinson 248

The first African American to receive a M.D. from Vanderbilt University was Levi Watkins, Jr. 246

The first five African Americans to receive M.D.s Pennsylvania State University were James Byers, Theodore Densley, Wade Johnson, Lewis Mitchell, and Janice McIntosh 247

The first major hospital in New York City named in honor of an African American was dedicated to Arthur C. Logan 247

William E. Allen, Jr. became the first African American physician to be awarded the Gold Medal of the American College of Radiology 247

William Rodney Wiley was the first African American to be appointed as biology department manager at the Pacific Northwest National Laboratory 94

1975

Curtis Cole, Jr. was the first African American athlete to receive an engineering degree at Old Dominion University 135

Daniel H. James became the first African American four-star general in the U. S. Air Force 366

Dave Bondu invented the slant golf tee 25

Donna P. Davis was the first African American doctor in the U. S. Navy Medical Corps 249

Eddie Charles Gay patented a cathode for a secondary electrochemical cell 321

Floyd Allen invented a low-cost telemeter for monitoring a battery and DC voltage converter power supply 321

Hugh F. Butts became the first African American deputy commissioner of the

New York State Department of Mental Hygiene 249

James B. Huntley patented an emergency fire escape mechanism 25

James Herman Mabrie III became the first African American otolaryngology resident at Baylor Affiliated Hospitals 249

Jeanne C. Sinkford was the first woman appointed dean of an American school of dentistry 70

John C. Norman completed the first partial artificial heart (LVAD) implantation in a human 248

Joseph Ausbon Thompson patented a moist/dry toilet tissue 24

Lillian Stokes was the first African American nurse to receive the Lucille Petry Award 70

Marion Mann became the first African American brigadier general in the U. S. Army Medical Reserve Corps 248

Maurice Rabb was the first African American president of the Chicago Opthalmological Society 250

Nathaniel John Mullen invented an asphalt paving vehicle 365

Paul J. Fox and Johnson B. Murray were the first two African American men to receive M.D. degrees from the State University of New York at Stony Brook Health Sciences Center 251

Samuel Blanton Rosser became the first African American to be certified in pediatric surgery 249

The first African Americans to receive M.D.s from the State University of New York at Stony Brook were Janice Lark, Mitchelene Morgan, Paul Fox, and Johnson Murray 251

The first two African American women to earn M.D.s from the University of California at Davis were Sandra Battis and Diane Pemberton 250

The first two African American women to graduate from the University of Colorado School of Medicine were LaRae Washington and Deborah Green 250

Virgie M. Ammons was granted a patent for a fireplace damper actuating tool 24

William K. Collins was the first African American president of the Association of Dental Examiners 70

Waverly J. Person appointed first African American director of the National Earthquake Information Center 323

William Childs Curtis patented an airborne moving-target-indicating radar system 366

1978

Alfred A. Bishop patented a flow distributor used in nuclear reactor cores 324

Alvin J. Thompson became the first African American president of the Washington State Medical Association 255

Augustus A. White III became the first African American to serve as chairman of a clinical department in a major teaching hospital 254

Barbara Lauraine Nichols became the first African American president of the American Nursing Association 73

Christian C. L. Reeburg patented a grease gun rack 25

Deborah Ratchford patented a for portable luggage carrier 25

Faye Wattleton became first woman and first African American president of Planned Parenthood 73

First text of its kind, Clinical Biomechanics of the Spine, authored by Augustus Aaron White III 255

Gerald Virgil Stokes became the first African American to teach graduate-level science courses at George Washington University School of Medicine and Health Sciences 95

Henry F. Henderson was granted a patent for a weight control system used in transport 137

Herman James Mabrie III was the first African American otolaryngologist 253

James C. Letton earned two patents for developing biodegradable soap agents 325

Jill Brown became the first African American woman pilot to fly for commercial airline 367

Joan Scott Wallace became the first African American Assistant Secretary for Administration at the USDA 25

Kenneth C. Edelin became the first African American to direct a major clinical department at Boston City Hospital 255

Kenneth Morgan Maloney patented an improved mercury vapor lamp 325

LaSalle D. Leffall, Jr. became the first African American president of the Society of Surgical Oncology 254

Lois Cooper became the first African American woman to earn a license in civil engineering in California 138

Mitchell W. Spellman became the first African American dean for medical services at Harvard University Medical Center 254

The first African American women to earn a M.D.s from the University of Massachusetts were Marcia Bowling and Vernette Bee 256

Tralance O. Addy patented a process for minimizing accumulation of static charges on fibers 325

Verdelle B. Bellamy became the first African American president of the Georgia Board of Nursing 72

1979

Doris L. Wethers became the first director of the Comprehensive Sickle Cell Program at New York's St. Luke's/Roosevelt Hospital 258

Frank E. Peterson became the first African American general in the U. S. Marine Corps 367

George Canty invented a photosensitive composite sheet material useful as a printing plate 327

Harold Amos became the first African American to chair the Department of Microbiology at Harvard Medical School 95

Hazel W. Johnson became the first African American woman promoted to general in the U. S. Army 75

Jacqueline Minette Jacobs patented a biocontamination particulate system 95

James Hall Porter founded the first minority-owned firm to receive contracts from the United States Environmental Protection Agency Laboratory 326

Jennie R. Patrick-Yeboah became the first African American woman to earn a doctorate in chemical engineering 326

Jerome Heartwell Holland became the first African American Chair of the Board of

Governors of the American National Red Cross 40

LaSalle D. Leffall Jr. became the first African American to serve as president of the American Cancer Society 256

LaSalle Doheny Leffall held the first national conference on cancer among African Americans 257

Leroy Maxwell Graham became the first African American elected to Alpha Omega Alpha Honor Medical Society at Georgetown University 256

Liz Johnson became the only African American of five selected to become a National Veterans Administration Scholar 73

Marcella A. Hayes became the first African American woman pilot in the U. S. armed services 367

Mary Munson Runge became the first woman and first African American head of the American Pharmaceutical Association 40

Robert Charles Stepto became the first African American chief of gynecology at the University of Chicago Medical School 257

Roland A. Gandy Jr. became a founding member of the Toledo Surgical Society 257

1980

Gloria Gilmer became the first African American woman to serve on the board of governors of the Mathematical Association of America 139

Guthrie Turner was the first African American brigadier general in the U.S. Army Medical Corps 259

John Brooks Slaughter became the first African American director of the National Science Foundation 138

John S. Trent discovered the use of ruthenium telraoxide with transmission electron microscopes 327

Lawrence C. Chambers became the first African American U. S. Naval Academy graduate to be commissioned a line officer 367

Leslie L. Alexander became the first African American chancellor of the American College of Radiology 259

Levi Watkins, Jr. became the first surgeon to implant the life-saving Automatic Implantable Defibrillator in a human 260

Maurice C. Clifford became the first African American president of the Medical College of Pennsylvania 259

Norma Sklarek became the first African American woman to be made a fellow of the American Institute of Architects 138

One of the first two African Americans to receive the Ph.D. in electrical engineering from Cornell University 139

Patrice T. Gaspard became the first African American elected to the Alpha Omega Alpha Medical Honor Society at Tulane University 258

Pauline Y. Titus-Dillon became the first African American woman administrator in the dean's office of the Howard University College of Medicine 260

Scott Spiral Knee Brace patented by Linzy Scott 260

Valerie Thomas patented a technique for a real-time, three-dimensional television system 138

Vernal Gordon Cave became the first African American president of the Medical Society of Kings County, New York 258

Vernice Ferguson became the first African American chief of the Nursing Department at the Clinical Center, National Institutes of Health 75

1981

Barbara McArthur became the first African American woman certified by the Board of Infection Control 75

Booker T. Whatley founded and edited the journal, The Small Farm Technical Newsletter 26

James E. West patented a technique for removing surface and high-volume charges from the high-polymer films 140

Jewel Plummer Cobb established the first privately funded gerontology center in Orange County, California 96

John Henry Allen, Jr. patented a computer-generated image simulator 140

Joseph G. Gordon II patented a projection display device 139

Mary Styles Harris was first State Director of Genetics Services for the Georgia Department of Human Resources 96

Raphael C. Lee was the first surgeon to win the MacArthur Prize Fellowship 261

Sabrina A. Benjamin became the first African American woman to receive a M.D. from the Uniformed Services University 261

The first African American appointed Director of the Michigan Department of Public Health was Bailus Walker, Jr. 261

The first African American graduates of East Carolina University School of Medicine were Natalear Collins and Brenda Klutz 261

1982

Carol Jean Hubbard became the first African American woman to earn a M.D. from Wright State University 262

David R. Hedgley Jr. was first to enable computer programmers to exhibit any three-dimensional object 141

Denise Annette Ford was the first African-American graduate of the University of Missouri-Rolla 328

Evan B. Forde became the first African American oceanographer to participate in submersible dives aboard research ships 328

Gladys L. Johnson became the first African American woman oral and maxillofacial surgeon 76

Godfrey A. Gayle became the first African American to receive a Ph.D. in biological and agricultural engineering from North Carolina State University 26

Irene Long became the first African American woman to be appointed chief of NASA Medical Operations 368

Jerome L. Wicks Sr. invented a door security device 26

Paul E. Belcher invented devices related to pulse magnifiers and remote AC power controls 141

Sally Thimms-Kelly and Alfred B. Kelly III patented wrist support braces 41

Samuel F. Lambert was the first African American president of the National Association of Power Engineers 141

Thomas P. Fraser was the first African American to be inducted into the South Carolina Hall of Science and Technology 97

Toothpaste containing pH-adjusted zeolites patented by Anthony L. Dent 327

William Lofton, Jr. became the first African American elected a fellow of the American Occupational Therapy Association 41

1983

Carl L. Wilson became the first African American appointed deputy director of the Department of Public Works for the state of Ohio 142

Chancellor A. Tzomes became the first African American to command a U. S. nuclear submarine 369

Doreen Palmer was the first African American woman to head a hospital's gastroenterology department 263

Frank A. Crossley patented a process for the refinement of titanium alloys 328

Gloria R. Smith was the first nurse appointed director of the Michigan Department of Public Health 76

Gregory Patterson became the first African American to receive a M.D. from East Tennessee State University 264

Guion Bluford became the first African American astronaut to fly in space 368

Jesse Belmary Barber Jr. became Howard University's first professor of social medicine 262

Kenneth A. Forde became the first African American elected president of the Society of American Gastrointestinal Endoscopic Surgeons 262

Laura Stubbs became the first woman engineering professor at the U. S. Naval Academy's Nuclear Power School 142

Lois E. Hill was the first African American to graduate with a M.S. from Clark College 329

Lori M. Campbell and Paul J. Smith became the first African Americans to receive M.D. degrees from the University of Hawaii, John A. Bumi School of Maui 263

Melvin E. Jenkins, Jr. became the first African American selected as a governor of the American Board of Pediatrics 263

Northeastern Ohio University awarded its first M.D.s to African Americans 264

Peter A. Dual was the first African American academic dean at San Diego State University 41

Richard L. Saxton patented a pay telephone with a sanitized tissue dispenser 142

Vallerie D. Wagner became the first African American woman to earn a M.S. degree in engineering from Tuskegee University 142

Virgil Pattman, Sr. became the first African American senior safety engineer at the General Motors Technology Center 141

1984

Bailus Walker, Jr. was the first African American appointed Commissioner of Public Health in Massachusetts 264

Clara Adams-Ender was the first African American nurse to be chief of the department of nursing at Walter Reed Army Medical Center 77

Clive Callender became the first and only African American member of the National Organ Transplant Task Force 264

Ernest Donald Walker, the only African American nurse on the United States Food and Drug Administration staff, retired 76

George Edward Alcorn patented imaging x-ray spectrometer 329

Harold P. Freeman became the first African American chair of the National Advisory Committees on Cancer 265

Ida Van Smith became the first African American woman inducted into the International Forest of Friendship 370

Isaac T. Gillam, IV, became first assistant administrator of commercial programs at the National Aeronautical and Aerospace Administration 369

Joan Murrell Owens became the first African American woman to earn a Ph.D. in geology 329

John S. Brooks patented an internal combustion engine spark timing control 370

Michael D. Griffin acquired several patents for a throttle positioning system for automotive engines 143

Neville A. Baron patented an apparatus and process for recurving the cornea of the eye 41

Ora Strickland became the first African American chair of the Board of Directors of the American Journal of Nursing 76

Queen F. Randall became the first African American and first woman president of American River College 143

The first dedicated comprehensive cardiac MRI analysis software package was developed by Roderic I. Pettigrew 265

1985

Albert M. Ware developed a forged aluminum design for use in high volume automotive applications 143

Anthony Michael Johnson acquired patents related to high speed circulate measurements, integrated optical devices, and photodetectors 330

Barbee Myers became the first African American woman faculty member at Pennsylvania State University College of Health, Physical Education and Recreation to earn a Ph.D. in exercise physiology and cardiac rehabilitation 42

Bobby L. Wilson patented a process for the hydroconversion of carbonaceous materials 331

Charles H. Epps, Jr. was the first African American selected president of the American Orthopedic Association 266

Deborah Ann Turner became the first African American woman certified in gynecological oncology 266

Donnie Cochran became the first African American to fly with the U. S. Navy's Blue Angels 370

Emergency escape apparatus patented by June M. Horne 27

Fifteen M.D. degrees awarded to the charter class of the Charles R. Drew University of Medicine and Science 267

Lincoln J. Diuguid patented a technique for increasing the burning efficiency of fuels 331

Lionel W. Young became the first African American chair of the board of the Society for Pediatric Radiology 266

Lonnie R. Bristow became the first African American elected to the Council on Medical Services of the American Medical Association 265

Michael D. Griffin received a patent for valve shaft end float control 370

Milton E. Brunsen was the first African American physician to complete a residency in obstetrics and gynecology at the University of Arkansas Medical School 267

Robert L. Kimbrough became the first African American president of the Chicago Dental Society 77

Welton I. Taylor became the first African American microbiologist to have a newly discovered species of bacteria named after him 97

William Frank King acquired over 30 U.S. and foreign patents 331

William L. Wade Jr. patented a porous carbon cathode for use in an electrochemical cell 332

1986

Agnes D. Lattimer became the first African American woman to hold the top medical post in a major hospital in a major city 267

Association for Academic Minority Physicians founded 268

Betty Wright Harris patented a spot test for an explosive called TATB 144

Everett Draper, Jr. became the first African American mathematics department head in the publishing industry 145

Harry C. Hopkins patented a device for power controller 145

Herbert W. Nickens became the first African American director of the U. S. Department of Health and Human Services Office of Minority Health 268

James E. Young obtained a patent for battery performance control 144

James E. Young patented a system for controlling a multi-cell battery 332

John L. Carter invented a distributed pulse-forming network for a magnetic modulator 332

John L. Mack patented a participant-identification recording and playback system 144

Lewis Walker patented a furnace 145

Ronald McNair became the first African American to die during a space mission 371

Rosalyn Sterling was the first African American woman certified by the American Board of Thoracic Surgeons 268

Samuel Dixon Jr. patented a subharmonic mixer 144

Wilbert Murdock patented a knee alignment monitoring device 42

1987

Benjamin S. Carson became the first neurosurgeon to successfully separate Siamese twins joined at the head 269

Beverly Coleman became the first African American woman to be a full professor of radiology at the University of Pennsylvania 268

Carolyn Armstrong Williams the first African American and first women's dean in an engineering school 145

Deborah Prothrow-Stith became the first woman appointed Commissioner of Public Health for the state of Massachusetts 42

Dennis Weatherby patented a lemon formula for dishwashing liquid 333

Frederick D. Gregory became the first African American to command a space shuttle 371

Gayle Smith-Blair became the first African American woman to receive a M.D. from Texas A&M University Health Sciences Center School of Medicine 268

John F. Williams was the first African American assistant dean of admission and chair of the admissions committee at George Washington University College of Medicine 269

Linneaus C Dorman invented an artificial bone material composed of an ivory-type compound 333

Melvin McCoy invented a vehicle support-type backpack 27

Shirley Tyus became the first African American woman pilot hired by United Airlines 371

William Harwell patented an apparatus for capturing an orbiting spacecraft 372

1988

Aubrey Carl Smith Jr. was the first African American manager of the Waste Management Operation of the Argonne National Laboratory 334

Bertram J. Fraser-Reid patented an economical method for linking single sugars together to form oligosaccharides 333

Carolyn Branch Brooks was a recipient of the First Annual White House Initiative Faculty Award for Excellence in Science and Technology 97

Delores Spikes became the first woman to head a U.S. university system 146

Em Claire Knowles was the first African American assistant dean of the Graduate School of Information Sciences at Simmons College 146

Eric A. Buffong presented the first eight cases of laproscopic vaginal hysterectomies in the world at the First North American/South American Congress of Gynecologic Endoscopy 270

James E. Millington patented a method of making styrene-type polymers 334

Michael Molaire patented a laminate adapted for use with to integrated circuit chips 334

Patricia E. Bath patented the Laserphaco Probe 270

Phillip A. Collins patented a bubble machine 27

Raven L. DeLoatch was the first African American chief of staff of Halifax Regional Hospital 270

Raymond L. Coleman patented a method and apparatus for testing electrical equipment 147

Sandra Cavanaugh Holley became the first African American president of the American Speech-Language-Hearing Association 43

Shannon L. Madison patented an electrical wiring harness termination system 147

Thomas E. Malone became the first African American to serve as Vice-President for Biomedical Research of the Association of American Medical Colleges 269

1989

Audrey Forbes Manley became the first woman named deputy assistant secretary for health in the U. S. Department of Health and Human Services 271

Edward D. Williams patented a protective mouthpiece 78

Elizabeth Ann Patterson became the first African American woman to head the Radiology Section of the National Medical Association 274

Evelyn Boyd Granville became the first African American woman mathematician to receive an honorary doctorate degree 147

Francis E. Levert patented a continuous fluid level detector 335

Gilbert Allen Cargill became the first African American enshrined in the Michigan Aviation Hall of Fame 372

Henry Scott patented a spinal traction and support unit 44

Jerome C. Scales was the first African American president of the Society of Pediatric Dentistry 77

Louis W. Sullivan became the first African American in George Bush's presidential administration 272

Meteorologist S. George Philander published his first text 336

Morris Leslie Smith was issued two patents for chemically treated paper products 335

Renee Jenkins became the first African American woman to serve as president of the Society of Adolescent Medicine 272

Richard A. Holmes became the first African American president of the Society of Nuclear Medicine 272

Robert Hilliard was the first African American elected President of the Texas State Board of Medical Examiners 271

Roscoe Michael Moore, Jr. was the first African American to serve as chief veterinary officer in the U. S. Public Health Service 43

Tyshawn M. James became the first African American to earn a M.D. from Marshall University 271

Walter Eugene Massey became the first African American president of American Association for the Advancement of Science 335

1990

Eddie L. Hoover was the first African American chair of the department of surgery at the State University of New York at Buffalo 274

Ezra C. Davidson, Jr. was the first African American elected president of the American College of Obstetricians and Gynecologists 275

Gary Holloway developed General Electric's first film-cooled, high-pressure turbine shroud 372

George Blevins Jr. was the first African American to receive a Ph.D. from the University of Arkansas 44

James Littles, Jr. became the first African American faculty member in the Radiation Oncology Department at the University of Michigan Medical School 275

Janet C. Rutledge was the first African American woman to earn a Ph.D. in electrical engineering from Georgia Institute of Technology 148

Maxie C. Maultsby became the first African American physician to author texts on rational behavior therapy 274

Percy Lavon Julian and George Washington Carver were the first two African Americans elected to the National Inventors Hall of Fame 28

Roselyn P. Epps became the first African American president of the American Medical Women's Association 274

Sylvester James Fletcher patented a modular-stackable front loading container 28

The first African American woman inventor to receive a patent for a fertilizer was Dawn Francis 28

Theda Daniels-Race became the first African American faculty member of Duke University's School of Engineering 148

1991

Alex Adu Clerk was the first African American sleep disorder specialist 276

Carl D. Virgil became the first African American man to receive the M.D. from the University of Nevada 277

Clay S. Gloster patented a method and apparatus for high-precision weighted random pattern generation 148

Donald E. Wilson was the first African American dean of a predominately white medical school 277

Edith P. Mitchell became the first African American woman to hold a Missouri Air National Guard squadron command 373

Gerald E. Thomson was the first African American elected chair of the American Board of Internal Medicine 276

Irvin W. Elliott patented a new anti-HIV compound 98

Kenneth Olden became the first African American director of the National Institute of Environmental Health Sciences and the National Toxicology Program 98

Valerie E. Taylor was the first African American woman to receive a Ph.D. in electrical engineering from the University of California at Berkeley 149

Vivian W. Pinn became the first director of the Office of Research on Women's Health at the National Institutes of Health 276

Wilburn Weddington, Sr.became the first African American appointed associate dean, Medicine Administration at Ohio State University 277

Zora Kramer Brown became the first African American woman to be appointed to the National Cancer Advisory Board 44

1992

Billie J. Becoat patented a dual-wheel driven bicycle 28

Charles L. Curry became the first African American appointed to the board of trustees of the American College of Cardiology 278

Edward S. Cooper became the first African American selected president of the American Heart Association 278

Energy conversion system patented by Thomas L. Cosby 152

George M. Langford formed part of the team of investigators who first demonstrated that special filaments responsible for muscle cell movement were also responsible for nerve cell particle movement 99

John W. Webster, III patented a method of comparing computer files to each other 149

Louis Freeman became the first African American chief pilot for a major United States airline 373

Mae C. Jemison became the first African American woman in space 373

Margaret H. Jordan was the first African American and first woman vice-president of Southern California Edison's Health Care Services 78

Margaret M. Patterson-Townsend was the first African American woman to own and operate a sleep disorder clinic 45

Marlon L. Priest became the first African American associate vice president for health affairs at the University of Alabama School of Medicine 278

Paul A. Stephens was the first African American president of the Academy of General Dentistry 78

Ricky Charles Godbolt became the first African American to win the Instructor of the Year Award from the U. S. Army 151

Robert M. Williams patented a method and apparatus for disinfecting medical supplies 44

Wanda Anne A. Sigur patented a method of fabricating composite structures 150

Wesley Leroy Harris Sr. became the National Aeronautics and Space Administration's first administrator for aeronautics 150

Woodrow C. Crockett became the first African American inducted into the Arkansas Aviation Hall of Fame 373

1993

Alphonso Michael Espy named first African American Secretary of the U.S. Department of Agriculture 29

Barbara Ross-Lee became the first African American woman to head a U. S. medical school 279

Beverly Parson was the first African American named National Program Director of the Year by the Arthritis Foundation 45

Clyde Johnson became the first African American to head the American Heart Association 45

David H. Reid III became the first African American national medical director of the U. S. Postal Service 281

Ellwood G. Ivey, Jr. invented the driver biosystem sensitized steering wheel 375

First African American commanding general of the U. S. Army Engineering Center 152

Frances Christian Gaskin patented a type of sunscreen 46

Gloria Jean Jeff became the first African American woman to be named associate administrator for policy at the Federal Highway Administration 152

Haile T. Debas became the first African American appointed dean of a predominantly white medical school 280

Henry W. Foster was the first African American president of the Association of Professors of Obstetrics and Gynecology 282

James D. Watkins was the first African American president of the Virginia State Board of Dentistry 78

Joycelyn Elders became the first African American and first woman to be appointed U. S. Surgeon General 279

L.D. Britt became the first African American Henry Ford Professor of Surgery at Norfolk (VA) State University 281

Roderick Wells became the first African American appointed to board of Louisiana Mosquito Central Association 99

Rodney Slater nominated as first African American head of the U. S. Federal Highway Administration 153

Ross M. Miller Jr. became the first African American president of the Los Angeles Surgical Society 281

S. Allen Counter was the first African American awarded the doctor of medical science degree from the Karolinska Nobel Institute in Sweden 279

Sheila K. Nash-Stevens patented an optical fiber holder 336

Warren M. Washington elected first African American president of the American Meteorological Society 336

William Avery Henderson became the first African American pilot to head General Motors' corporate fleet 374

Winton D. Jones was issued a patent for pyridyloxazole-2-ones, useful in the treatment of multi-drug resistant tumors 45

Winton Dennis Jones patented three chemicals used in the treatments of cancer and heart disease 45

1994

Charles Cartwright became the first African American to become a regional forester for the U. S. Department of Agriculture Forest Service 100

Charles F. Bolden, Jr. commands first joint United States/Russian space shuttle mission 375

Eve Juliet Higginbotham became the first African American woman to chair a university-based department of opthalmology 282

Evelyn Fields became the first woman from any branch of the U. S. military to command an ocean-going commissioned U. S. ship 153

Henry Thomas Chriss received a patent for a footwear additive made from recycled materials 337

James E. West acquired more than 20 patents in the field of electroacoustics 337

Jim Edwards Sr. and Jim Edwards Jr. became the first African American father and son pilots for a major airline 376

Kenneth Dwight Lewis was the first African American to lead a mission to remove a half ton of bomb-grade uranium from Kazakhstan 337

Patrice Clark-Washington became the first African American woman flight captain for a top airline service 375

Philip A. Carswell patented a programmable encryption device 153

Sylvester J. Gates Jr. became the first recipient of the American Physical Society Prize for Visiting Minority Professor Lectureship 338

William G. Anderson became the first African American president of the American Osteopathic Association (AOA) 282

1995

Bernard Harris, Jr. became the first African American to walk in space 376

Carolyn G. Morris became the first African American woman to hold the position of assistant director of the FBI 154

Clyde G. Bethea was the first to develop the technique of electric field-induced optical second harmonic generation 339

Darryl C. Hunter was the first African American to head a radiation oncology department for the Department of Defense 283

Francine Essien became the first African American to receive U.S. Professor of the Year Award from the Carnegie Foundation for the Advancement of Teaching 100

Gilbert Bryant Chapman II acquired a patent for an integrated utility/camper shell for a pick-up truck 154

Helen Doris Gayle became the first African American woman director of the National Center for HIV, STD, and TB Prevention of the U.S. Centers for Disease Control 284

James L. Sweatt, III, was the first African American president of the Dallas County Medical Society 283

James Winfield Mitchell patented a method of growing continuous diamond films 338

Lonnie R. Bristow became the first African American named president of the American Medical Association 284

Moses T. Asom acquired patents in the field of semiconductor devices 153

Raymond L. Johnson organized the first conference for African American Research in the Mathematical Sciences 154

Regina Benjamin became the first African American woman to be a member of the board of trustees of the American Medical Association 283

Shirley Ann Jackson became the first African American and first woman appointed to Chair of the Nuclear Regulatory Commission 339

The first African American woman appointed Health Commissioner for the City of Philadelphia was Estelle B. Richman 46

1999

OCCUPATION INDEX

ADMINISTRATOR

Austin, Wanda G. 155
Belson, Jerry 101
Benjamin, Floyd 48
Bessent, Hattie 71
Boutte, Etnah R. 35
Brown, Zora Kramer 44
Burbridge, Charles E. 226
Comer, James Pierpont 231
Debas, Haile T. 280
Dent, Albert Walter 35
Dual, Peter A. 41
Elders, Jocelyn 279
Ellis, Effie O'Neal 236
Espy, Alphonso Michael 29
Franklin, Eleanor L. 239
Fraser, Thomas P. 97
Garr, Dixie Tyran 156
Gayle, Helen Doris 284
Gaynor, Florence S. 66
Gillam, Isaac Thomas, IV 369
Harris, Jean Louise 212
Holland, Jerome Heartwell 40
Hunter, Gertrude Cera T. 226
Ireland, Charles 235
Jackson, Shirley Ann 339, 341
Jeff, Gloria Jean 152
Johnson, Clyde 45
Knowles, Em Claire 146
Lewis, Carolyn B. 48
Lomax, Eddie, Jr. 319
Manley, Audrey Forbes 271
Mitchell-Bateman, Mildred R. 221
Morris, Carolyn G. 154
Nickens, Herbert W. 268
Parson, Beverly 45
Patterson-Townsend, Margaret M. 45
Person, Waverly J. 323
Poussaint, Alvin Francis 232
Prothrow-Stith, Deborah 42
Randall, Queen F. 143
Richman, Estelle B. 46
Rogers Thomasina 48
Ross-Lee, Barbara 279

Santiago, Margaret 95
Satcher, David 286
Sinkford, Jeanne Craig 70
Slater, Rodney K. 153
Slaughter, John Brooks 138
Smith, Eunice Lewis 58
Smith, Gloria R. 76
Spellman, Mitchell W. 233
Spikes, Delores Margaret Richard 146
Standard, Raymond Linwood 37
Stanton, Robert G. 101
Sullivan, Louis W. 272
Thomas, Jesse O. 34
Thornton, Robert A. 305
Titus-Dillon, Pauline Y. 260
Tolbert, Margaret Ellen Mayo 340
Troutman, Adewale 47
Tunley, Naomi Louise 61
Walker, Bailus, Jr. 261
Wallace, Joan 25
Washington, G. Kenneth 214
Wattleton, Alyce Faye 73
Wells, Roderick A. 99
White, William J. 124
Williams, Carolyn Ruth Armstrong 145
Williams, Michael G. 157
Wilson, Carl L. 142
Wilson, Donald E. 277
Yancey, Asa G. 243

AERONAUTICAL ENGINEER

Harris, Wesley Leroy, Sr. 150

AGRICULTURALIST

Carver, George Washington 7, 14, 16, 18, 19, 28
Gayle, Godfrey A. 26
Spaulding, Major Franklin 17
Wharton, Ferdinand D., Jr. 38
Whatley, Booker T. 26

DERMATOLOGIST

ELECTRON MICROSCOPIST

ELECTRONICS ENGINEER

ENDOCRINOLOGIST

ENDOSCOPIST

ENGINEER

Turner, Allen H. 120
Turner, John R. 112
Turner, Madeline M. 14
Wade, William L., Jr. 332
Walker, Lewis 145
Walker, Madame C. J. 13
Walker, N. Lucius 126
Walton, Ulysses S. 56
Weatherby, Dennis 333
Weaver, Rufus J. 22
Webster, John W., III 149
Weir, Charles E. 305, 315
West, Edward H. 347
West, James E. 140, 337
Wharton, Ferdinand D., Jr. 38
Wicks, Jerome L., Sr. 26
Wiles, Joseph St. Clair 92
Williams, Edward D. 78
Williams, Paul E. 360
Williams, Robert M. 44
Winn, Frank 344
Woods, Granville T. 4
Young, James E. 144, 332

LAWYER
Albert, Albert P. 13
Pelham, Robert A., Jr. 12
Rogers, Thomasina 48

MATHEMATICIAN
Austin, Wanda G. 155
Bharucha-Reid, Albert Turner 119
Blackwell, David H. 122
Bradley, Lillian Katie 118
Browne, Marjorie Lee 113
Browne, Robert T. 107
Cox, Elbert Frank 108
Draper, Everett T., Jr. 145
Gilmer, Gloria 139
Granville, Evelyn Boyd 113, 147
Hedgley, David R., Jr. 141
Johnson, Raymond Lewis 154
Jordan, Wesley Lee 122
Mayes, Vivienne Lucille Malone 123
Reason, Charles Lewis 103
Wilkins, J. Ernest, Jr. 294

METALLURGIST
Crossley, Frank Alphonso 328
Parsons, James A. 291, 296

METEOROLOGIST
Anderson, Charles Edward 304
Bacon-Bercey, June 302
Philander, S. George H. 336

MICROBIOLOGIST
Amos, Harold 95
Hammond, Benjamin F. 93
Stokes, Gerald Virgil 95
Taylor, Welton Ivan 97
Wiley, William Rodney 94

MILITARY PERSONNEL
Ballard, Joe N. 152
Brown, Erroll M. 157
Brown, Jesse L. 364
Chambers, Lawrence C. 367
Cochran, Donnie 370
Davis, Donna P. 249
Earley, Charity Adams 111
Fields, Evelyn 153
Hayes, Marcella A. 367
James, Daniel H. 366
Lawrence, Robert Henry, Jr. 377
Mann, Marion 248
Mitchell, Edith P. 373
Paige, Emmett, Jr. 136
Peterson, Frank E. 367
Reason, Adam J.Paul 376
Turner, Guthrie 259
Tzomes, Chancellor A. 369

NEUROLOGIST
Bailey, R. Wellesley 187
Barber, Jesse B., Jr. 223, 262

NEUROSURGEON
Canady, Alexa 252
Carson, Benjamin S. 269
Greene, Clarence Sumner 209
Hyde, Deborah Maxine 252

NUCLEAR ENGINEER
Levert, Francis E. 335

NURSE
Adams-Ender, Clara Leach 64, 77
Allen, Esther Louisa 61
Allen, Karen 79
Bellamy, Verdelle B. 72
Bullock, Carrie E. 54
Carnegie, Mary Elizabeth 56
Carter, Carolyn McGraw 71
Dagrosa, Terry Williams 71
Daily, Alida Cooley 196
Daley, Phyllis 57
Dumas, Rhetaugh 68
Duncan, Elouise Collier 59
Felton, Geraldene 68

GENERAL INDEX

Page numbers which are *italicized* indicate illustrations.

A

Academy of General Dentistry 78
Acids, handling of 302
Acoustical wave filters 136
Adams, Christopher P. 46, 47
Adams, James Sloan 350
Adams, Numa P. G. 184
Adams, Walter Anderson 200
Adams-Ender, Clara Leach 64, 77
Addy, Tralance Obuama 313, 325
Adjustable shackle 128
Adom, Edwin Nii 242
Aeromycin 200
Aerospace Corporation, Electronic Systems
  Division 155
Aerospace medicine 368
African American patent holders, lists of 12
Air compressor, gas turbine 316
Air data sensor 363
Air purification system 311
Aircraft, monoplane 349
Airplanes
  air data sensor 363
  de-icer 353, 359
  emergency landing runway system 358
  folding wing 356
  mail delivery 355, 358
  parachute 351
  pilot-seat ejection system 363
  propeller 350
  radio beacon 359
  vertical ascent and landing 352
Airships 348
Akron General Medical Center 245
Alarm, train 346
Albert Einstein College of Medicine of
  Yeshiva University 218
Albert, Albert P. 13
Alcorn, George Edward 329, *329*
Alexander, Leslie L. 235, 259
Alexander, Virginia M. 182
Alexander, Walter Gilbert 173
Alexander, Winser Edward 130
Allen, Esther Louisa 61

Allen, Floyd 321
Allen, James Matthew 110
Allen, John Henry, Jr. 140
Allen, Karen 79
Allen, Raleigh H. 221
Allen, Robert T. 22
Allen, Thomas C. 354
Allen, William E., Jr. 189, 247
Almanacs 1
Alpha Delta Alpha Scientific Society of
  Clark University 291
Alpha Omega Alpha Honor Medical Society
  190, 256, 258
Alpha Phi Alpha Fraternity 192
Aluminum, forged 143
American Academy of Dermatology 236,
  241
American Academy of Family Physicians
  284
American Academy of Nursing 68
American Academy of Oral Medicine 79
American Academy of Orthopaedic Sur-
  geons 201
American Academy of Pediatrics 191, 272
American Association for the Advancement
  of Science 335
American Association of Dental Examiners
  70
American Association of Foot Specialists
  37
American Association of Pathologists and
  Bacteriologists 181
American Association of Physical Anthro-
  pologists 88
American Board of Cardiovascular Dis-
  eases 203
American Board of Dermatology and
  Syphilology 185, 203
American Board of Internal Medicine 191,
  208, 276
American Board of Neurosurgery 209
American Board of Obstetrics and Gynecol-
  ogy 185, 189